Enigma Books

Also published by Enigma Books

Hitler's Table Talk: 1941–1944

In Stalin's Secret Service

Hitler and Mussolini: The Secret Meetings

The Jews in Fascist Italy: A History

The Man Behind the Rosenbergs

Roosevelt and Hopkins: An Intimate History

Diary 1937–1943 (Galeazzo Ciano)

Secret Affairs: FDR, Cordell Hull, and Sumner Welles

Hitler and His Generals: Military Conferences 1942–1945

Stalin and the Jews: The Red Book

The Secret Front: Nazi Political Espionage

Fighting the Nazis: French Intelligence and Counterintelligence

A Death in Washington: Walter G. Krivitsky and the Stalin Terror

The Battle of the Casbah: Terrorism and Counterterrorism in Algeria 1955–1957

Hitler's Second Book: The Unpublished Sequel to *Mein Kampf*

At Napoleon's Side in Russia: The Classic Eyewitness Account

The Atlantic Wall: Hitler's Defenses for D-Day

Double Lives: Stalin, Willi Münzenberg, and the Seduction of the Intellectuals

France and the Nazi Threat: The Collapse of French Diplomacy 1932–1939

Mussolini: The Secrets of His Death

Top Nazi: Karl Wolff—The Man Between Hitler and Himmler

Empire on the Adriatic: Mussolini's Conquest of Yugoslavia

The Origins of the War of 1914 (3-volume set)

Hitler's Foreign Policy 1933–1939: The Road to World War II

The Origins of Fascist Ideology 1918–1925

Max Corvo: OSS Italy 1942–1945

Hitler's Contract: The Secret History of the Italian Edition of *Mein Kampf*

Secret Intelligence and the Holocaust

Israel at High Noon

Balkan Inferno

Hollywood's Celebrity Gangster

Calculated Risk

Arkady Vaksberg

The Murder of Maxim Gorky

A Secret Execution

Translated by Todd Bludeau

Enigma Books

Published in the United States by
Enigma Books
580 Eighth Avenue, New York, NY 10018
www.enigmabooks.com

Copyright © 2007 by Enigma Books

ISBN-13: 978-1-929631-62-9
ISBN-10: 1-929631-62-6

Translated from the Russian by Todd Bludeau

All photos courtesy of the David King Collection.

Printed in the United States of America

Library of Congress Cataloging-in-Publication Data

Vaksberg, Arkadii.
    The murder of Maxim Gorky : a secret execution / Arkady Vaksberg ; translated by
Todd Bludeau.

    p. : ill. ; cm.

    ISBN-13: 978-1-929631-62-9
    ISBN-10: 1-929631-62-6
    Includes index.

1. Gorky, Maksim, 1868-1936--Death and burial. 2. Authors, Russian--20th century--
Biography. I. Bludeau, Todd. II. Title.

PG3465.Z9 D43 2007
891.78/309

Contents

Foreword   vii

1.	Man or Myth?	3
2.	The Corrupting Poison of Power	11
3.	Smashed to Smithereens	25
4.	A Nail in the Heart	33
5.	Petty Intrigues	46
6.	In Search of a Bomb	65
7.	Face and Mask	85
8.	The Ladies Loved Him	95
9.	Poisoned by Anger	104
10.	On Deaf Ears	117
11.	Unsolved Mysteries	128
12.	Toothache	138
13.	A Dual Game	158
14.	Burned Bridges	172
15.	Death by Small Cuts	184
16.	Cords of Vanity	193
17.	A Stroll in the Gulag	213
18.	In Defense of Denunciation	225
19.	An Agent of Influence	235
20.	The Dead Man Returns	258
21.	A Feast in the Time of Plague	276
22.	Hunting Season	296
23.	Predator and Prey	314
24.	Everywhere a Conspiracy	327
25.	An Old Circus Bear	335
26.	Oxygen Deprivation	359
27.	Tragedy as Farce	375
28.	Maxim Gorky's Second and Third Deaths	389

Archival Sources   411
Bibliography   411
Index   414

Foreword

The last twenty years of Gorky's life are filled with riddles, contradictions, and many unanswered questions, but mostly with sorrow and high drama. Soviet propaganda was more than successful in its attempts to hide the truth about the life and death of the great writer. There is hardly another figure of equal renown in the past century whose life was steeped to such a degree in lies, falsifications, and suppression of the facts.

Since those most directly involved in the falsifications were connected in one way or another to Gorky's spiritual and physical destruction, and the dissemination of lies was promoted by official, state-sanctioned Gorky scholars, it was not easy to shed the ingrained stereotypes. Fortunately, the archives were opened slightly (then partially closed again) and this, along with a lifting of secrecy from many sources and documents, helped me get at least somewhat closer to the truth. The most difficult aspect was comparing what was previously known against what has been newly revealed. The resulting book presents to the reader a *different* Gorky, not quite similar to, yet not completely unlike, the one known by several generations of deceived readers.

The archives of the Federal Security Service (the FSB, the former KGB), the Russian Center for Preservation and Study of Records of Modern History (RTsKhIDNI, which includes the former archive of the Communist Party of the CPSS), as well as secret collections of the Gorky Archive provided the most useful sources. I consider it my duty to point out that the employees of this last archive are carrying out a very important mission, bringing to light extremely valuable documents, the suppression of which over decades can only be described as a crime perpetrated by the Communist regime against the whole world, for Gorky belongs to humanity and not to the Kremlin. Although I differ on many points with current Gorky biographers, it would be unfair not to recognize the service of those who reject the idea of a monopoly on the truth and instead help introduce previously unknown Gorky documents into the scholarly discourse.

This book is a documentary narrative concentrated on the last twenty years of an historical personality unlike any other. In many ways a book by one writer about another is necessarily subjective. But what else can any work by a writer be? In this book there is not one single fact that cannot be supported by a document or the carefully checked testimony of contemporaries. But the interpretation of these facts belongs, naturally, to the author.

The Murder of Maxim Gorky

A Secret Execution

1.

Man or Myth?

The entire life of this infinitely talented and enigmatic man, woven from blatant contradictions, consists of a chain of incredible chance happenings and mysterious coincidences, too improbable to reflect reality. If the word "chance" must be placed in quotation marks, then the same cannot be said about "coincidences": their abundance makes the life of the hero of this book read like drama with a boldly convoluted, even improbable, plot. This was especially clear when his life came to an end and the final note had sounded.

The former "Nizhny Novgorod petit-bourgeois" Aleksei Maksimovich Peshkov, famous throughout the world as the writer Maxim Gorky, died on the morning of June 18, 1936, not far from Moscow in an old estate that once belonged to the nobility that Stalin made available for him. This was that very same residence in which Lenin had passed away twelve years earlier. Was this some kind of stunt drummed up by the most masterly and malevolent of all playwrights that history has ever known? What kind of coincidence was this? The mustachioed leader was well aware of the relationship between the first Bolshevik tyrant and the "founder" of Socialist Realism. In sending the writer to the next world in that very same estate, where Vladimir Ilyich, who had banned him from Soviet Russia, died twelve years previously, Stalin clearly demonstrated the strange love he had for both of them, as well as that undying passion for sinister metaphors.

Along with this came another played by Lady Luck. By deeply symbolic coincidence, the place where Gorky spent his final days had long since seemingly borne his name, except without the soft sign in the middle.[*] In foreign languages, without the soft sign, this location bore the name of the deceased

---

[*] In the phonetic transliteration of Cyrillic spelling, the name Gorky should in fact be rendered as Gor'kii to show the soft sign (') in the middle. The name of the settlement, however, is Gorki. To non-readers of Russian, the distinction will be lost. And since Gorky is the *nom de plume* by which the writer is universally known, we use it, and not Gor'kii, here as well.—Translator's note.

not just "seemingly" but in reality: absolutely literally. Thus Stalin, who had conferred the name of the "great proletarian writer" on hundreds of schools, institutes, theaters, clubs, factories, libraries, streets, squares, and even the city of Gorky's birth, had no need to add to the interminably long list the location where Gorky finished out his life: his wise ancestors had done this for him.

There is still one more coincidence which, naturally, does not have any scientific explanation, but is also profoundly symbolic and sticks in the accounts of all the memoirists who subsequently talked about that unusually hot June morning: as soon as the heart of the writer stopped beating, several of the strongest peals of thunder were heard, followed by one flashing bolt of lightning after another, and a lashing, violent downpour; there is not a soul alive who would not have taken that as a cry from the heavens on the passing of the great son of Russia.

Stalin had been waiting for this moment. No matter which version of Gorky's death is considered the most likely one, Stalin had no doubt whatsoever that the writer's fatal hour with the inevitable was drawing near. When it did come, the dictator was immediately informed. Stalin assigned to his security chief, Karl Pauker, formally occupying the post of head of the operations department of the NKVD, supervision of the body's transfer from the outskirts of Moscow to the Hall of Columns in the House of Unions, where for twelve years final·respects had been paid to important Soviet corpses. The escort for the dead writer was accorded the same level of significance as the escort for a living leader. Less than two years remained before Pauker would be dispatched by the executioner's bullet in the basement of the Lubyanka.

As evening approached, Moscow Radio broadcast the official announcement on the death of the "great Russian writer, brilliant artist of the word, friend of the workers, and fighter for the victory of Communism." A commission for the organization of the funeral was created, with the participation of the then head of the Moscow Communists, Nikita Khrushchev. Of its ten members, five would be shot over the next three years. Five members joined the commission "for the formal acceptance of the literary heritage and correspondence of A. M. Gorky"—only one of them would escape the Great Terror.

Of the very closest circle to Gorky, those who stood near the grave in the final hours and minutes of his send-off to the next world, only a few would escape death in the Lubyanka. This will be discussed in greater detail in following chapters.

On the following day the doors of the Hall of Columns were open for all to pay their final respects to the deceased writer. Transportation was cut off around the center of Moscow and all adjacent streets. The line of people who wanted to file past the coffin stretched for many kilometers. According to estimates of the Moscow police, more than half a million people could enter the Hall in a single day.

Only toward the end of the day did Stalin show up to express his sorrow. Late in the evening, before the coffin was to be removed for cremation, several officials, including Nikita Khrushchev and Genrikh Yagoda, head of the NKVD—in all, eight people—stood as the final guard. Four of them would be executed in the very near future. A bit to the side was Lenin's sister, Maria Ulyanova, and the French writer André Gide, who had arrived in Moscow on the eve of Gorky's death. They had been allowed access to the coffin but not honored with being part of the guard.

The cremation took place during the night, and in the morning the doors of the Hall of Columns were again opened, this time to bid farewell to the ashes. Stalin, along with his inner circle of Molotov, Kaganovich, Ordzhonikidze, Andreev, Mikoyan, Zhdanov, and Chubar, kept the final guard of honor. Ordzhonikidze would commit suicide (or was he murdered?) within six months; Chubar would be shot two years later.

Stalin ordered the urn with the ashes to be interred in the Kremlin wall, even though he had been informed of Gorky's wish to be buried alongside his son in Moscow's Novodevichy Cemetery. Gorky's first wife and the mother of their deceased son, Yekaterina Pavlovna Peshkova, had asked Stalin to leave at least just a handful of ash for fulfilling the writer's will. She was told, "The Politburo does not consider it possible to satisfy this request."

About one hundred thousand Muscovites with special passes turned out for the funeral ceremonies on Red Square. Stalin and his henchmen personally brought the urn to Red Square and ascended the steps to their places atop Lenin's Mausoleum. Molotov gave the first speech: "After Lenin," he pronounced, stuttering, "the death of Gorky is the heaviest loss for our country and for humanity." Aleksei Tolstoy spoke next. While Gorky was still alive, Tolstoy was considered the second living classic; now he stood to be first. Sholokhov had not yet been moved closer to Mt. Olympus and arrived with the full expectation of being arrested. As befit the Soviet master of ornate language in such situations, Tolstoy exclaimed, bombastically and turgidly, "It is not with a funeral march but with a victorious song of life that we greet the great artist who lives among us and who continues to guide us with his eternal word."

André Gide spoke on behalf of the International Association of Writers. His speech was translated by the country's top journalist, Mikhail Koltsov, an employee of the special services who had Stalin's special trust. By rank he had no right to be standing alongside the leader on top of the Mausoleum. In three-and-a-half years, Koltsov would meet his punishment, later than the other participants of this solemn theatrical performance. Gide spoke not so much about

Gorky the person and not even simply about Gorky the writer, but he found justification and explanation for Gorky's position in the final years of his life, which had surprised many: before, emphasized Gide, writers stood against something, but "in this great country" genuinely revolutionary writers for the first time are not against, but for . . . Less than a year later, when Gide's book *Return from the USSR* (from "this great country"!) was to reach Moscow, he would be cursed, proclaimed a renegade and rotten agent of international capital, his name expunged from textbooks and encyclopedias, and his books removed from the shelves of bookstores and libraries.

For some time Gorky's death remained at the center of the public's attention: he was written about in newspapers as a person, and not as a "brilliant artist of the word" already cast in bronze. People from his closest circle shared memories of his final days. NKVD chief Yagoda was enraptured by Gorky's humanism; the greatest Soviet cardiologist of that time, Dmitri Pletnev, who had taken part in the daily doctors' briefing at the bedside of the dying man, talked about the strength of his soul, which on more than one occasion had conquered imminent death; the permanent house physician, Lev Levin, who did not leave Gorky's side for even a minute, wrote exactly what was expected of him: "Barely breathing. . . . he asked me to show him the newspaper in which the draft of Stalin's Constitution was printed." The draft had been published three days before his death, when all the members of his family and very closest friends had already been arriving to bid him farewell and when he was incapable of reading a single word.

A little more than a year-and-a-half later, at the last of the Great Moscow Trials, all three would be charged with Gorky's murder: Yagoda for political reasons, on the instructions of the "right-Trotskyite bloc" ("Gorky, as the best friend of comrade Stalin, must be killed"); Pletnev and Levin as the submissive executors of Yagoda's order. Levin and Yagoda were sentenced to be shot immediately; Pletnev would be given twenty-five years in prison, but would be summoned from there by Molotov, Kalinin, and Vyshinsky to report on the tortures he had endured and, finally, in September 1941, with the arrival of Nazi troops in Orel, where he was sitting out his punishment, at the order of Lavrenty Beria and approved personally by comrade Stalin, he would be killed among 156 prisoners of "the first magnitude" who had still escaped the executioner's bullet.

Gradually the real Gorky, although in the role of victim of the "killer doctors," would imperceptibly disappear from books and newspapers. He would become not a man but a myth, transformed into "the founder of Soviet literature," "the creator of Socialist Realism," the great friend of Lenin and Stalin (but Stalin, naturally, most of all!), an irreconcilable foe of "the enemies of the people," the creator of the Union of Soviet Writers . . . in short, he would be transformed into that bronze monument, which to this day stands near the Belorussky Station in Moscow, that same train station in which Gorky had arrived for the first time from emigration in 1928. He was canonized, occupying in both Soviet history and Soviet literature that place which Stalin assigned him and which did not change even after Khrushchev had overthrown the cult of Stalin.

A number of historical personalities, beginning with Lenin himself, had been transformed by Soviet propaganda into myths, squeezed into frames determined for them by Party ideologues. But probably no biography was subjected to such a mercilessly violent deformation as that of Gorky. Everything that did not fit into the strictly defined scheme was suppressed but anything that did see the light of day, more often than not from detested foreign lands, was contemptuously rejected and declared to be lies and slander. The fate of one of the most mysterious, dramatic, and contradictory personalities of the century was hewn, planed, and polished to the point of nausea, naturally evoking in anyone with taste and seeking truth, a staunch hostility to both the canonized personality itself and the works he created.

Gorky is multifaceted—many authors who have written about him, and first of all those who met with him personally, have noted this special quality of his. They faced an impossible task: to draw Gorky's image with some kind of definite trait—plus or minus—but the trait then slipped away, coming into irreconcilable conflict with reality. The stunning contradiction of Gorky's position, and, at times, the incompatibility of his own words and actions, is typical of the biography of this very complex individual. Duality, apparently, was his true essence. To grasp such an enigmatic nature is extremely difficult. Any attempt to use the yardstick of normal logic and so-called common sense is doomed to fail. Unless one rejects the fruitless attempt to squeeze Gorky into one of the predetermined groups—Leninists or anti-Leninists, "red" or "white," "pure or impure"—it is impossible, in any treatment of him, to discover this major paradoxical figure of the twentieth century.

Gorky's life and personality are no less interesting than his works. Maybe even more so. Even today many of his brilliant prose works elicit admiration, such as "My Childhood," reminiscences of Leo Tolstoy, and the final unfinished novel *The Life of Klim Samgin*. Clear and passionate, on the very edge of candor, even today his social and political writings from 1917–1918 must be read with deep admiration. His plays, without a doubt, have outlived their time and their author. If nowadays in the West they are given at all—or very rarely—in Russia the interest in his plays is not dying out. Every generation finds something in them it can relate to. Many are having their second, third, even fifth rebirth, attracting the attention of new directors and a new public. As these lines are being written, seven of Gorky's plays are currently running in Moscow theaters alone; even Chekhov is not staged as often as Gorky. Reviewing a 2004 performance of *Philistines* in the Moscow Art Theater, where a century before Gorky made his debut as playwright, the most popular Russian daily newspaper, *Izvestiia*, wrote, "Such amazing drama! How the characters are shaped, how the relationships are constructed, how the personalities are drawn—even those who only appear for a moment on stage! Such plays in the world's repertoire can be counted on the fingers of one hand."

But Gorky's creativity is by no means known in its entirety. Nowhere did it appear as fully as in his epistolary prose, the most important part of which was kept locked away in secret "cellars," under the strictest control of the secret police for many decades. This truly unique archive unveils Gorky the person and Gorky the writer in all his richness and variety, understand his tragedy, recognize the whole measure of his downfall and evaluate objectively his acts of humanity, that are worthy of admiration and respect, as well as the actions which left a black mark on his conscience.

Even a short list of documents hidden for half a century and accessible only now (and even then only partially!) for reading and research paints a picture of how the exceptionally complex, scandalously contradictory and essentially deeply tragic image of the writer, who by the end of his life ceased being a writer to become a "social figure" and a "fighter for the happiness of workers," was distorted and "straightened out" by proscription and silence. He had been transformed into a political figure and, in particular, as a pawn in Stalin's bloody game. Not only the leak of information—about Gorky and everything connected to him—from hiding-places in the Lubyanka, but even the most modest attempt, dictated by purely scholarly interests, to penetrate them were qualified as an encroachment upon a state secret of special importance and carried with it extremely severe sanctions.

Gorky's own correspondence and journal entries; the diaries and memoirs of his friends, colleagues and acquaintances; the secret dossiers of the OGPU-NKVD that were opened on Gorky and everyone in his circle; and the agency denunciations of people who hovered around him—both the deliberate plants and the volunteer snitches—were hidden from everyone caring about the historical truth. Among the items made available, even if only in a limited and partial way, are many letters from Gorky to Lenin; dozens to Stalin and his closest "advisors" (Molotov, Kaganovich, Voroshilov, and others); dozens to future "enemies of the people" (Zinoviev, Kamenev, Rykov, Bukharin); dozens, maybe even hundreds, to writers and scholars; a huge and truly staggering correspondence with Yagoda, which are impossible to read without shuddering;

more than 150 letters, opened and inspected, some of which never made it to their addressees but remained stitched to his Lubyanka file; the correspondence of people from his circle, containing extremely valuable information about Gorky; financial and medical documents that shed light on many dark pages of his life. An invaluable repository for those who want to know the truth about the life of the writer, concealed from unauthorized readers, about his tormented soul and about his milieu, is his correspondence with the "main" woman in his life, kept strictly off-limits by Soviet authorities, which finally became accessible. True, the texts which have reached us cannot be called "correspondence" in the strict sense of the word, since it includes her letters to him (carefully preserved by Gorky and kept in his archive), and not his letters to her. The exact fate of Gorky's letters to her remains unknown. But this vast epistolary legacy, even if truncated and concealed for decades, is of considerable interest, revealing what had been kept secret for several generations.

Returning to the correspondence of Gorky with the head of the Soviet Gestapo, Genrikh Yagoda, it should be reemphasized that reading it is a big strain on the nervous system, even if one approaches it with the completely detached and emotionally neutral attitude of the researcher. The mixture of bloodthirstyness and cheap sentimentality, the flattering and false demagoguery of Yagoda, and the reciprocal pathetic and paternal care about his health from Gorky, who had completely lost both his reason and vigilance, make this correspondence one of the most dramatic epistolary monuments of the Stalinist era. It seems that this prolonged epistolary connection between the writer and the executioner was kept hidden not only because of the odious nature of the name of Genrikh Yagoda, but also because Gorky himself comes off the worse in it in the sense that it creates a combined sensation of loathing and deep compassion.

A wealth of materials having the most direct relationship to Gorky's personality, his biography and, most of all, to its most enigmatic pages, is kept in files, closed until just recently, concerning Lenin and Stalin. It is precisely there that their correspondence, including, for example, Gorky's letters to Lenin of the pre-Revolutionary period, can be found. His evaluations and opinions already at that time by no means fit the framework, knocked together by the Party agitprop, as "the founder of Socialist Realism" and "great friend of Vladimir Ilyich." The cuts, which were made during an earlier publication of some of these documents, are not in the slightest bit less eloquent than the texts themselves hacked up by publishers.

The new material, blended with the old, makes it possible to see "another" Gorky—much more voluminous and complicated: powerful and helpless, cynical and naïve, repellant and touching, insightful and blind; an arrogant man, who presumptuously contrived to outwit the devil and who lost his luminous God-given talent in the devil's kitchen; a spoiled child of fortune, who had hopelessly lost his life.

The canonic image of Gorky, created over the decades, was in relative harmony, albeit somewhat shaky, within those documents that were accessible to all. Now it turns out to be in direct contradiction with it. But anyone who is not indifferent to the real Gorky needs only the historical truth, and more—a free attempt to make sense of events with all their contradictoriness free from any *a priori* idea and plan or hidden agendas.

To this day many important materials are, unfortunately, shut up in the secret files of archival repositories, and ostensibly not for political or ideological reasons, but by the will of interested individuals, predominantly the women close to Gorky. Everyone has the indisputable right to the secrets of his or her personal life. However, our knowledge of the truth connected to Gorky suffers severely as a result. Many more discoveries are still ahead of us, which will reveal a multitude of hitherto unresolved riddles.

2.

The Corrupting Poison of Power

When the stamp of "top secret" was removed from the few lines quoted below, and they were printed, their publication produced genuine shock waves. It was only one phrase, but it convincingly exposed the scale of the Soviet propaganda lie, which had shamelessly distorted the true relationship of "the great proletarian writer" to the even greater "creator of the Soviet state." As Gorky wrote to Vladimir Ilyich Lenin in November 1909:

> At times it seems to me that every person for you is nothing more than a flute on which you play one melody or another, and that you evaluate every individual from the point of view of his or her suitability to you, for the realization of your goals, opinions and tasks.

It should hardly be surprising that this passage was declassified only in 1993. Before then, publishers would insert parentheses and periods, indicating that the letter is published "with minor abridgements," and among the abridgements considered to be "minor" it was always precisely those lines, paragraphs, often entire pages, which erased the stereotype dictated by Party dogma. Just this one phrase about the "flute" (a paraphrase of Hamlet in the third act of Shakespeare's play) was enough to subject to doubt the myth of the "great friendship" between the "brilliant leader of the proletariat" and the "brilliant proletarian writer," about the unfailing admiration of the latter for the former and the boundless love of the first for the second.

Gorky underscored his estimation of Lenin even more clearly eight years later: ". . . a talented person, he possesses all the qualities of a 'leader,' as well as a lack of morals and a disdain and merciless disregard for the life of the popular masses, which is necessary for this role." Does it even need to be said that this evaluation—just as merciless as it is precise—was inaccessible to Soviet citizens for almost three quarters of a century?

These characteristics by Gorky add little to the image we already have of "Ilyich." On the other hand, they add a great deal to the image of Gorky. With amazing accuracy and long before the Bolshevik state revolution, he had seen through his "great friend" and, with incredible insight, had expressed his essence in just a few lines. This, however, did not stop him from actively participating in the glorification of a person who, not having worked a single day up to his forty-seventh year, lightheartedly played the flute, and who possessed, as has now been established by documentation, a very significant income from the property he inherited, enjoying all the pleasures of life of the European bourgeois, without the slightest hesitation to beg money from everyone "for the realization of *his* goals, opinions, tasks."

Without Gorky's direct participation, the strange alliance of one of the richest people in Russia, the industrialist Savva Morozov, with the Leninists could hardly have taken place. This "social paradox," as he was called, freed Gorky, after paying a huge pledge, from prison in January 1905 where the latter was being held for advocating armed insurrection, and then generously funded his "class enemies," whose victory realistically threatened not only his wealth but his life as well. Savva Morozov's nephew, Nikolai Schmit, another rich Moscow industrialist whose vast wealth also ended up in the hands of the Bolsheviks, entered Lenin's circle following the same path.

But Gorky did not limit himself to just the role of middleman. His play, *The Lower Depths*, enjoyed unprecedented success around the world, and the author's royalties brought him a huge income—so huge that Gorky, who loved, and had already become accustomed to living the life of luxury, could give away part of it for good deeds. Russian intellectuals, who ended up with extra money, even in small amounts, helped hospitals and schools, libraries and poor students. Gorky acted differently. On Lenin's advice, he made an agreement with Aleksandr Parvus, one of the darkest personalities in the history of Bolshevism, a swindler and, as it now turns out, a German agent. It is thanks to him that a few years later German money migrated into Lenin's coffers for the overthrow of Tsarism and triumph of the revolutionaries. This time his mission was much more modest.

Parvus acted as Gorky's literary agent, collecting money for the staging of *The Lower Depths* around the world and earning for himself in the process indecently large commissions of twenty percent. From the remaining eighty percent, three-fourths went to Lenin's party and only one-fourth to Gorky. But Gorky did not even get this sum: Parvus appropriated a significant part of it, simplemindedly explaining that he could not deprive himself of the satisfaction of strolling around Italian resorts in the company of one charming lady. This lady was the German Social-Democrat Rosa Luxemburg, whose name then thundered throughout Europe.

Gorky's generosity was all the more amazing because he had not only seen the essence of the Bolshevik leader, hidden from others' eyes, but also understood his far-reaching intentions. And in both an ideological and political sense, the antipodes of Lenin were much closer to him than from the milieu of Russian social democracy, liberals and humanists, schemers and dreamers attracted to European-style socialism, who found themselves in emigration. He was on different ideological poles with his savior and personal "banker" Savva Morozov as well. But already even then the Stormy Petrel* was woven together from uneasily combined contradictions: the eye saw everything correctly, the intellect gave a precise evaluation of what was seen, but the soul, for some reason, was pulled in a completely different direction.

He joyfully greeted the February 1917 revolution, with its overthrow of Tsarism and the triumph of the ideals of a democratic revolution, which the Bolsheviks immediately christened as bourgeois. In a letter to his old friend, the writer Nikolai Teleshov, he exclaimed, "We have lived to see the celebration of the Resurrection of Rus' from the dead!" He had no need whatsoever for either friendship or even cooperation with Lenin, who had returned from emigration (returning in mysterious fashion in a sealed train car through hostile Germany!). Everyone had his own goal: Lenin to seize power; Gorky to help the already existing power to become stronger and stand on its own feet. He was absolutely convinced that the revolution was genuine—genuine and desired.

Meanwhile, the war continued. The Bolsheviks shook the fragile foundation of the barely nascent democracy. Gorky saw his task as supporting science and culture, literature, and art, having finally found the highest good, which he valued above all else: freedom of the word and self-expression.

By that time he was already in charge of a monthly literary journal he had founded, *Letopis'* (Chronicle), and a publishing house, *Parus* (Sail). In only two years both the journal and publishing house had acquired a reputation of the highest standard. The best writers of the country and the world were published in *Letopis'*: among Russians—Blok, Bunin, Mayakovsky, Yesenin; among foreigners—Romain Rolland, Anatole France, Emile Verhaeren, H. G. Wells, Jack London. Less than a week after the overthrow of the monarchy, Gorky, concerned about possible acts of vandalism of art treasures, gathered in his

---

* This is Gorky's official Soviet nickname. It originates from his 1901 poem, "Song of the Stormy Petrel." There was probably not a single person in pre-Revolutionary Russia who didn't know it, and most likely by heart. The Soviets seized upon the imagery in the poem as the coming storm before the glorious revolution, and hence Gorky's moniker.

apartment the cream of St. Petersburg's intelligentsia. Without asking anyone, and relying strictly upon their own authority and understanding of social responsibility, those present founded the "Commission for Artistic Affairs" under Gorky's leadership. His deputies were the artists Aleksandr Benoit and Nikolai Roerich; Mstislav Dobuzhinsky was secretary. Immediately the rumor spread that Gorky wanted to monopolize the "administration of art" and even aspired to a ministerial post. A week later, other cultural figures, no less prominent in their own right, gathered for a protest meeting, and not in a private apartment but in the former imperial (Mikhailovsky) theater. From now until practically the end of his life, Gorky would fight on two fronts: against those who were an obstacle to culture (in his opinion, naturally) and against those who suspected some kind of pernicious agenda in his actions.

The Bolsheviks could not have dreamed up anything better. Whether Gorky was with them, or against them, their enemies would be the same: "the rotten bourgeois intellectuals."

Thus far all this was only visible, but not yet accomplished. In those first weeks and months of freedom, full of bright hopes, Gorky found himself at the peak of his glory and happiness. These were probably his finest hours, especially as far as his inner being was concerned. Never before, or after, had he experienced such an emotional lift. On March 20, the Academy of Sciences canceled its shameful, tsar-dictated act of 1902, which had rescinded Gorky's election to honorary membership of the Academy in the category of belles-lettres. As a sign of protest then, Anton Chekhov and Vladimir Korolenko removed from themselves the title of honorary academicians. On that same day, March 20, the academicians unanimously asked Korolenko to return to the Academy. Korolenko rejected the request: "A. P. Chekhov and I are in agreement," he wrote to the members of the academy, "which is that we cannot go in together." Gorky did not refuse the title of academician. Along with him, Stanislavsky, to whom Gorky owed his fame as a playwright, became an honored academician in the category of art.

One week later, taking advantage of Russia's newfound freedom, Gorky created two more organizations: the "Free Association for the Development and Dissemination of the Positive Sciences," along with the same Korolenko; Nobel Prize laureate and world renowned physiologist Ivan Pavlov; academician and professor of mathematics Vladimir Steklov; Nikolai Morozov, the oldest Russian revolutionary and scholar; other intellectuals; and the "Union of Art Workers," together with Fyodor Chaliapin, artists Mstislav Dobuzhinsky and Ivan Shukhaev. The demand of social engagement consumed him; each day new plans were born—and immediately realized. He drank the air of freedom that he had never breathed before.

He had already burdened himself with a multitude of different obligations, but it seemed he had the strength and desire for even more. On April 18, along with the famous Menshevik, economist and historian Nikolai Sukhanov, Gorky began to publish yet another newspaper, *Novaya Zhizn'* (The New Life), a landmark publication in the history of Russian journalism. The writers and politicians around Gorky's *Letopis'* were its initiators and regular contributors: in addition to Gorky and Sukhanov, these included Vladimir Korolenko, Ivan Bunin, Kliment Timiryazev, and others. They clearly defined the goal of the newspaper: cooperation of the revolutionary intelligentsia with the Provisional Government for the development of the country's industry and culture, as well as the creation of "a single social-democratic party," the realization of an idea, fatally unrealized under Russian conditions—the unification of the dissident democrats, fighting among themselves and poisoned by ambition, opposed to a cohesive and aggressive reaction.

But cooperation with the Provisional Government turned out to be impossible. Under threat of revolution from both the left and right, the government of Alexander Kerensky adopted a host of repressive measures, provoking, naturally, an immediate reaction in the pages of *Novaya Zhizn'*: true to its principles, its writers listened to the voice of conscience, not to the state of affairs. The Provisional Government closed *Novaya Zhizn'* (from the beginning of July and almost up until the middle of September it came out under the name of *Svobodnaia Zhizn'* [The Free Life]), which immediately gave the Bolsheviks a reason to come out in defense of the "poisoned" Gorky. The Central Bureau of Trade Unions, under Bolshevik control, adopted a resolution, calling for "branding the despicable calumniators, who in their bitterness dare to direct . . . weapons of malicious slander . . . against Maxim Gorky, the pride of Russian literature and the inexorable defender of the working masses."

Gorky did not bite at this flattery, not even at the appeal, so dear to him and contained in that same resolution, of defending the unfettered freedom of the press. He understood why his future oppressors so passionately defended the free word and tried not to meet with Bolshevik leaders at all, save perhaps for his old acquaintance Leonid Krasin who occupied a prominent position in the Party hierarchy, but always appeared to stand off to the side from the basic ruling nucleus. A true intellectual and highly educated engineer, Krasin managed to die happily in 1926, avoiding the inevitable fate of the Great Terror: he, no doubt, would have been one of the first to go.

Lenin expressed his attitude toward the authors of *Novaya Zhizn'* with his usual bluntness: "[their] predominant mood," he maintained, "is intellectual skepticism, hiding and expressing unscrupulousness." Meanwhile, *Novaya Zhizn'* and Lenin simply had different principles. How else could the organizer of the

Bolshevik revolution, which Gorky greeted with unconcealed contempt and the deepest hatred, react to the publications of those "New Lifers*"? It was hatred not only of the October revolution itself and for the Bolsheviks who had seized power, but most of all for their leader, about whose personal qualities and plans Gorky had no doubt: he had close knowledge of Lenin and his secret goal only too well.

This is what Gorky wrote in *Novaya Zhizn'* right after the Bolshevik uprising, which was immediately dubbed the "October revolution" by the mutineers:

> Lenin, Trotsky, and those accompanying them have already become envenomed by the corrupting poison of power, as evidenced by their disgraceful attitude to freedom of the word, freedom of the individual and to the whole list of rights that democracy fights for . . . Lenin is not an omnipotent magician, but a cold-blooded conspirator, who has no pity for either the honor or the life of the proletariat. The workers must not allow adventurers and madmen to heap upon the head of the proletariat disgraceful, senseless and bloody crimes, which not Lenin but the proletariat itself will pay for.

And in another one of his essays:

> The working class cannot fail to understand that Lenin is only carrying out some kind of experiment on their skin, on their blood . . . The working class must know that there are no miracles in reality, that hunger, the complete breakdown of industry, the devastation of transportation, long bloody anarchy, and after it a no less bloody and gloomy reaction, awaits it.

Both these and subsequent quotations from his *Untimely Thoughts*† (such is the name Gorky gave to a cycle of his publications) are surprising not only in their mercilessly precise analysis and just as precise foresight, but also in their unrestrained emotional force. We would hardly be wrong in recognizing that his seething fury was, to a certain degree, fury toward himself for having been so closely associated with a person whom he had figured out long ago but, as it turned out, not completely; for having done so much for the "cold-blooded conspirator," who became the leader of the adventurers, while sticking a knife into the back of Russian democracy; for having believed for so long in those

---

* From *Novaya Zhizn'*, which means "New Life"—Translator's note.
† *Nesvoevremennye mysli* in Russian—Translator's note. *Untimely Thoughts: Essays on Revolution, Culture and the Bolsheviks, 1917–1918.* Translated by Professor Herman Ermolaev, Princeton University (New York: Paul S. Eriksson, Inc., 1968).

zealots for the people's welfare realizing, finally, how cruelly he had been deceived.

Never—not before, not after—had Gorky's social and political journalism risen to such heights of uninhibited hatred; never had it been so merciless, bereft of even the smallest signs of hypocrisy. This is possibly the rarest of all instances when his writings allow for any criticism, save one: no one can reproach its author for being disingenuous. The persistently repetitious, transparent thought of his political pamphlets of that time; the painstakingly chosen words, style, intonation, temperament, breath, and much more—all this testifies to the absolute sincerity, almost unthinkable for Gorky, revealing, with total candor, the measure of his despair at the destruction of all hope.

Three days after the publication of the pamphlet containing the quotations cited above, Gorky returned to the theme and to the personality who provoked in him blind rage. Gorky wrote in *Novaya Zhizn*:

> Having imagined themselves to be Napoleons of socialism, the Leninists rant and rave, completing the destruction of Russia—the Russian people will pay for this with oceans of blood . . . This inevitable tragedy does not shame Lenin, a slave of dogma, and his myrmidons, his slaves.

Gorky's eternally opportune "untimely thoughts" reveal with merciless precision the simplest working, mechanism, through which Lenin realized his intentions:

> Life, in all its complexity, is unknown to Lenin. He does not know the people, the masses; has not lived with them, but he has learned—from books—how to raise this mass on its hind legs, how . . . to rouse its instincts to fury. The working class is to the Leninist what ore is to the metal worker.

In the first weeks after the Bolshevik revolution there was still hope that the mutineers would be destroyed, and Gorky, through his pamphlets, promoted this in every way possible. Although Lenin proclaimed the Provisional Government overthrown on October 25, it continued to function, something which Soviet historians have kept silent about for three quarters of a century. The minister of food, the socialist Prokopovich, released from jail, took upon himself the responsibilities as chief minister. The ministers of internal affairs (Nikitin); labor (Gvozdev); justice (Malyantovich); communications (Liverovsky); and agriculture (Maslov)—as well as the deputies of all ministries, including the deputy minister of education (the academician Vladimir Vernadsky), continued to carry out their duties.

Many of them, especially the minister of justice, the well-known St. Petersburg* lawyer Pavel Malyantovich, and the minister of enlightenment from the preceding Provisional Government, academician Sergei Oldenburg, were very close friends with Gorky. But he did not sign their appeal to the Bolsheviks entitled "Stop being the Jailers of Innocent People," basing his decision, evidently, on an elementary moral premise: you do not appeal to criminals, you fight them. His weapon was only the pen. Gorky's pamphlets stood out sharply from hundreds of articles of that time tarring the usurpers of power. The newspapers of the Constitutional Democrats, *Nash vek* (Our Century), *Russkie vedomosti* (The Russian Register), *Sovremennoe slovo* (The Modern Word), the SR (Social Revolutionary) *Zemlia i volia* (Land and Freedom), and the Menshevik *Novy Luch* (The New Light) and *Den'* (Day) continued to be published. While they were still being issued, there remained the illusory hope for a possible return to democracy. But the ban on advertising, which the Bolsheviks allowed only for their newspapers, was the first sign of sudden changes to come.

On the eve of the Constituent Assembly, the dispersal of which had already been planned, the Leninists organized a vulgar and, in essence, comic provocation. It was announced that the car Lenin was riding in had been shot at, and that the proletarian leader had been saved, thanks to the Swiss Communist Fritz Platten riding with him, who pushed his head down—this gave the authorities the grounds to call a state of emergency in Petrograd, flooding the city with armed units and breaking up demonstrations in support of the Constituent Assembly. The crowded (not less than 60,000 people) procession of the supporters of a democratic and free Russia was shot at by the Bolsheviks on the corner of Nevsky and Leteiny Prospekts.

Gorky immediately saw through the Bolshevist maneuver: "After some clown or bored loafer used a penknife to pick open the trunk of the automobile in which Lenin was riding, *Pravda*, taking the damage of the car's trunk to be an attempt on the life of Vladimir Ilyich, threateningly exclaimed: 'For every one of our heads we will take 100 heads each of the bourgeoisie.'" At the very end of the 1980s an expert commission of historians and criminalists, having studied all the documents, archival photographs, testimonies of contemporaries, as well as the topography of the site where the "attempt was made" on Vladimir Ilyich, concluded that it was not some clown or bored loafer who "used a penknife to pick open the car's trunk" but none other than the proletarian leader's chauffeur. Incidentally, even though this is important, it is

---

* St. Petersburg was renamed Petrograd in August 1914 by the tsar's government. In 1924, after Lenin's death, it became Leningrad. In 1991 the people voted to return to the original name of St. Petersburg.

not an overly significant detail: Gorky had given an absolutely precise evaluation of the events.

The Bolsheviks, meanwhile, clearly were not preparing to yield power, or share it with anyone. A pragmatist and a realist, Gorky understood that one could not live by hopes alone. He saw his mission as saving—this time from the Bolsheviks—culture, science, and art. But to do this, inevitably he had to enter into some kind of relationship with them. Anatoly Lunacharsky, Gorky's old friend from Capri, a graphomaniacal playwright who distinguished himself from the other Bolsheviks in Lenin's closest circle by his seeming intelligence and greater tolerance, was the People's Commissar of Enlightenment. Gorky summoned him from Moscow, where the Soviet government had already relocated, to Petrograd for a session of that same Union of Art Workers, which had been created one year earlier in a still free Russia.

Gorky's relationship with his former "Capri friend" by that time had become sharply strained. Gorky had already called Lunacharsky in his newspaper a "muddle-headed" people's commissar and chief Bolshevik supervisor for science and art. "I do not doubt for a minute," Gorky wrote to him, "that our personal relationship will prevent you from visiting me." He was right: Lunacharsky came.

The session took place in Gorky's apartment on April 19, 1918. Gorky demanded that a committee, elected by the Union, become "an executive organ for art"—in place of the board of the Ministry of Enlightenment. Lunacharsky spoke for Lenin and categorically refused: "We were," he announced, "against a political Constituent Assembly [formally, by the way, they were always "in favor of" it, advanced their candidates in the elections and received only twenty-five percent of all votes!], moreover we are against the Constituent Assembly in the area of art." The dialogue, not to mention any understanding, was a failure.

Gorky continued his vehement attack on the Bolsheviks. Following the removal of the government to Moscow, Bolshevism to him was encapsuled in the image of future Leninist advisor, Grigori Zinoviev, of the Petrograd Council, chairman of the Union of Northern Communes, of the Union of Commissars of the Northern Province or—more simply—the unlimited dictator of all northern Russia. He replaced Lenin in Gorky's irate tirades in the pages of *Novaya Zhizn'*.

> Mr. Zinoviev has "challenged" me to a verbal and public duel. I cannot satisfy the desire of Mr. Zinoviev—I am not an orator, I do not like public speeches, and I am insufficiently skilled to engage in a contest of eloquence with professional demagogues . . . Mr. Zinoviev contends that ... I "scratch the heels of the bourgeoisie." It is a coarse trick, but one cannot expect anything else from the

Zinovievs of the world. . . . Demagogues like Zinoviev corrupt the workers. . . . Soviet politics is perfidious politics regarding the working class.

To an even greater degree he felt the threat hanging over the intelligentsia. "In *Pravda*," he wrote, "various little beasts are setting the proletariat on the intelligentsia." This was his biggest sore point: this person from the bottom rungs of society, who had not received any education and had pulled himself up to the heights of culture by his own efforts, felt an almost sacred admiration for the intelligentsia. He saw its poisoning as a great tragedy which had befallen a barely freed Russia.

However, his attempt to enter into a dialogue with the Bolsheviks met with bitter reaction from the radically inclined and uncompromising figures of Russian culture. One of the people closest to Gorky (and no less popular in Russia), the writer Leonid Andreev, wrote in his secret diary, like the *Untimely Thoughts* hidden for many decades from Soviet readers, that

> . . . one cannot justify Gorky being chairman of the Commission for Art Affairs. The moral obtuseness of this chosen intellectual makes us fear for the future. Who cares about Lenin? Lenin will die and the fool will die, but what to do about these likeminded ones?

Gorky, however, continued with his line, indifferent to anyone. On May 14, he responded in *Novaya Zhizn'* to the latest Bolshevist attack on the free press.

> Soviet power has again suffocated several newspapers. . . . Destroying freedom of the word, the Messrs. Commissars gain no advantage for themselves and inflict great harm to the cause of the revolution. What are they afraid of, what are they faint-hearted about? . . . Have they really lost faith in themselves to such a degree that they fear an enemy who speaks openly, with a full voice, and that is why they are attempting to suffocate it?

Although Gorky continued to brand the "Messrs. Commissars," attentive readers detected in his pamphlets, if not a change in position, then at least less pathos. Perhaps fatigue from the fruitless battle was setting in, maybe he had simply exhausted the whole conceivable range of strong sentiments, or maybe as a pragmatist he felt the need to accept reality as it was.

Gorky rejected any idea that "Gorky is changing." As if answering his numerous critics on the right, he declared in the newspaper on May 30, categorically and in his former voice, "Everything that I have said about the barbarous, crude attitudes of the Bolsheviks, right up to sadism, about their lack of culture . . . about how they are conducting a revolting experiment on the people and annihilating the working class—all this and much else that I have said about 'bolshevism' remains in full force."

Those already negatively disposed toward him only did not accept his statement, but for some reason reacted even more. The next day that very same Leonid Andreev recorded the following in his diary:

> . . . it torments me that my hatred and contempt for Gorky (in his present phase) will remain *unfounded*. . . . I need to compile a total indictment in order to prove . . . Gorky's crime and the degree of his participation in the destruction and death of Russia . . . Will Gorky really remain unpunished, unrecognized, unexposed, and "respected"? Of course, I am not speaking about physical revenge, which is nonsense, but simply about truly respectable people judging him severely and decisively. If this does not take place (and it is possible that it will not) and Gorky comes through unscathed, then one can kiss life goodbye.

With amazing stubbornness, truly respectable people who expressed their position, and not only in personal diaries but also publicly, had already pushed Gorky at that—very early—stage into the open arms of the Bolsheviks, who, judging by everything, patiently waited for the desired and inevitable to take place. Patience, however, was not limitless—the Bolsheviks accelerated the course of events. On July 16, Lenin closed the newspaper of his "great friend," effectively shutting his mouth and in the process making it clear—not for the first time, true, and not for the last time—what he thought of him. Gorky found himself at a crossroads. But a month-and-a-half later fate was kind enough to help him cut through this puzzle.

On the evening of August 30, 1918, as Lenin was walking toward his car following a meeting at a Moscow factory, shots rang out. The wounded Lenin was taken to the Kremlin. Several days later his comrades (with his full participation, since he remained completely conscious and was in regular communication with his "companions") took the decision to unleash the "Red terror."

The day after the attempt on his life, Lenin received a telegram from Petrograd: "We are terribly anxious, we're worried, we sincerely wish you the speediest recovery, be strong in spirit. M. Gorky, Maria Andreeva." Right after the personal telegram, Gorky sent another one, this time seemingly more official, signed with his colleagues from the publishing house. The text of this telegram needs no commentary: "The insanity of people blinded by hatred attempted to cut short your life, dedicated to the liberation of working humanity. We genuinely wish you the speediest recovery and send our sincere greetings."

Finally, a few days later, Gorky arrived in Moscow and visited the recuperating Lenin. Unfortunately, there is no exact information about the nature of their conversation and the surroundings in which their meeting was held, the first one after a long separation and the deepest misunderstanding (if one can call what Gorky wrote about Lenin a misunderstanding). Gorky's future memoirs do not contain a single significant detail, save perhaps one:

> I came to see him, when he could still barely move his arm and barely move his wounded neck . . . [Lenin said that] the intelligentsia got him with its bullet. The passionate defender of the intelligentsia not only swallowed that remark, but subsequently quoted it sympathetically, as if to reproach himself.

What had happened? What reasons prompted the world famous writer, who had so concisely and frequently expressed his position with regard to the Bolsheviks and personally to the number one Bolshevik, comrade Lenin—what impelled him to make a sudden maneuver, which in nautical language is called a "hard come-about"? He later wrote, not very clearly, in his rough-draft notes:

> From 1903, I consider myself a Bolshevik . . . V[ladimir] Ilyich Lenin disturbed me and many Bolsheviks during the October Revolution with his fantastic rudeness. But Lenin turned out to be more brilliant than people thought . . . From 1918, from the day of the villainous attempt on the life of V. I., I again felt myself to be a "Bolshevik". . .

Thus, the total rejection of himself, of everything that he had written with such a measure of sincerity and passion, originated from the "shot of the SR [Fanya] Kaplan at Vladimir Ilyich." This shot, then, turned his soul upside down, opened his eyes, and gave him the opportunity to fully see the correctness of the proletarian leader and his own incorrectness at the same time.

Without even going into the details of the mysterious and dark history of that pistol shot, allow me to pose the question: what so shook the Stormy Petrel that it forced him to betray his ideals and principles (if, in fact, they existed)? As an opponent of violence, he could have—and, probably should have!—condemned this latest terrorist act. Like any normal person he could express sympathy for the victim, no matter how much he differed with him on questions on political issues. But how could this shot, no matter how "villainous" (Gorky's expression), change his views on freedom of the word; on reprisals against dissidents; on the dispersal of the Constituent Assembly; on the murder of prisoners; in general, on any issue, about which he had expressed himself so demonstratively, so clearly, so unambiguously?

Moreover, the villainy of the attack (taking on faith his canonic version) is highly dubious. Even the Bolsheviks recognized that it was a reaction to their policy of forcibly removing all other social forces from the political scene. When a person is in pain, he yells. The shot—even in the Bolshevik version—was the cry of a desperate people that any methods, acceptable for civilized society, to oppose evil, cannot be used. For all those who did not agree with the Bolsheviks, there remained only one possibility: to go submissively under the yoke. And what remained for those who did not agree to go under the yoke?

According to the logic of things, this is precisely how Gorky should have reasoned, had he remained that same Gorky with the amazing force of *Untimely Thoughts*. But for some unfathomable motives, a totally different logic began to guide him. It made an incisive and intelligent person blind and naïve. Not long before he had easily seen an elementary provocation in the January "attempt" on Lenin. This time such a thought did not enter his head. For some reason he was suddenly deprived of his critical intuition.

In the meantime, doubts as to whether it was the SR Kaplan who fired the shot and even if the arrested woman in general was the SR Fanny (Dora) Kaplan (Roidman), and not an individual who had been given this name, were immediately expressed by many people refusing to accept any Bolshevik version as the truth. Decades later, archival materials confirmed the long-standing hypothesis that the attempt on Lenin was nothing other than a Chekist provocation, aimed at unleashing the terror, justify a hunt for the most dangerous competing party to the Bolsheviks and, along the way, resolve their own, internal Kremlin, problems.

The true attempt was completely different, and the individuals suspected—Grigori Semenov and Lidiya Konopleva, employees of the Cheka (NKVD),[*] were known provocateurs and adventurers. The attorney general of the Russian Federation, for the sake of restoring the historical truth, on June 19, 1992, instituted a reenactment "concerning the terrorist act in regard to the Chairman of the Council of People's Commissars V. I. Ulyanov (Lenin) from newly revealed sources." The results of this "reenactment" are not known to anyone, and the "sources"—not juridical but political—have radically changed since then. Historians had already conducted their own "reenactment," proving the indisputable participation of Chekist provocateurs and the probable participation of precisely the individuals mentioned.

Gorky, of course, could not have known about all this, but did he not have even the slightest doubts? The main thing—how one shot—in a setting of

---

[*] All-Russia Extraordinary Commission, created on December 20, 1917, to combat counterrevolution and sabotage; abolished in 1922 and replaced by the NKVD (People's Commissariat of Internal Affairs)—Translator's note.

chaos and madness, when there is shooting every day and blood flows like a river—how could this induce him to completely alter his views, adopt a radically different position, reject his own self and, as a result, not feel—as evidenced by documents, the testimony of contemporaries and his own writings—the slightest pangs of conscience? No embarrassment whatsoever . . .

There is a rather widespread conviction that Maria Andreeva, who co-signed the first telegram of sympathy, played a significant role in this rather incomprehensible about-face. Before confirming or rejecting this version, it is necessary to address the delicate, but extremely important, issue of Gorky's relationships with the women who had occupied such a major place in his life. If we avoid this supposedly deeply personal question, we run the risk of not understanding many pages of his biography and greatly simplifying the explanation for the strange zigzags of his fate.

3.

Smashed to Smithereens

Not one page of this biography—not even those pages about his creative work or his social activity—can be understood without a view of his personal life along the way. Without knowing who exactly stood alongside him, nothing can be understood in Gorky's complex and contradictory life, full of riddles and blank spots.

It is one of those eternal truisms that women have played a great role in the life of any man, and this especially in the life of just about any writer. They played a very special role in Gorky's life, influencing his destiny. His complicated and difficult nature, noticed by everyone who met him, where it is seen as stubborn and stiff, unambiguous and impulsive, combined with defenselessness, and inclined to be influenced by those giving him support, inevitably required a woman's presence—in his daily life, in his heart and in his thoughts.

The entangled history of his romantic liaisons has still not been studied in full nor has it been written about, the real Gorky cannot be understood, without making at least a modest attempt to delve into the secrets of this history. This is not only because it is impossible in general to separate the personal from the nonpersonal in the life of such a person as Gorky, but most of all because the women who entered his life were never satisfied with the silent role of housewife, creating a hearth of peace and comfort for the husband; on the contrary, they had a direct influence on his literature, social status, and the positions he espoused. The abrupt shifts in these positions, which amazed his contemporaries and historians, also depended at times—and to no small degree—upon which woman he was with and the effect she had on the most sensitive strings of his soul.

The personal lives of Soviet celebrities, especially political celebrities (and Gorky belonged to that crowd), were always off-limits to Party historians. Did anyone have the right, even fleetingly, to touch upon Lenin's personal life? Or

Stalin's? Their "personal life" was reduced by biographers to the fact that each had "legal wives." And that was it! By Soviet standards, Gorky belonged to the same group. But his "personal life" in no way fit this Procrustean bed. He was "legally" married only once and did not divorce; other women, universally recognized as his wives and which he even referred to as such, turned out by this logic to remain anonymous. But they cannot be expunged from his biography either. One achieved the status of "friend and life companion," another of "secretary." Still others got nothing at all, as if they did not even exist. But they did, and now the time has come not only to name them (they were named long ago!), but to define the place they occupied in the writer's life and understand how they influenced his fate.

Incidentally, concerning the very first one, it cannot be said that she was actually ever named, except perhaps ephemerally, as an "object" of affection for the young man who had not yet found himself. Only in the 1990s were attempts made to get to the bottom of this "secret love," which Gorky himself did not make any attempt to conceal, and to learn the fate of this forgotten woman, whose hidden trace is present in both Gorky's creative work and inner world.

I am speaking about his first wife. Precisely that—first wife, not just his first love. In the short story "First Love," Gorky refers several times to the heroine, under the code name of "Olga K., as his *wife*. Her full name is Olga Yulievna Kaminskaya, née the baroness Gunther, the daughter of a physician from Nizhny Novgorod, and a nurse by training: Olga Yulievna earned her living as a midwife. She met Gorky, who was five years her junior, after having already been married twice. From her first husband, Foma Kaminsky, she had a daughter, also named Olga. With the second, a former deportee of Polish origin, Boleslav Korsak, she lived in a civil marriage but left him after she had become acquainted with her fellow countryman Aleksei Peshkov, at that time unknown, whom she called "Lyonya." There is not even any trace of the writer Gorky until the first publication of the short story, "Makar Chudra," under this pseudonym a whole three years later.

Their five-year romance is divided into two parts. At first a happy two years under a single roof when Olga helped Peshkov in his literary experiments, editing and rewriting his stories in her free time from work. The second when Gorky attempted to restore their collapsed marriage following his wanderings around Russia. Gorky's sharp pangs of jealousy were the reason for the couple's dissolution: Boleslav Korsak, desperately in love with Olga, showered her with letters and, although she did not reply, she nonetheless dared to read them, even in the presence of "Lyonya."

Many years Olga Kaminskaya's daughter, Olga Ivina-Loshakova, recounted her mother's tale:

> I was cleaning up in the dining room after our evening guests and, while shaking out the tablecloth, I saw an unopened letter from Boleslav. I put down the broom and began to read it. And suddenly I felt that Lyonya was there. I raised myself. He ripped the letter away and tore it to pieces. He grabbed a chair and threw it at my head. It missed. I ran out into the foyer and from there into the garden and the street. The blow was strong. The door frame was bent. . . . If I had not dodged it, Lyonya would have killed me. . . . Three days later . . . I decided to return home. Anuschka [the cook] met me with tears in her eyes: "Olga Yulievna! Save him! He hasn't eaten for three days. He just lies on the couch with his face to the wall and doesn't say anything." I entered Lyonya's room. He didn't turn his head. I got on my knees, put my hands on his shoulders, embraced him around the neck. He didn't say anything. . . . Anuschka brought dinner . . . He came into the dining room but didn't say a word. And for a whole month he was silent. Finally he said, "I asked you many times to have Boleslav Petrovich stop writing you these mournful letters. They prevent me from working. I took your daughter in our marriage; you took my literature as your own child. We don't need anyone else in our family." And he also said, "I want to be a real writer, but because of these stupid letters I can't work. If Boleslav is going to write you, then I'll remain just a newspaper hack, and will be known in public only as your insane lover."

Boleslav, however, continued to write and "Lyonya" decided to get rid of his Olga, setting off first for Samara and then, by way of various cities and villages, to Tiflis. In despair, Olga left for Paris to Boleslav but, as is often the case, nothing came of the attempt to revive the past, and a short while later she too was in Tiflis. By then "Lyonya" had become "Maxim Gorky." The former love was reignited with new vigor. "Lyonya" resolved to forget the past and start a new life. The interrupted marriage was renewed in Nizhny Novgorod, and lasted five years. They separated again, but this time for good.

Almost thirty years later rumors reached Gorky that Olga had died. It was then that he wrote the short story, "First Love," which recalled his version of their happy and unhappy marriage. The story enraptured Romain Rolland and Stefan Zweig, but was a painful surprise to Olga Kaminskaya, who was by no means dead, and read it in the journal *Krasnaia nov'* (Red Virgin Soil). To her it was like reading someone else's story because what had really happened and what had been transmuted into literature greatly differed from one another. Only now did she understand how the person, who had once been such an integral part of her life, viewed her and their relationship.

This offense was compensated, however, by one important detail: he unambiguously called Olga his wife, and official biographers can only agree with Gorky and, recognize the one who supposedly did not exist at all as the *first* and to recognize the one officially named *first* as *second*. It is not a question of arithmetic, but of justification: Gorky is interesting as he was, not as Soviet propaganda made him. Moreover, much of what was destined to repeat itself and develop later was clearly revealed in this first love, putting a stamp on the following stages of his life.

The woman recognized as his first wife, the only one who carried his name, became acquainted with Gorky a year after his final break with Olga Kaminskaya. This happened in Samara, where the woman worked as a proofreader for the local newspaper and where the writer, who had already gained fame, was published.

Yekaterina Volzhina was eight years younger than Gorky. She was born in the Russian part of the Ukraine, in Kharkovshchina, into a family of small gentry and belonged to a rather large circle of educated and well-read girls, touched by human suffering and known in literature as "Russian girl-students" who were obsessed with a desire to do whatever tangible good deeds they could, no matter how trivial.

A year later the "beginning," but already professional writer, and proofreader for the local newspaper, who had turned twenty, married. Katya Volzhina became Yekaterina Peshkova. Under this name she would enter history not just as the wife of a celebrated litterateur. For now she was still only the wife who gave her husband two children: a son Maxim in 1897 and a daughter, four years later, also named Katya, in spite of the superstition of naming a daughter after her mother. The omens came true: the daughter died in childhood, and all the parental love of mother and father were transferred to the son.

The glory of her young husband grew with unprecedented swiftness. He had been promoted into the ranks of Russia's top writers, becoming, at least in popularity, equal to Tolstoy and Chekhov, who were well disposed toward their young colleague. He was only a little more than thirty when he became an academician and was immediately stripped of this title by order of the tsar. This act, on the contrary, added to his fame. The best theater in the country—the Moscow Art Theater—had accepted his play *The Lower Depths* into its repertoire, the premiere of which took place in December 1902. Almost immediately it began its triumphant procession in theaters around the world.

Gorky had become acquainted with the troupe earlier in Yalta where, on a guest tour in 1900, *Uncle Vanya* was performed for its infirm author, Anton Chekhov, whose health did not allow him to travel to Moscow. Gorky was also living there at this time and for the same reasons, having left his wife and two children behind in Nizhny Novgorod. Embarrassed, though not without envy, he noticed how Chekhov was seeing two actresses, Olga Knipper and Maria Andreeva, at the same time, but it was Knipper who ended up as his wife. It could not have been Andreeva, not only because the extremely delicate Chekhov would never have intruded upon someone else's family life: he was not *her* man. But Gorky, it turned out, was. A year later, amid the intoxicating atmosphere of the theater where his play was being rehearsed, the Yalta acquaintance was renewed. Andreeva, the incomparable Irina in Chekhov's *Three Sisters*, was now Natasha in *The Lower Depths*—the appearance of the famous actress in his play who was obviously not indifferent to his attention spun his head even more.

Maria Yurkovskaya (Zhelyabuzhskaya after her marriage) and Andreeva on the stage, was four years older than Yekaterina Peshkova. She was married to a prominent government official named Zhelyabuzhsky, who held the civil rank of Privy Counsellor, which was equal to that of general. Like Peshkova, was the mother of two children, eight-year-old Yekaterina and six-year-old Yuri, who would later become a noted Soviet cameraman. The memoirs of contemporaries and her surviving photographs bear witness to the fact that in both life and on the stage this dark-eyed woman with golden-reddish hair stood out for her somewhat cold beauty, which made her all the more attractive. Finally, unlike her colleagues, especially those who had already gained professional success, she became actively involved in politics, completely unknown to anyone from her circle of friends: the famous actress Maria Andreeva was for the Social Democrats, moreover that wing which would soon call itself Bolshevik.

Gorky's social reputation as "a fighter for the oppressed and unfortunate," the sharp social tone of his play, as well as everything he wrote, the admiration of his lover, an actress—a personality!—which he could not, and did not want to, conceal—all this, apparently, not only brought them together but also allowed her to reveal herself to him in ways that were hidden to others. He saw in this rare combination of all the qualities that were dear to him that ideal of a woman to which he had always aspired. The affair began immediately and quickly evolved. In the very beginning of 1904, a split took place in Gorky's family.

The reverberations of the family drama can be found in a letter from Gorky, dated February 1904, to their mutual friend, Yelena Malinovskaya, distinctly dripping with another feature of his uncompromising character, which people are usually inclined to consider as egotism: decisiveness, inflexibility and readiness to try anything for the sake of a new sensation. As we will see later on, this may have been the only sphere where he rejected a double life—he acted only according to his own desires and without taking anyone else's opinion into account.

> As far as my relationship with Ye[katerina] P[avlovna] is concerned [he wrote Yelena Malinovskaya] this cannot be repaired with words, but would only make it worse. There is nothing I can say about her attitude toward me—it is abnormal now, that is, new for her and for me. She is somewhat late, all I want right now is one thing—solitude, rest. I assume I have the right to this. It's a bit incomprehensible to me as to exactly how I can prevent someone—in this case Ye[katerina P[avlovna]—from living her personal inner life?
>   . . . For me, the matter is clear—one of two people must sacrifice a particle of their ego for the benefit of the other, right? I would be deceiving myself and others if I were to take this upon myself—to willingly sacrifice without causing harm to myself—I can't do it now.

Realizing that the rift had already taken place and was irreconcilable, Peshkova and her two young children left for Berlin. Formally, the reason was for treatment, but in fact it was to save herself from a situation which had become unbearable. Gorky even promised to come after her, but he hardly believed his own words. In the meantime, the affair with Andreeva grew stronger, combining love with business. Andreeva drew Gorky more and more to politics.

The industrialist Savva Morozov was in love not only with the Art Theater, but especially with several of its employees—Maria Andreeva, most of all. Was this love only exalted and platonic? Who knows . . . ? In any event, she did not cease being the object of his affections. Gorky was desperately jealous when, in the fateful days of January 1905 (the shooting of the peaceful procession in Petersburg, known as "Bloody Sunday"), he could not tear himself away to Riga where the troupe was on tour but where Morozov had gone, either to accompany the theater, or Andreeva, or all of them at once. Whatever the case, he was now defined by his generous patronage of the arts, dictated by emotions not reason, let alone sober calculation, which many found astonishing. His new-found love for Andreeva and for Gorky, whom he regarded, against all logic, with deferential admiration, threw the industrialist into the arms of the Bolsheviks.

Through Andreeva and Bolshevik engineer Leonid Krasin, a Morozov employee with consummate professional qualities, the charm of an intellectual and the skills of a cold-blooded murderer and thief for the sake of his beloved Party (one historian glibly called him "head of the terrorist department of the Bolsheviks"), money from the capitalist's hands flowed into Lenin's coffers. Morozov's family was able to get him declared legally insane, thereby depriving him of the opportunity to throw his wealth around. Maria Fyodorovna's and Aleksei Maksimovich's interest in him immediately waned.

According to the accepted version, Savva Morozov, abandoned by everyone and driven into a corner, committed suicide with a bullet to the heart, which he had outlined in pencil beforehand to make sure he did not miss. New research, however, has put this version rather convincingly in doubt, and even rejects it outright. Morozov was probably murdered on May 13, 1905, in Cannes on France's Cote d'Azur, either by that same "intellectual" and charming Krasin, or with his close involvement. A year-and-a-half later, and just as mysteriously, Morozov's nephew, the industrialist Nikolai Schmit, would "commit suicide," leaving behind a huge inheritance and a will, according to the terms of which his younger sister Yelizaveta was to receive one third of his capital after her marriage. The Bolsheviks immediately searched for a suitable groom for the sixteen-year-old bride. "The matter is too important." Krasin wrote Gorky and Andreeva in Lake Placid with cynical frankness. "All sentimentality must be tossed aside." They betrothed a Bolshevik pimp, a certain Taratut, to the underage baroness and coerced her into giving her fortune to the party of the proletariat. This was all done with the complete knowledge of the "Stormy Petrel of the revolution" and consequently with his approval. And why not? After all, he had financed the party of murderers from his own funds.

Gorky sent a wreath to Savva's grave, entwined with a ribbon that bore the inscription "To a friend." Before Morozov died, he had transferred in timely fashion an insurance policy to Andreeva, bringing her 100,000 rubles—a gigantic sum in those years—60,000 of which she handed over to the Party. In essence, this was her joint contribution with Gorky to Lenin's fund. Everything had worked out very smoothly for Gorky: money in his pocket and his rival in the grave! Incidentally, it was not only jealousy that divided them. Although he helped the Bolsheviks (and not even the Bolsheviks at all, but his beloved woman!), Morozov wanted political reforms and a Western-style parliamentary system, and completely opposed to violence and revolution, which he spoke openly about to his great friend: candor had caused their split.

It is difficult to say whether Gorky would have gravitated toward Bolshevism without Maria Fyodorovna's involvement, or whether she, and only she, played a leading role in this. That her role in this was extremely significant is indisputable. Her guiding hand is evident on their trip together to the United States, on Lenin's instructions, to raise money (again money!) for the needs of the Party. Her hand, in turn, was guided by Lenin. In order to keep tabs on both, Lenin also sent his entrusted Bolshevik colleague, Nikolai Burenin, to the U.S., and to whom Gorky wrote the following enigmatic words on a photograph he had presented him: "To my comrade in the hunt for every kind of game."

This trip laid like a heavy stone on the soul. Newspapers raised a stink that Gorky, having abandoned his lawful wife and two children, arrived with an unmarried woman. Was there in this only a manifestation of a slumbering hypocrisy? Or a trivial pursuit for a newspaper scoop? Or still a politically hidden motive—after all, it was not too difficult to find out what the writer's earnings were spent on. No matter; the pair, shunned by a too moral society, were driven from the hotel where they lived, and had to find shelter among friends and admirers.

Besides money, the trip yielded at least two indisputable results: it produced in Gorky a firm hatred for America (it was then that he called New York the city of the Yellow Devil) and brought him even closer to Andreeva. For his sake, and his sake only, she suffered the nastiest insults, always wounding a woman more than a man, and even more so an especially sensitive actress.

Both Gorky and Yekaterina, whom he had abandoned, behaved in a dignified manner during this time. Gorky published the following announcement in New York newspapers: "My wife is my wife, the wife of M. Gorky. Both she and I consider it beneath us to have to explain ourselves on this account. Every one, of course, has the right to speak and think whatever they want about us, and all we have is the right to ignore the gossip." An even stronger slap in the face to the hypocrites was doled out by Yekaterina Peshkova, who sent to the *New York Herald* a telegram: "I am very indignant at this invasion of the personal and private life of an individual and amazed that Americans—citizens of a free country, who have created such widespread political freedom—are not free from prejudices, which have already died out with us in Russia."

The humiliation that Andreeva was exposed to in America on account of Gorky was all the more palpable for her. Because of him, she had left the best theater in the country, at the height of her success and with a realistic future of creative growth under the guidance of Stanislavsky and Nemirovich-Danchenko, and had become for everyone "simply" an unmarried wife, and for others, especially malicious puritans and fanatical protectors of high morals—according to their own interpretation, of course—something even worse: the concubine of a famous exile. For their life together Gorky and Andreeva chose Italy, the island of Capri, which had captivated them not only by its beauty and tranquility, but most of all by its climate, so suitable for Gorky's incurable tuberculosis.

4.

A Nail in the Heart

Gorky, meanwhile, did not interrupt his contacts with Yekaterina Peshkova. Melancholy about what could not be rekindled (it was as if he wanted to keep both, equally dear to him, at his side!), was heightened by the death of little Katya. The son—the only joy—remained with the mother and grew up without him. A letter from Gorky to Peshkova (December 1906) conveys his mental state:

". . . Could you come here, to Capri? . . .

You will have to meet the person who angers you. I know that this, most likely, will be difficult for you and her. And for me. People, even very good ones, continue to be divided into men, women, wives, writers, pallbearers—it is the source of all drama and foolishness.

But you see, I do not want to coerce you and I will not go against your wishes. If I say all this, it is for this reason: I do not live for my own pleasure at all and if I value my energy, I do not wish to expend it on dramatic scenes, and this is because I want and can use it for greater benefit. Is this clear?

I want to see Max.

Bring me a picture of Katya. How beautiful she was! Special somehow. She is like a nail in my heart.

If you agree to come to Capri, telegraph me, and I will rent a villa for you—how many rooms?"

The nail in his heart remained there forever, and it was not just because of the memory of his prematurely deceased daughter. The eight days that Peshkova and Maxim spent on Capri gave Gorky the opportunity to spend time with his young son, to whom he was increasingly drawn. For the first time since the separation, he could examine his "personal life once more." For both women these eight days were genuine torment, especially for Peshkova: she simply could not bear her "rival in love"—and not only, it seems, because the latter had "carried away" her loving husband, but because of the completely different direction she led Gorky.

Yekaterina Peshkova was also an active person—engagée, as it would be said today—who had also dedicated herself to the revolutionary cause. Her political sympathies, however, were for a completely different party: she belonged to the Socialist Revolutionaries. After she had been abandoned, she filled the void with social activity.

It is likely that at that time she joined a Masonic lodge for women. Gorky knew about this, which was something usually kept secret, and called her on more than one occasion—jokingly, not judgmentally—a "Masonka."

A bit later, in 1908, when the greatest police provocateur, the SR Evno Azef, was exposed, and the Central Committee of his party, as a result of this, was disbanded, Yekaterina Peshkova, together with prominent SR figures Ilya Bunakov-Fundaminsk and Andrei Feit, joined the "Provisional Delegation" Party, which replaced the Central Committee. This already speaks to the place which Peshkova occupied in the revolutionary movement and the direction her activity took. The rival who had captured Gorky "in life" was also her rival in thoughts, ideas and actions! Had he not met Andreeva and not pursued her, it is not clear with whom Gorky would have ended up, but it is impossible to separate the personal from the social in this fatal triangle.

Peshkova and Max were forced to emigrate, and again not only on account of the separation with Gorky and not only because sadness and restlessness drove her from her native country. She dashed about between Paris, where she mostly occupied herself with the SR émigrés, and Italy, where she found at least some peace of mind, feeling closer to her husband, for she had not abandoned hope of a reunion. She picked the seaside town of Alassio on the Ligurian Riviera as a place of seclusion for herself and Maxim.

The correspondence continued, as did the personal "contacts" when Gorky came to see his son from time to time. He never failed to give her money and attempted to steer their relationship, albeit from a distance, into a more peaceful channel.

> [. . .] please do not think," (he wrote her in February 1907) "that I can now relate to you with irritation and so on—for what reason?
>
> I have a very good—it seems to me—feeling toward you and in any case it can be called respect.

It is highly unlikely that assurances of respect could provide strong comfort to a loving woman and deserted wife, especially when accompanied by his offensive remark concerning her Party work: "I will not judge your activity, but in general I believe that in our time the activity of an individual—any—does not have great significance."

Nine days later he returned to the same theme, attempting somewhat to soften the inflexibility of his previous letter and show concern. Peshkova had dashed back to Russia, but Gorky did not want her and Max to be far away from him.

> [. . .] Your work? But what can you do with your lack of strength? You'll faint on the streets.
>
> Live here for awhile [in Alassio], try to improve your health, at least a little bit. If you think about work—it's all ahead and there's so much of it, that every slightest bit of valuable energy will be completely exhausted.
>
> [. . .] It seems to me that you're not taking a serious look at the work you're talking about, because this work, first of all, requires the presence of healthy energy and a healthy mind.

The correspondence continued, sometimes with one letter following another, sometimes with long interruptions between them. Its intensity, content and tone were influenced to a great degree, naturally, by the mood of the correspondents, the circumstances of everyday life and their relationships with other people. The letters of those months (winter 1906–spring 1907) testify to an impetuous elevation of suddenly awakened former feelings. Apparently in response to another very emotional letter from Peshkova, Gorky wrote to her in Nice (April 28, according to the Julian calendar used by the Russians, or May 11 by the Gregorian calendar used in Europe):

> My dear, kind friend—
>
> After your letter, there is much I want to say to you but I'm not going to write this. I'll say one thing: with a profound feeling of gratitude, with genuine respect, I kiss your hand. And, probably, for the first in my whole life I experience such a joyful, intimate, and pure feeling.
>
> [. . .] I have a great and unshakeable feeling of respect [again respect!] for you. I know that you are such a close, dear person to me. One of those people, to whom you don't need to speak words, for they even understand your silence. Thanks, dear Katya, thank you, my darling!

The awakened feelings mentioned above were more likely than not *feelings* only on one side; the other was limited by gratitude, which is also a feeling, of course, but a very different one. They both found themselves at another crossroads. The relationship between Gorky and Andreeva was beginning to crack, but not on the surface and not in a dangerous way. At almost the same time, another person had entered Peshkova's life—temporarily, but all the same entered it. By no means or by any parameters could he replace Gorky, but nevertheless someone had appeared, as evidenced by the hints contained in the secret cache of letters from Gorky to Peshkova and correspondence with his son. Without the benefit of irrefutable data, is there a point in trying to guess who exactly it was?

No specific events could have directly influenced the relationship between Gorky and Peshkova, but in such a delicate sphere as love it is enough sometimes for small things to change its intensity, make a man and woman more critical of one another, less tolerable and stable. In this particular relationship it was not trivialities, but, more likely than not, Andreeva's imperious nature, her implacability, obstinacy and demand that she be in charge that irritated the vulnerable and egotistical Gorky. Gorky could hardly have put up with her "leadership" for long.

The poet Vladislav Khodasevich, who would become friends with Gorky years later and become a witness to their relationship at a different moment, maintained that Maria Fyodorovna had spun myths on Capri, casting herself as a victim of love. According to the legend she created and then disseminated among the servants and local merchants, boatmen, and fishermen, she was a Russian countess who was banished from the country by an infuriated tsar for falling in love with a simple worker. I thought that Khodasevich himself, who could barely conceal his antipathy to the false countess, invented this legend. I was wrong.

In the summer of 1970, while visiting Capri, I met a charming seventy-five-year-old woman named Lika Riola, the daughter of a Russian mother and Neapolitan father, who remembered both Gorky and Andreeva well. She persistently referred to Maria Fyodorovna as "the countess Maria" and expressed unfeigned incredulity that "a Russian aristocrat could be so uneducated, even coarse at times." The islanders, insisted Lika, could not stand her and were convinced that she "loved only money and siphoned it out of Gorky, becoming hysterical when he could not fulfill her whims."

If Andreeva "siphoned off" money, it was by no means for herself, but for the Party coffers. And, in general, Lika most likely recalled a not too accurate, even totally inaccurate, exaggerated and one-dimensional image of Maria Andreeva. But it is important that it is precisely this image of the "countess" that impressed itself in the adolescent girl's memory and it is precisely the one she kept of her throughout her life.

Gorky suffered greatly from the separation with his son, understanding how important it is for a boy to have a man in his daily life. He reacted with dignity to the fact that someone had appeared and played with Max, compensating at least somewhat for the absence of the father. This person was

Aleksandr Mikhailovich Kovalenko, a mechanical engineer from the mutinous battleship *Potemkin*. During the uprising he went over to the side of the rebellious sailors and made his way to Switzerland via Romania. Kovalenko taught in a private Russian secondary school that opened in Geneva, founded mostly for the children of emigrants (later removed to Paris). Upon Gorky's advice, Max was also enrolled in that gymnasium. That is how they met.

According to the testimony of another teacher, Nikolai Semashko, the future Soviet people's commissar for public health, only two teachers were Bolsheviks; the others belonged for the most part to the SRs. More likely than not, Kovalenko was one of them, which brought him even closer to Peshkova, who at this time was in the Party leadership.

From Gorky's correspondence with his son, it is evident that Kovalenko was inseparable from Peshkova—mother and son—for several years and lived with them as one family not only in Paris but in Alassio as well. Max unfailingly conveyed greetings to Gorky from Aleksandr Mikhailovich. Gorky, in turn, never forgot to respond in kind. Gorky liked the fact that Kovalenko regarded Max as his own son—they went on long bike journeys together, built models, went to the theater, read books. In one of the letters, in which he told Max to bow before Aleksandr Mikhailovich not simply "in particular" but "still [that is, especially] in particular," Gorky observed, "He is a very good person and, obviously, loves you very much. Value this, my dear friend." Gorky did not send greetings to any other one of his son's teachers (including the Bolshevik Nikolai Semashko, with whom, ostensibly, he had more in common), and no one else appears in Gorky's correspondence. Gorky wrote to Peshkova in Paris:

> I think about you a lot! And it seems I love you this time, my dear girl. I am somewhat jealous. It prevents me from sleeping, but—it's nothing! That's how it should be.
>
> I kiss your hands, be calm, believe me—and, as you said to me, so I repeat to you: my feelings do not oblige you to anything.

The obvious change in intonation of the newly jealous and nostalgic Gorky did not extend, however, to his attitude vis-à-vis the political orientation of his "dear girl": ". . . Sometimes it makes me sick that you do not follow the same path I walk along, and that you are not with those people who right now are the most valuable and talented in Russian life. . . Our paths will converge, I believe this, I know this." "The most valuable and talented"—are these really Lenin's comrades-in-arms? After all, at this very same time Gorky had informed Lenin that he plays on the flute "one or another of his (Lenin's) favorite melodies." Incidentally, the crying contradiction in his estimations of people and his relationships with them is one of Gorky's characteristic traits.

The thought of a possible revival of their marriage was apparently on both their minds, and this hope had become all the more attainable as the rift in the relationship between Gorky and Andreeva grew deeper. Caught in a grip of contradictory feelings, Gorky sensed that, if he did not make a decision, he would lose both. As he admitted to Peshkova in July 1909:

> I got myself entangled. In essence, I do not have the right to speak about what I am thinking with anguish.
> This is not jealousy, but some kind of pity, a good kind of pity that's offensive to you.
> I kiss your hands.

Knowing her husband's indecisive character, Peshkova helped him make a choice. According to Gorky's letter, she had probably told him about the break-up with the man who had temporarily entered her life.

"And so, you severed the knot," Gorky wrote to Peshkova in August 1909. "As for me, not yet, although it is easier for me to do it internally, but externally it's more difficult."

As far as he was concerned, everything was already clear, but he could not transform this "internal" clarity into "external" action by himself: only Andreeva, who could understand with that same clarity and draw from it a practical conclusion, had no intention whatsoever of reaching *this* conclusion, even though she understood everything. In a hitherto unpublished letter to Peshkova (perhaps at the wish of descendants), Andreeva attempted to explain herself to her. Nothing came of it. As Gorky wrote in December 1909 to Peshkova in Paris:

> I am somewhat grieved to understand why you did not answer M. F.'s letter? It seems that you women are more unfair to each other than we men are to you.

He hastened to comfort her in the next letter:

> Personal matters are better, more definite. You will become convinced of this in spring. I'm not going to write. It is horribly difficult for me to read in your letters about how your moods fluctuate "from joy to despair." . . . It's also difficult for me, and I probably have much greater reasons for this than you.

Gorky and Peshkova not only wrote back and forth to each other, but even met from time to time: every now and then Gorky traveled to Paris and Alassio to see his son. Each new meeting did not cancel their hopes but rekindled them. The connecting link was the son—his father's love for him knew no bounds. Often without his mother and accompanied by some adult, the boy traveled to Capri—the mother did not prevent this, but any time the son encountered Maria Fyodorovna it was a blow to her pride and heart. Incidentally, it was at Capri that the twelve-year-old Max became acquainted with Lenin: Gorky summoned him to meet the person, who so skillfully "played the flute." This meeting would have a positive outcome for Max following "the great October Revolution."

The torturous uncertainty continued for two years, and there was no hope in sight. Joy truly was replaced by despair, but it had nothing to do with the "fluctuation" in her moods: how else should a woman react to such wishy-washiness on the part of the person she loved?

Andreeva had not surrendered her position. She still hoped to tie Gorky to herself. But a dramatic event put an end to this as well. Andreeva admitted to Vera Bunina, wife of Ivan Bunin, at the time still considered Gorky's friend (the Bunins were in Capri in November 1911), who was visiting Gorky, along with her husband, a little more than a year later that she had undergone "a small operation," which she endured "bravely and with great sadness—the hope of having a child from A[leksei] M[aksimovich], who was extremely agitated, had failed. The operation took place at home."

There is not the slightest doubt that Aleksei Maksimovich was extremely agitated. But to Peshkova he wrote (July 1910):

> My personal affairs are becoming a little bit clearer, and the ties are coming undone—in this respect everything is going pretty well.

No, the ties were not coming undone—the agony for all three kept dragging on. There was nowhere for Andreeva to go, no one to return to. Her artistic career had collapsed, and the directors of the Art Theater had no intention of including Andreeva in their troupe again, most likely because she had violated the basic principle on which the relationships in this theater were built: in creating it, Stanislavsky and Nemirovich-Danchenko had agreed that the stage occupies the main place in an actor's life and that everything needs to be subordinate to the interests of the theater, including one's personal life. Not for the sake of Andreeva, not even for Gorky's sake, did they wish to retreat from that principle. They were equally troubled by Andreeva's too noticeable activity in the political struggle. The social sympathies of the theater were obvious, but strictly alien to politics.

Thus, the possibility of Andreeva's return to Russia was extremely doubtful, for she would certainly have faced trial for her past revolutionary activities. Remain in Europe? What could she do, after having ceased being Gorky's wife? Andreeva's "social activity" had always led to supplying the Party with money. Savva Morozov was no longer among the living, and without

Gorky, even without his direct involvement in fundraising but who supported it by his mere presence alone, there was nothing she could do.

Nevertheless, the split was perfectly obvious and inevitable—Gorky had not only placed hope in Peshkova, but felt that her return was close at hand. From day to day he "fed" her with promises to come to her and their son; he was in a hurry to get going, while Andreeva continued to lead a life on Capri that both had already tired of. Gorky waited, in the hope that the knot would come undone on its own. He wrote on May 5 (18), 1911, to Peshkova in Paris:

> I beseech you, do not call, do not rush me. . . . I am not in a position now to say when I'll come . . . At the present time I do not possess the energy to take a decisive step, but I would ask you to let me experience this moment on my own.
>
> I do not personally feel a special need for anyone, but would like one thing: peace in which to work, and for this peace I am prepared to pay any price.
>
> I am very much alone. I don't say this as a complaint, but with amazement—very much alone!
>
> . . . I am very tired, overwrought and I'm desperately fed up with it all.

In another of his letters (from February 12, 1912, by the European calendar), "My personal life is revolting. You know, I never say anything about this and if I've begun to speak of it now, then it means it is really bad." But he had already begun to speak of it and in practically the same words—there was nothing new in all this. Almost a whole year had elapsed between the two letters, but they convey the sense of having been written only within weeks of one another. This is an unthinkably long period of torturous vagueness for this love "triangle," but all the more so for Gorky with his especially vulnerable nervous system. And there is hardly any point in mentioning that both women suffered.

There was a moment (May 1912) when Gorky himself was ready to abandon everything on Capri and go to Peshkova and Max. First to Paris, where his son was in school, and then to Alassio, when vacation began. These plans were so definitive, in fact, that he communicated the date of his arrival. As Max, who was just about to turn fifteen, replied to this news:

> My dear beloved, I still cannot gather myself from your letter, and there is nothing I can say about how elated I was when I learned that you will soon come.
>
> I already feel that you are getting nearer to us and that we will soon meet. Then we will both be happy.
>
> Well, farewell until then, my dear, I kiss and embrace you, I'm waiting.

The signature at the end was "Your expectant son Max."

Gorky came to Alassio and spent a whole month there, letting Andreeva know, rather eloquently though not directly, that the time for final decisions had already come. But, evidently, the strength to take the final step was not there. The waiting continued.

Everything was already clear to everyone, the words had been said and the decision taken—it was hardest of all for Andreeva, for not only did she have to "leave," but she had to leave for somewhere. She had just turned forty—and for such a vibrant, unusual woman of her disposition it was not so easy to start life over again, let alone after a "romance" with the world famous Maxim Gorky.

Nevertheless, she apparently did not abandon the hope of returning to the theater—her correspondence with an actor at the Art Theater, Nikolai Rumyantsev, confirms this: she was closer to him and his wife than to anyone else. Their trip to Italy gave her not only the moral, but also the formal possibility, to leave Capri while saving face: "formal" because, with Rumyantsev's participation, negotiations were held about the possible staging of Gorky's new play, *The Lycos*, at the Art Theater. Thus, to outsiders, her departure to meet up with the Rumyantsevs did not appear as a break-up. Gorky immediately reported to Alassio:

> M[aria] F[yodorovna] has departed.* We parted amicably. She took all her things with her and she will no longer return here.
>
> Do I need to come to you? Would it not be better for you to move yourselves here? Think about this. It doesn't seem to me that this would be very inconvenient for you: I live alone . . . there are few Russians here, they have all left. . . .
>
> Perhaps you will find it convenient to send Max here on his own for now, and you wait a bit? That is, of course, if you find it inconvenient to come now.

Yekaterina Pavlovna quickly moved to Capri, along with her mother and Max, only nine days after Andreeva left and after having waited at least five years for that moment. Doctor Ivan Manukhin, who knew Gorky well and had treated him, was convinced that Gorky had tried to glue the family back together exclusively for the sake of the son. "He loved him," Manukhin later wrote, "to the point of torture and sacrifice, but by nature he was not capable of torture and sacrifice, and family life *for the sake of the son*† did not flourish under the Italian sky." It was not possible to glue together what had been broken to pieces. The arrival on Capri of his friend and advisor on publishing matters, Aleksandr Tikhonov, along with his wife, slowed the inevitable development of events, but not for long.

* November 11, 1912.
† Author's emphasis.

Several months later, having lost everything, Gorky was forced to flee his home on Capri and try to find shelter during his wanderings. Andreeva again became his pillar—they met but did not get back together. The summer of 1913 was a period that was probably the most torturous for all three. And, of course, for a fourth, Max, who was already grown up and who understood everything.

At first, under the pretext of treatment, Gorky ran to Peshkova several times in nearby Naples, then, after exchanging letters with Andreeva, he joined her, and the four of them—with the Rumyantsevs—left on a trip to visit the Italian cities of Bologna, Rimini, Padua, Venice, Verona, Rome, back to Naples and so on. He was working on the play *The Zykovs*—one can hardly imagine how the ailing Gorky was able to write amid the July heat while traveling from one city to another, in hotel rooms, far from the conditions he was accustomed to.

The correspondence with Peshkova, who had remained in Capri, continued, but it was dry, businesslike and devoid of any emotion whatsoever. He asked that her return letters be sent to various hotels along his itinerary, but that they should be addressed not to him but to Rumyantsev. Was he simply protecting himself from curious eyes? Or was there some other hidden motive?

The one and only letter to his son during this period (most likely from Naples, undated) also stands out not simply because of its dry matter-of-factness—it does not resemble any other letter to Max during all the years of their correspondence—but because it contains none of his usual paternal feelings, not even "greetings to mama," which figured in every one of his letters.

> Dear Max!
> Please bring me some clean paper from notebook 10. Take it from my table, in the right-hand corner, but don't make a mistake, don't take stationery, but take this kind on which I'm writing, only big—writing—sheets.
> And please do not bend it or roll it up in a tube, but wrap it in newspaper and cardboard so that it does not get crumpled.
> It's a beautiful day here today, too bad you're not here.
> Until we meet.
>   A.

Gorky would return to Capri, Peshkova and their son to Alassio. Joyous news from Russia put an end to these labored geographical reparations: political amnesty was announced on the occasion of the three hundredth anniversary of the Romanov dynasty—it was rather scanty and very limited, but still . . . On the basis of this amnesty, the St. Petersburg court dropped the case against

Gorky for the publication of forbidden writings and participation in the events of 1905. There were no longer any obstacles to his return. The Russian consulate general in Naples issued Gorky an entry visa for Russia.

Gorky exchanged letters with Andreeva, who at the time was in Germany, and they met in Berlin to return to Russia together. According to the European calendar, the new year of 1914 had already begun, but by the Russian orthodox calendar the new celebrations had not yet taken place. They finally returned to St. Petersburg on December 31, and immediately separated: Gorky left for the dacha of one of Andreeva's relatives, protecting himself not so much from being tailed by the police (where could one get away from them?) as from annoying devotees and even more annoying reporters. Here, in this place of dachas in Mustamyaki, Finland, which, even though it was part of the Russian empire, had its own legal status, he waited for his internal passport to be "corrected" back home—Nizhny Novgorod—allowing him to receive all the rights of an inhabitant of the "motherland." Soon after, Gorky left for the suburbs of Moscow, staying at the estate of Ivan Sytin, one of Russia's biggest publishers.

Peshkova and Max, already back from Italy, were living in Moscow. Although Gorky settled down nearby (an hour ride by train) and even came to Moscow on more than one occasion, staying there for several days and taking care not only of business, but also visiting theaters, museums, exhibitions, and circus performances (always with Andreeva), there was no time to see Peshkova, or even their son. Apparently, the wound from the second separation was still fresh, making a meeting painful for all three. The letters of the father to the son, who lived nearby and was ready at a moment's notice to meet him halfway, reflect Gorky's uncertainty and depression. He asked Max in a letter dated January 22 (February 4), 1914.

> Are you somehow getting used to Russia? I am getting used to it poorly—everything is boring, there's no sun, the people are all unhappy, they rarely smile, laugh even less, move lazily, unwillingly. Birches grow everywhere in the fields. There are a lot of drunkards all around. And, in general, the difference is very sharp—I don't know how it seems to you—do you see it?

Depression from contemplation of the surrounding reality was heightened by a feeling of sudden and totally unaccustomed isolation. How he would extricate himself from this solitude will be mentioned later. One thing, though, was indisputable: there was no returning to the past. Andreeva, who finally understood that the Art Theater no longer wanted her, decided to return to her profession anyway: she simply had no other. She joined Nezlobin's amateur theater, then signed a contract with the troupe, well-known at the time, of the impresario Sinelnikov, and went with it on tour to Kiev. Peshkova and Max left again for Alassio. Gorky moved to St. Petersburg, which would soon cast off its German-sounding name and become Petrograd, where Maria Fyodorovna would look for a separate apartment for him on Kronverks Prospekt. Now he would divide his time between the capital and solitude at the dacha, receiving almost no one and finally enjoying physical and mental peace and quiet.

A sharp turn of events took place in the life of the two women, who had both desperately thrown themselves at Gorky and had both, in essence, lost.

Because of the First World War, Peshkova and Max managed, with extremely great difficulty, to return home via Constantinople and Odessa.

Some time later another person would enter the life of this much-suffering woman, who had also reached the age of forty: her comrade from the SR Party, Mikhail Nikolaev, who also occupied a prominent position. He was six years younger than Yekaterina Pavlovna and eyed her with unconcealed admiration. It would have been strange for a woman in her position not to have reacted favorably to such attention, but this, apparently, did not come easily to her. The lines from Gorky's letter in reply to her confused news reflected her turmoil: "What's wrong with you—matters of the heart are not in order? Or else I misunderstood your phrase about your personal life?" He understood correctly—in the sense that she was at a crossroads. Gorky really wanted her to "get settled" as it would remove his guilt complex.

Andreeva too—probably a bit later (no one knows the exact date, but most likely after the events of October)—had a "second breath." In Petrograd she became acquainted with a young lawyer, Pyotr Kriuchkov. Short, ruddy-cheeked and with a penchant toward putting on weight, he faded completely next to Andreeva's strength and unspent energy. He was seventeen years her junior, but had already married and divorced, leaving behind a son, and for her it was like repeating the fate of the person from whom she had just separated. Although Kriuchkov was listed as an assistant barrister, he did not take up legal practice but served in the Petersburg city council. Entrepreneurial, businesslike and with the manners of a clerk, he looked imposing, possibly, because of his passion for fine and fashionable clothes.

Gorky and Andreeva again "reunited," settled under one roof in the home on Kronverks Prospekt, where Andreeva moved with her children. The postal connection between Gorky and Peshkova was also restored. The son remained the bone of contention. Gorky wrote from Petrograd to Peshkova in Moscow, with marked politeness and in an atypical tone, on November 18 (December 1), 1915:

... I am going to ask you, to let Max come here for the holidays, for Christmas, and, if you do not have anything against it, to allow him to stay with me. M. F., as you know, is in Moscow and will be extremely busy for the holidays . . . M. F. only sees her children at breakfast and lunch. She is sufficiently well-bred to let anything bad happen.

Max had already turned eighteen and it was too late and hopeless to protect him from "bad influences." Moreover, he couldn't stand Maria Fyodorovna, and nothing could change his relationship to this rival. But the painful relationships of people, tormented by many years of nervous strain, could hardly be expected to follow cold logic and common sense.

Life, however, took its own course. Although Andreeva was in no hurry to advertise her new relationship, for Gorky, at least, it was no secret. Just as with Peshkova, it should not have troubled him—on the other hand, it should bring him joy. He succeeded in maintaining friendly relations with both—this brought into their relationship, finally, the certainty which had eluded them for so long, while removing the pain and anguish. Only one thing remained unchanged: the staunch enmity, if not hatred, of Peshkova for Andreeva and Andreeva's condescending magnanimity toward Peshkova. These two women would never become close and they would never find a common language.

5.

Petty Intrigues

Gorky could not live alone—he was simply not used to it—and there were no women around who might have replaced Andreeva. Brief attachments and attractions could not be better than what is commonly called domestic life. Gorky and Andreeva continued to live together in the apartment on Kronverks Prospekt—not even as old friends, who need each other's support, but simply as people accustomed to a life together. But she no longer had any influence over him. His *Untimely Thoughts*, in direct contradiction with Andreeva's thoughts, make this perfectly clear: she remained an orthodox Communist and kept her ties to Lenin and the Leninists, but there was nothing she could do to prevent Gorky from continuing his pamphleteering and social activities. Their life together at the time is convincing proof that ideological and political differences are no hindrance to a temporary union, as long as both parties are interested in maintaining it, even if for different reasons. If Lenin had the slightest hope, with Andreeva's help, of making Gorky "see the light," then he definitely would not have passed up the chance. But Lenin was a realist and extremely well informed of the nature of the amicable relationship on Kronverks.

Even more mysterious is what united Gorky and Andreeva in that truly historical telegram of condolence and caused Gorky to change, to everyone's surprise, his political orientation. To consider the Bolshevik version of the shot as the reason, even if he accepted it without any hesitation, is not possible. Wasn't this attempt the same life-saving occasion, which allowed Gorky to carry out his "political about-face," which he had decided upon long ago and was only waiting for the right moment? For the time being, he had been sharing the belief of many people in his circle that the end to the madness of Bolshevism would come very soon, almost any day now, and that there would be a return to the freedom which had suddenly washed over Russia in February 1917. But with each new day this conviction became less and less certain, and hopes were shattered in the face of harsh reality. Coldly pragmatic by his very nature, Gorky could not come to grips with what had already become evident to everyone else: against every rationale, Bolshevik power had stood its ground, it was going to be around for a long time, and therefore one had to adapt to it if one wanted to avoid the lamentable fate of the whiners and grudge-bearers.

Gorky was not prepared for such a destiny, but his former relationship with Lenin and his understanding of how much the latter needed him, gave him reason to assume that, even after *Untimely Thoughts*, their cooperation remained possible. For Lenin, there was no such thing as resentment: whatever serves the "cause of the proletariat" (more to the point, "my cause") is moral, he'd said more than once. To embrace the person who had only yesterday insulted him, but was now ready to be useful, was basic political expediency.

Andreeva could in this sense turn out to be a valuable informant and advisor: she could nudge Gorky to take that difficult step and guarantee that his offer would not be rejected. And for an even stronger guarantee, she would affix her own signature on a joint telegram, thereby showing their political connection, not their matrimonial agreement (who cared about their marriage in that context?!).

Not only did Andreeva contribute to Gorky's transformation, but Max also played a role in his sudden and decisive about-face. Without asking anyone, nor having informed anyone, Max had joined the Bolshevik Party in the summer of 1917; during the days of the October Revolution he participated on the side of the Bolsheviks in the battles for the Kremlin, and later enjoyed a very close relationship with Lenin. Since he was already twenty, he could make decisions on his own and take responsibility for his own actions. When the government relocated to Moscow, Max received a pass for unrestricted entry to the Kremlin and soon after became an aide to his commandant. Because the leader was usually too busy to see him, Max wrote to Lenin now and then, allowing us to rely upon documents instead of someone's biased reminiscences. There is a letter, for example, dated at the end of June 1918 (already June!) from Max to Lenin, containing such remarkable lines as: "Papa is beginning to get better—he's turning 'leftist'. Yesterday he even got into a heated argument with our SRs, who fled in shame after 10 min[utes]." "Our" is apparently a reference to people close to the mother, who continued not so much to cooperate as to be on friendly terms with likeminded individuals.

It was as if Max had ignored his father's journalistic fury, directed against those individuals with whom and for whom he now worked, and was now patiently waiting for Gorky's rage to run its course and cool off. For the time being he simply went about "his business": he worked for *Pravda*, the opposite of *Novaya Zhizn'*, traveled to Siberia to requisition bread from the peasants and "condensed the bourgeois," that is, participated in the forced expropriation of superfluous rooms—from the proletariat's point of view—from class enemies, transforming normal apartments into monstrous Soviet communal flats for the masses rushing into the capital from the provinces. He later joined the VChK ("Cheka"), the All-Russian Extraordinary Commission against Counterrevolution and Espionage, the very mention of which instilled immeasurable fear into millions of people. Vladislav Khodasevich supposed that his inclination to "Pinkertonism" had led him to the Lubyanka. Lenin deftly took advantage of this, advising the lad to go work for comrade Dzerzhinsky.

In 1918 Max was not yet working for Dzerzhinsky, but even so the paths of father and son swiftly veered off in different directions. It could not continue that way for long: a little bit more and the momentum would irrevocably place Gorky with the "enemies." The bullet that hit the leader turned out to be very propitious. Lenin accepted Gorky's proffered hand and (in a literal and figurative sense) clasped it with his own—still wounded and not responding well to physiological commands but still tightly gripping the state's rudder.

The telegram, as stated previously, had been sent on August 31. By September 1, the "temporarily unemployed" Andreeva became head of the theatrical department of the Petrograd Council, under the omnipotent Zinoviev, and by September 20 she had already been promoted. Andreeva's new position was officially called Commissar of Theaters and Performances of the Commissariat for the People's Enlightenment of the Union of Working Communes of the Northern Province. Translated from lofty revolutionary language to normal speech, this meant that Andreeva had become the main administrator of all theatrical organizations of the huge Petrograd region, encompassing five provinces to the north, south, and east of the former capital. Two automobiles were placed at her disposal, which in those days said much more to the population about the scope of her power than any official title, no matter how bombastic it sounded. It was obvious that both appointments hadn't come about because of Zinoviev's good will—he could not stand either Gorky or Andreeva—but on Lenin's personal instructions.

Gorky did not remain unemployed either. His proposal to create a new publishing house, Vsemirnaya Literatura (World Literature), was immediately supported. Gorky headed up this venture himself and the Soviet government undertook to finance it generously. He also led various commissions to provide money, food, and everyday assistance to workers in science and culture. His three-year activity, gigantic in force and sweep, encompassing the educational, publishing, organizational and social spheres, has been described and praised numerous times. The Committee of Workers of Culture, recently unsuccessful, was now in his own hands! It was not from vanity but from justification that he said, jokingly, "I'm no longer a person, but an institution." Gradually he became like a "social" people's commissar of culture or a middleman between the authorities and culture, equally recognized, in his own mind, by both sides.

So that nobody would think that the hand extended to the wounded Lenin was anything more than an emotional gesture or—even worse—a tribute to the current state of affairs, Gorky made a sensational announcement in *Pravda* on October 16, 1918, conclusively explaining his "new course" and delivering skeptics from the slightest illusions. Nothing reveals with such vividness the tragedy that suddenly overtook the author of *Untimely Thoughts* as these words: "If they had closed *Novaya Zhizn'* a year and a half earlier, it would have been better for both me and the revolution."

He said this in the days when the Red Terror raged throughout Russia, prisoners were publicly executed in parks and squares, and the overall number of those shot, simply for being "bourgeois" and without even fictitious accusations, affected thousands of people, according to official Soviet data. Moreover, it was said in that same newspaper, where, as we recall, by Gorky's own assertion, "little savages were setting the proletariat against the intelligentsia." As we shall see later on, Gorky would soon realize how hasty his obsequious and shameful declaration was: Lenin willingly took advantage of the "proletarian writer's" flexible conscience, but did not modify his attitude toward him.

Gorky's statement cannot be attributed to anyone's influence. Some kind of incredible mental turnabout had taken place in the writer, who always valued freedom of the word above all else and, in the eyes of the whole world, had only just fought so furiously for its ideals, to have suddenly resolved to sing publicly the praises of the noose tightened around the neck of the independent press by the Bolsheviks. Now he could make all the announcements he wanted, but no one could take him seriously any more, neither the Bolsheviks nor their enemies. Was there the slightest guarantee that Gorky, who had suddenly changed course, would not begin to say, with equal passion, the exact opposite of what he had said before, or publicly recant his former "mistake"?

Gorky's all-encompassing three-year, one-man cultural crusade has been written about in detail many times, and there is no need to repeat what has been known for a long time or to comment upon it. Volumes of reminiscences are devoted to his work in creating a publishing house for only the best that world culture had to offer; for assembling the writers and assisting those in need; for rescuing scholars who had fallen on hard times and saving the most important branches of science enfeebled from a lack of funds; to intercede on behalf of the humiliated, the despairing, and the persecuted. But the question that I was asked in Paris in 1968 by the writer Boris Zaitsev, who knew Gorky well and was part of the same literary circle as Gorky at the end of the nineteenth and beginning of the twentieth centuries, comes to mind: if such activity deserves a positive reaction, then why did so many of the best people indignantly condemn it, while others, who did not find within themselves the strength to refuse Gorky's help, detested themselves and could not forgive themselves their cowardice right up until their deaths? Without waiting for a reply, Zaitsev answered the question himself. The answer is important, and new information which we now have allows us to get closer to it, but still it does not make everything completely clear.

For that circle of intellectuals, whom Gorky was trying so energetically to help, there were two circumstances that were apparently especially odious: Gorky's flirtation with the authorities, from whom it was nauseating to receive any handouts, and Gorky's self-appointed role as savior. What in Gorky's eyes, and moreover in the eyes of Soviet historians, looked to be a life-jacket thrown out to drowning victims, was perceived by those being rescued as charity from a wealthy hand in exchange for loyalty, or at least in expectation of it. This was charity with factored-in reciprocal *gratitude*.

Whether this is in fact the case is insignificant. What is important is that this was the attitude of those people for whom the alms were intended. Their feelings and principles were not taken into account; it was believed that the most important thing for them was to survive, and the price to pay was unimportant. But an intelligentsia without dignity, prepared to belittle itself for the sake of life's most basic needs, is not an intelligentsia at all, yet it was precisely that intelligentsia that Gorky showered with his good deeds. How could he not have foreseen that his help would be rejected by some and accepted by others (who were, evidently, the majority), but squeamishly?

Gorky failed to take into account the most important factor on the psychological level. He could not have. And he did not want to! To the writers, artists, academicians and professors receiving Gorky's rations (flour, potatoes, sheepskin coats, boots, and so on), the hand generously distributing the goods belonged to someone who did not, under any circumstances whatsoever, fit the role of a wealthy patron of the arts. Only yesterday he was simply a *writer*, like all of them, but today he had suddenly risen above everyone as an omnipotent savior. To the multitude of those he saved, he was simply an impostor who had snuggled up to Soviet power, one of those who had overthrown the *legal* authority and proclaimed himself *the* authority. Dmitri Merezhkovsky wrote sarcastically at the end of 1920 from Paris, where he had emigrated:

> Gorky is allegedly saving Russian culture from Bolshevik barbarism. At one time I even thought the same way, and I too was deceived . . . But when I experienced

what Gorky's "salvation" means, I fled Russia. I would rather be caught and shot than be saved like that.

. . . At what price does Gorky "save"? At the price of *becoming demeaned*. O, not base and external, but inner, subtle, almost undetectable. Maybe he is unconscious himself of how he demeans people. He does this with "innocence." . . . In order to remain alive, I had to accept such handouts from other Bolsheviks, but I didn't want them from Gorky.

He surrounded himself with a courtly retinue of toadies and lickspittles; he doesn't even push them away, just drops them—people then fall into a black hole of hunger and cold. He knows that you can do anything you want to someone who is freezing and hungry with a piece of bread or a bundle of wood, and he does it.

Lenin is an autocrat, Gorky is the high priest. Lenin holds power over bodies, Gorky over souls.

Gorky is our "benefactor." But I am not alone, and all Russian writers, artists and scientists, when the noose is removed from their necks, will say in unison with me: may Gorky's good deeds be damned! . . . Gorky is not better, but worse than all the Bolsheviks, worse than Lenin and Trotsky. They kill bodies, but he kills souls.

It should be remembered, of course, that this pamphlet, stunning in its unrestrained venom, was written by someone who had never concealed his antipathy toward Gorky. But still the measure of his animosity is inconsistent with "what was done": Gorky, even if awkwardly, even if he did not fully grasp the subtleties of the intellectual soul, nevertheless did provide whatever assistance he could and did not starve or freeze his colleagues who had fallen on hard times. He made use of his connections, his possibilities and his ability to influence the new rulers, knowing how much they needed him—but not to harm people, but to do good! Is the naked hatred of Merezhkovsky, and of many others like it, though not as eloquent, justifiable?

Kornei Chukovsky's diary finally deserved glasnost several decades later. Unlike Merezhkovsky, he was truly close to Gorky, wrote enthusiastic articles about him and worked with him in various publishing houses and literary associations. As if apologizing to himself for his weakness, Chukovsky wrote in his diary that he was forced to beg Gorky to increase his rations; he was supporting a family of seven that had already forgotten the taste of a potato, wore socks without holes and shoes without soles.

It was not Gorky's fault, obviously, that the country had descended to such a deplorable state. However, Gorky clearly did not understand that charity—any kind in general, but moreover *this kind*—which the brilliant Russian intellectuals, yesterday his comrades, had to ask *him* for—was demeaning to them. On the contrary, he was proud and reveled in the opportunity to not be just a simple benefactor but a savior in the full sense of the word. This was too patently evident to others, but Gorky himself did not see it at all—he did not want to and, probably, could not see it. The chasm dividing him from the intellectuals he rescued grew even wider. The reaction to their belittlement increased. Some expressed it aloud; others, saving their own lives and the lives of their loved ones, kept it to themselves, only letting the anger build up without an outlet.

In summing up how much good Gorky did in those years and how the "bourgeois intellectuals" repaid him with ingratitude, it is simply impossible either to understand or explain that torturous duel between the two. If we consider abstract "proofs," then Gorky was correct and his critics were all wrong. The conflict, however, lay on the moral and psychological levels, where there is no right and wrong. If moral suffering has a price or if, in a century of grandiose social catastrophes, it has none at all is the issue. Is a hungry, cold person, pushed to the edge of the cliff, still able to retain his conscience and dignity, or do these categories exist only for those who are sated and have everything?

Gorky was not an intellectual, but he had joined a circle of intellectuals. He genuinely assumed, in accordance with the historical traditions of that milieu to which he belonged by birth, that the main thing was to be well fed, clothed and shoed, and that everything else would follow. The rescuer and the rescued did not hear each other; they spoke different languages and possessed completely different emotional structures. The helpless and impoverished intellectuals were dependent upon the parvenu who had obtained power—this alone carried with it an inevitable and dramatic conflict.

These issues do not seem to have bothered Gorky. He was guided by a completely different principle: he did what he considered necessary, convinced that he was acting correctly and bringing huge benefits to Russia. Without a doubt, no one else could do this under the prevailing circumstances. No one among the writers or scientists, who had begun cooperating with the Soviet authorities, possessed such fame and such authority. And, of course, no one had such access—even if somewhat illusory—to the leader himself. No one other than Gorky would have been given so many rights. No one "under" someone else would have been given so much money.

Not just careerists or the "crowd of worthless and self-interested flatterers," as Merezhkovsky's no-less-embittered wife, the poetess and essayist Zinaida Gippius, observed in her *Petersburg Diary*, cooperated with him. In addition to many writers, the greatest figures of Russian science, with high moral authority and irreproachable reputations were part of his entourage. Suffice it to say that food rations were distributed by Gorky to scientists in Petrograd and to world renowned academicians and professors: the geologist Aleksandr Fersman, the Indologist Sergei Oldenburg, the anatomist Vladimir

Tonkov, the pedagogue Albert Pinkevich, and others. This muddled the situation even further, confirming Gorky in the correctness of his actions and giving him the impetus to continue his cultural missionary work.

But he drew even greater energy from the resistance, which he encountered everywhere in the power structures. Not support, but resistance. This dramatic and paradoxical conflict consisted in the fact that neither one nor the other trusted Gorky: it was not only the intellectuals, whom he defended and saved, who looked upon him askance and saw in him someone who was meddling where he did not belong and expanding rights that did not belong to him without prior arrangement. The difference was that the reaction of the intellectuals was emotional and moral, while the authorities remained pragmatic: knowing Gorky's impulsiveness and unpredictability, Lenin wanted to extract the maximum benefit from him, while keeping him on a short leash, not giving him too much freedom and not having the Bolsheviks pay more than necessary for his services.

There was another circumstance—purely geographical, even technical—that had great bearing on his relationship with the authorities and on his entire social activity. Gorky lived in Petrograd, where the Academy of Sciences and all the scientific institutes (meaning the scientists themselves) were located. The basic circle of writers, artists, and musicians, on whom Gorky's care was lavished, also lived in Petrograd, the former capital, while the Party and the official apparatus were in Moscow. Little can be accomplished through letters and phone calls, especially with the technology of the time. Moreover, only personal connections and direct contacts could lead to some kind of concrete results within the quickly growing Bolshevik bureaucracy. That was the problem—Gorky had to travel to Moscow, sometimes on the most trivial matters.

No matter how these endless trips are portrayed, he found them demeaning. He went cap in hand, to ask, implore, cajole, and encountered an outwardly polite but, in essence, disparaging response. Andreeva, who was much closer to Lenin than Gorky, often called the Kremlin in advance of the next trip and obtained Lenin's agreement to be the first one, or maybe the only one, to receive the Petrograd "messenger." A car from the Kremlin was sent to the train station to meet him, and the dear guest was led into the foyer where Lenin came out to greet him with a kind and welcoming smile. For someone with a different sense of self, this would perhaps be flattering, but it drove Gorky insane. It was not the meetings in and of themselves that made him mad, but this forced method of conversation which he accepted with gritted teeth. He could barely endure his wounded pride, and did not allow anyone else to experience his feelings, not toward Lenin but to himself.

In Petrograd, real power was concentrated in the hands of Grigori Zinoviev, to whom Lenin, his close friend (if someone can be called Lenin's friend), had given unlimited authority. Zinoviev held Gorky in the greatest contempt, considering him to be a protector of the enemies of Soviet power and Gorky himself a covert enemy. Pretending ostentatious benevolence, he played dirty tricks whenever and wherever he could. As far as feelings were concerned, Gorky repaid Zinoviev in kind, but was unable to stop him in any way—on the contrary, he was forced to go to him, also hat in hand, to inquire about services that were within his area of responsibility and, even worse, to make sure that Zinoviev punctiliously carried out Moscow's orders. But Zinoviev failed to carry them out; instead, he procrastinated and came up with various reasons for delays, demonstrating what subsequently became so developed in the Soviet Union, the strength of local power over central authority.

Zinoviev's conflict with Gorky was explained not just by ideological and political motives, which only camouflaged the deepest personal animosities. It turned out that the interests of Gorky and Andreeva collided with the interests of the Zinoviev clan.

Zinoviev's wife, Zlata Lilina (Bernstein), had emigrated with Lenin and Krupskaya, as secretary of the Central Committee of the Bolshevist RSDRP* since 1908. In that same sealed train car, along with the Ulyanovs and the Lenins, the Zinovievs returned to Russia through Switzerland. This close relationship, combined with specific character traits, emboldened the Zinovievs with even greater self-confidence, which they displayed with particular zeal in regard to Gorky and enraging him in the process.

The drama of the situation became sharper after Zinoviev appointed Lilina to be head of the provincial department of people's education. In accordance with the administrative structure of the time, this allowed her to become an "overseer" of Gorky and Andreeva, throwing wrenches every step of the way. Without mentioning her personal "love" for Lilina, Andreeva once wrote to Lunacharsky, who was the People's Commissar of Enlightenment and above Lilina in the official hierarchy, but who feared her more than he feared fire: "He [Gorky] is so mad at Lilina that he cannot even hear about her. . . . You will immediately see how inconceivable or completely impossible it is to fight her."

Zinoviev's second cousin, Ilya Ionov (Bernstein), Lilina's brother, headed the publishing house of the Petrograd Council and, in connection with this activity, found himself in constant conflict with Gorky, considering him—not

* Russian Social-Democratic Workers' Party

without reason—as his competitor, taking that money, thanks to his closeness with Lenin, which could have been his.

Finally, Zinoviev's third cousin, the husband of his sister Liya Radomyslskaya, Samuil Zaks (who wrote under the pseudonym of "Gladnev") headed in Moscow the administration of Gosizdat,† a powerful concern, which then was the only national Russian publishing organization that belonged to the government: it was only under its control and with its participation that Gorky was allowed to develop his own publishing activity.

A fourth "Gorky-phobe" was added to this "troika"—Olga Davydovna Kameneva (Bronstein), Trotsky's sister. She was the wife of Lev Kamenev, the closest person to Zinoviev, who at the time headed the Moscow Council and was a member of the Politburo. Kameneva was in charge of the theatrical department of the People's Commissariat of Enlightenment and was, administratively, Andreeva's direct supervisor, the intervening link between her and Lunacharsky who, in turn, could not stand Andreeva since the days of emigration (they had both lived on Capri). All these petty intrigues reverberated in the most direct way on practical work; moreover, all intrigues and squabbles were passed off, naturally, as profound principal differences of opinion.

Like Lunacharsky, Kamenev regarded Gorky kindly, and even ironically. Both fiercely hated Andreeva, and she hated them just as much in return, asserting, and not without reason, that a professional actor would be better than Kameneva, who was nothing more than a "professional revolutionary" who had just managed to finish some courses in medicine, to lead Russia's theaters. Vladislav Khodasevich quotes Kameneva's words, very interesting in their candor, from February 1920, following a meeting with her in Moscow: "I'm amazed that you can associate with Gorky. All he does is cover up for crooks—and he is just as much a crook himself. If it were not for Vladimir Ilyich, he would have been in prison long ago!"

Another paradox was that Gorky suffered because of Andreeva, who had no influence whatsoever on him any more. Yet they lived under the same roof, and their joint telegram was proof of their supposedly common political positions and destiny in life. Hatred for the "crook" Gorky and the "crook" Grzhebin did not prevent Kameneva from proposing to their publishing house, which was called Z. I. Grzhebin Publishers, to publish feeble propaganda sketches, even though this powerful family could pick any publishing house of its choosing.

From this quartet, the one who raised Gorky's blood pressure most of all was Zaks-Gladnev, whom Gorky called, along with the whole Gosizdat leader-

† State Publishing House.

ship, "Hacks." Zaks especially despised him. Their conflict reached a crisis point after the Central Committee agreed to the creation of a private publishing house, with Gorky as the founder and director. The executive director was Gorky's old friend Zinovy Grzhebin, a well-known caricaturist, art collector and publishing figure.

Gorky's grandiose plans, in which he intended to saturate the book market with the best that world literature and world science had to offer, could not be realized because of the collapse of the typesetting industry. Gorky's idea to print books abroad and import them into Russia was therefore supported by the Central Committee. Legally, it was presented like this: Gosizdat orders Grzhebin's publishing house (that is, factually Gorky's) to print books *only* according to a list, preliminarily drawn up by Gosizdat together with the People's Commissariat of Enlightenment. In other words, under the guise of supporting Gorky, absolute mistrust was expressed in the selection of books for publishing—even their list, and not just manuscripts and books, was subjected to preliminary censorship. Only under this degrading condition, which Gorky had to agree to, did the Council of People's Commissars release to Grzhebin's publishing house a half million German marks "for the printing of manuscripts, books, and brochures."

Such an essentially humiliating condition provoked a stormy protest to the editorial board of Gosizdat and led to a further deterioration in the relationship between Gorky and Zaks. In a letter to Lenin, which has surfaced only recently, Zaks wrote about Gorky: ". . . he is preparing his future apostasy—if we will ever be shattered—right before our eyes. . . . It is especially sad and painful to me that you trust a person in whom I see the personification of your opposite."

The paradox, first of all, was that Lenin did not trust Gorky at all, but was compelled for tactical reasons to yield to him on some things in order to keep him in his political entourage. Secondly, and coming from the completely opposite flank, was an even more bitter mistrust toward him and all his publishing ventures on the part of many Russian writers who, because of utter impoverishment and impossibility to publish, were forced to sell their works to Grzhebin for next to nothing. "Grzhebin, Gorky's main agent," wrote Merezhkovsky, "bought up all of Russian literature for pennies, under the table, like a crook; one writer he didn't even pay with money but with rotten potatoes."

But there was a "third reason": people close to Gorky—Andreeva, Kriuchkov, and Max—reflecting the position of the elite to whom they were connected, were against Grzhebin. They also intrigued against him, attempting to influence Gorky. He stoically withstood this pressure as well.

Gorky suffered like any middleman who tries to appease the unappeasable and bring together those who cannot be brought together. Both groups regarded him with apprehension, if not worse. The Merezhkovsky camp hated and rejected him; the Leninists suffered him, trying to get him to submit. Only strangers to politicking and the intrigues of romanticism—more scientists than writers—were bewitched by his plans of universal education, in which he promised to bring world civilization to a huge, poverty-stricken, and generally illiterate country.

The biologist Boris Raito later recalled the meetings in Zinovy Grzhebin's apartment, which was used as an editorial office, with paintings by Benoit, Kustodiev, Sudeikin, and Levitan on the walls and eighteenth-century palace serving sets in cabinets of mahogany and Venetian glass: "It was a time of enthusiasm and grandiose plans, a time when it seemed to everyone that it was possible with one blow . . . to light up the whole country at once with the sheen of unprecedented culture. And from the windows (of Grzhebin's apartment) we looked out on Nevsky Prospekt, dark and desolate: frozen streetcars stood motionless, the Gostiniy Palace was empty and boarded up and people maneuvered about the snowdrifts in sledges."

This romantic feeling only elicited ironic jibes from the businesslike people in and around the Kremlin. Political plotters and pragmatists looked upon Gorky's battle against the Zinoviev clan and with everyone supporting him from a completely different point of view. Gorky's letters to Lenin, hidden in an archive for more than seventy years and which have only now been released, do not reveal any new behind-the-scenes details, but on the other hand they provide a complete picture of Gorky's attitude.

Here are only two excerpts, unknown to historians until the middle of the 1990s, from two of his letters to Lenin.

The first:

> Now all my work is going to rack and ruin. Let it be. I have performed several services for the motherland and the revolution and I am old enough not to allow any further mockery of me, or such careless and stupid regard for my work.
>
> I am not going to work or speak with Zaks and others like him. . . . I'm tired of stupidity . . .

The second:

> All possible accusations, wild tricks, and libelous obscenities have become such a common occurrence, have entered everyday life, that people have stopped reacting to it—this only amuses society.
>
> Another matter is Grzhebin.

. . . They poison him in the most revolting way. There is everything: slander, gossip, envy and malice—and no crime he would not be accused of. Grzhebin works like a fanatic . . . constantly risking, risking at times his life, for slander sometimes grows to monstrous proportions,.

. . . You, of course, think that it is easy to deceive me, that I am trustworthy and so on. No, don't worry, I know people just like you do. . . .

Grzhebin came from a family where they not only did not know books, but could not even speak Russian. His whole childhood was spent in terrible poverty and ignorance; he didn't know the alphabet until the age of 13.

It is his Jewish persistence and desire to 'come out among the people' that amazes me more than anything. . . . All this is worthy of respect, not persecution and poison. . . .

I know as well that if he had not been hindered at every step of the way, or caught up in all those insinuations, which his competitors and slanderers, or simply envious people, make use of—he would have created many valuable things.

. . . From the Grzhebin "affair" gradually came the Beilis Affair—small, but nonetheless rather vile. This last one especially fills me with indignation.

"This last one" seems to be very strange. Those who had poisoned Grzhebin (but who had aimed, of course, at Gorky—Grzhebin was just a convenient target for them) were also Jews. However, the Kremlin crowd knew that at a suitable moment they could play the "Jewish card," using in a certain milieu this fail-safe trump to create the necessary "public opinion": the Jew Grzhebin fleeces not only Russian writers, but also the Russian proletariat, squandering the money of the working people . . .

Gorky generally treated with special, almost fanatical passion, the Jewish question in Russia. In 1915, he called the Jews "friends of my soul"; on many occasions he signed appeals to the Russian people to defend Jews in everything and everywhere; he worked with the mayor of Petrograd, Ivan Tolstoy, in the "Russian Society for the Study of the Life of Jews," and organized charitable literary and acting soirees for the benefit of poor Jews and wounded soldiers of Jewish origin. One year before the October Revolution he wrote, "I am amazed by the spiritual steadfastness of the Jewish people, their courageous idealism, unwavering belief in the victory of good over evil, and the possibility of happiness on earth. As the old strong yeast of humanity, the Jews have always elevated its spirit, bringing into the world restless, noble thoughts, arousing in people a desire for something better."

February 1917 spawned in him hopes that it would bring an end to Russian anti-Semitism. October 1917 showed that anti-Semitism was being rapidly revitalized. In many ways this was because among the hateful Bolsheviks—and what is much more important, hateful not only to him!—were so many Jews.

But the vain attempts of some Jewish Bolsheviks to cynically play on these moods of an ignorant crowd provoked his even greater loathing.

It was hardly accidental (in any case, highly symbolic) that the last two essays in his cycle of *Untimely Thoughts* are devoted precisely to the Jewish question.

On May 20 (June 2), 1918:

> How disgusting is this anti-Semitism of these shiftless idlers!
>
> . . . I have already pointed out several times to the anti-Semites that if some Jews succeeded in obtaining the more advantageous and lucrative positions in life, it is because of their ability to work, the ecstasy which they bring to the process of labor, their love "for doing" and ability to admire what they are doing. The Jew is almost always a better worker than the Russian, and it's stupid to become angry at this, we should learn how to work. . . . No matter what kind of idiocy anti-Semites may speak, they do not like Jews only because they are clearly better, more adept and more hardworking than they are.

June 18 (July 1), 1918:

> . . . anti-Semitism is alive and gradually, cautiously, raises its vile head again; it hisses, slanders and sprays the poisonous spittle of hatred. . . .
>
> I'm convinced, I know, that the Jews in their masses, to my surprise, display a more rational love for Russia than many Russians. . . .
>
> The equation "Jew = Bolshevik" is a foolish equation, evoked by the zoological instincts of frustrated Russians. . . . I do not believe in the success of the slanderous propaganda of anti-Semitism.

Any signal about the infringement of Jews, any request to help them, even when they were subjected to persecution not just as Jews but simply as they were, provoked in him an immediate reaction. He reported to the despicable Zinoviev:

> . . . [T]hey write to me from Ukraine that my articles about the Jews, as well as the short story "Pogrom," are important and even circulate in mimeograph form.
>
> Do you not consider it necessary to propose to c[omrade] Ionov that he print about 200,000 books about the Jews and send them to the citizens of Kiev? . . . We have to hurry.[*]

He also wrote to Zinoviev:

> Dear Grigori Yevseevich!

---

[*] I was able to obtain the first publication of this letter only in 1998, even though the taboo on the name of Zinoviev had been removed ten years earlier.

Allow me to ask you to rescind the order by which Saul Moiseevich Ginzburg must clean out his apartment within a period of seven days.

This is physically impossible, as Ginzburg has a huge library containing up to 10,000 v[olumes], the majority of which are in the Jewish language and concern Jewish history.

Ginzburg is editing a four-volume historical collection, *What I've Lived Through*, as well as *A History of the Jewish People*, a work in fifteen volumes published by *Novy Mir*. He is also the editor of an historical journal in the ancient Jewish language called *Redvar*. Ginzburg is a scholar, the most serious worker on the history of his people.

Having to move out of his apartment will destroy—temporarily—all his work, not to mention that it will require a lot of money, which, of course, he does not have.

I earnestly ask you to instruct that Ginzburg be left alone.†

Even Zinaida Gippius, who despised Gorky with a passion, wrote in *Petersburg Diary* about one of his spontaneous manifestations of philo-Semitism. At one of the then numerous "conferences of sailors and Red Army soldiers," orators were found who sarcastically pointed out the small number of Jews in the army, and from the hall someone shouted: "Down with the Yids!" Gorky immediately shot back: "There are few Jews in the army because, in general, there are few of them." After this, writes Gippius, "he was showered with long applause."

Having detected an anti-Semitic strain in the poisoning of Grzhebin and, in general, of all his publishing business, Gorky became enraged. At least two circumstances had accumulated about this story, which touched him personally: his growing differences with Lenin and his overall authority, and the deepening conflict with Zinoviev and his family, which had already reached the boiling point.

Grigori Zinoviev comported himself like a dictator in Petrograd; unfettered by anything and anyone, he had burst to power allowing him to do whatever he wished. He did not feel piety toward Gorky, or to anyone in general no matter who it was; neither Gorky's stature as a writer nor his relationship with Lenin made the slightest impression on Zinoviev.

The first sharp clashes between them began when Gorky turned to the Bolsheviks, and his relationship with Lenin became like a second honeymoon for two people who have once again found each other after a long separation. Zinoviev carried out the "Red Terror" following the attempt on Lenin's life with such zeal that Gorky considered it necessary to warn him, as he had previ-

† This letter, too, was published for the first time in 1998.

ously warned the subsequently assassinated singer of the terror, the prominent Petrograd Bolshevik Moisei Volodarsky (Goldstein), that these "irresponsible actions" would only further incite anti-Semitism. Zinoviev, naturally, ignored him . . .

Fate forced them into contact with one another: Gorky depended formally upon Zinoviev, and Zinoviev morally upon Gorky, although to a lesser degree. There has not been much evidence to this day of their personal, let alone close, contact, but Kornei Chukovsky's recently published and extremely valuable diaries also shed light on this, as well as on the backstage alliance between the Party and intellectuals during those years.

November 13, 1919. An entry about a session, at which Gorky, Zinoviev, Ionov, and other Petrograd Bolsheviks were present.

> They were talking about the offspring of a rhinoceros that had died in the zoo. Gorky: "What are you going to feed them?" Zinoviev: "The bourgeois."
>
> And they began discussing whether to cut up the bourgeois or not. Seriously . . . Seriously! The question is, when were these people being genuine—when they pretended to be decent people, or now? [Gorky] spoke today with Lenin by phone. [Lenin] laughed. He always laughs. He promises to take care of everything, but asks: "How come you haven't been picked up yet? You know, they're planning to take [arrest] you [citizens of Petersburg]."

November 29, 1919:

> I was at Gorky's yesterday on Kronverks. Zinoviev was there. Near the entrance I was amazed by his wonderful car, a luxurious bearskin sleigh robe had been carelessly tossed on the seat . . . I waited for Zinoviev to leave. . . . Zinoviev walked past—fat, short."

No date:

> How repulsive Zinoviev is. I saw him at Gorky's. He does not shake hands with writers. He sat on the couch and did not even get up to greet us.

Gorky appears like a silent extra in these entries, not reacting to the discussion about the "carving" of the bourgeois or to the grand boorishness of the Petrograd dictator and the petty tyranny of ignoramuses, intoxicated with power, all happening before his eyes and with his personal participation. A subtle and refined person, he could not fail to see things as everyone else did, and it was impossible not to react to it, at least in his soul. However, the situation in which he had placed himself forced him to endure all this and put a brave face on a sorry business. Zinoviev saw very well that this was a game and a bad one at that...

Incidentally, the conversation that seriously amazed Chukovsky—about carving up the bourgeois—was by no means the joke *du jour* of a maniac driven mad by bloodlust. The verb "to cut" was fashionable at the time among the Party elite. Another entry of a visit by Gorky to Lenin in Moscow has been preserved:

> V[ladimir] I[lyich] sat down on the couch, very attentive, thinking of something and carefully looking over many documents, which lay on the table ...
> "What are you doing?" asked Gorky
> "I'm thinking about how best to cut through the kulaks who aren't giving bread to the people."
> "That's an original thing to do," remarked A. M.
> "We'll take away everything from the kulaks and destroy them, physically destroy them, if they resist orders from the government."

The author of this entry is one of Lenin's closest friends, Vladimir Bonch-Bruevich, who clearly agreed with his boss's bloodthirsty plans. But something else is sadder and more incredible: how did Gorky put up with all this? How could he have listened to this and not slammed the door in the literal and figurative sense? He could not tolerate peasants, both poor and rich (kulaks), but to "cut" them is something he would never have contemplated, not even in his worst nightmare. Yet he listened and made note of it. The years would pass before it would become clear that such patience, even for the sake of what he felt were noble goals, does not fail to leave a trace and an indelible stamp on the soul, gradually deforming one's personality.

Gorky felt dependent upon Zinoviev not only in public, but privately as well. It has to be assumed that a letter, dated February 17, 1920 (which I published for the first time in 1998) and quoted below, did not come easily, but there was no way out—only Zinoviev, and no one else, could resolve such a ticklish and important matter for Gorky:

> Dear Grigori Yevseevich!
> D[octor] Manukhin says that Max needs a month's rest. Upon his arrival in Moscow he must return to his job.
> Would it be possible for you—as a personal favor to me—to give Max a certificate that you are hiring him to work for you? At the end of his convalescence he will immediately show up in Moscow.

Grigori Yevseevich was very well disposed toward Aleksei Maksimovich! The request for a personal favor was complied with immediately. In agreement

with Zinoviev to deceive the Party and the Soviet government, Gorky had become his prisoner (Max, we should not forget, was then serving as a commissar
of general military training courses, under the auspices of the Cheka, that is,
with comrade Dzerzhinsky himself). He had made himself dependent, and
disliked it thoroughly!

It was a hateful role for Gorky—is that why he so quickly found a way to
remind Zinoviev that he was not "tamed" and that he should not expect slavish
obedience? Is that not how Zinoviev, especially nervous after the favor he had
done, perceived Gorky's ingratitude?

Gorky wrote a short play for the People's Comedy Theater (he called it a
scenario)—half vaudeville, half farce—in which the actor had the opportunity
to improvise. The performance based upon this play, called *The Plodder
Slovotekov*—a satire on Bolshevik verbiage, organically blended with official
bureaucratese—was directed by Sergei Radlov on the stage of the Zoological
Garden's Summer Theater. The actor Delvari, who had played the role of
Slovotekov, understood the author's intention very well (as, of course, did the
director) and, with his approval, enriched the text in the course of the
performance with the hot topics of the day. Zinoviev, who was present,
recognized Slovotekov in himself, although the same could be said of many
other Party bigwigs. The play was staged only four times to huge crowds, then
closed on Zinoviev's personal instructions. The tsarist censorship would not
have dared to act like that with Gorky the playwright. The Soviet censorship—
with the personal approval of a member of the Central Committee and a
candidate for membership to the Politburo—could do so.

Zinoviev did not remain indifferent to Gorky's attack, nor did he limit
himself to simply banning the play. Some clear signs from Zinoviev's officials
worked crudely—perhaps they purposely made it obvious—led Gorky to
realize that a complete inspection of his correspondence had started. In his
memoirs, published for the first time only in 1940 in the Russian émigré journal
Sovremennye zapiski (Contemporary Notes), Vladislav Khodasevich wrote that
"agents (of Zinoviev) opened and inspected Gorky's correspondence, including
letters from Lenin himself. These letters Lenin sometimes sent in envelopes,
sewn with a thread on all sides, the ends of which were closed shut with sealing
wax. But Zinoviev somehow managed to read them—Gorky told me this
himself later on." Khodasevich's memoirs were not documented and were
generally ignored because they mentioned the "enemy of the people" Zinoviev,
who supposedly never existed . . .

Only in the beginning of the 1990s this version—like tens, hundreds of
others—was fully confirmed. Gorky's opened and inspected letters were extracted from the KGB archive. If the letters from Lenin to Gorky had been

read, and then delivered to the addressee, then Gorky's letters to Lenin were in the cellars of the Soviet secret police. There is no evidence whatsoever that Lenin received several of Gorky's letters, beginning with the end of summer 1920—they were known only in Cheka-certified copies and preserved in the secret files of the Lubyanka. Gorky's bitter letters excerpted above ("I am old enough not to allow any further mockery of me, or such careless and stupid regard for my work"; "I'm tired of stupidity"; and others) are precisely those letters subjected to Zinoviev's inspection. There is absolutely no guarantee that Lenin read them, but they were read by Zinoviev, and in a political sense Zinoviev and Lenin represented at the time a single entity—Soviet power.

The collection of opened and inspected letters by Gorky in the KGB archive contains one more significant detail. In the certified copies of the seized letters there is a note: "To the file. Gorky's record of service," which is irrefutable evidence of one extremely important fact: at that time Gorky was already the object of a secret, but completely official, observation by an agency of the special services. A special file was opened on him, and this was only allowed at the time for "bourgeois," "foreign elements" or overt "enemies." It is not important which of these classifications Gorky fell under.

And still one more conclusion from this is extremely important: the letters to Lenin ended up in the secret Lubyanka dossier, bypassing Lenin—a fact that says a great deal and still awaits interpretation. What does this mean? That Dzerzhinsky and Zinoviev understood each other better than Dzerzhinsky and Lenin? That both wanted to shield the leader of the revolution from Gorky's putrid influence? Or was it something else? That this was done behind Lenin's back, and in some sense against him, is indisputable. Otherwise, his letters would not have been inspected.

But Lenin could not have known about the existence inside the Cheka of Gorky's "record of service" file. Lenin could not have *not* been provided with agents' information about Gorky's meetings with various people, about his telephone conversations, about his correspondence with others, or his statements about some important issue. To no small degree it is precisely these, and not just the candid Gorky monologues at the time of their Moscow meetings, that influenced Lenin's relationship to the "Stormy Petrel of the Revolution."

6.

In Search of a Bomb

Gorky could not stand being on his own, and he was terrified of solitude. Even though he emphasized many times in his letters to different people that what he dreamed of most of all was peace and quiet, and even though he genuinely believed this, the fact is that Gorky suffered tremendously without a woman around. He was amorously inclined.

Another woman who occupied a visible, if not as important, place in Gorky's biography as Peshkova and Andreeva, had come to know him very well at Capri but only become part of his life after his return to Russia. This was Varvara Vasilyevna Shaikevich (née Zubkova), appearing at times vaguely and obscurely—without any explanation whatsoever—in books dedicated to Gorky. What she was to him (friend? wife? lover? assistant? secretary? or "simply an acquaintance"?), has puzzled the most fastidious Gorky scholars. No description fits her, except maybe as "the wife of Gorky's employee."

The history of this affair, which was not as ephemeral as the others, is connected to a dramatic personal conflict in which Gorky and Varvara were the two "angles" of a notorious love triangle. The third player was her husband, who was also one of Gorky's closest employees in his publishing business, Aleksandr Tikhonov (Serebrov), with whom Gorky had not just a business, but also a friendly, relationship.

Varvara married Tikhonov in 1909, and already had a six-year-old son, Andrei, from her first marriage. Her first husband, Anatoly Shaikevich, the son and descendant of one of Russia's biggest bankers, Yefim Shaikevich, a Jew who converted to Russian Orthodoxy was, like many converts, no stranger to Judeo-phobia. Nonetheless, this did not prevent him from earning two university diplomas and becoming an erudite aesthete and a refined expert of the arts, most of all ballet. His impeccable taste in art, combined with unlimited resources, allowed Shaikevich to amass one of the most valuable antique collections in Russia. At the age of sixteen, while still a student in secondary school, Varvara was captivated by his sybaritism and married him, but by the time she was twenty she was already divorced, having suddenly discovered, much to her surprise, that she did not feel the slightest bit of love for her husband.

Gorky was living at the time in Capri, where Tikhonov and his young wife had come to visit. Shaikevich-Tikhonova (some sources call her by the name of her first husband, others by the second) was eighteen years younger than Gorky. She also had the exact same name and patronymic, Varvara Vasilyevna, as Gorky's mother, which probably lent a certain special flavor to his relationship with her. More importantly, she was pretty, a charming "simple lass" made even more alluring by the noble beauty of the Russian aristocracy, even though she did not belong to that class. She possessed alluring looks and lightness of manner; she was slender, elegant, and gracious, like a French or Italian woman. Everyone with any vague reminiscences of her (and, unfortunately, that is the only kind we have) spoke about this rare combination of qualities that made her stand out in a crowd.

No one knows exactly what kind of relationship Gorky had with Shaikevich-Tikhonova on Capri (there is some information that for a very short period there she filled in for Andreeva, following Gorky's second separation from Peshkova). The affair was renewed upon his return to Russia. Varvara Vasilyevna's daughter, Nina, maintains that she was born in February 1910, but another Nina, the writer Berberova, "transfers" this date to three years hence. "Ninochka's striking similarity to Gorky," she recalls, "confused those people who did not know about Varvara Vasilyevna's closeness to Gorky—if there were any such people. . . . What was rather coarse and simple in Gorky's face was transformed in her, thanks to the incredible elegance and charm of her mother, into a pretty turned-up little nose, light braids and a slim, supple body." An indirect confirmation of Berberova's statement is the fact that in 1912 the Tikhonovs arrived on Capri together: it is hard to believe that the mother would leave her two-year-old daughter at home.

This "triangular love"—alternating between Tikhonov and Gorky—continued a rather long time. Gorky did not hide his "close friendship" with Varvara from anyone: he was far from sanctimonious and hated cover-ups or conspiracies. He doted upon Varvara's epileptic son, Andrei, and helped with his treatment. There is a letter to Peshkova in which he asks Yekaterina Pavlovna to put Tikhonova in touch with a prominent Moscow psychiatrist, Professor Kashchenko, concerning her son. He also wrote and invited Max to Petrograd, saying that he could stay with the parents of Varvara Vasilyevna until Andreeva left for Moscow. This is more proof of a well-known fact:

Peshkova could accept any of her husband's women except Andreeva, for whom she felt nothing but revulsion.

This new affair of Gorky at times flared up, only to die out, but for the time being it did not exert any negative influence on either Varvara's marriage to Tikhonov, or to the relationship between the two old friends who continued to work closely together. The three of them traveled together to Moscow, sat on various publishing commissions and shared friendly meals. In August and September 1917 Gorky, along with the Tikhonovs and their two children—Andrusha and Ninochka—spent the happiest time in Koktebel in the eastern Crimea. It is possible to find out when Varvara lived with Gorky and when she was with Tikhonov. To call her Gorky's wife, even temporarily, would most likely be an exaggeration. Nina Berberova perhaps found the most accurate and elegant formula, not offensive to anyone: "At different times," she wrote, "different women sat at Gorky's dinner table playing the wife's role." Among them was Varvara Vasilyevna Shaikevich-Tikhonova.

This happened in Petrograd, on Kronverksky Prospekt, where Gorky lived in an apartment that was initially quite modest, but then made huge by knocking out a wall and combining two apartments together. As the number of occupants grew, it continued to expand. It is not easy to establish the exact number of rooms, but given the evidence we have it was not less than eleven. The individuals living in this apartment, by the simple logic of life, should not have lived under one roof. Maria Andreeva, who had found the apartment for Gorky, also continued to live there. Later on her secretary, Pyotr Petrovich Kriuchkov, whose true relationship with her was no secret to anyone, moved into the neighboring apartment. Nicknamed "PePeKriu" (an abbreviation of his first name, patronymic and surname), he took advantage of Gorky's sympathy; Gorky in turn was grateful to Kriuchkov—if anything for freeing him from superfluous complications in his relationship with Andreeva, making their separation less painful. Kriuchkov had abandoned his first family, leaving behind a wife and son, who would later die at the age of twenty.

Gorky himself occupied four rooms (bedroom, library, office, and space for his artworks). In the other rooms (except for the dining room and those belonging to Andreeva and Kriuchkov) lived the failed artist Ivan Rakitsky (nicknamed "Nightingale"), who was constantly around Gorky and completely dedicated to him; a girl of gentle birth with a difficult fate, Maria Geintse, nicknamed "Molecule" (subsequently a friend, then wife of the famous artist Vladimir Tatlin); and the artist Valentina Khodasevich ("Merchant Lady") with her husband, also an artist, Andrei Diderikhs ("Didi").

Valentina Khodasevich, the poet's niece, was hardly cut out for the part of "hostess," nor did she play that role, although a clear attraction is detected in the invitation which Gorky sent her in Moscow: ". . . Allow me, completely seriously and deliberately," he wrote her in the spring of 1918, "to propose the following to you: move to Peter.* You will have two fine rooms where you can work freely. If you need money, allow me to offer you as much as you need. Ivan Nikolaevich [Rakitsky] and Varvara Vasilyevna will take good care of you here—these are people who love you, respect your talent and want to see it flourish."

It should be mentioned that Valentina Mikhailovna had already been married for a long time, yet there is not a word about her husband, Andrei Diderikhs, in Gorky's invitation. They both moved to Petrograd, although "Merchant Lady" at first preferred to live with her aunt and not in the two rooms offered by Gorky. She and her husband subsequently moved into Gorky's apartment on Kronverksky, where she remained until the very end a loyal "friend of the home."

At first Tikhonova would show up whenever Andreeva left, and this happened frequently: Maria Fyodorovna spent long periods in Moscow. Incidentally, even then Tikhonova's appearance at Kronverksky was out in the open for everyone to see, including Andreeva. These two people, who were not very well disposed to each other, simply avoided undesirable contact. Having dedicated in January 1918 a collection of short stories to Varvara Vasilyevna Shaikevich, Gorky made it clear that their relationship was no secret.

The Tikhonov family had not disintegrated throughout all this; for awhile Aleksandr Nikolaevich and Varvara Vasilyevna even lived together on Kronverksky. Then the husband developed his own affair on the side, and thus the triangle became a square. Kornei Chukovsky's diary, for example, records the following entry: "In the evening, before the end of a session [of the publishing board], his lover came to see him [Tikhonov] in a beautiful fur, and waited for him in the office."

Outwardly everything appeared very proper. Gorky and Tikhonov continued to work together. When in 1919, the Gorky (in this case one can say Gorky-Tikhonov) publishing house World Literature gave a party in honor of Gorky's fiftieth birthday (Gorky had reduced his age by one year, therefore his fiftieth was celebrated in 1919 and not in 1918 as it should have been), Chukovsky wrote, "The Tikhonovs went all out, made many wonderful butter pastries and served tea† in goblets. Tikhonov sat a bit removed, and Varvara** sat next to Gorky, as befits the hostess. Andreeva was absent at this celebra-

---

* St. Petersburg.
† Instead of champagne.
** She worked in the same publishing house.

tion—a third person, as everyone knows, is always superfluous. But Tikhonov, although he was the third one here, was by no means superfluous...'"

By the way, this idyll (true, an idyll only to outsiders) did not last long. Soon after, Tikhonov kicked his wife out (and not only from the family, but from the business as well) and she definitely moved to Gorky's place. With her typically malicious bile, Zinaida Gippius relegates the split to the summer of 1919, adding that Gorky "showered [Varvara] with diamonds. . . . And now the boot-lickers . . . don't know whose boots to lick: T[ikhono]va, the abandoned wife, or Maria Fyodorovna." Another memoirist, Kornei Chukovsky, does not remember the diamonds but writes that Gorky "went with [Varvara] to second-hand shops, bought carpets and ivory *objets d'art.*" Not for her personally, it seems, but for their common home.

As long as it was their home, peace and quiet reigned: in contrast to Yekaterina Pavlovna and Maria Fyodorovna, Varvara Vasilyevna was a homebody type who loved the family hearth and tried to create the best possible domestic comforts for Gorky. She was supposedly an expert on literature; in any case, she more or less understood it. A short story by Kornei Chukovsky accurately conveys the domestic circumstances on Kronverksky when Varvara lived there. Nikolai Gumilev, who figures in this story, actively collaborated at that time with Gorky in his publishing and other cultural ventures.

As Chukovsky wrote in a commentary to his diary:

> Every Sunday, Gumilev would come for me, and we headed off on foot to the Petrograd side [that is, on Kronverksky] to see Varvara Vasilyevna.* Gumilev had two lures: he wanted to read to V.V. his new verses.† He believed that V.V. had a subtle understanding of poetry.** The second enticement was wine. V.V. had a stock of Italian wines. We walked along the magnificent dead city. The air was clean, as in the country . . . Only Gorky on Kronverksky had a heated bath—a wonderful luxury—there was no other bath within a ten-kilometer radius. V.V., listening to Gumilev's poetry, usually sat on the couch wrapped in a cashmere shawl. Gumilev sipped wine and puffed away on a long cigarette . . . [She] listened quietly, in silent rapture. This usually all took place at five o'clock or even earlier, at four.
>
> . . . Once during one of these festive occasions we heard some rustling in the next room. A minute later Gorky, stooped and more shy than usual, appeared. Awkwardly exchanging greetings with us, he said to Gumilev, "You read your verses excellently, especially this last one. Well, go on reading."

---

* An amazing detail: not to see Gorky, but Varvara Vasilyevna.
† During that winter he wrote a new poem every day.
** Gumilev worked with her at World Literature.

Calmly knocking the ashes from his cigarette, Gumilev replied:

"If you understood poetry . . . you would never have written a whole line of monosyllabic words."*

Gorky, who at the time had experienced a passion for Gumilev, shrugged and said timidly, "I'm no poet!"

Nikolai Stepanovich and I exchanged glances and hastened to say goodbye. They didn't try to stop us.

There is a reason for citing such a lengthy passage. Chekhov, as is known, said that a rifle hung in the first act of a play must absolutely be fired in the third. This would happen shortly thereafter. The "gun" would fire and unfortunately, not only metaphorically.

Thanks to the same Kornei Chukovsky, at the same time a new page opened in Gorky's biography that would have a lasting influence over the rest of his life. This page is connected with a woman mentioned by various sources with three different surnames that she used at various stages of her life. She, of course, is Maria Zakrevskaya, also called Countess Benkendorf after her first husband and the Baroness Budberg after her second. It is with the latter name that she became famous, thanks to Nina Berberova's novel, *Zheleznaya Zhenshchina.*† Berberova's book, in many ways extremely subjective and passionate, contains a multitude of facts from the life of this unusual and outstanding personality, thereby freeing us from the need to delve into the details of her head-spinning biography. But it is necessary to point out that without it the narrative that follows would be impossible.

Maria Ignatyevna Zakrevskaya (Mura, as everyone called her both in Russia and abroad) married Ivan Aleksandrovich Benkendorf, who came from a family of less-than-wealthy Baltic nobles and later served as secretary at the Russian embassy in Berlin. Although there did exist in Russia a distinguished clan of Zakrevsky counts, the family into which she was born was not related to them. Nevertheless, Mura always passed herself off as having been born a countess. This legend strikingly coincides with the one which, as we remember, Andreeva created for herself in Capri: the magic of noble origins thrills even those people who, it would seem, could get along just fine without attributing aristocratic roots to themselves.

After the revolution, Mura's husband was killed by peasants on his estate outside Tallinn while she was in Petrograd, protecting her apartment from

---

* From Gorky's "Song of the Nightingale," which students used to read aloud at the beginning of the twentieth century.

† *The Iron Lady* (in Russian only—Translator's note).

burglary and "consolidation." She managed to save the two children, a son and daughter who remained in Estonia, from reprisals; their governess hid them in a safe place. Her return to Estonia had been cut off, but thanks to the connections of her relatives and old acquaintances, she fell into a close-knit circle of foreign diplomats left behind in a country that had descended into chaos. Thus, she had to (more precisely, she managed to) become first the lover of the British ambassador R. Bruce Lockhart, and then of Sidney Reilly, the great British spy, who also worked in Petrograd under diplomatic cover. Participants in the "diplomats' plot," both these Brits were under the close scrutiny of Dzerzhinsky's Chekists. Mura was "removed" from Lockhart's bed following his arrest.

From British spies she passed into the hands of Soviet ones—literally: while in prison she went from being under investigation by one of the Cheka chiefs, Yan Peters, to becoming his lover, which more likely than not helped gain her release without any consequences. Without any means to support herself, she looked for anything to earn money. Someone told her that Gorky's new World Literature publishing house was looking for translators from English. Mura had a fairly good command of not only English but also French and German—the language she knew the worst, oddly enough, was Russian—and willingly grabbed at this straw. Mura knew Kornei Chukovsky, who worked in translation for the publishing house, from soirées she attended with her husband at the Anglo-Russian Society during the war. She turned to him.

Chukovsky did not ignore the request of the woman who instantly captivated him, but he did not offer her any translation work, for he would not allow personal sympathies to encroach upon such a sacred matter to him as literature. However, he did give her some kind of office work, a food card, and somewhat later, wanting to do something nice for her and help her even more, he introduced her to Gorky.

Gorky also did not give her any translation work, but instead suggested she "simply drop by," which she did, and soon after—several weeks later—she moved into Kronverksky. Varvara had only just moved out, but Mura established the very best relationship with Maria Fyodorovna, having intuited that such an initiative on her part would be kindly met. She never had any need—not then, not later—to be in conflict with rivals, and avoided it as much as possible.

In her memoirs, Mura's prosperous daughter, Tanya Aleksander, accurately describes what happened with Mura's arrival in Kronverksky: "This creature from another world captivated Gorky. There was something greater here than the charms of the imperial past: the initial physical attraction turned into something deeper. Gradually their relationship became warm and close." True, this "gradually" lasted less than a year.

Insofar as Mura immediately began to fulfill the functions of secretary—she typed for Gorky, translated his numerous letters to be sent abroad into three languages, and did all this for many years—Soviet interpreters were provided the fortunate circumstance of designating for her a "place near Gorky," without encroaching upon the "private life" forbidden by Bolshevik morality. She truly did fulfill the function of secretary, but by no means was it part of her job description: Maria Ignatyevna Zakrevskaya can justifiably be called the third (or, really, the fourth) wife of Gorky, beginning in autumn 1919. She was twenty-seven at the time.

Before she moved in with Gorky, Chukovsky noted one characteristic little scene that says a great deal. The incident happened at a literary session, which Gorky attended with Mura. ". . . Gorky, though he did not say a word to her, said everything for her, fanning out his peacock's tail in its entirety. He was very witty, loquacious and brilliant, like a gymnast at the bar" (diary entry from September 24, 1919).

Only on May 9, 1920, did Chukovsky allow himself to record in his diary: "Maria Ignatyevna has definitively moved in with Gorky." Evidently aware of the writer's inconstancy, Chukovsky (and not only him, of course) suggested that Gorky's latest attraction would be no more long-lasting than the previous one, but eight months after their relationship had become all the more stronger, he admitted that the new union looked firm. In that same entry about Mura and Gorky, Chukovsky writes, "They are terribly good friends—they have established a playful-polemical relationship—she jokingly hits him on the arms and he says, 'Ouch, ouch, ouch, how she fights!'"

The change in her status in Gorky's apartment—from temporary to permanent—became a reality and subject to evaluation not only by Chukovsky and other people close to Gorky, but also by the comrades at Smolny, where Grigori Zinoviev had set himself up with his numerous functionaries. It was precisely then that the Petrograd dictator delivered the cruelest and most belittling blow to the Stormy Petrel, from which he was unable to recover. The Petrograd Chekists stormed unexpectedly into Kronverksky. "By chance" Andreeva and Kriuchkov were not at home and their rooms were not searched at all. The officers barely glanced at the others, but they lingered for two hours in Mura's room, turning all her possessions upside down. Gorky was in a rage; Mura, barely able to stand, observed their excesses. The search did not yield any results; the "leather coats"* left with nothing.

---

* This term was the nickname given to members of the Cheka.

Zinoviev had already ordered a search of Gorky's place a year earlier, but Soviet historians had kept this episode, which destroyed the canonical version of the relationship between Soviet power and the Stormy Petrel of the Revolution, a secret for decades. Based on a denunciation, the Petrograd bosses discovered a whole arsenal of weapons stored at Gorky's apartment and stormed in to search the plotter's premises.

Gorky later discussed this episode in very colorful language with the American scholar A. Cahoon: "There were always twenty-five to thirty people at our table in Petrograd. One evening a detachment of Red Army soldiers showed up, looking for a bomb. The soldiers were hungry. So were we, such were the times. But it so happened that at eight o'clock that evening a friend brought us some wonderful potatoes, cabbage, three whitefish and a fine piece of suet. . . . We argued with the soldiers about their stupid search for bombs in my apartment, but at the sight of a frying pan they lost the ability to speak. 'Sit down, guys!' They all sat, even their leader. It was vaudeville! That period was a total mix of tragedy and vaudeville."

Instead of bombs, the uninvited guests discovered a collection of unusual museum-quality weaponry that represented no danger to Soviet power or to the Petrograd dictator personally. Because of this misunderstanding and the failure of the mission, Gorky's relationship with Zinoviev did not improve. With the second search—aimed at Mura—he had to exact revenge.

Zinoviev—and it cannot be discounted that it was genuine on his part— thought Mura was a British spy, just as Peters had figured her for a German agent. But Mura, of course, served only as the means—the blow was aimed at Gorky. Who could he use to defend himself against Zinoviev? Gorky rushed to Lenin in Moscow and invited him to come see him at Peshkova's. Lenin was not alone in swallowing his pride on that occasion; both Dzerzhinsky and Trotsky showed up with him. They must have known what the meeting was about.

This Bolshevik trio could not just shrug off Gorky, although their sympathies lay not at all with him but completely with Zinoviev. Who exactly was Gorky to them, supposedly offended by Zinoviev? An unbalanced hysteric, bewitched by a young adventuress or, even worse, a British spy who had turned his head? Even if she were not, Zinoviev had shown the correct vigilance, but the "proletarian writer," blinded by the attraction of a new skirt, had hindered Party workers and Chekists from safeguarding the revolution against the schemes of enemies swarming everywhere. Yet for form's sake they decided to meet once more, calling Zinoviev himself to Moscow for a face-to-face confrontation. Could Gorky have objected to this? *Audiatur et altera pars*[*] . . .

Zinoviev arrived and immediately simulated a heart attack. The confrontation did not take place. He was reprimanded and let go. Now he began to favor—to spite Gorky—Maria Andreeva, whom (especially as his wife) he previously could not tolerate. The more Gorky had distanced himself from Andreeva, the closer she became to Zinoviev. There was nothing genuine about this, only the desire to wound his implacable antagonist even more.

Life went on. Gorky's incandescent activity did not diminish by even one degree. First the House of Arts (formerly the private residence of the merchant Yeliseyev), headed by Gorky, opened on the banks of the Moika River. This was a club and a cafeteria and a dormitory all in one: Osip Mandelstam, Nikolai Gumilev, Vladislav Khodasevich, Viktor Shklovsky, and other prominent writers lived there. This was immediately followed, at Gorky's initiative and again under his supervision, by the opening, first, of the House of Writers on Basseinaya Street and then the House of Scientists on Millionaya Street, next to the Winter Palace, in the former palace of the Grand Duke Vladimir Aleksandrovich. The whole universe of Russian science at that time gathered at the House of Scientists. Food rations were distributed more generously in the House of Scientists than elsewhere. To become a member of at least one of these clubs was the best way to survive.

Gorky spoke about the real price of these rations in an entrusted (opened and inspected, of course) letter to Korolenko. After 2,026 rations assigned to the House had been parceled out, there still remained about 700 people "with major service to science" who had been left out. The reason, according to Gorky:

> The bosses don't like the House of Scientists, considering it to be a "White Guard organization"; the workers grumble that the bourgeois saboteurs are eating them out of house and home. . . . And it's becoming more difficult to live. . . . The death rate among scientists is terrible. . . . In addition, the workers have begun to make anti-Soviet speeches here and in Moscow—and this in the worker's state.[†] Anti-Semitism is flourishing and even more revoltingly than ever. Overall, it's not a pretty picture!

---

[*] Let others be heard. (Latin)
[†] The phrase does not smell of irony. Could it really be presumed that workers' power had been created in a country seized by a band of conspirators?

There was plenty of everything but, in reality, not much joy. Yet Gorky preferred not to whimper but to act. He helped "on his own" those to whom he was favorably disposed, without relying upon the generosity of the authorities. The writer Mikhail Slonimsky, one of the members of a group of young writers called the "Serapion Brothers," later said that he once went to see Gorky to arrange a meeting with the Serapions.

> He asked, "Do you have bread?" "We get it by ration cards." "Flour?" "There is no flour." "There's no butter either?" asked Gorky, already knowing the answer. He opened the drawer of his writing table and pulled out a large piece of butter, not less than two kilograms in weight and neatly wrapped in wax paper. "This is for all the brothers," he mumbled.

It has to be assumed that, even after such a gift, he still had something left over for himself and all the other inhabitants and guests of the apartment on Kronverksky.

Despite great difficulty as a result of sabotage from the Zinoviev clan, the publishing activity developed. Gorky devoted almost all his strength, time and passion to this business, which he called the most important in numerous signed documents and private correspondence. According to official Soviet history, it is bombastically called the "salvation of art treasures." It is time to solve this riddle of his life as well.

Gorky's admiration of the old masters who, at various times and in different countries, created works of art from wood, stone and metal, on paper or canvas, had appeared long before and was completely genuine. He differed little from thousands and thousands of people who have admired the talent of skilled artists and even collected their works, both for aesthetic and commercial reasons.

There is nothing strange about Gorky's passion for collecting manifesting itself rather late in life, during the chaotic period following the Bolshevik revolution. Prior to this, he had not really been settled and was constantly moving about. It just so happened that Gorky's acquisition of spacious quarters coincided with those troubled times. It was also the moment when thousands of works of art were abandoned or available for a pittance.

The rumors that Gorky was buying up extremely valuable works of art for next to nothing began to circulate in Petrograd in February–March 1918. Gorky was too visible a presence, known to everyone, for such activity to remain unnoticed for long. It caused indignation among most Petrograd intellectuals, preventing them from being objective about his journalistic activity in the pages of

Novaya Zhizn', where he expressed the same attitude, shared by his implacable critics, to the Bolsheviks and Soviet power.

Following his every move closely and venomously, Zinaida Gippius often touched upon Gorky's sudden fever for collecting expensive and beautiful things, which cost him almost nothing, in her diary.

> Gorky greedily buys up all kinds of vases and enamels from the despised bourgeois who are dying from hunger. (He went to look at a china collection in the apartment of the elderly E., an ailing intellectual liberal. And how he bargained!) Gorky's apartment looks like a museum, or an antiquarian's shop. . . . He sits for hours, cleaning enamels over and over, admiring his acquisitions . . .

> [According to the testimony of Doctor Manukhin] the apartment is a real museum, so filled is it with old things, purchased from people dying from hunger. Nowadays they will sell the last cherished family heirloom for a piece of bread. Gorky, along with sailors and soldiers who are rolling in dough, takes advantage of this.

This theme was like a thorn in her side, becoming an obsession and inciting her to return to the same subject over and over and with almost the same words. Embittered rage can blind one's vision, but at the same time these entries reflect, even if in extremely misshapen form, the realities of those days. In any case, we can see Gorky as he was seen then by the Petrograd intellectuals, who greeted the Bolshevik revolution with hatred. Month after month passed, but the entries remain the same.

May 18, 1918:

> Gorky . . . buys for nothing old and family valuables from the "persecuted" literally dying from hunger. Incidentally, he is not a "scoundrel," just a Bushman or Hottentot. But not with the innocent 'beads' as before, but with bombs in his hands which he tosses around—for enjoyment.

November 13, 1918:

> Gorky, it seems, has bought up all the antiques, so now he collects erotic albums. But he is misguided there, too. Someone told me, with naïve annoyance, "Gorky paid a thousand rubles for an album that costs 200 rubles at the very most."

For Gippius, and for those like her, Gorky is guilty either way, whether he "buys for nothing" or overpays by five times the price.

So what was the real story? This history of indulging his aesthetic passions on the troubles of others—was it the sad truth or the invention of gossipers who hated Gorky and were out to tarnish his reputation?

The fact that such desires were awakened in him and that he strove to give them a practical outlet in the Petrograd inferno is confirmed not only by his malignant critics, but also by those sympathetic to him, such as Yuri Annenkov, who knew Gorky well and recalled that Gorky's room and office on Kronverksky were furnished with Buddha statuettes, lacquered Chinese miniatures, Chinese colored sculpture and artistic masks of exceptional value. Nina Berberova states that Gorky also amassed an exceptionally valuable collection of jade. Kornei Chukovsky observes that not only Gorky at that time acquired unique antiques, but so did others from his closest circle. His diary for 1919 records this entry: "Tikhonov invited Gumilev and me over to his place to look at his Giorgione and Persian miniatures. Everyone collected according to his or her own taste. To own a Giorgione is something that Tikhonov could not have imagined before the revolution in even his wildest dreams."

Even if Gorky had tried to "cram" his whole apartment with antiques that had no value on the Petrograd market but nevertheless possessed true worth, he would have had neither the possibilities nor the energy. Not even a 100-room apartment could have accommodated all the riches lying about at that time. And there was still Moscow and hundreds of other cities, where antique furniture, paintings, graphic works, valuables, porcelain, and silverware were kept in once rich private homes, museums, and galleries. All this was in danger of being lost, of being drowned in the basements of the rabble on the crest of the "revolutionary" wave. Gorky cared about the welfare of the country.

Knowing the true state of affairs, he proposed in *Novaya Zhizn'*

> to devote two or three days to look over what is happening in the galleries of the Aleksandrovsky market, in the antique stalls of Petrograd and in the innumerable secondhand stores that have opened on all the city's streets. . . Not only are Russians robbing their own country, but foreigners too, which is much worse, for the Russian thief remains in the country along with what he has stolen, while the foreigner bolts with it back to his land where, at the expense of Russian carelessness, he fills up his museums and collections, that is, he increases the number of his country's cultural treasures, the value of which is immeasurable, just as immeasurable as is their aesthetic and practical significance.

At Gorky's initiative, the People's Commissariat of Trade and Industry, headed by his old friend Aleksandr Krasin, decreed on December 31, 1918, to establish an Appraisal and Antique Commission (OAK) for the classification and inventorying of luxurious and valuable objets d'art; Gorky was appointed chairman. Answering an inquiry from the Marx-Engels-Lenin Institute in December 1935, Gorky stated, "An expert commission was organized at my initiative and with the consent of V[ladimir] Ilyich for the purpose of selecting objects of high artistic or material value, left behind in the homes and apartments of émigrés, as well as preserved in special repositories. . . . These objects—paintings, bronzes, porcelain, crystal, carpets, and so on—were subject to theft by the servants of these émigrés—lackeys, doormen, caretakers—on orders of the antiques dealers who knew which valuables one noble family or another possessed."

This letter remained secret until the end of the 1980s and has never been published in its entirety to this day. Even the excerpt quoted above was published with several details missing. What danger could there be in this and other documents that revealed such conscientious activity on Gorky's part?

The explanation is very simple. Innumerable treasures, discarded against the will of their owners who were trying to save their own lives, or which remained after the liquidation of those individuals to whom they legally belonged, were cynically being stolen under the pretext of being safeguarded. It was the appropriation of other people's property on a national scale. To judge it from a moral position is meaningless: the seizure of power by the mutineers was amoral and illegal, and the appropriation of property from those overthrown was just the automatic and inevitable consequence. It was not just that the Bolsheviks did this that provoked fury but the fact that Gorky, yesterday's accuser of the Bolsheviks and yesterday's defender of civil rights and general human values, behaved the same way.

It was senseless to be angry at the Leninists—they were very good at "expropriation" even before the "revolution." But nobody expected this from Gorky. It was not some thug or fanatical commissar in a leather coat but the world renowned, handsome writer who would show up at someone else's home, from which some unfortunate fugitives had barely managed to flee, or whose inhabitants had just been carried away to the Chekist torture chambers. The goal was to save the remaining property, not for its rightful owner but for the faceless "people" of the Cheka, decided by Dzerzhinsky or his flunkies.

As Gorky remembered in the same letter dated December 8, 1935:

> The things that were selected, by the employees of the Expert Commission on apartments and repositories, were taken to rooms on the second floor of the Saltykova home on the Martian Fields. They were guarded by watchmen, provided by the Cheka. . . . The items . . . went to auctions, organized by the Cheka.

They went to auction, to be sure, only after Gorky and his team had determined what the Hermitage and other museums should, and should not, be given. It was not the selection that was the problem, but the fact, incomprehensible to his intellectual contemporaries, that it was Gorky himself who spearheaded this plundering of the plundered.

In the final analysis they were responsible for the welfare of Russia, for the preservation of its riches, for the salvation of its culture from barbarism. But Gorky assigned himself a monopoly to this salvation and, together with the authorities, realized his "right."

One essential detail did not escape the attention of his contemporaries: the expert commission with unlimited rights consisted of the Kronverksky inhabitants. Besides Gorky, it included the artists Ivan Rakitsky ("Nightingale") and Andrei Diderikhs ("Didi"), the husband of Valentina Khodasevich. Maria Andreeva was named commissar, and all official documents were drawn up with two signatures: hers and Gorky's. Andreeva's position would later be downgraded to something more concrete: "authorized deputy for the realization of artistic valuables."

Andreeva's functions prior to her appointment were carried out by Yuri Pyatigorsky, an employee of the People's Commissariat of Trade and Industry. He tried to take control of Gorky's commission, demanding to see the list of antiques taken to the warehouse by the inspectors, which on Gorky's personal orders, and without any documentation, were "distributed" afterward to "needy persons." Tens of thousands of works of art, not to mention a huge quantity of antique furniture, thus "drifted away" to parts unknown. Gorky responded to Pyatigorsky's basic demand with an inappropriately coarse letter in which he called his employees untalented and dishonest. "Let's speak bluntly," threateningly wrote Gorky, "what do you want? For the commission to cease its honest work, perhaps because it is disadvantageous to someone?" Everyone knew Gorky's commission was honest, but anyone attempting to control it was after some kind of personal gain.

At Gorky's request, Pyatigorsky was removed from his job and none other than Maria Andreeva put in his place, resulting in an amazing domestic quartet: Gorky, Andreeva, Diderikhs, and Rakitsky. Its unlimited power contained hidden values, both artistic and financial.

Even if none of these people can be suspected of improper behavior, it is still impossible not to be astonished at such a family grouping, absolutely incongruous for people belonging to an intellectual circle. There's no point in mentioning legality, because "revolutionary expediency" at the time *was* the law.

Another circumstance stands out. Gorky invested a great deal of passion, nervous energy and aggressive persistence into this work, devoting a huge amount of his time to it. On May 26, 1919, he wrote to the hated Zinoviev:

> The OAK proposes . . . in the course of the requisition and nationalization of apartments, private houses, palaces, as well as all kinds of warehouses and repositories of movable property up to and including safes, all government organizations and separate individuals as well . . . must summon, prior to the occupation of space. . . . members of the OAK for the inventorying and seizure of objects of artistic and historical significance . . . All organizations and individuals who have carried out the seizure of items without having observed the aforesaid, will answer to the full severity of the laws. M. Gorky.

The style and language of this letter, its revolutionary spirit, and—the main thing—its underlying task betrayed the author's true intentions and the underlying reasons for his uneasiness and profound changes in his consciousness, even in his way of thinking. Not for any other cause and never before had he ever allowed himself to write or, even more to the point, to think like this . . .

"The salvation of cultural valuables" became Gorky's *idée fixe*. During all these years the main theme of his numerous appeals to the authorities was the theme of Russian treasures that had to be assembled immediately. He wrote to Lunacharsky on April 3, 1920:

> Hunger makes people offer items of very high value and great artistic significance to museums, but the museums have no money.
> Then the owners of these items drag them to speculators and antiques dealers who hide them in such a way that they'll never be found.

The antiques dealers—professionals, as opposed to the dilettante Gorky, who are meant to do this kind of work—"hide artworks in order to return them to the market at their true value and only in such a way (how else?) preserve them for history, for culture. But Gorky, in pure Bolshevik fashion, offered a different method: requisition everything of value from the owners and hand it over to the government, which knows what to do with these treasures and can determine where they belong.

Thus began—at Gorky's insistence—the decades-long struggle of the Soviet authorities against people possessed by a genuine passion for collecting. Soviet power could not allow "private individuals" to encroach upon its monopoly to possess, use and dispose of anything having even the smallest commercial value. Gorky made the exception only for himself. Everything else had to go either to a museum or for export.

Thus, the idea of dealing antiques (mostly Russian but foreign as well—thousands of artworks of various schools and individuals had been collected by Russian collectors and wealthy people) also belongs to the writer Gorky. In October 1920 he proposed to Lenin that an Export Fund be created for the accumulation of hard currency from the sale of paintings and antiques and then use that money to buy up goods the country needed. Lenin supported the idea and by October 23, the Fund was already created. Who was chosen to run it? Gorky, of course. The newly appointed chairman of the Fund immediately directed that Rakitsky be sent abroad for the "establishment of ties with antiquarian firms" and that the antiques dealer Mikhail Savostin be made chief advisor for appraising requisitioned items.

Both the Cheka and the People's Commissariat of Foreign Affairs immediately opposed this. The deputy of the People's Commissariat, Maxim Litvinov, was dumbfounded that two individuals who were unknown in Europe would be sent there on such a delicate mission. He did not know that both were personally representing Gorky, and that this "representation" was more than sufficient. The chairman of the Fund appealed to Lenin, using strong inducements: he relied upon Andreeva, who was an even greater authority for Lenin than Gorky—Vladimir Ilyich personally gave her the Party nickname of "Phenomenon."

"M[aria] F[yodorovna] . . . asks you," wrote Gorky to Lenin on November 21, 1920, "to intervene in this matter in order to accelerate the departure of Savostin and Rakitsky." Gorky enlightened Vladimir Ilyich, who had no knowledge of antiques, promising fantastic enrichment from the sale of valuables stolen by the Soviets. He wrote that the "artistically rendered silver from the workshops of Sazikov, Fabergé, Ovchinnikov, and Khlebnikov are marketable items, which—owing to the cessation of production—have now become antiques . . . The value of these manufactured goods has increased several times." And, in an effort to enflame Lenin's imagination in language understandable to the leader of the proletariat, Gorky added, "We need to publish a decree about the confiscation of émigré property."

Gorky was too late with this advice! As far as confiscation and requisition were concerned, Lenin knew about this as well as Gorky. Five days before Gorky sent this truly historic letter—November 16, 1920—a decree had already been passed. Incidentally, it cannot be excluded that Gorky had imparted this advice to Lenin earlier, and Lenin, not waiting for the details in writing, followed this advice. In any case, Gorky is directly involved in one of the most loathsome crimes committed by the Bolsheviks—the fleecing of tens, even hundreds, of thousands of people, guilty only of having legally invested in works of art, thereby promoting the development of domestic culture and multiplying the riches of their country.

Not that long before, in the summer of 1918, Gorky angrily condemned in *Novaya Zhizn'* those by whose will or connivance works of art had left the country: the quote from this article was reproduced above. Now, with the same fervor—but secretly in correspondence with the leaders—he passionately argued for the need to trade Russian antiquity for filling the Soviet treasury. It is not incorrect to state that Gorky was the source of the shameful business in art for the sake of global Bolshevik ambitions! The earnings from the sale of antiques, plus the masterpieces of the Hermitage, plus the gold reserve, plus church utensils and more, was not used to support the people starving along the Volga, as claimed in the Soviet press, but to feed the "fraternal" parties, Moscow's main agency for subversive activities abroad, and for maintaining the *nomenklatura* and the punitive organs.

Gorky can be viewed as the forefather, initiator and main engine of this business. He floated the idea and it was realized. Everything else depended upon the skill of the Soviet merchants.

Gorky ran himself ragged in a multitude of activities, each demanding his complete attention and energy. The role of supreme protector, which he had voluntarily taken upon himself, caused silent irritation among those who believed that only they, by dint of their positions, were authorized to decide the fate of both science and scientists. The Bolshevik demagogy regarding "universal equality" prompted Gorky to convince Party leaders, reminding them of the benefit of the intellectual potential of the country and of skilled masters in their professions. Gorky wrote in 1920 to the Party officials responsible for science:

> If we make a talented metal worker clean cesspools, if the jeweler begins to forge anchors and the chemist is driven to working the earth, this is not only stupid, but criminal. It is criminal to spend the most precious energy of the people on trivialities, for this energy can enrich and make people happy only where it follows its very nature.
>
> . . . Workers of science must be valued precisely as the most productive and valuable energy of the people, and that is why we must create conditions for them, for the growth of this energy to be encouraged as much as possible.

Any mention of the superiority of the intellect and knowledge, art and mastery over darkness and ignorance, irritated people who had risen to power from nothing, with an extremely low education, and sometimes with none at all. The possibility of demeaning the intellectual without retribution satisfied their base instincts and elevated themselves in their own eyes. In turn, Gorky, protecting the greatest figures of Russian science, willingly or unwillingly satisfied his vanity by taking the role of savior, without whose intercession the flower of a nation was condemned to death. The rhetorical question of American essayist Boris Paramonov "was there not [here] the sweet realization of the Academy's dependence on yesterday's barefoot person?"[*] seems totally relevant.

The wave of arrests that claimed a large number of scientists and reached its first peak in 1919 (the mass arrests of members of the Constitutional Democratic party—the "cadets"—to which most of the Russian intelligentsia belonged, had begun) provoked Gorky's unrestrained fury. His letter to Lenin, hidden in the secret archives until 1993, speaks for itself. Lenin, in one of his letters to Gorky, had called him mentally incompetent:

> Yes, I am mentally incompetent, but I am not blind, I am not a politician, and I am not stupid, as politicians often are. I know that you are used to "operating the masses" and a person for you is a non-entity, but for me Mechnikov, Pavlov, Fyodorov are *the most brilliant scientists in the world*, its brain. You politicians are metaphysicians, and I am an insane artist, but more of a rationalist than you are.
>
> There is little brain power in Russia, we have few talented people and too many—too many!—crooks, scoundrels, adventurers. . . . I say count everything that has been accomplished by people of science during the time of existence of Sov[iet] pow[er]—. . . you will be amazed at the quantity and quality of work done by people half-starved, kicked out of their apartments, humiliated in every way possible, dragged into prisons.
>
> To eradicate the half-starved old scientists, stuffing them into prisons, exposing them to the fists of idiots crazed by the effects of their power is not business but barbarism.

Almost simultaneously Gorky wrote to "Yuzef"[†] Dzerzhinsky, Chairman of the VChK: ". . . I am reporting to you that I look upon these arrests as barbarism, as the destruction of the best brains in the country and I declare . . . that I have a hostile attitude toward Soviet power."

Gorky expressed himself even more clearly—and for the same reason—two months later in another letter to Lenin: "The Communists need to be thrashed. Ah, if you only knew what thieves they are! And what revolting bourgeois they will become in two–three years!"

All these letters from Gorky were obviously kept under the strictest classification until the end of the 1980s and, even after they were published (the letter to Dzerzhinsky in 1989, the letters to Lenin after the dissolution of the

[*] Referring to Gorky.
[†] Dzerzhinsky's name was Felix. Gorky's use of his Party pseudonym "Yuzef" in this case is very noteworthy.

USSR), were supplied with commentary intended to diminish their passionate anti-Soviet ardor . . .

Among those arrested were the most prominent representatives from all the branches of the sciences—heat technology engineers, chemists, mathematicians, botanists, physiologists, psychiatrists, Orientalists, linguists. Gorky's defense of these men elicited another attack of Lenin's wrath. The leader thought it necessary to respond not only to Gorky but also to Andreeva, presuming that she still had any influence over the Stormy Petrel.

Lenin to Gorky: "To waste yourself on the sniveling of rotten intellectuals . . . —shame on you."

Lenin to Andreeva: "We must arrest, for the prevention of plots, *all* Cadets and Cadet sympathizers (that is, preventively, even without any guilt). They are capable, all of them, of aiding the plotters. It would be criminal not to arrest them."

Gorky was unbowed:

> Vladimir Ilyich! I stand on their [the arrested] side and prefer arrest and incarceration in prison to participation—even in silence—in the destruction of the best, most valuable forces of the Russian people. For me it has become clear that the "reds" are just as much enemies of the people as the "whites." I personally, to be sure, prefer to be destroyed by the "whites," but the "reds" are not my comrades either.

Gorky's letters to Lenin circulated around Petrograd and Moscow, passed from hand to hand, as there was no one besides him who could publish them in that early version of "samizdat." Some copies even made it abroad, causing indignation among comrades from the "fraternal" European parties: they could not tolerate that the "great proletarian writer" and "singer of the revolution" would dare speak *like that* to his leader. Hurrying to repudiate the possessed fanatics and open the eyes of the blinded, Russian émigrés found themselves in the position of "slanderers" insofar as they could not imagine the originals of Gorky's letters, and Gorky himself, playing a dual game, refrained from publishing them. Only several years ago do the declassified documents make it possible to finally determine who did the slandering then, and who was zealous in his kowtowing diligence to serve the Kremlin.

7.

Face and Mask

Gorky's patience had run its course. In December 1919 he wrote to Lenin, without mincing his words: "I, of course, do not believe that the Russian people felt an active hatred toward the monarchy. No, they simply tolerated it, just as shamefully as they now tolerate the brutal and dull regime of Sov[iet] Power." The creator of the dull regime did not respond. What could he have answered? That he'd make a note of it and strongly keep it in mind if his memory still worked then? There was no common language and there would not likely be one.

Yet Gorky could not complete any tasks if he was completely out of touch with the regime and in communication with its hierarchy. The dull regime also could not, at least for the time being, refuse to acknowledge its accuser. When the propaganda photo-montage "Creators of the October Revolution" was published on the third anniversary of the Bolshevik revolution, Gorky, along with many people whose names have long since disappeared into the fog of history, was represented alongside a gigantic portrait of Lenin (but there was no place for Stalin). The man who had publicly exposed the jubilee of the revolution in all his incendiary passion was nonetheless represented as one of its standard-bearers, and Gorky accepted this obvious absurdity.

He shuffled back and forth between different extremes, unable to break with one world and enter the other. The whole time he tiptoed back and forth in a balancing act, trying to maintain, to the extent possible, good relationships with people who irreconcilably sat in hostile camps, to be the link between them and to feel, if not their respect, at least their "acknowledgment for services rendered." These attempts to be on good terms with everyone stood out like the proverbial sore thumb and were surprising to many. He had always been hospitable, and now people, who under any other circumstances would never come together, assembled around his huge table on Kronverksky.

Various memoirists essentially name the same visitors of his "revolutionary salon." It is strange to read but, thanks to this list, one can better understand what and at whom Gorky was aiming, what gave him satisfaction, and how he appeared to his visitors and guests. Lenin, Dzerzhinsky, even Zinoviev, could be seen in the same kind of camaraderie as the Menshevik Nikolai Sukhanov; or Fyodor Chaliapin, who despised the Bolsheviks; or Yevgeni Zamyatin and Boris Pilnyak, authors of veiled satires against Soviet power. The Chekist executioner Yakov Agranov sat at the same table with his future victims. Refined intellectuals did not immediately understand that the guests being introduced to them and with whom they were carrying on an enlightened conversation were none other than the pair then thundering across the entire country: Aleksandra Kollontai, the Valkyrie of the Revolution, and her common-law husband, Pavel Dybenko, head of the red sailors of the Baltic Fleet.

Petrograd was wrapped in cold and darkness and the corpses of people who had died from hunger littered the streets; but on Kronverksky, it was always warm and cozy, logs crackled in the fireplace, the many candelabra and torchère lamps created a pleasant half-glow, and burning tapers imparted to the friendly dinner parties an intimacy which, it seemed, had vanished forever. The table was not particularly distinguished by any great abundance, let alone elegance, but there was plenty of food and it was always tasty thanks to the housekeeper who was also cook. Chaliapin sang for the guests while Issay Dobrowen played the popular music of the time. Henrietta Rodzhers, an actress from the Mikhailovsky Theater, who would later marry Claude Farrère in Paris, entertained the guests with Russian and gypsy romances. The host himself, a great raconteur, regaled the guests with tales of his barefoot childhood and hungry adolescence.

Many contemporaries recalled that Lenin dropped by Gorky's apartment "for tea," but when did that happen? And why are there no details of it in all the vast Leniniana? The contradiction could be chalked up to the spotty recollections of the memoirists or to their reproduction of the rumors in circulation, but the fact is that no such rumors were going around then. However, there is other indirect evidence confirming that Lenin visited the former capital in 1919 and, perhaps, in 1920, and not only to take part in the second congress of the Comintern where he did, in fact, see Gorky. But this was in the Tavrichesky Palace where the sessions of the Congress were taking place, and not secretly at his home.

In her later years Valentina Khodasevich wrote her reminiscences, significantly devoted to Gorky. Her manuscript contains a story about how she—the only one among the guests of the apartment on Kronverksky at the time—witnessed Lenin's secret visit to Gorky. Following their conversation, Gorky led him out through the back door. Because of censorship, this episode was not included in the published text of her memoirs. But in 1993 Vyacheslav Ivanov, a well-known philologist who had assisted Valentina Khodasevich with her manuscript, was able to reproduce in print, from memory, the contents of the censored passage.

My prematurely deceased friend Vladimir Lakshin, who prepared the publication of Valentina Khodasevich's memoirs in the magazine *Novy Mir*, said exactly the same thing. Lakshin told me this in 1992, and I wrote it down immediately following our conversation. Not only this secret visit (or possibly visits) by Lenin but also the fear of Party censors, even during the Khrushchev "thaw," to reproduce the story of an eyewitness for discussion by historians, remains a mystery.

There is a version—thus far only a version—that Lenin used to travel unannounced to Petrograd to meet with Gorky in an effort to quell the conflict between them, when their relations had practically reached the breaking point. That notwithstanding, Soviet propaganda for decades had promoted the myth that Lenin disliked Gorky, and was even afraid of him (and Lenin was not afraid of many people!). While he did not want to lose such a prominent name, at the same time, Lenin already recognized that Gorky's name did not promote nor elevate the international prestige of Soviet power, but harmed it instead.

Infuriated by the endless carping, taunts, and bureaucratic red tape (most of all affecting his own publishing activities) which he encountered in both Petrograd and Moscow, Gorky wrote an official letter to Lenin in September 1920, informing him that he no longer wished to be "tormented" and "led around by the nose"; that he was tired of all the "stupidity"; and, abdicating all responsibilities which until then he had been carrying, refused "to work . . . in all . . . institutions where he had worked until the present day." "This decision has been thought through," he added.

Oddly, the Chekists' dossier on Gorky preserves not only the original of this—opened and read—letter to Lenin but the rough draft as well! The texts do not principally differ, except for one sentence, striking in its tone but, alas, incomplete, which did not show up in the letter: "It is better to perish from hunger than to allow all that . . ." How then did this draft enter the collection of opened correspondence? Gorky did not send Lenin the final version along with his jottings!

The logical conclusion, therefore, is that the rough draft was somehow stolen from him. Only a typewritten copy of the rough draft was kept in the archives of the Cheka, but someone took it. Did another secret search take place on Kronverksky? It cannot be excluded, although it is highly doubtful. Or perhaps someone from Gorky's circle, with access to all his papers, had copied the text? This hypothesis sounds more plausible. And, finally, there is a variant that the rough draft was confiscated a year after it was written from Zinovy Grzhebin, prior to his happy banishment from Russia. Another question triumphs over all the others: when did these papers fall into the hands of the Cheka? The reliability of the typewritten copies is confirmed by an employee of the "organs," Slavatinsky, who recorded two different dates alongside his signature: "21 March 1923" on the copy of the final version, and "21 March 1922" on the copy of the rough draft. One of them is an obvious mistake—in March 1922 neither Grzhebin nor Gorky were in Russia: they had left together. More likely than not, the Chekists had seized copies of Gorky's letters much earlier, which means that even after Gorky was beyond their reach, Dzerzhinsky's people continued to compile their dossier on the Stormy Petrel.

Gorky's moods were already rather obvious by autumn 1920. After having burned out and then somewhat cooled off, he retained all the positions that were so dear to him and was forced to continue this game, thinking one thing, saying another, and doing a third. This forced and complicated double game made him a nervous wreck and opened the prospect of an inevitable collapse.

The need to live simultaneously on several levels and play many roles at the same time helped create a new Gorky "image," which gradually became second nature. In fact, it puts everyone attempting to penetrate the mystery of this legendary person and separate the true face from the mask at a loss.

During this period he clearly did not want to look like a Bolshevik or even a "Bolshevizing" writer. At his birthday party at *Vsemirnaya Literatura*, he leaned over to Kornei Chukovsky and whispered, "They are making arrests again." Chukovsky commented, "He always said 'they' when speaking about the Bolsheviks. Always as enemies." The same diary cites an analogous opinion by other writers who were in close contact with Gorky. One of them, the critic and essayist Akim Volynsky, believed, for example, that "Gorky is a diplomat. With us he says one thing, but with them another. It is a very subtle form of diplomacy."

Everyone who came into contact with Gorky and observed him closely, trying to penetrate the secrets of his soul, recognized his two sides. Chukovsky's diary, made public only in the 1990s, lifts the veil on this mystery, painting a highly convincing, even if extremely subjective, psychological portrait of a man with whom he had been in close daily contact for almost three years. It is noteworthy that Chukovsky was also compelled to live a double life. He spoke and wrote in censored books the complete opposite of what he really thought of Gorky, entrusting his true thoughts only to his diary.

Gorky is meagerly talented, internally dull, exactly what is required these days. The old cultural milieu no longer exists—it died and it would take a century to revive it. They don't understand anything the slightest bit complex. Only refined people, and not commissars, understand irony. . . . That is exactly why Gorky is now an icon, because he is not psychological, but simple, elementary.

Gorky clever?! He's not clever, but simple-minded to the point of mental incompetence. He understands nothing of real life (incidentally, Lenin thought the same thing, but from a completely different viewpoint). If everyone around him [the ones he loves] are favorably disposed toward someone, [then] he instinctively and irrationally loves that p[erson]. If someone close to him (Mme. Shaikevich, Maria Fyod[orovna], the "merchant lady" Khodasevich, Tikhonov, Grzhebin) suddenly stops liking someone—it's over! He does everything for those who belong to *him*, signs any kind of paper, and becomes a pawn to them. Grzhebin can twist Gorky around his pinky. But everyone else is an enemy. . . . He was dragged into Bolshevism. . . . It's easy as pie to deceive him. . . . In his circle he is trustworthy and submissive. The profiteer Makhlin therefore lives on the same floor next to Tikhonov. G[orky] had this person freed from the Cheka, and saved him from the firing squad . . .

Even if Gorky was "simpleminded to the point of mental incompetence, even if he timorously succumbed to the influence of those around him, he still used those qualities to help whomever he could, even a real profiteer. Then and later, right up to the inglorious end of the Soviet Union, aiding specific in-dividuals and saving them from faceless power was a worthy deed, deserving only gratitude, regardless of the motives of the savior.

One can even say that during the revolution Gorky simply bet on several horses in order to win, whatever the outcome. So be it! But if he managed to save at least one person in that bloody horse race, does it matter what the goal was or with whom these bets were placed? One can use an historical analogy, popularized by the film *Schindler's List*. Did it really matter to those Jewish martyrs, rescued from the gas chambers, what goals Schindler was pursuing as long as he saved them from certain death?

The list of Gorky's good deeds is very long—under the circumstances it is unnecessary to discuss his feelings, or under whose influence he acted, and what was his goal. To distribute rations in a lordly manner in exchange for loyalty is one thing, but to save a person from the inevitable bullet is something else altogether.

In his memoirs the writer Boris Zaitsev repeated the rumor that Gorky had supposedly saved 278 people. "Where does such accuracy come from?" asked Zaitsev ironically. It seems that the "accuracy" in fact came from someone else, clearly not Gorky, in order to shed doubt about his participation in rescuing people. This number was lodged in Zaitsev's head. When we met in Paris in 1968, he repeated it in various ways, ridiculing the "meticulousness" with which Gorky "kept track of his good deeds," and emphasizing that part of Gorky's biography.

Zinaida Gippius (who asked Chukovsky, and more than once, to intercede on her behalf with Gorky) wrote about this even more maliciously:

> Gorky, in the depths of boorishness and almost villainy, intoxicated with power, nevertheless took "a Romanov" into his apartment, from prison, a member of the imperial family. He took him under the pretext of sending him to Finland, but he didn't do that and keeps the ailing person in his room full of antiques only to mock him daily. How despicable!

Her testimony, if it reveals anything, is only evidence of the extreme capriciousness and frequent unreliability of memoirs. Doctor Manukhin recalls the very same episode completely differently, and much more accurately, even though the paths of these people—Gorky and Manukhin—who were once close had long since diverged by then:

> In the fiercest, bloodiest period of the first years of the Bolshevik terror the Grand Dukes Pavel Aleksandrovich, Dmitri Konstantinovich, Nikolai Mikhailovich and . . . Gavriil Konstantinovich were arrested and imprisoned in the f[ormer] Exiles Prison on Shpalernaya Street. I appealed to Gorky many times to secure their freedom, because only Gorky, he alone, could do this at the time through Lenin.
>
> Thanks to Gorky's persistent requests, Lenin agreed to free G[avriil] K[onstantinovich], and the duke was taken to the private sanatorium of D[octor] Gerzoni. Soon after Gorky said, "So okay, they freed him. Now what? If he remains with Gerzoni, they'll kill him.* There is no other way out, I have to take him to my place. They won't dare touch him in my apartment."

Gavriil Konstantinovich was the son of the Grand Duke Konstantin Romanov, president of the Academy of Artists and a talented poet who published under the pseudonym of K. R. Gorky hid him and his wife, the ballerina Anastasia Nesterovskaya (the marriage was morganatic, as Tsar Nicholas did not consent to it) and their bulldog, on Kronverksky, and they ate at the same table with Gorky and his guests. "Gorky greeted us cordially," Anastasia Nesterovskaya wrote later, "and offered us a large room with four windows, completely filled with furniture. . . . Company often gathered [at Gorky's],

---

* The memory of how drunken sailors had killed the ministers of the provisional government, Kokoshkin and Shingarev, who were in the hospital, was still too fresh.

which took joy in our troubles and were grieved at our joys." The grand duke, however, was safe at Kronverksky. A little bit later Gorky—again from Lenin and Andreeva from Zinoviev—obtained permission for the grand duke and his wife to leave for Finland. Their lives were saved thanks only to Gorky, and they never forgot this.

The fate of the other grand dukes, Pavel Aleksandrovich and the eminent historian Nikolai Mikhailovich, whom Gorky also tried to save, turned out much sadder. Lenin, whom Gorky had specially gone to see regarding this matter, resisted for a long time, but nonetheless gave the "solicitor" a personal letter for Zinoviev with an order to allow the grand dukes to go abroad.

Strangely, Gorky took the letter at face value—if Lenin had really wanted to help, he could have contacted Petrograd then and there on a direct line. After he had returned, Gorky learned from a newspaper he purchased at the train station that Zinoviev had ordered his wards executed the night before. Who had informed the Petrograd dictator about Gorky's visit and the document which he had taken to Moscow? Lenin himself? A telegram, which Lenin sent afterwards to Zinoviev, ordering him to prevent Nikolai Mikhailovich's departure, is oblique but very convincing proof of this. Zinoviev correctly understood his friend's intention and reached the proper conclusions.

Manukhin was right: Gorky could not play the role of "intercessor for the persecuted bourgeois. . . . persuader, shamer." Nevertheless, he did this for several years. Incidentally, he saved Manukhin as well. Having become convinced of his method for treating tuberculosis (by irradiating the spleen), Gorky took a fancy to him and his bold projects, which held out the promise of deliverance from many diseases. "Manukhin must be given the opportunity to find a serum for typhus," he wrote to Lenin in March 1920, "but he can't do anything here." Dzerzhinsky, and especially Zinoviev, tried in every way possible to prevent Manukhin from going abroad, but Gorky persisted and Lenin finally agreed: Manukhin was given permission to emigrate to Paris.

Strictly speaking, there was nothing exclusive about Gorky's humanitarian activity. Everyone at the time looked for help among influential people, realizing that there was no other way to save one's skin. The archives of the Party bigwigs, which are now partially accessible, are filled with such personal requests. Every one appealed to someone with whom there was some kind of connection, however shaky or illusory it may have been: a drowning man will clutch at straws.

For example, a man by the name of Samuil Rozenfeld from Odessa, appealing for help from the then powerful Kamenev (whose real name was Rozenfeld), introduced himself as his "uncle on his papa's side," addressing him as "Dear Lev Abramovich." The dear "relative," however, was called Lev

Borisovich—the author of the letter having mistaken the name of his "brother." Alas, none of this is funny—everyone sought the tiniest salvation in the bloodshed. Gorky was one of them.

On September 4, 1919, Chukovsky wrote in his diary:

> I just saw Gorky crying. Sergei Fyodorovich Oldenburg was arrested—he exclaimed, "What can I do? I told those scoundrels, that is, *the* scoundrel [Zinoviev], that if they don't let him go . . . this instant, I'll create a scandal for them, I'll leave for good. . . . They can go to hell."

Chukovsky's testimony is completely trustworthy because an irate letter to Lenin (mentioning the academician Oldenburg, an outstanding Orientalist, permanent secretary of the Academy of Sciences and former minister of enlightenment of the Provisional Government), kept secret until 1993, was dated two days later—September 6, 1919:

> Several dozen of the most prominent Russian scientists (a list follows) have been arrested here. I consider it necessary to tell you my candid opinion: for me the wealth of the country, the strength of the people, is expressed in the quantity and quality of its intellectual strength. The revolution only has meaning when it promotes growth and development of these strengths. Scientists must be treated as carefully and respectfully as possible. . . . In saving our own necks, we cut off the head of the people, destroy its brain.
>
> It is clear we have no hope of winning nor the courage to die with honor, if we resort to such barbaric and shameful methods, which is what I consider the destruction of the country's scientific strength to be.
>
> What does this method of self-defense mean, other than despair, weakness, or— finally—a desire to avenge ourselves of our own mediocrity?
>
> I decisively protest against this tactic, which targets the best brains of the people, who are already spiritually impoverished as is.

Lenin's reply to Gorky's secret letter was also concealed in the archive for decades, and only excerpts were made available. This is perhaps one of Lenin's most terrible letters, revealing the force of an inveterate misanthrope's bloodthirsty sentiments previously carefully concealed. The worst of it is that Lenin chose a genuinely sacred figure of Russian democracy, Vladimir Korolenko, for his invective.

> The step of arresting the Cadets and near-Cadets was necessary and correct. . . . To mix the "intellectual strengths" of the people with the "strengths" of the bourgeois intellectuals is incorrect. I take Korolenko as an example. . . A pitiful petit-bourgeois, captivated by bourgeois prejudices! For such gentlemen . . . the

death of hundreds of thousands in a *justified* civil war against the landowners and capitalists elicits "oh"s and "ah"s, sighs and hysterics. The intellectual strengths of the workers and peasants grow and become stronger in the struggle to overthrow the bourgeois and its accomplices, intellectuals and lackeys of capital, imagining themselves as the brains of the nation. In fact this is not brains but shit. You allow yourself to be surrounded by precisely the worst elements of the bourgeois intelligentsia and fall for their whimpering.

Gorky replied with an extremely strange and muddled letter, though it was not its content but the manner in which it was addressed that set the tone: "My dear Vladimir Ilyich." This signified that Gorky accepted the cynical crudeness, if not outright boorishness of the tyrant, drunk with power and proclaiming himself leader of the world revolution, without flinching. He accepted the spit in his face—and wiped it off. Now anything could be done with him.

Lenin, a political pragmatist, reluctantly compromised, but only partially. Some of those arrested were set free. But Lenin did not hide his true feelings by any means.

To Gorky's argument, "They are arresting people who were your comrades only yesterday, and who hid you personally in their apartments during the Tsarist period," Lenin replied, according to Lunacharsky's memoirs, "Yes, praiseworthy, good people, and that is why they have to be arrested. They are praiseworthy and good, their sympathy is always with the oppressed and they are always against persecution. But what do they see now? The persecutor is our Cheka, the oppressed are fleeing Cadets and SRs. Obviously, their duty, as they understand it, compels them to become their allies against us. We must apprehend and disarm the active counterrevolutionaries."

Lenin "apprehended" them; Gorky saved them. When, in that same year 1919, the writers Yevgeni Zamyatin and Aleksei Remizov, the artist Kuzma Petrov-Vodkin, and others were arrested, Gorky immediately rushed to Zinoviev and eventually won their freedom. When another writer, Ivan Volnov, was arrested in 1919 in the north of Russia, Gorky obtained his freedom too. To this day his letters to the deputy of the People's Commissariat of Education of the Union of Northern Communes, Zakhar Grinberg, soliciting on behalf of the persecuted figures of culture, have never been published. There is little Grinberg could have done without Zinoviev's consent, but through guile and cunning almost every one of Gorky's requests was satisfied.

A multitude of very different people have subsequently considered it their duty to record Gorky's help—not to obtaining some modest blessings, but for saving their life. The maid of honor at the imperial court, Anna Vyrubova, whose name is unjustly and scandalously connected to the dark history of

Grigori Rasputin, admitted in a book published in Berlin in 1923 that Gorky saved her from reprisals and helped get her out of the country. The list of those whom he helped leave is very long. It includes Doctor Manukhin, the writer Aleksei Remizov, and many, many other names.

Badgered by local Soviet authorities in Sergiev Posad outside Moscow, the writer Vasily Rozanov turned to Gorky as his last hope:

> Maksimushka, save me from final despair, if not from the next world, then from its very edge . . . Maksimushka, I reach out for your hands. You know what it means to reach out for your hands? I don't know what to do. I will die, I will die, I will die . . .

The appeal was too late; he should have reached out for Gorky's hand earlier: Vasily Rozanov died.

In brief memoirs, written after Gorky's death, Fyodor Chaliapin maintained that intercession for those arrested and hounded "was the main purpose of his life in the first period of bolshevism." These words, uttered by someone who had already managed to become cruelly disenchanted with Gorky, bears witness to a truth which cannot be disputed.

8.

The Ladies Loved Him

People who otherwise could not count on any kind of support turned to Gorky not only for salvation from arrests and executions, but also in the hope of escaping hunger or to find shelter and clothing. Some legends relating to this activity have migrated from one book to another for decades. One was started by Valentina Khodasevich and endures to this day. The time has come to separate the truth from romantic sentimentalism.

This is what Valentina Khodasevich wrote in her memoirs about an episode from 1919:

> One morning the doorbell rang [on Kronverksky]. A young woman burst into the foyer, sobbing, and demanded she be allowed to see Gorky. Nightingale [Rakitsky] said that A[leksei] M[aksimovich] was working and could not be disturbed. . . . She . . . said that she had a suckling infant without any milk and that she had come to ask Gorky to help her get regular deliveries of milk for her child. As she said this, she came completely undone and began sobbing bitterly. Rakitsky realized that he had to do something to ease her grief. He fetched a brush, pan, and rag from the pantry and proposed that she wipe and dust the foyer while waiting for A. M., which turned out to be a good idea.
>
> When A. M. appeared during a break from his work, [the woman] repeated her story in a rational manner. He wrote a letter addressed to one of his comrades in charge of food distribution for Petrograd, and gave it to her. And for greater effect he wrote that it concerned his illegal child but asked that it be kept a secret. [The woman] left, shedding tears of gratitude. Nightingale asked her to come back some time and let them know if she was getting the milk, and at the same time to clean his room, because she is so good at it. He even got her to smile at this.

Evidently recognizing the ambiguity of this episode, Valentina Khodasevich considered it necessary to continue, embellishing it with what, in particular, subsequently became legend:

Many other women showed up with the same request. A. M., wishing to help them all, wrote letters, adopting their children in the letters until, finally, the comrade to whom he had written said that, unfortunately, he was unable to supply such a large number of Gorky's "children" with milk. And we laughed at A. M. and embarrassed him: "At your age, in your position . . . it's a bit awkward . . . so many children, and from different mothers." "I swear—I'll never do it again!" said A. M. and laughed until he cried.

This entire tale is completely at odds with a detail which Khodasevich relates a few pages later. On that same day, when the incident described above took place, "M[aria] F[yodorovna] spent a long time with Gorky and, after leaving the house in the evening, did not return to spend the night." Why did this funny incident, so typical of Gorky—as solicitor for the downtrodden and humiliated—annoy her so much?

The woman who had come that day to see Gorky was the poet Natalia Vasilyevna Grushko, who was twenty-seven at the time. Those who saw her (which is not very many) recall her sad, huge gray eyes. She had been formally married twice, and in the interim had had a short affair with the Russian writer Ignaty Potapenko, very popular at the end of the nineteenth and early twentieth centuries. Thirty-six years her senior, Potapenko was once friends with Chekhov and was involved in one of the most dramatic events in Chekhov's life. Lika Mizinova, who was in love with Chekhov, but kept at arm's length by the writer who liked her but did not respond to her ardor in kind, became Potapenko's paramour and bore him a son. This story appeared in Chekhov's *The Seagull.* Contemporaries were able to recognize, rather easily, Lika in the character of Nina Zarechnaya, and Potapenko in the writer Trigorin.

Gorky exacted a strange but clear revenge against Chekhov. But now with fatal inevitability his turn had come. The suckling infant in Valentina Khodasevich's story was not imaginary but actually Gorky's son, and not even the first but second. The young woman, without a real profession, and without the means to survive, remained alone. The well-known literary historian, Professor Yulian Oksman, who was very close to Gorky in the 1930s and worked with him in the Pushkin House of the Academy of Sciences, discussed this in detail. The playwright Leonid Zorin wrote it down and recently published his story, disguising Grushko's name with an initial.

Only specialists in Russian literature of the first third of the twentieth century would recognize the name of the poet Natalia Grushko. Her verses do not transcend the boundaries of traditional "women's" lyrics, and her plays (she also wrote plays) are amazing in their total absence of scenic sensibility, although one of them (*Blind Love*) was staged in the Imperial Petersburg

Theater. Nevertheless, she had the good fortune to remain active in the arts for many long years: one of her poems was set to music and performed by Aleksandr Vertinsky for decades. It spread throughout Russia on hundreds of thousands of records and even to this day is sometimes heard on the radio: "I'm a tiny ballerina / Always mute / But pantomime will speak more clearly / Than I can myself."

The legend of other women appealing to Gorky "with the exact same requests" and he fully acknowledging their children as his own so that the suffering mothers could get their milk rations, was set in motion precisely in order to hide the truth by presenting Gorky, who had renounced his children, as a philanthropist ready to perform a good deed even to glorify himself. No other letter from Gorky has surfaced except his letter to the Executive Committee of the Polyustrovsky Rural District Council, dated March 29, 1919: ". . . for your attention regarding milk for N. V. Grushko and her child, I sincerely thank you."

Incidentally, moved by the confidence Gorky had placed in them and letting them in on the secret of his bastard child, the comrades from the Polyustrovsky Rural District Council decided to apportion not only milk to the nursing mother, but together with the father of the child—Comrade Gorky—about a hundred pounds of sauerkraut. Gorky, straining to be funny, categorically protested: "Save it! I'll start speculating in that sauerkraut."

Thus the reason why Andreeva left the home, after having suddenly found out about something she apparently was not supposed to know, becomes all the more comprehensible. But she did not leave for long. Romance was not a novelty to the occupants of the apartment on Kronverksky, where everyone was used to everything and exhibited great tolerance to all.

Kriuchkov showed up at Kronverksky shortly after March 1919 without any hesitation whatsoever, settling in Maria Fyodorovna's half of the apartment and by no means serving only as her secretary. And Mura moved in right after him, but in Gorky's half, at the time still stubbornly calling herself by her maiden name of Zakrevskaya: the surname of her murdered husband—Benkendorf—which she formally used was definitely not agreeable with the new authorities.

The relationships of these people certainly did not settle into cozy, commonplace patterns: the husband threw out the wife, the wife left the husband. In their contacts with one another they were guided by other principles and a different morality, but without severing—no matter what the turn of events—their former ties, while switching, and not always easily, their affections and feelings.

That is the reason the judgments of Mikhail Sholokhov, expressed in the early 1960s to the American journalist Olga Carlyle—the granddaughter of Leonid Andreev (let us not forget that Andreev is the real name of the writer; Andreeva was the stage name of Maria Fyodorovna Zhelyabuzhskaya, who later made it her official name)—look so utterly primitive: "Over the course of many years and right up until his death, I did not see Gorky," declared the author of *Quiet Flows the Don*, unafraid of being caught in a lie, "because of the way Gorky treated Andreeva. [She] sacrificed everything—husband, career, money—for the sake of Gorky and the revolution. But Gorky dumped her and did not wish to have anything more to do with her. I could not forgive him for this."

Besides the vulgarity and sanctimonious thoughts, typical of the future Nobel laureate, Sholokhov is clearly lying here. He had forgotten what he himself had said only a few years earlier at a meeting with employees of the Gorky Archive on May 16, 1955: "After . . . the first meeting (1929? 1931?), I saw Gorky often. . . . Aleksei Maksimovich and I talked a lot about literature." These meetings, as he himself wrote to Gorky, gave him "a great surge of courage and desire to work."

He wished to see Gorky at Sorrento, but could not obtain an Italian visa. He flatteringly wrote to "dear Aleksei Maksimovich:" "Thank you . . . for your warm and attentive attitude toward me," "I shake your hand and strongly hope that the winds won't blow, that your bones won't ache, that your cough will not overtake you, that everything will be good for you there" (December 1932).

We have interrupted our narrative with this digression about the Nobel laureate and inveterate liar. Let us now return to the early 1920s.

Gorky once admitted to Yulian Oksman, "I was very unhappy with women." Oksman could argue with Gorky because of their friendly relations even on such delicate themes. Oksman objected: "You, who have been loved by such madonnas, can say this!" But Gorky obviously knew himself better than Oksman. "The ones I loved," he continued, "did not love me. The closer she was, the farther I felt. The farther she was, the more desirable she became." He did not say who, but Oksman knew perfectly well whom Gorky had in mind.

His love for Mura was hopeless from the very beginning. Even though she magically attracted men, Mura was different because of her rationalism, perhaps even calculation and reserve, which is often called coldness, although she was never at a loss for warm—even hot—words, both spoken and written. In this sense she was the complete opposite of Gorky, who was stingy with words both in his letters to his beloved women and in expressions of love—but not in his feelings. He was famous not only for his amorous exploits, but also for his extreme sentimentality, which led him to cry unabashedly even at the most trivial sufferings. This was by no means the manifestation of ordinary senile weepiness—he wept tears of tender emotion well before he had turned fifty.

Andreeva distanced herself even farther from Gorky—it can be presumed that, having lived through his affair with Tikhonova, she was completely broken by the news of Grushko, which had especially wounded her feminine pride. But she had already moved beyond Gorky. Her devotion to Kriuchkov was not ephemeral, and her hectic official and public activity did not leave room or time for any deep suffering. While fulfilling her functions as commissar, she tried not to forget her artistic calling. Together with Aleksandr Blok, Andreeva was occupied at this time with reorganizing a private Petersburg theater into a state theater, creating the Great Dramatic Theater that continued for eighty-five years and is now named after Georgi Tovstonogov. It made its début with Shakespeare, and the forty-nine-year-old Andreeva played her last role on stage as Desdemona.

Meanwhile, changes were taking place among the tenants at Kronverksky. The Tikhonovs moved out while Kriuchkov moved in; Valentina Khodasevich and her husband were living there. Andreeva's children moved in with her, but Maxim, who no longer needed his mother's permission, also stayed in his father's apartment for a long time. Incidentally, Gorky's final and complete break-up with Andreeva removed the reason for Peshkova's previously energetic resistance to her son living in that apartment.

Not immediately, but by degrees and with a kind of natural irrevocability, Mura began taking on the role of full-fledged mistress of the house. Her entry into the "commune" was further strengthened by her domestic nickname. Having told the inhabitants of Gorky's apartment that she had been born in the Ukraine, Mura immediately and unconditionally became "Titka" which in translation from Ukrainian to Russian means nothing more than "Auntie." As the lady of the house, she would receive the few foreign guests appearing at the time. The philosopher Bertrand Russell arrived with a delegation of English Laborites and trade unionists. Gorky, with a cold and strong cough, received Russell in bed, and Mura served them tea on a small table, simultaneously acting as translator. Gorky defended Lenin and the politics of the Bolsheviks, but there is some suspicion that Mura made this defense much more decisive by her translation. Russell had no doubts: Gorky "did everything that one person can do to preserve the intellectual and artistic life of Russia."

A bit later, at Gorky's invitation, H. G. Wells came to visit. The initiative had actually come from Lev Kamenev, who had met Wells in London, but Gorky willingly supported it. They had been acquainted a long time before, at least since 1907, and possibly even earlier, but only in passing. Wells had also met Mura, the wife of a Russian diplomat, at some cocktail party back in London, before the beginning of the war, and later in Petersburg. A fabulous soirée was rolled out for Wells on Kronverksky, as in the old days.

Chaliapin sang while Aleksandr Glazunov played his compositions on the piano; the young, imposing Kriuchkov, the lenses of his pince-nez sparkling, was especially attentive to Andreeva that evening. This salon atmosphere with its noncommittal conversations and light flirtatiousness was to Wells's liking. Mura had created it, an organic return to that already forgotten "other" life, supposedly vanished forever.

The Petrograd hotels did not function. They simply did not exist at that time. Soviet institutions were housed in some of them, others became the residences of new bosses, and a third—extinct and lifeless—was waiting for better times. So Wells stayed at Gorky's. Mura gave him her room and took the empty one next to it. On the eve of his departure Wells wandered into her room "by mistake in the middle of the night," having "lost his way" in the huge apartment. This visit would prove to be fateful for all three: Gorky, Wells, and Mura.

It cannot be excluded that Mura is to blame for those naïve judgments which Wells took away from his trip. "Gorky . . . is healthy and energetic," wrote Wells in his book, *Russia in Gloom*. "He occupies in Russia a completely special . . . exclusive position. [Although] he is no more a Communist than I am, he enjoys Lenin's solid support."

All this was not completely true, but Mura tried to convince him that it was in fact so. It was apparently not difficult to pull the wool over his eyes. When Gorky's conversation with two Petrograd Chekists, whom Gorky accused of making excessive arbitrary arrests, Wells interpreted it as "the convincing proof of freedom of speech" in Soviet Russia. Mura had evidently carried out her mission very successfully.

Mura's appearance in Gorky's apartment and the role which she began to play there did not upset Yekaterina Pavlovna Peshkova; on the contrary, it made her happy. There was no question of restoring her former relationship with Gorky—the line had been conclusively drawn where that was concerned. It was also clear that the question of a formal divorce would never come up at all; thus she remained, and would remain, not so much in the legal as in the historical sense of the word, Gorky's wife. She calmly put up with Gorky's romances—it was only Andreeva that she never forgave, and her relationship with her never changed.

Having pushed Andreeva aside from the position to which she aspired, Mura became, in Peshkova's eyes, her ally. Tikhonova, thanks to her soft character and unstable relationship with Gorky, could not pretend to the role of successor. Mura stood out because she was imperious and decisive; in this she resembled Andreeva, except that Mura was tougher and more stubborn in achieving her goals.

It was precisely to these kinds of women, and not weak-willed and tender ones, that Gorky gravitated. Kornei Chukovsky observed in his diary:

> Gorky was of weak character and easily gave in to the influence of others. Chekhov had an iron character, an indomitable will. Is that not why Gorky glorified strong, willful, powerful people, while Chekhov celebrated the weak-willed and helpless?

Major changes had also taken place in Peshkova's life, which to a great degree—both now and later—influenced Gorky in the circle of his acquaintances, his train of thought and decision-making. It had nothing to do with Mikhail Nikolaev becoming Peshkova's silent and almost invisible companion. He had no serious relationship to Gorky's life. Their later meetings were rare, and eyewitnesses left behind no recollections of them.

Peshkova had completely withdrawn from Party matters in 1917, after one year as a member of the central committee of the Social Revolutionary party. She did not break with them nor change her previously held views, but simply walked away, to take on different responsibilities, more onerous but much more tangible.

The Social Revolutionary party was doomed politically, and Peshkova had drawn her own conclusions in good time. Now she was dedicated to working for the Society for Aid to Freed Political Prisoners ("Pompolit" after February 1917) which later in a somewhat reconfigured form became the Political Red Cross (PKK). In the beginning (February 1918), Moscow and Petrograd each had their own committees. The Petrograd committee was led by Vera Figner, a veteran of the Russian revolutionary movement and a participant in the assassination attempt on Tsar Aleksandr II, for which she spent twenty years in the Shlisselburg fortress. In Russia her name was synonymous with honor, steadfastness and nobility. Peshkova headed the Moscow committee, which later became the All-Russian and even All-Union committee, changing its focus: instead of victims of tsarist oppression, the PKK shifted its focus to prisoners of Soviet jails and camps.

In its appeal to the peoples of Russia, the tasks of the committee were clearly stated: "The Red Cross has never allowed itself to judge single political parties and trends. It makes no distinction between anarchists or monarchists, since all individuals who have suffered for their political convictions or have been persecuted by the ruling regime for political reasons, have the right to expect the care of the Red Cross, which must by its charter protect their interests. If during the tsarist regime the Red Cross helped primarily the left parties, including the Bolsheviks, its obligations are now to help parties more to the right, including the monarchists."

Such an open declaration was daring and heroic.

Mikhail Vinaver, a lawyer and former Social Democrat (possibly a Menshevik) was Peshkova's deputy, and her closest employees were two other lawyers, Nikolai Muravyov and Pavel Malyantovich, famous in pre-Revolutionary Russia as participants in the noisy political processes. These individuals did everything they could to help, at least somewhat, the victims of the Cheka by giving them food, money, and advice, petitioning the authorities and, finally, providing information to the families of the arrested, who had no news about the fate of their loved ones from any other sources.

After the peace treaty was signed in Riga in 1921 between Russia and Poland, Peshkova became an official representative of the Polish Red Cross to care for Polish nationals living in Soviet Russia. Its main obligation in this capacity was to offer practical help to the Poles, as well as to Ukrainians and Belorussians who had formerly lived on territories given to Poland and who now, because of that treaty, wished to return there. Peshkova's direct and active participation resulted in more than one million persons being resettled in three years, but another million-and-a-half remained.

This work, naturally, was not simply under the control, but actually under the leadership of the Cheka (soon renamed GPU, an abbreviation for Main Political Directorate) and its omnipotent chief, Felix Dzerzhinsky himself, who was especially interested in this activity because of his Polish origins. According to reliable information, he designated Peshkova a representative of the Polish Red Cross and then personally directed all her work. The business and personal contacts between Peshkova and Dzerzhinsky could not help but give rise to many rumors, given the sinister reputation which the Cheka and its chief (nicknamed "Iron Felix" by the Bolsheviks) already had at that time.

However, the clue to this "connection," odd as it may appear at first, is very simple: Peshkova understood that without the support of a person in power on whom the lives of the condemned depended, the activity of the Red Cross was meaningless and could only mislead those who put their trust in it. It would be absurd to proudly reject "on principle" any close contacts with people with the ability to save lives. But a very high price was necessary: those who agreed to a pact with the devil become its prisoners and slaves of the System.

It is not clear who led Max to Dzerzhinsky, whether it was his mother or Lenin, or both. In any case the offer to serve Iron Felix did not contradict Gorky's mood. At the end of 1919 Gorky wrote to Peshkova:

Max strongly believes that life can, and must, be reconstructed in the spirit, and through the methods, used by Sov[iet] power. I don't believe in this, as you know, but I don't consider that I have the right to destroy the beautiful illusions of youth. He believes with reservations, but I don't believe with reservations. This does not mean that he and I completely agree, but I can understand him. . . .

These "beautiful illusions" led to an elevation in Max's social status. He continued to work in Dzerzhinsky's institution, but already in a different capacity. Iron Felix made him a diplomatic courier following Lenin's recommendation. Gorky did not know where to place his son, and turned to Lenin for help. Gorky had decisively tied his fate to the Bolsheviks, and Yekaterina Pavlovna, Maria Fyodorovna, and Max zealously served them.

But what about Mura?

9.

Poisoned by Anger

"Longing. Most of all for you. I think about you, you, you, you." These lines are from a letter by Mura, who was already far away. Now her kisses reached Gorky only on paper. Varvara again took her place at the head of the table.

In May 1921, Mura was in Estonia, which she jokingly called the "potato nation" and to which she was linked not so much by her first marriage as by her daughter and son who were both there. She left while Gorky was in Moscow, leaving behind a letter for him in Petrograd:

> I want you to feel that intense inner feeling that I think happens only a few times in life, that the love of this girl from Kobelyak* will be with you throughout the difficult, anxious, boring and dark hours of your life . . . You are my joy, my big true Joy, if you only knew how much I need you.

Without a doubt, she needed him. And so she thought about him, and only him.

Mura had long planned to visit her children, whose fate she knew nothing about, but the transformation of Estonia into an independent nation and the war that lasted so long on its borders cut "Estland" off from its former metropolis for a long time. Wells, keeping his promise to her, "dropped by" Estonia on his way back home and informed her, in a semi-encoded letter, that her children were alive and safe.

Not expecting a favorable decision from the authorities, Mura took a desperate step: she attempted to cross the Russian-Estonian border illegally but was apprehended. It is unlikely that she had informed Gorky of this move, since he would have certainly tried to dissuade her. After he found out what

* Her birthplace in Ukraine.

happened, he had to appeal to Zinoviev—there was no other way out: "Allow me once again to remind you of Maria Benkendorf—could you not release her into my custody? For the Easter holiday?"

Gorky's solicitation could provoke only one reaction from the Petrograd dictator: unconditional refusal, especially with the request to free her for Easter, which the Bolsheviks had officially canceled. Nevertheless, Mura was in fact free by Easter (which began on April 11) and already back in Gorky's embrace on the tenth. It was Andreeva and not Gorky who had influenced Zinoviev: her authority was indisputable. Andreeva did not dare write to Zinoviev, knowing his dislike for the Stormy Petrel, but instead wrote to Bakayev, head of the Petrograd Chekists:

> I respectfully ask you and the Commission of the Cheka to release into my custody Maria Ignatyevna Benkendorf, who attempted to cross the border somewhere outside Petrograd. It is known to me that she was going to see her children, ages six and seven, living under the care of an uncle and in very bad conditions in Estonia. I will bet my life that, having given me her word, she will not attempt to repeat this desperate undertaking, even for her children, therefore in the worst case scenario I give you my word to shoot me: knowing this and seeing my signature here, she will not lift a finger without your knowledge. She is a mother and a very good person.

Andreeva could hardly have surmised at the time how completely and uncon-ditionally Mura had pushed her out of Gorky's life.

Andreeva did not have to shoot herself. Mura did not place her guardians at risk, but left legally. Gorky apparently encouraged her into going, judging by these lines of her letter: "With eyes closed, I have come here, because you were able to convince me that it will be easier for you." For him, not for her . . . There is no reliable information as to how she received a passport and visa to cross the border, but Gorky most likely played a role in this as well: it is known that he sent dozens of such petitions, many of which were honored. But there are not any (at least not known) documented traces of a solicitation from him for Mura. It is almost certain that Andreeva again interceded on her behalf, having finally figured out the nature of the relationship between Mura and Gorky, and seeing an opportunity to distance them from one another. But Zinoviev (Andreeva could only appeal to him) considered Mura to be working for just about every known espionage agency, and her proximity to Gorky sharpened his hatred for both of them to an even greater degree. He would hardly have agreed to "throw a fish back into the river." More likely than not, Dzerzhinsky personally gave his permission at Peshkova's request, as she was in regular contact with him. Therefore, two of Gorky's former lovers, who despised each other, saved a third woman in the hope that she would disappear. Undoubtedly, Andreeva hoped for this to happen but not Peshkova.

In any event, obtaining a passport for Mura was impossible without personal contacts with powerful Chekists both in Petrograd and Moscow. Such contacts at a very high level were not something new for her following her previous arrests. We do not know the nature of the conversations she had in the offices of the Cheka, or under what conditions she was issued a passport. The Estonians, in any case, arrested her immediately upon her arrival in Tallinn, having suspected her of more than just an innocent connection with the Cheka. But after a few days she was let go again without any explanation, but allegedly at the intercession of an Estonian attorney and a complete stranger whose services she could not even pay.

The attorney in question had such a burning desire to help her that he had even found a fictitious bridegroom with an Estonian passport. This marriage automatically gave her the right to become an Estonian citizen as well and to travel throughout the country. What benefit did the participants of this operation secure from their "humanitarian" efforts? Why would the bankrupted Estonian nobleman Nikolai-Roger-Emil-Friedrich Budberg agree to a marriage if it did not even bring him a dowry? Some Gorky scholars, in an attempt to avoid such ticklish questions, assert that this was a simple "business" transaction: in exchange for his baronial title and Estonian citizenship, Nikolai was supposedly offered a "salary." Who paid for his maintenance? Mura's letters are filled with complaints about her extreme penury in any currency, and this is undoubtedly the case.

There is only one reasonable explanation to all these riddles: certain forces, who did not want to be known but who possessed powerful influence and money, intervened in Mura's favor. If true, then these forces were in London and were the two aces of espionage, R. Bruce Lockhart and Sidney Reilly, who already had a hand in Mura's fate. The only question is which of the two sides of this "great divide"—Moscow or London—were better informed about one another and who secured the final victory? All these questions remained unanswered, and it would have been odd if the special services of several countries had not racked their brains over the riddles Mura provided.

And so, just like in a fairy tale, Maria Zakrevskaya-Benkendorf became the Baroness Budberg, without having spent a single day with her new husband. In her capacity as baroness she told Gorky not to wait for her, as she was not planning to return to Russia. It cannot be excluded that such a plan had been agreed upon in advance, and even approved by those in Soviet Russia who supplied her with the documents for her departure.

But there is something else which is the most mysterious of all: Mura informed Gorky of her marriage *which had already taken place* several months before the marriage was in fact concluded. Can this be explained as harmless female cunning, the desire to nudge Gorky to leave faster to avoid losing his lover? Is there any point in searching for logic in her impulsive actions? Mura was not known for being impulsive—all her actions were not just rational, but well calculated and precise.

Mura had just left for Estonia when Varvara Tikhonova appeared again at Kronverksky. This woman, whom Gorky alternately pushed away and drew closer, was rather difficult. Both Shaikevich and Tikhonov already had their own families, but Varvara was homeless in the fullest sense of the word. Had it not been for her mother, Andrusha and Ninochka would have also been homeless and orphaned too. The grandmother's devotion to her grandchildren was such that after forty years of a sunny marriage she separated from her husband who could not bear the fact that his wife was actually encouraging her own daughter's "dissolute" life with Gorky, whom he detested.

Rumors that Varvara had returned to Kronverksky also reached Mura. She would hardly have relished the idea of relinquishing Gorky to her rival without a fight. But again: in this case the report of Mura's marriage (who could say that it was fictitious?) by normal everyday logic should not have pushed Varvara away from Gorky, but only brought her closer.

A sentence from Max's letter to his father muddies the water even further. While in Berlin, he had kept an active correspondence with Mura who told him all about her Estonian adventures. "Her family affairs are bad," reported Max, without being more specific.

What was hidden in this very significant phrase, which should not only have provided Gorky with information, but even soothed his nerves? Was Max trying to drop a hint that "Titka's" marriage was not going all that well and that all was not lost for Gorky?

All these musings, in the absence of indisputable evidence, are only hypothetical and required to solve the mystery; why did Mura deceive Gorky? Moreover, how could she, as we will see later, travel freely in and out of Estonia without an Estonian passport, after all that had happened to her? And why was she certain that Nikolai Budberg would keep his word and marry her, no questions asked, after a few months?

And why, finally, did she not do this since it would have truly rid her of all torments and transformed her from a suspicious beggar with a suspicious red Soviet passport into a respectable baroness and citizen of an independent republic? Why did she not go through with it right away, not grasp at this straw, but waited for something else instead of taking this already life-saving step?

Even more to the point: did she make the decision herself, or did she have to seek proper approval? Was she free to control her own destiny or were the interests of certain omnipotent institutions—and not only from Petrograd and Moscow but, perhaps, London and elsewhere—tied into a tightly bound knot, which even now, more than eight decades later, is still so hard to unravel?

Gorky took the news about the important event in Mura's life very seriously. Later, having learned that the marriage was only in the planning stage, he wrote to Max: "She wants to get hitched to some baron: we are all very much against it; let the baron find himself another fantasy, this one is ours!" Peshkova suggested he marry Mura. She liked this woman much more than she did Andreeva, and to the end of her days Peshkova maintained good relations with Mura; they corresponded with one another and exchanged gifts. Gorky replied, "Everyone very much liked your consideration concerning Titka,* but this woman has married some baron and, thus, you were too late to match her with me."

According to various sources in documents and memoirs, the notion of Gorky's possible departure abroad had already come up more than once on Kronverksky. Sending Max there under the guise of being a diplomatic courier was only the first step. After traveling once to Italy with the ambassador Vatslav Vorovsky, Maxim lived for awhile with his father in Petrograd and soon after left again, but got hung up in Germany before he could reach Italy.

From Rome he had written his father, "I don't really yearn for home." From Berlin he wrote his father again, a mysteriously worded, and not very grammatical, letter, with clumsy coded humor: "I have been living in Berlin for already a month-and-a-half . . . but I can't get to Rome. Thanks to the subtlety of the new diplomacy, dark forces in the guise of our representatives scattered about the countries of the planet have smeared my good reputation with false rumors, which do not permit me to move in the desired direction . . ." It was therefore not the Italians who blocked Max's entry, at least temporarily, into their country, as is commonly thought, but some of its "representatives," who even disseminated false rumors as well.

Maria Andreeva and Pyotr Kriuchkov left the country immediately following Mura and Maxim. They had been assigned to the Soviet trade representation in Berlin, she as head of the art-industrial department, created "for the export of artistic items"—in other words, to trade works of art and squander Russian treasures—he was playing the role of her secretary. Rakitsky also went as an expert in antiques. Lenin's personal assignment gave Andreeva an additional and even more important responsibility: to collect as much money as

---

* By "everyone" he meant Khodasevich and Rakitsky.

possible for the starving, impoverished country by using her foreign connections.

Thus, Gorky ended up alone in Petrograd. Mura and Andreeva were gone. Peshkova stayed in Moscow, living her very busy and intense life, and Varvara was a poor advisor and, under these circumstances, more a hindrance than a help. All this happened when Gorky's mental condition was exacerbated by new events which he could not ignore.

His mental state depended to a great degree upon the worsening situation in the country in general. At the end of the civil war the Bolsheviks had to face the question of what to do next; this was not the time to fight enemies but to bring life back to normal. The catastrophic impoverishment of the people was accompanied by a horrendous "turning of the screws": every one, the smallest signs of elementary freedoms, vanished. The intelligentsia was asphyxiated.

On the anniversary of Pushkin's death, Aleksandr Blok read an inspired speech, which turned out to be his last one, prompting Anna Akhmatova to call him the "tragic tenor of an era":

> Calm and will are needed by the poet for the liberation of harmony.* But calm and will are also denied. Not external, but creative calm. Not childish will, not the freedom to be liberal, but creative will and inner freedom. The poet dies, because he has nothing left to breathe, life has lost its meaning.

This speech reflected the sense of desperation that gripped everyone still harboring even the slightest hope that, with the end of the period of military Communism, something had to change. The Bolshevik leadership was also shaken by various party groups hoping, through utopian measures, to reduce the severity of the regime, at least for the "working class." But "a trade union discussion" and "a working opposition" only prompted the Leninists to turn the screws even tighter.

Dzerzhinsky was sympathetic to the attacks of those opposing the "general Party line; he did not support Lenin, who did not bring him into the Politburo, where there was a place for him. The GPU, however, remained the same as before. And Dzerzhinsky, in spite of all his disagreements with Lenin, assiduously fulfilled his role.

The uprising of the Kronstadt sailors (March 1921), taking the same positions of the Leninists as they overthrew the legal regime in Russia, was a spectacular blow to Bolshevism. Turning their own slogans against the Bolsheviks only emphasized the cynicism and demagogy, with which they had

---

* An echo of the famous farewell by Pushkin: "There is no happiness in the world. But there is calm and will."

duped and conquered Russia. It was expected that the workers, in whose defense the sailors had revolted, would also rise up. However, fatigue, apathy, and cowardice were predominant. The intelligentsia, on the other hand, was only morally on the side of the mutineers.

The Chekists, of course, were not idle. During the rebellion, a large group of Petrograd writers and scientists—including Aleksandr Amfiteatrov; Georgi Ivanov; Vsevolod Rozhdestvensky; the prominent economist and Menshevik Nikolai Rozhkov; and others—were arrested. A group of writers, led by Aleksandr Blok, petitioned for their freedom. Gorky sat it out, although there were several people among those arrested who were rather close to him: not only Rozhkov, for example, with whom he had looked in tandem for a way out of the crisis, but also Amfiteatrov, who had been his friend back on Capri and had worked with him in the *Vsemirnaya Literatura* publishing house.

Kornei Chukovsky wrote in his diary for November 7, 1921, about a session of the editorial board of the publishing house:

> [Gorky] has gone over to politics. And, as always, he talked nonsense. Naïve people, who barely know Gorky, at first attribute great significance to his political statements, but I know how authoritatively and ponderously he has repeated . . . the most absurd rumors and bluffs. . . . They began speaking about the arrest of Amfiteatrov. "I'm afraid it will be difficult to help him, what is he guilty of?"

Approximately one month later almost every one of those arrested (except Rozhkov) was freed. Moreover, *Vsemirnaya Literatura* did not intercede on behalf of its employee Amfiteatrov; instead, it sent a statement to the Cheka, signed by Tikhonov, requesting that the papers that had been taken from Amfiteatrov, but not Amfiteatrov himself, be saved, because these could be office materials belonging to the publishing house. In the language comprehensible to any official it meant that neither the publishing house as a whole, nor its director Maxim Gorky wanted anything to do with the fate of Amfiteatrov.

There is no reason to doubt what Gorky's attitude was to these arrests, but he expressed his thoughts to a small circle, rather than publicly. It was reflected in two comments recorded by Chukovsky: "Soviet power produces good avengers" and "Many [Bolshevik leaders] have a sick heart. It is self-poisoning by anger. A certain physiological factor."

Although his position to the mounting repression remained clear and un-changed, his personal activity as intercessor-petitioner had noticeably dimin-ished. He was indifferent to many such actions where he could have played a meaningful role. For example, he did not react to the woes of Stanislavsky, who had played a key role in his life and who had attempted through official channels to save his younger brother, arrested in the Crimea. The routine correspondence, drowned in the bog of officialdom, turned out to be fruitless. Stanislavsky's brother, Georgi Alekseev, and his three sons were shot, just as his cousin, the professor and ornithologist Vasily Bostanzhoglo, had been executed somewhat earlier.

Peshkova, along with Mikhail Vinaver, petitioned for the release of Aleksandr Izgoev. The philosopher had been confined to a camp "until the end of the civil war." There was no specific date, nor could there be—because of the civil war. Blok also got involved in trying to free Izgoev, but Gorky's name was not on the list of petitioners.

Fewer and fewer people turned to him for help. Some held back out of pride; others because they could see his fatigue and irritation; and still others recognizing that Gorky's intervention in their fate or that of their loved ones would have very little likelihood of success.

It was clear to everyone that Zinoviev's rancor and sadism could only worsen the situation of an unfortunate victim if Gorky was involved. In the past he had never been guided by such sober judgments, throwing himself headlong into providing even illusory help. Now he avoided trouble.

The slight reduction of his activity, perhaps, had to do with the weariness of his petitioning of the recognition that an irritated Lenin no longer had its former, even more so, effect on lower Party ranking leaders, perhaps.

At that crucial moment he did not seek weakness among the authorities for specific individuals, but wanted to redirect the general political trend. For this he had to remain on good terms with the authorities. The ideas of the reformers were always dear to him, and his relative proximity to Lenin, with whom his relationship alternated from hot to cold, seemed to hold out at least some hope.

Only recently has it become known from Gorky's declassified letters to Lenin that as early as 1919, Gorky suggested to Lenin that he introduce the "New Economic Policy" (NEP), but on one very odd condition. He forwarded to Lenin the appeal of Nikolai Rozhkov, who had undertaken "a hopeless attempt . . . to avoid the threatening consequences" of policies to the national economy. Rozhkov proposed "to seize power" back from the infuriated and hungry masses immediately, and through dictatorial means allow private business to develop without any discussions with the ultra-left dogmatists in the Soviet leadership. Gorky, in his accompanying letter supporting Rozhkov, wrote that the "allowance of private business" is possible only with the "personal [Lenin's] dictatorship, understanding by this the strictest centralization of power in your hands . . . We will be satisfied only on the condition that you take matters into your own hands and out of the hands of those blockheads, who cannot tell the difference between economic materialism and political idiocy."

The result of this appeal was Rozhkov's immediate exile to Pskov, a provincial city not far from Petrograd, but still not the worst fate at the time for a bold economist. Lenin treated Gorky the politician with the greatest irony and could not have cared less for his constructive proposals, but he tolerated them. Gorky evidently viewed this tolerance as a sign of hope. Finally, some two years too late, the NEP ("free trade") was introduced and the Leninist dictatorship, which Gorky had called for, was only too obvious.

Gorky's failed reformist efforts were incredibly naïve. They were usually announced either by a letter or another "observation," never exceeding the limits available to "publicly involved" Soviet writers who had seen themselves as statesmen but unable to renounce, as a purely emotional reaction, what they had seen. Here are just two sample recommendations from Gorky to Lenin:

> . . . I call your attention to the need to take decisive measures against adolescent crime . . . I propose organizing a "League to Fight Adolescent Crime," to which I will invite the most authoritative figures on matters of education . . .

(Wide-scale adolescent crime was the result of the long civil war, which turned millions of children into orphans, and no one, not even the most "authoritative figures on matters of education," could do anything without a radical change in the situation of the country.)

> Since the invasion of [White General] Yudenich, dozens of sackcloth sandbags, from which machine-gun nests and platforms were set up, are lying about rotting in the streets of Petrograd. The bags are ruined, yet the paper factories do not have enough rags.
>
> More than one million poods* of iron are rusting on the sites of destroyed wooden homes.
>
> In the process of knocking down houses the glass from windows and doors are not removed, but broken—nowadays window glass costs 1,000, 1,200 rubles—tens of millions of rubles are being wasted.
>
> It's not a question of money, of course, but of teaching people how to take care of their property!"

(The despised peasants actually took care of *their* property, and for this they were shot by the Chekists.)

---

* 1 pood equals approximately 36 pounds.

Gorky's relationship with the Kremlin, far from idyllic even before this, became all the more strained. By all indications it should have ended in an explosion. If in October 1919 Gorky wrote to Dzerzhinsky (need it be said that this letter lay in the secret archives until 1991?):

> I inform you that I view the arrests [you have carried out] ... as barbarianism ... and I declare ... that Soviet power makes me adopt a hostile attitude . . .

he now (July 1921) threw in Lenin's face:

> For some time now I have been convinced that a black but invisible criminal hand is operating cunningly and skillfully in Soviet Russia. Crooks prevail and are stealing . . .

Lenin always understood Gorky's allegories. Even if Gorky this time had only Zinoviev in mind, it would have been enough; after all, Zinoviev then personified Soviet power in Petrograd. Lenin, of course, could not let such a trenchant observation about the black hand of a triumphant crook pass without consequences.

Already by the fall of 1920 (and possibly even earlier), Lenin decided to quietly force Gorky, who had driven Lenin insane with his requests—usually not granted—to go abroad. When, many decades later, western liberals were incredulous at how Brezhnev and Andropov could exile from the Soviet Union tens, even hundreds, of the most active dissidents, they apparently were unaware of the fact that Lenin had established this tradition, and one of the first whom he chose to send into exile was Gorky. On October 20, 1920, in Peshkova's Moscow apartment, he told Gorky, "Don't go [voluntarily]. We'll send you." This "winged phrase" has been known for a long time—among Soviet historians it was always part of good Lenin jokes, dictated by his concern for the health of the great proletarian writer.

Lenin's letters to Gorky with a persistent offer to leave as quickly as possible, due to his spitting up blood, are also known. His letter to the people's commissar of health services, Semashko, where he asks "to appoint a special person . . . to send . . . *Gorky, Korolenko*, and others to Germany" sheds some light on Lenin's secret thinking.

Insofar as Lenin expressed his unambiguous attitude toward Korolenko ("this is not a brain, but shit"), then Lenin's humanitarian action, placing Gorky on the same level as "shit" and "others," becomes very clear.

But Gorky had still not made up his mind one way or the other. On the one hand, he had no idea of what he would do abroad or where and how he would live. After his fiery public activity and messianic hopes, life as a reclusive emigrant could hardly have made him happy, and the uncertainty of his relationship with Mura, who had become his strongest attachment, confounded everything.

Under these circumstances, he could have easily fallen under the strong hand of Andreeva in Germany once again, which was not at all what he wanted. Yet he was also not free to choose a country: so far none had canceled entry visas for Soviet citizens, even famous ones.

At the same time such seemingly incompatible events as the transition to the NEP and a sharp increase of the Red terror drew him into positions which he could not and, apparently did not, even want to refuse. The most important and responsible job, instilling new hope for even a short while, was to help the Russians perishing from starvation, and not just along the Volga, where the situation had become catastrophic, but in all other regions of Russia, including Petrograd.

This tragedy—the direct consequence of military Communism—rocked the world at the time. Numerous international committees, of which the largest and most active were the Aid Commission of the Supreme Soviet Entente headed by Joseph Nulance, the former French ambassador to Russia; the American Relief Agency (ARA), led by its director, the Secretary of Commerce, and future president, Herbert Hoover; and the Committee of the International Red Cross headed by its chairman, the Norwegian Polar explorer Frithof Nansen, collaborated with two Russian committees which had been set up at Gorky's initiative, on very different principles.

The official state committee headed by Politburo member Lev Kamenev (for seven decades official Soviet sources named the chairman as Mikhail Kalinin, who had absolutely nothing to do with it), but the public committees—All-Russian and Petrograd—played a significant role and included liberal-democratic figures who had enjoyed immense personal authority since pre-Revolutionary times, such as the eminent economist Sergei Prokopovich (former minister in the Provisional Government), his wife Yekaterina Kuskova (a close friend of Peshkova's who, like her, had joined a woman's Masonic lodge), and another former minister in the Provisional Government and one of the leaders of the Cadets Party, Nikolai Kishkin (the Kremlin bosses nicknamed this committee "Prokukish," from the first syllables of the names of these three leaders).

Among the other members of the committees, the names of the tsarist general Aleksei Brusilov, writers Aleksei Tolstoy and Boris Zaitsev, scientists Vladimir Ipatyev, Aleksei Karpinsky, Aleksandr Fersman, Nikolai Marra, Sergei Oldenburg, and others, widely known both in Russia and outside it, attracted attention. The presence of Leo Tolstoy's daughter, Aleksandra Tolstaya, in Pomgol (Committee to Aid the Starving) also increased its authority and gave its work a certain nobility.

Gorky was not only the initiator behind the creation of both the All-Russian and Petrograd committees, but also the guarantor that they would be allowed to act for the good of Russia and not for the welfare of bureaucrats.

Lenin again needed Gorky, as his name still meant a great deal abroad. The Bolsheviks feared for their power, expecting spontaneous outbursts by the infuriated rabble—an uprising of desperate workers who had not received either rations or salaries, or rebellions by the peasants, deprived of grain and cattle, throughout the country. Gorky was given a second wind.

In this critical moment he could truly help Russia, and he did everything within his power. Over the radio and telegraph he sent out appeals to Anatole France, H. G. Wells, Gerhardt Hauptmann, John Galsworthy, Anthony Sinclair, Tomas Masaryk, Vicente Blasco Ibañez, and other people of great moral authority with whom he could speak like a brother-in-arms or whose spiritual outlook he could influence. Gorky asked for help to save those who were dying—it was the most urgent task. Never before had Gorky felt that his country needed him so much.

Again the members of Pomgol felt themselves needed and detached from public life. And this frightened the Kremlin. It was easy to make use of well-known names in Russia and abroad to overcome the crisis, but any activity by these people elicited genuine fear: would the Pomgol turn into a parallel quasi-governmental structure? Pomgol's direct connection to foreign charitable or, even worse, governmental organizations would have ineluctably led the Kremlin leaders to those conclusions.

Tomas Masaryk of Czechoslovakia poured oil onto the fire. Reacting to a speech by Kishkin at a Pomgol session (the text was published in the foreign press), Masaryk announced:

> A new stage of development is beginning in Russia. We stand before events of immense importance; only half a year ago it would have been impossible for former ministers of the Kerensky government to criticize the situation in the presence of Soviet representatives; a bridge has been laid down between society and the Soviet government. An exchange of opinions has begun, and moreover, there is the possibility of cooperation between the opposition and the government.

Everything that evoked rapture in Masaryk brought horror to the Kremlin rulers.

This venture ended very sadly. Gorky had gathered the members of the Petrograd Pomgol at Kronverksky when, at Zinoviev's request, the police stormed in to conduct a search. Both public committees were disbanded after only five weeks, but not without succeeding with the help of international organizations to arrange for steamships and trains laden with food, clothing and medicine to arrive from abroad. A denunciation spread by the Bolsheviks within Pomgol about how Prokopovich gave an "anti-government" speech at a session was used as the excuse. The Bolsheviks determined what was "pro" and what was "anti."

In a letter to Stalin and other members of the Politburo, dated August 26, an enraged Lenin ordered

> today . . . to disband "[Pro]kukish" . . . arrest Prokopovich today. Send the other members [of the committee] out of Moscow, immediately today, one each to distant cities, where possible without trains, *under supervision* . . .
>
> To the newspapers we will give a directive: beginning tomorrow to mock the "kukishes" in hundreds of ways . . . Mock them with all our strength and poison them not less than once a week over the course of two months . . . Do not waver . . .

10.

On Deaf Ears

There could be no talk of wavering: Lenin might have had many short-comings, but this was not one of them. The invective began immediately. The arrests also would have commenced right away but that would have meant, according to Lenin's directive, shipping Gorky off to a distant city as well. After all, he was also a member of the committee (and he headed the one in Petrograd). But the Bolsheviks had already planned everything.

On August 24, Gorky wrote to Peshkova:

> . . . The Petrograd Soviet, in other words, Zinoviev, has ordered 'to cease immediately' the activity of the regional committee's fight against hunger. . . . I ceased and sent to Moscow my resignation from the membership of the All-Russian Committee.
>
> I was summoned today—politely—with the two bodyguards Bakayev and Yevdokimov [leaders of the Petrograd Cheka] to see Zinoviev for a "liquidation of the incident."
>
> I'm going [to Moscow] with my luggage in case I must travel from Moscow to Europe, where I have less and less desire to go.
>
> The arrests here are terrible. They are arresting people by the hundreds.
>
> This evening the whole city was rumbling with Cheka vehicles.

This letter, of course, was opened and read; thus Lenin and Zinoviev and the Cheka (which in effect was one and the same thing) knew in advance about Gorky's departure. That immediacy, with which Lenin ordered the arrests to begin, is explained precisely by the fact that they had to take advantage of the moment when Gorky was not in Petrograd. In his absence all the "kukishes" and other members of Pomgol were arrested. Vladislav Khodasevich, who had been in close contact with Gorky, reproduced his reaction to this unexpected misery twenty years later: "There were no limits to his shame and annoyance.

Noticing Kamenev in the Kremlin cafeteria, he said to him with tears in his eyes, 'You have made me a provocateur.'"

Gorky grieved even more at Kamenev's weakness of character because he had singled him out from the other Kremlin bosses. It was no coincidence that in September–October 1917 the chairman of the Provisional Government, Aleksandr Kerensky, conducted secret negotiations with Kamenev about joining his cabinet to create "a homogeneous socialist leadership of the country" and in the process marginalize Lenin and neutralize the conspiratorial ardor of the Bolsheviks by creating a split among them, a fact concealed by Soviet historians for more than eighty years. Lenin saw through this maneuver, but even then Kamenev made no move, depriving Russia of a historic opportunity. On this occasion, also, Kamenev showed his lack of courage and retreated—several years would pass before a weeping Gorky would forgive him for this.

Until then Gorky had resisted pressure from Lenin, who kept insisting that he go abroad for a cure and shake out some money from the "Western moneybags." At the end of July 1921 he wrote to Lenin that "there is no reason for me to go abroad" and asked him "not to rush my departure, and give me more freedom to act" (this letter, naturally, was made available from the secret archives only in 1994). The rapid succession of events, making Gorky foreign and superfluous in his own country, led him to consider such an opportunity. Lenin's advice began to appear very reasonable, but not at all for the reasons espoused by the Kremlin boss.

Two dramatic events had played out in those same days, compelling him to reach a final decision. Both were connected with the tragic fate that had befallen two of Russia's greatest poets, with Gorky involved in both but in different ways.

In the spring of 1921, Aleksandr Blok's health took a drastic turn for the worse. After having genuinely accepted Soviet power and sung its praises, although in his own key, in the poem "The Twelve," Blok had valiantly placed himself at its service in the full sense of the word. Needing the authority of his name, the Soviets included Blok in every one of the innumerable committees and commissions—at least fifteen of them—and assigned him to many positions, which were meaningless anyway but took away his time and energy. In particular, he became the chairman of the directorial board of the Bolshoi Theater, working with Andreeva, and department head at *Vsemirnaya Literatura*, where he worked with Gorky on a daily basis.

Tormented by this impossible burden and strangled by the lack of creative freedom, Blok became seriously ill. The doctors diagnosed him with asthma, infectious endocarditis, lack of blood circulation to the brain, a severe form of stenocardia and an acute nervous disorder, threatening to become a mental disorder. He had also developed scurvy as a result of constant malnutrition. Blok's internal condition is clearly and concisely recorded in his journal entry for April 17: "Life has changed, a louse has conquered the whole world, and now everything is going to be different from how we lived and what we loved."

On May 3, Gorky asked the people's commissar of enlightenment, Lunacharsky, to use his influence for Blok to go to Finland. Lunacharsky took his time and Blok's declaration got lost somewhere in the back offices: only the foreign department of the Cheka was in charge of exit visas. On May 29, Gorky repeated his request in a very strange letter to Lunacharsky: "Make it possible, I beseech you!" The leadership of the All-Russian Union of Writers in Petrograd, "firmly assured us that it speaks in the name of all Russian literature"; he appealed personally to Lenin, begging him to "urgently grant permission to A. A. Blok and his wife to leave for Finland."

Lenin did not answer the letter; Lunacharsky handed over Gorky's letter to the Central Committee only on June 10 and, apparently without any hurry, conducted some talks "at the higher echelons." The matter moved along with typical bureaucratic creakiness. On June 11, the Central Committee avoided deciding on the matter, agreeing only to "improve A. A. Blok's food situation." On June 28, the foreign department of the Cheka, without mentioning any petitions, informed Molotov, the Central Committee secretary, that the "Cheka sees no grounds to allow them [Blok and two other writers] to leave in the near future."

The news about Blok's sharply deteriorating condition spread throughout Petrograd and Moscow with lightning speed. Only on July 8 did Lunacharsky turn to the Soviet of People's Commissars and on the eleventh directly to Lenin:

> The matter of Aleksandr Blok, the famous Russian poet, and undoubtedly the most talented and the one most sympathetic to us, has become especially tragic . . . We have literally tortured him by not allowing the poet to leave and not providing him, at the same time, with basic satisfactory living conditions . . . Once again I protest against the inattentive attitude of the departments to the needs of the greatest Russian writers most energetically, and . . . I request immediate permission for Blok to go to Finland to receive medical treatment.

Only Vyacheslav Menzhinsky, who was considered the "most intelligent" among the Cheka leaders, reacted immediately. On July 11, he reported personally to Lenin:

Dear Comrade! . . . Blok's is a poetic nature; if any incident has a bad influence on him, he will naturally write verse against us. In my opinion, it's not worth letting Blok go, but to create good conditions for him somewhere in a sanatorium.

The issue came up at a session of the Politburo the next day. (The protocol of this truly historic session was declassified only in 1995.) Five members of the Politburo were present and examined the "petition of comrades Lunacharsky and Gorky in regard to allowing A. Blok to go to Finland." Stalin was not present. Trotsky and Kamenev voted "for"; Lenin, Zinoviev, and Molotov "against."

A desperate Gorky begged Lunacharsky to demand a review of the decision. On July 16, Lunacharsky sent another message to the Central Committee:

I can . . . say ahead of time what will happen as a consequence of [such] a decision. The highly gifted Blok will die in about two weeks . . . It will be clear that we have killed off Russia's most talented poet." He warned that he was sending a copy of this letter to "com[rade] Gorky so that the best writers in Russia will know that I am not guilty in any way in this (may the Central Committee forgive me for this expression) frivolous decision.

Lenin finally relented. On July 22 or 23, he sided with the minority, and Molotov abstained. Only Zinoviev refused to budge from his position. Blok was allowed to leave, but alone, without his wife. She remained a captive hostage.

Blok, confined to bed without her accompaniment and constant supervision, could not go anywhere—this was clearly understood by the Kremlin. Gorky telegraphed Lunacharsky on July 29:

Blok has acute endocarditis. The situation is extremely grave. . . . I ask you to petition for Blok's wife to leave. . . . Hurry, otherwise he will die." On August 1, Lunacharsky again addressed the Central Committee: "I append Gorky's urgent telegram . . . I ask you to consider it possible for the wife to leave.

On August 5, such a possibility was considered.
On August 7, Blok died.
In this whole tragic story, the most nightmarish details of which have only recently become known, it is unclear why Gorky used Lunacharsky as his conduit in this most urgent matter instead of writing personally to Lenin. Only in the rough draft of a letter, the identical text of which was intended not only for Lunacharsky but also for Lenin, is Blok mentioned, although Gorky had

appealed directly to Lenin, bypassing the middlemen, on other matters during those same months.

The "other" matters (the Pomgol arrests) apparently bothered him more, and he did not think it was a good idea to dump an avalanche of requests at the same time on Lenin. In any event, Gorky's energetic efforts to save the dying Blok are indisputable.

His activity in this affair is all the more ennobling since Blok's relationship with Gorky had sharply deteriorated at that time. On February 14, 1920, a surprised Blok reported to Kornei Chukovsky: "Strange! . . . Gorky expressed a completely unexpected opinion. I told him that . . . about one thousand workers are ill with spotted fever, and he says, 'The hell with them. That's just what they need! Swine!'" Blok himself wrote in his notebook on December 17, 1920, "Administration of the Union of Writers. Gorky's administration (for me heavy for a long time already)." Chukovsky confirms that Blok could not stand Gorky and Tikhonov before his death. No one, however, could reproach Gorky: he did what he could.

". . . Blok has died," wrote Yevgeni Zamyatin to Chukovsky on August 8 from the countryside, where he spent the summer. "Or more truthfully: he was killed by our cave-like, bestial life. Because it was still possible to save him, if he had gone abroad in time." Chukovsky confirms: ". . . all these swinish houses in fact ate him up . . . little houses with fleas, bedbugs, cucumbers, bathtub vodka . . ." The "little houses" referred to, of course, are a metaphor for the terrible faces of a brutalized crowd of savages, who crawled out from all their crevices and on whom the authorities relied.

It appears, however, that even Gorky could take it no longer.

His relationship with the authorities was at a dead end. Not one of his initiatives received support, practically all his solicitations were rejected and the death of Blok, whom the authorities literally destroyed before everyone's eyes by holding in contempt the prayers of his would-be saviors, was the strongest blow. He certainly could not have disagreed with Vladimir Korolenko, whose letter dated July 29 Gorky received on the eve of Blok's death:

> History will one day note that the Bolshevik revolution dealt with genuine revolutionaries and socialists in the same manner it did the tsarist regime, that is, purely as gendarmes. . . . At that time when the highest concentration of mental and moral strength was needed, [the intelligentsia] was forced to keep quiet.

Gorky had attempted to convince Lenin with practically the exact same words. But it fell on deaf ears.

At the same time, another tragedy was rapidly developing and already reaching its conclusion. On August 3, only four days before Blok's death, Nikolai Gumilev, who had worked closely with Gorky at *Vsemirnaya Literatura*, the House of Artists and other public organizations, was arrested in Petrograd. The arrest came in connection with the so-called "Petrograd Fighting Organization," a large group of mythical conspirators supposedly led by the prominent geographer Vladimir Tagantsev, a professor at the Petrograd University and Mining Institute. He had been in the hands of the Cheka since June.

An investigation was carried out by Yakov Agranov, who would later be part of Stalin's inner circle and occupy a high position in the NKVD (deputy people's commissar), infamous for his highly refined sadism and close friendship with great Soviet writers and artists and then, naturally, executed during the Great Terror. Agranov was still a student then, sharpening his extraordinary mastery of cruelty and falsifications on the Petrograd Fighting Organization affair.

More than 200 people were arrested, all accused of plotting to overthrow Soviet power: the Leninists imagined plots everywhere, and the Cheka assiduously supported the morbid fixation of the "Kremlin dreamers" (to use the phrase of H. G. Wells). Moreover, they were declared to be agents of French intelligence, serving some kind of "Center" located in Paris. Among the arrested were many older intellectuals, including some famous scientists. The arrest of the prominent chemist Mikhail Tikhvinsky, whose services to the Russian revolutionary movement were widely known (in his youth he belonged to the legendary group, Liberation of Labor), made a special impression.

Gumilev, like Blok, had accepted the October Revolution. Moreover, having surmounted great difficulties, he returned to Petrograd from England in the summer of 1918 and immediately jumped into that cultural work which Gorky had undertaken. Gumilev's arrest therefore caused the greatest bewilderment.

Investigators larded the case with contradictory "facts," which would eventually become a Chekist tradition. They gathered compromising material on Gorky and on Lenin himself. Agranov, for example, squeezed this out of Tagantsev:

> I visited [Gorky] about three times in his apartment. During these meetings various political themes came up in conversation . . . In particular, I learned from him Lenin's tragic view of the Russian people, which, in Lenin's opinion, is extremely pliable to any kind of violence and not well suited for nation-building.

On the other hand, the investigation demanded that the detainees make a confession that they had plotted the murder of Zinoviev and Gorky (two sworn enemies!!), as well as intended to "burn down factories, destroy the Jews and blow up monuments of commissars."

The widely disseminated version (according to Gorky himself, it was spread by Yevgeni Zamyatin and "confirmed" by one line in her dubious reminiscences *On the Banks of the Neva* by Irina Odoevtseva*) was that Gorky tried to save Gumilev and had even obtained his freedom from Lenin, but upon his return to Petrograd learned that the execution had already been carried out on Zinoviev's orders. Thus, was what had happened several years earlier when he saved the Grand Duke Nikolai Mikhailovich and has no relationship to Gumilev.

Some contemporaries and direct eyewitnesses whom I contacted confirmed that this version is false. It was put into circulation, if not by Gorky himself, then by his entourage in order to save the reputation of the "living classic." Anna Akhmatova told me about this in Leningrad in October 1964 in her Leningrad apartment, as did Yuri Annenkov in Paris in October 1966, and Georgi Adamovich in May 1968. Not one of them—I emphasize this—condemned Gorky; they simply rejected the falsification.

A large group of writers and actors, especially upset at being deprived of a second poetic genius of Russia after the death of Blok, visited Gorky and requested his energetic intervention. Gorky left for Moscow on August 9, thereby avoiding Blok's funeral which took place on the tenth. He stayed in Moscow until the fourteenth or even the fifteenth of August. It could be assumed that he went to intercede for Gumilev. However, documents bear evidence that his trip was connected with the same Pomgol affair, which threatened to become a scandal and affect Gorky directly, and with matters of the commission for improving the life of scientists which he also headed.

His "lost" letter to Lenin, which he sent to Peshkova, also promoted the version of Gorky's initiative on behalf of Gumilev: ". . . send immediately the appended letter to Lenin and Maria Ilyinichna,† this is very important." For some reason it had been assumed that Gorky had laid out his request in this letter concerning Gumilev.

But the "appended letter," it turns out, did not disappear at all. It was simply kept in Lenin's secret archive until 1995. Gorky had only played the role of intermediary, forwarding to Lenin a teary letter from a woman (A. Kadyan),

---

* Irina Vladimirovna Odoevtseva (real name Iraida Gustavovna Heinecke, 1895–1990)—poet, memoirist, and favorite pupil of Gumilev.
† Lenin's sister.

who knew the Ulyanov family well. The arrested Tagantsev was a nephew to this woman's husband.

Again the drowning victims clutched at straws and again the straws did not save them. Lenin replied to Gorky with a terse note, advising him to travel immediately to Europe for treatment, and as far as A. Kadyan was concerned, he ordered his secretary, "Write to her that I read the letter, have left on account of illness and assigned you to answer: Tagantsev is so seriously charged and with such evidence, that it is now impossible to free him." Forty years before this A. Kadyan and her husband had helped the Ulyanov family when Lenin's brother, Aleksandr, was arrested by the tsarist authorities and subsequently executed.

There is also mention of the Tagantsev affair in Gorky's "lost" letter. Here are a few lines from this very long letter, which Gorky devoted to him:

> The report of this "plot," printed in Petrograd newspapers, is so clumsy and so ineptly edited that it makes a very poor impression among some and elicits malicious glee among others. In general from the report it is clear that Tagantsev was provoked. People who know him unanimously speak of him as a stupid person. . . . And what about Mikhail Tikhvinsky? He's still in jail. These arrests of old Bolsheviks are scandalous.

That is all. Everyone is free to decide whether to call this a defense of Tagantsev, Tikhvinsky, and others who were arrested. There is not a single word about Gumilev in this letter.

It is now known that the entire affair, from beginning to end, was a provocation by the Petrograd Cheka and Zinoviev personally, a provocation which Lenin willingly went along with, having personally controlled the investigation and made the final decision. There was, of course, no trial and the "board of the Petrograd Cheka" pronounced the "sentence," as Lenin dictated. For a while he was on familiar terms with Tikhvinsky (a great rarity in the biography of the proletarian leader) and considered him as his friend, but now he had this to say about him: "Tikhvinsky was not arrested by chance: chemistry and counterrevolution are not mutually exclusive." No one tried to keep these words a secret; on the contrary, it became a truism and was quoted more than once to justify repressions against leading scientists or cultural figures.

Tagantsev, Gumilev, Tikhvinsky, and many other outstanding Russian scientists and intellectuals—sixty-one people in all, including sixteen women— were executed on August 24. Both the investigation and the "trial" were far from sluggish. However, several of the condemned, thanks to the intercession of various influential individuals, managed to get off. The geologist Yavorsky, the hydro-geologists Pogrebov and Butov were freed immediately or after a short delay—Krupskaya, whom their colleague, Professor Yakovlev, managed to reach, had petitioned for them. The engineer Nazvanov—the old Bolshevik and power engineering specialist Gleb Krzhizhanovsky, who occupied major positions in the Soviet apparatus, had personally appealed on his behalf to Lenin—also escaped the bullet. The only person for whom Gorky interceded (at the request of Vernadsky)—the chemist Aleksandr Gorbov—was also freed and managed to live well, working in his field of specialization for another twenty years.

In 1987, on the crest of Gorbachev's perestroika, when Bolshevik secrets were gradually revealed, the former senior advisor to the Prosecutor General of the USSR, Georgi Terekhov, who in the 1950s and 1960s was rehabilitating victims from the Stalinist terror, revived rumors about Gorky's intercession for Gumilev, publishing a short article in the journal *Novy Mir* that contained these lines: ". . . the materials of the criminal case against N. S. Gumilev contain an appeal by Maxim Gorky on behalf of Gumilev."

Unfortunately, the prosecutor's memory failed him. Since the real Gumilev case (volume 177, case number 214224 concerning the "Petrograd Fighting Organization") has ceased to be a state secret and all its 107 pages are known, it can be categorically stated that there was absolutely no "appeal by Gorky . . . on behalf of Gumilev." There is another document which the prosecutor had read thirty years earlier that he took as Gorky's personal solicitation.

Here is the complete text of this undated document, found on page 103, volume 177 (Gumilev dossier):

> To the Presidium of the Petrograd Provincial Cheka.
> Nikolai Stepanovich Gumilev, chairman of the Petrograd division of the All-Russian Union of Poets, member of the editorial board of the state publishing house *Vsemirnaya Literatura*, member of the Supreme Soviet of the House of Arts, member of the Committee of the House of Writers, teacher of proletarian culture and professor at the Russian Institute of History of the Arts was arrested by order of the Provincial Cheka in the beginning of the current month.
> In view of the active participation by N. S. Gumilev in all the aforementioned institutions and his great significance for Russian literature, the institutions mentioned below petition for the release of N. S. Gumilev into their custody.
> Chairman of the Petrograd Department of the All-Russian Union of Writers, A. A. Volynsky
> Comrade of the Chairman of the Petrograd Division of the All-Russian Union of Poets, M. Lozinsky
> Chairman of the Board for Administration of the House of Writers, B. Khariton
> Chairman of *Proletkult*, A. Mashirov

Chairman of the Supreme Soviet of the House of Arts, M. Gorky
Member of the Editorial Board of *Vsemirnaya Literatura*, Iv. Ladyzhnikov

The conditional language of behind-the-scenes petitions was well known at the Cheka. Gorky's participation in this very official collective letter, where his signature came fifth, between some unknown quantity and one of the members of his editorial board, had no significance. Moreover, he appears only in the capacity of head of the highly invisible House of Arts, which meant only one thing: he personally had not sent a petition. Both Zinoviev and the Petrograd Chekists knew perfectly well how Gorky behaved when he truly wanted to extract someone from their clutches. The investigation, it bears repeating, was run by Lenin—if Gorky had turned to him, Lenin would have come back with some kind of written inquiry, at the very minimum; at least, that was how it always took place.

For the Chekists, who had followed every one of Gorky's moves, Gorky's sudden departure on the twenty-first (according to other information, the twentieth) of August to the dacha near Beloostrov, near the Finnish border "for a rest," could not have gone unnoticed. At the most critical moment, with the clock ticking and only hours remaining, he distanced himself from "worldly affairs" and remained alone with nature until August 24, and only on the twenty-seventh, or possibly the twenty-eighth, when everything was finished, when the rumor of the executions all over of Petrograd, he left for Moscow.

Gorky did not react to this truly extraordinary event that happened immediately after Aleksandr Blok had been unmercifully killed (without a doubt, killed!) by the Kremlin leaders.

The futility of his efforts, which had become so obvious in the doomed struggle to save Blok, did not prepare him for a new duel with the authorities, which would have undoubtedly ended the same way. Lenin demonstrated how Gorky's vain efforts to save human lives infuriated him and how little he valued any one of his arguments in this regard. The Pomgol case had stunned Gorky and, thanks to Lenin, he looked like a provocateur, enticing people who trusted him into the Chekist pincers; this had broken him and thrown him into a depression. As a highly emotional individual who was unable to forget slights, he could hardly have dismissed the insult from Gumilev in the presence of his lover and younger colleague.

But it seems there was yet another reason worth all the others. Gorky could hardly have been unaware that such a fate—like that of Blok or Gumilev—could now affect him as well. No one, as it turned out then, was insured against a bullet to the back of the head—former services were no guarantee, no reputation was immune, no reasonable arguments were taken under consideration. He understood perfectly well and knew that he was under constant observation by the secret police. Even Mura, who was not getting his letters in Estonia and sensing that he, in turn, was not receiving the ones she wrote, conveyed to him in a letter she had the opportunity to send to him through a friend, "it's very clear that my letters and yours are of interest to someone."

It was time to clear out. Regardless of what he was saying aloud or writing, it was obvious that by the end of August he had already made up his mind to leave, as quickly as possible. He was simply out to save his life and hardly anyone could fault him for that.

This departure was a kind of escape, a break from all kinds of political bustle, allowing him to leave with some outward decorum. The assignments that Lenin gave him allowed for even more: to consider it a business trip, with the support of the authorities. The cost was not great: keep quiet up until the time of departure, refrain from any kind of activity, avoid various supplicants, most of all those who, looking for protection, pushed him into some actions or steps undesirable to the Kremlin.

He accepted this condition as obvious.

11.

Unsolved Mysteries

The fierce confrontation between the two "great ones" could not continue for long. No telegram of sympathy of any kind would have reconciled them and increasingly they could not stand one another. In 1918, the Bolshevik regime was hanging by a thread, and Gorky's support to the slightly wounded Lenin was needed. Now that the regime was stronger, Lenin felt that he was firmly in the saddle and the obstreperous Stormy Petrel was all the more an irritant, because with him the Dictator of All Russia had to play the role of democrat and humanist, to be a falsifier and hypocrite. Gorky understood this, and he was fed up with the senseless and demeaning game. Besides, he was not that brave a man and valued his life.

In short, one way or another, the wishes of Lenin and Gorky coincided. The longed-for dream of the Kremlin boss—to send Gorky packing across the border—was a dream he did not attempt to conceal at all, and it was close to being realized. Weary of the fruitless battle, having lost his apparent influence on Lenin, embittered at the Bolsheviks and, at the same time, distanced from and detested by their enemies, Gorky could not remain in Russia any longer, even if there were no threats to him personally. He could no longer, morally or physically, beat his head against a wall.

The feeling of his own helplessness left him dispirited. All his attempts to stop the terror, prevent the dissolution of Pomgol, and many other affairs failed. Vladislav Khodasevich remembered afterward that among Moscow's rulers "his authority was already practically equal to zero." Victims of terror and violence from all sides accused him of inactivity, and everyone in the Kremlin had long since tired of his "stinking humanism," alien to the proletarian sense of justice and morality.

Regardless of his genuine or imaginary guilt, the death of the two greatest poets, one after the other, was like a heavy stone on his soul, and he realized that all reproaches from the people in his circle would be directed against him. For several years he had practically written nothing except for the odd article and innumerable weepy letters. He could not force himself, practically or psychologically, to write under these circumstances.

He was also of that double life which did not promise him any sympathy— not from one group or the other. In the autumn of 1920 he confessed to Chukovsky (diary entry from October 3):

> I know that no one has to like me and they can't like me, and I'm reconciled to that. Such is my role. I often tend, in fact, to be dual. In the past I was never duplicitous, but now with our government I have to be cunning, lie, dissemble. I know there is no other way.

He dissembled not only with the government but also with its victims— from the conviction that "there was no other way." He had chosen this role for himself, but the daily hypocrisy could not go on forever: the moment comes when even the most talented actor must remove his makeup and go back to being himself.

In July 1921, when the desperate and unsuccessful battle for Blok was taking place, Gorky wrote sadly to Vladimir Korolenko that Lenin was deaf to his requests to defend innocent people, and Lunacharsky was "powerless to do anything." Gorky took Lunacharsky's positive participation in the Blok affair as a genuine desire to be on the side of the innocent. Yet that same summer Lunacharsky, in a secret letter to the Council of People's Commissars, offered to dupe Gorky, Chaliapin, the composer Glazunov and several other major cultural figures, after having promised to pay them in gold for loyalty to the Soviets. "In reality, we're not going to give away one single gold ruble," wrote the "main Kremlin intellectual" with captivating cynicism to his equally cynical colleagues. "For the maintenance of these individuals we will need the same academic rations plus a small sum of Soviet rubles. In so doing, we will not only put an end to the rumors about how we are starving the world famous Russian citizens within the boundaries of the RSFSR but, on the contrary, we will be able to show how much we care about culture."

Lenin preferred coarse and decisive actions to Lunacharsky's shiftiness and hypocrisy. In his language it was called "adherence to principles." On August 25, 1921—Blok had just been finished off and Gumilev executed—Lenin wrote to Lunacharsky with charming bluntness, "I advise you to put all theaters in the grave." The madman's brain, destroyed by syphilis, was already incapable of understanding a different lexicon. For the sake of the interests of the proletariat, he would have driven Gorky into the grave too, but he did not risk it:

he still recognized what Gorky meant both to Russia and the world. The same was true, incidentally, with Korolenko: he tried to hustle him across the border, also under pretext of seeking treatment, and even offered his salon car with all comforts, so long as he left.

Korolenko refused, tripping up Gorky with the following letter: "I heard that you are leaving the country. . . . Do everything *beforehand** that you can to change the system. Otherwise nothing will come of it. . . . Russia will die." That's the point: that "beforehand," that is, before his departure, Gorky could not change, or even slightly soften, the system while remaining in Russia. If he could have, he would not have gone anywhere.

In attempting to rid himself of the obnoxious Stormy Petrel, Lenin, as always, attempted to extract some immediate benefit from his departure. He did not want Gorky to remain in Russia, but at the same time he did not relish the idea of him being added to the ranks of émigrés. The assignment—to roust up influential people in the West to help out impoverished Russia—cut through the entangled knot in the best way possible. Gorky would leave but he would leave as an emissary for Soviet Russia, working for the good of the country. Collecting money, food, medicine—this was a convenient pretext and, moreover, a real and extremely vital matter!

Lenin's burning desire to send his "friend" abroad, as quickly as possible, allowed Gorky to lay out several conditions. One of them was non-negotiable: Zinovy Grzhebin, along with his wife and children, must be allowed to leave with him. The Cheka actively opposed Grzhebin's departure, but Lenin had to get rid of Gorky at any price. Besides, the price demanded was not all that high. Gorky's renunciation of solicitation, or at least a moratorium on it, was a much higher price. On October 3, the Politburo finally gave its consent for Grzhebin to leave.

In September and until October 10, Gorky remained in Moscow, staying in Peshkova's apartment on Mashkov Lane. Yekaterina Pavlovna herself was not in Moscow—she had left for Siberia, fulfilling her many arduous tasks for the Political Red Cross. He did not dare put up Varvara Vasilyevna and Ninochka, who had arrived in Moscow right after him, at Peshkova's. Zinovy Grzhebin gave them shelter in his publishing house: Varvara slept on the couch in the hallway and Nina on the publisher's own writing desk.

Gorky could not decide to leave on his own; his casting back and forth between several women had frayed his nerves and led to the loss of those who were particularly close to him. The time had come to define his position. Incidentally, he did not have much of a choice in the situation which had

---

* Author's emphasis.

developed—only Varvara was nearby. He proposed that she follow him to Europe. Together with Nina, of course. The grandmother had already managed to take Andrei Shaikevich to Germany via Riga.

It is possible that Gorky was not feeling well—that is how he himself explained his unusually long stay in the capital. But this was only a pretext. Warning Peshkova about his arrival in Moscow, he informed her that he was bringing along only the most important items in the event he would go abroad straight from there, bypassing Petrograd. It is a telling detail! He would have clearly felt uncomfortable in Petrograd.

What did he do in Moscow for a whole month and a half? Almost every day of his life has been traced by chroniclers down to the smallest details; September 1921, however, remains a blank spot in this chronicle. One thing is clear: without advertising it in any way, he was preparing to leave. More than just his psychological state would depend upon his decision (A short period? A long time? Or forever?): he had to bring order to a multitude of issues, including the mundane ones.

At two receptions—in August and later in October—Gorky transferred to the Petrograd Public Library a part (of course, only a part!) of his archive, including the originals of Lenin's letters, copies of his own letters to him and numerous manuscripts, a fact that testifies that he was leaving for a long time. Another part of his archive and the most necessary books from his library he kept for himself. Among the letters he took were those to him from Vladimir Korolenko and other documents which would later become objects of a search.

This already casts suspicion on the sincerity of his affirmation contained in a letter to Lenin (whom Gorky did not see during his month-and-a-half stay in Moscow) dated October 8: that he was planning to be gone for only three months in all. Lenin, however, was not so naïve as to believe it.

In an interview in 1989, before leaving for Moscow from the United States, Nina Berberova claimed that it had never even occurred to her or to Khodasevich to leave for long "from a starving, empty, terrible city" but only "for awhile, to eat to their hearts' content, rest a little and then return." But Gorky knew for certain that he was leaving, if not for good, then at least for a long time. He left, as Berberova said, "sick and angry at Zinoviev, Lenin, and himself."

Most mysterious of all is what Gorky did with his extremely valuable art collection. There is no doubt whatsoever that it had been assembled legally: numerous documents attest to that. The collection consisted of paintings, graphic works, sculptures, Chinese lacquers, bronzes, rugs, priceless ivory items, Asian and African masks, antique kitchen silverware, valuable Dutch china, Venetian glass and so on, not to mention jade works, Buddha statuettes, antique weaponry and other "trifles," the existence of which is not denied by partial memoirists or "objective" specialists. We will not engage in idle gossip, inventorying someone else's riches—the details are of interest only to confirm the reasons for his departure: temporary or permanent.

There is no argument about the jade, ivory, and works by Chinese masters: everyone agrees that he took those with him. Why did he have to burden himself with all this if he was planning to return after three months? Who would take *such* baggage along on a short trip?

But where is everything else? If he did not take out "everything else," then it had to go somewhere. Years later he would write "Didi" from abroad and tell him to take all the remaining books and works on Kronverksky to the Pushkin House (Institute of Russian Literature under the auspices of the Academy of Sciences). As we will learn from another document cited below, what remained was not that much. When did Gorky manage to liquidate a significant part of his property while spending a month and a half in Moscow—almost up to the day he left? If he did not liquidate it, does that mean he took it with him? And it could only have been with the permission of the authorities—otherwise it would have been impossible to take out of the country. But then the Kremlin knew of the real "terms" of his departure.

The existence of the letter to Diderikhs is known, but its exact text to this day is still classified. Does Gorky specify exactly which "items" are under discussion? Does this letter confirm which works of art remained behind on Kronverksky? In any event, this "property" did go somewhere. Any true answer is of great value, for it allows us to understand—better than any of his letters and statements—the thoughts with which he left Russia. His real plans, not the ones he spoke about openly.

This question is not new—it was quite actively discussed back then, but in the émigré press, naturally, not in the Soviet press. "In our solid émigré press," Gorky wrote to Peshkova in November 1921, "I read with sadness and envy that 'M. Gorky sold his treasures: antique silver, miniature, and so on.'"

With sadness and envy—what does that mean?

That, *unfortunately*, he had no such treasures of any kind? But this is absolutely untrue.

Gorky did not provide an answer. One thing is clear: the letter was not intended for future historians but for someone close to him who knew the truth. The obscurity of his words indicates only that something was hidden within them.

Another irrefutable argument in favor of one of the versions of his true plans is the indisputable fact that he prepared his departure in the strictest secrecy.

In spite of all his conspiratorial efforts, Gorky was expected abroad—the world press trumpeted the news that he had already left in July or August. Mura, who believed those canards, even rushed to meet him at Helsingfors, although the newspapers maintained he was already in Riga! But Mura, with whom, of course, everything had been planned in advance, knew that Gorky would leave through Finland. She was in a hurry . . .

Frightened that the information in the newspapers could be false, Andreeva wrote to Gorky from Berlin:

> Your arrival is absolutely necessary to help [in the collection of foreign money]; your non-arrival will be a disaster. [Émigrés] use everything they can to make trouble. Some (Bunin, Gippius, Merezhkovsky, and others), of course, will rejoice that you're not coming . . . These are only mongrels, of course. But there are also some big dogs that can cause a lot more serious harm.
>
> They look at you as an absolutely pure and reliable witness. . . . and your word about the solidity of the Soviet government, about everything they've done that's good . . . will be of huge importance here.
>
> . . . Just your appearance will be very important.
>
> . . . I am deeply convinced that you need to come, and as quickly as possible!

There is no doubt whose assignment Andreeva was carrying out. It was not in vain that Lenin gave her the following attestation: "Maria Fyodorovna is . . . ours, completely our person."

What kept Gorky in Russia, after he had already decided to leave? He insisted that Grzhebin also be allowed to go and take care of other official matters he could have done earlier. His illness could have only hastened his departure and not the delay: nobody in Russia at the time would have preferred treatment at home to going abroad, if that was even remotely possible.

Was he not occupied all this time with such a laborious matter as the liquidation of a portion of his collection and packing up the rest? No matter how much his biographers try to avoid this little mystery, replacing such "vile digging" with an analysis of the many problems tormenting Gorky at the time, one cannot avoid dismal daily life. Without answering the question as to where Gorky's treasures were buried, historians leave it as a gaping hole in his biography. The traditional Soviet response—that there were no such treasures—is absurd, because it is clearly false. New evidence has appeared, albeit very late, confirming that Gorky prepared his departure in complete secrecy.

Weeks before his exit when someone once close to him, Vladimir Ivanovich Nemirovich-Danchenko, asked Gorky to intercede on behalf of the Artistic Theater that was without money and missing part of its troupe, wandering about from country to country to survive. Gorky replied:

I look upon the matter with hopelessness—the wave of barbarism, self-interest and baseness is slowly but inexorably rising ever higher, threatening to strangle the remains of our shattered culture. . . . I'm afraid that it is inescapable, but I shall try nonetheless—as soon as I land on my feet—to speak with V[ladimir] Ilyich.

It will be a shame if the wonderful torch of Russian art will be extinguished, snuffed out by the thoughtlessness of some and the feral stupidity of others.

To talk about the fate of the Artistic Theater was much safer than to mention the fate of the arrested "enemies of the people." What prevented him? Was it the silent agreement to stop interceding for each and everyone?

But something else is more revealing. In the letter to Nemirovich, not one word is said about packing his suitcases, having one foot already in Europe or that he would hardly have a chance to speak with V. Ilyich . . . No changes were predicted in Gorky's status, and if something blocked him from taking action on Nemirovich's request (it was precisely action and not a declaration of sympathy he was waiting for), then it was only an indisposition. Did something stand in his way of meeting Lenin, given the fact that he was already in Moscow? Or at least write to him, like he had already done numerous times before? Incidentally, Gorky's letter to the boss, written eight days before his leave-taking is known: there is not a single word about the Artistic Theater.

A second example is even more striking. Chukovsky spoke with Gorky every day on matters concerning the publishing house, but even he did not have the slightest idea that Gorky was preparing to leave. He had sent Gorky a sixteen-year-old youth, the future theater historian Simon Dreiden, with a letter of introduction and discovered to his surprise that Gorky *had just* "left for treatment in Germany." Chukovsky was even more surprised than the young man: the head of the publishing house had left without warning or saying goodbye to anyone, with the possible exception of Tikhonov as "a friend of the house."

An exception was made for those closest ones in whom he especially believed. Such, in particular, was the young writer Vsevolod Ivanov, whom Gorky zealously protected and in whom he saw the hope of Russian literature. Ivanov belonged to the "Serapion brothers" literary group, which was a collective that would leave a trace in Russian literature from the 1920s through the 1950s. In 1992 the son of the late Vsevolod Ivanov, Professor Vyacheslav Ivanov, allowed himself to breach the secrecy and recount his father's story about how Gorky unexpectedly summoned several of the "Serapions" to see him before his departure:

When everyone was there, Gorky made a little speech, the nature of which was this: it is impossible to live in this country; he was going to arrange it so that everyone could cross the Finnish border and he proposed that they all emigrate. Not one of them agreed. Gorky left without them.

His departure was preceded by a new search. The whole apartment on Kronverksky was turned upside down. Mura was long gone, thus this search could not be because of her. The search produced no results and nothing was confiscated. The police left, without excusing themselves for the inconvenience. It is impossible not to connect this raid with the imminent departure, but what were the persistent Chekists looking for? Gorky was too tired to protest. He preferred to hold his tongue so that he could leave.

Gorky left early in the morning of October 16, several days after his return from Moscow with his prepared transit documents and, obviously, with agreement on how this departure would proceed. Kamenev had issued the foreign passport to Gorky, which was more than just a symbolic detail. Situated at the highest level of power and knowing what was going on, Kamenev understood perfectly well that, by banishing Gorky on Lenin's order, he was really saving him.

The day before he had said his goodbyes to everyone from whom he had no secrets. His closest friends—Berberova, Vladislav and Valentina Khodasevich, "Molecule," Diderikhs, Tikhonov—were there, as was someone else . . . There is indirect evidence that Natalia Grushko also showed up to bid farewell. Evidence of this is her poetry: "How you blanched at that moment / But how your eyes flashed / Who told me you're an old man? / Whom did your gray temples deceive?" As Valentina Khodasevich recalled later:

> The situation was such that nobody knew when and with whom they would see anyone else again, and especially with A. M., but for his sake everyone put on a brave and happy face. He was both happy and very sad and seemed even a bit distant. . . . Yes, it was a heavy evening, no one slept. . . . In the morning A. M. appeared in the hallway with his briefcase under his arm, very businesslike, stooped, pale, very thin, in a black overcoat and black felt hat, sat for a bit, removed his hat, looked somewhere off into the distance, waved his hand with the hat like a wing, stood up and quickly strode off . . .

A separate car came for Gorky, together with Varvara, Nina, and the Grzhebin family. Strictly speaking, Gorky had fully earned this "perk" from the Soviet authorities but, more likely than not, he needed a separate car not only for road conditions but because his luggage would hardly have fit into a sedan. He would have no problems with Soviet customs officials—Lenin's "parting wishes" safeguarded him. The Finnish inspectors could only welcome any contents in his luggage.

The road from Petrograd to the border took only one hour. Gorky and Varvara (in the transit documents she is listed as his secretary), tightly holding hands, did not utter a word. The carefree Ninochka played with her bracelet, covered in diamonds and rubies—Gorky had presented it to her before they left Moscow.

From Helsingfors station they went to the resort area of Munksnes, where Gorky's friend, the Petrograd antiques dealer Mikhail Savostin, had reserved several rooms for the guests in an elegant pension. Not one day passed before Mura appeared. For the second time, but this time on purpose, she had left Tallinn to meet Gorky.

From Mura's words, Nina Berberova explains the fabulous ease with which she moved about: she traveled in and out of Estonia because of the newly authorized representative of Russia (something like an ambassador), Georgi Solomon, who would soon become a refugee himself. Solomon's patronage of Mura can generally be believed: according to his own words (mentioned in his memoirs), he was extremely antipathetic to Andreeva, thus the possibility to help the one who had pushed Andreeva away from Gorky was probably to his liking. But here is the question: how could Solomon have given Mura a transit document? Does the representative of a foreign power have such authority? Did not some other, much more influential, hand get involved in this? Not from Moscow, to be sure, but from another capital . . .

Meanwhile in Moscow, relieved that Gorky was already far away, the punishment of the jailed members of Pomgol was speeded up. On October 20, five members of the Politburo decided their fate. Lenin, Stalin, Trotsky, Kalinin, and Kamenev were present. According to a report by the latter, the following decision was taken unanimously: "To sentence the remaining former members under arrest of the Committee for Aid to the Hungry to not less than a two-week exile to some of the nearby cities . . ." The decision was "top secret" and did not reach Gorky.

Gorky spent twelve days in Helsingfors—from October 17–29—then, having changed his route, he left for Berlin via Stockholm. Earlier it was assumed that he would travel through Tallinn and Riga.

The sudden change could hardly be explained because it afforded greater comfort in travel. The situation he was in was truly unenviable. Varvara had burned all bridges behind her, entrusting her fate to him. Hers and Nina's . . . The unexpected intrusion of Mura, who had become, or was soon about to become, an estranged wife, upset all the best-laid plans. Mura was much stronger than Varvara and had far greater influence on Gorky. He found himself between two fires, already knowing who would win the battle for his heart. But he could not admit this victory at the time in Munksnes. The trip through "Mura's" Estonia was equivalent to recognition of her victory. As a weak-willed person, he preferred to put off the dramatic finale, letting time do its deed.

The conditions under which his journey took place are related in a very short letter to Peshkova from Berlin dated November 8, 1921:

> To be sure, the comrade journalists gnaw and bite me and hunt me down in every way possible. . . . This began in Helsingfors, continued in Stockholm, continues here. Torturous and stupid. Besides journalists—spies—Finnish, Swedish, German, *and most of all and ruder than all of them—Russians—left and right.*

A fragment of this letter had already been published in 1966, but the words set off in capital letters were cut by the censor. Only in 1995 was the text restored. The meaning is in these words: the comrade journalists and comrade spies had been sent by the Lubyanka on the heels of Lenin's emissary, to track his every step—Moscow had no faith in him whatsoever, and Gorky had no hope of escaping its surveillance or have any privacy. And he knew this well himself.

Kornei Chukovsky, without betraying the fact that Gorky had left without saying goodbye, wrote to him ten to twelve days after his departure: "I wanted to give a lecture on your works in Moscow, but it turns out this is now *impossible*" (Chukovsky's emphasis). Why impossible? Why did the works of the "great proletarian writer" and even his name itself suddenly become seditious in Soviet Russia barely after he had crossed the border? It would have seemed that neither a trip abroad for treatment, nor to collect money and food for the starving souls along the Volga, could cast a shadow on the living master, whom Lenin had discarded.

The question is rhetorical: the game played on both sides was no secret. There were no assurances that Gorky, having left the country, would remain unwaveringly loyal to the Kremlin, or that he would soon return home "unsullied."

12.

Toothache

From Helsingfors, Mura did not continue the journey with Gorky but returned to Estonia. They had long conversations in Munksnes and Helsingfors, but there are no reliable accounts of what was said. She had not yet become a baroness but once she did she would acquire legal status, and it would only help their relationship. Tormented by the unknown and defeated by her logic, which brought him no peace, Gorky was suffering but did not betray his feelings.

After a two-week stay in Stockholm, Gorky, Varvara, and Nina arrived in Berlin. They were met at the station by Max and Rakitsky. Max was accompanied by a charming young lady, whom Gorky already knew about. Max introduced her as his wife, though formally she was not, but this did not bother Gorky, as he was in a similar situation himself.

Nadezhda Alekseevna, whom Max had already nicknamed—in the tradition of Kronverksky—"Timosha," had befriended Max a long time before, but, apparently unconvinced of his feelings and the seriousness of his intentions toward her, had married an engineer named Sergei Sinitsyn while Max was expropriating bread from the peasants and "condensing" apartments. The daughter of a well-known Moscow urologist, Aleksei Andreevich Vvedensky, she had lost her mother while still a schoolgirl and soon her father as well, and needed to bring order into her life. The marriage turned out to be unstable, possibly because Max had suddenly reappeared and whisked her away with him.

His personal and maternal ties to the "upper echelons" were such that, without any help from Gorky and even without his knowledge, Max obtained a foreign passport for his wife, and for her girlfriend too, Chaliapin's daughter Lidiya, and her husband. Maria Andreeva had already arranged a German visa for all of them in Berlin. Now Max informed his father for the first time that he was married.

Before his father's departure he had managed to travel to Italy at Lenin's personal initiative, as can be seen from the letter cited below. Vatslav Vorovsky, the Russian ambassador to Italy, wrote from Rome on September 7, 1921:

> Dear Vladimir Ilyich!" As you wished, Maxim Peshkov, Gorky's son, is here. The question now is what to do with him. For the lad's own good he should sit and study but then we would have to give him some kind of stipend. . . . One little hitch—Max has got himself a wife, whom he took out of Russia and brought to Berlin. . . . Since you took such an active participation in his dispatch to Italy, speak with whomever necessary and send . . . instructions, whether to issue to M. Peshkov pending new instructions so many liras, and at the expense of which institution (the Spanish king, for example).

Behind the jocular tone is a sense of irritation. What function was "this lad" supposed to carry out and whose ward was he to become, with a young wife in tow? An impoverished country, swollen from hunger, where thousands of unfortunate souls were dying from famine every day—yet the Soviet treasury had to pay out from its budget to Maxim and his wife (and not at the expense of the Spanish king!) valuable lire for hotels, restaurants, and beaches in glorious Italy!

Thus, unable to wait any longer for Timosha in Rome, but also not allowing anyone to sit him down for studies, he returned to Germany and met his father, beaming and basking in the love of his beautiful bride.

Timosha (from lack of habit, Gorky called her Nadya for some time) was a stunning creature. She was twenty and stood out for her genuine simplicity, cheerful disposition and unquestionable upbringing and intelligence, giving her a special charm. Both Max, who had never lived in a real family, and Gorky, who had never had one either, were attracted by Timosha's serious attitude toward domestic life and her ability, even under nomadic conditions, to create peace and comfort. Gorky took a liking to her right away and accepted her into his family.

In November 1915, he had written to Peshkova, "I think that the woman who will fall in love with Max will be very happy." It is difficult to say whether Timosha was truly happy, but her husband and father-in-law were indisputably so: she had brought into Gorky's family precisely what it had been lacking.

It was a rather simple matter to get a divorce according to Russian laws at the time, but a person had to be in the country and not abroad to make it happen. Yekaterina Peshkova, at the request of Max and Timosha, took all the responsibilities upon herself. Many months later the necessary documents were produced, and Max and Timosha were legally married at the Soviet embassy.

Among the greeters at the Berlin station were Varvara's mother and Andrei. They lived in the Stern pension on Kurfürstendamm and Varvara, grabbing hold of Nina, preferred to go directly there from the station. Gorky had to move in by himself in a different pension, rented ahead of time by Max for *three persons*, also located on the Kurfürstendamm. From time to time Gorky, creating the illusion that nothing had happened, would pay visits to his "secretary."

The latest act in the long drama was unraveling, but all the participants—and Gorky most of all—tried to drag out the finale. More than anything Gorky was afraid of losing Nina; the mailman brought her presents from him daily. A book inscribed "To Nina Aleksandrovna Tikhonova from a person who loves her very much. Maxim Gorky" made an especially strong impression. Nina Aleksandrovna, even by her own recognized date of birth, would have been eleven years old at the time. Already by the second day following this unexpected gift, Varvara rushed Nina off to the Suderod spa in Harz. The girl, who was very attached to Gorky, was told that Aleksei Maksimovich was ill and in need of treatment . . .

Indeed, Gorky was ill. Thrombophlebitis and even the indisputable signs of scurvy were added to his normal coughing up of blood: Gorky had not suffered from lack of food in Petrograd, but his daily nourishment lacked calories and vitamins, filling his belly without any benefits. Gorky needed a proper diet and medical attention. Instead, he again plunged into his daily routine, only in different circumstances in different surroundings.

Berlin at the time was the center of Russian emigration, as Paris would later become in the 1930s. Around half a million Russian refugees were living in Germany, with at least three hundred thousand of them in the capital itself, according to various calculations. There was a Russian theater, seventeen publishing houses, dozens of restaurants, three daily and five weekly newspapers. The popular Landgraf Café had been transformed into something like the Petrograd House of Arts—here Russian writers, artists and journalists met on a daily basis. Among the regular patrons of worldwide renown were Pasternak, Mayakovsky, Tsvetaeva, Yesenin, Pilnyak, Ehrenburg, Andrei Bely, Aleksei Tolstoy, and many others. Gorky did not pass up the Landgraf either and became the center of overall attention.

It was very difficult for Gorky to define himself politically, but the logic of émigré life required such a definition. Gorky was unable to do so—not only "for external consumption" but also for himself. His letters and statements of that period are filled with contradictions, and to the uninitiated it would probably seem that they were written and uttered by completely different people.

Almost as soon as he came to Berlin, Gorky renewed his correspondence with Lenin, conducted, as was all his correspondence with Russia, through the Soviet trade representation where Andreeva worked—that is, through diplomatic channels. A letter to Lenin dated November 22 was, for example, kept secret until 1993. Tenderly addressing Lenin, twice even, as "dear V. I.," Gorky assured him that the book which he intended to write "will be an apology of Soviet power," whose successes "completely justify its sins, intentional and unintentional." His letter is filled with sympathy: "Excuse me if I say that I am very much worried about you—how were you not raked over the coals for your economic policy?"

Why was such a letter classified back then? Because it contained such lines that did not frighten Lenin but were too "prickly" for his successors: ". . . to see hundreds of Soviet idlers, living in clover off the 'treasury.' . . . How much money is spent in vain by the country, whose population is wasting away from hunger! Is there really no other way to arrange it, to do it a bit better?" It is strange that it never occurred to him that the "stipend" which Vorovsky had extorted for Max and his wife in fact belonged to those expenditures which were depleting the treasury.

By displaying touching concern for Soviet power, Gorky nonetheless did not bother to conceal from dear Vladimir Ilyich what he thought about it: "The number of idiots in Russia is significantly greater than during the old regime— maybe this is because it seems that they did nothing at the time but nowadays they're in power." Lenin, who was definitely no idiot, had put them in power. This especially irritated Gorky: precisely in such a context was a new Russian tsar needed?

Gorky expressed himself somewhat differently and with much greater precision in his letters to Romain Rolland, with whom he began corresponding immediately after he had left Russia. This correspondence only became accessible in Russian in 1995, and four years earlier in French. Recalling the "heavy" dramas he had suffered in Russia, which had been "called into being . . . by dull and cold reasoning fanatics and cowards," Gorky continued:

> It would be mistaken to think that the Russian revolution is the result of activity by the mass of the Russian people. . . . The intellectual strength of Russia is quickly diminishing—during these four years dozens of scientists, writers and artists have died—V. Korolenko, an interesting writer and wonderful person, has just passed away, and not long ago our greatest poet A. Blok died, as did another, Gumilev . . .
>
> Never before had words such as honor, humanism, and kindness had such significance and weight—as they do today—on this terrible day, threatening the

destruction of a person, whose soul has been developed over centuries through torment of the heart, sufferings of the mind.

In another letter he wrote: ". . . Enthusiasm and faith are exhausted, strength, capable of organizing Russia as a European nation, has vanished." Only those whom Soviet power mercilessly destroyed could be this strength— both correspondents could hardly have failed to understand what they were talking about. But they preferred to avoid definitions.

This somewhat lofty and extremely literary style which both had chosen, on the one hand, kept them, as litterateurs, from sinking to the level of banal politicization and, on the other, turned each of their letters into a small essay allowing them to read each other's true thoughts. It is also highly possible that Gorky's letters reached Rolland in distorted form. Gorky did not know a single foreign language; Max, who, in spite of the legend, did not have a very good command, to put it mildly, of the art of translation in both directions, translated Gorky's letters (and those to him) that winter.

Gorky gave an interview to the émigré newspaper *Poslednie novosti* (The Latest News): "In principle I completely share Lenin's theory and strongly believe in the international socialist revolution"; to the Jewish writer Sholom Asch, for publication in the Yiddish-language newspaper in America, *Forverts*: "I'm not a Bolshevik and not a Communist; on the contrary, I am fighting against them now. Earlier, perhaps, I was closer to them, but now I am very distant."

Who can say in these contradictory statements where Gorky was being genuine? No matter how absurd, probably in both.

To the Danish newspaper *Politiken* he said, "Russia is a country of half-savage people." Avoiding the opportunity to discuss the Soviet regime openly, he concentrated all his anger at the Russian people, making it clear that it was not so much the Bolsheviks themselves and not even their opponents, but only the populace that was guilty of Russia's woes. In a brochure entitled *On the Russian Peasantry,* hidden from the Soviet readers for more than seventy years, he wrote:

> I think that a feeling of special cruelty, cold-bloodedness and, as it were, experiencing the limits of human tolerance toward pain is a characteristic of the Russian people.
>
> A diabolical sensitivity is felt in Russian cruelty, there is something subtle and refined about it.
>
> If the facts about cruelty were an expression of the perverted psychology of individuals, then one might not need to speak of them; in this case they are

material for a psychiatrist and not for a writer describing the everyday affairs of life. But I have in mind . . . the collective amusement of a person's torments . . .

Who is more cruel: the Reds or the Whites? Probably they are equal, because both one and the other are Russians.

Gorky accused the peasants most of all of anarchism, a revulsion toward work and a senseless existence, devoid of any ideas or goals, ignorance and bestial instincts. This stance suited the Leninists, because in the presence of such a dismal view of the Russian people they turned out to be the force attempting to reshape it: to illuminate it with an idea, point to a goal, ennoble and educate it. Emigration, with its political factions, had a completely different view of the abandoned country and the Russian people, now the object of grandiose social experiments. In Gorky's bitterness it saw not only slander against the population of Russia, in the midst of a fratricidal war, but also a desire to avoid all accusations against the Bolsheviks.

Gorky meticulously carried out Lenin's assignment in seeking foreign money, but Lenin was not satisfied with the results of his efforts and demanded even greater activity. Tell Bernard Shaw, he wrote to Gorky, "to take a short trip" to America and join Wells who was supposedly already there, "so that both can take it upon themselves to help collect donations for the starving." These strange directives to people who were not subordinate to anyone, did not upset Gorky at all; he accepted them seriously, introducing only a slight correction to the tactics: ". . . to write to B. Shaw," he answered Lenin, "is useless: this old braggart is always trying to be witty and is full of skepticism."

Gorky had no plans for the immediate future. He was at a crossroads and continued the same work he was engaged in before his departure.

His health was destroyed, working conditions in Berlin were impossible, the housing he wanted cost an arm and a leg, and the daily hassles were as time-consuming as in Petrograd.

His relationship with Varvara was falling apart, and his relationship with Mura in suspended animation; she did not want to lose him, but at the same time she was not in a rush for any kind of permanence. The marriage in Tallinn had still not taken place, and she needed him for a number of obvious reasons.

Constant contact with Andreeva, working in Berlin, was also no gift: Gorky had never felt such a need for mental (and physical) peace before.

On the advice of doctors in the first days of December 1921, Gorky left for a sanatorium situated in the village of St. Blasien, in the Black Forest near the Swiss border. It was assumed that he would live and receive treatment there by himself: contact with Varvara was limited to the occasional letter. But more often than not Max and Timosha came to see him, as did, of course, Nightingale (Rakitsky) and Peshkova, who would travel to Berlin to see her friend Mikhail Nikolaev, who had found a job there.

Kriuchkov came no less often, and not only as Andreeva's emissary—his desire to handle all publishing matters was clear. Gorky, it should be remembered, did not have a literary agent, did not know any foreign languages, could not conduct correspondence on his own and contacts with foreign publishers demanded specialized skills. He naturally needed an assistant, and not just any dilettante. Kriuchkov possessed all the necessary qualities and was considered *one of his own.*

It is highly possible that, using Kriuchkov, Gorky wrote to Lenin on December 25 from Saint Blasien, suggesting he "appoint agents for raising [funds] in all countries . . . which . . . would stimulate the matter. . . . I would highly recommend M[aria] F[yodorovna] for this role, and also Maria Ignatyevna Budberg, a very energetic and educated woman who speaks five languages."

Maria Fyodorovna, as is known, was "our, completely our" person—here Gorky's recommendation added nothing to Lenin's previous position. In reality, the recommendation concerned only Mura: Gorky had to give her such work so that they could be united in a common cause. Kriuchkov clearly did not object, for he already knew who could, and who could not, be entrusted with such an important assignment.

Probably the most important visitor to see Gorky in Saint Blasien was a person, about whom nothing has been said so far and who played a very unique and important role in the life of Gorky and many of his contemporaries. This person's name was Zinovy Alekseevich Peshkov.

He was born with a different surname—Sverdlov—and was the younger brother of Yakov Sverdlov, who for a very short time until his sudden death in 1919 occupied the second position in the official Soviet hierarchy as chairman of the Central Executive Committee (TsIK). Both Gorky and the Sverdlovs were from Nizhny Novgorod and knew each other long before they each became famous. In 1902, in order to enroll in the Imperial Philharmonic School, Zinovy converted to Russian Orthodoxy. Gorky was his godfather, giving him his name at his christening: Zinovy Mikhailovich Sverdlov became Zinovy Alekseevich Peshkov, the adopted son of the Nizhny Novgorod petit-bourgeois Aleksei Maksimovich Peshkov, *aka* the writer Maxim Gorky.

Zinovy emigrated to America, where he had met Gorky when the latter had visited there with Andreeva in 1906. Then, after knocking around the world awhile, he moved in with Gorky at Capri. The relationship with his adoptive father, as was typical with Gorky, went through all the stages from complete adoration to total loathing. These poles are unambiguously indicated in his letters to Peshkova, in 1907 and 1911.

> . . . I have seen no end of people, but nowadays I feel that Zinovy, this small and rigorously upright person, is closest to me; he is therefore hated everywhere.
> This beautiful lad has recently behaved incredibly boorishly to me, and my friendship with him is finished. It is very sad and heavy.

Even after he apologized to his godfather, Zinovy did not earn his forgiveness: "Zinovy is a lout," claimed Gorky in a letter to Peshkova. "His tears are the tears of the guilty."

The fallout occurred on the basis of Zinovy's latest love interest, the Russian Kazakh Lidiya Burago, whom he was in a hurry to wed. In general—his whole life!—he had an unusual weakness for women, and his choice was always characterized by irreproachable taste. Just among Zinovy's more prolonged attachments were an Italian queen, the daughter of the millionaire J. P. Morgan, the Princess de Broglio, Countess Combette de Comon, the writer Edmonde Charles-Roux, and before that the Russian-Georgian beauty Salomé Andronikov, to whom Tsvetaeva, Akhmatova, and Mandelstam dedicated poetry and whose portraits were painted by Serebryakov, Somov, Petrov-Vodkin, and Shukhaev. Zinovy managed to take out of Russia, gripped in a civil war, not only the famous artists Sorin and Sudeikin, but also Salomé Andronikov, who, grabbing only a small suitcase, threw herself into the unknown at his very first call.

By that time he had already survived the First World War as a volunteer in the French Army, acquired French citizenship and lost an arm in battle. Officer Peshkov had carried out the duties of his government in China, Japan, and Manchuria, and met with his adoptive father in Petrograd, where in 1917 he was a member of an official French representation during Kerensky's administration. Gorky forgave him all his previous transgressions after seeing the crippled soldier covered in military decorations. Gorky knew that Zinovy had afterwards been accredited to both Kolchak and Vrangel—two accursed foes of Bolshevism—which lent more weight to the invitation he had sent him almost as soon as he went abroad.

The version of Zinovy taking the initiative for their meeting is refuted by Gorky himself, who in plain terms reported to Lenin in the same letter of December 25, 1921:

> A few days ago I summoned Zinovy Peshkov from Paris, my so-called adopted son and cousin of the Sverdlovs—he was elected secretary of the International

Commission of Aid [to Russia] and is rather influential in this matter. . . . The urban and rural communes of France are giving money very generously and willingly. . . . Schools give good amounts, and workers from the ports of Le Havre and Marseilles are loading an entire steamship; the rich south of France is making very broad sacrifices . . .

Apparently, Lenin also knew that Sverdlov's cousin was definitely not among the friends of the Bolsheviks. But to Lenin it made no difference from where or from whom the money came—this is what Gorky had in mind when he let him know he had summoned Zinovy.

Zinovy spent Christmas in Saint Blasien, and, after ringing in the New Year with Gorky in the Russian tradition, left for Paris on January 2. According to his official status, Zinovy was on duty, attached to the Foreign Legion stationed in Morocco. He could hardly have gone anywhere without the permission of his superiors, even for the Christmas holidays. He had to submit a report and receive permission. But more likely than not his true superiors belonged to a completely different, and much more influential institution, from which he did not get permission for a trip, but instructions to carry it out. And, like all such instructions, it was accompanied by an order to keep his trip a secret. It is difficult to explain why Gorky complained when journalists, having found out about Zinovy's arrival, photographed him without his permission—both on his own and with his adoptive father. At Gorky's demand, the police confiscated all negatives taken by the journalists.

These seemingly minor details lend even greater significance to both the discussions Gorky had with him during the Christmas holiday, and the report where these discussions were summarized. Zinovy's report to French Minister of Foreign Affairs de Peretti is dated January 6, 1922, meaning that he submitted it immediately upon his return. A short summary of the report, addressed to an unknown individual (French intelligence? only this can explain the lack of an addressee on the report), was published three times in Russian: in 1976 in two Russian émigré publications and in 1993 in the Russian press. Professor Nikita Struve was the publisher. I quote fragments from this extremely valuable document from a Russian reprint.

. . . Gorky says that the situation in Russia is much worse than they imagine in Europe, and that it is getting worse every day, in spite of all the efforts of the Bolsheviks to make believe that the opposite is true. In his opinion, the state of affairs is disheartening and hopeless. Disorganization and dissolution are the norm everywhere—political, social, and economic. Some people are afraid that if the Bolshevik government falls, anarchy will set in, but could it be any greater anarchy than what already exists in Russia? . . .

The government is simply incapable of organizing. All its plans, all its intentions, which they loudly proclaim to the world, are empty; their published statistics are absolutely worthless . . .

Lenin spent his whole life abroad; he doesn't know his own country, and Gorky spoke about this more than once. But Russia in and of itself is completely indifferent to the leader of Communism. Lenin says that in his hands it is timber for setting the bourgeois world aflame. Gorky answered him, "This timber is from damp wood, capable only of emitting smoke and suffocating those who ignite it."

Gorky draws a hopeless picture of Russia's condition; he does not offer any plan of action. He awaits the collapse of Bolshevism and the resurrection of the country to its native strength.

Gorky left Russia after having sold all his property.

His total ignorance about the true state of affairs in Europe and his mistakes in judgment about it are eloquent witness to the success of the systematic lie, practiced by the Soviet regime.

Gorky believes that venality and bribery are created and supported by the regime. They are everywhere, permeating all organs, infecting the population.

Gorky's view of the Russian people is extremely pessimistic.

There is no doubt as to the authenticity of this document, because all other known documents and testimony confirm that these were exactly Gorky's opinions then about Lenin, the Bolsheviks, Russia and her people. Its style reveals with absolute certainty that the author of the report had a very close relationship to the intelligence services and is reporting on the given assignment. But something else is more important: Zinovy, to whom Gorky spoke completely candidly and truthfully, testifies to the fact that his adoptive father had left Russia *for good*—or until the fall of the Bolsheviks, which he was secretly hoping for. There is even a concise answer to the question previously raised: he had liquidated all his property in Petrograd and brought with him only the least cumbersome and most valuable items. Major Peshkov had reported to his superiors the undisguised truth about his adoptive father.

Gorky, however, continued his double game. Who was he deceiving when he assured Lenin that he would return to Soviet Russia in about three months? He told Bukharin that he was going to live in Germany "until the end of July (1922) and then return to Russia." To Madeleine Rolland, Romain's sister, he cited that same time frame—the end of July or the beginning of August—in a letter. Was he deceiving his correspondents or himself? Or did he believe what he wrote? It can hardly be considered a coincidence that Lenin sent Bukharin abroad "for treatment" precisely to Saint Blasien, moreover, to that same exact sanatorium where Gorky was recuperating. "The Party favorite" and its "enfant terrible" became friends, strolling along the paths of the sanatorium's park.

Bukharin even gave Gorky the familiar nickname of "Beautiful Whiskers" and attempted to find out Gorky's plans for the future by eliciting his candor.

How was Gorky going to combine all his plans to return (Where? After all, all his property had been sold or given to the Pushkin House and there was no one remaining among his friends in Petrograd—he had taken them all out!) with a search for comfortable lodging in Germany or an attempt to leave for the French Riviera, where the climate was similar to what he was so used to in Italy?

Right at this time (the beginning of 1922), it so happened that, in response to his request, French writers, scientists, and public figures unleashed a campaign for the authorities to issue a visa to the Stormy Petrel of the Revolution, so that he could settle in the south of France. An appeal published in the journal *Clarté* was signed by Anatole France, Romain Rolland, Henri Barbusse, Eduard Herriot, Marie Curie, Jules Romains, Georges Duhamel, Charles Vildrac, Victor Marguerite, Jean-Richard Bloch, and other equally well-known individuals. It would be awful to assume that Gorky had led them on, while really having completely different plans. And it is no coincidence, of course, that Gorky, allowing for the possibility of a move to France, unsuccessfully attempted to master the rudiments of the French language in 1922. Could this casting about mean that he was simply waiting, hoping for the collapse of the USSR which he had discussed confidentially with Zinoviev?

His relationship to the Soviet Russia he had left behind is found in one of Mura's letters from Tallinn. Judging from the context, it is a reply to his confidential statements in a letter to her which has never been seen:

> I want so much, without stopping, without end, to speak to you about Russia, which now, from a distance, I feel and see better than before. No, no, it will not perish.* It is terrible, it is horrible, that many Russians are dying, but Russia will not die. It is going through a severe, cruel trial. But, in a rotting Europe, is not what is happening in Russia better?

Gorky was not prepared to agree with her, but that influence, which she already had over him, was becoming clearly defined.

Not one of Gorky's statements, not a single one of his lines among hundreds (and possibly even thousands) of his letters, can be taken separate from his statements to others. Depending upon his mood, his attitude to the addressee, the events taking place in the country and the world, the dynamics of his relationships to those closest to him, he could express himself differently about the same subject, leading objective historians into a dead end and immea-

---

* An obvious rebuttal to Gorky, who had affirmed the death of Russia.

surably rejoicing those who are biased, for each had the opportunity to find in him what they wanted to see.

"It is no good abroad," he assured the young Konstantin Fedin, a writer from the already mentioned group of Serapion Brothers, in 1922, "for it is slowly, but inexorably, rotting. . . . Everything here is naked, shameless and pitilessly exposed." But to a different "Serapion," Lev Lunts, he must have written something completely different. Lunts responded to his letter (lost, unfortunately) with the following words: "The desire to leave has begun to burn within me again with renewed force." And when, already deathly ill, Lunts did manage to leave, Gorky greeted him (this letter has been preserved) with the words, "I was so happy that you got over the border . . ."

Finally, by preliminary agreement with Gorky and, it can be said, at his insistence, Fyodor Chaliapin, then still his close friend, left Russia at the end of June 1922. Formally it was "for treatment and a guest tour" and even with the title of People's Artist of the Republic bestowed upon him by the Soviet government, but Gorky understood that this great son of Russia was leaving his homeland forever.

His likeminded friends who remained in Soviet Russia after Gorky's departure felt themselves orphaned and bereft of support. He knew this, but did not alter his decision. At the end of the summer of 1922 a letter arrived in Berlin, written by one of his closest friends, the academician Sergei Oldenburg. It was not a request, but an entreaty!

> I am sending you this letter to call you back to Russia. I feel that it will not be easy for you. . . . Your word, the trust which the masses have in you, is needed now more than ever. . . . In the current attitude of the authorities in Russia toward people of science and culture in general, Russian culture has been placed, temporarily of course, on the edge of destruction . . . I know that I summon you to a difficult path . . . The main thing is that you are in Russia so that your voice will be heard here, in Russia.

Gorky did not see the sense of his return: he certainly knew that if he were to live in Russia, his voice would not be heard there. He did not reply to Oldenburg's letter.

It is relevant to ask two questions. The first is whether Lenin, who had so strenuously pushed him out, wanted him to return? Where would he be staying if he were to return to Russia? Could he really not have known, for example, that immediately following his departure from Petrograd all three of his favorite institutions had been closed: the House of Scientists and House of Art at the beginning of 1922, and the House of Writers already by the end of 1921? This alone made him understand how much he was rejected and how vain his attempts would have been to return to his previous activity.

In bringing up his impending return to different individuals, he knew that his entire circle, with the exception of Peshkova, were already abroad. With Lunacharsky's assistance, both Khodasevich and Berberova had left; his publishers Ladyzhnikov and Grzhebin were also here, and Mura was refused entry back into Russia, even if she had direct contact with Iron Felix. Mura was not so naïve that she did not understand that no contacts offered her even the slightest guarantee, and that only idiots could believe the Lubyanka: to be a free person in a free society is much better than an honored captive in a despotic one. She would not have returned to Russia for anything, and would not allow Gorky back there either. And Gorky already could not imagine life without Mura.

It had been agreed that she would stay with him, but for now she went around several European capitals with an Estonian passport, arranging her— and his!—affairs. Having completed the course of treatment at the sanatorium, Gorky returned to Berlin, and in May 1922, rented a house for the summer in Heringsdorf, a four-hour journey from Berlin and not too far from the Baltic port of Swinemunde. Mura had finally arrived as someone else's wife according to her passport, but Gorky's wife for all intents and purposes. Her move-in as mistress of the house would take place within a few months.

From Heringsdorf, he followed the unfolding of one of the most infamous provocations by the Soviets during the Lenin period—the trial of the Social Revolutionaries. It would have been unthinkable that, after observing this political farce which threatened to turn into a bloody tragedy, moreover participating in the campaign to save the latest victims of the Bolshevik terror, he could have given serious consideration to the possibility of returning to Russia.

The basis for reprisals against former comrades in the revolutionary struggle was a falsified brochure by those same two Chekist provocateurs, Lidiya Konopleva and Grigori Semenov, who were involved in the attempt on Lenin's life back in 1918 and the execution of Fanny Kaplan: for some reason Gorky had believed back then in their provocation, but this time it evoked in him a decisive protest.

The "repentant" provocateurs accused their party comrades, the Social Revolutionaries, of a conspiracy against Soviet power, and Lenin retaliated against the leadership which had still not managed to emigrate. As soon as information about the impending trial appeared in the Soviet press, a campaign began in the West in defense of the accused. Anatole France, who had just sacrificed his Nobel prize for the victims of starvation in Soviet Russia, appealed in March—"in the name of humanity, in the name of the highest interests of the world proletariat"—to Lenin's government "not to carry out, against the political enemy, any actions which could be interpreted as revenge."

Lenin did not heed that appeal.

Trying not to overly excite the liberal-minded Communists of the "fraternal" parties, as well as other European "leftists" who could still be appeased, Bukharin and other Bolsheviks, who had arrived in Berlin for an international congress of socialists, gave their word that the death sentence would not be imposed upon the defendants. Moreover, they gave assurances that even the public prosecutor does not demand such punishment. The price of these promises was well known to everyone and confirmed by both Lenin and the people's commissar of justice, Kursky, who announced that the court was by no means bound by Bukharin's obligation.

At the initiative of the prominent Russian Social Democrat (Menshevik) and Lenin's former friend Yuli Martov, Gorky joined the campaign to save the SRs. Martov asked one of the Menshevik émigrés, Fyodor Dan, to personally deliver his letter to Gorky, "so that he cannot help but respond, cannot put it off and, if necessary, you can 'exert pressure' on his fragile willpower." Although Gorky at this time was conducting negotiations with Soviet authorities about guaranteeing him a financial base (more about that below), he immediately responded to Martov's request. At the beginning of July, Gorky wrote to Anatole France, asking him to appeal once again to the Soviet government, "pointing out the inadmissibility of the crime." He was completely justified in calling the trial against the SRs a crime, which "had taken on the cynical nature of a public occasion to murder people who had genuinely served the cause of liberation of the Russian people."

Anatole France expressed total support with his Russian comrade-in-arms, but with a slightly different motivation that was probably more comprehensible to the Kremlin murderers, but offensive to the moral sensibility of a conscientious person. "Like you," he wrote to Gorky, "I believe that their sentence will have a heavy resonance on the fate of the Soviet Republic." But the fate of the Soviet Republic didn't interest Gorky—he had defended people who were completely innocent and honest—people, in fact, who had fought for the freedom of their country and its people, unlike the Bolsheviks who had greedily seized power, and whose lives were in real danger.

Gorky did not know where to knock in order to stop the impending reprisal. He decided to turn personally to "the representative of Soviet power." Not his "friend" and permanent correspondent, Vladimir Lenin, but Lenin's deputy in the Soviet of People's Commissars, Aleksei Rykov. To a significant degree, the choice of the addressee was determined by the fact that Lenin was sick (he had suffered a stroke at the end of May), although at the time he could still speak and was still involved in daily affairs. The fact that Rykov temporarily sat in for Lenin at sessions of the Soviet of People's Commissars, and that he and Gorky had met in Berlin, where the former had gone for treatment, played a role. But it seems that Gorky in general did not want to enter into correspondence with "dear Vladimir Ilyich."

> Aleksei Ivanovich!
> If the trial of the Social Democrats will end with murder, it will be premeditated murder, vile murder.
> I ask you to inform A. D. Trotsky and others* that this is my opinion. I hope that it will not surprise you, for during the revolution I pointed out to the Sov[iets] a thousand times† the senselessness and criminality of destroying the intelligentsia in our illiterate and uncultured country . . .

The reaction to Gorky's statement was purely Soviet in spirit. Leading Party publicists Karl Radek and Sergei Zorin abused Gorky in the newspapers *Izvestiia* and *Pravda*, calling him "a petty bourgeois hanger-on of the Russian revolution," "a philistine" and so on, assigning him his place "practically at the bottom." The crowning touch was the statement calling Gorky "a toothache in the jaw of the proletariat," which must be "filled or removed." *Pravda* declared that Gorky "harms our revolution. And harms it greatly."

In spite of these warnings, the trial went on as planned. The widespread international campaign, joined not only by Romain Rolland and Gerhardt Hauptmann, H. G. Wells and George Bernard Shaw, but also by Albert Einstein, Marie Curie, Bertrand Russell, George Brandes, Georges Sorel, Sidney Webb, and many other world renowned figures in science and culture, was ineffective.

Both Russian lawyers and foreign socialists, who came with the approval of the Soviet authorities to defend the accused, were subjected in Moscow to such scorn and mockery that they were forced to abandon the trial and leave the main defendants without any defense. The only thing they managed to accomplish was the commutation of the death penalty handed down to the twelve defendants.

There was no reaction at all following Gorky's appeal, except for one line from Nikolai Bukharin (he was then in Germany) in a letter to Lenin, who had recovered, dated September 7, 1922: "I read [in the foreign press] Gorky's nasty letter. I thought of lashing out at him in the press [about the Social Revolutionaries], but I decided that it would be too much." Russian commentators in the

---

* Undoubtedly referring to Lenin and Zinoviev; no other "others" were of any interest to Gorky.
† He had "pointed this out" not to the Soviets, but to Lenin personally, whose name he again avoids here.

traditional Soviet style assessed this reaction in 1994 as follows: "And even on this occasion Lenin displayed maximum caution and tact toward the writer." There may have been a lot of everything else, but there was truly more than enough tact.

Could this trial, which had exerted such a depressing influence on the entire civilized world, strengthen Gorky in thinking he had made the correct choice and that the road back to Russia was cut off for him? The evolution of the regime was perfectly clear. Hopes of loosening up society, engendered by the NEP, were shattered in a collision with Soviet reality. The especially repugnant role of the two-faced Lunacharsky, who appeared during the trial as one of the accusers, could only amaze Gorky, especially since then and later (right up to the 1990s) intelligence, education, culture, humanism, and a multitude of other worthy qualities continued to be attributed to Lunacharsky.

This legend had very little in common with reality. Gorky had never had a high opinion of Lunacharsky, but he nevertheless singled him out from the mass of Party apparatchiks, appealing to him both as an equal and a person of the same "blood group." From his behavior during the trial of the Social Revolutionaries, Gorky saw how mistaken he had been. But in reality there was no one more humane, more cultured and more educated than Lunacharsky within the Soviet leadership. Bukharin appeared at the trial as a defender of the accused, but his speech was even more scathing than the speeches of the accusers. The trial exposed the true face of the "liberals," depriving those who still wavered, and believed in something, of any illusions.

The final blow to such illusions was the event which occurred immediately following the trial.

The trial ended on August 7, and already by the ninth the "troika" picked out by the Politburo two months earlier, consisting of Lev Kamenev, People's Commissar of Justice Dmitri Kursky and Dzerzhinsky's deputy Iosif Unshlikht, prepared a list of intellectuals subject to exile abroad. Lenin had given the order to draw up such a list and carry out the exile—before he had his stroke on May 25, which pinned the leader to his bed for more than three months. On June 1, a new Criminal Code went into effect, defining exile abroad as the second most severe (following the death penalty) punishment for the execution of a particularly dangerous crime against the state.

Nonetheless, it was assumed that the court would choose this punishment. However, the "socialist sense of justice" did not allow taking into consideration such "bourgeois prejudices." By order of the Central Committee, the GPU took upon itself the rendering of the final decision. Dzerzhinsky's institution practically doubled the list compiled by the "troika" to about 160 people.

This was preceded by a careful selection, according to a scheme worked out by Dzerzhinsky himself: "All of the intelligentsia needs to be divided into three groups, approximately: 1) writers, 2) publicists and politicians, and 3) economists. . . Information is to be gathered by all our departments and collated in a department devoted to the intelligentsia. There should be a file on every intellectual."

Those chosen according to this scheme had in their "file" the obligation never to return to the territory of the Soviet Union; in the worst case, and they agreed in writing to this, they would face a firing squad without trial. Each of the exiles was allowed to take with them "one winter and one summer coat, one suit, two pairs of underwear, two shirts, two nightshirts, two pairs of socks, two pairs of shoes." Accompaniment was prohibited, but some people—alas, not more than ten—showed up anyway at the Nikolaevsky banks of the port of Petrograd. Among them was the artist Yuri Annenkov, who would become an émigré a bit later.

Under these conditions the best minds of Russia, its pride, its creative and spiritual potential—the brains of a great people (in Lenin's terminology, "not brains but shit")—were exiled. Philosophers made up the majority of the group, and the steamship that transported them to Europe was called "the philosopher's boat." Together with them into exile went the greatest economists, psychologists and lawyers, "thrown out from the territory of the RSFSR" (such was the formulation of the official announcement for the press).

The list of those individuals who already had, or soon would acquire, worldwide fame included Nikolai Berdyaev, Semyon Frank, Sergei Bulgakov, Ivan Ilyin, Lev Shestov, Nikolai Lossky, Fyodor Stepun, Vasily Zenkovsky, Ivan Lapshin, Boris Vysheslavsky, and Aleksandr Izgoev. The dean of Petrograd University, Professor Lev Karsavin; the historian Aleksandr Kizevetter, corresponding member of the Russian Academy of Sciences; the sociologist Pitirim Sorokin; and the writer Mikhail Osorgin were also sent packing. The leaders of the ill-fated Pomgol, Yekaterina Kuskov and Sergei Prokopovich, shared the same lot.

Lenin personally amended and added to the list. The late historian Dmitri Volkogonov has already made note of the fact that Lenin carried out the selection as Krupskaya was busy trying to teach him simple math exercises involving the multiplication of two-digit numbers by single digit numbers, suitable for a seven-year-old child, which the leader, judging by the notebooks that have been preserved, was not in a condition to solve.

It is highly possible that the leader of the revolution solved the mathematical exercises, far from his circle of daily interests, with extreme difficulty, but there are absolutely no signs of illness (except perhaps mental) in his selection of "tossing out onto the Western trash heap" the most brilliant among the Russian intellectual elite. . . . It is true that not a single Party boss during the Soviet period experienced such violent hatred toward the intelligentsia as did Lenin. Confined to his bed and practically lapsing into childhood, Lenin wrote in a letter dated July 17, 1922, carefully hidden in his "secret archive" that became worthy of publication only after perestroika: "to send abroad mercilessly" "all of them—out of Russia," "to arrest several hundred and without announcing the motives—leave, ladies and gentlemen!" "We will purge Russia for a long time."

In his pathological hatred toward the exiled "shit," Lenin, unfortunately, was not alone. In an interview given to the American journalist Louise Bryant, the widow of John Reed, on August 30, 1922, Trotsky shared responsibility with Lenin for this purge:

> Those elements, which we are exiling and will exile, are politically insignificant on their own. But they become potential weapons in the hands of our possible enemies. In the event of new military complications, they, in spite of all our pacifism, are not excluded—all these irreconcilable and incorrigible elements of ours will become military and political agents of the enemy, and we will be forced to shoot them according to the laws of war. That is why we preferred on our own, during a peaceful period, to send them out ahead of time, and I express the hope that you will not fail to recognize our premeditated humanism.

Having become acquainted with this revelation, Gorky had every reason to believe that he had been shown premeditated humanism. This version—that under the guise of punishment the scientists, condemned to death if they had remained in Russia, had in fact been saved—turned out to be very marketable. Historical experience has shown that exile truly did translate into salvation for them. The overwhelming majority of those exiled lived until the 1950s and 1960s, instead of perishing in the middle or end of the 1930s as they most surely would have. But there are no signs of Lenin's recognition of the humanity of this step, such as his farsightedness that allowed him to predict with accuracy the coming Stalinist terror.

On the contrary, something completely opposite appears. In his final memoirs Gorky wrote that in 1919, that is, two years before the "philosopher's boat" sailed off to Europe, Lenin told him, "It is bad for these people.* The smart ones among them understand, of course, that they have been ripped up from their roots and can never grow again in this soil. But transplantation to Europe will not satisfy the smart ones. They will not get used to it there."

---

* I.e., nonconformist intellectuals.

Thus, he had undoubtedly viewed exile only as a punishment, a justifiable retribution, not to mention an act of sanitation, liberating the pure Soviet earth from bourgeois trash. He rejected all attempts to save someone for the good of domestic science and culture. In order to soften him somewhat or overcome his veto, great efforts had to be applied, and this alone already speaks for itself.

The persistence of influential intermediaries allowed some to be saved. The publisher and critic Aleksandr Voronsky managed to save the writer Yevgeni Zamyatin, who did not want to leave Russia: he admitted his mistake and with immense difficulty managed to leave some ten years later. The ideologist of Proletkult (Proletarian Culture) and at the same time a physician, philosopher, and economist, Aleksandr Bogdanov (he would die soon after, experimenting on himself), solicited on behalf of two professors, V. Fomin and I. Kukolevsky. Major Kremlin chiefs Osinsky, Vladimirsky, and Smolyaninov removed from the list the professors Kondratyev, Rybnikov, and Yurovsky, who eight years later would become members of the mythical "Working Peasants' Party," sent off to the Gulag, and then executed. Others "were saved" because they had already been in the Gulag. Vladislav Khodasevich was also on the list of those exiled, but he managed to "get" himself out earlier and met the refugees in Berlin.

Gorky already knew at least by September 1922 about the new wave of arrests and the subsequent banishment of those arrested—he reported this without comment in a letter to Aleksei Tolstoy. His position was obvious even without commentary. "The country, deprived of its intelligentsia, is moving backwards," he wrote of the events that had taken place in Russia. The thought is not subject to dispute, but it was expressed weakly, in un-Gorky-like fashion, inadequate to that drama which had befallen the country.

Was he not crushed by the immeasurable audacity of the tyrant, did he not see himself among the passengers of the "philosopher's boat"?

Lenin would scarcely have included him in the general list, but he would have definitely driven him into a corner. If Gorky had remained and not expressed his protest—not formally but passionately—his name would have been crossed out forever not only to Russian, but also world, public opinion. Had Gorky expressed it, Lenin would have exiled him, and not with "honor," like a year before, but on completely different terms . . .

The ship had still not set sail from Petrograd when Gorky acquired a new German address. A German address, not a Russian one. During the fall, winter, and spring seasons he moved to the resort town of Saarov, east of Berlin, an hour and a half away. Talk of returning stopped: after everything that had happened, it would have been simply absurd to discuss such an idea.

But there were more than objective reasons for that. Mura categorically demanded that "no secretaries be brought along." Varvara, as already mentioned, was listed in documents as secretary when she and Gorky left together from Petrograd. For Gorky, this question was already resolved. Having found her way to him, Mura felt she was the lady of the house to an even greater degree than before, and not in a precarious existence but on stable and solid ground, and Gorky could not resist this in any way. On the contrary, with her help he once again acquired a mental peace of mind, which only the creative impulse could return to him.

13.

A Dual Game

Gorky fled Soviet Russia in order to find peace and quiet, but he found no peace of any kind abroad. The main reason now was not the horrible atmosphere of Soviet constriction and mendacity, but the problems he confronted in Germany. It would soon become absolutely clear that he would have to leave Berlin because, as usual, he needed treatment and creative solitude. Berlin is "a small little city," wrote Khodasevich, "provincial, but very restless." Trivial Party scuffles were the rule of the day; empty chatter and bitterness flourished.

The confused entanglement of his personal relationships, the uncertainty of his status which he had chosen and the endless conflicts in the émigré community which pressured him to take sides—all this exhausted him to such a degree that he was ready to escape just to get away from it all. Moreover, he was constantly under the surveillance of the Cheka, which had already succeeded in penetrating all European capitals, especially Berlin, the Russian émigré center at that time.

Varvara and Ninochka were still in Berlin—a painful situation. Gorky had essentially ruined the family, torn Varvara away from the husband who still loved her, taken her abroad and cast her into loneliness in a strange land and without any money. She was not yet forty at the time. No one ever heard a word of reproach from her. If not for the assistance provided by Anatoly Shaikevich, who had emigrated, and the sporadic paid translations from Tikhonov in Moscow, the family would have lived a very pitiful existence.

Gorky was in no hurry to restore *this* union. He wanted to get together with the grown-up Ninochka, whom the mother never let in on the nature of her relationship with Gorky. Clutching at this straw, Varvara did not permit Ninochka to see him, relying, perhaps, on the growing strength of his feelings that would unite all their lives.

In vain! Gorky reconciled himself to this separation, satisfied with rare meetings with Andrusha Shaikevich. Varvara did not prevent these meetings from happening, since Gorky felt only sympathy toward Andrusha. On the other hand, Mura hastened to solidify her position at "the other end of the table."

For the time being Gorky basked in the peacefulness of this charming German "godforsaken place," where the peals of thunder from Moscow or Berlin failed to reach him and where he could experience genuine bliss from contact with a sheet of paper and his dearest friends, who were with him but did not pester him with their constant presence. The greatest paradox was that the two main women in his life—Yekaterina Peshkova and Maria Andreeva—coming in turns to Saarov, did not pull Gorky in different directions.

Andreeva's strong Bolshevik position did not tolerate changes of any kind. Throwing herself completely into the work of the Political Red Cross, Yekaterina Pavlovna was in constant contact with Dzerzhinsky without whose assistance, let alone protection, she would not have been able to do anything for anyone. Her stories about the "wonderful Felix Edmundovich" echoed those of Andreeva about "dear Vladimir Ilyich" and, complementing one another, exerted the same influence on Gorky, pulling him toward the now distant Kremlin.

It does not seem, however, that Gorky was swayed by all this. Although Max reported to his mother on December 3, 1922, "We're thinking of moving back to Russia in the spring or in the middle of summer, if Dad's health is good," Gorky looked differently upon the country he had left behind.

On December 7 of the same year he wrote to Romain Rolland, "Storms and Communists are howling in the motherland. . . . When fanaticism is cold, it is colder than frost." Was Gorky really drawn to frost and snowstorms instead of the warmth he loved so much?

On April 21, 1923, in a letter to Rolland, he answered this question very clearly: "I don't feel the slightest desire to return to Russia. I would not be able to write if I have to spend all my time repeating the same refrain: 'Don't kill.'"

Meanwhile a kind of rumbling—and even more to the point, a schism—was taking place: several prominent émigré writers had applied to return to Russia, brushing off any fear and indignation of those who remained. In the spring of 1922, Aleksei Tolstoy published an open letter in the Berlin-Russian newspaper *Nakanune* (On the Eve), calling upon his fellow countrymen—writers and scientists—"not to grow numb in the cellar of emigration," but "to go to Russia and beat your own small nail into the battered Russian ship." A year later he was back in Moscow. Boris Pasternak, Andrei Bely and Ilya

Ehrenburg also yearned for home, inevitably deepening the rift between those who stayed and those who returned, and demanding, like it or not, that everyone take one position or the other and not sit on the fence.

It was precisely this need to choose that Gorky found unbearable. He did not want to return, nor did he want to express solidarity with those who resisted joining with the Bolsheviks. His desire to remain his own person and not join with anyone else was understandable. But this cast him both outside emigration and the Soviet environment.

In Moscow he was feared and despised; in Berlin and Paris he was also hated but tolerated. Again, he was a stranger everywhere.

Here in Saarov, peace of mind and the desire to work had returned. He returned to the writing table and hatched a crazy dream: to skirt Soviet censorship by publishing in Germany a literary and scientific-educational journal, which would be allowed free access to the Russian market. Moscow, in an attempt to maintain relations with Gorky, who thus far had not defined his position, had assured him through the Soviet trade representation in Berlin (where Andreeva and Kriuchkov worked!) that there would be no obstacles to his ideas.

But these promises were just bluff: any literature written with a free hand, reflecting ideas of freedom and humanism, was in and of itself anti-Soviet and therefore not welcome back home. In addition, it mattered to the Kremlin leaders who actually created the published works: a number of authors— Russian and foreign—had been placed on black and quasi-black lists. It turned out that almost everyone invited by Gorky to participate in his new journal *Beseda* (Conversation) ended up on those secret lists.

In the spring of 1923 the journal finally appeared, advertised more abroad than in the Soviet Union ("the goal of the journal," Gorky wrote to H. G. Wells, "is to acquaint Russia with the intellectual life of Europe"). Before the very first issue, which included Rolland and Galsworthy along with other famous personages, the journal was banned in Soviet Russia under various pretexts. Instead of the promised several thousand copies, Moscow bought no more than twenty to thirty copies for "special" (secret) stocks in the biggest libraries.

According to information that reached Gorky in a roundabout way, only Kamenev of all the influential Moscow leaders was in favor of allowing *Beseda* into Russia. Two years later, with his hopes completely dashed, Gorky decided to close down *Beseda* and wrote to Vladislav Khodasevich: "[They have decided] not to let in [the journal], so that Gorky will come back home. But he is not going back. He is stubborn too."

What Gorky expected is unclear. After all, he was receiving reliable information on a rather regular basis about what was going on in Russia. And he reacted to it as, for example, in this letter to Khodasevich (1923): ". . . From the news which boggles the mind. . . Nadezhda Krupskaya has forbidden the reading of Plato, Kant, Schopenhauer, Vl[adimir] Solovyev, Tennyson, Ruskin, Nietzsche, L[eo] Tolstoy . . . and many other such heretics in Russia."

Concerning his reaction to the Soviet lists of seditious literature, which preceded Hitler's banned lists by ten years, Nina Berberova remembered:

> When he found out that Krupskaya had drawn up a list of books to be removed from libraries, including the Bible, the Koran, Dante, Schopenhauer, and about one hundred other authors, he resolved to renounce his Soviet citizenship and write about "Madame Ulyanova's insane confiscations" in the London *Times* with unconcealed outrage.

Among the authors *madame* found unsuitable was Jules Verne, whose only sin was that in his predictions of the future there was no place for a Communist utopia.

After waxing indignant for awhile, Gorky cooled off and did not send his letter to the *Times*. It is possible that money from Moscow had reached him in time, or that someone with influence on him—more likely than not the pragmatic and sober Mura—had stopped him from taking this fatal step.

Beseda was destined to fail, but only Gorky, with his tireless energy and need for action, refused to accept it. He was furious but, while cursing Lenin and the Bolsheviks and knowing perfectly well with whom he was dealing, he was also completely dependent upon them. Most of the money came from Moscow, and he was incapable of starting life with nothing.

Not that long before, Gorky had voluntarily invested hundreds of thousands of marks in the Party treasury of the Bolsheviks, but no one was planning to repay that debt to him. It had simply been "forgotten" and "written off," and Gorky did not dare demand his money back, on which Lenin had lived like a lord in France, Switzerland, and Austro-Hungary, and now had control over millions the victors had seized. There was nothing Gorky could do except count on the Kremlin's "help" in the form of royalties on the books he had written. The money the author earned was a scrap mercifully thrown from the baronial table.

The Kremlin was prepared to "help materially." In 1921, Lenin had already decided to support Gorky, knowing his longing for a life that would allow him to live as he pleased, as well as maintain his unemployed son (and now his family too), plus the invariable "spongers" and numerous guests. Having barely set foot on German soil, Gorky immediately complained to Lenin that "everything is expensive as hell here."

When Gorky had been pushed abroad, the question of his financial well-being had not been raised. Now Lenin reacted immediately.

On December 12, 1921, he wrote to Molotov "for the members of the Politburo":

> . . . Gorky left . . . without any money and is hoping to receive author's royalties from Stomonyakov [the Soviet trade representative in Berlin] for the publication of his books [Gorky does not mention one word about this in his letter!]. Krestinsky [the Soviet political representative in Berlin] thinks that Gorky should be included among the comrades treated abroad at the Party's expense . . . I propose to carry out Krestinsky's proposal through the Politburo to include Gorky in the number of such comrades and make sure he is fully guaranteed the necessary amount for treatment.

As expected, the Politburo approved. On December 21, it was decreed "to include comrade Gorky in the number of comrades getting treatment abroad and to charge comrade Krestinsky with making sure that he is completely guaranteed the necessary sum for treatment."

The emphasis on the word "treatment," of course, is no accident. "Treatment" was nothing more than a Party euphemism to explain why the Stormy Petrel had emigrated and to justify giving him money from the Party treasury. There is no mention of author's royalties—the Kremlin simply decided to make Gorky completely dependent upon it.

This demeaning position did not suit Gorky, if for no other reason that it would not have gone unnoticed by the other émigrés who followed Gorky around as zealously as the agents from the Lubyanka. The ruble was an inconvertible currency, and Soviet Russia at that time did not pay royalties to anyone in hard currency, except maybe to a very select few individuals. The Kremlin found it more direct and convenient to put Gorky on the dole; a royalty would have created the illusion of money honestly earned.

On February 17, 1922, Maria Andreeva wrote to Lenin, asking him to accelerate the decision about publishing Gorky's works. ". . . Aleksei will not take allowances or loans," she wrote. "He left without a kopeck. Everything that he had has been spent, and to live here, especially to get treatment, is incredibly expensive."

Again Lenin reacted immediately. On February 23, he ordered "in all ways possible to expedite Gorky's receipt of money. If there is the slightest friction, tell me." There was, of course, no "friction": the Politburo took the decision to "acquire from M. Gorky author's rights on his works [and] immediately begin financing Gorky." On June 13, this deal was signed in Berlin.

Gorky repaid Vladimir Ilyich with a sharply worded letter about the trial being prepared against the Social Revolutionaries—the very same letter which Lenin would later call "nasty." The situation was paradoxical: he had driven himself into the Bolshevik cage, having made his well-being dependent upon Moscow, but he still did not allow the door to be locked.

Mura had already stopped wandering around Europe. She was there and apparently planned on staying with him. His best friends were also nearby: Andreeva and Kriuchkov, or Peshkova and Nikolayev, would come to visit. Max and Timosha were inseparable at home—temporarily but all the same at home—just like Khodasevich and Berberova, to whom he had become attached.

He felt the admiration, even adoration, of those who were dear to him— only in such an atmosphere could he draw the energy to work. Zinovy Grzhebin, who was also in Berlin, had a son and named him Aleksei in Gorky's honor and asked him to be the godfather; now, besides Zinovy Sverdlov, Gorky had another godson.

As in the best Petrograd times—mostly on weekends but sometimes for the whole week—guests arrived at the quiet lakeside of Saarov, left during the winter, and again, like not all that long ago on Kronverksky, the atmosphere of a coachman's inn that Gorky loved came to life again. Sitting at a long table, he amused them for hours with stories about the past and whatever came into his head on the spot. Among the guests, incidentally, was Elsa Triolet, whom no one knew at the time, but who had sent him her short story at his request and received an invitation to spend several days in Saarov.

Having yearned for pen and paper, he now wrote a great deal and with pleasure. Removed from daily Soviet reality, he became balanced, relaxed, and free. Writing came easily, as a process in and of itself, and not as a political goal.

Contemporaries remember that during that winter (1922–1923) he cursed the Bolsheviks, complaining about Soviet censorship, which had virtually killed his journal *Beseda*, made plans for life abroad—and wrote. It was during this period that he wrote *My Universities*, the short story "First Love," and many sketches for a book of memoirs, *Observations from a Diary*. The creative impulse had returned. Short stories including "The Experimenters" were banned by the Soviet censors, the first for pointing out what, in Gorky's opinion, is peculiar to the Russian people—their ineradicable cruelty—and the second for criticizing the arrests of innocent people and the crushing of freedom of speech.

While spending the winter in Saarov, Gorky should have decided what to do further. According to Max's plans, he was getting ready to go back to Russia.

But Gorky had different ideas. Having found out that several posts in Petrograd were still listed in his name (for example, chairman of the commission for improving the life of scientists), he removed himself from all these honorary positions.

In June 1923, Gorky moved to the Black Forest and settled in the village of Hunterstal, not far from Freiburg. He was going further south, feeling the need for a warm climate. The thought of the Russian cold was equated to spiritual coldness, alienation, bitterness, and severity, which turned into cruelty.

He dreamed of Italy, the only country he loved. Even the spiritual torments he experienced there did not make him anti-Italian. But the path to Italy was still closed—the stormy political events in that country leading to Mussolini's rise to power did not give much hope. Each step closer to the Italian border made him feel that he could again go to his "eternally favorite" place someday.

There was another hidden reason behind this dream: there were practically no Russian immigrants in Italy, at least no immigrant "community" life, which in and of itself promised peace and a break from the environment he so despised where "storms and Communists howl."

His relationship to emigration failed, since it did not allow for "sitting on the fence" but demanded definition, irreconcilability and unambiguousness of political values; any deviation from its rules was interpreted as covert Bolshevism. Gorky, with his political odiousness and revolutionary past, was not permitted to change. Having escaped the Kremlin press, he automatically—and inescapably—fell under the émigré press, something he could not accept.

The latest paradox in Gorky's life was that he had emigrated without feeling like an emigrant. His attitude to the Russian Diaspora was to keep a "polite" distance from it.

"What a disgusting, rotten public this is!" he wrote to Peshkova about *all* Russians in Berlin on November 18, 1921, right after his arrival. "The rotten public" felt his attitude and repaid him in kind. He pretended not to read the émigré newspapers, filled with bilious attacks on Gorky—in fact this press reached him on a regular basis, embittering him more and more.

He had never concealed his resentful attitude toward the entire Russian people, personified for him by the peasantry. But his colleagues—writers, journalists, artists, those whom he called the Russian intelligentsia—made him even more furious. If everything that he wrote about them from the turn of the century were to be gathered, it would be material more fit for psychoanalysts and psychiatrists than historians.

All these writers are mentally ill, pitiful, perverted, to hell with them all!

I would recommend keeping a greater distance away from the émigrés—what a crowd they are! They horrify me and evoke a feeling of revulsion—they're sick, hysterical, helpless, and inexpressibly mean, to hell with them all!

[Russian writers] are capable of poisoning the strong and healthy—what rubbish they all are, what filth.

. . . the unhappy Russian intelligentsia, it seems, will soon rot from . . . perversion, into which it sinks with ever greater zeal.

. . . our intellectuals are foul, weak, and puny. . . .

The exalted Russian intelligentsia has become lost, bankrupted and suffocated! . . . I feel toward these effaced individuals only contempt and pity, as toward greedy beggars, who, crowding around the gates of a rich man, fight for the alms they expect. But alms will probably not be their lot—the servant will simply come out and drive them all away with a dirty broom.

I don't understand how it is possible to become so strongly decomposed and rotted during life. . . . Cemetery, corpses, and organic decomposition.

Those who have come here from Russia are herds of rams, lambs and swine. Where do these dead people come from? They stink extremely badly and behave even worse. . . . They're stupid to the point of tears.

I'm in a foul, irritable mood. People disgust me; it seems that the best of them are shiftless, untalented and useless; all the rest are liars and scoundrels.

Such quotations can go on and on and on . . .

It is true that all these excerpts are from private letters, but clearly Gorky is more candid in them than in public, and they convey more accurately his genuine thoughts and feelings. It is impossible to hide them, even if he tries to rein in his contempt. "Viper," "filth," "monster," and "degenerate" are words he used to describe well-known political figures and writers he did not like when he went on personal attacks. It was exactly those whom he so bitterly and vulgarly branded that Gorky accused of bitterness and was puzzled as to where their animosity toward him originated . . .

He could not remain anywhere émigré life flourished, and especially not in Germany. As Italy was still off-limits, Khodasevich and Berberova advised him to go to Czechoslovakia. It was strange advice, considering that even then Prague was one of the centers of Russian emigration. Perhaps this is why the

Khodaseviches suggested he spend the winter months not in Prague but in Marienbad (now Marianske Lazny), which emptied out in the off-season.

A visa was needed to enter Czechoslovakia. Khodasevich and Berberova obtained them without difficulty, but Gorky had a problem: his reputation was complicated, scandalous, and mysterious. President Masaryk got personally involved or, more precisely, it was Rolland who intervened for Gorky: Masaryk, after a visit with Rolland, promised to remove the obstacles. However, Masaryk declined a personal meeting with Gorky, and the police continued to track him the whole time until he reached his destination.

Here in cold, empty, and uncomfortable Marienbad, in the desolate Maxhof Hotel where, besides Mura, Max, Timosha, and Nightingale, who had accompanied him, and Berberova and Khodasevich, who brightened up his loneliness, many more guests could have been accommodated, Gorky immediately began working on the novella *The Artamonov Business.*

Far from the turmoil of the outside world connected only by the occasional letter, he worked enthusiastically and quickly. Marienbad's winter climate did not agree with him and there were no clinics anywhere to treat his tuberculosis. Soviet propaganda circulated the absurd version from Leninist times that Gorky had gone there for treatment.

Actually, Gorky was waiting for an Italian visa, but the refusal of the Soviet ambassador in Rome to help him confirms that the Kremlin knew Gorky was "stuck" in Europe for a long time, and his talk about a speedy return was only a smokescreen to preserve his status. In fact, he was not an émigré or on a business trip, or a tourist, or even anyone's guest, but simply Maxim Gorky, a stateless person without a homeland and without a permanent place of residence.

On January 22, 1924, Gorky received a telegram from Yekaterina Peshkova in Moscow: "Vladimir Ilyich has died telegraph text of inscription on wreath."

The return telegram was sent the following day—he had spent the whole day and evening deep in thought. "On the wreath write farewell friend," was his laconic reply.

Yekaterina Pavlovna carried out his instructions right away. "Farewell, friend! M. Gorky" was written on the ribbon framing the huge wreath that Peshkova personally placed on Lenin's grave.

For the second time Lenin had strongly entered his life, fatefully turning it around. The first time was when, after Lenin was mysteriously shot in August 1918, the zealous opponent of the Bolsheviks suddenly decided to cooperate with him. Now the death of the leader was going to destroy his peace of mind and, no matter how much he rebelled against it, force him to define himself one way or another. He simply could not be silent and neutral like "someone on the sidelines."

Gorky had just written to Rolland (January 15, 1924):

> . . . I am not returning to Russia, and I feel more and more like someone without a homeland. I am even inclined to think that I would have to play a terrible role in Russia—the role of opponent to everyone and everything, and because of my lack of constraint in speech, thought, and action I would find myself in the awkward position of a person who beats his head against a wall, wishing to break it . . . My arguments [with Lenin] awakened a spiritual hatred for each other.

It cannot be said any more clearly than that! Now (March 3, 1924) Gorky again wrote to Rolland: "Yes, my dear friend, Lenin's death is for me personally a great blow. . . . I loved him. Loved him with anger. . . . He was a very great Russian person." And, at the same time, in *Russkii sovremennik* (Russian Contemporary), an émigré journal, he wrote: "It is probable that more people were slaughtered under Lenin than during that of Taylor, Thomas Munzer, and Garibaldi." Such was, in Gorky's own confession, this "great Russian person," whom he loved, albeit "in anger."

These lines were written when he had already finished the first draft of his reminiscences about Lenin, entitled in laconically Gorky style "A Person." Mura immediately set to work on them, having correctly calculated how much money their publication in many languages would bring. Kriuchkov rushed over from Berlin, with the same goal in mind. Orders came from Moscow, one after the other, for reminiscences about Ilyich. They were ready by the beginning of February.

> Vladimir Lenin, a true great Person of this world, has died. This death has painfully struck at the hearts of those who knew him, very painfully.
>
> But the black line of death will emphasize his importance even more sharply in the eyes of the whole world.
>
> And if the storm cloud of hatred toward him, the storm cloud of lies and slander around his name grows thicker, it would make no difference: there are no forces which could darken the torch raised by Lenin in the sweltering pitch darkness of a panic-stricken world.
>
> And there was never a person like this who so truly deserved immortality in the world.

The scandal erupted immediately. Through Mura's efforts Gorky's reminiscences about Lenin were published right away in various languages in many countries. But they were not favorably received in Moscow: the canonical image of Lenin the leader had already been created, and the Kremlin had already downgraded the relationship between the "leader" and the "Stormy Petrel" to "friendly." Gorky's sketch did not fit into this scheme. Tikhonov, who ran the *Russkii sovremennik* journal, in which it was supposed to have been published, pleaded to make corrections in order to indulge both the censors and the new Kremlin bosses.

Gorky's reaction is unknown—his return letters to Tikhonov have been lost, or destroyed. Perhaps they will be found: not all hiding places have been searched and, of course, not all have been opened. In any event, the text published in Russia did not coincide with the text published abroad. Besides the words quoted above about Lenin the murderer, there were descriptions that Gorky introduced about Lenin, the "thinking guillotine," and about Lenin's "logic of the ax" (in another passage he compared Lenin's logic to the "blows of a hammer"), and none of this was said in judgment but welcomed as destroying something "which should have long since been destroyed." No matter how "ax-like" Lenin's logic was (and this is still a very soft definition), he always expressed himself with coarse and concise bluntness, to the point of cruel and unjust cynicism, but Gorky obscured the issue with his ambiguous "dialectical" paradoxes.

There are at least six, even seven, known versions of Gorky's memoirs about Lenin. He was editing them all the time, adding here, subtracting there, right up to the beginning of the 1930s. And not just because the changing political landscape demanded it, but because he could never clarify his position.

Now it is possible to view the censor's redaction of the first draft. Such lines as ". . . a leader, who—to one degree or another—would not have been a tyrant, is impossible" were removed.

It is difficult to say whether Gorky's intention was to defend Lenin in this passage or, on the contrary, to accuse him. Either way, it was not included in the published Russian text. Many other lines did not make it either. Gorky, who valued every one of his phrases and carefully selected every word and knew its worth, voiced no protest on that occasion.

He subsequently crossed it out on his own. Comparing the first version of his memoirs about Lenin with the very last one, it is difficult to believe that they are one and the same work, belonging to the pen of the same author.

The recent events which had ended tragically with the deaths of Gumilev and Blok, Mikhail Tikhvinsky and the grand dukes sat like a splinter in his brain, and he returned to them in his reminiscences.

> Very often I overwhelmed him [Lenin] with requests of various kinds and at times felt that my solicitations on behalf of people elicited Lenin's pity for me. He

asked, "It doesn't seem to you that you're occupying yourself with nonsense, trifles? . . . You're compromising yourself in the eyes of the comrade workers."

. . . Nonetheless, I cannot remember a case when Ilyich refused my request. If it happened that they were not granted, it was not his fault . . . It is possible . . . it was someone's* mean-spirited unwillingness to alleviate the fate of valuable people, to save their lives. . . . The enemy is as cynical as he is cunning. Revenge and spite often act out of inertia. And, of course, there are mentally ill sick people taking comfort in the sufferings of their neighbors.†

Moscow closely observed the Stormy Petrel and noticed how he had sharply changed course once again, but was in no hurry to draw final conclusions. Speaking at a soirée in memory of Lenin, Trotsky expressed Moscow's official position: "[Gorky] did not understand Ilyich, approaching him with that intellectual, petit-bourgeois sickly sweetness, more typical of Gorky in recent years." Such statements could hardly have moved Gorky—physically and mentally—closer to Moscow.

According to Kornei Chukovsky's diary, it was exactly at that time, the spring of 1924, that he was again banned from giving a lecture on Gorky's works: it was not clear *which* Gorky Chukovsky was planning to talk about: the Soviet writer or the refugee writer. Everything remained the same: Moscow gave Gorky money but treated him with caution and suspicion; as an émigré he was cursed and reviled.

The animosity with which the émigré crowd greeted the first rather restrained version of Gorky's reactions to the death of Lenin grew day by day, having a huge effect on the writer's wounded soul. The émigrés' attitude to him became more irreconcilable, yet he had created it himself, suffered from it and did everything to deepen the rift with the émigré environment. Emigration doggedly pushed Gorky into the embrace of the Soviets.

It is precisely the theme of Lenin and emigration that was the most painful for him at that time and is invariably present in his letters addressed to his closest friends. In trying to convince them of his correctness, he essentially convinced himself. After he had completed the first version of his memoirs, he tested it out on Andreeva, who was devoted to Lenin and, because of it, was not indifferent to what Gorky thought about Lenin and what he wrote.

I wrote and—I was flooded in tears. I did not even grieve as much for Tolstoy. And now I am writing and my hand trembles. His premature death has shaken everyone, everyone. . . . Only this rotten emigration pours its poison which, incidentally, is incapable of infecting healthy blood. . . . It is awful to see how

* None other than Zinoviev.
† An unquestionable dig at Zinoviev.

Russians become wild, bestial, and stupid when they are uprooted from their land. Especially revolting are the degenerates Aldanov and Eichenvald.* It's a pity that both are Jews.

Lenin's departure is the greatest cause of unhappiness [for Russia] in one hundred years. Yes, the greatest . . .

In those very same days (the beginning of February 1924), he wrote to Peshkova:

> Before Lenin's death, in spite of all the abomination and mediocrity of the émigré press, I nevertheless felt a kind of pity, sympathy and so on toward emigration in its overall mass. But their attitude to Lenin's death, an attitude full of putrid, morbidly rabid enmity, completely cured me of these sentiments. . . . Days full of bitter, savage rejoicing. Never has human stupidity and malice revealed itself before me with such magnificence. . . . It is very difficult to watch unburied corpses decompose so fast.

Gorky's subsequent evolution was already, in essence, predetermined. He could not remain for long in the marginal position of someone torn from one shore and unanchored to another. His indefatigable energy and thirst for action demanded an outlet, as well as a need to be in contact with a wide circle of people. In this sense émigrés were completely out of the question. He did not know any foreign languages, and traditional Western "good manners" were something completely alien. Because of his nature, he could not carry out Pushkin's command, "Live alone!" Thus, a "course set for Moscow" was inevitable.

Intelligent people in Moscow apparently understood this, and therefore did not rush him into defining himself once and for all. He was still not submissive. A cruel power struggle had begun inside the Kremlin. It is not difficult to guess whose side Gorky took (more accurately, would have taken): in any case not with Zinoviev who turned out to be for a very short moment on par with Stalin. For the time being Gorky's life abroad suited everyone. He had already begun "to turn red"—all that was needed now was to wait patiently until he "ripened."

The process of "ripening" did not promise, however, to be short and pain-less. Gorky was afraid that the new Kremlin bosses (he had considered Trotsky and Zinoviev to be his enemies) could interpret his tears for Lenin as testimony of a complete and unconditional surrender. A month and a half after Lenin's death he wrote to Peshkova on March 3, 1924:

---

* Writer and literary critic, respectively.

. . . If "influences" would have worked on me, then I surely would have submitted long ago to V[ladimir] I[lyich], who possessed a great ability to influence, and I would now be nibbling on diamonds, cavorting with ballerinas and driving around in the very best automobiles, only for real and not in my imagination . . .

These words, conveying his true thoughts and feelings with greater sincerity and expression than the *pathétique* of published memoirs, were not published until 1993. And it is easy to see why: they completely destroy the official image of Gorky as the friend of Lenin and the Bolsheviks.

14.

Burned Bridges

Gorky's fear that the publication of his memoirs about Lenin would prevent him from securing an Italian visa turned out to be groundless. When the Soviet ambassador in Rome managed to get an audience with Mussolini to obtain a visa for Gorky, Il Duce asked whether "this Russian troublemaker" was writing anything new. Upon hearing that he was penning his memoirs, Mussolini supposedly calmed down: "Well, if it's just memoirs, then I will allow it. Whoever writes memoirs is finished as a writer."

At the end of March 1924 a report reached Marienbad that permission for the trip to Italy had been granted, but on one condition: he could settle wherever he wanted except on Capri. Rome suspected that his presence alone could awaken among the native islanders their former political activity.

Gorky did not object: he had many other favorite places in Italy even without Capri. The choice fell on Sorrento, where he hastened to immediately with all his belongings, via Prague and Vienna, with a short stop in Naples. Khodasevich and Berberova had left Marienbad, which they had grown sick of, even earlier in order to join up with Gorky in Italy.

Just before his departure a telegram arrived from the despicable Ilya Ionov in Moscow, congratulating him on the publication of the first sixteen-volume collection of Gorky's works in the Soviet Union: "To the innumerable threads connecting you with Russia, new ones are added all the time . . ."

The "threads" felt more like a chain binding Gorky to the Soviet wheel. The man who arrived in Sorrento was inordinately fatigued from everyday life, repulsed by emigration, with no ties to the West nor any comfort in the European milieu while he remained connected—morally and materially—to his Kremlin benefactors. There could be no talk of returning to the Soviet Union, especially now when beloved Italy had finally opened its doors to him and

Zinoviev and Trotsky ruled in Moscow. Stalin seemed not to exist just yet—for Gorky he was still not the leader, but simply "one of . . ." But the connection with Moscow had been established and was strengthened every day.

This was facilitated by publishing matters in which he was personally involved. His publishing house, *Vsemirnaya Literatura*, where Aleksandr Tikhonov played an active role, continued to issue books. Tikhonov also published the "independent" literary journal *Russkii sovremennik*, which was supposedly a supplement to the journal *Beseda* published in the West.

Gorky was still hoping that *Beseda* would be allowed into Soviet Russia: the NEP was in full swing, and from a distance this seemed to promise creative freedom as well. Gorky had finished the *Artamonov Business* and was about to begin his final novel, *The Life of Klim Samgin*. It would have been difficult to have better working conditions than those in Sorrento.

The people he needed most were with him. Now, finally, Gorky had acquired a real family and not a surrogate. Mura, Max, and Timosha, of whom Gorky grew fonder by the day, were all together under one roof. In Germany and Czechoslovakia Gorky had undertaken to "educate" Timosha—he chose books for her to read and discuss, accompanied her to exhibitions and museums (Timosha suddenly discovered a yen for drawing) and bought her art albums.

This show of love for the daughter-in-law stood in contrast to his elevated but somewhat intangible love for his son. Never, not even during their brief meetings, which Max—first as a child and later as an adolescent—had so longed for, had he lavished on his son as much attention as he did now on his son's wife. In Sorrento, where time was plentiful and the mood favorable, Gorky's care for Timosha became all the more touching. Here he told the young couple unambiguously that he wished for the continuation of his lineage.

Lenin, in sending Max abroad, had ordered him to be inseparable from his father and assist him in his work (or, more to the point, influence his political orientation). This role, for a relatively short period, was clearly to Max's liking. He had no profession to speak of, no education, nothing specific to do. Thus, what Gorky feared most had happened, and he was guilty of it to a significant degree: Max had turned out to be a *nobody*.

Back in 1908, Gorky had written to Peshkova, "Let him not be the 'son of a writer'—this unfortunate variety of the superfluous man."* Max in fact did become this "unfortunate variety." "Capable of everything, but doesn't do anything," "incapable of working seriously"—these characteristics testify con-

---

* Reference to a frequent character type in nineteenth-century Russian literature, introduced in Turgenev's *Diary of a Superfluous Man* (1850). The character is well-educated and idealistic; he sees the injustices of the world around him, but either cannot or will not do anything to effect change.

vincingly that, as far as his son's possibilities and future were concerned, Gorky was not mistaken.

Hundreds of pages have been written by Soviet scholars and memoirists to prove that Max performed an extremely useful mission by dedicating his life to his father and serving as his assistant and secretary. This hardly corresponds to the truth. The role of true secretaries was fulfilled by Mura and PePeKriu; Max might have put up and taken care of the guests who came to Sorrento, while trying to handle his father's financial matters and jealous of Mura and Kriuchkov, who limited his immense expenditures. Max knew how to throw money around and loved doing it—flattered by his attention, slavish writers later hastened to call this activity the "generosity of a good soul."

It was believed that Max spoke several languages fluently, and even knew Italian dialects. This, mildly speaking, is a great exaggeration. While growing up in France and Switzerland, he attended a Russian school, played with Russian children and did not have local friends his age. His stay in Italy (in Alassio on the Ligurian coast) was also spent isolated from the surrounding environment, exclusively in a domestic circle; there is absolutely no evidence that he attended an Italian school, had any close Italian friends his age, or even once mentioned in a letter to his father that he was mastering the Italian tongue, except perhaps in Sorrento where, as an adult, he could understand the Neapolitan dialect to some degree.

But there is evidence that refutes the legend of Max the polyglot. The rare translations of newspaper articles, and letters from and to his father, which he did in the presence of Mura, were so inaccurate that they elicited at times completely non sequitur responses from Gorky and his correspondents, resulting in awkward situations and the need for additional explanations. An example of a translation he did for his father (the international committee's appeal to Gorky against repression in Russia) proves that he had only an approximate understanding of French and hardly any better mastery of Russian literary language. Several years later in Moscow he translated an article from Italian for his father's almanac, but it could not be published until after Gorky himself had completely "reedited" the translation.

Vladislav Khodasevich, who had lived more than a year with Gorky and his close friends as a single family, wrote about the thirty-year-old Max, married and already balding, that "in terms of development it was difficult to see him as being more than thirteen years old." Unsure what to do with himself, Max took up tennis and motorcycling and race car driving, stamp collecting, detective novels, the circus, and western films.

Everyone who knew the family closely made note of Gorky's total love for Max. It may not have been so much love as a complicated feeling spawned by a paternal guilt complex toward his abandoned and underachieving son.

Gorky himself called Max "a Soviet prince," referring to the sumptuous and idle life the Kremlin provided him. Another domestic nickname for the "prince" was more naturalistic: "the singing intestinal worm." It picturesquely depicted his thinness and habit of singing *canzones* at picnics, domestic carnivals, and the boisterous feasts that he organized practically on a daily basis. Long since inclined to copious alcohol binges, he had settled down somewhat after marrying a young woman from a well-bred, intelligent family, but in Italy he "loosened up," giving free reign to his former ingrained habits.

To everyone and in everything he was a "good guy," as many wrote of him, who got along well with people and was fond of "drag racing" in expensive automobiles. Leaving his wife alone during his prolonged excursions, his partying associates were usually guests of his father who came to visit more frequently from faraway Russia.

Unable to control the Soviet prince's taste for *la dolce vita*, Gorky wrote to Peshkova in June 1925:

> Max, by his egotism, does not pay her [Timosha] sufficient attention and it would be good if you wrote him—only please don't mention me!—and let him know that a pregnant wife, moreover a good one, demands caresses and care. . . . He doesn't want anything, except his car; he rides off somewhere every single day . . .

From time to time Peshkova would come to Sorrento, at times on assignment from Dzerzhinsky, with whom she worked very closely and not only on official business. In one of her trips she brought Max an unexpected invitation from the Lubyanka chief to return to Moscow and go to work for him again. In 1918 Max had received a stamp collection from Dzerzhinsky confiscated from some "bourgeois" for his successful service to the Cheka. This time Iron Felix was promising him a car in advance.

Gorky immediately figured out the guileless intention of the Lubyanka: they did not need Max, of course, but his father! "And after they've slaughtered them all there," he asked Peshkova, "then what?" He was still hoping that *they* would be the ones slaughtered; Peshkova was convinced that *they* would get rid of everyone who hindered *them* . . . "They think that I will come after him," said Gorky. "But I won't go, not on your life!"

This was most definitely not the moment to try and entice Gorky to come back: in Leningrad, as Petrograd was now called, Aleksandr Tikhonov had been arrested and forced to shut down the publication of *Beseda*. At first that same

Ionov had driven Tikhonov from his job at *Vsemirnaya Literatura*. Gorky telegraphed from Sorrento: "I am categorically opposed to Tikhonov's removal." To which Ionov replied with disarming frankness: "If I feel some kind of enmity toward someone. . . . it will be difficult for me to work with such a person."

Tikhonov's removal was followed almost immediately by the closing of the publishing house and his arrest on Ionov's denunciation. The reason was not reported. "The wildest rumors are going around the city," wrote Kornei Chukovsky in his diary. One such rumor, totally absurd, being spread by the Chekists was that Tikhonov had allegedly helped a group of writers and editors employed at the publishing house to cross the Finnish border illegally. The truth spilled out soon after: Zinoviev thought that Tikhonov was hiding Lenin's letters to Gorky in which he was mentioned.

Gorky's fury knew no limit, but his letters and telegrams in defense of the arrested did not produce the desired consequences. At his request, Peshkova interceded on his behalf to Dzerzhinsky in Moscow. "Our asses" is what Gorky called the Kremlin leaders during those days, according to Khodasevich.

"My relationship with Moscow," he wrote in February 1925 to a Russian émigré scientist, "is becoming all the more rotten, and contacts all the more rare." Even after Tikhonov was freed after almost four months in prison, the "contacts" did not become any warmer or more frequent. "I was extremely distressed and indignant at what happened with you," he wrote Tikhonov after the latter was released from prison.

The news of Tikhonov's arrest reached Varvara as well. Both she and Nina had moved to Paris by that time and settled into a small apartment not far from the Gare de Lyon. Pride prevented her from asking Gorky for help but the situation soon became hopeless: money stopped coming from Tikhonov. Her gas and electricity were turned off for nonpayment, local shopkeepers stopped selling them food on credit and eviction was inevitable. At her mother's call for help, Nina turned to Gorky. By that time Gorky had already done everything he could to free Tikhonov, but Nina's letter produced the desired consequences: he sent three small amounts of money to Paris, literally saving the mother and daughter from perishing.

Peshkova also honored Gorky's request to ask permission from Dzerzhinsky for Tikhonov to come to Sorrento for a rest. He arrived with his new wife, the same made-up young petit-bourgeois who had comforted him during Varvara's dramatic peregrinations from her husband to Gorky and back again.

Nothing personal now separated the former friends; they only had woes in common. *Beseda*, which never entered the Soviet Union, was no longer being published, and a bit later *Russkii sovremennik* met the same fate, strangled by the censors.

Nonetheless, Gorky wrote to Bukharin (June 23, 1925): ". . . I want to go home. I'll go to Russia, to the Volga, to the country, to the Urals and all over!" However, to Rykov, a year before this, he had written something very different: "Thanks for the invitation to move back to Russia,* but I'm going to wait a bit on this."

It does not appear that he deliberately lied to either one or the other. It was simply that his mood changed under the influence of "current events"; his soul was troubled and torn. And yet he never had worked with such a feeling of independence and freedom as he did in Sorrento, stubbornly protecting himself from any attempts at influence, most of all from those closest to him.

> To convince him of something [recalled Nina Berberova] was impossible because he had an amazing ability of not listening to someone he didn't like, or not to answer when he was asked a question he could not answer. . . . You had to listen to Gorky and be quiet. Perhaps he did not consider his opinions as infallible, but he did not want to have to resolve or reexamine anything, and he probably couldn't: if you touch one thing, another begins to fall, and pretty soon the whole building collapses, and then what? Let it stand as it had originally been built.

The paradox is that he constructed a great many of these "buildings"—his evaluations of people and phenomena, likes and dislikes, changed many times, and often very quickly, and each time he considered the latest "building" as unshakeable, as if there had never been any collapses at all. Everyone could choose which Gorky was more to his or her liking.

Khodasevich and Berberova left Sorrento for Paris, where the émigré cultural elite were gradually moving. Back at the villa Il Sorito, where Gorky was now solidly entrenched, someone new appeared: on August 17, 1925, his granddaughter Marfa was born.

Peshkova came for the birth and left immediately after. With the blessings of Dzerzhinsky, she was even busier at the Political Red Cross. This is one of the mysteries that remains unsolved to this day! Was this a trap, ensnaring, with Peshkova's help and thanks to her good reputation, the victims of the terror, who trusted her completely and revealed their innermost thoughts, or a genuine attempt by Dzerzhinsky to lighten the lot of those who suffered from his *oprichniki,** or simply a decorative shield creating the illusion of "proletarian humanity"?

---

* Made after the death of dear Vladimir Ilyich!
* Armed members of the *oprichnina*, a special administrative elite under Tsar Ivan the Terrible

Thousands of prisoners who had fallen under the Red Wheel across the vast expanses of Russia waited for "Auntie Katya" or "Mother Hen," as she was called in all the camps and prisons, or "political isolation wards" as they were now called. She crisscrossed the country in a car specially assigned to her, bringing letters and clothing to the prisoners, receiving their complaints and solicitations in return, which were then forwarded to the proper departments along with her notes, at times even personally delivered to high-ranking offices. People with an irreproachable moral reputation recommended her to their friends and acquaintances in trouble as a person of "good will and great possibilities" (from a letter by Maximilian Voloshin).

In August 1925, Gorky told the Russian poet Vyacheslav Ivanov, who was visiting him and who had settled in Italy, that Yekaterina Pavlovna "makes use of her great influence on Dzerzhinsky and company" and can "get anyone a foreign passport without difficulty." With Peshkova's help, her deputy Mikhail Vinaver managed to inform the West about the atrocities taking place in Soviet political camps. She played a key role in the repatriation of inhabitants of former Russian territories now part of Poland. For this activity she was awarded the Honorary Badge of the Polish Red Cross. Twice a year she traveled to Poland on official business, where she was always enthusiastically received.

Was there not some kind of profound, internal tie between this mission of hers and her relationship to the Pole Dzerzhinsky who, perhaps, was not the simple one-dimensional figure he had been portrayed for many years by Soviet apologists and foreign subversives? Even Nikolai Berdyaev, exiled from Soviet Russia, whom Dzerzhinsky once personally interrogated, remembered him with obvious sympathy: "There was something soft in his manner and appearance, good breeding and courtesy came across."

There is reason to believe that she fulfilled personal and highly confidential assignments for Dzerzhinsky, the details of which are not to be found in the official press, nor in the secret archives. Once from Sorrento, for example, where she had bought Dzerzhinsky an expensive tortoise-shell mouthpiece as a gift, she made an unannounced visit to Prague to see her long-time friend Yekaterina Kuskova, whose hatred for the Soviets had not abated since Lenin had her exiled from Russia aboard the "philosopher's boat." It was obvious that Peshkova would not have summoned the courage for such madness without the permission, or even direct orders, from Dzerzhinsky.

All this must be considered when evaluating one, possibly involuntary, step of Gorky's that turned out to be truly inauspicious and led to the next—abrupt and fatal—turn in his life.

On July 20, 1926, Felix Dzerzhinsky died unexpectedly, and at the time there was no explanation for the cause of death, just as there still is none to this day. It cannot be excluded that he was helped into the grave, as had happened just a year earlier with Mikhail Frunze, the people's commissar of defense and one of the probable leaders of the Party who had remained above political infighting. We should recall that seven years earlier Gorky had sent Dzerzhinsky a spiteful letter: "Soviet power makes me hostile toward it."

Now, having learned of Dzerzhinsky's death, Gorky reacted in a letter to Yakov Ganetsky, who was then a member of the board of the People's Commissariat of Foreign Trade—a person not that close to him but who had been actively involved in resolving Gorky's money problems. The choice of this addressee was possibly determined by the fact that Ganetsky was also a Pole and Gorky, in expressing his feelings, counted on Ganetsky's special understanding.

> I am totally shocked by the death of Felix Edmundovich [wrote Gorky]. I saw him for the first time in 1909–1910 [on Capri, where Dzerzhinsky, fleeing the tsarist authorities, had gone for a respite], when he made an unforgettable impression of emotional purity and solidity on me. From 1918–1921 I got to know him rather closely, and spoke with him on a very sensitive subject several times [the bloody Chekist terror]; he was often burdened with many problems . . . Thanks to his mental sharpness and fairness, many good things were accomplished. He made me both love and respect him. And I understand perfectly Yekat[erina] Pavlovna's tragic letter where she writes to me about him: "There is not a more wonderful person, infinitely dear to everyone who knew him." My soul is troubled and heavy . . . No, how unexpected and premature and senseless is the death of Felix Edmundovich. What the devil!

Several days later—August 11—the two leading Soviet newspapers, *Pravda* and *Izvestiia*, reproduced the text of this letter under the heading "Maxim Gorky on Com. Dzerzhinsky." The question of whether it was proper to publish a personal letter without the author's permission while still alive evidently never troubled the Soviet publishers. Ganetsky, a Party functionary tightly bound to both the Central Committee and the Lubyanka, had obviously informed Stalin about this spontaneous manifestation of feelings on the part of the exile in Sorrento, and the Kremlin fox resolved to take advantage of this fortuitous and unique opportunity.

The reaction of the entire émigré crowd did not take long: Dzerzhinsky embodies the Bolshevik terror. All the Cheka's cruelties, all the barbarity of the executioners, both great and small, were personified in this individual with the sunken cheeks and goatee. It is easy to imagine what and how the émigré press of all stripes wrote about yesterday's defender of the injured and insulted, who until recently had excoriated Lenin and all Bolsheviks in general.

The writer Mikhail Osorgin—one of those who had also been exiled from Russia on the "philosopher's boat"—chose to bypass the press and sent Gorky a personal and very respectful letter (extracted from the secret archive only in 1995):

> . . . The state murderer, an executioner with initiative, is not a person but a perversion of the idea of a person and I cannot find in myself any human love, or justification, toward him. . . Dzerzhinsky was the "axe of the state," that is, the perversion of a person. You can write about him in literary fashion, but the word *love* does not apply to him. His name in Russia will be forever cursed by simple, real and genuine people. If it is otherwise, then we are not people . . . I am very saddened that your letter was published—it is an easily understandable letter, written to friends about a common comrade. . . . It weighs terribly on the nerves of mothers, wives, children and brave people.

All bridges between Gorky and the émigrés were now thoroughly burned. Punishing himself for his hastiness, he could not even protest for it would have been a blow to Yekaterina Peshkova and to everyone whose fate depended upon her.

Gorky unambiguously expressed his reaction to this Jesuitical trick by the Moscow "comrades" in a letter to his Prague correspondent, Dalmat Lutokhin: "I am very angry at myself for putting her opinion about Dzerzhinsky in my letter." About his *own* opinion, let alone the unauthorized public use of his personal letter, he said nothing. Rationalizing, however, he confirmed to Lutokhin what he had written to Ganetsky:

> [Dzerzhinsky] very highly valued . . . Peshkova's work, protected her from provocations, and Yekaterina Pavlovna was truly wounded by his untimely death. She . . . told me many things which further elevated F[eliks] in my eyes.

He did not respond to Osorgin's letter or to any other such letters overall. Instead, his reaction to them was "What scum these émigrés are, and how quickly they rot."

Now Gorky had no other fate—at least psychologically—than to return to Moscow . . .

To be sure, he did not want to go there, or go anywhere for that matter. He turned down Chaliapin's invitation to stay with him at his villa in Normandy, just as he declined all other invitations which would have required him to travel.

His connection to the outside world came only through the mail, and almost everyone who wrote him, and to whom he wrote back, lived in the Soviet Union. The logic of events pushed him more and more to look only in one direction. He still retained his sense of reality and realized perfectly well what was in fact taking place in Soviet Russia, although the dramatic zigzags of the severe power struggle could hardly have been comprehensible to him.

Out of habit, several Russian writers continued to seek intercession from the patriarch in Italy, who had already lost any influence with the Soviet authorities. Nevertheless, he was still *Maxim Gorky*, and this name still meant something. Persecuted by local authorities, the poet Sergei Klychkov wrote to Gorky about his troubles and asked for protection. The letter reached its destination. Gorky responded—and was successful: "The local executive committee," Klychkov reported to Gorky, "has been ordered to keep its hands off me." "It pleases me," Gorky answered, "that, in spite of everything, the Russian writer still remains as spiritually independent as he had been . . . Nobody here understands how difficult your life and your heroic stance are. In saying 'you,' I exclude many people who do not write what they should, but only what they are ordered to write."

These letters were unquestionably opened and read, thus giving the Lubyanka and the Kremlin an opportunity to follow the evolution of his thoughts and feelings. Other correspondents, even ones very close to him, understood that exchanging letters with Gorky would automatically place them on the Lubyanka's list and therefore refrained from contact with the disgraced half-émigré, in spite of the need for it. When, for example, Didi (the artist Andrei Diderikhs) was arrested in 1926 in Moscow, his wife Valentina Khodasevich decided not to "bother" Gorky, but to use the services of Isaak Babel instead, who had his own contacts inside that same sinister institution. Didi was freed shortly thereafter.

Such a fateful episode—Gorky's opinion of Dzerzhinsky—coincided with the period when the issue of his finances came up; he could only expect money from Moscow and nowhere else. If he still displayed pride and did not overly advertise his dependence on the Kremlin's dole, before now he simply stood with an outstretched hand, which completely excluded the possibility of any confrontation with his donors and creditors. Incidentally, the living classic never bothered to remind anyone that the underground Bolshevik party and its boss lived grandly for whole years on Gorky's personal money and on the funds he raised for them.

Before moving from Marienbad to Sorrento, Mura had rationally advised him "not to argue with the Bolsheviks," from whom, she said, "you have to squeeze out more"—after all, foreign publishing houses could never have provided him with financial security. "I hate the Bolsheviks no less," the highly pragmatic Mura assured the writer, "but there is no other way out. Let them beat each other up, and then we'll see."

Pride, scrupulousness, and the fear of losing his independence had stopped him in the beginning from contacting high-ranking Moscow leaders. Instead, he complained only to Kriuchkov, who gradually took all financial matters into his own hands: "If I am owed money for a book, send it because there's no more of it," he appealed to PePeKriu immediately upon arriving in Italy. But in 1926 the author of the angry pamphlets about the Yellow Devil (his term for despicable gold in his sketches from long ago about America) began pestering the Moscow leaders directly about his impoverishment.

In letters not only to Ganetsky, but also to Rykov, at that time the number-two man in the government (chairman of the Council of People's Commissars), he drew a gloomy picture of his impecunious condition, asking that the money be sent faster. Neither one answered—it is possible they were waiting for the supplicant to fall to his knees—although Gorky supposedly enjoyed a good relationship with Rykov (they had met in Germany).

Instead of being ashamed of this humiliation, the decrepit mutineer simply sank even lower. Gorky wrote to Aleksandr Voronsky, editor-in-chief of the journal *Krasnaia nov'* in June 1926:

> A few days ago, *Gosizdat* sent me 1,500 dollars. . . . I've already gone through this money, having used it to pay off debts, various shopkeepers, housekeepers, and so on.* I will ask *Gosizdat* to give me ten thousand. . . This will allow me to pay off all my debts once and for all, live with peace of mind for a few months and work without having to worry about money. Perhaps I might even go somewhere for a week and relax. During the four years of living here,† I haven't gone anywhere, not even to Rome, four hours away. . . Could you not intercede on my behalf for them to send me the money?

No one gave him ten thousand—they gave him two thousand, thereby making it clear that he was on their leash and that he would have to earn the next portion. Loyalty alone was already insufficient. So far there were no enthusiastic outbursts, but Gorky's numerous letters to Soviet writers, opened and read, bore evidence that he had already turned "slightly pink" and was quickly and inexorably "reddening." It was now only a matter of time. . .

The money was spent with lightning-fast alacrity and already by November of that year Gorky again debased himself before Ganetsky: "I would greatly

---

* Naturally, Gorky kept silent about the money wasted by Max.
† He had lived in Sorrento only two years by then.

appreciate it if you were to intercede on my behalf for two thousand dollars in addition to the two which I already received." The Kremlin's tactics were clear: to dole out neatly packaged financial infusions to the former Stormy Petrel so that he did not completely lose spirit and run into the arms of imperialist sharks, and to entice him with future prospects while paying a reduced price for services rendered.

15.

Death by Small Cuts

The financial problems desperately gnawing at Gorky, the sudden loss of that creative mood which he had so yearned for and the everyday problems (Timosha's illness immediately following the birth of his grand-daughter and the protracted repairs on his new Sorrento dwellings which forced them to relocate temporarily to Naples) all fatally coincided with a drama of the heart that also affected his mental state: his relationship with Mura had radically changed. It is difficult to judge the details behind it, and is there even a need to? Nevertheless, it can be said that the main reason was Mura's constant departures—not her absence itself, at times prolonged, which also upset him—but his understanding of the factors leading to it. Even the trips to see her children seemed (and they were!) only a convenient pretext to hit the road. Mura lied or, in the very best case, simply concealed something which, in the context of their seemingly friendly and trusting relationship, was essentially a lie as well.

Fortunately, several letters from this period—Gorky to Mura and Mura to Gorky—have been preserved, giving us the opportunity, if not to learn the intimate details, then at least to understand his emotional state, to get to the bottom of his ideological makeup. With him, one is inseparable from the other. A few fragments of this correspondence deserve close reading in chronological order.

Mura to Gorky on October 23, 1925:

> . . . Do not doubt, you cannot doubt how strongly, with no second thoughts, I loved you then in Russia. And these feelings continued in Saarov and Freiburg. And then I felt, probably, gradually, because I don't remember exactly when, that I was no longer in love with you. I love you but I was not in love. There wasn't that—ah, what makes birds sing and makes you see *God* in your head. It was awful for me—this I remember—so awful that I can't say. Here, I thought, is a person I so desperately need, who also needs me, he loves me, he is close to me forever, I

have so much tenderness for him, but there's no rapture. I struggled with this for a long time, I convinced myself that none of this is important, that this demon can be strangled, but it kept on growing. My dear, you cannot imagine how I hated, and still hate myself for this. It was not a desire of sexual intimacy with anyone else—oh no, this I know very well, but an attempt to sense my life being illuminated again with that wonderful kind of love that gives everything, but demands nothing, love for which alone it is worth living. I had this with Lockhart and I had it with you—but it's gone—does this mean my life is over? I never looked for a "man"; I always needed one thing only: that feeling of happiness. But without it, what am I good for, how can you need me? Yes, finally, it was insulting to take your rapture of love—and not be in a condition to sing with you as one voice, not feel excitement from your caresses. My dear friend—God knows if I have left you to suffer—I have paid for this a hundred times over with my own suffering.

Gorky to Mura on December 21, 1925:

It seems you are very cautious in your attitude toward me. To be sure, it is sad for me to know this, because sincerity vanishes in the presence of caution. It's a pity, it's sad, but nevertheless useful to know that your sincerity is waning so quickly, although you assure me of the opposite. . . . I'm no less self-centered than you, I want you to be inspired with the philanthropy of a surgeon and not be tormented like you have tormented me this whole past year. In the last few months it has been especially onerous and frivolous.

Mura to Gorky on December 29, 1925:

It is very difficult for me to answer your last letter from the twenty-first, because this time it sounds simply hostile, and I am at a loss, I seek your former attitude to me. You were the one who instilled caution in me, but as for the "the frivolity with which I have tormented you," I cannot agree. But I am not going to prove the opposite . . . Your words "the philanthropy of a surgeon" make me ask you: would it not be better for you to be just as "surgically" open with me?

Gorky to Mura on December 30, 1925:

You understand me so poorly—and it's only getting worse—that I find it necessary to explain my view of our relationship one more time and in a somewhat "simplified" form, which you, as an intelligent woman, should not take offense at. . . . I told you many times before that I am too old for you, and I said this in the hope of hearing your truthful "yes!" You did not dare, and do not dare say it, and this has created for both you and me a completely unbearable situation.

Your attraction to a man younger than I and therefore more worthy of your love and friendship is completely natural. And it is absolutely useless for you to conceal the voice of instinct with the fig leaves of "fine" words. What is this for? . . . You ask: what should we do? I'll say it again: we must separate. Maybe temporarily— that's your business, your decision, but—in my view—we must separate. This will be better for you, you will not have to split yourself in two, not have to resort to thinking up little lies "out of concern for me," you will not have to restrain and distort yourself. It will probably be somewhat easier for me; my work requires basic conditions of peace of mind, but with you, with the relationship we have created, that will be impossible for me. After all, I love you, I am jealous and so on. Sorry, maybe you don't need to be reminded of this . . . How heavy, how terrible, all this is.

Mura to Gorky on April 19, 1926:

> So it means that I did not instill in you during the winter the certainty of my attitude toward you? I didn't try, you say? Well, I think you have to agree that this is not completely fair. . . . I also think you will understand . . . that from now on my life . . . is consumed with concern for your emotional peace of mind . . . I told you that I decided not to see R. any more.* With all my strength I am trying to lead my life, for my own peace more than according to my natural taste and I must say, glory be to the Almighty, that it is beginning to work out for me.

This dramatic epistolary novel could go on and on, but these fragments are probably sufficient. What, perhaps, worked for Mura, did not work at all for Gorky, no matter how much he tried to console himself with rational words. None of the women who occupied such a major place in his life, with the exception of Yekaterina Peshkova, brought him peace of mind, not even temporarily. To be sure, there was joy, amusement and high spirits—but not peace of mind. Instead, there was all the noise, anxiety and troubles one could ask for. No matter which standard is used to measure it by, Mura was undoubtedly the leading culprit in this regard.

Moreover, he never concealed his attitude toward Mura from anyone and spoke about it with characteristic frankness in letters to others: this "person, to whom my intimate, spiritual life is open" (to Stefan Zweig); "a person whose opinion I trust very much" (to Romain Rolland). No other love of Gorky's was so deep and lasted so long. No other brought him so much suffering, becoming, despite Mura's will, a kind of death by small cuts. And with no other woman did he feel so lonely, lost and even helpless.

In tracking how his views, judgments, evaluations, and moods changed—at times even inexplicably—those heartfelt sufferings and mental torments, which this sick and no longer young man felt at the crucial stage of his life, must always be kept in mind.

---

* The publishers of this correspondence presume that she is referring to Robert Bruce Lockhart.

As Gorky neared his sixtieth birthday in his Sorrento paradise, he managed the chaos of his personal life, which not all that long ago had been so entangled and stormy, but which had seemingly acquired—after Mura rejected his advice and did not leave him even temporarily—some parameters which promised him, if not exactly peace, then at least the desired clarity.

Mura had already solidly entrenched herself as his wife, living with him and submissively carrying out the many duties of a true helper. She handled all of Gorky's correspondence in several languages and organized the reprinting of his manuscripts: Gorky wrote by hand, there was no Russian typist in Sorrento, nor even a typewriter, and neither Max nor Timosha would have been capable of handling such "rough" work. Mura took complete responsibility for everyday matters. This kind of work, natural for any woman constantly living under the same roof with a man, allowed (and to this day allows) practically all Soviet and Russian specialists to call her the "writer's secretary." It's not difficult to guess how Gorky would have reacted to such concern about his "moral image" and to such a sanctimonious "definition" for a woman who spent more time with him like a wife than any other.

The first chapters of his novel, *The Life of Klim Samgin*, dedicated "To Maria Ignatyevna Zakrevskaya," were published in Moscow in May 1927. No one knows why he chose the maiden name of his favorite woman for the dedication, since she had already changed it twice by then, but it was probably his way of repudiating Mura's dubious (if not altogether false) title of baroness and all her other previous connections to the various men in her life. Or perhaps he simply believed that "Zakrevskaya" sounded less exotic to Russian ears? Whatever the real reason, it was impossible for decades to explain to Soviet readers the identity of this woman, the recipient of the great proletarian writer's dedication of his final novel.

Her frequent absences were extremely painful to Gorky. It was believed she traveled to Estonia to see her children. Who knows, though, where she went, and why? The affair with Wells, which had flared up again in Petrograd, continued—sputtering out or blazing anew—and it was inevitable she needed to see him to keep it going. This romance, far from being a secret for only the two of them, was painstakingly concealed from Gorky, but perhaps he simply pretended not to know, so as not to ruin his long-last acquired serenity.

It is highly likely that more than just affairs of the heart made Mura travel. In spite of her sworn promises she continued to meet with Lockhart, her old flame, in various European capitals, but this person, tightly connected to the British special services also tied Mura to them as well. To this day we do not know precisely what contacts she had with Iron Felix: the version that she traveled from Italy for meetings with Dzerzhinsky's agents (Estonia was an excellent location for this) is very plausible. Italian counterintelligence certainly took this version very seriously—it was not a coincidence that during one of her returns in 1925 Mura was subjected to a very demeaning and prolonged check by "customs inspectors" at the border. They turned her luggage upside down and, naturally, did not find what they were looking for: if Mura did have secret meetings with Moscow's emissaries, then her mission did not consist of bringing something forbidden into Italy. However, they did confiscate her correspondence with Gorky.

This was not the first scandal involving Mura. Earlier the villa had been searched. Even now the legend lives on in Russian "Gorkiana" about the fascist black shirts transgressing the peace and good name of the great writer. Several years before, when Zinoviev's emissaries had burst into the apartment on Kronverksky, upturning up Mura's room, his Italian "colleagues" were interested only in Mura and not at all in her common-law husband. The search took place in a villa rented by the writer Maxim Gorky and this allowed him to "protest resolutely." More to the point, the embassy protested on his behalf. Soviet ambassador Platon Kerzhentsev managed to obtain an audience with Mussolini and the latter, without admitting what had prompted the police visit, promised to leave the "honorable *signor* Gorky" alone.

Yekaterina Pavlovna regularly came to Sorrento—usually twice a year—spending about three weeks with the family. "I have the friendliest relations with her," said Gorky to Vyacheslav Ivanov. "Like with Maria Fyodorovna Andreeva," he added. "I've managed to avoid any drama with my closest women." In reissuing his *Tales of Italy*, he never removed the former dedication to this woman with whom he spent many creatively and spiritually rich years of his life.

Andreeva, according to everyone who saw her in the mid-1920s, was as beautiful as ever. Her thick reddish hair, without any strands of gray, and proud head on her upright, supple figure gave her, as before, an air of importance; the fashionably narrow shoes, rings and tastefully modest jewelry (rich and fancy was never her style) testified to the fact that she was full of life and still felt herself to be an attractive woman, not just some ordinary Soviet operative carrying out important tasks for the Party.

Her nostalgia for the past, inseparably linked to Gorky and their time together in Italy, was reflected in a letter she sent immediately after he settled in Sorrento. "Dear, dear Lyosha,* remember me sometime in a good moment, when you are gazing out at the sea or up at the starry sky, when it is velvety, and know that I firmly, faithfully love you, and that I only want to remember

---

* Diminutive form of Alyosha, itself a diminutive of Aleksei.

what was good." The reconciliation, so clearly expressed in this letter, was because she had "a quiet haven" in the person of Kriuchkov, who was completely tied to her by his career and position and continued to live and work with her in Berlin.

Yet in less than a year this relationship, which had seemed so solid to her, was irreparably broken. This is reflected in a letter from Andreeva's close friend Aleksandra Kollontai, who had just gone through a similar situation herself, to their mutual friend Zoya Shadurskaya, also working in Berlin:

> You have to tear yourself away internally from persistent love for a man. This is what Maria Fyodorovna has to understand. You have to be able to admit to yourself that at our age it's not possible for them to fall in love with us. There are many other things that bind men to us: outbursts of desire (*charme*, such as Maria Fyodorovna has, does not diminish with the years), comfort (we know how to create it), a flattering self-love and so on. But none of this is love, not that love which we had (in our youth).
>
> What can we do to avoid suffering from this? My advice: isolate yourself internally. I am one, he is another, completely different. Live with all sides of your rich spiritual "I" (and M[aria] F[yodorovna] is rich, very rich!)... And do not create illusions for yourself.
>
> ... If you think of building a life at our age based upon relationships with "them," you will get only sorrow, humiliation, slings, and arrows. You have to teach yourself to be alone, internally alone. Do not count on anyone and least of all on "them"! ... Tell this to M. F. Let her learn not to expect anything. Exactly that: do not expect. Honesty with oneself! Let M.F. ask herself: does she want to have her K[riuchkov] "whole" and "forever"? I don't think so.

This letter was written in June 1925, when the union with Kriuchkov had already crumbled beyond repair. More likely than not, Kriuchkov had decided on such an abrupt end not just for understandable reasons of a deeply personal nature. By that time he had already ceased to be Andreeva's silent partner, liberating himself from this dependence, placing himself fully at the disposal of Iron Felix. Kriuchkov felt his power and the possibility to shine on his own.

The role of Gorky's assistant, secretary, and litigant, as well as intermediary with the many organizations in the Soviet Union and abroad, and in fact the writer's overseer, controlling and directing, as much as possible, every one of his moves, was ready-made for him. Gorky accepted him in this role: he needed Kriuchkov now much more than he did Andreeva. He accepted him and his young wife Yelizaveta Zakharova, who had come between Kriuchkov and Andreeva. In letters to PePeKriu, Gorky now began calling him "my dear friend."

Grateful that the "dear friend" had smoothed his separation from Andreeva, Gorky had promoted him in a letter to Peshkova back in 1921 as a "very decent person." Now he simply needed him. Acutely desirous to have visitors from Russia who not only compensated for his not being there, but who also supported his typically messianic feelings and his sense of self-importance, Gorky could rely wholeheartedly on his "dear friend": he knew that Kriuchkov was omnipotent, that only he could supply the guests with foreign passports, necessary visas, money for living and everything else necessary for the trip.

Was he aware that these good deeds implied a selection, which Moscow carried out mercilessly, eliminating questionable visitors and sending their agents or "trustworthy people"? Did he sense an invisible hand showing him that even abroad he remained dependent and deprived of his freedom?

It is likely he did understand this. But he went along with it, as he needed less and less freedom, preferring peace, comfort, and guaranteed financial security.

On October 12, 1927, a second granddaughter, Darya, was born. No one knows exactly who gave rise to the rumor that this was not his granddaughter, but his own daughter. This version has been widely disseminated and is no secret. It is highly unlikely that any evidence will ever be found to confirm or refute it, and therefore it will remain only a rumor.

Nonetheless, this rumor originated somewhere. No one ever doubted Marfa's "origin," but the whispers about Darya not only did not fade with time, but grew in ever greater detail. The publishers of Kornei Chukovsky's diary in 1995 still did not print his entry from 1938 in full, when Chukovsky met Timosha's sister, Vera Alekseevna Gromova, in Kislovodsk in the Caucasus. In relating to Chukovsky how Gorky "spoiled one granddaughter [Darya], but mistreated the other," the girls' aunt hinted at the reason for the difference in Gorky's treatment of them. If anyone knew the truth, it would have been her.

An oblique confirmation of this by no means indisputable version is that in group portraits Gorky is always holding Darya, not Marfa, on his knees, and that his special feelings toward his daughter-in-law were no secret to anyone. At his insistence, the artist Pavel Korin gave Timosha drawing lessons, although her ability in fine arts was modest at best. In any case, it was not at all up to the level of the teacher, who was used to students of a completely different caliber. Having done literally nothing to "educate" his son, Gorky tried extremely hard to compensate with his daughter-in-law . . .

Meanwhile, Max took a very careless attitude toward Timosha's interests and anxieties. He would often go away for long periods, preferring the society of guests and casual acquaintances to her. Gorky, in turn, frequently found himself without female attention when Mura was away, and there was no one around to replace her. Max and his wife had moments of silence, the exact reason for which can only be conjectured, while Timosha found comfort with her father-in-law—he alone understood her and never failed to give her moral support.

A month after the birth of Darya, he wrote to Peshkova, who had come for the birth and returned to Moscow ten days later: "He [Max] and Timosha had a little fight, but now everything is quiet. Tender, soft, etc. Don't drag him back to Moscow. We'll come together." Now he was writing about his return not just for the sake of diversion, but was in fact preparing for it.

But before this he took an important step toward achieving the care and solitude he needed more than ever. He remembered the person who earlier—long ago and for a long time, albeit with interruptions—had lived as a full-fledged family member, close assistant and friend, but never as anything more. Now he felt an acute need for her presence. Whether Andreeva had reminded him (as is often believed), or he remembered on his own makes no difference. The main thing is that he remembered and began writing to her. The woman in question here is Olimpiada Dmitrievna, known simply as Lipa.

Lipa Chertkova was forty-nine years old at the time. In her youth she had worked as Andreeva's housemaid and as a costumier in the Art Theater. When Andreeva left her family and became Gorky's companion, Lipa remained with her and just as naturally became part of her new family. Before this she had suffered a great tragedy: both her husband and son died on the same day from cholera. In 1901 she had helped Andreeva in her conspiratorial revolutionary activities and in 1905, during the Moscow armed uprising, Lipa carried out both their assignments, fearlessly standing at the barricades, delivering weapons and written messages, and participating in battles as a nurse. She was interrogated by the police about Gorky's connections with the mutineers, but they got nothing out of her.

As he went off into exile, Gorky, unable to bring her along, was concerned about her survival. For this she needed a profession. Gorky subsidized her studies in medical school, where she became a nurse and obstetrician.

When Gorky and Andreeva settled into the apartment on Kronverksky after their return from emigration, Lipa again ended up with them. She had caught the keen eye of H. G. Wells, who did not forget to send her his regards and thank her for everything. Gorky could not take her along when he went abroad a second time, but he remembered that there was a woman in Russia genuinely, unconditionally, and inseparably devoted to him. In January 1927 he began corresponding with her—the reason was a sketch he was working on about Savva Morozov, whom Lipa had met a number of times. Gorky asked her impressions of him.

This was just a pretext: Gorky never made use of the reminiscences of other people in his memoirs, and there is absolutely no trace whatsoever of Lipa's presence in the sketch about Savva Morozov. In April their correspondence continued: Gorky unexpectedly asked Lipa to gather up some books he needed. It was unexpected in that Lipa was never before, or after, his literary secretary and in general had never done such work. Peshkova, Tikhonov, or someone else in Moscow or Leningrad could have handled this assignment much more successfully. But there was something else much more suitable for her talents behind this assignment: to come to Sorrento and help Timosha, who was expecting a child: Darya.

With Kriuchkov's assistance, Lipa came—and stayed. From then on, and until his final breath, she and Gorky would never part.

16.

Cords of Vanity

On the third anniversary of Lenin's death—January 21, 1927—*Pravda* published a facsimile of Gorky's note, undated, to an "unnamed addressee":

> His [Lenin's] superhuman will has not vanished; it remains incarnated in people on earth.
>
> The work which he inspired and began cannot be set aside, and it can hardly be interrupted, even temporarily. The world had waited for this person, the person had appeared, showed the way, and people will follow this path to the end with the bright image of the immortal leader before them.
>
> M. Gorky.

There was nothing unusual in these bombastic and highly speculative maxims—Gorky had always expressed himself that way and had always, with the exception of the brief period of *Untimely Thoughts*, indicated where the deceased leader would fit in world history. What is startling is the publication itself—in life, and not posthumously: the thriving author of the "note" could have "stated" who his "unnamed addressee" was, explain for whom it was intended, for what reason and why it was written and how the "note" (if it really was one) ended up in the newspaper.

It was then assumed that what really happened was that he had approved and probably even proposed the publication in this form to show his uninterrupted cooperation with the Soviet press in such an unobtrusive manner.

Meanwhile, its purpose and intentions are perfectly clear: the systematic "assimilation" of Gorky to Soviet reality was underway, and the groundwork for his return was being prepared. Lenin definitely did not need him in Russia. Their relationship had deteriorated. If one ignores Soviet lies, the truth is that they simply despised each other during Gorky's last year in Russia. The exile Georgi Solomon, who had occupied major posts up until 1922 in the People's

Commissariats of Foreign Affairs and Foreign Trade and who had met with Lenin many times, remembered his comment about Gorky: "Very conceited, loves money. A great poseur and hypocrite." Gorky—as mentioned above—repaid Vladimir Ilyich in kind. Stalin did not have any prior *personal* relations with Gorky and calculated, not without justification, that he would find an ally in him in his power struggle against Trotsky and Zinoviev.

In truth, Gorky had no *personal* relationship with Stalin. But he could hardly have forgotten what Stalin, enraged by his *Untimely Thoughts*, wrote about him ten years earlier: "The Russian revolution overthrew a lot of big names. We're afraid that their laurels will not allow Gorky to sleep; Gorky may have been fatally dragged into the archive, what the heck, let him do what he wishes! The revolution cannot pity or bury its corpses." There is no denying Stalin's candor or imagery. Now the author of these devastating lines and the one whom he spoke of with such truculence, preferred to pretend that Stalin had never written anything of the sort. It was better that way for both of them.

Gorky feared not just being in need, but also afraid of being forgotten, of losing his readers in Russia. He gradually grew accustomed to the idea that Russia had to be accepted as she was by History. He did not seek, nor could he have ever found, even if he wanted to, a place for himself in the West, and Stalin understood this very well.

Beginning in 1927, a campaign started to lure Gorky back to the Soviet Union. Mayakovsky set the tone with his poem entitled "A Letter from the Writer Vladimir Vladimirovich Mayakovsky to the Writer Aleksei Maksimovich Gorky." This political, and by no means poetic, démarche was all the more unexpected since they had not been on speaking terms for several years.

Soon after the revolution, Kornei Chukovsky hastened to inform Gorky of a rumor that Mayakovsky had infected a certain young lady known to both of them with syphilis. An indignant Gorky immediately made this vulgarity public, defending the honor of the disgraced woman in such a strange manner that in fact he humiliated her even further.

His action provoked, naturally, a stormy reaction from Mayakovsky (and from the "victim" too). The details of this scandalous history would lead us too far astray—what is important here are not so much the details as the fact itself. When the two writers met in the Landgraf Café in Berlin, where Gorky was being honored, Mayakovsky stood and cried out, "There is no such writer in literature; he's dead!" and demonstratively walked out.

Mayakovsky's "letter" began with the memory of this incident: "Aleksei Maksimovich, as I recall, something like a fight or argument took place between us. I left in worn-out pants, and you in a carriage with springs."

As if seeking reconciliation, Mayakovsky exclaimed, "It's a great pity, comrade Gorky, that we don't see you as we are building our days." Indignant at the fact that he was still "in Europe, where each citizen reeks of peace, gluttony, and foreign currency," Mayakovsky got to the point: "I know that the authorities and the Party value you and would give you everything—from love to apartments. Prose writers would sit before you at their desks: Teach! Rule!"

He could hardly have promised the emigrant (that's exactly what Mayakovsky called Gorky) such specific worldly goods, so valued by his addressee, without instructions from above.

There was no answer from Gorky but he took note of the offer made to him. He was particularly flattered by the prospect of "ruling" over prose writers from the heights of a teaching position, a role in which he felt especially comfortable. But the situation was not so clear-cut: endless debates continued in the Communist Academy as to whether Gorky could be considered a proletarian writer, and Lunacharsky attacked him publicly. A fight broke out over Gorky but Stalin let it pass, preferring for the time being to stay on the sidelines.

Gorky's letters to his Soviet correspondents, sent through diplomatic channels via the Soviet embassy in Rome and the consulate in Naples, which greatly alleviated the task of opening and reading his letters; they were studied closely in Moscow where the proper conclusions were able to be drawn. Those passages from his letters, which were not at all intended to be read by others, reflected his inner change and helped the authorities work out pressure tactics: ". . . I wanted to go to Russia so that I could curse Europe from there. I can't do it from here, they'd kick me out right away, and this means that I could not finish the book [*Klim Samgin*]. I think that this is my last book, and then I'm going to take up journalism" (June 1927); ". . . if it weren't for the novel, I'd leave for Russia right away" (July 1927).

That same summer, in connection with upcoming new elections, a list of candidates to full membership in the Academy of Sciences of the USSR was published. Many readers were surprised, as was Gorky himself, to see his name on the list. The plan was to move him from honorary academician into the ranks of the "full members," although this status hardly carried more prestige— it is no accident that twelve years later Stalin would become an honorary and not a full member.

Gorky's name looked strange on this list because he was still considered "almost" an émigré. Formally, Soviet authorities remained neutral, as if respecting the traditional independence of the Academy. Only in 1996, when all the documentation connected with those elections was extracted from the archives, did it become known that the Politburo of the Central Committee refused to support Gorky. The overall list of candidates had been divided into three groups: "VKP [All-Russian Communist Party] members," "candidacies closer to us," and "acceptable candidacies." There was no place for Gorky on any of these lists.

The directive was carried out: not one candidate outside the secret list of "recommended" and "acceptable" was elected. Most surprising of all was that a person very close to Gorky, the permanent secretary of the Academy Sergei Oldenburg, whom Gorky had defended on several occasions from persecution and had fished out of a Bolshevik prison, was in collusion with the authorities. Incidentally, this did not save Oldenburg: after fulfilling the orders of the Kremlin, he was immediately expelled from his post by the Kremlin.

The process of prying Gorky away from the Russian émigré milieu went on at the same time. Vladislav Khodasevich, once one of his closest friends who had lived under the same roof with him in Germany, Czechoslovakia, and Italy, published an article, "Maxim Gorky and the USSR," in the émigré journal *Vozrozhdenie* (Renaissance), in which he spoke ironically about Gorky's false promises to return—promises which could not be kept because of his alleged poor health. The arguments of two opposites—Mayakovsky and Khodasevich—coincided. Gorky did not expect anything else from Mayakovsky, but the article by Khodasevich was like a knife in the back, only strengthening his desire to return.

Many major western writers, whose opinions Gorky valued, had also markedly cooled off toward him. This was not directly connected with the articles that Gorky wrote for the Soviet press: having played at fashionable "leftism," these writers could only welcome the transformation of Gorky from émigré to "normal" Soviet writer. The hospitality showed him by the Mussolini government was bewildering, as was the fact that he never criticized the Fascist regime, saving his invective for the much more democratic regimes in America and Europe.

The events that happened soon after could only prod Gorky into making a final decision. In November and December the Left opposition was completely destroyed. Gorky's "sworn friends" Zinoviev and Trotsky lost all their power and found themselves in exile. One of the main obstacles preventing his return to Soviet Russia had now been removed.

In the summer of 1927, Zinovy Peshkov arrived in Sorrento to see Gorky for what was probably their final meeting. It is said that they met later but nothing confirms such a meeting. Zinovy used to visit Gorky every year; for six years Gorky was easy for him to contact. From France and the Levant, where Zinovy served in the High Commissariat, it was a short distance to Italy—so what happened between them? Why did their correspondence begin to wither ending altogether in 1930? The most logical assumption is that Zinovy encountered a *different* Gorky, someone who surprised him not so much by the strange plans for his future life as by his totally unacceptable opinions. Gorky's journalistic writings, soon be published regularly in the Soviet press, exposed the chasm between Zinovy and his adoptive father after so many years of spiritual and mental proximity. There was most likely another reason as well: the abrupt about-face by the recent émigré and opponent of the Leninist regime forced the secret police, to which Zinovy was connected, to reexamine its relationship. It was virtually impossible to receive the kind of information from him that interested these organs.

Stalin, while not betraying any personal involvement in the well-conceived operation, systematically lured Gorky into his nets. Knowing that Gorky was very favorably disposed toward Artemi Khalatov, with whom he had once worked on the commission to improve the lot of scientists, Stalin added to Khalatov's previous posts the position of director of *Gosizdat*, making his contacts with Gorky close and natural. At the outset he decided to please the writer with a generous gift. "Khalatov sent me a fish four feet long," exclaimed Gorky.

He could still allow himself to speak ironically of the extreme zeal of the Moscow seducers, but his choice had been made. This became perfectly obvious after he had betrayed his colleagues, who had sent out a distress signal from Russia, with stunning animosity and unconcealed hatred.

Vikenty Veresayev, a writer from Gorky's circle in pre-Revolutionary times and a well-known Pushkin scholar, laid the groundwork.

> There is a general languishing [he addressed the *urbi et orbi*] along practically the entire front of contemporary Russian literature. We cannot be ourselves, our artistic conscience is violated all the time, and our creativity becomes more and more two-tiered: we write one thing for ourselves, another for publication. . . . Such a systematic constraint of the artistic conscience is costly to a writer. . . . It is a terrible thing to say, but if Dostoyevsky appeared among us now, so removed from contemporary trends but at the same time so needed with his white-hot incandescence, even he would have to pile up on his writing table the manuscripts, one after another, of his novels with the forbidden stamp of Glavlit.

In July 1927 the Russian émigré newspaper *Poslednie novosti* (Latest News), published in Paris, sent an appeal from Moscow entitled "To the Writers of the World," signed by an anonymous "group of Russian writers." This howl of despair revealed the mechanics of the murder of freedom of speech in Communist Russia. "Do you know all this?" the authors of the letter asked the "writers of the world"? "Do you feel the horror of the situation in which our tongue, our language, our literature, is condemned? If you know, if you feel it, why are you silent?"

The letter was addressed not to Russian colleagues in exile, but to foreign colleagues, whose authority in both their own countries and in the world at large was extremely high. But they generally did not know about the existence of the "cry of the silent," as one Russian émigré journalist called this letter. Not a single French newspaper or any other non-Russian-language newspaper published it.

After fruitless attempts to turn the attention of the West to the cry emanating from Russia, Ivan Bunin and Konstantin Balmont were able to get *their* open letter to Romain Rolland published in the small circulation Paris newspaper *Avenir*. Calling their addressee "a great humanist" and "the conscience of the French people," they quoted the letter of the Russian "anonymous writers" and appealed to the "just, kind and courageous heart" of Rolland. The latter turned to Gorky—trusting only his opinion.

Expressing doubt that "writers [in Soviet Russia] could write [an appeal]," Gorky immediately, in typical fashion, pounced upon the émigré colleagues "who dared to bother" Rolland. "I have known Balmont for a long time," he wrote. "He is an unintelligent person and, as an alcoholic, not completely normal." About Bunin he could only say that he was in "enfeebled bitterness." As far as Soviet writers were concerned, in Gorky's opinion they were much happier even under censorship than writers "in bourgeois countries."

Mayakovsky spoke out in Moscow with a poetic panegyric to the suppressors of the word: "With our censorship we will circle around the white lies of anti-Soviet propaganda to make room for the truth." Did not these hymns to the censors have Bulgakov in mind, as "a fish who had given public assurance that it doesn't need water"?

Relying on Gorky's opinion, Rolland published a response in the journal *Europe* entitled "To Konstantin Balmont and Ivan Bunin": "I make my choice without hesitation in the duel now taking place between revolutionary Russia and the rest of the world." Although Rolland's letter was reprinted in the Soviet Union, Gorky continued to convince Rolland of his correctness. Four years ago he had been indignant at Krupskaya's action of "cleansing" the libraries of the classics of world literature—now he objected that such a "cleansing" had its place. Returning to Blok's death, he called this incident "a sad mistake" but right away defended the murders: ". . . as you know, conditions did not permit the workers and peasants to increase the number of their enemies abroad— they began driving them out of Russia about two years later." Again it fell "to the disturbers of the peace": "out of all the talents of the poet [Balmont], only the habit of inventing and lying remained"; and Bunin, according to Gorky, "together with his friends, whipped up the civil war."

Rolland was jarred by his aggressive bitterness—he tried to cool his friend's anger, but Gorky reacted with barely concealed fury: "I doubt the right of such a person [Balmont] to give you lessons on social morals and how to control your opinions [he unconditionally left this right to himself]. Do you think I am speaking of him cruelly? I've said less than I could say."

Gorky's conceited opinions were in stark contrast with Russian, even world, literary traditions. But no one managed to out-shout Gorky with his still unshakeable authority—Stalin could chalk up one more point in his favor. The only practical result of this desperate action by daredevil writers was a ban by Soviet censors on all of Bunin's books, even those published during the Soviet period. He would remain off-limits to readers in his own country for almost forty years.

In this situation, having already demonstrated his complete loyalty, Gorky could allow himself to display some free thinking. Nadezhda Krupskaya in *Pravda* crushed Kornei Chukovsky's stories in verse, which had become favorite reading among several generations of Soviet children. The censors had also found allusions in his tales of the tragic fate of the tsar's family; now the widow of Vladimir Ilyich noted a similarity to Neville Chamberlain in Krokodil, a positive hero in one of Chukovsky's tales. "Krokodil," she continued indignantly, "kisses the feet of the Hippopotamus tsar! He opens his soul to the tsar! . . . He dares to say, 'I give your people freedom! . . . What does all this nonsense mean? What political meaning does it have? . . . This is bourgeois rubbish."

Kornei's twenty-year-old daughter, Lidiya Chukovskaya, wrote to Gorky: "From childhood I know that a writer hit by misfortune has to ask Gorky to defend him . . . I don't know how to fight against poison. I appeal to you and strongly hope that you will help to restore justice."

Gorky was given the opportunity to show his independence and deny the rumors of his joining the ranks of the conformists. Moreover, he knew very well how far Krupskaya (Deputy People's Commissar of Enlightenment) was from genuine culture, from literary taste, from everything known as education. He wrote an article in defense of Chukovsky, and *Pravda* immediately published it. "It is a very strange and very unjust review" is how he qualified Krupskaya's critical attack. Stalin was rubbing his hands in glee: he had the pleasure of "dealing a blow" to Krupskaya through the proletarian classic. Their interests coincided. . .

Four years later it was not Chukovsky's daughter but Chukovsky himself who turned to Gorky for help, and not for ideological literary reasons but for an everyday matter. "My daughter [the younger one] is dying," he wrote to

Sorrento. "I have spent everything I have on her treatment, and now I do not even have money for medicine." Chukovsky was not paid royalties for his published works. He begged Gorky, "Appeal to their conscience so that they will feel ashamed." Gorky wrote indignant letters to the publishers, and the money was immediately transferred to Chukovsky.

Gorky once again regained the reputation as an omnipotent humanist.

Mail to Gorky from Rome and Naples was now being delivered in sacks as if by an invisible but obvious wand; thousands of readers from all corners of the Soviet Union, writing on envelopes "Maxim Gorky, Italy" (or sometimes "Island of Capri" and even "Island of Cyprus"!), were pelting him with questions along the lines of "Why does our beloved writer not return home?"

Gorky did not see in this increased correspondence any signs of a prepared scenario, conceived by Stalin and carried out by Yagoda. He took the sudden wave as a spontaneous and genuine manifestation of readers' sentiments. He wrote back to one such "reader" in March 1928: "I have no differences with the Soviet Union, as you probably know from my articles [in Moscow newspapers]." This letter "by chance" made it into the Soviet press . . .

Unaccustomed as he was abroad to boundless praise, Gorky was hooked on the readers' "spontaneous" appeals. He liked the agricultural collectivization campaign, just underway, that would turn the "half-savage, stupid, heavy people of the Russian villages" (his expression) into "an agricultural proletariat." Stalin had gained Gorky's favor in advance, binding him through his vanity. The boss knew the power of ambition, and Gorky was taking the bait.

Correspondence with tens, hundreds, even thousands of readers, begging him to return to his native land, again "by chance" coincided with Gorky's sixtieth birthday, reported in the papers a year in advance. The greatest world writers had been personally alerted. Not only were Moscow's politicians trying, but Mura did her part as well: traveling ahead to Germany, she was pushing all the right buttons, sending letters everywhere and getting in touch with the necessary people. Like no one else, Mura knew how to whip up such "publicity" and she tried, to the extent she could, to melt the ice that, by Gorky's fault, had formed between him and his greatest colleagues in America and Europe.

At the end of March, Gorky was showered with congratulations, filling him with self-importance. "In the name of American writers and artists," wrote Upton Sinclair, Sherwood Anderson, Theodore Dreiser, and others, "we congratulate you, a genius of world literature and a teacher of life . . . You are . . . a powerful life force in the new Russia, for whose freedom you, a celebrated fighter, have always fought and still fight." Greetings were sent by John

Galsworthy, Bernard Shaw, Knut Hamsun, Thomas Mann, Heinrich Mann, Gerhardt Hauptmann, Romain Rolland, Selma Lagerlöf, Georges Duhamel, Leonhard Frank, Arthur Schnitzler, and Lion Feuchtwänger. Stefan Zweig, in addition to an enthusiastic greeting, dedicated a new book to Gorky, *Three Singers of My Life* (literary portraits of Casanova, Stendhal, and Leo Tolstoy). "I cordially congratulate my old friend and great artist Gorky." A similar telegram, the text of which was probably composed by Mura, came from H. G. Wells.

Those heartily congratulating Gorky not that long before had openly and unambiguously announced what they thought about the persecution of people and freedom of thought in Bolshevik Russia. Having received news about mass executions in Soviet camps, the American journalist Isaac Don Levine asked eminent Western intellectuals to express their opinion on these atrocities. Thomas Mann wrote, "Karl Marx would turn in his grave if he knew what was going on in Soviet prisons and camps." Selma Lagerlöf wished "success to those who help the unfortunate Russian revolutionaries, dying in prisons and exile." H. G. Wells, here unquestionably with Mura's help, proclaimed, "The suppression by force of the political opposition, which does not resort to force, is a crime on the conscience of the government . . . Russian prisons are just as revolting as they were before."

Gorky, one of the most visible European intellectuals, was not among those who condemned Bolshevik terror this time. On the contrary, he approved! And this is how he justified his approval: "The people have a right to vengeance and cruelty, insofar as there is cruelty in the self-defense of the people, surrounded by secret and open traitors, their irreconcilable enemies. This cruelty is provoked, and justified." Others, such as Rolland, Shaw, and Sinclair, did not simply hold their tongues but categorically refused to engage in "anti-Soviet agitation." Gorky must have thought he was in pretty good company.

The burning sympathies addressed to him showed that the *former* writer, accepted by the world, could only quietly wait for death in places familiar since childhood. The honored classic began to prepare to take the road home.

This was the only way Stalin wanted him. And that was how he arrived.

"What do we want from Gorky?" Such was the title of an article by Bukharin in *Pravda* in anticipation of his arrival. Conditions were placed upon him—something completely unacceptable in principle for the former Gorky— but the great fighter for freedom of the written word accepted them. So just what did they want from him? "To seize the [petit-bourgeois] as necessary, rub it against the wool with a strong masculine hand, and rub it in such a way that the petit-bourgeois turns sour but not true readers who, on the contrary, will successfully roll up their sleeves to get down to work even more quickly—would this really be such a bad thing?" The significance of Bukharin's imagery concealed what was known only to students of Soviet terminology at the time: those who did not want to participate in campaigns announced by the authorities, who shunned political action, who did not want to be sucked into the nets importunately cast by the Kremlin and the Lubyanka, were called "petit-bourgeois."

Gorky took the bait again. He had always hated the bourgeois. But there was no specific content to the term—it could be used at will by giving it any meaning they desired. The petit-bourgeois from his outstanding play of the same name had nothing in common with those on whom the Soviets hung this label. But Gorky did not feel the difference, or, better, he did not want to feel it.

The trip was in preparation for more than one month. In creating the necessary groundwork, Gorky continued now and then, but rather intensively, to publish in Soviet newspapers. Rapturous odes in honor of the "zeal of socialist construction" were combined with rants against the Russian emigration.

The model was the same: accuse the émigrés of bitterness with hatred and contempt. In an article published in *Pravda,* he called the outstanding Russian historian Sergei Melgunov "a worthy candidate for the executioner;" Dmitri Merezhkovsky a "small and soulless person;" all his opponents "foul Lazaruses, whom Christ would not resurrect." He predicted that "they will all soon lie in the grave" and added that "it was time to do this." As far as Soviet Russia was concerned, "an attempt is being made to reshuffle life. . . on the foundations of reason, fairness, and beauty."

Stalin sent messengers to Gorky to remove any impediments still preventing him from taking the final step. In October 1927, the "litterateur" Boris Volin visited him. This Party functionary would soon become famous as one of the heads of Soviet censorship, the notorious Glavlit. There is absolutely no information about the nature of their conversation but it can easily be assumed that Volin gave Gorky some advances against the unhindered publication of everything he considered necessary.

The visit of Yakov Ganetsky, highly respected by Gorky since 1917, was of even greater significance. Ganetsky, as is known, was directly involved in the return of Lenin and company from Switzerland to Petrograd by equipping the Bolsheviks with German money to overthrow the government. He subsequently played an important role in Gorky's finances as an émigré, and almost certainly came with guarantees "on the financial front" in the event of his return.

Moscow was preparing for Gorky's return too. In November 1927, a government commission for Gorky's jubilee celebration (similar committees were created in dozens of cities around the country) was created, which then turned into a greeting committee. It included two members of the Politburo, Bukharin and Tomsky, two People's Commissars, Lunacharsky and Semashko, and other high-ranking officials. To one of them, Ivan Skvortsov-Stepanov, Gorky had written from Sorrento:

> On behalf of all the people prematurely and innocently killed, I implore you: don't do it! I want to visit various places both known and unknown to me as a detached observer . . . Who needs this celebration? You? You don't need it. Me? I'm already "burdened with popularity" without it . . . Moreover, I intend to live for a long time and it would be more grandiose if the committee puts on a celebration in '38.

Who needed this celebration? It is difficult to believe that Gorky did not have an answer to this question. It benefited those attempting to extract political capital out of Gorky's return to the Soviet Union—Stalin needed it, and Gorky had to have known this. Lenin had driven him out of the country, Stalin had brought him back and just that alone said everything.

Until then their paths had not crossed at all. Stalin's name is not even mentioned in *Untimely Thoughts*, nor is it mentioned in his later journalistic writings. But Gorky, not calling him by name (Stalin was still a very minor figure to him at the time), prophetically created in one of the final chapters of *Untimely Thoughts* (June 1918) a generalized psychological portrait of the future tyrant:

> More than anything he is ashamed of himself because he is not talented, not strong, and people have insulted him. Like a sponge, he is completely filled with a feeling of revenge and wants to repay one hundred-fold the insults he has suffered . . . He relates to people like a mediocre scientist relates to dogs and frogs, destined for cruel scientific experiments. . . People to him are material, the less spiritual they are the more convenient they become.

Had Stalin recognized himself in this portrait? If he did, then he preferred not to notice. Neither he nor Gorky ever remembered what Stalin had written about the writer in 1917: "The Russian revolution toppled many authorities. It can neither pity nor bury its scoundrels." The toppled "scoundrel" had been resurrected, and there was no need to stir up the past.

In May 1928 Gorky set off—not for good, but only to have a look. Accompanying him were Max and Lipa, while Timosha and the children (Darya was only seven months at the time) remained in Sorrento. For Mura the absence of Gorky was a good reason to spend several months in Europe, mostly in London with Wells.

The journey took them across Germany. At the Berlin train station Gorky was met by Maria Andreeva. They had not seen each other for five years, but the meeting did not rekindle any emotions—everything had fizzled out long ago.

On May 27, 1928, at the Soviet border, a delegation of writers and all kinds of officials awaited the honored guest. A personal salon car had been sent for him. In Minsk, Smolensk, and other cities along the way, crowds of thousands waited to see Gorky, even if his train arrived in the middle of the night. It appeared to him as a spontaneous expression of universal love. What he did not know was that the whole ritual of meeting the returning "prodigal son" had been discussed and confirmed at a session of the Politburo ten days before.

The festive meeting in Moscow stood out for its exaggerated pomposity. Rykov, head of the government, and Politburo members Bukharin, Voroshilov, Ordzhonikidze, People's Commissar Lunacharsky, members of the Central Committee, a delegation from the Art Theater headed by Stanislavsky, and a huge group of writers were at the station. Tens of thousands of people had gathered on the square near the station where the meeting took place. Lined up along the sidewalks, Muscovites in their Sunday best greeted the cortège of vehicles heading toward Mashkov Lane, where Yekaterina Peshkova lived: her apartment became Gorky's temporary residence.

He managed to rest only two hours, after which he immediately headed for the Bolshoi Theater for a ceremony in honor of the tenth anniversary of the Communist University. Here he met Stalin for the first time. The handshake was firm, Stalin's smile bewitching: many people have remarked that Stalin, when he wanted to, had the ability to make even the most inveterate skeptics fall in love with him. But by that time Gorky was no longer one of them.

Krupskaya, having forgotten the recent offense, delivered a fiery speech. She thanked Gorky for the fact that he, "such a close, such a dear friend of ours, spent his first day here among us." There were other speeches in a similar style—the anniversary of the Communist University had become Gorky's anniversary.

Following the ceremonies, and having had his fill of listening to encomiums, he visited Lenin's mausoleum on Red Square, and then asked to be driven around the city. He cried the entire time from emotion and excitement. Three days later he again visited the mausoleum, went inside and stood awhile near the sarcophagus, contemplating the relics of the person who had sent him out of Russia in 1921.

Gorky took the outbursts of joy accompanying him every step of the way very seriously. And to many people at the time they appeared to be genuine. Only now, when the evidence of the past, hidden away for many decades in secret archives, has been made public, the old story may be properly corrected. Those who spoke at the time were very far from reflecting his or her own true thoughts. For example, the diaries of Mikhail Prishvin, a writer with the reputation of being a "bard of Russian nature," far removed from politics, loved by Gorky and loyal to him, have been published. Their thick correspondence supposedly confirms this.

In his diary Prishvin wrote something completely different from what he was writing to Gorky:

> The anniversary [of Gorky] didn't come from the public . . . but from the government just like all Soviet holidays. The government can say today "Kiss Gorky" and everyone will kiss him, tomorrow they'll say, "Spit on Gorky" and everyone will spit . . . If there is no change in policy soon, Gorky will turn into nothing.

On his visits to factories, newspapers, institutions, and other establishments, Gorky gave speeches but avoided two issues. He said nothing about the so-called "Shakhtin trial" taking place at this time—a falsified (now proven with documents) court case against "saboteur engineers," representing the first rehearsal of the bloody show trials of the 1930s. At various gatherings Gorky was often asked to give his opinion of the trial, but he remained silent.

He also assiduously tried to avoid recognizing Stalin as the sole ruler, preferring instead the term "a collective Lenin" (after Stalin's death, Khrushchev and others used this invention of Gorky, introducing into the political dictionary the concept of "collective leadership"). Evidently, the political forces were still unclear to him, and the sympathies he felt toward Stalin's main opponents—Bukharin and Rykov ("the two Ivanoviches" as he liked to call Nikolai Ivanovich and Aleksei Ivanovich)—now and then dampened his enthusiasm.

Apparently, things were not so simple. Prishvin recorded in his diary Gorky's confession: "I'm a resourceful person, so why shouldn't I use everything they do for me?!" Prishvin assumed that Gorky dreamed of "creating Soviet public opinion and beginning a renaissance of the country." In his diary Kornei Chukovsky also observed that Gorky knew on which side his bread was buttered and that his statements should not be taken too literally. Concerning Soviet reality, Chukovsky wrote that Gorky "speaks just as enthusiastically in private conversations . . . as he does in the newspapers, but with a lot of mockery that cancels all his zeal."

His days in Moscow were filled with events, organized by the inseparable Kriuchkov. On June 23, Gorky took an excursion around the capital that had been planned for him long before: in disguise and wearing make-up, he strolled along a route he had worked out with Kriuchkov and Max, who was also part of the masquerade, having donned a false moustache, beard, and wig. The strollers visited cheap tea houses and beer halls and ate at a train station. It appears Gorky was convinced that he had tricked the authorities and had seen life as it really was. Actually, everywhere he went "comrades in plainclothes" were already waiting for him. They also took part in the sham, pretending to be service personnel. A specially prepared meal for the guests at the train station diner was abundant, cheap and tasty.

The walk gave Gorky genuine satisfaction. "I saw many interesting things," he wrote to Timosha, "and I will probably repeat this method of observation more than once." Max also reported to Timosha the enthusiastic impressions of his "uninhibited" father: "The streets are as clean as in Berlin. An urn stands near the entrance of every building, into which the smokers throw their butts and the spitters spit." He also liked the fact that loudspeakers blared on the streets from early morning until late evening, and brass orchestras played constantly in the squares.

Many writers sought to contact him, but the wall Kriuchkov had constructed around Gorky was practically impregnable, though some got through nonetheless. Only a meeting with one writer was absolutely out of the question: Gorky categorically refused to meet with Mayakovsky. The mere mention of his name enraged him. Was the old insult the reason? It would have been more in character for Mayakovsky to still be offended at something from the past, but Gorky could not forgive his Berlin escapade, nor the lines of poetry that had wounded his vanity. Mayakovsky never once appealed to him with slavish letters, never sought his protection, never asked his advice on how to live and write. Gorky did not like such colleagues.

The chairman of the Moscow City Executive Committee (the "mayor" of Moscow), Konstantin Ukhanov, invited Gorky to his dacha, specially set up to entertain the important guest. There he and Max became acquainted with another guest known to them only by name and through correspondence: Genrikh Yagoda. He was first deputy to the head of the Cheka, Yvacheslav Menzhinsky, but actually the true head of the OGPU. Yagoda enchanted Gorky with his modesty and soft smile. He attended the meals and helped light the campfires Gorky loved so much. After a few days he could already consider himself a friend to both father and son. . .

Henri Barbusse, who was in the Soviet Union at the time, visited Gorky outside Moscow. His driver was Artemi Khalatov: this was the first meeting of the two comrades who immediately discovered a common language.

After one more stroll around Moscow from three o'clock in the afternoon to midnight—again wearing absurd makeup and a wig—Gorky traveled around Russia. Everywhere he was met by crowds and the brass orchestras he admired. It was very hot, more than 100 degrees, with the wind blowing up clouds of dust. Gorky stopped in at a colony of former orphans and adolescent criminals; visited the Dneprogas construction site and spent six days traveling in the Crimea, and then headed for the Caucasus (Baku, Tiflis, Yerevan). From there he journeyed along the Volga and, after changing steamers, followed a path from Stalingrad to his native Nizhny Novgorod, stopping for two days in Kazan, also connected to memories of his youth.

While he was on the road, the court in Moscow, led by the relatively unknown Andrei Vyshinsky, handed down a death sentence to the eleven defendants in the "Shakhtin" trial, five of whom were shot, while forty-four were sent to the Gulag. The newspapers cursed them in print, but Gorky did not react at all.

Max, PePeKriu, and Tikhonov joined him on his trip, constantly at his side, along with many Chekists assigned to him as administrators, assistants, chauffeurs, cooks . . . They controlled his every step and sent reports back to the Kremlin. In Gorky's tireless speechmaking there was still no place for Stalin, though one had already been found for the "Party"—soon one would replace the other.

He said one thing, but then saw and thought something else. Chukovsky recorded in his diary Tikhonov's recounting of their trip along the Volga: "[Gorky's] impressions of Russia are terrible: everyone is impoverished, gloomy, crushed. He wanted to get out in Tsaritsyn [Stalingrad] but took one look at the crowd waiting at the dock and decided against it . . . Gorky is in bad hands."

After his return to Moscow, he settled in at the dacha on the former estate of Savva Morozov, which retained the name of "Morozovka" and had been turned into a house of rest: "a combination Chinese pagoda, medieval castle, and a steamship," as Max described it. The dacha had been emptied of vacationers and placed at Gorky's complete disposal. The meetings with Yagoda continued, becoming a weekly ritual. Their business relationship had somehow unwittingly been turned into a personal one. Yagoda assiduously and relentlessly had entered their life. Yes, *their* life, the father's and the son's. Gorky's sentimentality allowed him to vaguely remember his fellow countryman from Nizhny Novgorod who had lived not so far away, and helped the professional Chekist gain the writer's favor.

At the very end of August Gorky went to Leningrad, again incognito: putting on makeup and disguising himself in strange clothes was clearly to his liking.

On this occasion there was at least some justification, delivering him from tiresome visitors: Gorky's temperature had risen, accompanied by sharp pains in his stomach. The doctors diagnosed appendicitis, but decided against an operation. Lipa announced that she would take care of Gorky on her own. Either she helped, or it was the doctors, but by two days later Gorky was already feeling better. He booked two rooms in the Yevropeiskaya, the best hotel in the city. Kriuchkov's approval was required for anyone to get an audience with him.

Chukovsky was let in. Gorky, Max, and those with them, wrote Chukovsky in his diary,

> sat . . . at a table with *hors d'ouevres*, vodka, wine—Gorky ate and drank a lot, happy that he had fooled everyone who had not recognized him . . . But, you know, he was tired of it all [said Gorky]. In every city, at every train station it's as if the exact same people are standing and saying the exact same thing in the exact same words.

Chukovsky repeated the story of a writer to whom Gorky complained, "I'm honored everywhere I go. I'm an honorary baker, an honorary Pioneer. Today I'm going to visit an insane asylum, and they will make me an honorary insane person, you'll see." He mocked this spectacle yet willingly took part.

The flood of letters he received contained not only enthusiasm but also insults. Many people who for many years had considered him to be a moral authority were now amazed at the changes in him. The rapturous defense of Soviet reality did not square in their consciousness with the name of Gorky the living embodiment of nonconformity. It was strange for them to read trivial Party agitprop under his signature, conspicuous only perhaps in their fiery zeal and other elements of the Gorky style. Some of his correspondents, unable to restrain their indignation and choosing indelicate words, bluntly told him off.

Gorky did not hold back. He answered those whom he called "mechanical citizens of the USSR" and again in the traditional style of Gorky the publicist, the one which until then he had been in his polemics with the Russian émigrés.

His bilious letter was published simultaneously in *Pravda* and *Izvestiia*. Now it would become the norm: almost all his letters in this genre would be published simultaneously in the two leading papers of the country, becoming in the process Party directives, along with those of comrade Stalin. No other author was given this honor: Gorky and Stalin ended up together at the apex of an invisible pyramid.

Gorky saw Stalin a few more times, once even intimately, at the Maly Theater for a performance of the play *Lyubov Yarovaya* by his old friend Konstantin Trenev. The play, naturally, was a panegyric to Bolshevism and a denunciation of "counterrevolution," serving as an example of what was now the norm. Following the performance, a table was set in the foyer—Stalin, Gorky, Peshkova, Max, and Trenev discussed literature, art, and "our common goals."

Gorky felt even greater sympathy for "the wonderful Georgian." This is exactly how Lenin referred to Stalin in a letter to Gorky fifteen years before. His shy smile and deliberate speech, combined with that special strength, was a combination that Gorky had always instinctively found attractive. Their closer union was seen by both of them as inevitable and desirable.

The common aesthetic positions, which in Soviet reality became political positions—although it is possible that Gorky did not realize this—brought Gorky closer to Stalin. Gorky, in the opinion of people who were in close communication with him, understood nothing about fine arts and painting, despite his unquestionable concern for people of culture and his passion for collecting. He especially hated the avant-garde which he simply considered trickery. His attitude toward the avant-garde carried over not only to Malevich and Tatlin but to all representatives of "revolutionary art" in all spheres. He could not stand the mention of Meyerhold, just as he could not tolerate Khlebnikov and Mayakovsky, the latter not only for personal reasons, but also for his poetry: it was completely foreign to Gorky, both in form and content.

Meanwhile, it was precisely the revolutionary avant-garde that occupied leading positions in art after the Bolshevik seizure of power. This was its hour of triumph. Its representatives not only acquired complete freedom of creative self-expression (alas, for only a very short period!) but also occupied key posts in the government offices in charge of art. Stalin had no need for it at all—he associated the notorious "avant-garde" with the "revolution," which the new master of the Soviet empire secretly detested, although thanks to it he became not simply the tsar of all Russia, but also the "Earthly God." Gorky's aesthetic views fully coincided with Stalin's political intentions—in this matter the classic willingly subordinated himself to the leader, not seeing any subordination at all in the Kremlin's support of his genuine antipathies.

Nevertheless, Gorky did not want to appear completely subservient. He decided to show his independence, having defended Isaak Babel from slander by the illiterate Soviet "commander" (later marshal) Semyon Budyenny, who called Babel "a literary degenerate" and saw in his novellas the "artistic spittle of class hatred." Gorky's belated, and very restrained, response was published in *Pravda* where Budyenny immediately published his "reply to a reply," again protesting against "Babel's supercilious slander."

In a fit of temper, Gorky wrote a sharply worded rebuke, which was not published at the time:

> Comrade Budyenny, allow me to tell you that . . . having ridden into literature on a horse and criticizing it from there, you become like those reckless critics who ride roughshod over literature in carts of poorly mastered theory. For criticism to be correct and useful it is necessary that the critic be either culturally above the writer or—at the very least—stand on the same cultural level.

This was a very strong and precise blow, both in essence and form. The new Gorky was reminiscent of the old Gorky from not that long ago. But that same Artemi Khalatov, who was close to Stalin and, in addition to everything else, a member of the editorial board of *Pravda*, advised Gorky to take "a softer" variant: "Criticism is useful if the critic is objective and attentive to young growing forces."

Gorky agreed! Stalin could chalk up one more point to his advantage, not because he wanted to defend Budyenny—he knew the real worth of this "hero of the civil war" better than anyone—but because he saw in Gorky's acquiescence a true sign of his readiness to yield further.

Among the many letters from Mura that have survived, there is one dated July 5 (she was living at that time in Kalijarvi, Estonia, with her children) in which it is clear that Gorky, feeling the need to remain in the Soviet Union for good (he liked it so much here!), made it contingent that Mura move there as well. The need for her constant presence was so great that to lose Mura would have been completely unbearable for him. If he had thus far accepted her constant junkets "to Europe" from Sorrento, had somehow become used to this, then the move to Moscow would have meant her total loss: from there she would not have been able to run around in carefree fashion to different countries several times per year. There was only one solution: to move here together with him. For good.

> This is very difficult for me to do, my dear friend [she replied], because of my children, and I think that this cannot be explained by moral cowardice... Personally for me—and believe me, I am being perfectly open about this— Europe, as I see it, when I leave you, has very little to offer and makes me

depressed, but . . . nevertheless I think that it is more honest for me not to return. . . . I understand perfectly well that your life abroad now—especially after this trip—is absurd. This can only be done to complete that work which would be difficult for you to finish there. And this thought, meaning separating from you, is very, very tormenting, my joy, believe me! But when you come back, you and I will think of something, so that this separation will be as little a separation as possible and does not interrupt our relationship so dear to me.

Many things become clear from this letter—Mura's cunning, the secret, un-expressed thought and the most important task. The pretext about the children is naïve—Mura did not live with them anyway and only visited them. And, of course, she knew perfectly well that there would be nothing to prevent her from taking trips to Estonia (closer to Moscow than to Sorrento). It would have been more complicated to go to Berlin where, as can be judged by a plethora of evidence, she regularly met Lockhart, and to London where H. G. Wells awaited her. She definitely did not want to break with Gorky, but she diligently worked at pushing him to make the permanent move back to the USSR. Gorky fulminated, searching for a way out of this unclosed circle.

The time to leave finally came. It was necessary to soothe the Soviet population that the great proletarian writer was returning to Italy, by no means of his own volition, but because evil doctors were sending him there for treatment. The Lenin model was repeating itself, but this time with a farcical variant. On the eve of his departure *Pravda* published the conclusion of a conference of specialists, transforming his trip back to Italy into a major medical event:

> During his stay in the USSR, Aleksei Maksimovich, who suffers from tuberculosis of the lungs and myocarditis, experienced some exacerbation of active pulmonary tuberculosis . . . That is why, with the coming of autumn, when the number of influenza illnesses can increase, the further stay in Moscow of Aleksei Maksimovich, who in recent years has become accustomed to the warm climate of Italy, would mean great danger to his health. Comrade Gorky must therefore leave immediately for Italy, from where he can return to Moscow [not come back, but return!] not earlier than May 1929.

The "exile" himself knew well before his arrival that he would be leaving Moscow in the fall without any medical recommendations. But he played along with this charade (leaving only upon doctors' orders!), thereby entering into silent collusion with the authorities at the same time. From Vyazma, the first large station the train pulled into early in the morning, he sent a telegram to *Pravda*:

Farewell, comrades. I go unwillingly. It is difficult to imagine returning to a life more peaceful than the one I led in the Soviet Union. It is a pity that physical infirmities have prevented me from fully expressing those good spirits I picked up from you. Farewell until May. Sincerely yours, M. Gorky.

Max was more candid: on the eve of departure he wrote to Timosha, "Everything is finished. Hooray! We are leaving in a week. Everything is ready and there will be no delays." Father and son exchanged places: Gorky had become "red" and blinded, while Max's eyes had been opened. And, in contrast to his father, he had no need to lie or pump himself up with strained enthusiasm.

Gorky and Maria Andreeva, 1906.

André Malraux *(left)* and Gorky.

Zinovy Peshkov and Maria Andreeva. Petrograd, 1917.

Gorky and G. Yagoda, 1934.

P. Kriuchkov, Gorky, and G. Yagoda, 1935.

Yekaterina Peshkova *(back left)*, Mura Budberg *(back middle)*, Timosha *(front right)*, Maria Andreeva *(back right)*, Darya *(front left)*, and Marfa *(front middle)* paying final respects at Gorky's funeral. Moscow, June 20, 1936.

Professor Dmitri Pletnev. 1932.

Stalin and Gorky. Moscow, 1932.

Stalin and Politburo members Molotov
(far left), Kaganovich *(behind Molotov)* and
Ordzhonikidze *(behind Stalin)* carry the urn
containing Gorky's ashes. June 20, 1936.

Gorky, 1932.

Gorky and Max, 1922.

Gorky *(second from left)* with Stalin *(third from right)* at the Lenin Mausoleum. May Day 1933.

André Malraux and Vsevolod Meyerhold. Moscow, 1935.

Max, in his OGPU uniform. Moscow, 1918.

(Left to right) Timosha, Yekaterina Peshkova, and Mura Budberg.
Sorrento, 1925.

Varvara Tikhonova. 1913.

Valentina Khodasevich. 1916.

Lenin and Gorky. Petrograd, 1920.

Yekaterina Peshkova. 1935.

Gorky and Romain Rolland. Moscow, 1935.

Varvara Tikhonova and Nina. Berlin, 1922.

Fyodor Chaliapin with his wife Maria Petzold.

17.

A Stroll in the Gulag

While the "peaceful life" of Moscow existed only in letters and telegrams, true peace and quiet awaited him at home in Sorrento, in his study surrounded by his closest friends, far from the hustle and bustle, in the country he loved so much, where everything brought joy to the eyes and the soul. Even Mura, who had traveled around the capitals of Europe visiting her secret friends, was there awaiting her "infinitely dearest" and "infinitely beloved." It was time to make the final decision: at his age there was no longer the time to delay, and yet Gorky was still not ready to take that final step. Very delicately and unobtrusively, Mura pushed him toward the idea that his place was *there*, not neglecting to add at the same time that for her it would be an irreparable loss, because that was no place for her and never could be. She was concerned most of all about his interests only.

Gorky wavered and pondered. The bitter political struggle continued in Moscow, and no one could predict who would win. To return as an honored guest meant that he would be forced to take sides.

As it turned out, Stalin's main adversaries were personally much closer to Gorky ideologically than Stalin himself. This can now be reliably stated from letters that have come to light. He was simply friends with the "Ivanoviches" (Bukharin and Rykov), and on very close terms with Kamenev. Furthermore, the final obstacle separating Gorky and Kamenev had fallen: the latter had left his wife (Trotsky's sister), who had caused Gorky no small amount of misery during the Petrograd years, and taken up with a young editor at an academic publishing house, Tatyana Ivanovna Glebova, who would soon bear him a son, Vladimir. Driven from government positions, Kamenev was appointed ambassador to Rome after his latest confession. Until the 1990s there was absolutely no mention of any meetings between Gorky and Kamenev in Italy, nor could there be since scholars and biographers of Gorky did not mention his contacts with "enemies of the people." Moreover, neither Gorky nor Kamenev advertised their meetings.

They more than just met: Kamenev and his new wife spent several days with Gorky in Sorrento and their subsequent correspondence, while the married couple relaxed and underwent treatment on the island of Ischia, touched upon both literature and politics. This can be deduced by Kamenev's still unpublished letters, just as Gorky's letters to him are believed to "be missing." It means that Gorky did not keep copies of his letters, and Kamenev, to protect Gorky, most likely destroyed them. From Kamenev's preserved letters it is clear that they discussed the sharpest political issues of the day in their correspondence. In very circumspect but easily decipherable statements, Kamenev wrote that the "matter undertaken by the Old Man" (meaning Lenin) had evolved, adding unambiguously: "If is he lying about the business as a whole, then it should be no surprise as to how 'well' and 'fine' it is going. In spite of all the bitterness among the arguing parties, the struggle has continued thus far and, I assume, there will continue to be an unforeseeable interval of tolerance."

How naïve these "friends and advisors of Vladimir Ilyich" could be! The "unforeseeable interval" did not even last eight years from that moment. The opposition, mostly educated and erudite, of European persuasion, were much closer to Gorky than the lowly cultured, if not barely literate, yes-men within Stalin's closest circle—and, of course, than Stalin himself. Gorky had probably figured on the victory of those closer to him, but he did not exclude the other possibility either. His intellect told him to sit it out, but his heart was pulling him back to Moscow, into a situation of total worship.

Gorky had already begun preparing for his final trip. A portion of his library—not the most indispensable but important nonetheless—had been readied for shipment to Moscow and was now sitting in Berlin awaiting his further instructions. According to his closest friends, the conversations about whether to return or not were conducted practically on a daily basis, before he came to the safest solution: he would make one more "reconnaissance mission."

In Moscow, meanwhile, the Stalinists had racked up one victory after another over their adversaries. The total and forced collectivization of the countryside had been established, and the overthrown "Bukharinites" were out of their posts. Bukharin himself was expelled from the Politburo and the Comintern and removed from his position as editor-in-chief of *Pravda*. His closest ally, Mikhail Tomsky, was stripped of his positions, and Rykov was hanging by a thread. Stalin had complete and undivided power.

Gorky had to be aware that mass repression of the technical intelligentsia, which he had always admired, had begun in the Soviet Union. Peshkova had told him about this during a visit to her son and granddaughters, as did Pyotr Osadchy, a great Russian engineer of that time who, while on an official trip to Italy, took advantage of the opportunity to see Gorky. The need to defend those humiliated had not disappeared—he recalled his newly found relationship with Yagoda when informed of the persecution of a married couple in Yakutia with whom he had become acquainted on Capri in 1912. The letter "to dear Genrikh Grigorievich" in their defense was a trial balloon to see whether or not it would work.

But of course it worked! The request was so trivial (the husband and wife had been deprived of their right to vote), that it would have been absurd not to indulge the "suppliant." Gorky had already begun paying for it by closing his eyes to the ever-growing wave of repression, the atmosphere of dread and the campaign against the "saboteurs," that is, to everything that had become the norm in Soviet Russia. He even justified his non-intervention with a certain philosophical spin.

He outlined his credo in a letter to Kuskova, who had reminded Gorky of his opposition during the first years following the revolution and was astounded at his abrupt change in position:

> You have the habit of not keeping quiet about phenomena that rouse your indignation. I not only consider myself in the right and can be quiet about them, but I even consider this ability among my qualities. Is this amoral? Then let it be.
> The fact of the matter is that I most genuinely and unequivocally hate the truth which is ninety-nine-percent abomination and lies . . . I know that this truth is harmful to 150,000,000 Russians and that the people need another truth . . .

It would have been useless to remind him that it was not "another" truth he had defended in *Untimely Thoughts*, but the only one that exists in reality, and that is exactly how he had acted in fighting the suborners of the truth in 1918–1921 or when interceding on behalf of the arrested Social Revolutionaries in 1922. By radically changing his positions, he always cited not just moral but also philosophical principles, defending them with a fiery zeal that betrayed a growing guilt complex.

This guilt led him to ignore the arguments of his opponents, to always consider himself correct ahead of time, and to recognize his own "mistakes" only when such an admission ended in victory, not defeat. Even though he knew the truth, he willingly replaced it with fiction to the advantage of this new turn in his fate. While composing the latest draft of his memoirs on Lenin, Gorky wrote about Lenin's efforts to expel him from Russian in 1921: "For more than a year he insisted with incredible stubbornness that I leave Russia and it surprised me that he, completely consumed as he was by his work, remembered that someone who was ill needed a rest." It is precisely this Christmas tale from Gorky about the "great humanist" that was known around the world to this day.

In November 1928, a list of candidates for the Nobel Prize in literature was published. Along with John Galsworthy, G. K. Chesterton, Thomas Mann, Sinclair Lewis, and others, two Russians made the list: the émigré Dmitri Merezhkovsky and (who? A Soviet writer? An émigré writer? A writer on his own terms, beyond any identification?) Maxim Gorky. This was both flattering and depressing: it did not suit him to be thrown in with a "trained flea, elevated now to philosopher." Moreover, he recognized that his treacly panegyrics in praise of Soviet power would hardly earn him the sympathies of the Nobel Committee. Previously he viewed the award with supercilious irony, therefore repudiating the possibility of receiving it, but, like any writer, secretly hoping for it.

The Russian émigrés had ceased being indignant at Gorky; now they simply detested him. Ivan Bunin removed the dedication to Gorky from his poem "Falling Leaves" (1900), announcing that he had made this dedication "at Gorky's shameless request." Concerning Gorky's old pamphlet about Anatole France, Bunin had this to say: "In all of world literature there is nothing like it in terms of boorishness and stupidity, or in the insolence of a brute full of himself."

The émigrés had pushed Gorky out of Europe, driving him into the arms of Stalin. He had not resisted, and passionately desired to end up in Stalin's embrace. All that remained to be agreed upon was the price. But Stalin never cared about the price—if he wanted something, he would find a way to pay for it.

Possibly the only émigré who regarded Gorky with the same affection as before was Chaliapin. Preparing to go to Rome, he wrote to Gorky in December 1928: "I wait with joy the opportunity to see you and be together with you again, my dear beloved Aleksei Maksimovich." The meeting took place in April 1929. Gorky made a special trip to Rome, along with Max and Timosha, to hear Chaliapin perform in the opera *Boris Godunov*. They passionately embraced and both wept. Neither one had a closer friend. . . Following the performance, a typical Russian dinner was held in the old "Biblioteca" restaurant. Chaliapin sang tirelessly for the person with whom the best days of his life had been inseparably linked.

Gorky tried to talk Chaliapin into returning to Russia, but to no avail. In order to "save the good name" of the artist, Gorky (in a letter to Rolland) and to Timosha had spread the rumor that Chaliapin was dying to go home, but his second wife, Maria Valentinovna Petzold, had allegedly declared, "You will go to the Soviet Union only over my dead body." Later, when this rumor reached Chaliapin, he was compelled to refute it. He reminded everyone what he had distinctly told Gorky as to why he was not returning to the Soviet Union. It was not from fear of possible sanctions! "I fear the whole system of relations, I fear the 'apparatus,'" he explained.

By then the classic propaganda model was solidly entrenched in the Bolshevik press, as was the falsified historiography, namely that all the most outstanding Russian émigrés "were dying to go home," but that there was always something that prevented them from doing so, be it illness, age, the intrigues of relatives, or machinations of foreign intelligence services. The simplest explanation—their distaste of Communism and their desire to return only to a free Russia—somehow did not exist.

Another meeting took place immediately following the one with Chaliapin: Nina Tikhonova came to see Gorky in Sorrento. After she had settled in Paris with her mother, she took up ballet. A true Russian beauty with a charming, spiritual face and slender, supple figure, she was accepted into the ballet school of the famed Olga Preobrazhenskaya and in her first years became prima ballerina of the "Russian seasons," dancing with Tamara Karsavina, Ida Rubinstein, Bronislava Nizhinskaya, Leonid Myasin, and others. Guest tours took her to Naples and from there, taking advantage of a brief respite between performances, she went to Sorrento.

The half day spent at Il Sorito left a heavy mark on Nina. Gorky was gloomy and uncommunicative, clearly burdened by the presence of the person whom he "loves very much." Nina recalled many years later:

> Before my departure from Paris mama handed me a sealed envelope: "Give this to Aleksei Maksimovich." I forgot the letter in my hotel in Naples . . . When I told Gorky this, he answered very quickly, "It's okay, it's okay, it's not important," and rejected my offer to send it to him by mail. His reply surprised me. The half day spent at Il Sorito was not at all what I was expecting. At first Timosha showed me in too great detail the home and the garden and the view of the sea and the shore. Finally, Aleksei Maksimovich appeared. I felt an unpleasant awkwardness in the conversation.

Instead of conversation he proposed that Nina listen to his recently acquired recordings of Russian choral songs and "became too excited, even getting tears in his eyes: 'How great they are!' Not a word about us or Paris. . . I was disillusioned and perplexed. It's not the way I was used to seeing Gorky."

Max came to her rescue. He offered to take Nina to Naples in his brand new sports car. "Along the twisting roads of the shoreline," recalled Nina, "often littered with rocks which had fallen from the cliffs, he drove with a kind of daring recklessness." The following day he and Timosha went to see Nina's performance and went backstage to express their admiration. "At home [in Paris], unpacking my suitcases," Nina concluded her reminiscences of this most bitter episode of her life: "I handed mama the forgotten letter. Her face was impassive. She smiled."

Neither Varvara nor Nina ever saw Gorky again.

On May 26, 1929, Gorky again left for Moscow. With him were Max, Lipa, and Nightingale, as well as Timosha and the children. Mura had again departed for London.

While Gorky was traveling, Stalin had prepared a gift for him, which Gorky found out only upon his arrival. The Central Executive Committee of the USSR, something like a Soviet quasi-parliament, had decided to increase its staff by one member *personally*. When the train crossed the Soviet-Polish border, the delegation meeting Gorky handed him a certificate of membership to the Committee and a chest medal to commemorate it. Thus, he had already been formally transformed from an independent writer into a Soviet statesman, accepting the gift with tears in his eyes.

This time the Moscow program was not as full, and there was no talk of disguises—Gorky decided to refrain from taking walks along the streets. He left for the village of Kraskovo outside Moscow, where a large dacha in a pine forest had been placed at his disposal next to other dachas belonging to the big Kremlin bosses, in whose tight circle he spent his time. The vodka flowed like a river (his neighbor, Politburo member Valeriyan Kuibyshev, was especially fond of it) while *shashlik* grilled over a fire in the garden and animated conversations lasted late into the night. The life of the party was Genrikh Yagoda.

Like other chiefs of the Soviet secret police, he did not at all give the impression of being a monster. There was even something soft and unprepossessing in his outer appearance. Without any special effort he presented himself as touchingly sentimental and weary, overburdened from excessive work, consumed with the common good, dreaming only of gaining the understanding and sympathy of people dear to his heart. During the last year Gorky had become such a dear and close friend. Now Max and Timosha also entered his innermost circle.

Not only nostalgic reminiscences about their native city connected Gorky to Yagoda, but also cold calculation: the fates of those for whom he might intercede depended upon Yagoda. Max, an "old" Chekist, easily found a common language with Yagoda, who tried to satisfy all his whims and even anticipate his wishes, offering him what he already knew he would like. Captivated by Timosha's feminine charm, which distinguished her from the usual society of Party ladies, Yagoda—this "punishing sword of the revolution"— whose very name instilled horror in millions of people, fell in love with her like a little boy. However, he was able to prevent his emotions from spilling out. The role of friend to *both*—Timosha and Max—allowed him to preserve and develop his relationships with the entire Gorky retinue.

Having correctly figured out the nature of the relationship between Gorky and Lipa, Yagoda displayed increased attention to her as well, tenderly calling her by the nickname Gorky created, "Redhead Lapa."* It was as if the extended Gorky family had grown by one more: the "dear friend" and fellow countryman Genrikh Yagoda.

The program for Gorky's stay in Moscow was already less taxing than the one from the year before, but he would still show up at various events, attracting general attention and heightened interest. He spent a day at a gathering of Young Communists from all over the country in Dynamo Stadium in the company of several Soviet leaders and called upon them to "be strong, healthy, and beautiful in life." He took part in a strange event, the All-Union Congress of Atheists, where he was supposed to deliver a speech, but the presence of Mayakovsky ended any interest: he categorically rejected any participation with this poet, no matter the cause.

The highlight of this year's program was a trip conceived by Yagoda. Following a stopover in Leningrad, Gorky traveled to the sinister "Solovki"— not long ago the most picturesque of monasteries, built on an island in the White Sea and turned into the first Soviet concentration camp by Lenin. This was also the beginning of the creation of the enormous Gulag Archipelago. "The Solovetsk Concentration Camp of Special Designation (SLON) was at the same time both a road leading into hell (beatings, torture, and mass execution of political prisoners took place there from the very first months of the camp's existence), and a show window of Soviet humanity: in the 1920s prisoners at Solovki published their own journal, *zek** actors had their own theater, musicians their own symphony orchestra, and scientists their own "hearths of culture." It was precisely to this Potemkin village that the creator of romantic myths, on whom Yagoda placed great hopes, had to be accustomed.

Yagoda abstained from taking the trip, despite wanting very much to go; Timosha was also taking this excursion to the death camp. But there was no

---

* A play on words: "Lapa" is Russian for "paw."
* Colloquial name for a Soviet Gulag inmate, an abbreviation of the Russian word for "incarcerated."

room for the Cheka boss: a multitude of complaints was expected, which would have been embarrassing before the Great Intercessor, and Yagoda would have had to make decisions on the spot.

Yagoda's closest colleague, Matvei Pogrebinsky (Motya), head of the suburban Moscow children's "labor colony," that is, a camp where underage criminals were "reeducated," accompanied Gorky, who had become acquainted with Motya during his visit the previous year to this colony, which he found fascinating. Forced to stop on the return trip to Leningrad because of an aggravation of his illness, but hastening to send a written report to Yagoda about his excursion to Solovki, Gorky wrote about Motya: "the nicest . . . governor, a person of indomitable energy. He is a good fellow. The more I know him, the more I like him." He had found the exact word: the GPU employee Gorky met truly was the "governor," meaning the tutor and educator of the famous sightseer.

It was in the middle of the white nights, even lighter in those regions than in Leningrad. A view of the fantastic beauty of the monastery, transformed into a torture chamber, appeared before Gorky from the steamboat. Enraptured by the outstanding creation of human hands, he wept at all the grandeur and vacillating enchantment of the landscape,. Timosha shared his awe. Yagoda had supplied her with a GPU uniform: black leather cap, leather jacket, leather riding breeches, and high narrow boots. She was striking and even more dazzling than usual.

Years later, dictating her reminiscences, Nadezhda Peshkova (Timosha) left these impressions about this unusual excursion:

> From the sea, the Solovetsk Monastery is like a fairy-tale city.
> We acquaint ourselves with the life of the Solovetsk camp. I go into a museum, built in one of the churches. Everything that remained after the monks left had been collected: many old icons and various church crockery.
> We all go to Sekir Mountain. There is an incredible view of the lake from there. The water in the lake is a cold dark blue, around the lake there is a forest that seems enchanted, the light changes, the tops of the pine trees sparkle and the smooth lake seems fiery. Even the stillness is amazingly beautiful. On the way back we pass peat bogs. In the evening we heard a concert. We dined on Solovetsk herring, small but amazingly tender and tasty; it melts in the mouth.

And that is it. Her memory apparently retained nothing else.

Gorky was more impressionable. He "recorded" at every campsite, leaving his entries in the book of comments. In the control journal of the head of Sekir Mountain, which included isolation cells and torture chambers that Timosha writes about enthusiastically, Gorky, upon seeing an entry by some GPU inspector that said "Found in good order during the visit," added, "And, I would say, excellent." And he signed it.

Gorky left an entry in the main logbook which did not "make it into" the collection of his writings:

> I am not in a condition to express my impressions in a few words. I don't feel like it, and besides it would be shameful to succumb to stock praise about the outstanding energy of the people who, being vigilant and tireless guardians of the revolution, are able, at the same time, to be wonderfully brave creators of culture.

For Gorky's visit the political prisoners were taken to the other end of the island, where access was off-limits. He was shown almost exclusively criminals who expressed the greatest satisfaction at their fate. But when he entered the foyer of the Solovetsk theater without a Chekist retinue, the *zeks* threw themselves upon him with notes—he collected them by standing next to the wall and putting his hands behind his back. What became of those prisoners (shot to death, heightened punishment, solitary confinement) was recounted by Timosha, but whatever she said did not make it into the published text of her reminiscences and remains hidden to this day.

Most likely by coincidence he met a prisoner of conscience whom he knew well: Yuliy Danzas, a professor of the history of religion at Petrograd University and a descendant of Pushkin's second in his duel with George-Charles Dantes. For some reason she was not packed off into the island's interior, and had the opportunity to see the high-ranking guest only in the foyer of the camp theater. In March 1920, Gorky had appointed Danzas to be director of the Petrograd House of Scientists. After his departure abroad she was arrested with a group of other Catholics and sent to Solovki. At least she should have given him a hint, but she hardly had a chance to talk to him about the kind of performance he was about to enjoy!

The notes Gorky had received and all diary entries that he had taken to the island disappeared immediately after his departure: two of his suitcases were stolen! Yagoda explained this as the work of professional thieves. One suitcase was later returned—instead of papers there was a small box with ashes. The ominous symbolism was too obvious: Gorky understood it and drew the proper conclusion.

The incident with the suitcase, like many other incidents connected to Gorky, is murky and filled with contradictions. From Timosha's unpublished reminiscences it is clear that the suitcase with Gorky's manuscripts did not disappear right after his visit to Solovki, but on "one fine day" when Gorky, Timosha, and other individuals accompanying them were already in Abkhazia (more about this below). A letter from Gorky to Stalin, dated November 29, 1929, also bears evidence of this. Only "about two months later," confirms Timosha, "the suitcase was returned;* some shoes were inside, but the little box that contained his manuscripts had only ashes. And Yagoda explained that they† became frightened and supposedly burned the manuscripts. And there were a lot of notes!"

Absolute rubbish!

He could not expose the farce which had been set for him in advance—he had already been given a crude but unambiguous hint about this. But who could have made him admire this hell camp—publicly, passionately, and for the whole world—with typical Gorky pathos? As to what Solovki in fact was, he certainly knew from Yekaterina Peshkova. The *zek* V. Svechnikov, who had miraculously escaped from there, managed to cross the border and who had met with Gorky on Solovki, published a tale of the camp in the Russian-language Berlin newspaper *Rul'* (The Rudder). Gorky read this eyewitness report and wrote his comments in the paper's margins. Can one say that he did not know, see, or understand anything, when the truth about this inferno had already been mentioned many times? Could not any halfway intelligent person know when he was being hoodwinked?

"I would very much like to see you as soon as possible," Gorky wrote to Yagoda right after his return from Solovki to Leningrad, "in order to share with you what I think." He "shared" this soon after not only with Yagoda but with the whole world by including his panegyric to Solovki and the whole Soviet camp system in the cycle of his travel sketches called "Around the Land of the Soviets."

The schedule of trips around the country had been drawn up a year in advance, but one part of the itinerary looked very strange: Gorky planned to go to the Caucasian shore of the Black Sea in the high heat of summer. There could hardly be a worse place than that in all of the Soviet Union for his health. The debilitating humidity was considered fatal not only for patients with tuberculosis but also for those the least bit susceptible to the disease. The climate, combined with the tiring trips, doomed Gorky's health to a sharp deterioration.

There was no reason for Gorky to make this suicidal decision, no reasons relating to Gorky's traditional interests could be found there either. The official

---

* By whom? How? To whom?
† The thieves, apparently.

Mura in the presence of a dozen guests around the table. Gorky did not forgive such transgressions. In letters to other writers he wrote nasty things about Pilnyak. "This person disgusts me. . . He writes like a minor detective," is how Gorky characterized Pilnyak in his typical free and easy style in a letter to Aleksei Chapygin.

But in 1929, Pilnyak, just elected chairman of the All-Russian Union of Writers, became the victim of defamation for his novella *Red Wood*, published in Berlin by Petropolis publishing house. In the typically vulgar denunciatory manner of Party journalism at that time, critics immediately called him a counterrevolutionary, knowing, like everyone else, what the consequences could be of such an accusation. According to the testimony of friends, Pilnyak, sensing reprisals, was on the verge of suicide.

Gorky decided to intervene, but in such a way as not to change his relationship to Pilnyak. "We have developed a foolish habit," he wrote, "of elevating people to the heights of praise, and then soon after casting them into the mud. It should be remembered that we are still not all that rich in our own people that we can just throw anyone to the devil and reject individuals capable of helping us in our difficult and magnificent endeavor." This was only an oblique and highly dubious defense, but Pilnyak was left alone.

For another persecuted writer he tried to intervene, not obliquely but directly. This was Yevgeni Zamyatin, with whom Gorky had successfully collaborated in the difficult but happy Petrograd times. Unable to publish in the Soviet press, Zamyatin resorted to Gorky's help in order to obtain a foreign passport. Gorky displayed total sympathy and even dared personally to speak with Stalin. This time the conversation went nowhere. Then he turned—and not for the first time—to Yagoda, who said, "Well, if he will insist, we'll let him go, but then there is no coming back." A confession was demanded of Zamyatin, who refused, and the matter remained open.

Gorky's subsequent request to reintegrate the writer Vladimir Zazubrin to the Party in order to give him the possibility to publish and lead a normal literary life was denied. Zazubrin was denied reentry to the Party, and Gorky was not informed as to the reason why, but Stalin, of course, did not forget about this solicitation and reacted to it in his usual style: in 1937 Zazubrin was shot.

chronology of his life with a list of his "works" during these Caucasian-Bla
Sea days is completely blank!

Yet for some reason he went. And not one single physician assigned to h
and responsible for his health tried to prevent it. A letter from Nadezh
Alliluyeva to her husband Joseph Stalin, who at this time was vacation
nearby in Sochi, sheds some light on this mystery: "I heard that Gorky went
Sochi and is probably staying with you, alas, without me—it is very pleasant
listen to him." From this statement at least one thing is indisputable: Gorky
met with Stalin a year earlier, not only officially but also in a domestic sett
But something emerged from this as well: Alliluyeva understood immedia
why Gorky had left for Sochi . . .

The next round of correspondence between Stalin and Gorky indicates
they had also met during the writer's second trip to Sochi. Or was it onl
Moscow, in October, right before his departure? Why is there such a
around a seemingly simple fact? Gorky probably did not want it to be kn
that he had gone to see Stalin—to the detriment of his own health—and
that Stalin had come to him. Stalin did not want to attract attention to his
à-tête meeting with Gorky in the heat of his battle against the "Ivanoviche
it might not be interpreted in the best way and could be used by his po
enemies.

A very reliable opinion says that Gorky's support inspired Stalin to u
take the merciless collectivization of the countryside but that he also caut
him against the danger of demanding excessive sacrifices. The consequer
this was Stalin's article, "Dizzy with Success," that heaped blame fo
expenses of collectivization on zealous Party bureaucrats on a regional
Where else but in Stalin's Caucasian dacha could they have conducted a
hurried, detailed private conversation like that? Why else would Gorky
traveled to these torrid regions? Finally, it is simply inconceivable that,
only a few kilometers away from Stalin, he would not have met with
But—and this cannot be explained—even he pretended that Stalin
nowhere near.

The retribution did not stop. After stopping off for one day in
(Tbilisi), Gorky continued his journey along the Georgian Military road.
car he spat up blood and returned to Moscow in critical condition. All
trips were postponed.

After a few weeks he had sufficiently recovered to complete his N
affairs. One of them concerned the fate of Boris Pilnyak, who had bee
oughly poisoned in the press; Gorky could not pretend that he had not r

He had no great love for Pilnyak since Petrograd when, in Gorky
ment on Kronverksky, Pilnyak had made some unflattering commer

18.

In Defense of Denunciation

All these skirmishes had completely exhausted Gorky. He barely made it back to the villa in Sorrento, where he began working on a new draft of his memoirs of Lenin.

The previous one had ended like this: "Vladimir Lenin died. His heirs in thought and will are alive." Now he added, "Alive and working just as successfully as no one had ever worked in the world." The facsimile of the fifty-third typewritten page with this insert and Gorky's signature was reproduced many times in print, even in school textbooks. The name of the main heir—comrade Stalin—is not mentioned in the final version of the reminiscences, but soon he would have an opportunity to correct this omission.

Gorky even considered apologizing for his first version: "What was written [about Lenin] shortly after his death was done in a state of depression, hurriedly and poorly. Some things I could not write about for reasons of 'tact,' which I hope are now understood." As to what "tact" he is talking about (and to whom) remains "completely incomprehensible." Something else is important: Gorky had completely revised his views. Many people, in fact, had predicted this but hardly anyone could have imagined that the turn would be as sharp and as candid. It did not simply coincide with, but was conditioned by, the change that had taken place in society and in the country.

The meetings with Stalin in 1929 took their relationship to a whole other level. They did not become friends (this word in general was inapplicable to either one), but they did draw closer. This is clear from their correspondence, only recently declassified. Gorky's unconditional and enthusiastic evaluation of forced collectivization came as a strong support, both morally and politically, for Stalin. Gorky wrote to him from Sorrento:

> . . . After the Party has so decisively placed the country on the rails of collectivization, the social revolution will acquire a genuinely socialist character.

This is practically a geological shift and, what is more, immeasurably greater and deeper than anything the Party has done . . . The task of reeducating [the peasants] in the shortest amount of time is the maddest of tasks. And, yet, it is being practically resolved . . . In general, everything is proceeding excellently. Much better than could have been expected.

How exactly it was resolved is well known. Moreover, it was already known then. . .

His beloved "Ivanoviches" were, on the contrary, resolute adversaries of collectivization, this greatest tragedy which befell Russia. Even for them Gorky found the appropriate words, creating the illusion of being on the side of the "right." Who knows where lay the falsehood and where the naïve attempt to reconcile the irreconcilable and preserve the appropriate "decorum"?

In late autumn of 1929, preparations for Stalin's fiftieth birthday began. The distribution of political forces had still not been settled, so not everyone reacted to the initial stage of the new leader's deification with equal enthusiasm. Yagoda even went so far as to express his indignation at a session of the Moscow committee of the Party: the Bolsheviks, he said, had never practiced "elevating the individual above the masses."

Far from Moscow and out of the loop, Gorky sent Stalin an extremely dry telegram: "Congratulations. I firmly shake your hand." However, on the day of the birthday, December 21, all newspapers called Stalin "the leader of the world proletariat." The headlines of the jubilee articles spoke for themselves: A TRIED AND TESTED LEADER; LEADER OF THE WORLD OCTOBER REVOLUTION; LEADER OF VICTORIOUS SOCIALISM; ORGANIZER OF THE UNION OF REPUBLICS; LENIN'S GREATEST THEORETICIAN. Gorky quickly corrected his negligence, congratulating Stalin a second time: "I congratulate you once again on your half century of life service. A good service." "Life service" Of what? It is impossible to say.

The new relationship he was developing with Stalin allowed him to adopt a role he had tried to play with Lenin: to give useful advice to the authorities. "The compositions 'of their own correspondents' of the bourgeois press," he wrote to Stalin, developing his favorite idea about the saving benefit of a lie, "are not so frequent or harmful to us as are the facts and conclusions of our own self-accusations. By emphasizing the facts negatively, we give our enemies large quantities of material which they skillfully use against us."

Stalin himself used the opportunity to demonstrate his "loyalty" to the truth and only the truth:

We cannot do without self-criticism. No way we can, Aleksei Maksimovich. Without it, stagnation, rotting of the apparatus, the growth of bureaucratism, and subversion of the creative initiative of the working class are inevitable. Of course, self-criticism gives ammunition to the enemy. In this you are absolutely correct, but it also provides ammunition (and a stimulus) for our movement forward. . . .

Stalin's latest demagoguery concealed his goal: "self-criticism" then consisted of annihilating the followers of Bukharin, exposing their "mistakes" everywhere, and by "rotting of the apparatus" Stalin had in mind the Party officials who shared the views of the hated opposition.

Yagoda corresponded even more actively with Gorky. If the correspondence with Stalin can be called warm, then with Yagoda it was already hot. "My dear Genrikh Grigorievich," Gorky addressed Yagoda. "Dear kinsman Aleksei Maksimovich," wrote Yagoda to Gorky. In one letter Yagoda even reminded Gorky that, while he was in Moscow, he had called him his "intimate friend." Gorky did not object—it was expected. "Warmest Wishes" is how Yagoda ended his letters, and this already speaks volumes to the degree of their relationship.

Gorky had hardly left Moscow when Yagoda was promoted to head of the OGPU.* It can be said with certainty that the brilliant operation he had carried out in the duping and domestication of Gorky was far from complete—total possession of the Stormy Petrel was the desired dream of the leader, and the dream came true. The upward career path, which objectively took place thanks to Gorky, raised Yagoda's feelings to his "intimate friend" even higher, and the image of Timosha, stuck in his heart and was inseparably linked with Gorky, imparting a sentimental nuance to their official relationship.

"Timosha . . . troubles me," as if by chance Yagoda hinted to Gorky. "She has totally, totally forgotten me." We now know that there was correspondence between them but, according to the wish of N. A. Peshkova, it remains classified for many years. Max was also in contact with Yagoda. From indirect information it can be ascertained that they did not entrust anything serious to paper, but their letters apparently reflect the nature of their relationship developed within that triangle. However, this correspondence is also classified for the time being.

It seemed that the friendship with Yagoda would help him intercede on behalf of persecuted individuals, but there was no more than a handful of such appeals, and each time for a comparatively trivial reason, while thousands of prisoners were ignored. Now he preferred to act in a new capacity and, more to

---

* Joint State Political Directorate (also known as All-Union State Political Administration), the successor of the GPU, created on November 15, 1923.

the point, in a different way. The most accurate word to describe this is *denunciation.*

From the rather large number, two stand out.

The first is connected with Romain Rolland and is therefore of special interest.

Rolland, together with a large group of French intellectuals (among them Paul Langevin, Georges Duhamel, Luc Durtain, Jean-Richard Bloch, Charles Vildrac, and others) had risen to the defense of the Italian anarchist Francesco Gezzi, arrested in Moscow, who had earlier been granted political asylum in the Soviet Union. Besides Rolland, none of the French intellectuals enjoyed such a close relationship with Gorky so, naturally, it was Rolland who turned to his friend for a personal request to help.

This normal and obvious initiative was received, unexpectedly for Rolland, by Gorky with hostility. It was not so much his negative attitude in and of itself toward Rolland's request that was surprising as his reasons:

> Now, when the Soviet government decisively tackles the issue of replacing private ownership of land with the collectivization of agriculture, the instincts of our peasants, in all their obviousness and anarchic morals, assume very violent forms in certain places. Anarchists and individualists are taking advantage, naturally, of this state of the peasants' mind and spend time instigating unrest. Therefore, there are arrests.

(This is a reverse translation from the French to the Russian by Mura. It was precisely in such form that the addressee read the letter.)

Rolland took Gorky's reply only at face value, stating, "I'm talking about one thing, and you're talking about something completely different." He responded immediately:

> I am an independent person, never concerned whether someone likes it or not but who is capable of seeing and saying ruthlessly what he sees and what he foresees. I have not stopped defending the USSR in France. Therefore, let not my friends and me be forced into silence!

Max translated the letter to Gorky inaccurately, as was usually the case; so inaccurately in fact that a bitter scandal almost ensued as a result. Gorky was filled with indignation when he found out that his French colleague had decided to speak about him "ruthlessly." Meanwhile, to speak *sans management* means "to speak point-blank," "without beating around the bush" or something similar, but not to "speak ruthlessly." Gorky took on faith Max's inaccurate translation and reacted immediately!

The fate of this letter is very mysterious. In the complete collection of correspondence between Gorky and Rolland, published in 1991 by the Paris publisher Albin Michel, not only is it missing, but there is no mention of it, nor has it ever been published in Russian. Yet it exists in the Gorky archive in Moscow under archive number PGin-60-6-172. What is known is half of one phrase from a letter dated February 4 or 5, 1930: ". . . I too can speak ruthlessly, but only to the enemies of Soviet power." It can be assumed that Rolland's wife, Maria Kudasheva, about whom more will be said in later chapters, handed the original over to the "Moscow comrades." But why were there no copies for the Rolland archive in Paris? And why such a mystery about this one letter?

It appears that the relationship between the two friends was on the verge of collapse. This assumption is plausible judging by Gorky's comment in a letter to Rolland dated February 26: "Your last letter elevates him [Gezzi] too much, and I daresay that I must cease correspondence with you because of such a tone." The sharpness of this epistolary discussion seems all the more absurd because Gorky's reaction was completely inadequate to Rolland's request; he could have at least answered his "French friend" that he had communicated it to Moscow, but was unsuccessful in getting it approved. Who would have condemned him for that?

In the meantime, Gorky did not limit himself to correspondence with Rolland on a relatively minor matter, which had also turned into an issue of primary importance. Only now has a secret, previously unknown factor been revealed: at the same time as he "rebuffed" Rolland, Gorky was corresponding on the exact same issue with Yagoda. How he "supported" his French friends can be judged after reading the text of Gorky's letter dated February 6, 1930:

My dear Genrikh Georgyevich,[*]
Roman Rolland sent me on 26 January 1930 a letter in which he very eloquently lectured Soviet power about fairness. He proposes that I solicit the release from prison of the anarchist Francesco Gezzi and his return to France.

I sent my reply—I append an excerpt and, as you can see, there is nothing offensive to Rolland in it. But he took offense and sent the short letter attached on 3 February 1930. I responded to this loud and arrogant letter as well.

I turn to you now with a question: is it not possible to banish this Gezzi from the Soviet Union? To be sure, it needs to be done—if it can be done—not for the sake of Rolland's satisfaction but simply for the sake of avoiding any sour and dirty tears.

It is possible that all these demeaning escapades against his "highly esteemed friend," taking place, incidentally, behind Rolland's back, are all only a

---

[*] Mistake: it should have been "Grigorievich."

means, with the help of which Gorky wanted to win clemency for Gezzi from Yagoda. This time it failed. Yagoda did not answer directly but through his employee PePeKriu, saying that to free Gezzi was "by no means impossible," and that his prison term had been exchanged for exile in Suzdal, not far from Moscow.

Nevertheless, a denunciation, and one with a choice of terminology insulting to Rolland, was not a method to achieve the desired result. Another incident that even more convincingly testifies to Gorky's voluntary collaboration with the chief of Soviet secret police provides evidence of this.

Boris Pasternak asked Gorky for help. He wanted to go abroad with his wife and son to recuperate, relax, and see his family (his father was the well-known artist Leonid Pasternak, and his sisters lived in Europe). Since nothing had come of his own efforts, he turned to Gorky, remembering the legend that used to go around Petrograd: the great solicitor will never refuse to help his brothers-in-arms.

Gorky was blunt in his reply to Pasternak: "I cannot fulfill your request and very much advise you not to ask for a trip abroad." He then considered it necessary to immediately report to Yagoda:

> Pasternak is asking me to solicit for this trip—with his wife and son—abroad. I answered him that I am not going to solicit, that I cannot. I attach herewith the feuilleton of the scoundrel Kaminsky. I am very surprised that this louse was allowed out of the country.

The journalist and writer Anatoly Kaminsky, allowed abroad, refused to return and published an innocuous piece in the émigré press about Soviet literary morals. Equating Pasternak's request directly with Kaminsky's action, Gorky unambiguously warned Yagoda that the former (because of his "weak will," as he called it) could follow the example of the latter. Gorky's "signal" was not motivated by any considerations of noble tactics. It was *simply* a denunciation, pure and simple.

Gorky's letters to Yagoda, when read in chronological order, demonstrate how quickly and irrevocably yesterday's Stormy Petrel had evolved at the start of the 1930s. It was as if he were attempting to prove his loyalty no matter what and the absence of any cunning, no matter what secret thoughts were concealed in his words and actions. Only this can explain the persistent theme throughout his letters to the head of the secret police, namely, hatred toward the "saboteurs," who were being so valiantly exposed and so justly punished by Yagoda's institution.

Incidentally, he began this theme with imprecations against the non-returnees, whose numbers grew sharply following the beginning of arrests in

Moscow. The refusal of several Soviet diplomats to return home and their denunciatory publications abroad of Soviet abuses at home prompted Gorky, in a letter to Yagoda, to such flights as, "My mood is such that I feel like punching faces."

Already tattletelling in the next letter on his "visitors from the USSR" (although not called by name, they could easily be identified by Yagoda), who were in a "sour and fearful" mood, Gorky fervently congratulated Yagoda and his colleagues "for their new and huge service to the Party and the working class." He was speaking of the two, totally sham, trials being prepared in Moscow against the "Promparty," which never existed, and the "Union Bureau" of the Mensheviks, also a work of fiction.

Among the defendants in both cases were people whom he knew well: for example, the engineer Osadchy, who had just been his guest in Sorrento; or the economist Nikolai Sukhanov, with whom he published the newspaper *Novaya Zhizn'*, where *Untimely Thoughts* was published.

Gorky wrote to Yagoda:

> Along with hatred toward them, the pride of your work and joy in the fact that the working class has such a vigilant, loyal guardian of its life and interests is inspiring.
>
> It does not surprise me that Sukhanov, a boy with sickly self-pride and the psyche of a swindler, ended up in the dock for criminals.
>
> I would very much like to attend the trial, look at the mugs of these has-beens and listen to their speeches, but I'm afraid I don't have the strength for it.

Yagoda quickly sent Gorky a specially prepared selection of materials of the preliminary investigation intended only for the delegates of the next Party congress, in which the defendants admitted their guilt in committing the most heinous of crimes, including the planning of terrorist acts, "organizing famine," sabotage, diversions, and other evil deeds. The idea that these so-called confessions "in one's own hand" might be false, having been extracted under torture or blackmail, never seems to have occurred to Gorky, although probably no newspaper in the West probably would have written about it.

After familiarizing himself with the materials, he hurried to make Yagoda's day with a new letter:

> I read the confessions by the sons of bitches about the organization of terror and was extremely shocked. If they had not been such abject cowards, they could have shot S[talin]. And you too, I hear, walk and drive carefree along the streets. It's a strange attitude to life, which, first of all, is a business and what a business we have!

I read the minutes of the trial. It is very difficult to define that complicated feeling which the trial provokes in me: revulsion toward these people, and rage, and joy that they are at last destroyed. I would really like to come to Moscow to the trial and look at these crushed scoundrels. What a swine that Osadchy is!

Everything that Gorky expressed so colorfully in his personal letters to Yagoda he also repeated in his journalism intended for the rest of the world. He devoted several articles to the trial against the so-called "Promparty," where the chief defendant, Professor Leonid Ramzin, had been specially recruited by Yagoda's employees in the role of provocateur (documents from the recently declassified KGB archive provide evidence of this). On orders from the OGPU, Ramzin, a member of both the board of Gosplan and the Supreme Soviet of the Economy of the USSR, admitted to being the ringleader of the nonexistent Promparty, which supposedly included fifty people, with another five hundred sympathizers. Among those sentenced were world renowned scientists and professors.

Gorky accepted all these falsehoods exactly the way the OGPU presented them to the world. His article, published simultaneously in *Pravda* and *Izvestiia*, as already was the tradition, has entered history with its title immediately transformed into a formula, justifying the repressions: "If the enemy does not surrender, he must be annihilated." (*Izvestiia* entitled the article, "If the Enemy Does Not Surrender, He Will Be Destroyed.") "Against us," wrote Gorky, "is everything that has outlived the time allotted it by history, and this gives us the right to consider ourselves to still be in a state of civil war. The natural conclusion: if the enemy does not surrender, he will be annihilated." In conclusion, he threatened to strike "a final blow to the head of capitalism" and throw it into "a grave, dug for it in good time by history."

The annihilation of the hard-working peasantry (they were all accused of being "kulaks"), the deportation of millions of peasants to Siberia and the north, and enforced collectivization were the cause of terrible starvation that killed millions of people. The guilt was placed on a few dozen engineers and scientists, allegedly "harming" the country consciously in order to sow dissatisfaction against Soviet power. This scenario, neatly embroidered by the NKVD, was figured out by numerous people in both the USSR and abroad, but was completely misunderstood by Gorky. Insofar as there is no basis to consider him completely blind or of having lost his ability to think critically, it is proper to conclude that he willingly closed his eyes to the truth and took the poison Yagoda and his henchmen concocted in the kitchen of the Lubyanka.

When the "trial of workers and peasants," as Gorky pompously called the latest bloody spectacle in Moscow, sentenced the "saboteurs," the League for the Defense of Human Rights sent their protest signed by, among others, Albert Einstein and Heinrich Mann. This gave Gorky the excuse to refuse cooperation with the "International Union of Democratic Writers," only because it included these "gentlemen humanists," as he disdainfully referred to them.

"The indescribable infamy of the actions of the forty-eight [defendants] is well known to me," Gorky wrote self-assuredly in an "open letter" to Rolland, Upton Sinclair, Bernard Shaw, H. G. Wells, and other "humanists"—again published in both *Pravda* and *Izvestiia*.

> The organizers of the famine, provoking the justifiable wrath of the working people against whom they carried out their base conspiracy, were punished by the unanimous demand of the workers. I consider this punishment totally legal... It is completely natural that the combined might of the workers and peasants crush their enemies like fleas.

Logically, his addressees should have recoiled in horror from their Russian colleague, who continued to consider himself a writer and who proudly welcomed the collective punishment, while lecturing his famous brothers-in-arms around the world on the rules of elementary morality. Alas, this did not happen.

Incidentally, he had hastened in vain to inform the Western "humanists" about the sentence (five of the defendants were sentenced to be shot). Yagoda's scenario had foreseen a lighter sentence which was, in particular, promised to Professor Ramzin ahead of time in exchange for implicating himself and his comrades. This planned act of mercy, with its far-reaching propaganda goals, agitated Gorky even more than the "betrayal" of the scientists. He expressed his dissatisfaction in letters to the Kremlin leaders, which have now become known. For example, to Voroshilov he wrote, "I am somewhat bothered by the mitigation of the sentence against the saboteurs, [insofar as the workers] had demanded capital punishment." He wrote the same to Bukharin: "The trial of Ramzin and Co. upset me, evoked disgust and a desire to punch the faces of the traitors . . . I am indignant that the sentence did not correspond with the mood of the working masses and this makes me dissatisfied."

However, to Romain Rolland, who continued to be troubled by the fate of the defendants, he joyously reported on the humanity of the falsifiers at the Lubyanka: "I know that all the sentenced saboteurs in the case against the 'Promparty,' now in custody, are living and working in excellent conditions, correcting the damage they have wrought. Ramzin even reads lectures to engineers at the Thermal Institute."

The idea of a "betrayal" by scientists and technicians was like a thorn in his side, prompting him to return repeatedly to the same topic, punishing himself for having been favorably disposed toward, and a passionate defender of, "that group." In a letter to Krupskaya he confessed that he had not listened to the advice of Lenin, who "at every good opportunity tried to convince me not to 'solicit' too much and often mocked my attempts 'to defend the persecuted.' In essence I understood the 'repressed' to be only here, beyond the borders of the USSR." He expressed his new understanding in the latest version of his memoir of Lenin: "To be sure, after a host of facts in connection with the basest sabotage by specialists, I was obliged to reevaluate—and have reexamined—my attitude to the workers of science and technology."

His reevaluation went so far that he quickly composed a play about the saboteurs called *Somov and Others*, where the characters are the saboteur Troekurov, the conspirator Bogomolov, and Somov's wife, Lidia, who "lost her connection to life." ("In my sleep I see that I must write the play 'Saboteur,'" he wrote to Yagoda.) Beyond its political topicality, the literary and artistic level of this play was such that not a single theater was willing to stage it. Incidentally, he could not bring it to a conclusion like his main novel, *The Life of Klim Samgin*. Gorky's creative activity now manifested itself mainly in aggressive or laudatory newspaper articles.

And he was still working in the denunciation genre—these came to light only recently. The latest he sent to Yagoda: ". . . Romain Rolland renewed his correspondence with me . . . Rolland's 'sympathy' [toward the USSR] is already poisoned by narrow-mindedness, as you will see from my letter to him, a copy of which I deem necessary to send you." He was referring to a letter dated the same day as the denunciation to Yagoda (November 2, 1930):

> It seems to me, Rolland, that you could make a judgment about the internal affairs of the Soviet Union with greater calm and fairness if you were to consider one simple fact: the Soviet regime and vanguard of the working party are in a state of civil war, that is, a class war. The enemy they are fighting—and must fight—is the intelligentsia, which is trying to restore the bourgeois regime and the rich peasant who, defending his private property—the basis of capitalism—prevents collectivization: they resort to terror, to the murder of state farm workers, to burning collective property, and other methods of partisan warfare. And in war people kill.

19.

An Agent of Influence

Almost until the end of the 1920s, Gorky was the most translated Russian writer. Not a single émigré author—not Bunin, not Merezhkovsky, nor Kuprin—could compete with Gorky by the number of translations, to say nothing of the authors who lived and worked in the Soviet Union. These writers were not translated that often, although they were translated quite willingly and sometimes above and beyond the level they deserved because people in the West really wanted to understand just what this miracle of post-revolutionary Russia was. In terms of the number of overall translations, only Ilya Ehrenburg, another semi-émigré like Gorky, who lived constantly abroad but remained a Soviet citizen and wrote for the Soviet press had caught up to Gorky. In the free world both he and Gorky were called "Soviet emissaries."

By the beginning of the 1930s, they switched places. Ehrenburg was translated and published more and more, while the interest in Gorky, whose works in translation did not disappear, of course, suffered a noticeable decline. Gorky knew this and was upset by it, especially since Ehrenburg was someone he disdained completely. "Ehrenburg is a cynic, a nihilist who has never written anything serious and never will," affirmed Gorky in his typical unqualified style in a letter to Dalmat Lutokhin. Writing to someone else, he was even harsher: "Shameless prevarications! Stupid little nihilism."

Besides envy (both in number of copies and in popularity at home and abroad, Ehrenburg ran neck and neck with Gorky), there was another reason for such passionate animosity. Ehrenburg was a "Westerner," a European through and through, while Gorky did not know or understand the West, much less like it. As far as America was concerned, he reviled it as much as possible. With Germany he was only somewhat acquainted, if it can be called that: he found it uncomfortable and cheerless. He had been whipped up in his enmity toward the West by such "leftists" as Rolland. "I reproached you," he wrote to Gorky, "because you see only the smile of France, and I want you to see its teeth as well." Where had Rolland seen Gorky contemplating French good nature? In fact, he had expressed himself very clearly on this point, calling Paris a "den of thieves," "dirty, cold and unhealthy," adding that he "is somewhat afraid of Paris."

If he loved anything, it was not the West and not Europe with all its diversity, but only Italy. And not even all of Italy, but just *his* little world which he had created there—the heavenly climate, the benevolence of the people around him, the view of the gulf, the harmony of nature and man and the beauty so pleasing to the eye in everything, right down to the smallest details. But aesthetics did not put food on the table. The exigencies of daily life compelled him to look toward his only source of money which, if the Master of the Kremlin so desired, might not reach all the way to Sorrento.

In the Soviet Union everything had miraculously changed. In the overall output of world and Russian classics, including all contemporary foreign and Soviet writers, every twelfth published book was his: 19,000,000 copies in total in less than five years. There would not likely be a single author in the world with that kind of reach. And this in addition to the fact that a system to transfer royalties abroad did not exist.

In order for even one ruble to be converted into hard currency and sent abroad, special permission was required from a so-called "hard currency commission," under the auspices of the Politburo's Central Committee. Actually, the Kremlin made all such decisions: the archives record dry and laconic official documents about sending Gorky five or ten thousand gold (meaning hard currency) rubles, which were very large sums in those days, and yet only a minimal part of what Gorky was legally owed.

His yearly excursions to Moscow had become a tradition, but in 1930 Gorky was unable to make the trip. One lung had stopped working altogether, and tuberculosis had developed irreversibly in the second. He was so weak that he could not go anywhere. The émigré press, closely following his every move and every line he wrote (just as every spoken word), hastened to report that he had again separated himself from the Soviets. This was only wishful thinking that the émigrés hoped to present as reality and very far from the truth. They would never make their peace with Gorky, but all the same they wanted him to be at odds with Moscow.

He was not at odds with Moscow; there was no reason to be, for Moscow looked after him as best it could. The money was now flowing smoothly both from a new collection of his works and individual publications, as well as excerpts from his unfinished *Life of Klim Samgin* and the completed *The Artamonov Business* appearing in magazines. Moreover, Moscow was convinced that his final trip home was not far away and had prepared for him a *home*, in every sense of the word.

Vladislav Khodasevich, who knew and understood Gorky as well as anyone, wrote an essay at the end of the 1920s entitled "Maxim Gorky and the USSR," which contains a subtle psychological riddle: it was not tuberculosis at all that detained him in Italy. In fact, Gorky had become "Sovietized" right before one's eyes, but he nevertheless wanted to sit on the fence for as long as possible, so as not to lose face in the West. This, of course, is what happened, but he could not go on like this forever. Gorky already knew that sooner or later he would return for good. And Moscow knew this as well, automatically extending his Soviet passport.

Stalin had decided to turn a gaudy merchant's mansion in the very center of Moscow on Malaya Nikitskaya into a permanent residence for the one person whom he considered his equal. By May 1930 the reconstruction of the mansion had still not been completed, but the following year Gorky could already move into his new and completely free home—the government picked up all expenses for its upkeep.

He was still clearly at a crossroads. As before, he wanted to be *there*, but did not want to leave *here*. It was not only and not so much a need for money (now there was enough money) that prompted his concern for the fate of his truly priceless collection of antiques. A portion of valuable bronzes was still being kept by Chaliapin, to whom it would not be so easy to turn after their meeting in Rome. Gorky nonetheless wrote a letter for Mura to give to Chaliapin for its transfer. The letter did not find its intended recipient (at first Chaliapin was out of town, then on tour in South America) and was lost. Other Gorky letters given to Mura shared the same fate.

Another, much bigger, part of the collection remained in bank vaults in Berlin, along with a part of the archive, and Mura had access to the vault. She probably handed over the archive, with Gorky's permission, to Kriuchkov, and the latter spirited it away to Moscow. It can be said with certainty that this was not the most valuable (in the sense of "explosive") part of the archive, which Gorky fearlessly turned over to "reliable hands." What was taken was most likely not the entire contents of Gorky's vaults, but only the most valuable items in terms of money at that time. An inquiry from Mura in Berlin to Gorky alludes to this: ". . . what should I do with the ivory and jade? There's a whole suitcase of ivory—I'm afraid it will be difficult to bring it to Sorrento.* And there's another whole suitcase of jade. Have you thought of selling it? But you have some of the items and the appraisal will therefore be incomplete."

---

* Because of customs control at the border.

If Gorky had wanted to take the ivory and jade with him to Moscow, then all conditions for sending his baggage by diplomatic transport would have been guaranteed. But he still did not want to do this—at least not then. Either he did not have the intention of returning for good or, allowing for such a possibility, he preferred to turn the collection, obtained through not entirely legal means, into hard cash.

His correspondence with Stalin was growing, though the letters mostly flowed from Sorrento to Moscow. Not all his thoughts pleased Stalin, but all received support. In particular, Stalin supported Gorky's idea to create a multi-volume *History of the Civil War* and joined the editorial board himself as a rank-and-file member under Gorky's direction, while he most likely detested Gorky's main argument: "The direct participants of the civil war . . . are getting old and decrepit, dying out, and we are gradually losing the living witnesses of the past." Did this not also refer to Stalin himself? Psychologically, Stalin was already pre-pared for his own immortality. The prospect of decrepitude and dying out, which Gorky had stated with implacable mercilessness, did not fill him with optimism. And he was certainly not going to give Trotsky any credit as the genuine creator of the Red Army, which the "living witnesses of the past" knew full well, nor mention others in comparison to whom his true role in the civil war looked modest at best.

The thick correspondence with Stalin did not prevent Gorky in the slight-est from carrying out an equally intensive correspondence with his enemies. The most active correspondents were the "Ivanoviches": Bukharin and Rykov. These letters were preserved until only very recently in top-secret funds of the Kremlin archive. Gorky's letters to them are in sharp contrast regarding con-tent, and, more importantly in tone, language, and emotional feeling, to his letters to Stalin.

The "Ivanoviches" were more sympathetic to him than all the other partici-pants in the internal Party struggle thanks to their enthusiasm, lively minds, and erudition which for Gorky, a voracious reader, was a quality of extreme importance. This sympathy, however, did not prevent Gorky from differing with them on the main question which, at least externally, separated them from Stalin and had become a litmus test for personal loyalty to the new leader. Bukharin and Rykov were decidedly opposed to the mad tempo of collectivization. Gorky, on the contrary, remained true to himself in seeing his old ideas practically realized by Stalin's attack on the peasantry.

Gorky greeted with unfeigned joy Bukharin and Rykov's confession at the Sixteenth Party Congress (1930), when they admitted their "mistakes" and declared their agreement with the "general line of the Party" (meaning with Stalin): after all, he had willingly admitted his old sins—both real and imaginary—not seeing in this any wounded pride. Why wouldn't the Ivanoviches do the same? He did not relish having to choose between Stalinists and anti-Stalinists; he wanted reconciliation and was glad that it happened—or so he thought.

"I embrace you and shake your hand. Cordial greetings to Aleksei Ivanovich [Rykov]," Gorky wrote to Bukharin. Informing Rykov about his desire to "go see you [Rykov and Bukharin] right now, to look at you, to shake your mitts," he exclaimed. "You are truly dear people and—if you'll beg my pardon!—I love you very much and am amazed by you in general." (May 10, 1930.)

Here are two more excerpts from his letters to Bukharin:

> My dear and accursed deviator . . . I strongly clasp your hand, embrace you strongly and genuinely love you, dear Nikolai Ivanovich! [July 23, 1930]

> I embrace you very strongly. And Aleksei Ivanovich too. You have both lived through a lot during these years, I know. But—excuse an old man's "sentimentality"—I have come to love and respect both of you more. It's a fact. [December 11, 1930]

The letters from the Ivanoviches often reached him from someone passing through or were sent from outside the Soviet Union. Gorky punctiliously responded to his repentant friends through diplomatic channels: Max took his letters to the Soviet consulate in Naples. All were opened and read and the text was on Stalin's desk. Stalin was therefore completely informed of this exchange of rapturous enthusiasm and he understood perfectly well why Gorky had come to love and respect his enemies *even more*. Only a very naïve person would have failed to realize back then that anyone who disagreed even slightly with Stalin or was not on his side became his sworn enemy forever.

The NKVD's net, in which Gorky was already entangled in Moscow, grew even thicker. Yagoda's flattering letters only created an emotional and psychological foundation to fully draw Gorky into this web. Kriuchkov (PePeKriu), bound by strong ties to the OGPU, was officially designated his secretary—all of Gorky's publishing and financial matters, as well as all his correspondence, were now going through him. Kriuchkov spent a long time in Sorrento, sometimes with his new wife Yelizaveta Zakharova; she then occupied the modest post of secretary to the editorial staff of the journal *Krestyanka* (Peasant Woman)—no match for the high-ranking Maria Fyodorovna—but anyway a nice and fundamentally simple young woman. In character she yielded nothing to Maria Fyodorovna.

Not a single person from the Soviet Union could get to Gorky without first passing through Kriuchkov: he handled foreign passports, entry and transit visas, even dispensing of money for stays abroad. Thus, all visitors passed through the Lubyanka, thereby becoming either informers or "persons of trust." Only Kriuchkov could determine their status. In letters to him, as to Yagoda, Gorky referred to him as his "dear friend." Kriuchkov's unfortunate relatives, who had lived through the Great Terror as children, violently defend his "good name" by citing the fact that Gorky wrote him such warm letters and thanked him many times for helping him in his work. Indeed, he did write and thank him. Yet the letters to Kriuchkov are nothing compared to those to Yagoda: there Gorky displayed such affection which—on paper at least—was not conferred upon any of his obvious friends. Does this mean that we must now turn away from the historical truth and see Yagoda and Kriuchkov only through Gorky's eyes?

During Kriuchkov's absence, Mura and Max handled all of Gorky's mail and other affairs. Therefore, it can be assumed that the Lubyanka had some idea (incomplete, probably) even about the letters Gorky did not send from the Soviet Union.

It is doubtful, however, that Mura was a very diligent and thorough informer. She had to maneuver and think about the future. Friendly meetings in various European cities (mostly Berlin) with her old lover, the British spy R. Bruce Lockhart, her closeness to H. G. Wells and the realistic hopes that it would become a tight bond, did not stop her zealous service to Moscow. But fear of the Lubyanka's omnipotence and ability to reach any point on the globe also influenced her actions.

One thing is clear: while her services were used in Moscow, she was distrusted. The Lubyanka, as is known, did not even trust those who knowingly served it faithfully.

Stalin needed full information and absolute sway over his newly embraced Sorrento friend. This task could partially be carried out by Yagoda's messengers, who had visited Gorky as guests. One of them, Matvei Pogrebinsky, the closest person to Yagoda, was dispatched to Sorrento under a false name and on special assignment, the exact nature of which can only be conjectured. Without a special need, there would be no reason to send a high-ranking figure from the OGPU on such a risky journey. There were no apparent reasons for Motya's trip to Sorrento, which lasted four whole weeks! Not only was Gorky not surprised by this conspiracy, he even played into it. He did not betray the Chekist secret entrusted to him. Confirming in a letter to Kriuchkov, who was in on the secret beforehand, that the operation was successful, Gorky employed a euphemism: ". . . Policeman has arrived." "Motya knows what is going on,"

Yagoda confidentially reported to Gorky in a letter that traveled by diplomatic pouch. "He has a lot to tell you."

What did Motya know? What did he have to tell Gorky? Why organize such a dangerous trip in Europe, unusual even for the Lubyanka, to bring Gorky material for a screenplay about young criminals? Was the masquerade with falsified documents, placing not only Motya but Gorky himself at risk, required in this case? In the event of the slightest slip-up, his name would be directly linked to an OGPU intrigue. In less than four months he would again be leaving for Moscow—was it not easier to discuss his creative plans at a dacha outside that city? We know nothing about any concrete results from the mysterious visit by the "Policeman."

This was initiated by the Soviet secret services, and specifically by Yagoda. His passion for Timosha had not abated; on the contrary, the separation only strengthened it. The secret penchant for operations by the sinister organization, combined with the secret love of its chief, was diabolically drawing Gorky into its web. It is possible that he allowed himself to be drawn into it, and, without realizing what he was becoming party to, was already involved. If one accepts the hypothesis stated below regarding the relationship that existed between Yagoda and the "Ivanoviches," as well as the subsequent fate of Pogrebinsky, it cannot be excluded that the tale of "Motya-Policeman" was exactly that. Then Yagoda's ardent love for the hermit of Sorrento will acquire a more exact and fuller explanation.

Other guests, who were allowed to visit Gorky (not all, it should be assumed), were useful to the Lubyanka in different ways—some as voluntary informants, believing (genuinely or not) that they were doing a good deed. The writer Lev Nikulin, a worldly playboy and a person of talent, a pleasant collector who mastered languages and had good contacts abroad, was one such frequent visitor at Sorrento.

Regularly taking trips to France for treatment at a time when very few Soviet people had such a possibility available to them, Nikulin met there with émigrés and, upon his return, according to his Parisian "friends" the historian Boris Suvarin and the artist Yuri Annenkov, wrote up reports about his conversations with them. Gorky considered him a "Soviet Pierre Benoit" and rashly predicted that Nikulin "will stand taller than all the French schemers." Aleksandr Tvardovsky, on the contrary, considered him a charlatan and was much closer to the truth. The accumulation of indirect information allows us to conclude that the "Soviet Pierre Benoit" was one of those stool pigeons around Gorky whose agent pseudonyms will be cited below.

Yagoda's nostalgic letters turned more sentimental—he bared his soul in expressions permissible only to an intimate friend: "I miss you very much. . . .

Now all I do is work, and my nerves are shattered. . . . . It's sad without you."
Gorky answered him in the same vein:

> Your words . . . distressed and even outraged me. They are the result of a bad
> mood, my dear Genrikh. One has to fight this bad mood, it must be overcome; it
> is "unbecoming" of such a masculine person and steadfast revolutionary as I know
> you are. I cannot imagine any other reasons—except extreme fatigue—that could
> have knocked you out of the saddle. You must take it easy, get yourself back in
> shape. Damn it, how good it would be if you could come here! We'd take care of
> you!

Gorky wasn't unable to imagine "any reasons at all" for Yagoda's "bad
mood." The backstage Kremlin intrigues, in which the chief of the secret police
had to take a very direct part, could hardly promote a good mood, regardless of
how they turned out. At that time everyone was feeling the sword being held
over their heads. In the struggle between the Stalinists and the "rightists"
(Bukharin, Rykov, Tomsky), Yagoda had taken the side of the latter. Now, as
chief of the OGPU, he had to fight against his likeminded colleagues and their
followers: the Bukharians, even after the confessions, continued to be treated as
enemies "of the general Party line."

Gorky's fanatical passion for receiving and writing letters is widely known.
His correspondence with Moscow (with the Soviet Union to be more specific)
makes up many volumes—even now, after these volumes have been published,
the unpublished letters are so numerous that they would take up more than one
volume. Politics is not the main theme—Gorky acted mostly as tutor-teacher to
those writers who flocked to literature. His animosity and anger toward real
talent, which could probably have competed with him for the literary Olympus,
combined with delight and clearly inflated praise that he distributed to the
dubiously gifted and not overly ambitious.

Now, after some sixty to seventy years, it can be determined how reliable
his predictions were. It is useless to name names: they are already long forgotten. But Gorky gave hacks and graphomaniacs evaluations that would have
fit Dostoyevsky or Chekhov. Incidentally, he did not spare the classics either.
Nina Berberova, who knew Gorky well, said,

> Russian writers of the nineteenth century were mostly his personal enemies. He
> hated Dostoyevsky; Gogol he despised as a physically and morally sick person; he
> twitched with anger and jealousy at the mention of Chaadayev and Vladimir
> Solovyev; he mocked Turgenev. There was something about Leo Tolstoy that

upset and troubled him. Of course, he considered him great, the greatest, but he loved to speak of his weaknesses.

Nevertheless, he did recognize unquestionably talented contemporary writers, although begrudgingly and with many reservations, while any complete hack elicited his admiration to the point of tears. This betrayed a strong complex of envy and jealousy, combined with a need to be a trailblazer of talents who would in turn be eternally grateful to him and would never eclipse him. Succumbing to momentary euphoria from the most mediocre of travel sketches, he reported, for example, in one of his letters that its author "rubbed the nose" of Maupassant, even though the poet Nikolai Tikhonov, who subsequently squandered his talent as a functionary in the Union of Writers, did not measure himself by the same yardstick. Even the most meticulous historians of Soviet literature do not know his essays today.

On the other hand, Gorky did not stand on ceremony with those unpleasant to him. When news about Mayakovsky's suicide reached Sorrento, he responded (from a letter to Bukharin dated May 10, 1930), "And here Mayakovsky stopped. He picked the right time! I knew that person and—I did not trust him." As if the latter, having shot himself, had committed some kind of base act! No one else reacted to the tragic demise of the poet so despicably. His written response to this tragedy embarrassed even those who never liked Mayakovsky's poetry. Tucked away until recently in the Lubyanka archives, a diary from one of his contemporaries records the expressions of other writers about that shameful gesture: ". . . Gorky is a jealous and petty little person . . . He should catch diabetes—that would serve him right." "An inappropriate reaction to an inappropriate act!" (This diary, incidentally, fell into Yagoda's hands and was reported by him to Stalin. Nothing happened to the writer who had wished diabetes upon Gorky.)

Even more impressive is the incredibly absurd story that is part of the "Gorkiana" known as the "Chaliapin episode."

In 1926, the Leningrad-based publishing house Priboi issued the memoirs of Fyodor Chaliapin, published ten years earlier in Gorky's *Letopis'* journal. Four years later the book was delivered to France, intended for the Russian émigré market. Soviet Russia had not signed a single copyright convention, and therefore any foreign publisher could now freely translate a book into different languages and sell it. The enraged Chaliapin filed a lawsuit against the Soviet government in a French court. Since the publisher did not have the consent of the author to the publication of the book and had paid him nothing, Chaliapin demanded compensation in the amount of two million francs.

In purely legal terms, Chaliapin's suit was rather shaky. French courts were forced to take into account that Soviet Russia was not bound by any international obligations to defend copyrights. The property (including copyrights) of émigrés was nationalized, which also had to be reckoned with. But in this case it was not a question of the translation, but of the sale of part of the edition of the book, written and previously published in Russia and now reissued in the USSR, and brought to France simply as an imported product. Therefore, the suit was not against the Moscow publishing house but against the Soviet trade representation in Paris that represented a monopolistic Soviet foreign trade organization and trafficked, according to Chaliapin, in illegal goods.

From a formally legal point of view, however, the situation was by no means as clear-cut. Chaliapin had had correspondence with the Leningrad publisher, where the point could be made that in principle he did not object to the publication of his book. Finally, *Priboi* had the status of a "cooperative"—the state (in this case, the trade representation) bore absolutely no responsibility for it. But morally Chaliapin was unquestionably correct. Thus, all the more incredible was Gorky's unexpected reaction to his close friend who only a year ago, with genuine tears of joy and tender emotion, had embraced him in Rome, confessing to indestructible, brotherly love.

He published articles in *Pravda* and *Izvestiia*, insulting to Chaliapin, about the history behind Chaliapin's memoirs and even proposed to Valeriyan Dovgalevsky, the Soviet ambassador in Paris, to help in rejecting Chaliapin's lawsuit. Gorky maintained that he was the author of the book and that the magazine had already paid royalties to Chaliapin. What else could Chaliapin claim?

Gorky, just like any author around the world, received royalties for each new edition of his old works. The money from his numerous reprints was the source of his lavish lifestyle. As far as authorship is concerned, it was proven through documents that in the summer of 1916, in the Crimean town of Foros, Chaliapin had dictated his memoirs to a stenographer and Gorky had edited them, that is, done the usual job of an editor which does not confer upon him any legal rights whatsoever to co-authorship. Nonetheless, for every foreign edition of his memoirs, Chaliapin had punctiliously given Gorky half his royalties.

He wrote directly to Gorky, "If I cared about and worried about the financial aspect of this book, then it was so that you would receive several thousand dollars which, as I had presumed, would most likely not be unwelcome to you."

The dispute was heightened because the trip to Foros and co-authorship of the memoirs had been Chaliapin's idea as a pretext to take Gorky to the Crimea, saving him from the bad Petersburg weather and the bustle of the capital, both detrimental to his health. On April 14, 1916, Chaliapin, not knowing, of course, how events would unfold fourteen years later, wrote to his daughter Irina that Gorky

> feels in terrible health and must absolutely spend time in the warmth of the sun, but due to his irresponsibility and involvement in various social activities he will of course never do this. So I have decided to propose the following to him.
>
> I'm going to write a book of my reminiscences, and he will edit what I've written. We'll publish it in his journal . . .
>
> He liked this idea very much and decided to come with me to the Crimea.

For the friendly service extended him by Chaliapin, Gorky now repaid him with a stream of insults and the defense of his enemies. In a letter to Yagoda he called Chaliapin "a brute." Dovgalevsky introduced Gorky's letter to the Paris court. It would have been better had he not done so: Gorky looked absolutely foolish with his absurd arguments, and the Paris court awarded Chaliapin ten thousand rather than two million francs in recognizing the merits of his lawsuit. Gorky had suffered a cruel fiasco. At first, it looked like an impulsive act by someone who misunderstood the situation. But only at first glance. . .

The world was already accustomed to Gorky's unexpected actions, but this surpassed everything. The reason could only be the fear of uncovering circumstances that would have shown Gorky in a poor light and damaged his reputation. He did not fear "public opinion" in the West, and the émigrés even less; he was only interested in what Moscow would think of him and attempted to mitigate any undesirable consequences for him. Otherwise, there is no way to explain the extreme gesture of denouncing practically his last close friend, depriving himself of getting more money in the process and getting nothing in return.

Getting nothing? This is the mistake he made. Had not Gorky sold Chaliapin's memoirs to *Priboi*? There are serious reasons to believe this version. *Priboi*'s version differs from the one published in *Letopis'*, but corresponds to the typewritten original, one of which remained with Gorky, the other with Chaliapin; there was no third copy. Then how, if Chaliapin had not handed over the manuscript, did it end up with the Leningrad publisher?

There could be other reasons prompting Gorky's improper reaction to Chaliapin's suit.

He had to fear that, by denying help to the "Soviet government," he might be cut off from Moscow's generosity. After all, it would not have cost Stalin anything to close the pipeline through which thousands of gold rubles were delivered from Moscow to Sorrento.

There is yet another explanation: by going to court Chaliapin decisively blocked his friend's intention of returning him to Soviet Russia—Gorky had not concealed his plan and more than likely he had managed to convince Stalin of its reality. By attacking Chaliapin (and also assuring Stalin that only pressure from his wife and his closest circle made him decide), Gorky defended himself. He did not need to win at the "trial" in Paris but with Stalin.

And with Stalin he won. What was a loss to the Parisians compared to such a victory?

Gorky's relationship with the OGPU became more and more enthusiastic. Was this a real or feigned attitude? One would like to believe that the far-sightedness of his previous days had not completely abandoned him, that his ears had not ceased to distinguish false notes. But reality indicates otherwise. He attempted to adapt his enthusiasm to artistic forms too persistently—and unsuccessfully! He compensated for this artistic failure with the epistolary genre, which flowed more easily.

Many times he returned to the play *Somov and Others*, and each time became convinced that nothing would come of it. His pen resisted the false intention. At least preserving the ability to evaluate critically his own work, he announced his failure with bitterness and bewilderment. He wrote to Stalin that "the play about the saboteurs is not working." How could Stalin help him? Only with what he had at his disposal. He ordered that "OGPU materials" be sent to him, an order Yagoda willingly carried out. Gorky greedily read the falsified documents, assuming they were the real thing. In a letter to Stalin, he called the GPU

> a truly tireless and vigilant guardian of the working class and the Party. . . . I know that hatred has grown in you against the enemies and pride at the strength of the comrades.

As if fearing he would not be believed, he branded with ever greater passion the so-called traitors and saboteurs the Lubyanka had chosen for its victims: the extremely talented Kondratyev and Chayanov, the scrupulously honest Sukhanov (his recent friend) and many others. He never tired of calling them scoundrels, miscreants, blackguards, and the like, regretting only that the dictionary of synonyms was not larger. Even Stalin reigned him in, telling him "not to get too worked up about it" as these "scoundrels don't deserve it."

But Gorky knew no restraint. This passionate agent of influence assured the West:

Inside the country the most cunning enemies are organizing famine against us, the kulaks are terrorizing the collectivist peasants with murder, fires, and many other perfidies—everything that has outlived its time is against us, and this gives us the right to consider ourselves still in a state of civil war. Hence there follows a natural conclusion: if the enemy does not surrender, he will be destroyed.

Stalin closely followed the evolution of the former Stormy Petrel's views and promoted the hardening of this tendency in every way possible. His paranoia—not imaginary but genuine—and becoming more acute with every year was unquestionably accepted by Gorky. Gorky's concern for Yagoda's valuable life was discussed in the previous chapter. Now this fear spread to the general secretary, and all the more so: the life of this comrade was even dearer to Gorky. He signaled to Stalin in December 1931:

They are successfully hunting you. It must be assumed that their efforts are growing. And you, dear comrade, as I heard and saw, do not handle yourself very carefully . . . I am absolutely convinced that you do not have the right to conduct yourself so. Who will take your place if these scoundrels get you? Don't be angry, I have the right to worry and to advise. In general, all leaders of the Party and the country should be a little more concerned about protecting their lives. Everything is unfolding worrisomely and some riff-raff know how to wait for the right time to strike a deadly blow.

Not so long ago Gorky had taken nothing on faith, thinking on his own, and clearly expressing his opinions. Now he was a different person: he was hostile toward any information from the West, while any propaganda from the East was the ultimate truth. "The letters and newspapers from the Soviet Union," he assured Stalin in February 1932, "do an excellent job of lifting the contemptible political fog in which one lives here." He was becoming more and more red from one day to the next.

Only recently have the reminiscences (written and oral) surfaced of the only person who was equally in close contact at that time with both Gorky and Stalin and knew about their relationship better than anyone else. Only a small circle of specialists—at best—might know his name, and yet he was a key figure in Soviet journalism and Soviet literature at the end of the 1920s and early 1930s.

Ivan Gronsky became the editor-in-chief of *Izvestiia* in 1928 and also ran the literary journal *Novy Mir*, apparently enjoying Stalin's trust at the time. He addressed him informally and even had the right to call him by the familiar "Josef." He was allowed to attend all but the most secret sessions of the Politburo. Stalin also assigned him to exert a daily influence on Gorky when the latter was in Moscow. Therefore, Gronsky's stories, classified until the beginning of the 1990s and recreating hitherto unknown details of the relationship between Gorky and Stalin, can be considered firsthand evidence.

"Stalin," said Gronsky, "was an artist at playing up his friendship with Gorky, when in fact he did not trust him. It was a very subtle game. What is incredible is that Gorky, the writer and 'engineer of human souls,' thinks he understands human nature, but Gorky was never able to figure Stalin out."

One passage from Gronsky's memoirs is of special interest: "At one of the sessions, a very small one," Gronsky told employees of the Gorky Museum and Archive, "Stalin said, 'Gorky is a very ambitious person. This has to be taken into account. Gorky must be bound to the Party, using everything, including his ambition.' And Stalin attempted—successfully—to bind Gorky to the Party . . . But, at the same time, Stalin was afraid of Gorky." In another conversation, this time alone with Gronsky, Stalin told him, "Gorky influences the consciousness and minds of millions of people in our country and abroad. And we need to preserve . . . this asset. But Gorky is an artist, a person of moods and emotions, and these emotions can lead him astray . . . he can . . . cause great damage to the Party."

It was precisely this dual attitude that Gorky encountered on his third trip to Moscow from Sorrento in May 1931. In the center of Moscow, on Malaya Nikitskaya, the restored mansion of businessman Stepan Ryabushinsky (designed by the famous Russian architect Fyodor Shekhtel) was placed at his disposal, along with its superintendent, OGPU officer Ivan Koshenkov, and a staff of secret agent guards and servants. Stalin no longer had to find a place and reason to see Gorky: he could visit his "great friend" at any time, which he did, even at times with his wife Nadezhda Alliluyeva. Not a single "unauthorized" individual could get in without the special permission of Kriuchkov, the true boss of this "Kremlin asset."

From time to time Yagoda stopped by as well, though not as frequently as he would have liked. Recalling this, Gorky wrote to him after returning to Sorrento: "You came infrequently to Nikitskaya, but I enjoyed each visit very much. I am very 'used' to you. You have become one of my 'own,' and I have learned to value you. I really love people of your type. There are not many of them, incidentally."

What *type* of people was Gorky referring to here? His letters to Yagoda are generally filled with mysteries, but *this* one is probably the greatest of them all. Yagoda was not distinguished by any extraordinary human qualities, so what made him so special in the eyes of Gorky, who was quite capable of judging character? Why would Gorky place Yagoda among people of a special and rare type? Was it the strange combination of merciless cruelty, monstrous cunning, and political intrigue carried out with sincerity, sentimentality, affected hypochondria, and adroitly peddled lyricism, which impressed the impressionable Gorky? In answer to Gorky's lines about their meetings on Malaya Nikitskaya, the chief of the secret police exclaimed,

> How splendidly I have become attached to you. I was not aware of my own qualities, but if they existed, then I had forgotten them . . . How fast we live, and how brightly we burn. I've become weaker in my nerves and have grown very old. You will still write, yes? I embrace you strongly.

It was not so much Gorky Yagoda was attached to, as it was Timosha. The passion was still there, but he had to keep it in check, otherwise the result could be disastrous. He was able for a while to hide his personal interest from Stalin, who had ordered him to follow Gorky, by combining it with business: there is not the slightest doubt that Nadezhda Alekseevna (Timosha) carried out the OGPU's delicate assignments and was present at Gorky's side as one of his "own people" on behalf of the secret police.

Nonetheless, Yagoda's "lyricism," addressed to the charming young woman who was so strikingly different from the other Kremlin wives, was too obvious. One of the first to notice was his wife, Ida Leonidovna Averbakh, also from Nizhny Novgorod. Moreover, Ida was the niece of Yakov Sverdlov, meaning she was also related to Zinovy Peshkov: thus Gorky and Yagoda were already bound by family ties!

Ida's brother, Leopold, was also a well-known figure. As head of the notorious Russian Association of Proletarian Writers (RAPP), he excluded from literature everyone who did not share its ultra-left, sectarian views. He and Gorky had a common "mission": the leadership over literature—more precisely, over those who created it. Averbakh even traveled to Sorrento and made a good impression on Gorky.

Yagoda wanted to befriend the young Peshkovs and, at the same time, get rid of Max's irritating surveillance, which precluded any possibility of being alone with Timosha. Thus, he conceived and pulled off a tricky operation benefiting both himself and Max: he sent him beyond the Polar Circle on an expedition aboard a ship belonging to the Lubyanka, named *Gleb Bokii*. The main object of the trip was to visit the Arctic islands, including the island of Vaigach.

Max was given a childhood friend, Kostya Bleklov, as his traveling companion. "Max had surrendered himself to a carefree life," Bleklov later recalled, "where childhood dreams of virgin forests and adventures on an uninhabited island came true." The exotic nature of the expedition was obvious although, aside from admiring the ice floes and having his photograph taken while standing on them, there was not much for Max to do and yet, in thrall to the exotic, he was in no hurry to return to Moscow. The OGPU stooges, following their orders, did what they could to prolong the Arctic voyage, making it as enjoyable as possible.

Gorky, in the meantime, had completely withdrawn into his own affairs and was seemingly not at all interested in anyone's lyrical experiences. This is probably because Lipa guaranteed total peace, and all the other women had left him of their own accord. The correspondence with Mura, naturally, continued; it was dry and businesslike, in spite of the fact that every one of her letters ended with what had become a triviality: "I very, very tenderly embrace you, my beloved." The addressee knew the true price of words too well and was able to distinguish the pro-forma hugs and kisses from genuine hugs and true feelings. He understood—and suffered.

Andreeva had requested a transfer to Moscow. Having been left completely on her own in Berlin, she felt herself abandoned by everyone there and detached from public life. The People's Commissar of Foreign Trade, Anastas Mikoyan, had appointed her to manage the export of Russian handicrafts, which were in great demand in the West. To support her, Gorky had offered to buy up the drawings of the Palekh masters (sketches for the famous lacquered boxes produced in the village of Palekh) with his royalties and sell them for a high price in Europe, thereby turning a profit for the common good. But he did not want to meet with Andreeva—they called each other infrequently and exchanged fewer letters.

Varvara Tikhonova, meanwhile, scratched out a pitiful existence in Paris. The modest sums that Nina earned were not enough to support a family of four. Andrei had become seriously ill: tuberculosis was now added to his epilepsy, and there was nothing left for treatment—saving up whatever money she could, the mother sent him to the country. Varvara was forced to work as a salesclerk in a food stall belonging to the brother of her first husband, Fyodor Shaikevich. Instead of a salary, she was paid in leftover unsold products, which would keep until the following day. Nizhinskaya's latest venture, featuring Nina, had failed, and she worked as a secretary in a dark and damp garage. For failure to pay rent, the family was evicted from their apartment and grandmother, daughter, and granddaughter moved temporarily into an attic provided by their Parisian friends.

In desperation, Nina risked asking her mother to turn to Gorky for help, but was categorically turned down. It was impossible even to think of any help from Tikhonov—the money transfers from Moscow had long since dried up. As before, Gorky supported Tikhonov as best he could, recommending him to

Khalatov, head of *Gosizdat*, "as a very good bookkeeper." He gave the same reference to Peshkova's friend, Mikhail Nikolaev, stating that "people of this kind need to be utilized"—advice that Khalatov diligently followed.

Since there was no news from Varvara and Nina, Gorky could have assumed that everything was fine with them. It turned out that all the women in his life had found "quiet harbors" after the fierce storms they had been through. Not all the women, though—Natalia Grushko found herself in a precarious situation—without her family, without means for subsistence, without publications (her writings did not interest anyone in the slightest) and with two adolescent boys on her hands. Her second husband, the nephew of the great playwright Ostrovsky, had died, and soon after Potapenko passed away as well.

Grushko clutched at a straw and wrote to Gorky. We can find traces of these events in his letter to Khalatov: "I am overcome by letters from the author Potapenko's widow—a copy of her letter is attached. He did not leave behind one widow, it seems, but six or so. Doesn't it seem to you that some of her works . . . could be published?"

As in that distant incident with the milk, all the way back in 1919, he phrased his request in a purposefully disparaging way, thereby removing the possibility of suspecting him of any kind of personal compassion. Khalatov could scarcely have known what motives guided him, but he honored the request. One novel by Potapenko, now forgotten by everyone, was published, and Gorky's conscience was clear.

Besides the private dwelling in Moscow, Gorky was also given a personal residence outside the city. It was that same baronial estate in the village of Gorki outside Moscow where several years earlier the paralyzed Lenin had died. There was something mystical about these two destinies, so solidly and paradoxically linked to one another. However, it was not Fate, but Man that choreographed the drama. Stalin had picked out this wonderful dwelling for Gorky in a densely forested park outside Moscow, with inevitable reminders to the new occupant about the person who had died there. The version that Stalin had ended Lenin's life was a very popular one at the time and could not have escaped Gorky's attention. His private thoughts on these rumors remain a mystery . . .

As in any good drama, the plot had an extra intriguing element: up to 1917, the mansion had belonged to the widow of Gorky's former friend Savva Morozov; after his death she married Moscow's mayor, General Reinbot, and the estate was confiscated by the Bolsheviks. Thus, Gorky had settled in chambers stolen from the widow of a person who had rescued him financially numerous times, allowing him and Andreeva to live in the lap of luxury for several years.

Almost as soon as he moved into this residence from the humid and dusty city, Gorky began to feel worse. He was coughing up blood. The best Kremlin physicians were dispatched to look after the patient. Lev Levin, to whom Gorky became very close during his trips to Sorrento, attended to him around the clock. Levin served the OGPU as did, incidentally, everyone who worked in the Kremlin's healthcare system. Precisely because he was treating Gorky, Levin was especially close to Yagoda, regularly reporting to him on his patient's condition.

This time the outbreak of chronic illness did not last long, and Gorky was soon able to return to work. His interests were fully concentrated on literature—some writers he helped, others he cast aside, using a classification system known only to him, virtually deciding the fate of many of his fellow writers. He again acquired the longed-for right which he had used in troubled times—after reconciling with Lenin and up until the latest (and final!) falling-out with him.

Pilnyak was still not allowed to leave the country, but he did not appeal to Gorky for help. Gorky's animosity toward him became even greater. Pilnyak wrote to Stalin personally, bypassing the patriarch "middleman," and unexpectedly received permission. On the other hand, storm clouds were gathering over another *enfant terrible* of Soviet literature, Yevgeni Zamyatin. Gorky's intervention this time was successful: Stalin allowed Zamyatin to leave. He would soon end up in Paris.

Before Zamyatin's departure Anna Akhmatova came from Leningrad to bid him farewell. She subsequently told her close friends what he had told her in confidence: he had gone to say goodbye to Gorky, who responded rather strangely: "Go, go, but we'll see which of us will win—this one [he made a gesture depicting Stalin's moustache] or our Ivanoviches." If anyone else besides Gorky had made such an announcement, Zamyatin would have thought that he was being provoked.

In the private residence on Malaya Nikitskaya, Gorky arranged a meeting between Stalin and Sholokhov, trying to help the publication of the latest volume of *Quiet Flows the Don*. Sholokhov was being attacked at the time from different sides. A rumor was spreading that the manuscript of the first parts of the novel had been stolen from a dead White officer. The third part of the novel was about the Cossack uprising against the Soviets. Without even delving into the question of authorship, Sholokhov's interpretation was at odds with the official version and, moreover, there was the danger that the description of that uprising could be viewed as similar to the peasant rebellions against the continuing collectivization.

With Gorky's support, Sholokhov managed to convince Stalin that the Cossacks had by no means acted against Soviet power but against Trotsky's "exaggerations," as a result of which the Cossacks "rolled downhill into the camp of the counterrevolution—this is the essence of the tragedy of the people." The purely demagogic conclusion suited Stalin perfectly, and he allowed the book to be published.

Gorky racked up one more victory on this trip. His old acquaintance, the lawyer Pavel Malyantovich, a very well-known minister in the last cabinet of the Provisional Government, was a victim of repression. On May 10, 1931, he was sentenced to ten years in the camps, but the intervention of Gorky, Yekaterina Pavlovna, and others saved him from inevitable death at hard labor. The camp was replaced by three years' exile.

Writers immediately felt that Gorky's influence in publishing and in just helping them get by was enormous and much more effective than under Lenin. Can they be accused of seeking his support in critical moments? Even the egotistical and proud Boris Pasternak, who had forgotten how Gorky had reacted in the past to his request for travel abroad, decided to solicit his help again. He accurately described Gorky's relationship to him as "the spirit of a mysterious power from afar through a secretary" (from a letter to his wife dated May 28, 1931).

It was precisely through Kriuchkov that Gorky, without Pasternak's request, asked that the manuscript of his new prose work for publication abroad, with payment of royalties within a week. Pasternak joyfully accepted this manna from heaven, but the gift turned out to be a bluff. There was no publication. "No one had made him say anything," sadly commented Pasternak on the situation; nevertheless need drove him a second time to seek Gorky's patronage.

The complex circumstances of his personal life (divorce, living with his brother) left Pasternak without an apartment—in the Soviet Union, as is known, an apartment could only be "obtained," not bought or rented. "You have sufficient authority," a humiliated Pasternak wrote to Kriuchkov, "and you do not need to bother Aleksei Maksimovich. Help me in this, without turning to him. I want to speak with you."

Understanding that his letter would be reported anyway to the person he asked not be bothered, and knowing Gorky's relationship to him, Pasternak had to resort to self-abasement: ". . . all these years I have fought against empty and soulless formalism . . . in my poetry." He even promised Gorky, through Kriuchkov, to write a novel in which it would be "decisively revealed if the opinion as to whether I am foreign in spirit to our times is justified . . ." At such a high price Pasternak got his tiny two-room apartment, and Gorky could record this good deed on the plus side of his ledger.

He again found himself in that same situation, which—consciously or not—he had always wanted: to be in a position to influence authority and alleviate the suffering. He wanted to influence only for the good and only help worthy people. But good could only be what he himself considered it to be, and he alone decided who was worthy and who was not. The lesson taught him during the Petrograd years had not sunk in, and he still did not understand that for all his imaginary influence he had to pay tribute through subordination to the "general line of the Party." The people, who had not completely lost their worthiness and to whom he provided services in such fashion, look upon them not just with a feeling of gratitude but also of humiliation.

The difference was that the times had radically changed. The people who could have told him directly to his face what they thought about him were no longer around. Genuine thoughts could only be—at huge risk—entrusted to a carefully concealed diary or the closest of friends. This is why it could have honestly seemed to Gorky that he was truly loved and honored, and even many of those "mechanical citizens," who did not share the overall enthusiasm and anonymously expressed in their letters what they truly thought about him, were just the dregs of society deserving contempt. The "Damoclean sword of the Revolution" would surely fall on them.

A week before leaving for Italy, Gorky was paid a visit by Stalin and Voroshilov, who arrived already tipsy; at Gorky's place they imbibed even more. To visit someone "just for the sake of it" was not Stalin's habit—every visit had some ulterior motive. This time the motive was to create the reasons for facilitating Gorky's quicker return.

Stalin showed himself to be an expert on Gorky's work. Instead of a general expression of admiration, he asked his host to read "something" from his writings and immediately specified exactly what it was that interested him.

The leader's choice fell on a composition, forgotten by everyone, from the early Gorky, entitled "The Maiden and Death," a work belonging to an obscure genre (the author called it a "fairy tale"), remarkable for its revolutionary romanticism and heightened pathos. There was probably no special meaning behind this request other than Stalin having read this "poem" and remembering it. "The Maiden and Death," was banned by tsarist censorship back in 1892, and was published in *Novaya Zhizn'* in 1917, among his *Untimely Thoughts*, which Stalin read on a regular basis and which, he had promised Gorky in *Pravda* to cast him "into oblivion," since the revolution "is incapable of pitying and burying its corpses."

With tears in his eyes, the author read his poem through to the end and the inebriated Stalin, taking the book from Gorky's hands, wrote his summation on the final page of the "fairy tale": "This piece is stronger that Goethe's *Faust* (love conquers death)." Voroshilov was even more eloquent: "From myself I will say that I love M. Gorky as my own and as my class of writer who spiritually defined our movement forward."

What was hidden behind this almost comic incident? Was it just drunken horseplay, an attempt to tug at the heartstrings of an extremely sentimental writer, or was there a more concrete and official goal, in true Stalin tradition?

There is a version that seems convincing, based upon the evidence, that Stalin had secretly dreamed of having Gorky write a book about him. "Bring me Koba's [Stalin's nickname] biography or materials about it," Gorky telegraphed to Kriuchkov, and the latter replied that the materials had been sent by diplomatic pouch through Kursky, the Soviet ambassador to Rome. Artemi Khalatov wrote to Gorky about this a month later, in January 1932: "We have sent you materials for I[osif] V[issarionovich]. Write me if you need more materials and when you think you will give it to us."

Obviously verbal agreement about such a book already existed; Khalatov writes about it as a done deal and the question about whether Gorky was planning to write it is beside the point; now it is only a question of when. They could have come to an agreement on this only when Gorky was in Moscow, and Stalin, pretending that he did not know anything about his present, assiduously charmed Gorky—and charm was something Stalin knew how to do.

Let there be no doubt that Yagoda and the other "fellows" from his closest circle, especially his deputy "for culture," Yakov ("Yanya") Agranov, influenced Gorky in this matter as well. Gorky also tried very hard to honor his promise. A secret section in his archive preserves the rough drafts of the future biography of the leader: two crossed-out pages of a manuscript with the phrase "Josef Vissarionovich Dzhugashvili was born in the city of Gori [Georgia]" and brief information about the Caucasian landscape, most likely extracted from an encyclopedia rather than from his own recollections.

Beyond a doubt he made an honest effort, trying to put sentences together and mercilessly crossing out hapless passages. On this occasion the heart was stronger than the hand: Gorky could not squeeze anything more from himself.

At that time another highly mysterious incident took place involving another attempt to get Gorky to write a laudatory essay about Stalin. This time the initiative supposedly came not from the Kremlin but from overseas. New York publishers Ray Long and Richard R. Smith had made an offer to Mura to be the translator of a series of books (numbering almost fifty!) on the achievements of modern Russia. The plan was to publish a collection of articles on "Russia Today," which would also include Gorky's profile of Stalin and Stalin's own story of his work and the prospects of socialist construction in the USSR.

At the beginning of March 1932, the publisher not only signed the contract, but sent Gorky a check for $2,500 as an advance ($500 of which was earmarked for Mura as the translator). Upon submission of the manuscript, the advance would have been doubled and the authors were also guaranteed royalties of fifteen percent on sales! Long even visited Gorky in Sorrento to discuss their future cooperation. The incisive Gorky immediately saw in the unusual activity, not to mention the extreme generosity of a publisher nobody knew, more than just an ordinary desire to publish a profitable book. He wrote to Stalin, "[Long] has arrived specially from New York to Sorrento for negotiations about this venture. I think that for a small and personal matter this is too great an 'investment.' The financial conditions he offers are abnormal, even for major publishers in America." It was obvious that some political forces wanted the publication of the book: Gorky naïvely thought that "progressive" Americans, interested in recognizing the Soviet Union and befriending it, were behind it all.

Spiridonova maintains, and with good reason, that the entire escapade was not only initiated but even organized—and probably financed—by Moscow. The Presidents' Archive of the Russian Federation (the former Politburo archive) contains a remarkable document—the instructions ("wishes") that Long gave Gorky about what he should write about Stalin: "His modesty and motivations. His ability to select people for responsible posts. What his reward is for a job well done, and what the reprimand is for one poorly executed. Do not forget that his personality arouses great curiosity and that you are the only person capable of describing him to the people of America as he truly is."

It is unthinkable that Gorky could allow any publishing house to dictate the content of his future works to him, let alone get him to agree on what to write. Yet on this occasion Gorky not only accepted the conditions, but was even prepared to carry out his obligation in record time—one-and-a-half months, as he gleefully informed Kriuchkov in a telegram. Then an unexpected bottleneck occurred: after mulling it over, Stalin refused to participate in the project. According to the official version, the reason was his dissatisfaction at the premature advertisement of the book that the publisher had placed in the *New York Times*, and an even earlier announcement in the London *Evening Standard* that a book by Stalin was forthcoming, in which he "tells about his life, explains his relationship with Lenin and Trotsky, and talks openly about how the USSR relates to Great Britain, the U.S.A., and Japan." Stalin, apparently, was not preparing to write anything of the sort, and could have written only lies for all the issues as listed. The Politburo made a decision: "In view of Long's attempts to distort the character of the agreement with comrade Gorky . . . it is hereby resolved to decline the offer from Long and to suggest to comrade Gorky to motivate the refusal on the basis of the impossibility to fulfill the agreement within the specified period, in view of the comrades' busy schedules." Gorky willingly participated in the reply.

The real reason for the collapse of the meticulously planned action was something very different. Stalin had placed exaggerated hopes on Gorky becoming his biographer—how could he stop the work Gorky had begun with such ardor for some other nonsense? How could a newspaper announcement, which only attracted the attention of the future American reader to his persona, have affected him? Regardless of what Long had announced, Stalin would have written only what he pleased. It seems that his "dissatisfaction" was only a pretext for refusing to cooperate. It is highly probable that he had reliable information to the effect that the job was going badly and that the quality left much to be desired—in other words, Stalin was not getting the results he had expected.

In any event, it was he, not Gorky, who broke the contract (to Mura's extreme distress the unpaid check was returned to the publisher) and this effectively killed the plan for a book about Stalin by the great proletarian writer Maxim Gorky.

20.

The Dead Man Returns

Gorky decided to make his next trip to the Soviet Union a longer one. "To live outside the Soviet Union," he affirmed to Rolland in a letter dated February 20, 1932, "is becoming more and more difficult." But he immediately denied the feelings by making absurd accusations in the characteristic style of the Lubyanka:

> . . . the signs of moral enlightenment among half-corpses in their relationships to the Soviet Union are clear; I have just been informed that there are something like 7,000 emigrants who have expressed their desire to return to their homeland. But here's the question: why, for what purpose? To defend the freedom of their country or to unite the former wealthy classes in the struggle against the working class?

Did the simplest thought never occur to him, that maybe for normal people the *goal* might not be a struggle against anything at all, but merely to return to one's abandoned home?

The Moscow press continued to denounce the latest "enemies"—Gorky reacted in the same spirit, but in pure Gorky fashion. "With rage, but also with joy," he wrote to Artemi Khalatov, "I read . . . about the saboteurs. When will this rotten swine finally be slaughtered and destroyed? And the GPU truly deserves a medal—the best of them—comradely gratitude of the working class."

In praising the terror, he even found a theoretical basis to justify it: "Class hatred should be cultivated as an organic revulsion toward the enemy, as toward a creature of the lowest type. . . . I am absolutely convinced that the enemy is truly a creature of the lowest type, that it is degenerate, physically and 'morally.'" Insofar as he had expressed these same ideas not only in private letters, Gorky actually became a propagandist for the Stalinist regime, continuing to fulfill the functions of an agent of influence. The Stalinist regime established in the country was perceived by him (or he forced himself to perceive it, which is essentially the same thing) as the practical realization of his long-standing socialist views.

Of course, Gorky was not in on the secret scenario of the terror unleashed in the country; he could not know that Stalin decided who was an "enemy of the people" and why. Gorky took on trust what was happening, believing in general the documents of the Lubyanka, sent to him on Stalin's orders. Even such obvious fabrications by mediocre Lubyanka compilers, like confessions of the arrested about their meetings at the end of the 1920s with the former textile manufacturer Pavel Ryabushinsky, who had actually died in 1924, did not put him on his guard. Did he not notice, or did he pretend not to notice? The main thing is that he swallowed it hook, line, and sinker, precisely as Berberova had written: so as not to destroy a certain "edifice" he had constructed in his mind.

Gorky did not limit himself to general observations, but willingly attacked individuals. From Sorrento he would impart authoritative recommendations on how to act toward those he classified as "creatures of the lowest type." Into this group fell the relatively young scientist Aleksei Losev, one of only a few top-notch Russian philosophers not sent into exile aboard the "philosopher's boat." His freedom-loving ideas and attempt to interpret the role of Christianity in the history of culture were rejected by the Bolsheviks, and were not to Gorky's liking. He attacked the author in *Pravda* with a mocking and humiliating, if not downright criminal, article entitled "Concerning the Struggle against Nature," thereby condemning Losev to the hard labor hell of the Gulag.

> The manuscript copy of Professor Losev's illegal brochure, "Addendum to the Dialectics of Myth," says the very same thing that is printed in the daily press of politically active émigrés, traitors of the working people in the past and ready to betray it once again in the future. . . . If the professor were even the slightest bit a normal person, he would understand [what a scoundrel he is] and hang himself. . . This professor is clearly insane and obviously barely literate. . . What can these pitiful, vain, rotten little people do in a country where a young master—the working class—is operating with unbelievable success? . . . There is nothing for these people, who were too late to die but are already rotting and infecting the air with the stench of decomposition, to do in it.

However, Yekaterina Pavlovna, who still worked in the functioning Political Red Cross, had a different opinion of the professor and his work. She used all her old contacts in the OGPU to obtain the release of Losev, trampled and hastily sent to the grave by her husband. A year-and-a-half later the professor was freed and even had his sentence rescinded. Now this "insane, barely literate, and rotten little" professor is recognized as the creator of a scientific school and an outstanding Russian philosopher of the last century. During the Gorbachev period—in 1986—an elderly Losev received the highest official award: the State Prize of the USSR.

An unusual event preceded Gorky's arrival this time. According to recently declassified journals from Stalin's secretariat, the leader received Kriuchkov twice on March 27, 1932. Civil servants at that level did not generally have access to Stalin, but here an exception was made twice on the same day, clearly for some extraordinary reason. The first time Kriuchkov spent twenty minutes in Stalin's office, and the second time, in the evening, almost an hour-and-a-half. Moreover, on both occasions the general secretary and PePeKriu met in private!

This anomaly is easily explained—a magnificent gift was being prepared for Gorky's arrival. Stalin had disbanded the Russian Association of Proletarian Writers (RAPP), headed, as has already been mentioned, by Yagoda's cousin, Leopold Averbakh, in favor of a single Union of Soviet Writers. From the very beginning it had been conceived as a "ministry of literature" with all the bureaucratic structures and trappings, and the person to head it, naturally, could only be the patriarch himself, the living classic recognized by the world. This is what Stalin and Kriuchkov discussed.

Gorky usually left Sorrento in May, but this time he set off a month earlier. On the eve of his departure he received a letter from Maurice Thorez, proposing that Gorky quit the editorial board of the French magazine *Le Monde*, which, in the words of Thorez, takes a "supra-party" position that "hinders the ideological work of the French Communist Party among the intelligentsia." Earlier it had been precisely the "supra-party"—or more precisely "external party"—position that Gorky liked, as it allowed him to remain true to himself, not dependent upon any dogmas or binding him to any discipline.

Now his views had radically changed. He obediently fulfilled the requests of the French Communist leader, reporting to *Le Monde* that he was leaving the editorial board and its staff because the ideas defended by the journal "sharply contradict my views as a Bolshevik and Communist." Naturally, Gorky did not say on whose instructions he made this announcement. He also kept silent about when he had again become a Bolshevik, that is, a member of the Party bearing that name: from time to time he proclaimed himself to be a member although, close to the Party since 1905, he did not renew his membership in 1917 and had in fact dropped out.

Gorky left for Moscow with his entire family, including Lipa and Nightingale, constantly at his side, and Aleksei Tolstoy, who had spent the winter in Sorrento. It was assumed that Tolstoy would spend less time with Gorky but he overstayed his welcome, and not just because of the wonderful climate, comfortable quarters, and a sudden creative outburst.

Timosha had acquired yet another admirer: a husband "with experience" and the father of many children. Tolstoy, who suffered from obesity and shortness of breath, fell in love with the kind of ardor reserved for youth and could barely conceal his feelings. The situation at home was already tense enough without this additional complication. Max and Gorky had to have been shocked at Timosha's strange romance with the all-powerful chief of the Lubyanka, on whom both were dependent, each in his own way. At least Yagoda was far away in Moscow, but the new admirer lived right there in Sorrento, and they saw each other on a daily basis, like members of a single family.

Mura, as usual, took advantage of Gorky's trip to spend time leisurely in London: both Wells and Lockhart were waiting for her there. This did not prevent her from following Gorky's movements almost every day, both on his way to Moscow and in Moscow itself, or to regularly send business letters to her "dear friend," always ending with the traditional "hugs," sometimes "strong," sometimes "tender" and sometimes both at once. She did not even conceal her meetings with Wells, mentioning in passing that she had seen this one and that one, in addition to Wells, "who is preparing to write you."

Following a brief stay in Berlin, Gorky set off for his homeland. A special railway car was sent for him in the small border town of Negoreloe. Meeting him halfway was a large delegation led by Aleksandr Serafimovich, once close to Gorky's literary circle and at the time a very popular writer. Yagoda (who modestly signed as Genrikh Grigorievich) and Leopold Averbakh had sent a short telegram to the special car: "Greetings. We Kiss You" (a common expression among Russian men at that time). The familiarity of the telegram upgraded their relationship from semi-official to intimate and friendly.

Gorky became a star in Moscow, craved by those hungry for his patronage and support. Only one of the visitors to the mansion on Malaya Nikitskaya dropped out from the ranks. Not a he, but a she . . . Having written to Kriuchkov and received his consent, a shadow reappeared to Gorky—someone he had already managed "to bury" in the past: Olga Kaminskaya, his first love, and his first wife . . . She was no longer Kaminskaya but Olminskaya—Olga was an actress in the provinces, traveling from city to city, barely making ends meet: she had absolutely no acting talent and her life had not been a success.

Visitors to the Gorky Museum are aware of several details concerning this visit (from an entry by Margarita Volina).

> For Kaminskaya's arrival A. M. ordered that a room be prepared for her on the second floor. She arrived, but she did not go upstairs. He took her into his study where they talked for more than two hours. Kaminskaya left [she lived in Moscow in a communal apartment on a miserable pension]. Gorky locked the door. And when he came out, he was terribly sad. His granddaughters remained with him. Playing with the girls, Aleksei Maksimovich became distracted.
>
> Gorky was gloomy when Kaminskaya left. She returned home in profound despair.
>
> "Alesha thought that I had come to beg," she told her daughter, "and shouted at me: 'Olga Yulievna! Maybe you need money? I'll send you money!' I answered, 'No need to.' I looked at him and said, 'Your eyes are still the same . . . deep blue.'"

After having thought it over, though, Kaminskaya wrote to Gorky asking for help. Gorky ordered Kriuchkov to put the request through, and money followed shortly thereafter—at first from Gorky personally, then from the government. It was not much: Olga and her daughter were assigned a so-called "personal pension of local value." But at least it gave her something to live on. Gorky was not mentioned at all in the designation of the pension—someone who was not in the know would never have understood why that money (even though extremely modest, but a privilege nevertheless) was being awarded to these women. And Kaminskaya's connection to Gorky was completely erased; at most she is mentioned in the notes to "Story of a First Love."

Everything continued as in his previous trips: his admiration for the "grandiose successes" and curses for those who "harm and slander." Present at the May Day parade and then at a parade of athletes (both times, naturally, he stood next to Stalin, above Lenin's Mausoleum), Gorky was completely enraptured. The marchers, filling up Red Square, carried hundreds of portraits of the mustachioed Stalin in his modest military shirt.. Stalin kidded about these signs of worship and deification, as if excusing the weakness of people who needed idols. In an equally half-joking gesture, typical of him, he suddenly proposed to Gorky to become the people's commissar of enlightenment. Gorky begged off, claiming that he did not possess administrative qualities.

Gorky's own plans for himself were even more grandiose than merely being the director of schools and kindergartens. He had been nurturing the idea of creating a unique medical center, which would concentrate on prolonging human life and make man immortal in the future. This self-taught person without any formal education, but who was incredibly well read, did not think of it as a utopian fantasy at all—he was a science fanatic, believing in its boundless possibilities.

During his previous visit Gorky had held talks with Lev Fyodorov (Ivan Pavlov's closest colleague) and Aleksei Speransky, famous physicians and physiologists at the time, about creating an institute for the study of man, subsequently transformed in their conversations into something more mysterious and even downright sinister: the Institute of Experimental Medicine. Medicine that does not heal, but rather experiments or heals while experimenting on a sick patient. Gorky's draft for the creation of an "institute of broad biological study on healthy and sick persons" specified that its task is "to undertake all attempts for the specific introduction of a method of Marxist dialectics in biology and medicine."

The idea of carrying out a revolution not only in social life but also in physical life, to enter into a duel with nature, encroach upon its laws and overcome them by "force of reason" acquired by "a working class freed from oppression," became an *idée fixe* for Gorky. Now he had to sell his passion for it in informal meetings to those in power. Gorky could obtain anything since Stalin needed him and believed in him.

Not only Stalin, but also those in his closest circle now became habitués at the mansion on Malaya Nikitskaya. Regular visitors were Voroshilov, Kaganovich, Kirov, Ordzhonikidze, Zhdanov, Bubnov, and the top commanders of the Red Army, including Budyenny, who tried to forget how Gorky had publicly stung him about Isaak Babel, author of the cycle of short stories, *Red Cavalry*, which Budyenny disliked.

In confidential conversation it was not difficult for Gorky to get the leader and his "advisors" interested in his grandiose idea that promised—*them* first of all!—long life. Preparations were made for the creation of an "experimental center," unlike anything anywhere in the world, and all plans for future experiments were agreed to by Gorky, forcing him to dig deeply into the most complex issues of the different sciences. For him, though, this was mostly enjoyable.

Kriuchkov followed his every step. Only Max was a burden. Yagoda again decided to entertain Max by sending him to the north, to that same island of Vaigach, which had become a penal colony for the most serious political "criminals": the work conditions were so severe that even the Lubyanka sent only the hardiest and healthiest there. But Max was provided all comforts, while drinking in the Arctic exotica and feeling like a hero who could overcome incredible difficulties. "Under these circumstances," related Max's friend Konstantin Bleklov, who had accompanied him, "[he] felt like a fish in water.

There was not a trace of that moodiness and agitation that often overcame him in Moscow."

Why was he moody and troubled in Moscow? There were no visible reasons for it . . . He probably knew (no doubt he guessed) what was going on between his wife and Yagoda, or, with his characteristic insouciance, he did not pay much attention to their relationship, certain of his partner in life and proud of the fact that the monster whose very name frightened children regarded Timosha with such respectful tenderness. He could hardly have turned down a romantic journey, organized especially for him at such a high level and inaccessible to anyone else. And he probably did not want to . . .

At that time in the country the early rumblings could be felt announcing the coming storm, later called the Great Terror: rumors of secret show trials against "dissidents" were circulating not only in the Soviet Union, but around the world. Gorky, it has to be assumed, did not pay attention to those rumors—he had the most informed source in Genrikh Yagoda. Dissidence in literature especially attracted Gorky's attention.

The trial of the Siberian writers, who had emphatically rejected the Soviets and elected their idol, the "White" dictator of Siberia, Admiral Aleksandr Kolchak, who had been shot by the Bolsheviks, was then beginning to unfold. Among them was a very talented young poet, Pavel Vasilyev, whom Gorky would subject to merciless, annihilating criticism in one of his articles. Gorky's fury turned out to be disproportionate to the accusations which he publicly launched against Vasilyev. Now, as the documents of that secret trial have finally become known, it is easier to understand the sources of Gorky's anger: Yagoda could not have failed to acquaint his friend with the testimony of the accused during the investigation, as well as with the writings that had put them on trial.

One of the most important points of the indictment was the troglodytic anti-Semitism of all the accused who, as many like-minded individuals, identified Bolshevism with Jewry: at that time the persecution of Jews had not yet become part of Stalin's policy—on the contrary, the fight (to some degree for show) against anti-Semitism was viewed as an organic part of the struggle against the counterrevolution.

As far as Gorky was concerned, even the smallest hint of anti-Semitism always provoked his immediate and sharp reaction. It is easy to imagine what feelings he experienced, reading the verse of the accused Pavel Vasilyev:

> A Greenland whale, ruler of the ocean
> Once swallowed a greasy-haired Yid
> He began darting about here and there

> On the third day the ruler was exhausted
> But he could not digest the Yid
> And so, Russia—O, the comparison will be terrible
> Like the whale, you will die from indigestion.

Gorky changed his political positions and aesthetic orientations, his personal relationships, habits, and tastes numerous times, but in one thing at least he remained consistent and implacable: he despised anti-Semitism and branded anti-Semites with the most abusive words in his vocabulary.

He did more than just denounce and brand: the desire to help the persecuted had not disappeared. Yagoda listened to his requests: Julia Danzas, who had run into him in Solovki, was immediately freed and even managed to meet with him at Malaya Nikitskaya. Kriuchkov wanted to be present during their conversation, but the sly Gorky found an excuse to send him on some urgent errands, and so he had to send Aleksandr Tikhonov as a spy.

Everyone close to Gorky was viewed by the Lubyanka as potential employees, for it was deemed undesirable to allow anyone not already connected to the Lubyanka to see him. By OGPU standards Tikhonov was already seen as having committed some "sins," had already been in prison and experienced the omnipotence of the Soviet secret police. It was therefore not particularly difficult to influence him.

The fate of Julia Danzas continued to trouble Gorky—he had managed to get permission for her to visit her brother in Berlin, but she had failed to return. Before leaving, she again went to see Gorky. On parting, he whispered to her—for her information (more likely, for future generations): "Soviet literature is nothing more than the grimace of a galvanized corpse." Decades later this message of his reached the descendants: the notes of Julia Danzas, preserved by her family, were published in the mid-1990s.

Gorky was troubled to an even greater degree by the fate of the leaders of the opposition, Kamenev most of all, who had been expelled from political life. Kamenev was exiled to the town of Minusinsk in Siberia, where Lenin had once been sent by the tsarist authorities. The tragicomic analogy did not deter Stalin—on the contrary, it gave him special satisfaction. During his previous trips Gorky had obtained permission for Kamenev to do literary work: numerous contracts had been signed with him for writing, editing, and compiling guides, even creating a screenplay for a film. But Gorky had different ideas for Kamenev, and got permission for him to return to Moscow. Stalin "loved" Kamenev with a truly incandescent love, but he needed Gorky then and honored his request.

Gorky's health, in the meantime, remained critical. Again he began coughing up blood and again his temperature rose, forcing him to remain in bed and sharply limit his visitors. However, he insisted that the doctors not stop his trip to Amsterdam for a congress held by a group of European intellectuals (primarily Communists). The Soviet delegation was considered to be a trade union, headed by Nikolai Shvernik, leader of the Bolshevik "trade unions." Gorky was part of the delegation. Other delegates had just as "close" a relationship to the trade unions as Gorky: the standard-bearer and torch-bearer of world revolution, Karl Radek; Central Committee functionary Elena Stasova; one of Gorky's favorites, Professor Lev Fyodorov; and the elderly academician Abram Ioffe, an outstanding physicist, were part of the delegation and clearly for cosmetic purposes.

Already in Berlin, the delegates learned that Dutch authorities had refused them transit visas. In the first place, Radek would have been *persona non grata*, and the Western secret services would have had little difficulty in unmasking the agents masquerading as translators and reviewers. An attempt to transfer the congress to Paris did not succeed, either: the French authorities made the same decision as the Dutch. Gorky announced that he did not want to go to either Amsterdam or Paris. He could not have gone there anyway—in Berlin his health had deteriorated to such a degree that Mura quickly rushed there from London to take care of him. After spending several days in a sanatorium and barely recovered after an acute attack, Gorky hastened his return to Moscow.

Max, who had already returned from Vaigach, was waiting for him, and Gorky sent Romain Rolland the photographs he had brought back. In the accompanying letter he wrote, ". . . after I had visited Murmansk and Solovetsk islands in 1929, I returned here again, with the same joy and for an extended stay. They say that those who have seen the northern lights and the sun that never sets during the day or night over several months get used to the polar night very easily." Such were the impressions he brought back from Solovki.

Meanwhile, a grandiose show was being prepared in Moscow, with a single goal in mind: to bring Gorky back home once and for all and indissolubly link his name with that of Stalin. Three days after his return from Berlin the newspapers announced that the government had created a commission to celebrate his birthday.

Strictly speaking, no anniversary was planned for Gorky: he was born in March but the jubilee was set for September. The occasion was the fortieth anniversary of the publication of his first short story, "Makar Chudra," in a provincial newspaper. If such a "date" had not been conveniently found, Stalin would have come up with another.

On September 22, he summoned Kriuchkov to a meeting lasting almost five hours! With Stalin were the closest among his inner circle—Molotov, Kaganovich, Stalin's secretary Grigori Kanner—and many other lower level officials. They discussed plans for the celebrations, practically according them the status of national holiday. The reverence at the state level surrounding Gorky truly had no precedent in world history.

It began with a text discussed and adopted at a session of the Politburo on September 24, in which the Central Committee welcomed the "greatest revolutionary artist, a fighter against tsarism, against capitalism, for the international proletarian revolution, for the liberation of workers of all countries from the yoke of capitalism." It appears nothing had been omitted.

Immediately, the signal for the celebrations was given everywhere. Every day the newspapers reported on meetings, gatherings, conferences, and other mass activities devoted to the event, an occasion of great joy for the entire country. The Kremlin hand-picked miners, from the Donbass, who had requested that the Order of Lenin be conferred upon Gorky. The Party and the government decided not to refuse the miners their request and confirmed the decree, awarding the Order of Lenin to the "great proletarian writer and comrade Maxim Gorky for his literary services to the working class and to the workers of the Union of Soviet Socialist Republics."

Comrade Stalin was even more generous than the Donbass miners. The Order of Lenin was just the beginning. It was also decreed that a literary institute be founded in Moscow and named after Gorky to teach young talents—"in the first place . . . from among workers and peasants"—to become writers. Throughout the entire Soviet Union stipends, as well as a fund for "awarding the best literary works in the languages of the peoples of the USSR," were established in Gorky's name, and his name was conferred upon the best theater in the country, the Anton Chekhov Moscow Art Theater, celebrated by Chekhov's *The Seagull,* and featuring its emblem and not the emblem of the Stormy Petrel, on its historic curtain. Both founders of the theater, Stanislavsky and Nemirovich-Danchenko, were traveling abroad at the time. Not only was their opinion not asked, they were not even informed, and only learned of the joyous news through the press. The dumbfounded Stanislavsky reacted with a cold telegram: "The conferring of your name took place at the end of our friendship." Nemirovich sent an even colder note a month later.

The signal had been given—Gorky's name was momentarily turned into a way for those seeking to distinguish themselves by outdoing others in glorification. The Bolshoi Dramatic Theater in Leningrad, created in part Aleksandr Blok, was named after Gorky. Stipends and prizes in Gorky's name were established everywhere, even in schools "for students, who . . . will set examples in the study of native language and literature." Recalling that the young Alesha Peshkov had once worked in a bakery, the trade union of flour grinders resolved to build a rest home for bakers in Gorky's name in the Crimea and make available there "two cots for worker correspondents and working authors."

The main Moscow-Tver railway was also named after the person who now walked around in an embroidered skullcap typical for Central Asia (as he now depicted himself in photographs), having transformed himself from the "Stormy Petrel" into the "great proletarian writer." The same fate befell the main place where Muscovites liked to go to for a stroll: the Central Park of Culture and Rest simply became Gorky Park. Kronverksky Prospekt in Leningrad was renamed Gorky Prospekt. Over the course of a few days, streets in his name appeared in all cities of the country, large and small. Even in tiny villages, where there were no streets at all, some kind of "site" was immediately found which could be properly renamed, so as not to lag behind others, and show loyalty to the "Party line."

The most valuable gift of all came on September 25 when the main ceremony was held at the Bolshoi Theater. "The appearance of the stage of the Bolshoi Theater was extraordinary," *Pravda* told its readers. Its reporter had seen many meetings on that stage, but never had there been anything like this. "The leaders of the Party and government sat here and there with writers and poets." Stalin arrived with his advisors. Henri Barbusse appeared late. "They were met," announced the reporter, "with stormy applause, turning into an ovation. Barbusse shook Gorky's hand and sat at the table of the presidium."

The stream of rapturous glorification continued for several hours. "Teacher and brother!", Barbusse addressed Gorky, folding his hands in prayer. "Teacher, because he is a brother!" Stalin did not give a speech but his wish for "many years of life and work to the joy of all workers, and of fear to the enemies of the working class" was read aloud. The advisors addressed Gorky informally, in the Party manner, wishing him "many long years of elevating the masses in the struggle for the total victory of Communism." Of the fourteen people who signed this greeting, seven would be executed very soon thereafter, one would commit suicide, and one would die a mysterious death.

Foreign greetings, specially prepared by the Moscow emissaries, were made public. Without their initiative, who could have sent out greetings on the occasion of a date no one knew to observe, and in this case clearly unknown to anyone in the West? Had anyone really retained the cheerful memory of the day long ago when a tiny Gorky novella appeared in the Tiflis newspaper *Kavkaz*? The salutations from Romain Rolland, Stefan Zweig, Upton Sinclair, and

Bernard Shaw, among others, were met with stormy applause. Even *Le Monde*, after a slap in the face from Gorky, congratulated the celebrant.

Among the flood of greetings perhaps the most emotional one was signed by Yagoda, along with his wife and her brother Leopold Averbakh; a top OGPU figure, Semyon Firin; and three writers who were openly linked to the Lubyanka. Addressing "the dearest and the nicest," "the most beloved," and "the best writer of the new mankind," the authors promised that "each of us will always give his life for the good of the Party." They kept their promise: five of the seven who had signed this message were executed in less than five years.

When all the greetings had finally been read, Politburo member Pavel announced the main "gift of the country to its great son": henceforth Nizhny Novgorod would be renamed Gorky. The exhausted participants of the celebration rose from their chairs, put their hands together for the umpteenth time and hoarsely shouted "hurrah!"

Finally, the celebrant himself was given the floor. Cutting through the roar of ovations, he said, "I'm too old to be modest. . . . Is it possible that there could be such an honor anywhere else in the world? . . . It's impossible. The small temple of capitalist society has collapsed, its acoustics are bad and the dynamics are lousy."

He cried from habit and confessed, "I feel like teaching in my old age." He had always wanted to teach since his youth. Now such a right was officially being given to him, the absolutely free right to convince his fellow Soviet citizens why they need to love "our Party, its excellent strength, intelligent, unwavering, strength." With these words he ended his speech.

Not everyone, however, was blind, and not everyone bowed submissively to the official enthusiasm. Some only pretended to participate in the general enthusiasm, while others preferred to be quiet and hide on the sidelines, entrusting their thoughts to paper, an enormous risk in and of itself.

Mikhail Prishvin made an entry in his diary that reached his descendants only in the mid-1990s:

> Gorky's anniversary. Behind the backs of Tolstoy and Chekhov, taking advantage of their simplicity, walked this cunning impostor of Russian culture. And now, when everything with Russian truth and conscience is gone, when everyone is walking around in rags and you won't find a piece of sugar on a single kolkhoz, even on a holiday when small children will never see a roll or anything sweet, our father, gorging himself on Italian jams, enjoys another celebration of himself for everyone to see. It's as if Gorky is gradually casting off the barefoot humanitarian attire, the nut cracks open, and the very kernel of a Russian lout appears. . . . What will remain? A third-rate writer, an insignificant publicist, and an equally insignificant orator.

. The published part of the correspondence between Gorky and Prishvin takes up many pages. Gorky deservedly marveled at Prishvin's lyrical novellas and essays, devoted to the beauty of Russian nature. Prishvin, albeit less frequently, repaid him in kind, calling Gorky's works "a great event in Russian culture." His letters were always filled with deferential respect toward their addressee, and flattering references to Gorky, and more often than not with some kind of request that hardly anyone could have honored without Gorky's intervention. After the entry cited above in his diary, Prishvin would present to the "cunning impostor of Russian culture" his new books with the following inscriptions: "To Maxim Gorky from a pure heart" (in one book) and ". . . with brotherly love" (in another).

They were all lying to one another; they thought one thing, said and wrote something else, and did a third . . .

Mura was now more absent than present in his life. He called her to Moscow, but she answered with a mysterious phrase: ". . . for me to come there from here [London], a small 'psycho-technical' difficulty exists, which I will tell you about when I see you." Who knows what she told him, if she told him anything at all? The "psycho-technical" difficulty could be Wells, but it could also be something completely different: the open transformation of *persona non grata* into *persona gratissima* could create problems for the Lubyanka, which had still not worked out the corresponding legend, or the mechanism for issuing visas. Nevertheless, and again from London, Mura sent by mail assurances of her undying love: "I tenderly think of you uninterruptedly during this separation, my dear friend, and I really want to be with you." Did he believe these hackneyed words or had he already become reconciled to reality? We can only guess.

The time for his departure was nearing. Only a few doubted that this separation would be his last; there was nothing more left for him to do in Sorrento, or abroad in general. All ties with *that* world were permanently severed. Someone whose name in his own lifetime now adorned cities, steamships, institutes, theaters, schools, libraries, factories, kolkhozes, clubs, and thousands of streets and squares in his native country, could assume that now, finally, he possessed enough power to help influence the path along which that country would travel.

A mansion by the sea, one of the old Crimean summer estates in the small town of Tesseli near Cape Foros, was immediately restored for him. The climate here was very much like Sorrento, even better in some ways; for example, the absence of sudden winds and a rainy season, even briefly. From here he could better teach and guide in an effort to humanize the Soviet system.

He left, with Stalin's consent, to liberate Kamenev and return him to active work. Several days before his departure, the hard currency commission under the chairmanship of Politburo member Yan Rudzutak discussed, along with the question of exporting bread (from a country paralyzed by mass hunger!) and cellulose, the matter "concerning the additional issuance to OGIZ [General State Publishing House] of 10,000 rubles in hard currency for the payment of royalties to M. Gorky," with a positive decision, naturally. An agreement in principle for the creation of an institute of experimental medicine was also secured. Gorky could feel, with total justification, that he had achieved what he wanted.

The question of Stalin's biography remained open—the leader, apparently, understood that he could not expect anything from Gorky and gave it up as a lost cause. "Gorky will write the best book about Stalin," Isaak Babel, in Paris, wrote assuredly to Boris Suvarin (an historian, one of the founders of the French Communist Party, and who had broken off all ties with it). Babel was wrong.

Incidentally, did Stalin even want Gorky to write his biography? More precisely, did he want it all along or did he later reject this enticing idea? After all, in a biography created by an author, Gorky no less, there would inevitably be subjective judgments and assessments, making selections that, even though laudatory, would nonetheless be subjective. Details about domestic and daily life would be required—something Stalin could not tolerate. He would not have been able to proofread and edit Gorky between the lines. In his eyes "the best book" could turn out to be the worst.

Stalin had a backup plan and apparently, with this goal in mind, on October 7 he received Henri Barbusse, who spent twenty minutes in his Kremlin study, accompanied only by a translator. This was enough time to decide the matter in principle. The onus had been lifted from Gorky, but Stalin never forgave anyone for such offenses. It is possible that he too was glad to rid himself of Gorky's capricious authorship; but Stalin should have decided this—and not Gorky. The master was patient and knew how to wait things out, but in any event did not forgive the slight.

On the eve of his departure there was a little performance in two acts by the Soviet press called "historic."

The first act was given on October 16, 1932, when Stalin, Molotov, Voroshilov, Bukharin and Postyshev, under the strictest secrecy, appeared at Gorky's private residence in the city. They had come to meet with a group of carefully selected Communist writers, to sense their mood and give orders as to how they should all comport themselves during an upcoming session of the

Party leadership with a wider writer's circle, including non-Party-affiliated. Something took place at this meeting, which all participants (those who survived) kept silent about for decades—even a single mention of it could elicit a bullet in the Lubyanka's basement. Literary critic Korneli Zelinsky recalled the episode from the words of Aleksandr Fadeev in his memoirs, kept in deepest secrecy, and published many years after his death. Neither Fadeev nor Zelinsky could have made this up—they would have paid dearly for it. And there were other participants at the meeting still alive who could have refuted them.

According to Fadeev and recorded by Zelinsky, a slightly tipsy Bukharin sat next to Stalin. Suddenly Bukharin grabbed Stalin by the nose and said, "Well, tell them some lie about Lenin." Gorky was aghast and everyone else froze in horror. Stalin, however, was not offended and even more likely embarrassed. He pleaded ignorance: "Better you should do it, Nikolai. Tell Aleksei Maksimovich how you slandered me, about how I supposedly wanted to poison Lenin."

Why had that specific subject entered his head? Bukharin had not given him any reason whatsoever for such a choice. The need to find an "outlet" for this theme, which was like a thorn in his side, can only be clarified with a Freudian explanation.

Bukharin related how Stalin, back in 1923, suddenly reported at a session of the Politburo that Lenin had asked him to bring poison on a visit so that he, Lenin, could commit suicide. No one, according to Bukharin, believed Stalin. It was immediately suspected that he might be preparing an alibi for himself in the event of Lenin's poisoning. Stalin allowed Bukharin to finish before telling his side of the story: Lenin was suffering from his illness, which he learned was incurable, and had turned to Stalin because he was more trustworthy than anyone else and was considered the "cruelest member of the Party." "Stalin announced this with pride," was how Fadeev concluded his plausible story.

This episode had immense psychological importance—only now that everything has been revealed can we explain it. The issue is not even that Bukharin had signed his death sentence that evening—he had probably already done so much earlier. The eyewitness accounts of Fadeev and Zelinsky give us an insight into the kinds of thoughts constantly swirling inside Stalin's head, which "subjects" he mulled over and how it was all stored away for several years until fatally condemning to death some of the participants at that evening's performance.

The second act was played out ten days later: another large group of writers met at the dacha on Malaya Nikitskaya. The majority had no idea that they would be meeting not just with Gorky, but with Stalin himself. Gorky, Kriuchkov, and Yagoda had selected them with extreme care. It was assumed that the best of the best had been chosen, even though Pasternak, Akhmatova,

Bulgakov, Mandelstam, Pilnyak, and Platonov were not among them—these writers were not considered the best. Babel probably would have been included, but having finally obtained permission after a four-year interruption to go abroad, he was in Paris where he assured Boris Suvarin that, after Stalin, Gorky was the "second figure" in the Soviet Union. Nevertheless, among the graphomaniacs and hacks at this get-together were names somehow still connected to literature: Valentin Kataev, Vsevolod Ivanov, Mikhail Sholokhov, Samuil Marshak, Lidiya Seifulina, Yuri German and, of course, Lev Nikulin and Leopold Averbakh.

When everyone present at that meeting had passed way, the last one alive, Yevgeni Gabrilovich, shared his impressions of Stalin with historian Eduard Radzinsky:

> He was a small man in a dark green jacket of light thread, reeking of sweat and dirt. His thick black hair, falling onto his small forehead and pockmarked face, pale from constantly working in his study, remained in my memory. He was very animated like all short people and often laughed—he would burst out laughing under his moustache and there was something sly and Georgian in his face. But when he was quiet, his bushy brows, slanting upward, gave his face a severe and inflexible expression.

Stalin was accompanied at the meeting by the people he had brought with him ten days earlier, except that Bukharin had been replaced by Kaganovich. It was here that Stalin called writers "engineers of human souls"—this aphorism immediately received widespread dissemination and has been used countless times since then, even without citing its author. It was also here that the new slogan "socialist realism" was used and became reality. According to the most recent information, Stalin had personally announced this compulsory style for all such "engineers" at a session of a Central Committee commission to set up a congress of writers. Only "realism" in the service of "socialism," or more precisely, "the general line of the Party," was approved.

Gorky's long-held idea about the existence of two truths—a thought which he had strongly defended more than once—was therefore confirmed. Literally two weeks before this meeting he had haughtily lectured Vasily Grossman, referring to him in the third person:

> The author says, "I wrote the truth." He should have asked himself two questions: the first is which truth? The second is why? It's known that two truths exist and that in our world the base and dirty truth of the past quantitatively predominates. . . . Why does he write? Which truth will he affirm? Which truth does he wish should triumph?

The prevaricating pharisees were thus given the opportunity to poison any honest artist, accusing him of writing an untruth or even of writing the *wrong* truth, of not being in harmony with the "method of socialist realism."

Now, with new available evidence, it is clear that it was not Gorky who authored this concept, but that he accepted it and even sanctified it with his authority. Thus it is not at all difficult to see why the patent on this "classic" term was attributed to him. Stalin did not object.

Still unaware that Stalin had set aside unthinkable rewards for the loyal writers, some began begging for them then and there. To Leonid Leonov's morose hint that he did not yet have a dacha, Stalin replied immediately, "The dachas of Kamenev and Zinoviev are free, you can have one." At that moment these dachas had not been vacated, but Stalin knew that they would be and was not unwilling to inform his literary servants about it. He apparently did not consider his writers as being anything more than lackeys.

Since Bukharin was not there, he could not do anything unexpected. Someone else did that. This was Georgi Nikiforov, a mediocre writer, but an honest and decent person. A Party member since 1919, he was present from the beginning and, apparently, felt comfortable in the pseudorelaxed atmosphere that existed there. When one of the participants proposed a toast to comrade Stalin,

> Nikiforov, who was sitting across from him and having already profusely paid tribute to the hospitality of the host and to Stalin, who generously filled his neighbors' glasses with vodka and cognac, stood up and screamed for everyone to hear: "Enough! We have already toasted the health of comrade Stalin 47,000 times! I bet even he's sick of hearing it!"[*]
>
> Stalin also rose. He extended his hand across the table to Nikiforov and squeezed his fingers, looking at him ironically and unkindly. "Thank you, Nikiforov, you're right. Enough already!"

Stalin did not forget anything. His hand, which could only reach Nikiforov's fingers across the table, reached his temple seven years later: Nikiforov was shot in 1939.

On the eve of his departure from Moscow, Gorky found an excuse to send Stalin a loyal note so that the latter would not think that the two embarrassing moments that Gorky had witnessed would somehow influence his relationship with the leader. The note ended with these lines:

---

[*] This is again from Korneli Zelinsky, who this time was not repeating someone else's words, but what he had seen and heard for himself.

With a feeling of profound respect and strong sympathy I embrace you, dear comrade. Be healthy, take care of yourself. Sincere greetings to Nadezhda Sergeevna.

Dear Nadezhda Sergeevna had not long to live.

21.

A Feast in the Time of Plague

The question of the permanent return to Moscow had been decided, or so it seemed, but the discussions as to whether it meant breaking with Italy forever continued at Sorrento throughout the winter. Mura was very much involved, since a final move would undoubtedly spell the end of her extramarital union with Gorky. The end, in essence, had already come, and it was now burdensome to both to continue going about business as usual. It was strange, really: precisely in these truly fateful months, when the final stage of Gorky's life was being determined once and for all, Mura was often gone for long periods.

And yet, what was so strange about it? Wells, who was fed up with her meanderings and had no intention of sharing his woman with Gorky, was waiting for her in London. There was no love lost between Wells and Gorky, even though they continued, just in case, to express their former admiration for one another. Mura wanted to cut this knot as quickly as possible; there was nothing for her with Gorky anymore. She was going to be forty-two and it was time to take care of the second half of her life.

Her whole behavior—intelligent, precisely calculated, and opposed to any submission to authority, which was detestable to Gorky—testifies to the fact that she was consistently pushing him to make the final move to Moscow, a decision he should have made himself. "Write to me here about your plans," she wrote to him from London, emphasizing these words in boldface. Even though she left Gorky alone in these decisive months, she did not withhold words of love and loyalty in her letters while moving back and forth between England and Estonia, with stops in Berlin and Paris along the way: "There is a lot I want to tell you, but you already know everything, my beloved treasure."

He truly did know everything. There was also no future for Gorky in continuing their relationship. He understood this intellectually, but not emotionally. Even through the somewhat cloudy mirror of Mura's letters and without the benefit of seeing, unfortunately, Gorky's texts, one can understand how shaky he felt without her support, used as he was to always having her advice about everything and amazed at her ability to keep her head no matter what twists and turns life threw her, and make decisions rationally and quickly. An unbelievably weak and dependent person, he felt strong only when leaning on her. But life forced a sober assessment of the future. In spite of his still formidable energy, sublimated in organizational plans instead of creative activity, he felt incredibly tired and needed nothing more than peace, a safe harbor. He found it with Lipa. If he had understood that this was all he needed, his entire life could have turned out differently.

Only now, after his correspondence with Yagoda and many accompanying documents have become accessible, it is possible to understand the important role the chief of the Soviet secret police played in the formation of Gorky's views during these crucial years of his life and the strength with which he influenced him, turning Gorky not simply into a passionate propagandist for the Kremlin's policies, but also into a fiery troubadour of the escalating terror. Yagoda regularly sent Gorky secret Lubyanka documents about the discovery of the latest "conspiracies" and the unmasking of purported "terrorist acts," which Gorky accepted as the gospel truth. His tirades against the enemies, foreign spies and all kinds of saboteurs were more than just a tribute to flat propaganda tasks—he actually made himself believe in the truth of this myth or, rather, Yagoda (or Stalin through Yagoda) had manipulated him, and he simplemindedly believed.

He had barely returned to Sorrento when news arrived about the sudden death of Stalin's wife, Nadezhda Alliluyeva. Did Gorky know that this was a political suicide and, perhaps, political murder too? The foreign and émigré press were full of contradictory reports, making it difficult to draw a precise conclusion, but one thing was clear: there was no smoke without fire.

Gorky did not wish to get involved in the details, accepting the mysterious death of the young woman simply as fact and worthy of an expression of sympathy to the grieving husband. "I squeeze your hand tightly, dear friend and comrade," he telegraphed to Stalin, leaving it at that. However, several days later—Mura and Wells were in London—he decided to place a completely different spin on it, which should have signified the latest and, probably, the most important turn in his life. He sent Stalin a long letter.

> I am convinced that you, Josef Vissarionovich, do not need a verbal expression of my profound sympathy and feeling of respect toward you, a person of extreme masculinity and great spiritual strength. I will say, however, that I would really like

to live in Moscow during these times, which are undoubtedly very difficult for you. . . . Life here is dreary. I left Moscow unwillingly, with much greater strength than before. In the spring I will move once and for all to the Soviet Union and remain until the end of my days. This has been decided.

In fact, nothing had been decided at all, but now it may have been too late. Moscow had recorded his words.

Secret information prepared by the OGPU regarding the "counterrevolutionary group" of Ryutin and his comrades was delivered to Gorky. The official report about their imminent "exposure" appeared in the Soviet press only on January 3, 1933, but already by the end of November 1932 Gorky, in a letter to Yagoda, expressed his knowledge of the incident, which had so frightened Stalin:

> . . . I can't brag about my mood. My mood is anxious, in my dreams I see ugly faces and they are grunting "Ryutin, Ryutin." Some kind of diabolical and sour nightmare.

Martemyan Ryutin, who had never occupied any important posts in the Party hierarchy (for a short time he had been a candidate to membership in the Central Committee and headed one of the Moscow district committees), belonged to the ranks of "romantics of the revolution," still believing in old utopian illusions about the emancipation of the working class and the triumph of true democracy under the Soviets. He had not become, and did not want to become, a Party apparatchik led to the trough and making use of its gifts. Remaining a "Marxist-Leninist," and believing that Stalin had corrupted the sacred revolutionary ideals, Ryutin boldly accused him of corrupting and betraying the revolution.

His brilliant political pamphlets, widely known only at the end of the 1980s (the leaflet "To All Members of the Great Communist Party [Bolsheviks]: Read and pass along" and the brochure "Stalin and the Crisis of Proletarian Dictatorship," which became known as "Ryutin's platform"), were, in essence, the only attempt within the Party to speak out against Stalin's despotism without any demagogic camouflage. There is no evidence, however, that the authentic text of this passionate and argumentative Party journalism (Party, and not enemy!) by the "grunting" Ryutin had reached Gorky, who knew Ryutin's political position only from those files that Yagoda had selected for him, and he had no grounds to doubt the honesty and fairness of his dearly beloved Genrikh Grigorievich. There is, however, one circumstance casting doubt over the actual sincerity of his simplemindedness.

In letters to Stalin and his advisors, Gorky had given full expression to his enthusiasm for the great leader, his loyal advisors, and the policies they were enacting with an iron hand. Why these panegyrics were kept secret until the 1990s is truly incomprehensible. It would have seemed that Stalin should not only have published them, but made them mandatory in the school curriculum! Did his subtle and refined ear detect something immensely false in these excessive glorifications that betrayed something other than the words on the page?

It was both impossible and unreasonable to prevent Gorky from publishing his ebullient articles, since they had such a positive propaganda effect. One example is a description of Stalin in the article, "The Truth of Socialism":

> An excellently organized will, the penetrating mind of a great theoretician, the boldness of a talented master and the intuition of a true revolutionary who knows how to subtly delve into the complex qualities of people, cultivating the best of these qualities, and who mercilessly fights against those who stand in the way of good people to develop their best qualities, put him in Lenin's place.

The groveling inarticulate language betrays the absolute insincerity of this babbling enthusiasm. Stalin, who indeed possessed "the intuition of a true revolutionary," must have felt the mendacity of these raptures. Such drivel in private letters was already too much!

Here, for example, is how Gorky reacted in a letter to Stalin in regard to a plenum of the Central Committee about the results of the first Five-Year Plan and "work in the country" (the triumphant account of the destruction of the peasantry and the annihilation of millions of people through famine and deportation):

> I read your powerful and wise speech at the plenum with a feeling of the deepest satisfaction and amazement. I am absolutely sure that it will evoke a powerful echo among the world of workers everywhere. Its calm and strongly restrained form conceals such resounding thunder, as if you had compressed all the noise of construction of the past years into your words. I know that you do not need praise, but I think that I have the right to tell you the truth. You are a great person, a true leader, and the proletariat of the Soviet Union is fortunate that at its head is a second Ilyich by strength of logic, by inexhaustible energy. I strongly shake your hand, my dear, respected comrade.

Or here, from a letter to Lazar Kaganovich (the number two man in the Party hierarchy), written at the same time:

> . . . It has probably never happened in the world that political speeches reached such musical harmony and power as those at the plenum in 1933. If I were a composer, I would write an oratorio in the image of these speeches. Our

musicians are deaf, the devil flog them. How is it possible not to hear the new melodies in that grandiose creative noise which excites the entire world of the working people and causes shrieks of fear and hatred among its enemies? What symphonies can be created from the clash of the international with the national! In the summer I am going to speak with musicians about the need to write new music.

In the same letter to Stalin, Gorky offered to establish literary prizes for compositions that glorified the Party's policies, increase their amount and "to confer Stalin's name upon these prizes, for it originates with you." "I resolutely object," the leader quickly answered Gorky with characteristic petulance.

Why was this correspondence so classified? After all, it confirmed Gorky's boundless loyalty to Stalin, his total support of the general line and, if that were not enough, the exemplary modesty of the leader, beloved by everyone. In these letters not a single word had to be cut in accordance with the rules of Soviet censorship. Only Stalin detected the parodying nature of Gorky's exaltations.

As evident from the newly opened archives, a stream of anonymous opinions from Soviet citizens, shaken by the metamorphoses which had taken place with Gorky, as with other turncoats—Aleksei Tolstoy, for example—reached the secret police. Recently a denunciation made to Stalin and Yagoda by an "old Bolshevik" and director of the Literary Museum, Vladimir Bonch-Bruevich, who had received an anonymous letter in doggerel entitled "The Baron of Sorrento in three quatrains, has been discovered. The quatrains themselves are lost, gathering dust in an archive, but the commentary by Bonch-Bruevich is available: "The OGPU should be given the most energetic instructions to apprehend these scoundrels, who allow themselves to send such calumny through the mail against Aleksei Maksimovich" (to Stalin); "It would be very good to put the screws on these people" (to Yagoda).

Whether the screws were put on this nameless tattletale we do not know, but others were caught and punished: any criticism of Gorky began to be viewed as a counterrevolutionary crime—with all the negative consequences.

The growing flood of angry readers' letters, on the one hand, and the strengthening influence of the Lubyanka, on the other, compelled Gorky to prove that he was not sitting on the fence, that he didn't hold a grudge, that he was worthy of the trust and all the honors bestowed upon him. Only this can explain the letter in which he suddenly, after almost a year, reacted to Chaliapin's autobiography, *Man and Mask*, in which the author speaks bluntly about his recollections of life under the Bolshevik yoke.

This letter was probably not sent, otherwise it would have been found long ago in Chaliapin's archive, which carefully preserved everything connected with his great friend. In Gorky's own archive there is his rough draft with a strange note in his hand: "3 copies. One on cigarette paper." No reaction from Chaliapin has been found, apparently because there was none, the reason being because he never received this letter.

Judging by the "rough draft," the letter is so crude that it casts doubt that Gorky was the real author of these insane lines:

> It seems to me that you are lying, involuntarily, but because of your flabby nature, and because it is useful to the crooks who surround you that you lie and compromise yourself in every way. They force you shamelessly to lie by taking advantage of your greed for money, your low level of literacy and deep social ignorance. Why do they need this? They are your parasites, the lice that drink your blood.

The style leads us to ask: under whose direct or indirect dictation he wrote this? The notorious "three copies" were undoubtedly intended for those who were interested in this letter and whom Gorky dared not ignore. The hand of Yagoda (and naturally of Stalin!) lurking behind the curtain is very clear.

Incidentally, his sentimental Lubyanka friend constantly offered him his hand very openly. Hurrying to Moscow and fearing that Gorky might have reconsidered, Yagoda poured out his soul to him. On March 18, 1933, he wrote to Sorrento,

> Like a chained dog, I lie at the gates of the republic and tear the throats of anyone who raises a hand against the tranquility of the Union. The enemies have crawled out from under all the cracks, and the struggle has expanded like never before ... True, there is something worth living for and something to fight for. I am very tired, but my nerves are so tense that I don't notice the fatigue ... For the time being I am hanging on.

The scoundrel knew that these banalities on the meaning of life and the goal worth fighting for would bring tears to Gorky's eyes.

The final winter in Sorrento was filled with guests (perhaps they had heard that the hospitality on the banks of the Gulf of Naples was going to be shut down) and an atmosphere of impending separation from all that had been so dear to Gorky: he had spent the happiest years of his life in Germany, Marienbad, and here, most of all.

An especially large number of guests had come for New Year's: besides his family and regulars, there was the writer Vsevolod Ivanov (Gorky's favorite among all the "Serapion Brothers") with his wife Tamara (recently Isaak Babel's close friend and the mother of his son); the artist Vasily Yakovlev (who had studied drawing and painting with Timosha); Doctor Dmitri Burmin, who temporarily replaced the permanent physician Lev Levin and immediately provoked Gorky's extreme dislike; and Party historian Isaak Mints, with whom Gorky had worked on *A History of the Civil War*. Anxiety and sadness mixed with the traditional cheer, warmed by the jokes of the inexhaustible Max and the carefree laughter of the grandchildren. Although nothing final had yet been decided, the feeling that changes were at hand cast a pall on the holiday mood. Not only was the separation impending, but Gorky also admitted that another page of his life was turning, possibly the final one: apart from politics, there were still such important "things" as health and age.

Already preparing himself not just for a trip but for a move, Gorky was especially keen to events in Moscow and attempted to bind himself to them even more. Leaving Moscow, he let Kamenev know that he had to ask forgiveness from Stalin—in exchange, the leader promised to show mercy, meeting Gorky halfway. Kamenev obeyed and Stalin did not let him down.

In February 1933, Kamenev wrote a confessional letter from exile (unpublished to this day; I offer a brief excerpt):

> Dear comrade Stalin! I turn to you with an urgent personal request: help me liquidate this most stupid period of my life, which led me in the fifteenth year of the proletarian revolution to a complete break with the Party and the Soviet state. . . . I . . . had not thought that among us is there one person, who, like Lenin, is capable of becoming the focal point of an ideological, practical, and organizational leadership of the Party and state. History has shown that such a person was among us, and the Party without hesitation and upheaval found him and showed that it was you . . .

Stalin ordered that the letter be copied and sent to all Central Committee members and candidates for membership. Kamenev's repentance had satisfied him and, fulfilling Gorky's request, Kamenev was recalled from exile and appointed director of the "Academia" publishing house.

Such an act of benevolence had to come at a high price, but it does not appear that this price was all that burdensome for Gorky. Knowing that every word of his letter to Yagoda would be shown to Stalin, he did not fail even here to emphasize his enthusiasm for the leader's wisdom. "J. V. [Josef Vissarionovich] presented to the plenum and the world a powerful short speech," Gorky wrote to Yagoda, "an outstanding speech!"

Something greater than simply a need to compliment the leader was behind this heavy emphasis in letters to various people about his enthusiasm for Stalin's speech. Gorky triumphed from the fact that his long-held and innermost views on the "peasant question" in Russia were not only confirmed at the state level, but had now become part of life itself, making him a prophet. That is why his invocations to Stalin on this stage could hardly be considered cynically slavish. He genuinely wanted to bind himself to Stalin's wheel, hoping thereby to realize his messianic intentions. So much had already happened, why not something more as well?

That "something more" was the most grandiose of all: the All-Union Institute of Experimental Medicine (VIEM), which was being organized at full speed. The physicians, biologists, and physiologists assigned to work there had already begun conducting experiments on which so many hopes were placed. At least one remarkable incident attests to the strength and influence of these people who had promised to conquer old age and enjoyed the powerful support of Stalin and Gorky. When Molotov began offering Professor Speransky some advice at Gorky's house, Speransky sharply cut him off with words unthinkable coming from anyone else: "You still haven't learned how to run the government and already you're arguing about the human organism." Molotov fell silent . . .

Gorky himself had announced the most important task of this institute in a letter to Olga Skorokhodovaya, a young deaf, blind, and mute woman who had learned to read and write, which only reinforced his belief in the unlimited possibilities of science. This is what he wrote to her in the first days of 1933, when he sent his praise to Stalin:

> I think that the time will soon come when science will ask so-called normal people: do you want all illness, deformities, imperfections, premature decrepitude, and death of the human organism to be studied precisely and in detail? Such study cannot be achieved by experiments on dogs, rabbits, or guinea pigs. We need to experiment on humans themselves, we need to study the human organism, the processes of intercellular feeding, blood circulation, the chemistry of the nervous system and in general all processes of the human organism. Hundreds of human units will be required. This will be a true service to mankind and, of course, more important and useful than the destruction of tens of millions of healthy people for the sake of a comfortable life for an insignificant, mentally and morally degenerate class of predators and parasites.

It is now reliably known that Gorky's idea for the creation of the VIEM was influenced by English philosopher Bertrand Russell's book, *The Scientific Outlook* (1931). The British creator of "prognostication" could hardly have prognosticated how unexpectedly his ideas could be transformed. The insane thought of experimenting on "hundreds of human units," for the illusory sake of prolonging the life of selected oligarchs, does not square with the iconic image of Gorky the humanist. Yet the quoted letter, in which Gorky makes no attempt to hide his true thoughts, speaks for itself.

To the best of anyone's knowledge, VIEM did not engage in experiments on people: it had too many employees to keep such a secret, if it indeed existed. . . But constructive ideas do not just vanish: Gorky's friend Yagoda realized them in a different institution. The nightmarish laboratories of the NKVD (subsequently the KGB) conducted "experiments" with different types of poison on people condemned to death, and the Lubyanka was very success-ful in this activity—we will return to this later. Some of the greatest scientists affiliated with the work of the executioner's laboratory began their careers at VIEM.

Now, when a mass of previously unknown documents, mostly from Gorky's correspondence (and this is still only part of it!), have become rela-tively accessible, two basic themes clearly occupied the writer, preparing for his final return, more than all others: the creation of the VIEM and the search for innumerable enemies preparing to destroy the Soviet Union and kill its glorious leaders. Gorky even attempted to draw children into his "anti-saboteur" cam-paign. "The struggle against small saboteurs—weeds and rodents—has taught children how to fight against large, two-legged ones," he wrote. "It is worth-while to recall the achievement of the Pioneer, Pavel Morozov."

The myth about the fourteen-year-old adolescent from a distant Siberian village, "Pavlik" Morozov, who "exposed" his own father for hiding bread from requisition and was allegedly killed for this by his own grandfather and grandmother, was loudly propagandized in the Soviet press. The name of the glorious Pioneer who sent to prison almost his entire family, "outside his world outlook," grew into a legend and a symbol for encouraging and rewarding denunciations for sixty years.

Of course, Gorky could not have known what transpired much later on: "Pavlik" was not a Pioneer at all, but a local hooligan despised by the entire village who had taken revenge against his father for leaving his mother; in gen-eral, the story was concocted by reporters creating necessary myths for propa-ganda. Nonetheless, taking the model developed by the propagandists, Gorky could not have failed to realize that he was participating in the willful poisoning of "sons" against "fathers" for the sake of notorious "class interests" and propagating an atmosphere of total denunciation by everyone against everyone.

Why, with all that was going on in the Soviet Union, was Gorky so hooked on the "fight against enemies"? This consciously created hysteria suited him—the seeds of hatred had fallen on well-tilled soil. Was that because Yagoda had prepared it? Gorky wrote to him at the end of November 1932, on the occasion of the fifteenth anniversary of the Lubyanka:

> Dear Genrikh Grigorievich, You know how I relate to the work of the comrades [from the GPU], how highly I hold their heroism, amazing in its fearlessness, and also amazing in its modesty. The time is near when lying tongues of the enemies will turn numb and all that they have slandered will be forgotten, like the shadows of night are forgotten in the light of day. Then, in simple and honest language, history and its writers will recount the selfless service of our heroic proletariat concealed under the three letters GPU . . . I firmly shake the hands of all the comrades I personally know, and my heartfelt greetings to all GPU employees. . . .

The correspondence with Yagoda continued. Gorky's angry and incandescent bombast was in odd harmony with Yagoda's intimacy and lyricism, as if these two correspondents had switched places.

> . . . In about another 4 months* we will see each other if I will still be standing. The desire to see you is huge, and at times simply necessary. You do not know how lonely I am. . . . I embrace you strongly and kiss you. Just as ardently I kiss Lapochka,† do not forget to do this.

In another letter from the same period:

> You are not here, dear Aleksei Maksimovich, a whole four months . . . I am now practically alone . . . So far I'm managing. I sleep so little that I sometimes fall asleep at the table. But this is not that important. It's a pity that I have aged so much during this year. Come and I will tell you so much that we will have to spend more than one evening together . . . Come sooner! I really would like to see you. Apparently, you have decided that I do not exist, but you could have written at least one small note. . . . I strongly embrace and kiss you. Yours, G.

"G" was clearly being unfair. Gorky had written to him, without the lyrical asides, but with some sentimentality: "You have become one of my 'own' and I have learned to value you. I very much like people of your type. There are not many of them, by the way." Much more often, though, he wrote about the "mongrels of a terrorist stripe," who inevitably "will come to us from abroad" in order to bomb and shoot. He wrote that he believed in the "infinite baseness of mankind" and that the enemies of Soviet power evoke "cold fury" in him. About the victims of the falsified show trials, the materials of which

---

* Yagoda had counted the days to their meeting.
† Gorky's nickname for Lipa, overheard by Yagoda.

Yagoda obligingly sent him, Gorky responded in letters to his dear friend exactly as the latter wanted. ". . . There is revulsion toward these people, and fury and joy that they are destroyed at last," Gorky assured the country's number one executioner, not forgetting to express his admiration for his activity: "The indefatigability of your energy is amazing. You are carrying out a huge job."

Yagoda had no need whatsoever to heat up the anger already bubbling within Gorky; on the contrary, he had to appear to Gorky in contrast to the "mongrels" as a philanthropist worn out by the struggle, a lonely sufferer, profoundly unhappy from the burden which he had to take upon himself and his infinitely loyal friend. From a reading of their correspondence this entire game betrays itself at every line, every word—what kind of blindness could have deprived Gorky of the power to discern what had become so obvious?

In Moscow it was already understood that he was completely tamed, and this inevitably changed the attitudes toward him, although gradually, not right away. The Moscow literary bureaucrats, to whom every one of his words not all that long ago was the supreme truth and any directive was unquestioningly carried out, now made decisions on their own, indifferent to the hermit of Sorrento's opinions.

Gorky personally chose three new short stories by Babel ("Oil," "Dante Street," and "Froim Grach"), whom he held in high regard, for his almanac *Year XVI*. Nevertheless the editorial board, headed by Stalin's favorite, Aleksandr Fadeev, rejected them all, in defiance of Gorky's judgment: "The stories, in my opinion, are unsuccessful, and it would be better for Babel himself if we do not print them." Less than six months before, no one, under any circumstances, would have had the audacity to defy Gorky's opinion on purely literary matters.

But no matter how hard the censors tried to clean it up, two truly mocking fables by Nikolai Erdman and Vladimir Mass ("A Session on Laughter" and "The Law of Gravity"), for which their authors were arrested soon after, made it into the almanac. The almanac was one of Gorky's favorite offspring and therefore, to avoid darkening his arrival with an unpleasant surprise, the censorship was dropped. His return was more important than anyone's satirical barbs.

Before leaving Sorrento, Gorky received another letter from Romain Rolland in which the latter asked him to intercede on behalf of the French "anarcho-Trotskyist" of Russian origin, Viktor Serge, arrested in Moscow. Gorky had met the man back in 1919 in Petrograd but knew him then as Volodya Kibalchik, a relative of the famous Russian revolutionary hanged in 1881 for his participation in the murder of Tsar Aleksandr II. Volodya's father was a French Communist and had returned to France with his son following the October Revolution.

During Party discussions at the end of the 1920s, Serge always took Trotsky's side, which led to his arrest on more than one occasion. After the latest arrest, the French Left stood up for his defense. Rolland had no personal sympathy for him but believed, however, that Serge's arrest could hinder the creation of a single anti-fascist front and influence the attitude of the European intelligentsia toward the Soviet Union. Gorky promised Rolland to seek all the necessary information in Moscow, and nothing more.

The main question—to return for good or just for another summer—had seemingly been resolved. Again the word "seemingly" becomes necessary, because notwithstanding a concisely formed opinion, Gorky had not made a final decision, despite the assurances he had given Stalin. He was inclined toward remaining in Moscow permanently—but only inclined. And he had prepared himself for it by getting used to the idea. But the inevitable question was what to do with the huge archive he had amassed during these years.

Gorky's almost maniacal correspondence with hundreds of people (a genuine treasure trove for historians!) allowed him to gather an enormous quantity of letters to him and many rough drafts of his letters to others. His decisive turn toward the USSR, the enthusiastic attitude toward Stalin, the friendship with Yagoda, the appeals to mercilessly destroy the rapidly multiplying "enemies"—even all this did not allow him to hand over those individuals who throughout the years had turned to him in trust. Among his correspondents were many emigrants, the majority of whom had absolutely no intention of enlarging the Lubyanka's files with their own letters.

This concerned a solid group of Gorky's Soviet correspondents—politicians and statesmen, writers and theater people. Having made it abroad and liberated themselves temporarily from the vigilant eye of letter openers and readers, they took it upon themselves to share their thoughts and feelings with Gorky, who, in their opinion, was insufficiently informed. It is mostly the correspondence from 1922–1926, when in the minds of the majority Gorky was still an expatriate who nevertheless had an influence on the policies of the Soviet government that falls into this category.

According to the well-informed Nina Berberova, it was precisely those years spent under the same roof with Gorky that saw letters from many anti-Stalinists who then belonged to the highest echelons of Soviet power, including Bukharin and Rykov. There were also letters from Babel, Stanislavsky, Nemirovich-Danchenko, and Meyerhold, all of whom had revealed to Gorky something completely different from what they said aloud and wrote in the censored Soviet press.

For example, Nemirovich-Danchenko, who lived in San Remo as a half-émigré (he had unsuccessfully attempted to secure a long-term contract in Hollywood, which would have guaranteed him a life abroad) conducted a thick correspondence with Gorky, asking for advice on the same question that troubled the addressee: to return, or continue to wait? When he made the decision to return, he had no money for the trip or for repaying his debts, and Moscow did not particularly loosen its purse strings: Nemirovich was not Gorky. In March 1933 Nemirovich traveled from San Remo to Sorrento to seek Gorky's advice. Their relationship was complicated but Nemirovich went reluctantly all the same. He was going to stay in a hotel, but the generous Gorky put him up in his home. He advised him to return, promised to solicit on his behalf but, as in 1921, after having promised, he did nothing. This whole saga—there were a great many just like it or similar to it—was reflected in the correspondence, which could have given the proper authorities rich material for their highly valued work.

Max proposed to burn all these letters. It is easy to understand why: he did not want to betray his father; but he was afraid of keeping his father's secrets from the Lubyanka. Gorky rejected the idea. The possibility of entrusting the archive to Zinovy Peshkov was discussed, but this was also rejected: Max and Timosha, as well as Mura, who supposedly played no active role as an "interested party" in the discussion, were against it. It was assumed that the owner of the archive would have the opportunity to do as he pleased. Later . . . What this "later" meant everyone understood—including Gorky.

As far as Timosha and Max were concerned, they more likely rejected the idea of giving it to Zinovy, for other reasons. Moscow would *in fact* lose control in the broadest sense of the archive with him, and *in fact* it became inaccessible even to them; for this alone such an option was unacceptable. Gorky succumbed to the pressure but probably for other, purely personal, reasons. Zinovy had stopped coming to Sorrento for several years and had virtually broken all ties with his adoptive father.

Zinovy's Soviet biographer explains very unconvincingly that the French officer did not want to discredit the master of Soviet literature by his presence. The reason, it seems, lies elsewhere: Zinovy's disappearance occurred right after Gorky had made his splashy return to the USSR and started an especially virulent attack against Russian emigration.

The dark history of the suitcase with hundreds of letters and his accompanying comments, which Gorky had wanted to bring with him to Moscow, gave rise to many rumors, originating in a clearly implausible story from Berberova regarding its subsequent fate: we will return to this episode later. But one thing appears beyond doubt: part of the archive was entrusted to Mura and taken out of Sorrento in March 1933 when she visited the villa of Il Sorito for the final time.

Timosha and Max knew about the contents of this suitcase and Kriuchkov most likely knew too, meaning that Yagoda was informed as well. The secret, therefore, was not really a secret at all. But the originals of the letters were, of course, of much greater interest than the story of their content. Thus the hunt for them was unavoidable and in and of itself promised a dramatic, if not tragic, outcome. Moreover, a significant portion of the early correspondence remained in storage in a Germany rapidly turning to Nazism—in the vault of the Dresden Bank, the key to which in all likelihood also remained with Mura.

Kriuchkov had taken care of everything, having been in Sorrento in April and left for Moscow to prepare a worthy reception for Gorky. The last visitors to the house in Sorrento turned out to be Gorky's old favorite, the poet and future great translator of English poetry, Samuil Marshak; Isaak Babel, deeply respected by Gorky; and, of course, Lev Nikulin, who had successfully combined his talent as the "future Pierre Benoit" with the function of an active observer for the Lubyanka. Nikulin, who had rambled about from Italy to Paris bringing him, in his words, "incredible despair," rushed to accompany Gorky once he learned that Gorky had decided to return. "I am not a burdensome companion, and I will be a good guide for you in Istanbul," he convinced Timosha from Paris. The grandchildren, along with their Swiss governess and under the watchful eye of Nightingale, had left by train for Moscow a year earlier. Along with his servants and people accompanying him, Gorky embarked in Naples on the Soviet trade steamer *Jean Zhores,* with specially appointed, luxurious staterooms for its eminent passengers.

Mura met Gorky in Istanbul, where he spent only a few hours. There were no signs that the door would slam shut behind him, nothing was said, but everything indicated that he could be detained in Moscow for a long time. It seems that Mura had made a specific trip to say goodbye to him—could anyone guarantee that there would not be any obstacles to their future meetings?

His dream came true: he returned home in an aura of glory, deified in life and elevated to a pedestal. A mansion in Moscow, a mansion outside Moscow, a mansion in the Crimea, innumerable personal services and life "under Communism" awaited him: the state took over his maintenance completely. So why was he filled with anxiety, why was he sick at heart, why was the whole atmosphere of bidding farewell in the last piece of the free world for him—the port of Istanbul—shrouded in insurmountable melancholy?

All his previous arrivals had been met with festive rituals. This time the arrival was considered a return and perceived differently. Nevertheless the city of Odessa organized a triumphant meeting for him that erased his anxious thoughts. The same in Kiev. As always, enthusiastic crowds consisted of "organized," that is, specially prepared, "representatives of the workers." At the stopover station of Konotop, a delegation of Soviet writers, including his favorite, Vsevolod Ivanov, awaited him, as well as the detested graphomaniac and martinet Panferov, a favorite of Stalin's. The delegates accompanied him the rest of the way, bringing him up to date with the latest events on the literary front. From the abundant paradise of Sorrento, Gorky had immediately, while still on the train, entered an atmosphere of heated squabbles and intrigues.

A crowd of many thousands had gathered on a square before the Kiev station (then Bryansk). The prodigal son, *aka* the great proletarian writer, *aka* the best friend of Comrade Stalin, had returned home.

Immediately after arriving, Gorky went to work but not, unfortunately, at his writing table.

His first act was crowned with stunning success: at his insistence Professor Aleksei Zamkov, the husband of Vera Mukhina, the sculptress of "Factory Worker and Collective Farmer," which would soon adorn the Soviet pavilion at the World's Fair in Paris, was freed from exile. Zamkov was the creator of "gravidan," made from the urine of pregnant women, which supposedly had a "rejuvenating effect" and purportedly restored male potency. The idea was highly alluring to the decrepit Kremlin leaders. Gorky himself had asked Zamkov in 1929 for a course of treatment. The professor returned to Moscow after a three-year expulsion on May 15, and already on May 17 Gorky attended a session of the Politburo where it was resolved to create an Institute of Urogravidanotherapy under Zamkov's direction.

Gorky's latest bout of flu, with complications for the lungs, did not prevent him from carrying out the events he and Yagoda had concocted, the main one being a trip in August of one hundred twenty writers to the canal connecting the Baltic and White Seas. This was a construction project using only prisoners, both criminal and political. Although far from uncommon, this particular project was characterized by one thing: the Lubyanka not only did not conceal the fact that it was using slave labor but was even proud of it.

In the language of those years this was called "re-forging," that is, purposefully transforming the enemies of Soviet power into its friends with the help of encouraging labor: "shock" work resulted in premature liberation or a shortening of the sentence. This was still not quite the Gulag, but its decorative propaganda façade.

It is now known that from an economic point of view the canal was an absolutely useless construction project. This was already clear to the hydroelectric engineers and specialists back then, but for the benefit of propaganda it was built at a feverish tempo, moreover by hand: this was not a construction but a dig! It cost the lives of tens of thousands of prisoners, but that was not publicized. Yagoda had invited the eminent guest, personally selected by his dear friend, for the canal's inauguration.

Besides the obligatory Lev Nikulin, Vera Inber (Trotsky's cousin who, in defiance of logic, enjoyed the Lubyanka's complete trust), Aleksei Tolstoy and other signers of the "re-forging," writers with a decent reputation such as Mikhail Zoshchenko, Viktor Shklovsky, Vsevolod Ivanov, and many others also took the trip. One of the participants of this unparalleled excursion in a specially marked train, the writer Aleksandr Avdeenko, made an entry in his diary about this feast in the time of plague: "We eat and drink as much as we want and don't pay for anything. Smoked sausages. Cheeses. Caviar. Fruits. Chocolate. Wine. Cognac. And this in a year of famine!" Judging by the responses of everyone else, the trip to the prison camp was like a merry walk to a foundling hospital.

The event concluded with a meeting in a city outside Moscow, where the still enslaved *zeks* had come in order to continue their "shock work" at a different Gulag construction site: they had begun to dig a canal which would directly connect the Moscow River with the Volga. Gorky, present at the ceremony, broke down in tears and gave a speech.

"Poor devils," he exclaimed touchingly, "you don't know yourselves what you have done!" Calling his audience "human raw material," he explained to them that it "is immeasurably more difficult to work that than wood." He promised the *zeks* and the OGPU agents overseeing them that a book would be written about their "inspired work," and it was, only a few months later before it was realized.

The thirty-six participants of the trip, personally selected by Gorky, timidly agreed to become troubadours of the Gulag and issued under his editorial direction the fundamental work, the "Stalin Canal," in which Gorky called— for the umpteenth time—the person whose name adorned the canal a great theoretician and talented master. Stalin was already used to Gorky's praise. In the summer of 1933, he could read in *Pravda* and *Izvestiia* his latest oath of fealty: "The iron will of Joseph Stalin, the rudder of the Party, magnificently corrects any deviations from the true course and very quickly cures . . . the crew of the Party's vessel." Everyone knew which medicine was used to effect this cure. Gorky, it turned out, had approved the methods of Stalin's treatment.

We remind the reader once again of what is truly a fatal moment in the final coil of Gorky's fate. To this day there is a version, according to which Gorky's return in 1933 had already been determined in Sorrento and that

Gorky knew exactly that he would remain for the winter—and forever—in the Soviet Union. The information now available, however, turns this into a dubious claim. Berberova maintains that the "house in Sorrento was liquidated" and the belongings shipped to Moscow, meaning a line had been drawn across the past (more than eight years!). That is what happened in Petrograd when he had fled in 1921. But did the same happen in Sorrento?

As is clear from Kornei Chukovsky's diary, Aleksandr Tikhonov told him in the fall of 1933 that "Gorky *does not want* to leave for Sorrento." If he had returned for good, then such a question could be raised. More important is the testimony of Lev Nikulin. This person was very close to Gorky and knew much more than others who were no less close, and in a somewhat veiled form was able to say in his memoirs what others preferred to keep silent. "A. M. has decided not to return to Italy anymore," he stated, making it clear that another alternative existed. "The doctors are afraid that the abrupt change in climate and our severe winter can harm Gorky, but he already cannot leave Russia in the winter." "Already cannot" is a rather ambiguous expression: he can not because he himself had made such a decision, or he can not because he *can not?*

In 1993, the reminiscences of Professor Vyacheslav Ivanov were published. As mentioned in a previous chapter, he was the son of the writer Vsevolod Ivanov, a close friend of Gorky's. The professor's irreproachable memory and moral reputation rules out the possibility of error; according to the information of his well-informed father, he asserts that "in the autumn of 1933 . . . citing the opinion of doctors, Gorky was not allowed to go to Italy."

There is even more convincing, and more eloquent, evidence. Mura Budberg, who knew everything, was directly involved in the decision. In April 1933 she wrote to Gorky from London, answering his letter which we do not have: "So my dear friend, you are going so soon and you want to—for a long time? That is, right up until autumn?" How clear it all becomes! From what Gorky wrote to her and from what she knew herself, Mura understood that he was going to Moscow "for a long time," "right up until autumn." He had not made any other decision—otherwise he would have let Mura know.

In the middle of June Mura expressed a desire to come to Moscow and see Gorky for two or three days and "breath the air" (the "air of freedom," which she was deprived of in London), and she was just about to go from Estonia when she suddenly wavered. "When are you going to Italy?", she asked him on July 25. "If it is soon, then, perhaps, I can come see you—is it worth it? Then better I should meet you in Sorrento?" So much clearer! Only at the end of September did Mura finally understand which decision he had taken: "What I have been awaiting anxiously for four autumns now has happened, knowing that this would shake me up. My dear friend, what can I say to you about this?

I perfectly understand that you will remain in the Soviet Union . . . Before my eyes it is dark and terrible in my soul . . . What will you do with Sorito?" And a bit later, "Still, I don't understand a lot." If Gorky in May, and even later, until September, had a firm intention to stay, he would not have concealed this from Mura.

Here is one more eloquent line. In constant correspondence with Romain Rolland, and having informed him two days before his departure from Sorrento about his trip to Moscow, Gorky did not tell him that he was talking about his usual summer trip, but about a final return and that he now had a different address. Correctly interpreting his letter, Rolland sent to Gorky his latest letter (December 1933) and was surprised to have it returned, marked "addressee not found."

Finally, the evidence that his return had been planned in the fall is that Gorky retained the home he had rented in Sorrento, as well as numerous books and other items (it would have been easier to put them on a Soviet ship leaving from the port of Naples than to ship them later by rail through several countries). The servants continued to clean and maintain the huge house and garden in expectation of its master, whom they awaited, as always, toward September-October. They were kept waiting . . .

On orders of the Kremlin, Gorky exchanged Italy for the Crimea, he was already in Tesseli no later than the beginning of October. Only Lipa from his former circle was with him. "The quiet harbor" was now a daily reality. Correspondence continued to trickle down to him, but it was far from the previous torrent and, moreover, it first passed through Kriuchkov's control. Different authors sent their works. News came about the performance of his plays. Right after *Yegor Bulychev*, with which the Vakhtangov Theater had marked his anniversary the year before (Stalin showed up for the play, taking part in the ovations for Gorky), it now staged *Dostigayev*. A performance of the same play was staged in Leningrad in the theater bearing his name. The Moscow Art Theater rehearsed *Bulychev*.

Gorky showed up at the rehearsals and saw the episodes already prepared under supervision of the censor, Osif Antovsky. The latter saw that Gorky was satisfied and asked him, somewhat impudently, "Do you think it normal that Russian workers sing the 'Marseillaise'?" Gorky immediately agreed that, in fact, this did not belong anywhere. The foreign "Marseillaise" was replaced by the Russian "You fell a victim . . ." The number of performances of other Gorky plays in the country's theaters reached astronomical proportions.

Each bit of news was happier than the previous. But there was no escape from the ennui overtaking him. He felt alone and detached from a life quickly rushing past. In Italy he had not experienced similar feelings nor sensed *such* a detachment from life, although Sorrento was farther away from Moscow than the Crimea. For some reason the correspondence with Yagoda ceased. There was a sense that Gorky had been completely forgotten.

He assiduously reminded everyone about himself. In November he wrote to Lazar Kaganovich, head of the Moscow Party committee, demanding that churches be handed over to the capital's sculptors as workshops and for preserving "sculptural Leniniana." He categorically demanded that "the church of Nikola in Zvonarny Lane, the church on Gorky Street in Balashevsky Lane, the church on the corner of Varvarka and Old Square, on Solyanka, on Pyatnitskaya, in the Podkolokolny Lane, near the former Khitrov Market, be given to the Union of Sculptors."

Such demands went to the authorities who willingly carried them out, which in turn continued to feed Gorky's ambitious dreams and supported the illusion that he was still riding high.

Gorky must have been stunned by the sensational information from Stockholm: in 1933 the Nobel Prize for literature was awarded to Ivan Bunin! Along with Merezhkovsky and Kuprin, Gorky had been among the list of candidates for several years; Bunin entered this list much later, only in 1930. Like any writer who has found himself in such a position, Gorky had been counting on such an award, especially when another Nobel Prize laureate like Romain Rolland was strongly advocating for him. If Gorky had simply not been awarded the prize, it would have been a lesser blow than a prize conferred upon a former friend. This was a writer whose talent, even detached from his native land and from the environment of his language and his readers, grew stronger with every year and won him recognition around the world.

Had the decrepit Stormy Petrel not hurried back to Moscow and not exalted the Bolshevik terror, but told the world at least the slightest truth about it, then the Nobel committee would hardly have ignored him. Several well informed Swedes (the Soviet ambassador Aleksandra Kollontai reported this to Moscow) maintained that such a decision was highly probable, but the academics had made a different choice. The poor Kollontai, crushed by fear, afraid that she would be thrashed for lack of vigilance, assured her bosses that the decision of the Nobel committee was "only an expression of the stupidity and enmity toward us." Oh no, this was not a question of politics, but a question of morality, without which literature does not exist in general.

As there was now no turning back, he had to extract as much benefit as possible from the situation in which he had placed himself. This was not a primitive, selfish benefit—he personally had no needs—but a global benefit for his fatherland. Hurried preparations were underway for the opening of the next—seventeenth—Party congress. Gorky, preparing to promote the reconciliation of Stalin with his recent opponents, had placed great hopes on it. What could he have done from Tesseli?

Mura arrived in Tesseli on December 10, having obtained a visa (which she had asked Kriuchkov for), apparently, in Rome—although on the eighth she was still in Vienna, where she had spent several weeks "on business" and from where she sent Gorky a telegram (still expecting "the possibility from one day to the next"). Incidentally, who knows where and how she obtained it? It is very difficult to follow Mura's mysterious movements from one European capital to another from the available materials. Maybe only the intelligence services of the countries following her knew for sure.

It does not appear that this lightning-quick visit brought Gorky any joy. "My dear friend," Mura wrote to him from London, celebrating Christmas with Wells and expecting an equally happy New Year's celebration, "how many different and vivid experiences these four short days* have brought me, and I am glad that I was with you. Everything has become very simple and good."

Maybe for her it had, but had it become "simple and good" for Gorky too? The ephemeral stopover by the woman with whom he had been inseparably linked by the memory of happy years in Sorrento only further heightened the feeling of isolation in a gilded, comfortable cage.

After ringing in the New Year in Tesseli, Gorky immediately left for Moscow.

---

* Mura had already hurried back by December 14.

22.

Hunting Season

On January 26, 1934, Gorky joined the guests at the opening of the Seventeenth Party Congress. His dreams, it seemed, were about to come true. Kamenev, restored to the Party (like Zinoviev), was given the opportunity to make a confessional speech at the congress, allowing him to return to active work. The Ivanoviches even had the honor of being elected candidates to membership in the Central Committee. Of course, this was nothing compared to the position they had formerly held in the Party, but nevertheless it testified to their presence in political life.

Immediately after the congress, Bukharin was appointed editor-in-chief of *Izvestiia*. Rykov remained a member of the government as People's Commissar of Communications. A bit later (in April) Zinoviev joined the main ideological organ of the Party, the journal *Bolshevik*. Kamenev, without losing the Academia publishing house, was to become the director of another organization created by Gorky, the Institute of World Literature, which, naturally, would be named after him.

None of this was remotely comparable to their former influence, which spoke more about the "employability" of disgraced leaders than their full-fledged return to the ranks, but Gorky, highly capable of mitigating Stalin's severity, was energized by his new strength: it meant he was correct in choosing his cause of action; it meant he had a beneficial effect on Stalin, which would be good for the entire country!

The material available today allows us to confirm the long-held version (originating with Bukharin) that Gorky had organized a meeting at his house between Stalin and Kamenev. It probably took place shortly before the congress, sometime in the middle of January, explaining why Gorky had hurried back to Moscow from Tesseli. Kamenev supposedly professed his love for Stalin, charmed him with his candor and promised not to oppose him in anything. If this is true, then Gorky alone could have made their reconciliation possible.

This and other similar facts, the whole atmosphere of the country immediately after the Seventeenth Congress, held out the hope that after cruel years of struggle against the opposition, the peasantry, the "saboteurs," and other "enemies of the people," a period of liberalization had finally begun. Stalin, it seems, tried to instill such hopes, and Gorky had encouraged him to take this step. All the victims he had denounced in order to gain some influence on the leader now seemed justified.

Strictly speaking, it is not very clear why the liberal Party members, let alone the Russian intellectuals, could believe that an era of liberalization had started (or was about to). Isolated acts of mercy stood in stark contrast to the new wave of mass arrests begun the year before and increased in the new year, affecting very prominent individuals in scientific and literary circles—the greatest historians, philologists, and musicologists, including many academicians and members of the Academy of Sciences, as well as professors from Moscow, Leningrad, and other Russian universities.

In the long list of those arrested (the majority of whom were subsequently shot) were several brilliant Slavic scholars of worldwide fame: Vladimir Peretts, Mikhail Speransky, Nikolai Durnovo, Afanasy Selishchev, and Grigori Ilyinsky—all members of the Academy of Sciences.

Rumors were spreading very quickly. Not only did this reality not elicit a reaction from Gorky, it barely registered with him. It seems that he selected only what strengthened, not destroyed, his hopes. Moreover, the facts allowing him to make an optimistic prognosis also had their place.

For example, an inconspicuous, fundamentally important change in the Organizational Committee, preparing for the congress of writers, had taken place. In mid-1933, following Gorky's final return, Stalin removed Gronsky from the post of head of the committee, turning the "patriarch" from an honorary chairman into a real chairman, making him an acting figure instead of a decorative one.

The removal of a gloomy dogmatic figure from the top ranks had to be a clue to the coming changes, but this was very deceptive and misleading evidence. The real tone in the Organizational Committee was set by Party apparatchik Aleksei Stetsky, Party publicist Vladimir Stavsky, and, most of all, Aleksandr Fadeev, an author of some talent who was inordinately ambitious but lacked the talent for leadership. Gorky did not immediately recognize the real intentions of this aggressive troika, or those of the graphomaniacs swarming around them aspiring to high office. But he expressed his attitude to the writers' intrigues by systematically failing to show up at sessions of the Organizational Committee.

There were no obvious signs of his disgrace. His directives were still listened to and his projects examined with the same respectful attention; and new articles, incredibly similar to one another and not containing a single, slightly original or unexpected thought were published; but the inner ear of the writer could not have failed to notice that something had changed, that something was happening.

That "something" did not relate to him personally, but reflected the invisible secret battle going on within the highest leadership. Gorky's true sympathies were known to Stalin just as he knew that his former opponents who, at Gorky's insistence, had supposedly confessed and were now employed, would not be loyal to him anyway.

Right after the end of the Party congress, the results of which Gorky could have considered as his victory, a trial balloon was released to temper his euphoria. The untalented "Cossack" writer, Aleksandr Serafimovich, who was bitterly jealous of Gorky and clearly angled for his position as "patriarch," published a work in praise of Fyodor Panferov, one of the writers who had burst to power, and whom Stalin was favorable to but Gorky hated. Serafimovich especially glorified Panferov's "manly strength," knowing full well that any praise of "manliness" would drive Gorky mad.

Gorky responded sharply to Serafimovich, addressing his accusations not so much to him as to Panferov. The graphomaniac who—in the words of Gorky—"was in too much of a hurry to achieve glory and the rank of proto-pope in literature" joined a group attempting to squeeze the master out of the effective leadership of the future union of writers. Gorky called Panferov's "manly strength" the "instinct of a minor proprietor, expressed . . . in forms of zoological savagery."

What followed was a "response to the response." In a rambling tone, Serafimovich rejected all of Gorky's arguments, reminding him that "our goal . . . is to show . . . the great victory of the deeds of Lenin and Stalin."

When four years earlier provincial Siberian newspapers spoke disrespectfully about Gorky over what was, in essence, a trivial matter, Stalin proposed that the Central Committee adopt a special decree and severely punish the "guilty," equating their statement to an anti-Party action. On this occasion there was no Kremlin reaction at all—Gorky was given to understand that his untouchable status had expired.

In Italy, he occupied the position of master vis-à-vis the Kremlin; in the Soviet Union, he was its slave. Stalin no longer feared losing the Stormy Petrel. Lenin had unsuccessfully attempted to tame him through persuasion; Stalin accomplished the same without any special effort, through good deeds and flattery. The main goal—getting him to return—had been reached. But Gorky nonetheless remained Gorky, and in his new capacity he was still more dangerous than useful, and as obstinate as ever.

The Lubyanka agents meticulously reported Gorky's utterances, which did not correspond at all to Stalin's moods and desires, and his meetings and conversations with leaders of the former opposition. Bukharin was a regular at Malaya Nikitskaya, often spending long hours there and leaving only when Stalin was expected to show up.

Bukharin was more than just friends with Gorky—they teased each other and joked around like heroes of Russian folk tales, exchanging jabs and acting out comic scenes for their own amusement. Stalin understood what such "informal" relations could mean in the future.

A more direct reason for the change in attitude toward Gorky (more precisely, for the first step in the change) was, apparently, the position he occupied in connection with the dissolution of RAPP and the replacement of Averbakh's group with that of Fadeev-Panferov, much closer to Stalin in origin, mentality, national "attitude," and many other factors. But the true reason went deeper than that.

Averbakh was essentially Yagoda's alter ego. However, Yagoda—and here is the greatest riddle that historians are only beginning to solve—in the internal Party struggle (at least at the end of the 1920s and beginning of the 1930s) did not support Stalin but the "right-wingers": Bukharin, Rykov, Aleksei, and Tomsky—people who were much closer to Gorky than to "the great continuer of Lenin's work." Back in 1929, Yagoda was among those who spoke out against enforced collectivization. Most likely it was Yagoda who, resisting the executions of Communists (under Lenin such a measure was still considered unacceptable), saved Ryutin from execution in 1932—Ryutin would otherwise have been long gone because of his passionate anti-Stalinist pamphlet.

In continuing to publish glorifications to Stalin, Gorky by no means advertised his true sympathies. In January 1932, in letters to Stalin and Kaganovich, he expressed admiration for the "general line of the Party." He wrote to Rykov who, like Tomsky, had delivered an allegedly confessional speech at the plenum of the Central Committee: "The genuine . . . courage [of your] speeches, their clear wisdom and feeling of personal worth . . . with which each word is filled, makes them the most valuable documents . . ."

He added, "[I find myself] in constant alarm for each of you, people whom I sincerely respect, love and value as the best revolutionaries who ever were, true and happy creators of a new world . . . I firmly clasp your hand, dear Aleksei Ivanovich."

When Gorky expressed his sincere feelings, his language changed completely and the words and corresponding intonation followed appropriately—it suffices to compare the letter to Rykov with the letters written simultaneously to Stalin and Kaganovich. Yet most striking of all was this; Gorky did not send his letter directly to Rykov but to Kriuchkov, accompanied by a very eloquent note: "Pyotr Petrovich, please deliver the enclosed letter personally to Aleksei Ivanovich. I append a copy of the letter, but I strongly request that you do not show it to anyone."

Why had Gorky decided to acquaint Kriuchkov with a copy of his letter? Did he not know where Kriuchkov worked and which organization paid his salary? Then for whom was this letter supposed to remain a secret, and for whom the opposite? There was no one closer to Kriuchkov than Yagoda; he would have shown him Gorky's letter even without the author's request. "Do not show it to anyone" could only have referred to Stalin.

Thus it turns out that Yagoda and Kriuchkov were in the camp of the "right-wingers," with Averbakh too—without Yagoda he would not have existed one day. In defending Averbakh, Gorky was defending *the anti-Stalinists!*

Naturally, he knew the price Averbakh and all former RAPP members had to pay, as evidenced by their revolutionary phraseology and the barracks discipline they had implanted in literature. But he could control (or comforted himself with the illusion that he could) the Averbakh faction. The horde of self-assured hacks, who had replaced them with Stalin's help, was completely alien to him and did what they wanted in Gorky's name: no matter what they decided, everything supposedly emanated from him, as chairman of the organizational committee.

At the very end of April, approximately the twenty-seventh or twenty-eighth, Max left for Leningrad. Marfa and Darya, together with Yekaterina Pavlovna, were sent to Tesseli just before, but Gorky, who should have traveled with them, for some reason stayed back in Moscow: "I decided to linger somewhat," Timosha flatly reports him saying, in her dictated memoirs, "and besides I had urgent business." What kind of business was this? To judge by the published *Chronicle of Gorky's Life*, there is no mention of anything urgent, let alone serious, that would have prevented him from going to the Crimea.

But the next sentence is more intriguing: "Max and I remained with him." With him—that means in Moscow. But it is now known with absolute certainty that, having seen his mother and daughters off, Max did *not* remain in Moscow but left for Leningrad.

Why did he go there? Why did Timosha remain silent about this in the approved-for-publication version of her reminiscences? According to Valentina Khodasevich, who was living in Leningrad, Max immediately called her from a hotel immediately upon arrival, saying that he had "come for several days. . . . Soon after he [again] called and said that he had to leave immediately [!] for Moscow—he was called away on business. He promised to return to Leningrad in the next few days."

Apart from this, there is absolutely no information as to why he went to Leningrad in the first place—now it appears that even his hasty return is also mysterious. Who "called" him that he dared not disobey? What was the reason and cause for the call? Why did he have to return "immediately"?

When Max became ill, and Yekaterina Pavlovna was quickly summoned from Tesseli, Gorky wrote to ten-year-old Marfa and seven-year-old Darya that their papa "had fallen ill . . . caught a cold at the airport, is lying in bed and coughing." What is important here is not the calming tone of the letter, but the mention of Max having caught a cold specifically at the *airport*. Max, indeed, had returned from Leningrad by plane (apparently on April 29), but practically the entire day of May 1 he stood on Red Square in good health, observing the military parade and procession with Gorky and other leaders atop Lenin's mausoleum.

In the same memoirs Timosha, contrary to the information from her father-in-law, reports that Max caught a cold while fishing. Indeed, on May 2 (May 3, according to other sources), he had gone to the NKVD dacha at Serebryany Bor, just outside Moscow, with Kriuchkov. After fishing, he returned home shivering. Why such contradictions?

"It is very nice here," wrote Gorky to his grandchildren right after Max had become sick, "even better, probably, than in the Crimea. The days are clear, sunny, warm but not hot, the birch trees and the lilacs are beginning to bloom, soon lilies of the valley will appear and it will be spring—excellent!" Meanwhile, Max was sick precisely because during those days Gorky had waxed so rhapsodically about, it was either cold according to some reports or, on the contrary, "extremely hot" according to others.

Max got sick after spending some time laying on the ground on a rubber raincoat provided by Kriuchkov, or on a garden bench, "sweaty and without a shirt, for two hours," according to others. Kriuchkov's daughter from his liaison with Alma Kusurgasheva, Alla Pugacheva, cites her mother's memoirs, according to which, and contradicting Timosha's story, the heavy drinking did not take place at Serebryany Bor, but in Gorki. Max drank cognac on the river bank not with Kriuchkov, but with Pavel Yudin, thrust upon him as an "advisor." After drinking, they had taken a nap on ground that had only recently been cleared of snow; Kriuchkov "quickly ran down the stairs to the river, woke Max up and brought him home." The endless inconsistencies in these details can only lead one to think that "witnesses" reproduced not what they personally saw or knew, but the variations of a version forced upon them, which they then produced, convinced of its authenticity. The main version of the story had been determined, but the details had not been worked out.

The physicians immediately summoned to Max—the same Lev Levin and the same Aleksei Speransky—came up with the identical diagnosis: lumbar pneumonia.

The agony lasted one week. Max died on May 11.

A day earlier fate had presented Yagoda with yet another gift: Vyacheslav Menzhinsky, the nominal chief of the NKVD, passed away from paralysis of the heart. Yagoda had been his deputy and now a direct path opened for him to the People's Commissariat. On the twelfth and thirteenth, he was present at two consecutive funerals which, it seemed, had decided his fate—professional and personal—all at once.

The rumors that Max's death was no accident began circulating immediately. How is it, people said in Moscow, that a perfectly healthy young man suddenly dies, and the best doctors in the country are unable to save him? But Max was not "perfectly healthy" at all, even though this argument continues to be repeated by almost everyone who looks at the history of this tragedy, either in detail or superficially.

On the contrary, Max was undoubtedly a sick person—he had been ill all his life. He was not even two years old when a drunken nanny carried him upside down to keep him from crying and yelling. He was close to death when Gorky found her—he beat her and drove her out. It is highly probable that Max's mental deficiencies can be traced back to this act of barbarism.

Back in 1905 Gorky had asked Yekaterina Pavlovna, in a letter from Kuokkala, Finland, "How is Max's heart?* Better? I would like to hear something from you." Apparently there were grounds for worry. Gorky's letters to Yekaterina Pavlovna in later years are filled with anxiety about his son's health. He wrote to her about a nervous breakdown, about anemia, about a poor memory, about an incessant cough, and again about a "weak heart." In one letter he writes with even greater detail: "Max's health really worries me—he catches cold much too easily, easily and frequently . . . His father is a person with damaged lungs. The inheritance from his mother's side is not so good either."

---

* The child was eight at the time.

In the 1920s and 1930s, Gorky was troubled most of all by Max's penchant for alcohol. Incidentally, this expression is too polite—Max gradually and irrevocably turned into an inveterate alcoholic. "It was very difficult," Gorky reported to Yekaterina Pavlovna from Sorrento in February 1932, "to get him to quit wine and tobacco . . . He should get serious treatment."

He did not get treatment, and he did not stop drinking wine. Kriuchkov, robust and no match for Max, literally made a drunkard of him—there is plenty of evidence that from the very early morning both "friends" emptied one bottle of cognac after another. Quite often they drank as a threesome: Max, Kriuchkov, and Yagoda. It did not take much to persuade Max—he was always ready for hard liquor.

Gorky understood that his son was doomed, but remained steadfast. He took the death silently. Stalin and his "advisors" came to express their condolences two hours after Max's heart stopped. Gorky interrupted Stalin: "There's nothing more to say."

The funeral was held at the state's prestigious Novodevichy Cemetery on the next day. Who had made this decision? Who was in such a hurry and why?

We will probably never find out. On May 13, Isaak Babel wrote to his mother and sister in Paris: "Yesterday Maxim Peshkov was buried, a terrible death. He . . . had been swimming in the Moscow River* and contracted an inflammation of the lungs with lightning speed. The old man barely moved at the cemetery, it was impossible to look at him, so heartrending it was."

Among those who sent telegrams of condolence were not only Romain Rolland, Henri Barbusse, and Stefan Zweig, but also Chaliapin. His was the only one Gorky did not answer. In a return letter to Rolland he mused with cold detachment:

> [Max] was talented. He possessed his own kind of artistic talent, like that of Hieronymous Bosch, he was drawn to technique . . . He had a sense of humor and the good instinct of a critic. But had no willpower, he was all over the place and did not manage to develop a single one of his talents.

In less than four years Yagoda and Kriuchkov, together with Doctor Levin, would be accused of killing Max. In contrast to other stunning "revelations," causing a multitude of puzzling questions, this one, on the contrary, was perceived as being highly likely.

The diary of the house superintendent at Malaya Nikitskaya, Ivan Koshenkov, preserved in the Gorky archive, states that it was immediately sus-

---

* Yet another version.

pected at home that Yagoda was the "cause of Max's illness." And not just at Gorky's home but "all Moscow" knew the degree of Yagoda's mad passion for Timosha. This passion had stood the test of time: the strange and malicious romance had lasted for almost six years. Max alive stood as an unconquerable obstacle in the path of Yagoda's lust, regardless of whether it led to nothing more than adultery or to something more.

"To have an affair" with *such* a man was impossible, since one word from Gorky to Stalin about it would have been enough for Yagoda to lose his head. To send Max on another excursion to the Arctic (or Far East, or Central Asia, or anywhere else) was also risky, and for what purpose? Both Yagoda and Timosha were too visible for their relationship to remain secret.

Yagoda could not get rid of Max without Kriuchkov's personal involvement. Despite their hatred for one another, these two "bottle buddies" were, however, close and in contact on a daily basis so that, no matter what operation was conceived, only Kriuchkov could have guaranteed its execution. Naturally, we can only make all these assumptions today since the Supreme Court of the USSR in 1988 judged the accusations against Kriuchkov to be unfounded. In the euphoria of perestroika this was the only correct decision.

Judging by all the documents and evidence now at our disposal, Max hated Kriuchkov because he could not accept his role at home. But he could not deprive him of this role either. Kriuchkov, without a doubt, had figured out Max's attitude toward him and, of course, knew about Yagoda's "secret" passion. How could he have done his chief a bad turn? Not only did he depend upon him completely, but he could also free himself from years of mounting bitterness and believe that he was better suited to be Gorky's secretary than Max; that he truly helped the writer better than Max; and that he protected his interests much better—after all, the son squandered his father's money recklessly and indiscriminately while he, Kriuchkov, saved him money! And what did he get in return? No thanks and no prospects of any kind. When it came time for Gorky to leave this world, Max would be the one and only heir; while Kriuchkov had nothing to look forward to. Max would definitely eliminate him from all matters connected with his father's legacy.

That would have been Kriuchkov's reasoning, if Yagoda enlisted him as an accomplice in murder. He could not have had any special fear: Yagoda remained the omnipotent chief of the secret police and Kriuchkov, as an employee of the "organs," was aware that this institution regularly removed undesirable individuals—both at home and abroad—and not a single action by the Lubyanka had ever been exposed, for this would strike an irreparable blow to both the prestige of the NKVD and the overall prestige of the USSR.

If one accepts this hypothesis, a number of questions remain. For Max to catch a cold did not automatically condemn him to die. Having undertaken this operation with Kriuchkov, Yagoda had to be certain of its success, otherwise it lost any meaning and only caused additional problems. Even in those days pneumonia was not necessarily a death warrant. Could Yagoda, taking aim at Gorky's son, simply rely on fate? Did he have to help it along somehow?

Doctor Levin was obviously drawn into it as well. Judging by the accusations subsequently leveled against him, his task was *not* to treat Max, or to treat him incorrectly. However, there were other physicians besides Levin around Max, in particular Aleksei Speransky, who was absolutely loyal to Gorky. He was also connected to some degree to the NKVD, but he was not close to Yagoda. Could Yagoda have enlisted him, too, in such an incredibly dangerous operation?

Speransky's subsequent successful career leads one to think that he was not involved, otherwise a reason would certainly have been found to remove him as a witness, just as the three other physicians who had taken part in Max's treatment were removed: Professors Dmitri Pletnev, Aleksandr Vinogradov, and the head of the medical clinic at the Kremlin, Iosif Khodorovsky. The latter two died under mysterious circumstances in prison before the beginning of the trials of Yagoda, Kriuchkov, and the "killer doctors" in March 1938.

Incidentally, there is no mystery here: they were liquidated by the very same means as others had been. "Medical murders" were already at that time part of the Lubyanka's regular repertoire.

However, according to testimony by Koshenkov, the domestic servants were unhappy that a "new method of treatment" had been used on Max. What was this method? Neither in the documents "strengthening" the official Soviet version, nor in those refuting it, is there anything said about this "method." But *new* methods, not applicable to Max, were in fact generally being "indulged in" by the VIEM, where Speransky was one of the directors.

Does this mean that he was involved in Max's demise? Or were the mysterious "new methods" the handiwork of Dr. Levin? Or had Dr. Vinogradov brought some kind of "mixture"? Such a mixture, according to Lipa, was actually in her medicine cabinet, but Vinogradov had only given his for Max to drink. It is possible that it was the *very same* mixture Lipa had, but his family and close friends could not call such a substitution a "new method of treatment."

In 1964 Yekaterina Pavlovna was visited in Moscow by the American journalist Dan Levin, an expert on Soviet Russia. He had known Yekaterina Pavlovna since the 1920s and could rely upon her candor. In his book, *Stormy Petrel: The Life and Work of Maxim Gorky* (New York, 1965), he relates how

Yekaterina Pavlovna reacted to his question about the death of Max: "Don't ask me about this. If I start talking about it, I won't be able to sleep all night."

Fate led me to Levin in Paris in 1968. During our discussion, we talked about this episode. The dialogue about Max did not end with the quote cited above. Yekaterina Pavlovna touched her ears, letting him know that their conversation was being recorded. Then he made a gesture depicting "liquidation" and asked only, "*Da?*" Peshkova nodded and left the room to compose herself.

In any event, we can assume that Yagoda had taken care of him instead of letting "nature" run its course. "We cannot wait for favors from nature—it is our task to take them from it," as Ivan Michurin, beloved by the Bolsheviks, once said; it became one of the most popular aphorisms of the Stalin era. That Yagoda may have taken these words literally leads to another link in the chain of indirect clues.

Why had Max gone fishing at the NKVD dacha? (Among the many versions of how he spent May 2 or 3, there is also this one: Max had not gone fishing but hunting. But what kind of hunting could there be within the city limits? Was the purpose of this rumor to deflect attention from Serebryany Bor and move the "action" away from the Lubyanka dacha?) It is very obvious that at this "site," hidden from everyone and from all witnesses, anything could happen; for example, like spraying a drug to weaken the body's resistance and cancel the action of any medicines used for a specific illness. In this case the treatment can be viewed as correct, not arousing anyone's suspicion, but also not yielding any result. We will shortly return to the question of what the pharmacological capabilities of the NKVD were.

The basic question, however, remains the same: if this was murder, then what was its main goal? Yagoda's personal interest, and to a lesser degree that of Kriuchkov, is obvious and understandable. The fact that Kriuchkov himself would never have dared undertake such an action on his own is also clear. Was there not something bigger, much bigger, behind it?

The official accusation brought against the murderers (or pseudomurderers) four years later does not stress a personal motive either, in light of how shaky it is, nor would it have improved upon the bloody political show conceived by Stalin with far-reaching consequences. Therefore, it was necessary to remove Max to reduce Gorky's importance and weaken his health even further, since he was so attached to his son and would have taken his death very hard.

If Gorky had to be removed, the Lubyanka had many ways of doing it. Then why such complications with an even higher risk? As we now know, after Max's death there was no deterioration at all in Gorky's already seriously ill condition—had Yagoda not foreseen such a possibility?

Finally, and this may be the most important point of all, why did Yagoda "cut down" his friend Gorky, already under his control and tirelessly praising the dirtiest and most scandalous acts of the Lubyanka?

On the one hand, all available information supports the version that Max was killed; on the other, the motives of the murder and its mechanism are complex.

Everything, however, falls into place if we look at different—and hidden— criminal sources.

Why did Max suddenly go to Leningrad in such secrecy, and who hastily called him back from there and why?

Why has everyone remained steadfastly silent about his trip to Leningrad prior to his death?

Why did Dr. Levin, testifying at the trial as to how Kriuchkov intentionally had let Max catch cold, insist that this episode took place in *April* when it is reliably known that the "fishing expedition" took place on May 2 or 3?

The attempt to erase the trip to Leningrad from Max's life is obvious, just as everyone close to him played into the hands of those who attempted to keep it quiet. Only Gorky "pierced" the conspiracy, having unwittingly mentioned the airport in a letter to his granddaughters: how and why had Max suddenly turned up there? Such a tactic of keeping silent about a seemingly trivial episode is well known to criminologists: it means that it is the key to the mystery.

Relying upon the recollections of his father, Professor Vyacheslav Vsevolodovich Ivanov proposes a hypothesis worthy of close examination. He says that Max had gone to Leningrad on a special assignment for Gorky to see Kirov to discuss a plan for the possible removal of Stalin from the post of general secretary.

Rumors of such an operation (to be sure, without reference to Gorky) and the hopes placed on Kirov as a possible successor to Stalin, appeared precisely at that time. These rumors, as all rumors disseminated under the Bolsheviks, must be taken with utmost seriousness: in a totally closed society, under a harsh totalitarian regime, oral evidence serves as an extremely important source for historians—they should not be brushed aside under any circumstances, but correlated to other sources and considered part of the overall wealth of information at our disposal.

The account Vsevolod Ivanov gave to his son is especially important: Ivanov was very close to Gorky and was present at all group meetings with Stalin that Gorky had organized.

What could have been the purpose of Max's mission? Probably just to inform Kirov of Gorky's position. Opponents of the version, according to which Stalin was implicated in Kirov's murder, prove that Kirov did not oppose Stalin at all but, on the contrary, that he was among the Stalinists.

They are correct. But this in fact made him the most promising candidate as a potential successor for the position of general secretary. Not one of the oppositionists at that time could have replaced Stalin. Only Kirov, because of his personal qualities, presented himself as more loyal, more patient, and more well-balanced; he was a popular and influential Party figure who could calm the hysteria in the country, establish a reconciliation desired by Gorky and free it from the permanent confrontation and fear instilled from above. This would have enacted Lenin's rejected testament, which had proposed replacing Stalin not with a political opponent, but with a more patient, more loyal and less capricious individual.

It is no accident that even the academician V. I. Vernadsky, so cautious in his conclusions, wrote in his secret diary (published only in the mid-1990s) that Kirov "stood out sharply among those untalented and bureaucratic rulers." This was how he was viewed by many inside and outside the Party, and his candidacy, undoubtedly, would have satisfied and reconciled everyone.

Max was clearly supposed to have confidentially reported this idea to Kirov from Gorky. Gorky and Max would not have dared take such a step without Yagoda's consent or, at least, without his knowledge; they both understood perfectly well under whose control they were and under no circumstances would they have acted behind Yagoda's back. Moreover, without Yagoda's participation, this scheme had no future: Stalin would never have voluntarily relinquished his post, and such an idea, or one approximating it, could have been realized only by force of arms. No matter how he regarded Stalin, Gorky was by no means a simpleton or a political schemer or—even less—a suicide.

If this is so, then Max left for Leningrad not only under assignment from Gorky (and perhaps only under the pretense of such an assignment), as Vyacheslav Ivanov presumes, but most of all from Yagoda, and could only be recalled by him. It is difficult to imagine him timidly answering to anyone else in such a situation. Whether Yagoda personally called him in Leningrad or Kriuchkov did so on his orders is irrelevant.

In such a case, the mystery about this trip is explained. Something happened and the plan fell through; circumstances forced Yagoda to make changes. The hasty murder of Max is then directly connected with this mysterious "something." As the most dangerous and key witness, he had to be liquidated immediately! Not because he was "close to Gorky" but because he was himself at the center of a failed operation.

Everything else, including Yagoda's personal motives, led to the fatal solution but was not the main reason. The whole chain is now apparent; what exactly happened unexpectedly must still be explained.

This "something" could only have been Stalin's intervention. No one else could force Yagoda to undertake such abrupt measures and change a carefully set plan so quickly. Perhaps this was not a change in plan but, on the contrary, the exact realization of it? And the recall from Leningrad and what followed was all dictated by Stalin, and no one else! That is why Yagoda was so bold and why the operation, successfully concluded "from the inside out," brought him and Kriuchkov the supreme leader's temporary head-spinning benevolence, reviving the most ambitious dreams: Yagoda was promoted to the post of People's Commissar of Internal Affairs.

The fact that Kriuchkov made Max "catch cold" was not discovered four years later but then and there. The uncompromising measures, of which Stalin was a master, should not have been delayed. Something completely different occurred. People were afraid to say it aloud but at that time everyone knew very well what could be revealed and what could not.

Gorky could not have known the details of the intrigue unfolding behind his back; he had simplemindedly written about the airport, although he could have avoided giving the girls any information and not specified where Max had picked up his cold. But all letters had been sent through Kriuchkov, meaning they passed through his censorship and it was important to Gorky that Yagoda should know: the family accepted the necessary version about the *cold*. Max at that time was still alive and Gorky was hoping that he would get well.

Levin, who stated that he could not contradict the omnipotent Yagoda (Levin's non-complicity in Max's death is completely obvious) was later blamed and supposedly justifiably: as personal physician to Stalin and members of his family, could he really not have exposed the crime as it was being hatched and disarmed Yagoda? The accusation would have been founded except for one extremely important point: no matter what directives he received from Yagoda, Levin knew from whom only an order (let's say it more delicately: a recommendation) could come—he could not have complained to Stalin about Stalin himself! All he could do was timidly obey.

If our hypothesis is correct, other doubts in this extremely dark history are removed in exactly the same manner. At the trial Kriuchkov explained his participation in the murder by a desire to seize Gorky's literary heritage after his death—this would supposedly have brought him immense wealth.

The absurdity of such an "explanation," accepted by the prosecutor Andrei Vyshinsky, is also patently obvious: how could Kriuchkov have become the heir in the place of Yekaterina Pavlovna (Gorky's legal wife), two grandchildren and Timosha, who would inherit, along with Marfa and Darya, a portion of Max's rights? Moreover, Gorky's legacy—and Kriuchkov knew this better than anyone else—would become "national property," that is, devolve to the state.

At a public trial some kind of *motive* is required for the accusation to hold up. It could be dubious as long as it was understood to everyone. For Kriuchkov, it became the mythical battle for Gorky's patrimony, and for Yagoda it was jealousy. Neither one could say what the real motive was, which is why Yagoda so stubbornly evaded the persistent questioning of Vyshinsky and the judge, Vasily Ulrikh. No matter how much they demanded a confession from him for his role in Max's murder and an explanation as to why he did it, Yagoda obstinately repeated, "I cannot answer this *here*," and "Allow me not to answer that question." Vyshinsky, naturally, allowed it.

Yagoda's stubbornness is usually interpreted as nobility: the motive for Max's murder was only his love for Timosha, but he did not want to drag the name of his beloved woman through the mud. This interpretation is only partially acceptable—it was no accident that Vyshinsky willingly played into Yagoda's hand, hoping that everyone who heard the dialogue between executioner and victim got exactly that impression. Yagoda's sudden request to give testimony about the episode at a closed trial session also helped promote this.

No one, however, has focused attention on one very important circumstance: in the exact same way ("Allow me not to answer this question") Yagoda reacted to all attempts by Vyshinsky to induce him to testify about different episodes, concerning a plan to "change the Soviet leadership." "I cannot answer you on this question"; "It was not at all like that, but it is not important"; "I know how it really was, but I cannot talk about that *here*"—this is how Yagoda deflected Vyshinsky's questioning and not only when the conversation concerned Max's death.

What did Yagoda say at the closed session? We do not know. The archive does not contain a single stenographic or protocol note. Even Aleksandr Nikolaevich Yakovlev, a member of Gorbachev's Politburo, the second person in the government and head of a commission especially established for the investigation into all of Stalin's crimes—that is, someone to whom all archives without exception were made available—stated that there are no documents about the testimony Yagoda gave at the closed session.

The session is "closed" only to outsiders and not to trial participants, nor to those who are legally charged with studying and verifying the evidence of the case. The transcript (at a minimum) or a shorthand report at closed sessions should be maintained in as much detail as during open sessions.

Why was such a transcript not kept? And did this closed session really take place? The details of the relationship between Yagoda and Timosha did not interest Vyshinsky and Ulrikh, because those details were of no significance for a fabricated case; the rest remained a mystery even for them.

At the beginning of my legal career I worked as an assistant to Ilya Davidovich Braude, a very prominent lawyer at the time who defended Dr. Levin at that trial. Even then the secrecy surrounding the closed session of the trial attracted my interest. I found no rumors about an affair between Timosha and Yagoda—by the mid-1950s they were already muted; Gorky's biography did not interest me then; and the thick tome of the shorthand report seemed to me complete and reliable. Only one link appeared to be missing: that of the closed session. Only a few lines in the "shorthand report" alluded to it: Yagoda stated that he killed Max for his own "personal aims."

I asked Braude what in fact was said at the closed session. I was certain that he would decline to answer, citing the ban on revealing secrets. Instead, he said something completely unfathomable: "I did not take part in that session."

An attorney not taking part in a trial session! Especially one for the defendant directly connected to the episode, for the sake of which the doors of the court were closed to the public! I asked Braude no further questions. When I compare his reply with everything else, my doubts as to whether this "closed" session even took place increase.

The romantic relationship between Yagoda and Timosha was definitely an integral component of the tragedy. But Yagoda was hiding from the public and from everyone in general and could not say who the *main* actor was.

It was impossible to say Stalin's name aloud. Yagoda had *him* in mind when he interrupted Ulrikh, who had extracted from him the necessary "confession of the accused" for the public trial: "You can put pressure on me, but don't go too far. I will tell you everything that I want to say, but . . . don't go too far."

This mysterious response—more like a cry from the soul—did not make it into the "shorthand report" of the trial, but it was reported by American journalist Walter Duranty and other foreign observers present at the trial.

It was reproduced almost verbatim among those present in the courtroom by Sir Fitzroy Maclean, at the time secretary of the British embassy in Moscow. He and I discussed this at great length in London in February 1988—I had written down Yagoda's comment in the version as recalled by Maclean: "You don't have to pressure me, nothing good will come of it. I will say what I can, but nothing more. Don't make me go too far."

How did Stalin find out about the true reasons for Max's trip to Leningrad and what exactly did he know? The version that Yagoda had betrayed his like-minded colleagues and allies and had deserted back to Stalin, figuring that victory was secured and that the time had come to change "trains," is the only one that provides an answer to all the riddles of the tragedy.

When exactly did Yagoda make his fatal turnabout? Did it not happen immediately after Max left for Leningrad? And weren't all the moves thought up by Yagoda in advance, with Max's stay in Leningrad only confirming the revelations which he reported to Stalin? Had he not conceived very carefully and cunningly the whole operation in which Max was nothing more than a decoy? Yagoda thought he had brilliantly planned everything; Stalin was even more cunning and more insidious than all the conspirators put together. The trap which Yagoda had prepared for Max, for the "Ivanoviches" and for everyone with them, had been sprung on himself.

It is worth mentioning the episode recalled by NKVD resident "General Aleksandr Orlov" (Lev Feldbein), who refused to return to Moscow and to his inevitable death, in his book *The Secret History of Stalin's Crimes*. To induce Yagoda to make a "confession," Nikolai Yezhov (Yagoda's successor) sent his former subordinate Abram Slutsky (head of the foreign department of the NKVD, that is, counterintelligence) to his jail cell. A dialogue took place between them, later reproduced many times in the literature of the Great Moscow Show Trials. In the context of what has been said above, it takes on a new and very significant meaning.

> You can write in your report to Yezhov [Yagoda told Slutsky] what I say: "God probably does exist." I have not deserved anything from Stalin other than gratitude for loyal service; from God I should have earned the cruelest form of punishment for violating his commandments a thousand times. Now look where I am and judge for yourself whether there is a God or not.

This version answers the logical question of why Yagoda, if he was on the side of the "conspirators," did not take advantage of the fact that the whole security of the Kremlin, as well as the personal security of Stalin himself, was under his control. He did not take advantage of it because he betrayed his supporters, although they could only rely upon him. Yagoda's greatest service to Stalin consisted precisely in the fact that he had revealed all the plans of his opponents and had returned completely to Stalin's side. He therefore resolved many problems for himself. The removal of Max, who turned out to be a victim of Kremlin-Lubyanka intrigues, was one such "solved" problem. But only one . . .

Kirov probably never even knew what designs Gorky, or "someone" in Gorky's name, had on him. Had he known, then obviously he rejected them, just as he had rejected similar offers expressed by others (and even, as is now known, he reported them back to Stalin with amazing naiveté). But the simple fact that stakes had been placed on him and that he was indeed a very suitable figure for such a role made Kirov a dangerous man. It makes no sense to restate the complex details of the history of his murder, which as before is filled with numerous contradictions that have more blank spots.

It was precisely then, at the end of spring 1934, that Kirov's fate was sealed. Not because Kirov himself wanted to replace Stalin (it is possible and more likely that he did not), but because those who counted on Stalin's replacement were too numerous and too influential.

With the removal of Kirov, their whole plan automatically collapsed: there was no one equal to him. In the environment of that time only a Stalinist could replace Stalin. The old opponents did not stand the slightest chance. Only Kirov among the Stalinists possessed the comprehensive qualities of a leader, and he was the only one against whom *no one* would have protested. With his liquidation, the path was opened to the liquidation of those who had dreamed of change, and had prepared for it.

The shot rang out on December 1, but the smoke was already rising as Max lay in agony, nearing the end of his life. Chronology and logic complement one another.

23.

Predator and Prey

Many people have wondered what made Gorky change his calling, turn his back on literature and dabble in politics when there were no politics as such, only blind subjugation to Stalin's will. He apparently thought otherwise. He still believed in his messianic hopes, still hoped to turn the Kremlin in the direction of peace, without upheaval and, of course, without blood. As to how far removed his utopian dreams were from reality, and how far his pseudo-friendly relations with the dictator were not influencing him, but, on the contrary, how he was being choked in Stalin's embrace, Gorky was unable to understand. Or, even if he did suspect it, he drove these thoughts from his mind.

There is a very plausible version that he not only appealed for reconciliation on the Kremlin Olympus, but even had a plan to make it happen. According to this version, Gorky intended for the "hero of the civil war" and future marshal, Vasily Blukher, to replace Stalin as general secretary of the Central Committee, while Stalin would head the government under the condition that Kamenev and Bukharin become members of the cabinet, and Gorky himself would take on the portfolio of People's Commissar of Enlightenment. Of course, anyone can play around in his imagination, changing political landscapes or revamping governments, as he pleases. As always, Gorky remained a romantic idealist, without realizing what games he was playing and how he was being manipulated by a truly experienced and mercilessly cruel adversary.

There is a version which subsequently became an aphorism: "Aleksei Maksimovich Peshkov took precedence over the writer Maxim Gorky," in the sense that the instinct of the former petit-bourgeois from Nizhny Novgorod was stronger than the artistic drive and political maturity of a world-renowned writer. The independent, proud, and farsighted author gradually turned into the mouthpiece of authority, reconciled himself to it, and cast off independence. "He made himself forget," as the playwright Leonid Zorin writes, "that a writer should not, does not, dare allow himself to become a servant, even if he is given the private residence of Ryabushinsky." Nevertheless, Stalin knew that a blind man can learn to see at any moment, and that something like that had already happened with Gorky. A prisoner can rebel, and this was no common prisoner—it was impossible to deal with him as he had dealt with others.

There were no visible signs of a change in Stalin's relationship to Gorky. Stalin was never impulsive or rash; on the contrary, he painstakingly thought through every decision and took his time in carrying them out, especially when it concerned Gorky. Ivan Gronsky made this claim on the basis of his personal observations:

> Stalin was afraid of Gorky. Gorky was so great and his authority around the world so indisputable that it was impossible to touch him. And Stalin knew perfectly well that he could manipulate whomever he wanted, pounce on anyone he wanted, but not on Gorky.

Of course, Stalin could not subject Gorky to a dressing down, deprive him of positions or expel him from his mansions, let alone arrest him. What Stalin *could* do required time, skillful tactics, restraint, patience, and a complex and carefully conceived game plan—in other words, everything that did not burden Stalin in the least but gave him special pleasure. He loved to "toy" with his victim for awhile like a true predator with his prey, in no hurry to enjoy his meal right away.

On the same day that Max became fatally ill—May 4—the Politburo appointed Kamenev director of the Institute of World Literature. Stalin continued to visit Malaya Nikitskaya, and the two carried on their usual emotionally charged conversations. Less than two weeks after Max's funeral *Pravda* and *Izvestiia* published Gorky's latest article, "Proletarian Humanism."

He truly had not lied when he told Stalin on May 11, "This is no longer a topic," referring to the death of his son. He was busy with a completely different theme: the "historically and scientifically founded proletarian humanism of Marx-Lenin-Stalin, genuinely common to all mankind." There were no obvious reasons for the choice of that specific theme at precisely this time, but it undoubtedly concealed some inner meaning. "This is true philanthropic teaching," exclaimed Gorky in the style of provincial propagandists, reminding the proletariat that it was brought up "on the ideology of Marx and Lenin, truly and wisely realized by its leader Stalin." Two months later German émigré writer Alfred Kurella, living in France, asked Gorky to write something for the

Communist press; Gorky advised him to reprint "Proletarian Humanism," adding significantly, "Comrade Stalin very much approved this little article."

To keep Gorky from heavy thoughts and specifically from participating in a writers' congress, he was sent on a trip along the Volga. "I embrace you very tenderly, my dear, my most valuable treasure!" wrote Mura from London, and soon after joined him to share the melancholic joy of this Volga voyage. It was very hot and Gorky almost never left his stateroom where he had a fan; but in the evenings, when the heat died down, he came out on deck to breathe in the Volga air so dear to him. He did not go ashore and barely saw anyone. The return to Moscow was timed for the arrival of an important guest: after a fifteen-year break H. G. Wells returned to the country of the Bolsheviks.

Mura accompanied Wells to Estonia, where she remained with her children awaiting his return. Wells asked her to join him as his interpreter. "Don't you know that I'm not allowed entry into the Soviet Union?" she said, rejecting his offer. Their joint arrival in Moscow would be too much of a challenge to Gorky, which is not what she wanted at all. But Konstantin Umansky, a future ambassador to the United States who replaced Mura as interpreter, knowing nothing of these intrigues, let slip that she had been here "only a week ago." Gorky went even further: Wells learned from him that in the past year Mura had visited him on more than one occasion. It is possible he even said—especially to tease his hated rival—that she had journeyed with him along the Volga. The surprised Wells nevertheless maintained his composure.

Having guessed or realized that her secret had been exposed, Mura sent Gorky an unusually restrained letter from Estonia filled with hints and innuendo.

> All this trouble is still not over, but it is settling down. In my thoughts I am always with you, especially after the visit to see you. Everything here seems unreal, devoid of meaning. It is harder to live here. My dear friend, how are you? You know how difficult it is for me to write you. Neither you nor I like certain words. But you truly feel how strong and indestructible this closeness is to you.

Could Gorky not have discerned empty rhetoric and insufferable falsehood in these inarticulate banalities?

Wells tried to carry out his program in Moscow and Stalin was the first one he visited. His book *Russia in the Shadows* contained references to a multitude of leading Soviet writers but he did not mention Stalin. On the contrary, Trotsky, Kamenev, Zinoviev, and Rykov appeared on just about every page. Stalin, naturally, did not point this out to Wells, but he had taken good notice of it.

Now the lord of the Kremlin had to dislodge the names he despised from Wells's mind and become the protagonist of his new book, but it was a labored conversation. While Stalin spoke of successes, Wells stubbornly steered him toward a single-minded dialogue about freedom of speech and the freedom to create. At the time Wells was head of the International PEN Club, and his goal was to convince the dictator to allow Soviet writers to join.

Stalin listened suspiciously at first, then with deliberate interest. "He did not understand me," Wells wrote after he had returned home. In fact, Stalin had understood him all too well and only pretended to be unfocused. How else could he have reacted, hearing these words from Wells:

> Our organization insists upon the right of free expression of opinions, including those of the opposition . . . However, I do not know if such broad freedom can be possible here [in the USSR].

When Wells was given a recording of the conversation by the interpreter, Konstantin Umansky, for review, those lines were omitted. Wells restored them, demanding that Stalin confirm they had been said. Stalin confirmed it. That was as far as "self-criticism" went.

Having obtained nothing from Stalin, Wells decided to try his hand with Gorky, whom he met the following day. Gorky invited a few writers, as well as the People's Commissar of Foreign Affairs, Maxim Litvinov and his English wife, to his dacha outside Moscow. Yagoda had already managed to warn Gorky of the nature of the conversation, as well as Stalin's conclusions. Wells was hoping to draw the Soviet writers to his side and seduce them with his odd ideas.

Yagoda also opposed Wells's proposal, since many members of the International PEN Club had already signed an appeal to the Human Rights Defense League, protesting recent court verdicts in the USSR. Gorky agreed. "Why should we help Russian émigrés return home," he rebuffed Wells. "So they can carry out anti-Soviet propaganda here?"

Gorky's relationship with PEN was conflicted and contradictory, just as his entire behavior was in general in the 1920s and 1930s. Back in 1922 the first president of PEN, John Galsworthy, had invited him to a ceremonial dinner as an honored member of the club. At that time honored guests included Anatole France, Romain Rolland, Thomas Hardy, Maurice Maeterlinck, Knut Hamsun, Gerhardt Hauptmann, George Brandes, Selma Lagerlöf, and many other luminaries. Gorky found himself in good company and gladly consented.

A year later he found out that his "accursed friend" Merezhkovsky and other exiles were among the PEN members, and that Pilnyak, whom Gorky found highly undesirable, liked the idea of creating a division of the club, even in Soviet Russia, causing an immediate change in Gorky's attitude toward the organization. Now the situation had become even more complicated: PEN intended to create a center for "writers in exile," which would include those who had fled from both Nazi and Soviet despotism. Such a campaign did not suit the "new" Gorky at all.

A year earlier Wells had presided over a PEN congress in the Yugoslav city of Dubrovnik, where Mura joined him after parting with Gorky in Istanbul. Writers arrived from a multitude of countries, representing their national centers: Benjamin Cremier and Jules Romains from France; Filippo Tommaso Marinetti from Italy; Ivo Andric and Desanka Maksimovic from Yugoslavia; Maria Maierova from Czechoslovakia; Elisaveta Bagryana and Dora Gabe from Bulgaria; Jan Parandowsky from Poland; Mikhail Sadoveanu from Romania; and many other writers well known beyond their own countries. As always, Gorky was invited, but his path led to Moscow.

At the suggestion of German antifascist writer Ernst Toller and the American Sholom Asch, who wrote in Yiddish, a resolution was proposed to condemn the sadly famous book burning organized by the Nazis in many German cities on the evening of May 10 was proposed two weeks before the congress opened. This medieval action—the public burning of books—shook the entire world. However, the official group of German delegates abstained from voting, essentially underlining what Stalin had told Wells: "We cannot allow heretical thoughts in our country."

Praising the end of freedom of speech and approving the destruction of "seditious" books was so inconsistent with the charter of the International PEN Club that Hitler's writers were asked to leave the session and the German PEN Club was unanimously excluded from the writers' community and disbanded. Having rejected the principles of the PEN Club and dismissing its activity, Gorky had managed to appear, along with Soviet writers, to be no better than their Nazi "colleagues," although no one had the slightest doubts about his militant antifascism.

Realizing that he had embarrassed himself, Gorky reflected that he had no responsibilities and that it was "not up to him to decide." As with Stalin, Wells's conversation with Gorky ended in a stalemate.

According to one of the participants of the meeting, the editor and journalist Ilya Shkapa, "Gorky received the guest from London with a kind of icy politeness, barely concealing his inner alienation." No doubt the history with Mura had something to do with his attitude. The relationship with her had definitively unraveled, but he preferred to be the one to initiate the break.

Wells stung him with everything, not the least of which that he was independent and could do as he pleased, without having to look over his shoulder.

Gorky now found himself in a position diametrically opposed to what he had glorified in the past. He characterized Wells to Shkapa as a "haughty gentleman who pretends to a lot, but understands little," and he said that his book *Russia in the Shadows* "smells of mothballs."

Wells responded in kind in his statements about Gorky, not in private conversations but in his travel notes. Observing that Stalin "never breathed fresh air in his life and did not even know what it meant," he cited his despondency at his meeting with Gorky, who is "fiercely convinced of the correctness of Soviet patriotism and even rejects—among other freedoms and human rights—birth control and a woman's right not to have children." He wrote these lines on a charming Estonian lake where he spent two quiet and peaceful weeks with Mura, the same Kalijarvi, from whence she had written to Gorky at the time, "I strongly and tenderly embrace you, my dear friend."

She embraced Gorky strongly and tenderly on paper, and Wells, at the same time, in the flesh.

The day for the opening of the first congress of the Union of Soviet Writers was drawing near. Several writers' associations in different regions of the country had sent Gorky to the congress as their delegate. He was given number-one status and every conceivable sign of protocol attention was shown him, but other people—people whom he cared nothing for and profoundly despised—were handling the preparations for the congress.

The RAPP team was no better than the one it had replaced—simply a different literary "mafia." Incidentally, it was not Stalin's intention to shove the RAPP aside; after all, they were Yagoda's people and he could still be very useful to him. Stalin conferred with both groups behind Gorky's back, acting in tune with his traditional method of intrigue. At one of those closed sessions he said, according to Gronsky, "We did not know that Gorky wishes to be chairman of the Union of Writers. Had we known, we would not have appointed him. Do you have any assurances that, as chairman, he will follow the Party line? I don't." Stalin had instilled in Gorky the thought that he saw no one else but him as head of the Union.

Gorky did not change his plan. He insisted that the disgraced Bukharin and Radek be given the right to speak at the congress with the two leading speeches and that Kamenev be head of the Union. Stalin agreed reluctantly to the first request and only partially to the second: the Politburo confirmed Kamenev as a member of the administration of the Union of Writers and—to compensate for this "demotion in rank"—obliged the academicians to nominate him for active membership in the Academy of Sciences during the next election. This decision can be considered irreproachable in its precision: the lulling of vigilance was carried out brilliantly, and Gorky became even more emboldened in thinking that he was destined to be a peacemaker.

In the minds of the "liberals" the congress gave way to genuine euphoria: the absence of Akhmatova, Mandelstam, Bulgakov, and Platonov was compensated by the presence of Babel, Zoshchenko, Pilnyak, and Pasternak, who was even allowed a place on the presidium alongside the Kremlin favorites. Gorky was celebrated as a true patriarch of literature.

Many foreign guests came for the congress, including Louis Aragon and Elsa Triolet (who had enjoyed a relaxing time on the Black Sea shore of the Caucasus), Jean-Richard Bloch, André Malraux, Rafael Alberti, Oskar Maria Graf, Vitezslav Nezval, Moa Martinson, and many others. Their speeches were translated from different languages not by professional translators but by their colleagues—Pasternak, Ehrenburg, Ilyanber, and Tretyakov—which confirmed the high cultural level of the Soviet literary elite.

Lubyanka employees and volunteer informers crammed into the Hall of Columns, filled its lobbies and all seats designated for the delegates and guests of the congress, and grabbed many copies of an underground leaflet addressed to the foreign participants. The majority of the foreigners did receive this leaflet, but only a few handed it in to the secretariat of the congress. Judging by the text, the sheet had been written by a person with a mastery of literature and more likely than not by a number of writers. The authors, as far as can be judged by the archival materials, were not identified.

Here are several passages from this leaflet:

> We Russian writers are like prostitutes in a brothel with the only difference being that they trade their bodies and we our souls; just as for them there is no way out of the brothel except through death by hunger, the same is true for us . . . The obligation to inform on one another is removed and we inform on our friends, families, acquaintances . . .
>
> In your countries you organize various committees to save the victims of fascism . . . But why do we not see any activity from you in saving the victims of our Soviet fascism carried out by Stalin; these victims, truly innocent, are greater, much greater, than all the victims on the whole planet taken together since the end of the world war.
>
> Do you understand the game you are playing? Or, perhaps like us, you are prostituting your sensibility, conscience, and duty? But then we will not forgive you for this, never forgive you.

Gorky was not shown this leaflet; otherwise he would not have been able to restrain himself from a resounding rebuke to the scoundrels and slanderers.

Then he would have been in his element. This cry from the soul by anonymous authors, alas, was addressed to the wrong crowd: the foreign guests convened in Moscow were people with a clean conscience who belonged to that circle of the leftist Western intelligentsia, which, seeing "certain shortcomings" in the USSR, could not argue with it about anything, believing that it was a real force in the battle against the threat of fascism.

It should not be thought by any means that only "prostitutes" and cheer-leaders had gathered in the auditorium. Many speeches at the congress stood out for their freedom of expression and thought, and their weakly veiled allusions were easily decoded.

"It cannot be permitted," said Ilya Ehrenburg, "that the literary critique of a work instantly influences the social position of a writer, who should not be dependent upon literary [i.e., Party] criticism."

Yuri Olesha, whose sway was very great with writers, unambiguously spoke out against the martinet-like coarseness with which "proletarian" writers slighted intellectual writers, forcing them to slavish agreement with invective: "Worst of all is to belittle one's self, to say that I am nothing compared to the worker or Young Communist. How would it be possible to say such a thing and continue to live and work?"

"Do not sacrifice your individuality for the sake of position," exhorted Boris Pasternak. "The danger is too great of becoming a literary dignitary. Move further away from such flattery!"

Isaak Babel used a simple metaphor: "We speak unbearably loudly about love here . . . If it continues like this, we will soon have to proclaim our love through a megaphone like referees at football matches." The applause in the room spoke to the fact that the metaphor was understood and approved.

The hero of the year, Otto Yulevich Shmidt, who led a polar expedition and almost died in the Arctic before being rescued by Soviet pilots, went even further in his speech: ". . . our work does not need buttoning up, or pressure, or exclamations; it does not need the intervention of the leader with the masses. These are not our methods at all. I do not want to say it, but these are foreign methods of a neighboring state." And again the hall reacted with applause at this direct comparison of the Soviet regime to the Nazis, striking in its audacity and boldness.

The foreign guests were much more reserved in their criticism, much more subject to the diktat of self-censorship, but their praise of Soviet power and its leaders was several degrees higher than those of their hosts. Aragon outdid everyone by calling for the creation of an "international socialist culture . . . under the banner of Marx, Lenin, and Stalin." Jean-Richard Bloch, who did not limit himself to complimenting the hosts and delivering a mean-spirited caricature of the French reader, reminded his Soviet colleagues that they ran the risk of "gradually turning into social parasites, as in ancient times when a writer's duty consisted of supporting the monarchy: 'How wonderful you are, how wise you are, how great and just.'" The room went numb and preferred to ignore this negative prognosis altogether.

When Bukharin took the floor to report "on poetry, poetics, and the tasks of poetic creativity in the USSR," the writers greeted him with a loud ovation. Naturally, he immediately announced that the ovations should be addressed to "the great Party" he represented. He highly praised Mayakovsky and sharply criticized Pasternak, but all the same it was clear that the future of poetry lay with the latter and not the former. Without mincing his words, he correctly evaluated the mediocre poets who had passed themselves off as the standard bearers of Soviet poetry.

Following the end of his speech, the shorthand report noted the "stormy applause of the entire auditorium, turning into an ovation. Shouts of 'hurrah.' The whole auditorium rises." Upon returning to the presidium, Bukharin, deathly pale, leaned over to Gorky and whispered, "Do you know what you have just done? You have signed my death sentence." Did he really not understand that this sentence had been signed long before?

Although Bukharin spoke in the name of the Party, he concluded by saying that "the key points of the speech were examined and confirmed by the responsible agencies." The hosting poet, well informed of the true distribution of forces and skilled in the ways of the Kremlin, pounced upon him. The so-called Young Communist poets and the former friends of Mayakovsky were in an uproar. One of them, Semyon Kirsanov, accused Bukharin of trying "to lead poetry astray from the struggle and participation . . . in the class war . . ."

Gorky did not offer a single word in this "discussion." Feeling their power, the demagogues and hacks crushed the speaker who had been brought to the dais by Gorky himself. He had even approved Bukharin's speech. Thus, all the abuse was directed at him personally. But he kept silent . . .

Karl Radek took into account the situation into which his friend had fallen, and in his own speech on contemporary foreign literature avoided any kind of heresy. He praised those who required it and railed at those whom he had been ordered to attack, including André Malraux, who was rebuked for "not clearly" expressing on whose side he really was—"with us" or with someone else. "The fact that I came here," Malraux assured Radek, "means that I am with you." After these words, the shorthand report notes, "Noisy applause which did not die down for a long time, the entire auditorium rises to greet Malraux; Malraux stands and bows."

Of course, the main act was played not in the glimmering Hall of Columns of the House of Unions, but behind the scenes. While the speeches were being given, a struggle for the leading posts was in full swing.

Gorky had understood before the start of the congress that he was destined to become a mere curtain behind which the Party bureaucrats and the graphomaniacs serving them would plant *their* "literature," *their* morals, and *their* rules of the game. On August 2, before Stalin left on vacation, Gorky sent him a letter which became known only in the 1990s. He pointed out that the tone at the Organizational Committee was being set by apparatchiks, like future "philosopher" Pavel Yudin. He wrote:

> The ideology of this line is unknown to me, but leads to the creation of a group seeking to control the Union of Writers. This group, with "a will to power" . . . of course, is capable of leading but, in my opinion, has no right to an active and necessary ideological leadership of literature . . . due to the intellectual weakness of this group, as well as its extreme illiteracy . . .

The tone of the letter must have puzzled Stalin. Although Yudin was his creature, Gorky was completely straightforward in his assessment of him: "My attitude toward Yudin is even more negative. His loutish cunning, lack of principle, duplicity and cowardice is revolting to me. Recognizing his personal fecklessness, he tries to surround himself with people even more insignificant than he is and hides among them." Gorky again to Stalin:

> Dear sincerely respected and beloved comrade . . . I earnestly request that you release me from chairmanship of the Union [of Writers] on account of poor health and my extreme overload of lit[erary] work. I do not know how to be chairman, and am even less capable of sorting out the Jesuitical cunningness of the politics of these little groups.

Stalin did not reply to Gorky's letter, but gave orders from the Caucasus, where he was on vacation. He included the majority of those whom Gorky had recommended to become part of the leadership in the Union of Writers, but he did not exclude anyone from the list of those called "barely literate and insignificant." Now, having heard everything the future leaders of the Union had to say at the congress and seen how they conducted themselves, Gorky made a final attempt at rebellion. Stalin was not in Moscow; Gorky's undated letter, sent on August 30 or 31, was not addressed to anyone in particular, just "To the Central Committee of the Party." Of course, this letter was also hidden in the secret archives until the 1990s.

Writers who do not know how to learn, or do not wish to learn, but are accustomed to play administrative roles and strive to secure command positions for themselves, are in the minority. . . . Their speeches at the congress . . . revealed their professional illiteracy . . . However . . . these people will be introduced to the Administration of the Union. Thus illiterate people will be in charge of people much more literate than they are . . . Personally, I know these people to be very adept and experienced at "creating" various internecine conflicts, but I absolutely . . . do not believe in their sincerity. Therefore, I refuse to work with them for I value my time and I consider myself to be completely in the right not to spend it on trivial "squabbles" . . . This circumstance . . . all the more urgently compels me to ask you to free me from my obligations as chairman of the administration of the Union of Writers.

The spirit of the absent Stalin was invisibly present in the Hall of Columns. Apparently, his personal representative, Andrei Zhdanov, who had only just been appointed as one of the stranglers of science and culture, conveyed Stalin's decision to Gorky. There was nothing left to but to accept it. Gorky naturally, became decorative chairman; Aleksandr Shcherbakov (future secretary of the Central Committee) became the Central Committee's observer, and Fadeev and Panferov the lead violinists in the orchestra.

Veniamin Kaverin, to whom Gorky had once promised a great literary future, recalled many years later that Gorky opened the congress with "an exhausting three-hour speech; he began practically from the first human on earth." All the foreign guests also remembered later that Gorky's speech was unbearably boring. On the other hand, other Soviet and foreign participants showed up in a state of completely unjustifiable euphoria. Klaus Mann recalled:

As far as oratory is concerned no one could compete with the two Frenchmen, Louis Aragon and André Malraux: they thundered with the enthusiasm of Danton, joked with the wit of Voltaire, and were ironic with the elegance of Anatole France, while Gorky, chairman of the congress, wheezed out with great effort flat patriarchal jokes in a whistling falsetto. Ilya Ehrenburg, sophisticatedly skilled, cleverly resourceful, and somewhat windy, was much more intelligent and entertaining. The pensive and noble poet Boris Pasternak, the adroit raconteur Aleksei Tolstoy, the pedantic but highly intelligent and zealously achieving Bukharin, even Karl Radek, that red-bearded schemer and intellectual master of the sleight-of-hand—all of them brought more to the explanation of literary and cultural-political issues and were more original in their statements than the tired and honorable old man, petrified in his glory and already near death. Nonetheless, Gorky was greeted with shouts by the crowd.

On August 20, the whole constellation of foreign guests, along with several of their Soviet colleagues personally selected by Gorky, had the honor of being invited for dinner at his suburban residence. Neither Stalin nor Voroshilov was present at this meeting, but Kaganovich and Molotov showed up, surrounded by second-rank Kremlin bigwigs. Kriuchkov greeted the guests, his whole demeanor showing just who was in charge here. Veniamin Kaverin remembered, "I had seen Kriuchkov before, but on this evening I was especially struck by his repulsive appearance. He had a red beefy face and short fingers which picked at his long stringy red hair. He comported himself like the master of the house."

Klaus Mann did not take his eyes off Gorky.

Having known and described extreme poverty and darkest indigence, [he] was in princely luxury: the ladies of his family greeted us in Parisian evening dresses; the fare at his table stood out for its Oriental sumptuousness. Before dinner he answered all questions that the foreign delegates asked him. We heard something about the situation and tasks of the writer in a socialist state, definitions and postulates of no great staggering originality. Then there was a great deal of vodka and caviar.

Kaverin was more observant:

. . . It seemed that none of the invited guests interested him. Gorky was quiet and in a strange way this silence spread to everyone, despite Kriuchkov's efforts. . . After coffee, when everyone stood up from the table and retired to the parlor, Nikulin began to sing to the accompaniment of a guitar. This was disgusting and not just because he shamelessly and even, I would say, indecently, grimaced . . . Suddenly I caught Gorky's dark, sidelong poisonous glance—pale and colorless— from under his drooping eyebrows. He [Gorky] soon left without saying goodbye to anyone . . . And as if a burden had suddenly disappeared, the tension was lifted as soon as he left.

Through its agents the NKVD gathered the writers' opinions about the congress, including statements about Gorky. It is impossible, of course, to vouch for the accuracy of the denunciations, but the quoted statements by the writers correspond to their judgments of the literary patriarch, known by even more reliable sources. Ilya Selvinsky, a very popular poet in the 1930s, said, "Gorky is a breeding-ground of clannishness. At Gorky's banquet it was important who sat closer [to him]. The spectacle was so disgusting that Pasternak could not stand it any longer and left." Lev Kassil (one of the most popular children's writers in the 1930s) said:

It was generally difficult to have any illusions under Gorky's leadership. If he has his own politics, then it is determined exclusively by personal moments: what a pitiful, vengeful old man he is . . . He does not forgive anyone for anything.

Boris Pasternak opined,

You get the feeling that there is some kind of bitterness inside Gorky against everyone. He does not understand, or else pretends not to understand, the significance every one of his words has, that resonance which echoes right after one of his speeches. Gorky's nuances are as subtle as a truck's rumble.

Not all that long ago Gorky had been a canonized, untouchable sacred cow—such statements could hardly have passed without consequences—but the time of unconditional fealty had already passed. Not the slightest signs of dissatisfaction from above, concerning such daring statements, were found.

The activity and conclusion of the congress was officially recognized as a great political victory. But in essence it spelled the end of Gorky: broken and repentant after several attempts at rebellion, not only did he no longer present any kind of threat, he did not even offer any interest. He had played his role; he was not fated to play any other.

Exhausted and wilted, he left for Tesseli.

24.

Everywhere a Conspiracy

Gorky nevertheless managed to place in key positions the people he trusted: Kamenev, Pasternak, and Zoshchenko were in, but already during the first weeks after the congress it became clear to everyone that the administration, like its chairman, was nothing more than the latest Soviet fiction: all true power was concentrated in the hands of apparatchiks without the slightest relationship to literature. Shcherbakov pretended that he was unable to make a single decision without Gorky's instructions, and Gorky played into the charade in complete seriousness.

"We got a call from the NKID [People's Commissariat of Foreign Affairs]," Shcherbakov wrote to him from Tesseli, "asking us to give our conclusion with regard to Soviet writers joining the PEN Club. I declined to discuss this subject. You have to give the final word."

Both understood it was a game but continued to follow its rules. "Wells has already played a little swinish trick," replied Gorky, probably having in mind the publication of his Moscow impressions. "They say he plans to do something solid. We'll have an answer for him."

Gorky had clearly drawn a conclusion from all the recent events. To remind them that he was not a tame "chairman of the Union," but *Gorky,* was something he dared not do. He remembered, naturally, not just the slap in the face he endured for his obstinacy during the preparation and carrying out of the congress, but most of all the tragedy that ended with Max's death. The need to demonstrate not just his loyalty, but also the strongest ideological steadfastness, is clear in all his correspondence of this period with various Kremlin leaders.

While Stalin was relaxing in the Caucasus, Gorky pestered Kaganovich, his stand-in, with letters, trying to get a response. Romain Rolland complained that some local hooligan had attacked his sister, and Gorky asked Kaganovich if it would be possible to invite Rolland and his family to settle permanently in the Crimea. ". . . This will be nice for him," assured Gorky, "and will make a very good impression on writers in Europe." Kaganovich answered by telegram: "I spoke with the comrades we doubt how he will react and need to explain the matter."

Rolland was actually not planning to exchange Switzerland for the Crimea, and the question was moot.

Gorky also began asking Kaganovich to tighten censorship: ". . . There is the danger of infiltration . . . of the ideology of the Mensheviks and SRs. This danger would be removed through closer participation in the work of the party organization. . . ."

Kaganovich had not managed to react to this request, very strange for any writer, when Gorky came up with a new initiative. In the evening Moscow newspaper he read an innocuous item about the opening of the Pushkin Café, with a room for dancing, on Pushkin Square. A letter was quickly dashed off to Moscow to "dear Lazar Moiseevich":

> This escapade is completely unacceptable and compromises Soviet power. As a citizen of the country that is creating a new culture . . . and as a writer of literature and chairman of the committee celebrating the hundredth anniversary of the pre-mature death of the great poet, poisoned by "the noble mob"—I protest in every possible way.

Gorky had found something that brought him joy—the opportunity to ruin someone's life! Kaganovich sent a return telegram to Tesseli: "Your completely correct suggestion to change the name of the café was accepted by the Moscow committee [of the Party], and those guilty were punished."

The popular French singer Gilbert Bécaud, in composing his wonderful little song "Nathalie" thirty years later, apparently did not know that the Pushkin Café of his imagination and nostalgic reminiscences had disappeared because of Gorky back in the 1930s.

On June 30, 1934, Hitler's closest advisor and rival Ernst Röhm was shot to death. Exactly five months later Sergei Kirov was murdered in Leningrad. Only the most insightful saw the analogy. On November 7 Gorky's favorite, Karl Radek, the best informed and most unprincipled Soviet publicist, wrote a prophetic article in *Izvestiia* in the form of a dialogue with Machiavelli. Addressing the notorious Italian, the author wrote,

... We will not give back to the fascists your idea of dictatorship ... Our proletariat ... can still learn something from you, such as how to unite the politics of the lion with the politics of the fox, and it will enthusiastically ... read your words: "When speaking about the salvation of the motherland, all notions about what is fair and unfair, what is merciful and cruel, what is glorious and what is shameful, must be tossed aside. You need to forget about everything and act only so that its existence is saved and its freedom remains untouched."

The prophecy, as we know, came true—"all notions" were tossed aside. Once he received the news of the murder, Stalin immediately dictated a law creating "troikas" to accelerate the investigation of an "anti-terror case" with neither a plaintiff nor defendant, with no possibility of appeal of the death sentence, depriving those sentenced of the right to a pardon, with the sentence to be carried out immediately.

On December 1, Gorky saw from his window unknown persons hiding behind trees and bushes in the park surrounding the Crimean dacha. If they were protecting him from evildoers, there was no need to hide; on the contrary, he would have been told that he was being reliably protected, but from whom, from what?

Didn't Gorky understand what was going on in the country, what was about to follow this shot? If thousands of others (we now have documented evidence of this!) understood this, then he should have as well. But how could he have expressed his awareness in a practical way? He had no other possibility except to sing along in unison with everyone else.

On the death of Kirov, he reacted as follows in an article for *Pravda* and *Literaturnaya gazeta*: "A wonderful person has been killed, one of the best leaders of the Party, an ideal example for the proletariat and a master of culture ... The success of the enemy speaks not only to its abomination, but also to the inadequacy of our vigilance." This was written on December 2 and published on the fourth. No "investigation" had been conducted, but everything was already obvious to Gorky: "the success of the enemy."

A bit later he elaborated the same theme in another article. "Kirov was killed, and it was revealed that the enemy is constantly sending dozens of murderers into our country to hunt down our leaders." Nothing had been "revealed," even according to Stalin's interpretation of the killing, but Gorky understood where this interpretation was heading and went ahead of events that were developing very quickly.

He had not managed to send the latest (the last, as it turned out) official letter to "dear Lev Borisovich Kamenev" with a request to attend to the condition of the Tomsk University library, when books were the last thing on his addressee's mind. Kamenev was arrested on the night of December 16–17; Zinoviev had already been arrested the day before. At the end of December a secret trial was conducted against Kirov's assassin, Leonid Nikolayev, and his "accomplices," who had absolutely nothing at all to do with the murder. They were executed immediately. On January 16, 1935, a guilty sentence was handed down against Zinoviev and Kamenev, accused of having created a so-called "underground Moscow center," of deceiving the Party, of making false confessions at the Seventeenth Congress and plotting Kirov's murder.

On the following day both Zinoviev, whom Gorky could not stand, and Kamenev, whom he greatly respected, appealed to him in writing from prison, seeing in him, as before, as perhaps the only person capable of preventing the inevitable.

"Aleksei Maksimovich," Zinoviev wrote,

> I have not had personal nor written communication with you for a long time and it often seemed to me, honestly speaking, that I personally did not take advantage of your friendship in the past. But many people write to you, one could say everyone. The reasons for this are understandable. Thus, allow me as well, now one of the unhappiest people in the whole world, to turn to you . . . You are a great artist. You are an expert of the human soul. You are a teacher of life . . . I ask you to think for a moment what it means for me now to sit in a Soviet jail . . . Most of all I fear ending up in a mental institution. That would be the most terrible punishment . . . Help me, Aleksei Maksimovich, if you think it possible!

Kamenev's letter was distinguished by greater restraint and severity:

> To the burden of what I am experiencing, it would be infinitely bitter for me to add the thought that you doubt the truthfulness and sincerity of my behavior toward you, the truthfulness of what I told you during our meetings.

He did not ask anything for himself, but asked only that his wife not be forgotten. "It will be hard for her. In time of need support her spiritually, strengthen her courage." It is now known that both these letters never reached Gorky; they ended up in the archives of the Lubyanka. Only many years later were they transferred to the secret part of the Gorky archive, where they were kept under lock and key almost to the end of the twentieth century.

After he returned to Moscow, Gorky unsuccessfully attempted to get through to Stalin and Yagoda. Neither would come to the telephone. It was possible to communicate only through Kriuchkov, who invariably answered that both high-ranking comrades were overloaded with work. He was right. Kriuchkov did report that Gorky wished to intercede on Kamenev's behalf, but this was already clear to everyone even without his report. However, on the evening of March 3, 1935, as recorded in the entries of Stalin's personal secretaries, Gorky officially visited Stalin in his Kremlin study and had a one-on-one conversation with him lasting an hour and five minutes (from 8:25 p.m. to 9:30 p.m.). This was the hour when Gorky was usually getting ready for bed. As to what the two partners discussed, there is absolutely no information available. Moreover, in the several published volumes of *A Chronicle of Gorky's Life*, where, it seems, his entire biography has been tracked hour by hour, where even his most insignificant meetings were noted, there is not a single word about this Kremlin get-together.

That stark entry in the secretary's ledger deserves some kind of answer. What is concealed behind such a beguiling secret? Why did Gorky visit Stalin, instead of the other way around, as had been the case many times—moreover, not on "a house call" but on official business? Did they talk about Kamenev? Did Stalin quietly recommend to Gorky not to get involved in something that he might later regret? Is there another way to decode the meeting between the supreme leader of all peoples and his great and devoted friend? We can only guess at the reasons why there was nothing mentioned in either *A Chronicle of Gorky's Life* or in any other source about one more meeting that remained classified until the end of the last century: Stalin's visit to Gorky on April 11, 1935. What could have been the secret about that one as well? After all, his other visits had been broadly reported while Gorky was alive and after his death.

This visit was preceded by a public attack on Gorky that was completely unexpected for both the writer and his readers. He could not reject critical attacks after writing in a letter to Politburo member Andrei Andreev that "I'm not against arguments, I'm for them. At the Union of Writers, unfortunately, no one argues anything." After that they began arguing, not just at the Union of Writers, but around the world. But can jeering be called argument? After Lenin's death the Soviet press had not indulged in such unbridled baiting.

David Zaslavsky was assigned to launch the attack. In the not-too-distant past he had been a prominent Menshevik and a member of the Central Committee of the Bund (All European Workers' Union), which had resolutely opposed the Bolsheviks. In 1917 he led a bitter campaign against Lenin, publishing extremely scandalous articles about him being a German spy. Very few branded Lenin an agent of the Central Powers and he called Zaslavsky a scoundrel, a well-known slanderer, a gossip, and a villain, condemning anyone who would agree or help Zaslavsky. Soon after Lenin's death, and to everyone's amazement, Zaslavsky became one of the leading publicists of *Pravda*, the central organ of the Party. For a non-Party person to achieve that position was unthinkable, and even more for a recent, vocal, and passionate opponent of Bolshevism. In 1934 Stalin himself recommended him to the Party—and Zaslavsky was proving that the leader had not put his trust in him for nothing.

He first pounced on the Academia publishing house (meaning on Kamenev) for publishing Dostoyevsky's novel *The Demons*. Zaslavsky characterized it as "a dirty little pasquinade aimed against the revolution." Insofar as Gorky was in charge of the publishing agenda, and Kamenev his main protégé, the blow was directed squarely against Gorky.

Zaslavsky did not even conceal whom he was attacking. Gorky was referred to in the article with the transparent and malicious title of "Literary Mold." Gorky took the bait on the obvious provocation, and *Pravda* gladly offered him the opportunity: "I am against the transformation of legal literature into illegal that is sold under the table."

Zaslavsky reacted with lightning speed:

> If, for the sake of consistency, to become acquainted with the ideology of the class enemy, according to Gorky, one should print not only the old junk from the 1860s and 1870s, but also contemporary rubbish . . . From such suggestions it follows that it is beneficial to publish an edition of counterrevolutionary literature by Trotsky, Zinoviev, and Kamenev and to open the floodgates to literary sewage.

Panferov took the opportunity to settle scores with Gorky and immediately joined Zaslavsky. In an article published in *Pravda* right after, he reminded Gorky how he had always praised "slanderers and double-dealers" and supported the "class enemy." Everyone understood who was behind this campaign against the "untouchable" Gorky. Moscow's informed readers knew that the direct order to Zaslavsky to write the article had come from Nikolai Yezhov, Stalin's closest henchman, who would replace Yagoda a year-and-a-half later as People's Commissar of Internal Affairs. Moreover, Lev Mekhlis, *Pravda's* editor-in-chief, who had previously served as Stalin's personal secretary, refused to print Gorky's reply to Panferov and his objection to Zaslavsky. It was made perfectly clear to Gorky that he could enjoy polite respect and a comfortable life on one condition: that he leave the political stage and shut up!

This "polemic"—mysterious for the average reader, but very clear for informed people—was happening during the days when a new sinister event took place: Politburo member Valeriyan Kuibyshev suddenly died. Gorky had been in contact with him and knew that he did not support the repression and opposed the most drastic measures. Kuibyshev was an alcoholic who suffered from obesity, Basedow's Disease,[*] and heart problems, yet his sudden death—a month-and-a-half after Kirov's murder—appeared to be more than just a coincidence.

One news item followed another. At their secret trial Zinoviev was sentenced to ten years in prison, Kamenev to five. Hardly had the first sentence been pronounced when a second immediately followed: Yagoda's efficient employees had uncovered a so-called "Kremlin plot"—Kremlin apparatus employees, mostly workers at the library it turns out, were concocting the murder of Stalin and his closest advisors. The head of the "plot" was Kamenev once again (Stalin clearly had a soft spot for him), and practically his whole family was singled out as co-conspirators. On the night of March 19–20, both wives—Olga Davydovna Kameneva and Tatyana Ivanovna Glebova-Kameneva-Afremova—his brother, artist Nikolai Rozenfeld, his brother's former wife Nina and their son Boris were arrested. Some were sent to the camps, others were exiled. Lev Kamenev's sentence was increased from five to ten years. If on March 3, during his meeting with Stalin at the Kremlin, Gorky truly had attempted to intercede for Kamenev, then the arrest of his wife and the sentencing of both can be considered a fitting response from the leader to Gorky's misplaced good intentions.

Gorky's public pronouncements honoring Stalin, however, did not lose any of their previous enthusiasm. "The intelligent and vigilant leadership of the Leninist Central Committee, headed by a person who truly deserved the deepest love of the working and peasant masses" was written not at the time of their daily friendly libations, but when Stalin was avoiding his persistent phone calls (January 1935). Since then his ecstatic words of praise had become even more fervent. While the former love had evaporated, the game continued. Forced to write exaggerated praise for the great Party and its brilliant leader, Gorky had to understand what was really happening in the country.

Another detail should be pointed out. Gorky's visit to Stalin's office was preceded by that of David Kandelaki, who left there, according to the ledger, at 8:25 p.m. Kandelaki was very close to Stalin, and a friend to the brother of his first wife, Yekaterina ("Alesha") Svanidze. Not long before this he was appointed trade representative to Germany, where he undertook highly secret negotiations with Hitler's higher-ups (including Göring) in an attempt to build bridges between Moscow and Berlin. Rumors of these negotiations were then circulating everywhere and had reached Gorky's ears as well, eliciting his horror: he saw in the closeness of the two dictators an inevitable crawl toward

---

[*] A common form of hyperthyroidism characterized by goiter and often a slight protrusion of the eyeballs; also known as exophthalmic goiter.

world war. Was this what he discussed with Stalin, and the reason their meeting was shrouded in secrecy? Or was his visit right after Kandelaki's no more than a coincidence, but deeply symbolic in any case? The mystery still exists, but it is time to end the myth about "striking changes" in their relationship. The form may have changed, but the content remained the same.

One can only guess at what had happened to his soul, but documents testify how he appeared to the outside world. One of his main correspondents was now Aleksandr Shcherbakov, an overweight curmudgeon who had become one of the Party's leading ideologues. In letters to him (February–April 1935) Gorky demanded that a monument be erected immediately in Moscow to the Pioneer and stool pigeon Pavel Morozov and that the "vacant dachas" of Kamenev and others who had been arrested be made available to those writers who were Gorky protégés.

In the same vein, probably the one that is most striking is the denunciation he sent to Shcherbakov about "Crimean youth," who "have found themselves for a long time under the influence of a group of counterrevolutionaries." He was referring to schoolchildren who were studying in a literary group under the auspices of the Sevastopol newspaper *Mayak kommuny* (Lighthouse of the Commune). A law had just been passed making all forms of punishment, including the death sentence, possible for adolescents, starting at the age of twelve—Gorky immediately showed his vigilance and understanding of the new situation in the country. "We did not succeed in eliminating the influence of the 'opponents,'" he grieved; ". . . therefore . . . people from Moscow ought to be sent here." The signal was received: "people from Moscow" were sent, the literary group was duly disbanded and its members arrested.

25.

An Old Circus Bear

Gorky was usually not in a hurry to leave Moscow. At least there was some kind of life and he was in contact with people and did not feel completely cut off from the rest of the world, and where, besides everything else, it was best to spend the summer in its suburbs than in the sultry Crimea. Still, he was planning to leave in May, at the end of the Crimean spring, but some unknown event led him to change his plans.

At the end of April 1935 he left for Tesseli without waiting a few more days to be present at the May Day celebrations he loved so much. The year before he had stood three times on the tribune atop Lenin's mausoleum, and once even had the opportunity to witness a truly unique event. On that day, June 19, the crew of the polar expedition aboard the icebreaker *Chelyuskin*, who, after crashing into the ice had spent several weeks on a drifting ice-floe before being rescued, were greeted as national heroes. They had been rescued, and Stalin had organized a grandiose celebration for both rescuers and rescued, the "highlight" of which was the appearance over Red Square of the largest airplane in the world, an eight-engine behemoth built by Anatoly Tupolev from the design of journalist and pilot Mikhail Koltsov. The "propaganda" airplane was named the *Maxim Gorky*. In addition to cabins for the crew and seventy-two seats for everyday passengers, it had magnificent staterooms with beds for elite passengers, a printing press, a photo laboratory, an electric generator, several powerful radio antennae, a telephone network, and a buffet with a huge samovar.

The airplane flew over the square during the parade, and thousands of people froze in amazement and horror when the gigantic metal bird descended so low in order to drop hundreds of thousands of leaflets over the crowd below that its wings (with a span of 206 feet) almost touched the supreme leader and Gorky.

On May 1, 1935, a repeat of this grandiose spectacle was expected, but at the last moment it was cancelled, and the demonstration flight of the *Maxim Gorky* was moved back two-and-a-half weeks to coincide with the annual "air show," beloved by Muscovites, held at Tushino airfield outside Moscow. Tens of thousands of people always showed up at this event to admire the masters of the aerobatic arts.

On the eve of the show the *Maxim Gorky* completed a training flight with honored guests aboard, including Antoine de Saint-Exupéry, who was full of enthusiasm for the aircraft; Henri Barbusse; and Arthur Koestler, who also happened to be in Moscow at the time. A professional pilot, Saint-Exupéry was not only a passenger but also co-pilot during the flight. The airplane's builders, along with their wives and children—forty-seven people in all—were invited to participate in the parade flight the next day.

For some reason the organizers of the celebration thought that the appearance of the gigantic plane by itself would not produce the desired effect. In contravention of the rules, three different types of airplanes, without any practice on the ground or even a preliminary training flight, were also sent aloft. One of the country's best pilots, Nikolai Blagin, was to accompany the *Maxim Gorky* on a small I-5 fighter plane and perform highly complicated loops around it, without a radio connection to a control panel on the ground.

This was an absurd task and not a single ace in the world could have performed a "figure eight" around the wings of the enormous airplane, owing to their difference in speed. Thousands of people stood on the airfield and anxiously watched the pilot attempt to carry out his assignment.

The third attempt was fatal. Blagin cut into a wing of the *Maxim Gorky* and the monster crashed to the ground. There were no survivors.

The flood of condolences to Gorky was greater even than to the families of the victims. "Together with you I deeply grieve," Aleksandr Shcherbakov telegraphed to Tesseli, using the traditional expression of sympathy at the death of a dear one. "The 'Maxim Gorky' has died," wrote the newspapers. From over-usage the quotation marks disappeared altogether so that the phrase read as "Maxim Gorky has died!"

It seems that he felt he was attending his own funeral. "The absurd destruction of the 'Gorky' airplane," he wrote Shcherbakov, "has made me howl like a wolf." "I am troubled that . . . the destruction of the airplane has shaken you so much," Shcherbakov expressed his sympathy a second time. The death of the son and the demise of the *Maxim Gorky* were of the same rank.

What really happened remains a mystery to this day. Several days later Anatoly Tupolev, the airplane's designer, was arrested, even though he had nothing to do with the tragedy—it was not the *Gorky* that crashed into the fighter plane, but the other way around. And even if it had, why would its builder be responsible? His colleagues were told that the crash of the giant plane did not incriminate Tupolev. Was the catastrophe and the arrest only a coincidence?

The Soviet press—writing on orders, naturally—was up in arms against "air hooligan" Blagin, and the voice of fighter pilot Mikhail Gromov, who had tested this very same airplane, joined the chorus. But two of the seven Hero of the Soviet Union pilots—Mikhail Vodpyanov and Mavriki Slepnev—refused to sign the collective condemnation once they realized that there was something fishy about the matter.

Four months later an apocryphal "last will and testament" of Nikolai Blagin appeared in the Russian émigré press, wherein the kamikaze pilot admitted that he had consciously committed a terrorist act: "Tomorrow I will fly my winged machine and ram it into the airplane which bears the name of the scoundrel Maxim Gorky. In this manner I will kill dozens of Communists."

The coarse forgery was obvious, and now has been proven beyond a doubt: the "will" was written overseas. Besides, if Blagin had really wanted to "crash" into the mausoleum and destroy Lenin's mummy, along with the leaders standing on the tribune, including the "scoundrel" himself, then why would he have decided to kill his closest friends, together with six of their children, ranging in age from eight to fifteen?

So who gave the order to perform a "figure eight" with that predetermined outcome? And why was no one held accountable for the criminal aerial stunts above residential buildings? This question was not even asked. Was there some connection between this event and the secret decree of the Central Committee adopted six days earlier (it has not been published to this day) about the creation of a "Special Safety Commission for Members of the Politburo" headed by Stalin? Or was that just another coincidence?

It is very likely that Gorky's premature departure to the Crimea was the reason for canceling the May Day flight. Some kind of show had been prepared but in Gorky's absence it was meaningless.

The key to solving the Tushino tragedy, possibly, lies in Stalin's decision several days later. Donations were being gathered for the construction of four more airplanes just like the one that crashed, only with different names. The vacancy left by the *Maxim Gorky* would now be occupied by an even bigger *Joseph Stalin* and, in slightly smaller dimensions, *Vyacheslav Molotov*, *Klim Voroshilov*, and *Mikhail Kalinin*. The leader made it clear that the flagship of the air force could only be the same as the flagship of the country. Gorky, who had practically experienced a rehearsal of his death, reacted to Stalin's eloquent gesture two months later with the following words: "Long live Joseph Stalin, a man of huge heart and mind . . ." Stalin, in turn, coined a popular expression in the style of Gorky's aphorisms: "A person is the most valued asset in our country."

In the middle of June an international congress of writers in defense of culture was planned in Paris, organized by French leftist authors. The congress was financed by Moscow; the Kremlin's emissary, Mikhail Koltsov, handed the money over to the organizers. Gorky was planning to take part in it, although he had written to Shcherbakov, "I am becoming decrepit. My ability to work is dropping . . . For some time now I have a fear of going blind. It's an idiotic disease; however it does hinder me. My heart works lazily and capriciously."

On April 19, the Politburo confirmed the names in the huge delegation of Soviet writers, with Gorky the appointed leader. Sometime later, at his insistence, his favorite Vsevolod Ivanov was added to the delegation, which included names unknown outside Soviet Russia. On June 8, Gorky was issued a foreign passport. It appeared that his desired goal of going abroad was close to realization, and that the traditional reason to prevent him from going—doctors' orders—might not have worked, since his desire to participate in the congress was so great that he would have ignored their advice anyway. A search began to find a solution to the situation, and it was found.

Romain Rolland had been planning for a long time to visit his great Russian friend. Gorky had proposed that they participate in the congress and then travel from Paris back to Moscow together. To the joy of the Kremlin, though, Rolland did not want to come to Paris. "The soil in Paris is rotten," he wrote to Henri Barbusse. "Sooner or later it will poison everyone who steps on it." He had dreamed of holding the congress in the Soviet Union. "Moscow should, in my opinion, remain the center of the great new movement," he wrote to Gorky.

Stalin was afraid to hold a gathering of writers from around the world in Moscow—who knows who would have wanted to come? And who could guarantee their behavior? Paris, with its broad Soviet participation, but minus Gorky, was the preferred option. The situation could not have turned out any better: the arrival of Rolland alone in Moscow could ruin Gorky's trip to Paris if both events were in conflict.

At the key moment Gorky received a letter from Maria Kudasheva, Rolland's wife. It is too categorical, too tendentious and too purposeful to not be part of Stalin's plan:

> [Rolland] is very happy to meet you and in fact he waits for this more than anything else. But it would be better if the meeting takes place in an intimate and

easy setting, without tension, not in a hotel among strangers and when he would be tired! . . . Would it not be better to have the most favorable conditions for it, free it from anything external that can interfere with it! . . . After all, there is Moscow. Is that not a better place for a *first* meeting?

Many years later the son of the French writer Georges Duhamel, Bernard, while preparing his father's diaries for publication, spoke with Kudasheva. "Maria," he wrote, "denies that the Soviets manipulated her," although in conversation with him she referred to a certain Moscow "friend" who, perhaps in a slip of the tongue, she even called her "chief." However, Bernard Duhamel stated that collaboration between Kudasheva and the "Soviets" in general "cannot be discussed." In the very best case, he specified, it could have been "as ordinary blackmail."

I also had the opportunity to have a long discussion with Madame Rolland in May 1968. Maria Pavlovna told me essentially the same thing she told Bernard Duhamel, only in more general terms, and as if she were justifying herself: "I already knew before going to see Rolland [from the Soviet Union] that nothing could be concealed from the GPU." She repeated this several years later, only more openly, to Russian writer Boris Nosik: "When I was sent to visit Rolland, I did not know if he would leave me at his place or not." At the time this declaration could not be related to anything, but now, after the publication of previously classified Gorky documents, it becomes much more tangible.

Working in the 1920s as a technical employee in the French embassy in Moscow, Kudasheva could not avoid having "friendly" relations with the Lubyanka, which used her to "mix" with the French leftist cultural elite—and writers mostly—that came to Moscow. She attempted to seduce Paul Claudel, and flirted with Charles Vildrac, Georges Duhamel, and Luc Durtain, trying to draw them into honeytraps and by no means without the consent of the Lubyanka (and possibly on its direct orders). She initiated an epistolary romance with Rolland, obtaining his permission to come see him.

"Do you know Maria Kudasheva," Romain Rolland asked Gorky on April 5, 1928, "who writes me from Moscow and whom Duhamel and Durtain told me about? She was their devoted guide in Russia. Now she is simply in love with Bolshevism . . ." What did Gorky know about Kudasheva, whom he had seen once in the Crimea, other than that she indulged in poetry and once belonged to a circle of literary bohemians? Nevertheless, he ardently supported the young lady who was "in love" with Rolland and even asked his friends at the Lubyanka to allow her to go see the great elderly man. But that was exactly what they wanted . . .

In order for the plan to succeed, the illusion had to be created that the sinister institution, on the contrary, was opposed to the trip. Kudasheva could never have avoided orders from Moscow, even if she wanted to. Despite all its politeness, her letter to Gorky was fundamentally peremptory in tone. Rejecting Kudasheva's offer, Gorky refused to meet with Rolland in Moscow or forced him to go to Paris, which the latter for some reason (or due to someone's influence; perhaps from Kudasheva herself?) stubbornly opposed.

Gorky found a compromise: on June 8, as soon as he was handed his foreign passport, he telegraphed Rolland that he was going to Paris and was leaving his Moscow home at his disposal where he expected to meet him at the beginning of July. Gorky was straining to get to Paris, even if it meant canceling the meeting.

Stalin's plan was about to fail, so he had to resort to a tried and true method: Gorky "by chance" and "unexpectedly" came down with bronchitis. Rolland, in the meantime, was preparing his trip to Moscow. Aleksandr Arosev, a diplomat friend of Molotov, was sent to meet him halfway. Fearing that Rolland would postpone his arrival by at least a few days, the organizers suggested that Arosev go directly to Switzerland to fetch Rolland, who resisted, so they agreed on Warsaw. Rolland had been given advance notice that the ailing Gorky was waiting for him in Moscow, even though Gorky was still convinced he would be going to Paris.

Stalin's need to play "hide and seek" was so great that two more emissaries were dispatched to meet Rolland along the way: Kriuchkov and Dr. Levin. They awaited their guests at the border station of Negoreloe. By then the main Soviet delegation was already in Paris. Gorky was not among the delegates (the doctors had restricted him to his bed). Panferov, his supposed replacement, was there instead. Stalin had put everyone in their place with unique insidiousness.

The Paris Congress opened on June 21.

Rolland arrived in Moscow on the twenty-third.

Gorky (coming from Tesseli) showed up only on the twenty-eighth.

Prominent writers had gathered in Paris. Although Thomas Mann, H. G. Wells, George Bernard Shaw, Upton Sinclair, and several others did not show for various reasons, 230 writers from thirty-eight countries accounted for an impressive and prestigious collection of left-wing intellectuals. Heinrich Mann, Bertold Brecht, Aldous Huxley, Selma Lagerlöf, Lion Feuchtwänger, and Max Brod, along with their French colleagues André Gide, André Malraux, Aragon, Paul Eluard, and many others passionately denounced not only fascism, as Moscow had assumed, but also against every kind of suppression of freedom of speech, and violence against human beings. To compensate for Gorky's absence, Stalin, at Koltsov's request, also sent Babel and Pasternak after the delegates had left; even their participation represented a lesser evil in his eyes.

Gorky was not forgotten in Paris. The working-class suburb of Villejuif, under communist control, named one of its boulevards after him; five thousand people showed up for the official opening. André Gide was master of ceremonies and the mayor of Villejuif, a publicist and member of the French Communist Party's Politburo, gave a speech, as did Louis Aragon, Leon Moussinac, Luc Durtain, and other French left-wing intellectuals. Mikhail Koltsov represented Gorky. A telegram was sent to Gorky, who would have preferred to represent himself at the ceremony.

Gorky's failed trip coincided with another dramatic story being played out in parallel. Timosha was being drawn further and further into more sinister "love" nets. Following the death of Max, Yagoda felt on top of the situation. His dacha was not far from Gorky's residence and, under the guise of going to his own place, he showed up instead almost every morning for breakfast at Gorky's, leaving his car a distance from the house and casually cutting across the field from the gates to the main entrance.

Gorky did not come down for breakfast—after waking he would follow his long-established routine of working in his office until lunchtime. The children remained in Moscow, attending school (Marfa was in the same class as Svetlana Stalin and even sat in the same row with her). Yagoda and Timosha usually had breakfast together. In the evening he would show up again for dinner. He sat in front of her and they exchanged meaningful glances back and forth for everyone to see. There is eyewitness testimony of Timosha's frequent visits to Yagoda's office in the Lubyanka. A housekeeper at one of Yagoda's dachas on the Leningrad highway later explained how the Lubyanka chief would often stop there for about two or three hours in the company of a young woman she described exactly as being Timosha. Kriuchkov reported on an investigation of major amounts of hard currency that Yagoda had given to Timosha through him just before his own dethronement; Yagoda did not want money to enter into their relationship. The testimony of anyone under arrest in an investigation within the Lubyanka must be taken with utmost skepticism; however, some parts may be true. The sinister art of the masters of torture consists of building their own fantastic constructions on actual facts interpreted to suit their purpose. The detail about money logically connects to an indisputable truth.

At the same time Aleksei Tolstoy also experienced a cruel attack of unrequited but persistent love for Timosha. He was a constant guest in Gorki and Tesseli, where Timosha often accompanied Gorky. In the evenings he drank with Kriuchkov, obsequiously making him cocktails and complaining about his job. It often turned out that both pretenders for the heart of the young widow were present at the dinner table.

Tolstoy's "secret" love was no secret to anyone, and especially not to Yagoda. He was smart enough not to have any displays of jealousy; on the contrary, he brought his unsuccessful rival even closer to him. Yagoda willingly acquainted him with the secrets of his institution, which was highly valued, and, as Tolstoy admitted in one of his letters, Yagoda had given him "incredible material" for a new novel. To cap it off, he secured permission for him to buy and bring a car into the country without having to pay import taxes; broke him of the habit, in order to avoid unpleasantries, of interceding on behalf of arrested writers; and did many other useful things for Tolstoy.

Two people saw the development of this romance with anguish and utter helplessness: Gorky and Tolstoy's wife, the poetess Natalia Krandievskaya, who remained with her children at the Tolstoy home outside Leningrad. "Compliments to Timosha," she wrote her husband in Moscow, " ... but don't forget that you have a family ... Your loving wife who misses you very much."

Tolstoy suffered two serious heart attacks, but this did not cool off his youthful ardor. Gorky carefully attempted to reason with him:

> At fifty you cannot act like a thirty-year-old ... You should also drink wine in moderation ... and all contact with other women should be limited to communication with your own wife—which is established and sanctified by the canons of the Orthodox Church.

It could not be said any clearer than that, but Tolstoy was unable to "limit his contacts."

In May 1935, while all the agonizing commotion surrounding Gorky's trip to Paris was taking place, Yagoda organized another trip to Europe—not for himself, but for Timosha and Yekaterina Pavlovna. It might have appeared as if they were simply being allowed to take a break following the loss of a son and husband. In fact, the trip had very specific objectives. Gorky's home and property were still in Sorrento. When he left Italy in 1933, he had not burned all his bridges behind him. In her memoirs Peshkova writes that she went to "liquidate the remaining property of Aleksei Maksimovich" (Yagoda gave them two thousand dollars to pay off their debts).

Timosha had a different purpose: she wanted to spend time in London and talk Mura into relinquishing Gorky's archive. Its fate—the so-called "suitcase"—remains mysterious to this day, but in the summer of 1935 it was still in

Mura's possession. Now Timosha, the only person from Gorky's circle who did not have a troubled relationship with Mura, was supposed to carry out a very tricky—and possibly even fatal—assignment. But on whose behalf: Gorky's or Yagoda's?

A "group of artists" was cobbled together as a decoy. Timosha supposedly had been involved with art in the past so her presence in the group would not raise any eyebrows. The well-known artist Pavel Korin, whom Yagoda tried to use in every way possible, was assigned to assist her and given the assignment to be Timosha's teacher—on the trip he also acted as her chaperone, protecting her from obnoxious admirers.

And there was someone to protect her from: Tolstoy had latched on to the group! Yagoda, knowing full well that Tolstoy was destined to fail on this romantic front, did not place any obstacles in his path. The trip coincided with the congress in Paris, and Tolstoy was part of the delegation, giving him the right to move freely about in Europe. Perhaps Timosha had given him some hope back in Moscow. Mura's lines in a letter to Gorky from London, sent at the end of June, make an allusion: "Concerning Timosha's 'faux pas,' I agree with you, but this, of course, is unthinkable and she is 'tormenting herself.'" The overly demonstrative importunities of the "red count" pursuing the young widow roused Timosha to reach an understanding with him in London. Having finally realized that there was no hope, Tolstoy left her alone. Timosha's meeting with Mura, who had her own plans regarding Gorky's inheritance, also ended without results. Besides their mutual admiration for cocktails in Parisian cafés and London pubs, Timosha had nothing to brag about afterwards.

Rolland was already in Moscow when Yekaterina Pavlovna and Timosha left Paris for Sorrento. On the way they stopped in Fréjus, not far from Grasse, where Bunin lived. Yekaterina Pavlovna had once been very close to his wife Vera, who did not come alone to see her friend, but was accompanied by her husband. Bunin listened in silence to the tales of the guests about their happy life in the Soviet Union, said simply, "You have become Bolshevized," and left.

Having settled their debts and sold Gorky's property in Sorrento, both ladies returned to Moscow on July 13. Tolstoy's melancholy did not last long. Krandievskaya and her children left home; but her place was immediately filled by his secretary, the twenty-six-year-old Liudmila Barsheva. After several weeks she would legally become Countess Tolstoy after leaving her proletarian husband, the prose writer Nikolai Barshev, whose first literary experiments were highly esteemed by Gorky. Nikolai Barshev would later be arrested and executed on March 30, 1938.

Arosev beseeched Rolland to stay in his apartment, knowing how important this visit was for Stalin personally, at the same time elevating himself in the eyes of the leader. Although Arosev had a small three-room apartment in the "house on the embankment,"* Rolland did not dare refuse his persistent companion but, "just in case," he booked a room in a hotel. The "just in case" immediately came to pass: unable to close his eyes for two nights because of an invasion of bedbugs, Rolland called a taxi in the middle of the third night and, without waking their hosts, fled to the Savoy Hotel, where an apartment with several rooms awaited them.

The struggle for the "body" of Rolland continued: Arosev begged him to return, assuring him that he had exterminated the pests; Gorky summoned him to his own suburban Moscow residence; and Rolland himself preferred to stay in the hotel. On June 28, Stalin received the guests. The official ledger has been preserved with the following entry: "16:00–18:00: com. Arosev, com. Rolland and com. wife of Romain Rolland." For two hours—an inconceivably long time for Stalin—he patiently showed courtesy and a favorable disposition, emphasizing many times that he was at "the complete disposal" of his dear guest. The conversation, however, did not give him any satisfaction: Rolland began to speak about Viktor Serge, who was continuing to serve out his exile; about the mass executions of the "conspirators"; and the recently passed law that allowed sentencing children as young as twelve. Stalin vaguely justified himself, referring to the "severe laws of the class struggle," and then interrupted the conversation by saying "We'll meet at Gorky's." Arosev recorded notes of the conversation and sent them to Stalin for his approval, but the latter refused to publish them.

The following day Rolland was driven to Gorky's urban palace and a day after that, following a parade of gymnasts which both attended, to his suburban Moscow residence. Bukharin joined them for lunch on July 4, charming Rolland with his intelligence, simplicity, "youthful soul," and beautiful knowledge of French. At the same time he puzzled him with a very mysterious and ambiguous phrase: "We have to constantly maneuver and adapt ourselves, for everything is relative and subject to change." Gorky nodded his head in agreement.

In the middle of lunch, Bukharin suddenly had to leave in a hurry: a call had come in from Moscow warning that Stalin, together with Molotov, Kaganovich, and Voroshilov, would be arriving in the evening. In parting,

---

* Reference to Yuri Trifonov's famous novel, *The House on the Embankment*, which first appeared in January 1976 in the journal *Druzba narodov* (Friendship of the Peoples). Built in 1928–1931, the huge complex overlooking the Moscow River had a theater, cinema, two stores, and apartments for the Party elite. It was also known as "Government House."

Bukharin exchanged a few friendly jabs with Gorky, and Gorky kissed him on the forehead. He had barely left when the table was set for the more important guests.

Stalin was in a good mood, constantly pouring wine for Gorky, forcing him to drink without pause, deliberately indignant at Kriuchkov for acting like master of the house, and showing off his humanism by condemning the unjustifiable measures which—without his knowledge, of course—the Lubyanka used against innocent people. There was no mention of the Paris congress, as if it had not even happened.

The author and director of the program prepared for Rolland was Yagoda, with Kriuchkov as its executor. Every day, without any agreement from the host and guest, construction workers on the Moscow metro system, parachutists, Young Communist activists from Moscow, Pioneers from Armenia, and so on came to Gorki. Composers performed their works for hours, followed by ninety writers reading their poetry and prose in Russian. With only one day off for a breather, Yagoda brought in 150 underage criminals who also read poetry, sang songs, and danced. Rolland was simply fenced off from any undesirable meetings. In spite of his requests, neither Pasternak nor Shostakovich was allowed to come to Gorki.

Yagoda cajoled Rolland as much as possible, trying to worm his way into the French writer's confidence. He told him fairy tales about the wonderful conditions of life in Stalin's camps and how former prisoners are "re-forged" into law-abiding citizens. He "secretly" allowed Rolland to read Viktor Serge's manuscript about the history of Western anarchism, confiscated during Serge's arrest, and even promised to give him a copy. On parting, however, instead of the promised manuscript he gave Rolland a bouquet of flowers.

"An enigmatic personality" is how Rolland characterized Yagoda in his Moscow diary which, according to his wishes, was made public only a half century later. "He appeared to be a refined and elegant person . . . But his police functions instill horror. He speaks quietly, calling black white and white black, and looks at you in amazement with honest eyes if you begin to doubt his words." Rolland's Moscow diary also contains an entry about how unnamed people—simply called "others"—try to impress upon him how soft and kind Yagoda is, how tired he is and how he has aged in recent years because of his excessive work load. It is not Gorky's voice that he was referring to; Rolland would have mentioned him or Kriuchkov. Was Timosha this "other"?

With the arrival of the women, life in Gorki became more humane and pleasant. Timosha enthroned herself at the head of the table, and the Rollands immediately felt at home. She is "very pretty, cheery, simple and charming," Rolland recorded in his diary. (Kaverin had a different impression of her:

"cordial and indifferent.") When Timosha was absent—she was often away in Moscow *on business*—her place was taken by Yekaterina Pavlovna. Only she spoke French, which liberated Kudasheva from translation duty and made the conversation freer; Kriuchkov, who was constantly at their side, did not know French. "Bitterness is concealed in [Peshkova's] smile," Rolland wrote in his diary.

The bitterness stemmed from the premature loss of her son, which she could not get over. Once, when she was alone with Rolland, she confessed that she despised the circle around Gorky. She meant Yagoda and Kriuchkov. Even more dispiriting was the fact that all her activity for the Political Red Cross was now frozen and that Yagoda not only did not help her but actually sabotaged the job. Gorky was also resolutely against her working there: "You cannot get mixed up with state affairs." He did not lift a finger when the Society of Former Exiles and Political Prisoners was closed, to which Stalin and Voroshilov and other Soviet "leaders" formally belonged—all he managed was to get permission from Stalin to hand over a portion of his library to the Union of Writers.

Rolland might not have believed Peshkova had Gorky not defended before him several strange—to put it mildly—decisions by the Soviets. For example, he considered it an indisputable fact that "Kremlin librarians" were preparing to murder Stalin: a secret trial had just ended, known since as the "Kremlin case," the same one where an additional five years were tacked on to Lev Kamenev's prison term. Thus, a person whom Gorky had long respected over the course of many years, whom he had rescued from exile, and for whom he had just (!) obtained prestigious academic posts, he now suddenly considered a potential murderer! There was something to Kamenev's fear, expressed in his last letter to Gorky from prison . . .

The selection of students to enter college according to social indicators also troubled Rolland. Gorky objected, "If you have to choose, who would you sacrifice—the majority or the minority?" Gorky did not answer the counterargument, "Then why are you outraged by Hitler, who wants to eradicate the Jewish minority?" "There is pain and fear in his eyes," Rolland noted in his diary.

Lipa had overheard this conversation. Taking Kudasheva off to the side, she whispered, "Gorky thinks the same as you, but he doesn't dare say it." She had found someone to trust! Let there be no doubt: Gorky's secret thoughts, voiced by Lipa, reached the ears of those who were especially interested in them. What was Gorky afraid of? Microphones? Or any one of his guests, no matter who it was?

From the partially accessible NKVD file on Gorky it is clear that several authors—regulars at the Gorky home—were writing denunciations, signing them with their agency nicknames: "Altaisky," "Zorin," "Sayanov" . . . Rolland was also mentioned in these denunciations. The French guest told Gorky about a book by Boris Suvarin,[*] just published in Paris, where he wrote that Stalin had participated in robberies at the beginning of the century to enrich the Bolshevik treasury. On May 21, 1968, Maria Pavlovna Kudasheva, whom I visited in her apartment in Montparnasse in Paris, told me, recalling this episode, "Gorky could not interrupt his guest, but his eyes were filled with anguish." In his *Moscow Diary* Rolland concisely described the atmosphere which the almost totally blind man could not see: "Those independently minded, but capable of prudently holding their tongues, have vanished. One cannot speak too loudly. He who bares his soul gives himself away."

Rolland was also convinced that authority must always be urged to be humane—in the final analysis those kinds of appeals might work. So that there would be no doubt that he shared the French writer's opinions, Gorky published an article in *Pravda* before Rolland's departure and undoubtedly translated for him by Maria Kudasheva: "The humanism of the proletariat demands inextinguishable hatred . . . by the regime of the capitalists, their lackeys and parasites . . ." He added that "the proletariat of the Soviet republics, led by . . . the inexhaustible, ever growing energy of Iosif Stalin, creates a new culture, a new history of mankind's working class."

The sad and significant paradox was that Rolland, against whom the Gorky of Sorrento had written humiliating denunciations to Yagoda, turned out to be for the Gorky of Moscow, the only connecting thread to the free world.

The day to say goodbye arrived. Gorky had tried to talk Rolland into moving to the Soviet Union for good. Was he worried about Rolland? Or did he dream of having at least one close person near him? "In essence, he is a weak, very weak person," Rolland precisely diagnosed in his diary. "I love him very much and I am very sorry for him. He is very lonely, even though he is almost never alone. It seems to me that if he and I could be alone together (and the language barrier did not exist), he would embrace me and sob silently for a long time." Quick and to the point, Rolland had called Gorky a person who "will carry the heavy burden of sadness, nostalgia, and regrets."

It is worth citing a more complete quote from Rolland's diary, striking in its exactitude in piercing Soviet reality at that time and of Gorky's condition, which Maria had forbade him to publish and which saw the light of day only after her death:

[*] Also known as Boris Souvarine

> Having drowned in the storm of popular ovations, Gorky became intoxicated... He does not want to see but he does see the mistakes and the suffering, and at times even the inhumanity of what is happening. In essence, he is a weak, very weak person, in spite of his appearance as an old bear . . . He has allowed himself to be locked up in his own home . . . Kriuchkov is the only go-between for all of Gorky's contacts with the outside world . . . One has to be as weak-willed as Gorky to submit to control and surveillance at every second. The old bear has a ring in his nostrils . . . An unhappy old bear, crowned with laurels and showered with honors!

A terrible but amazingly accurate image of the crumbling and helpless bear, led around on a chain dancing for the amusement of the crowd, allowing his master the opportunity to earn a good living from his debasement.

Gorky and his whole family accompanied Rolland to the station. Only Yekaterina Pavlovna was in the car with Rolland. Kudasheva was in a separate car with Gorky. Peshkova did not need a translator. But who could say for sure that the driver did not understand French? It was there in the car that she told him openly what Rolland had already understood on his own: Gorky was in a cage and no longer capable of getting out of it.

It was a painful farewell. Gorky looked at the departing train for a long time. Bukharin stood next to him. The leaders did not show up, since Rolland was no longer needed. Arosev had been sent a year earlier on a special business trip abroad. Now Rolland had someone else—Kriuchkov—accompanying him to Warsaw. Tipsy from wine and self-aggrandizement, he boasted that he was reading all of Gorky's correspondence and did not bother taking notes of his conversations with him, insofar as he "can control the notes of others." Rolland was convinced that he was one of the "others," and that his diary had been read and photocopied. Kriuchkov was alluding to something else: he could read the denunciations of all the agents surrounding Gorky, because Yagoda gave them to him.

Gorky spent three weeks in Gorki, meeting infrequently with writers who came to visit. He was then taken on another boat tour along the Volga, with Timosha, his granddaughters, their governess Magda, Lipa, Valentina Khodasevich, Kriuchkov, and Dr. Levin. The prominent guests—more precisely, Timosha—were accompanied by Yagoda, and Matvei Pogrebinsky, that same "Motya the Policeman" now appointed NKVD boss of the Gorki *oblast*, as far as Stalingrad. The steamer was named *Maxim Gorky,* just like the airplane that crashed.

During the course of the whole two-week excursion he never once went ashore when the vessel was moored at port. Using their motor boats, a few local Party bosses came aboard to report their "grandiose successes." Gorky was wilting from the heat and oppressive humidity. "Above us," recalled Valentina Khodasevich later, "often hung a gray blanket of storm clouds, but it did not rain, and it seemed that this gray cover was about to suffocate us. The ship was shaking from the engine working noisily without interruption . . . The cutlery bounced up and down on the table." The hold was crammed full of oxygen cylinders—without them Gorky simply could not breathe. But he kept to himself in his stateroom, avoiding any contact, and not just because practically the whole crew was staffed with Lubyanka employees. Anyone could sense the atmosphere reigning on the ship. Yagoda apparently ordered that a door be cut out in his stateroom, connecting it with the adjacent one, designated for Timosha.

Vladimir Yakovlevich Lakshin, previously mentioned, told me that Valentina Khodasevich's memoirs contained a story, excised by the censor, about Dr. Levin sitting on deck, buried in heavy medical books. Khodasevich once asked him what was bothering him so much. "We treated him correctly," replied Levin with some embarrassment, referring to Max. "I don't understand why he died."

Was that a naïve attempt to deflect suspicion from himself? A suspicion growing stronger as he attempted to understand the secret of Max's death? Did he realize his own guilt, even unwillingly? Or was there something else?

Henri Barbusse lived in Moscow for a long time but very rarely saw Gorky. If Gorky had only wanted, Barbusse would have gladly moved to Gorki, where there were always many vacant rooms, but Gorky clearly did not want this. The book entitled *Stalin*, whose author was supposed to have been Gorky, was written (or merely signed?) by Barbusse.

Unlike Gorky, Barbusse traveled unhindered to Paris to take part in the writers' congress. He then returned to Moscow, crowned with success and rewarded for a job well done. He did not meet up with his great fellow countryman and colleague in Moscow either: perhaps aware of the complex relationship between them, Rolland's "organizers" kept him away from Barbusse. Besides, Barbusse was busy preparing for another assignment: to sing the praises of the upcoming Seventh (and last, as it turned out) Congress of the Comintern in Moscow. This Congress was of great significance, signaling a change in tactics in the strategy of world Communism, to backing the unification of leftist forces in a "popular front"); but beyond that it created powerful support of "like-minded individuals" for Stalin in the period immediately preceding the outbreak of the Great Terror.

Recognizing the benefit he had brought to his Moscow friends, Barbusse decided to fortify his success, not unreasonably counting on their gratitude.

Moving into the same Savoy Hotel from which Rolland had recently checked out, he began setting up appointments with the leaders of the Comintern, to convince them to financially support the "united anti-capitalist front," to which he was closely tied. In other words, he simply demanded money for services rendered. The nominal head of the Comintern, Georgi Dimitrov, forwarded Barbusse's carefully detailed estimate to Kaganovich and Molotov; all papers were returned to the Comintern with an anonymous but very eloquent decision: "Limit amount of subsidy in view of Barbusse's excessive requests."

This slap in the face practically meant that Barbusse had already done his duty and that the Kremlin no longer had any need of his services. The writer, who was well known not just in France and the Soviet Union, was refusing handouts. On August 26, after some wine and shellfish, Barbusse felt sick. He was taken to the Kremlin hospital with a temperature that had suddenly shot up to 104 degrees. Cut off from everything, he worked on crossword puzzles. Four days later he died from "symptoms of lobar pneumonia." The diagnosis was the same as the one given for Max, even though Barbusse did not go fishing, did not go for a swim in the icy water, and did not lie for a few hours on the damp ground. Dr. Levin was among those who signed this latest "death certificate."

Why did Stalin need the death of Barbusse? The assumption that it was because of the writer's gravitation toward Trotskyism is absurd—he had published only a few articles in the spirit of Trotskyism, which had provoked the dissatisfaction of the French Communist Party and the Comintern. The narrow vision of the dogmatists disturbed Stalin; he clearly discussed this with Ivan Gronsky: "Barbusse is political capital, but they are squandering it." Stalin could hardly have feared Barbusse's critical attitude to the trial of Zinoviev and Kamenev. First of all, the May 1935 trial had not yet been planned and, secondly, he knew that Barbusse would not have raised any objections.

Perhaps, then, the reason is in the slavish book *Stalin* Barbusse had signed, where one reads the following description of the leader, composed (prompted, perhaps?) by Barbusse's secretary, the German Communist writer Alfred Kurella, who had fled Germany, later to become secretary for ideology in the German Democratic Republic: "No matter who you are"—Soviet (and not only Soviet) citizens memorized these words in study groups about the rudiments of political knowledge—"your destiny is in the hands of this person with the mind of a scientist and the face of a worker dressed as a simple soldier." It could not have been said any better than that!

The mystery surrounding this unexpected and mysterious death becomes even thicker when we discover the fear of leaked documents unknown to us, which clearly frightened the top comrades in Moscow. Documents that turned up in the briefly declassified Comintern archive of G. Dimitrov before it was closed again attest to this.

The executor of the delicate assignment was André Marti, a member of the Central Committee of the French Communist Party and a deputy in the French parliament; he practically lived uninterruptedly in Moscow as secretary to the executive committee of the Comintern. Every Soviet schoolchild at the time knew the name of this "internationalist hero," who had led an insurrection in support of the Red Army. He would subsequently be labeled a renegade and expelled from the French Communist Party in 1952 and his name became anathema in the Soviet Union. Marti had the blood of thousands of Spanish republicans on his hands.

On August 31, the day after Barbusse's death, he dashed off the following to Dimitrov, a copy of which was sent to the Lubyanka:

> Secret Report.
>
> 31.8.35: I headed to the Savoy Hotel, room number 16 at 13:10. Comrade Annette Vidal, secretary of comrade Barbusse, handed me some files, a list of which is appended hereto.* Informing me in detail on the contents of the files, she singled out those pages (around ten) several times, which she identified as personal documents.
>
> She noted, incidentally, that maximum political advantage from Barbusse's death could be extracted if he were buried in Moscow.
>
> Then she . . . specified that many documents, in particular, invoices . . . were hidden in three different places in France. She promised upon her return to Paris to do everything possible to hand over all documents to the Party . . .
>
> I left my room at 14 hours 16 minutes.
>
> Comrade Susanna Tilge, stenographer of the secretariat of the E[xecutive Committee] of the C[omintern] was present at the conversation.

Neither the text of the "report" nor his specific style (such punctuality: "14 hours 16 minutes"! As if he left the meeting not as a writer but some kind of important spy, where every second spent in his company is laden with significance!) requires any commentary. But the postscript to the denunciation, where a fragment of the shorthand report of the conversation is produced (the cited text belongs to Annette Vidal) is very interesting:

> The documents must be confiscated. I believe that immediate measures must be taken in Paris so that we get those documents, and only when we have them all can we relax. The documents are in the desks of a few comrades. It never

---

* No such list or any files were found in the Comintern archive. Apparently, the only copy of the list, together with the files, was sent to the Lubyanka and buried in the secret archives.

happened that I left these papers unguarded for even a few hours. But nobody knows what has happened to them now.

What terrible secrets was Barbusse hiding that had alarmed the Moscow comrades so much, and which French comrades were holding them? The very fact of enlisting a great writer to take part in some dubious, if not downright subversive, Moscow operations and his readiness to carry out conspiratorial assignments is the important discovery.

Stalin decided not to extract "maximum political advantage" from Barbusse's death—less than maximum was enough for him; after all, Barbusse had done what Gorky could not, or did not want to, do: he signed a syco-phantic panegyric to the Leader in a book that Stalin immediately had removed from shops and libraries because it contained too many names of the "enemies of the people" who had once been his "loyal comrades." An urn containing the ashes of the hastily cremated Barbusse was sent to France for burial.

Gorky declined to be present at the farewell ceremony for the man who three years before, his hands laced in prayer, had turned to him and said, "Teacher and brother! A teacher because you're a brother." Possibly because he guessed what the former writer had become, he did not particularly want to be considered his teacher. To Rolland he wrote, "Last respects were warmly paid to Barbusse and he was sent back to his native land with ceremony. I was not at the funeral because of the awful weather and I don't feel well: my legs ache, I'm coughing up blood and, besides, I can't tear myself away from my desk. There is a lot of trivial but necessary work."

The more acutely he felt his solitude, the more often his thoughts returned to Mura. He had understood a long time ago that he had lost her; he suffered and was angry, realizing that, even if she were present, he could not be as can-did with her as before. But he desperately needed her anyway. This can only be viewed, unfortunately, from Mura's letters—his letters, as previously men-tioned, have disappeared. She wrote to Gorky:

> I really want to come, and I know that I need to, but I don't know how to do it right now. Some "dark forces," unexpectedly stronger, now seem insur-mountable... Don't be angry with me and do not blame me, my dear and only person. This is not at all easy for me, as you might think. But I will come, of course. Maybe a bit later.

And in another letter: ". . . it's terrible for me after your words: is there a need to write at all? This, and in general the whole tone of your letter, doesn't coincide with that emotion and love with which I constantly think of you. And you know this." It is not so much her emotion and love that shine through these lines as it is Gorky's despair!

A few days before Gorky's departure for Tesseli at the end of September, he was visited by the journalist Ilya Shkapa, who wrote in his memoirs several years later:

> The phone began to ring in the room next door. Kriuchkov left for a few minutes. We remained alone. Suddenly, bowing toward me, Gorky said, "What is happening, my friend? . . . I am very tired. It's like I'm surrounded by a fence that I can't climb over. Surrounded . . . Imposed upon . . . I can't go backward or forward! This is so unusual! . . ." I did not manage to say anything before Kriuchkov returned. Suddenly Gorky bowed and kissed me on the forehead. I saw his eyes, all wet, and could barely restrain myself. We said goodbye.

A few days later Shkapa was arrested and spent twenty years in the Gulag. Was there a connection between this episode and his arrest? If the arrest had been planned in advance, Kriuchkov would have also been informed in advance and Shkapa simply would not have been allowed to see Gorky.

Not long before this Kriuchkov had summoned him to the NKVD's safe house. A certain person in an NKVD uniform was waiting for them. "You work with Gorky," he said, "and you know who comes to see him, with whom he corresponds. You have to help us, periodically letting us know what interests us." Shkapa did not give a straight answer—his reply was considered a refusal. The Lubyanka did not forgive that.

In September 1935 Gorky arrived in Tesseli. His granddaughters stayed behind in Moscow. Only Lipa never left his side.

From time to time Timosha stopped by, staying for a while before hurrying back to Moscow. Kriuchkov also behaved oddly by remaining for long periods in Moscow as well. The need for his vigilant eye was fading. Gorky would be unable to take any kind of "undesirable position" while in the Crimea: his mail was controlled, as were the visits of his guests. A large brigade of guards and domestic "help," led by an NKVD officer, had been hired for this. Unlike Sorrento, the number of guests here over a period of eight months was just a handful.

Yekaterina Pavlovna spent two days in Tesseli.

And Mura, one.

Mura's trips to the Soviet Union after Gorky had been locked up in his cage from 1933 to 1936 remain one of the greatest unsolved mysteries in

Gorky's biography to this day—and not just Gorky's. Various sources claim there were no less than six visits, but probably more; all of them surrounded by the greatest secrecy. Until the 1990s there was no mention of even a single trip in all the vast literature on Gorky. But now, when the taboos have supposedly been lifted, we still do not know the exact timing of these visits, their duration, and purpose.

Some of them may be dated through indirect details here and there. For example, it is now known that Mura was present at Aleksei Tolstoy's reading in Gorki of his short story, "The Golden Key," sometime during the first ten days of March 1935.

Why all the secrecy? The Kremlin ideologues had decided on a function for Mura with Gorky: secretary. In that case, how could the visits by the "secretary" have affected him? Who supplied Mura with entry visas? Why, when she was so afraid of crossing the Soviet border for some twelve years, did she suddenly become so daring? What attracted her to Moscow after she had grown so close to Wells? Was Wells informed of these visits? From his published autobiographical notes he clearly did not know at first; but having found out (in 1931 while in Moscow), he was stunned. Did anyone else, besides the Soviet comrades and Western intelligence services, know about them?

Even Nina Berberova, Mura's biographer, mentioned the possibility of only *one* visit to Moscow (the final visit during Gorky's life). But she only made up false versions of that single trip, and did not even suspect that there were others.

To be sure, without the direct participation of the Lubyanka, Mura could not have traveled to Moscow freely. Only the Lubyanka could guarantee the secrecy of those trips: there were no leaks—even in the USSR! Neither Mura herself nor Yagoda, apparently, concealed from Gorky the relationship that bound the "iron woman" to Moscow. Incidentally, Gorky was not blind; he could draw conclusions from what he saw, if he wanted to . . .

Of course, he could not have known that Yagoda, via Kriuchkov, had given Mura a large sum of hard currency without any receipts. Was this simply a bonus? Compensation for past or future expenses? In the unending chain of riddles here is riddle number one: Mura's encounters with Stalin in Gorky's home. That Stalin was seen there with her is in one of Gorky's letters to him, hidden away until 1993. Is it possible that the Leader failed to ask who was the lady sitting at the head of the table like a member of the family was, taking part in the general conversation?

Through many facts that have now become known, it can be stated that part of Gorky's archive, kept by Mura, was gradually transferred by her to Moscow's hunters of secrets during these visits, though probably not the most important part, which up until the summer of 1935 she undoubtedly withheld, otherwise Timosha and Peshkova would not have been sent to persuade her to make an "amicable deal" with the Lubyanka.

Mura's final visit to Tesseli (to Tesseli, not Moscow!) ended in a quarrel. It is likely that she had asked Gorky either for formal power of attorney for the right to use his archive, or a last will and testament to her advantage in order to dispose of it after his death. He refused.

Was it only because their love was already gone? Otherwise it is difficult to understand what could have made Gorky end their long private conversation with such a stormy reaction, after which Mura, having spent only one day in Tesseli and not having said anything to anyone, left for Moscow. Without a doubt, the fate of the archive troubled both Gorky and those close to him more than anything. Stalin and Yagoda may have exaggerated the importance of the letters and notes but they were not too far from the truth.

Gorky knew better than anyone else what he was worth in political, financial, and historical terms, which is why he took all the fuss around him to heart. He clearly did not yield to the solicitations of the Lubyanka—not only the death of Max but also the "archive" question and Mura's mission played an important role in the abrupt cooling-off of his relations with Yagoda after 1934.

At the beginning of December Stalin presented Gorky with one more gift by publishing in *Pravda* his answer to a letter by Lili Brik. Mayakovsky's muse and lover, who for good reason was considered his common-law wife, was distressed by the fact that the name of Vladimir Mayakovsky had been completely forgotten. Stalin understood what dividends he could reap from the dead poet—as much as he was wary of a living, unpredictable, and unmanageable one. He understood, and said: "Mayakovsky was, and is, the best, most talented poet of our Soviet era." This was a blow not only to Bukharin, who a year earlier in the name of the Central Committee had considered Pasternak to be the best, and not only to Pasternak, whom the press immediately began to trample and poison, but mostly to Gorky, since his relationship not only to Mayakovsky personally, but to his poetry as well, was known to everyone.

Gorky did not answer Stalin's statement, but two days later in a letter to one of the literary bureaucrats, the poet Aleksei Surkov, he ironically explained the "music of hatred" in Mayakovsky's poetry by the fact that Mayakovsky "was tall and became angry that there was no comfortable place for him to stand—the ceilings hindered him." Gorky knew that this mean and unfair comment would be reported to Stalin through Shcherbakov.

Meanwhile, preparations for the first of the three Great Moscow Trials were being made at full speed inside the Kremlin. Stalin had personally extracted through blackmail from the broken Zinoviev and Kamenev, who had lost every notion of reality, their consent to confess at the public trial of having been spies, traitors, and terrorists preparing to kill Stalin, the beloved leader of the people, along with all his closest advisors. This was necessary, he explained to the Old Guard Bolsheviks and friends of Vladimir Ilyich, in order to present Trotsky to the whole world as a direct agent of fascism. In exchange for such a confession—for the good of international Communism—Stalin promised to spare their lives. Zinoviev swore that he and his comrades had only discussed the possibility of replacing Stalin with another Stalinist, and only within the boundaries of Party democracy, and had not thought about anything else. Stalin insisted on his version. The defeated surrendered.

To keep him from getting involved, Bukharin was sent to Paris at the end of February 1936 to purchase the Marx archive taken out of Nazi Germany. It is possible that Stalin had hoped he would not return. Bukharin would then have been located and killed, and his act would have provided all the "arguments" needed for the terror already in preparation.

In Paris, Bukharin met with a prominent Menshevik and historian of the Russian revolutionary movement, Boris Nikolayev, and another important Menshevik, Fyodor Dan. He told them what was going on in the USSR and about the new constitution he had drafted with Karl Radek, with Stalin's approval. Among other things, it provided for the creation of a second Party, a "Party of non-Party members" or a "union of intellectuals." According to his plan, this union would be called upon to "constructively" help the ruling Party, reflecting the interests of other social groups besides laborers and collective farm workers, and even to take part in elections to the Soviet "parliament" with a separate list. It was presumed that Gorky and the academician Ivan Pavlov would head the list, along with other non-Party individuals with worldwide prestige: Aleksei Karpinsky, president of the Academy of Sciences of the USSR, academician Vladimir Vernadsky, and others.

While Bukharin was on his way to Paris, Pavlov unexpectedly passed away. He was an older man but full of energy and in good health; nothing led anyone to believe in his sudden demise. Karpinsky died right after him. Both were known for their enmity to the Soviets. Describing Lenin as "a pathological type of the resolute criminal," Pavlov openly said, "If what the Bolsheviks are doing to Russia is an experiment," then he would "even regret submitting a frog to it."

In August 1934, in a letter to one of the People's Commissars, Pavlov condemned the "years of terror and unrestrained arrogance of power," and Gorky, defending his good name, explained Pavlov's acerbity by the fact that the scientist is surrounded by "people who have poisoned him with lies, rumors, and slander."

Rejecting this defense, Pavlov, in December 1934, wrote to Molotov as soon as the wave of mass arrests began, provoked by the murder of Kirov: "We lived and live under an endless regime of terror and violence. Those who viciously sentence to death masses of their own kind and carry it out with satisfaction, as well as those, taught by force to participate in this, can hardly be feeling and humanely thinking creatures. Have mercy on our country and us."

Stalin knew about the idea of the "Party of those without a Party," presented to him as a means for the unification of all social groups, but supposedly approved it at first. "Not even suicides would think about organizing a second party during the "Great Terror," says physician and journalist Viktor Topolyansky today. It does not even matter that this idea came in 1935, *before* the "Great Terror."

In the final analysis Stalin did not agree to this, although he allowed the blind fanatics some hopes. An echo of the original idea was the cliché he came up with soon after for Soviet election campaigns, in which "candidates of the indestructible bloc of *Communists* and *non-Party individuals*" participated.

It is obvious that neither the initiative itself originating from Bukharin and Gorky, nor the candidacies of future "leaders of an allied Party" could have suited Stalin. He knew the moods of Pavlov and Karpinsky, just as he did that of Vladimir Ivanovich Vernadsky. This outstanding geochemist and political figure was a permanent member of the Central Committee of the Party of Constitutional Democrats (Cadets), deputy minister of enlightenment of the Provisional Government, had fled abroad from the Bolsheviks, and returned only in February 1934—right after the Seventeenth Congress!

What did he hope to achieve? Even today this question is left open; Stalin asked it as well. In Vernadsky's secret diary there is this mysterious entry: ". . . the failure to reach power by people from the GPU—Yagoda." It confirms the scenario discussed in connection with Max's death. The tragic events of 1936 were possibly an echo of that fatal step when Yagoda's nerves weakened, and he betrayed a certain secret plan to Stalin. The quote cited above immediately follows a description of Kirov who, according to Vernadsky, "stood out sharply . . . among the untalented and bureaucratic rulers" of the USSR and after an even greater charge: "Stalin's dictatorship should have been reined in." This retrospective entry was made by Vernadsky on November 16, 1941, but his diary was extracted from a hiding place and published only in the mid-1990s.

Regarding a plan for the creation of a "second Party," I can add one more piece of information from firsthand knowledge. My uncle, Professor Matvei

Vaksberg, occupied a prominent position in the "All-Union Association of Workers of Science and Technology for the Promotion of Socialist Construction" (VARNITSO*), patronized by Gorky and headed by the academician Aleksei Nikolaevich Bakh. This was the prototype of the "Party of those without a Party," as more than ninety percent of the members of VARNITSO were. My uncle was scientific secretary in charge of the Association's journal, *Front nauki i tekhniki* (The Front of Science and Technology). He was accepted as a candidate for membership to the VKP(b), but never moved up to full membership, which was highly distressing. Bakh comforted him: "Don't hurry; very soon you will be needed in a non-Party capacity, and you are destined to play an important role in the new union."

Bakh revealed to him Bukharin's project, calling it Gorky's, however, and emphasizing that the idea came from Gorky, who had convinced Bukharin. In the spring of 1936 a meeting of a "steering group" of the future union with Gorky was proposed—my uncle was invited to it—but the meeting never took place. Matvei told me about this in the 1950s when, after having served his time in exile, he was rehabilitated and returned to Moscow.

Almost the same thing, and in practically the exact same words, came from eminent geneticist Vladimir Pavlovich Efroimson in the 1980s, regarding his half-century-old conversations with academician Nikolai Vavilov, about Gorky's project of a "second Party." He did not remember if the academician was intended for membership and leadership in that Party but, in Vavilov's words, many employees of the institute he ran were on the lists.

The position of Kaganovich and Yezhov, who actively resisted the suspicious idea of a "foundation" of a Party of the intelligentsia, was closer to Stalin than the Bukharin-Gorky position. And he reached the necessary conclusions on his own.

---

* Vsesoiuznaia assotsiatsiia rabotnikov nauki i tekhniki dlia sodeistviia sotsialisticheskomu stroitel'stvu.

26.

Oxygen Deprivation

A world celebrity honored in his own country as the greatest (not like Lenin, but like Stalin!) could literally not take a single step of his own free will. The choice was limited: either Moscow or Tesseli. To remain in Moscow meant signing his own death sentence, but even if Gorky had wanted to, it would have been prevented because any form of suicide was unacceptable. The only choice was to accept the Crimean incarceration, where even the weather in winter was not at all like what he had been told: gusty winds and constant temperature fluctuations hampered his breathing. "This Crimea . . . is a capricious thing," he wrote in one of his letters. "Fog, wind, heat, and cold—all in the same day. And in order to breathe normally, I must have oxygen at home..." It was not just the weather that irritated him. There, he again turned into a hermit. The "oxygen" he refers to is in the literal, medical sense of the word, but it had a broader meaning as well. The "oxygen deprivation" he experienced was that of an enforced lock-up, tearing him away from his usual surroundings where he was able to breathe. It was suffocating and made life unbearable.

Not all that long ago in Sorrento he had avoided all kinds of fuss, enjoying his freedom from daily worries; now the isolation of Tesseli only brought melancholy. There was none of the free spirit of Sorrento, the mental peace, creative fervor, and even happiness filling every day and every hour. In Sorrento he had always been surrounded by a crowd of people, and his house was filled with guests whose presence did not hinder, but helped, his work.

Now there was oppressive silence all around. Max had died, his granddaughters lived far away, and as for Andreeva, Gorky did not want to even hear her name! Yekaterina Pavlovna was busy with her job, trying to save her favorite child, the Political Red Cross, from being disbanded. Stalin, who hated and despised all these idealistic fighters and revolutionary romantics, had just closed the Society of Former Political Prisoners and the Society of Old Bolsheviks, along with all their print organs, and the PKK awaited that same inescapable fate. Mura's visits (she showed up again in December 1935) did not bring joy but only anxiety. As far as Timosha was concerned, Gorky, even though unaware of the details, knew the essence: she had become someone he now had to fear. The mark of doom was her "friendship" with Yagoda—where could she have turned, where could she have avoided his fiery passion? Any man who spoke with her or smiled at her might be subject to arrest. She was completely in Yagoda's power. It is now known that she informed him about everything that was said at home, including what members of the Politburo said in her presence.

As Gorky felt the march of events unfolding in Moscow, he felt the need to make himself known, to show his former power and unswerving loyalty. ". . . The 'Chekists' have a difficult job," he wrote in one of his latest articles (his work on a novel was going nowhere and he could produce only articles), "those same 'terrible Chekists,' whom the bourgeoisie of all countries depicts as people devoid of all humanity . . . The humanism of the proletariat can be seen clearly in the work of the Chekists."

The insincerity permeating every line of these forced articles is apparent in the wretched vocabulary, the primitive style, and the absence of argumentation, replaced instead by simplified declamation. But no one needed sincerity; what was needed was a poster-like, one-dimensional text—and, of course, the signature of "M. Gorky."

Fear of the "organs" appeared in another incident involving Gorky. On his recommendation Yagoda sent the "proletarian writer" and former orphan Aleksandr Avdeenko to the Moscow-Volga canal construction site so that, fortified by new impressions, he would rewrite his novel *The Capital* (about the construction of a factory in the Urals) in a different way, singing the praises of the "heroic labor of the Soviet Chekists." A general's-rank badge was pinned on the young and not very literate lad from the Urals in the employ of the NKVD. *The Capital* became *Fate*, but Yagoda did not like the new version either: the author was captivated by the psychology of the *zeks* to the detriment of those who had been "re-forged"; in his work they came off as faceless and colorless shadows. The disgraced general was promptly booted out of the Chekist ranks.

The novel was far from being fine literature, but that was not what infuriated Yagoda: the author had not justified the hopes placed in him. Gorky already had a grudge against Avdeenko, who had joined Panferov's sycophantic chorus praising Stalin in *Pravda*. He sent Avdeenko an openly insulting letter which, along with the response to it, was kept in the secret archive until 1989.

Very often you write that you do not have a clear idea, and this speaks of your frivolous attitude to the job . . . You are riding into literature on the backs of others . . . The word "fate" should have no place in the Soviet lexicon . . . It [should be] clear to you how insignificant your novella is and how insignificant is its main hero, an unsuccessful candidate for kulaks and extortionists.

The author put up with the criticism of his work, but refused to be humiliated and trampled. As Avdeenko replied:

I thought about your letter for a long time. Unbelievable irritation and profound unhappiness drove your pen . . . How quickly you devalue people . . . It's bitter for me, Aleksei Maksimovich. I should not have to write to you about a Person, about human worth.

Could Avdeenko have known that not only irritation but also a terrible fear of Yagoda was driving Gorky's pen on this occasion?

He had spilled out his irritation in letters to Politburo members Andreev, Postyshev and Ordzhonikidze. He accurately observed the quick transformation of the Union of Writers into a feeding trough for the chosen and a punitive tool against "renegades," which he methodically and consistently identified to "the advisors of comrade Stalin." The cantankerous tone Gorky was using could only instill anger in his addressees.

The last straw in the dialogue of the deaf between the Kremlin and the Crimean exile was his letter to Stalin in response to an editorial in *Pravda*, entitled "Confusion Instead of Music," coarsely denouncing Dmitri Shostakovich's new opera, *Katerina Izmailova*. Gorky, of course, usually preferred a completely different kind of music—classical, melodic, and accessible to any ear. The fact that he acknowledged the genius of the young innovative composer, considered unworthy by the authorities, is to his credit. Gorky had already expressed his admiration for Shostakovich's music in general and this opera in particular before Stalin complained about it. Without hearing it in its entirety, he ordered the composer be defamed, and those instructions were carried out immediately.

The complexity of the music, "incomprehensible to the people," was the official reason to accuse the composer of "formalism." Yet the real reason behind Stalin's wrath was not the music but the libretto. Stalin had seen an allusion to contemporary Soviet reality in Shostakovich's reworking of the novella, *Lady Macbeth of Mtsensk*, by Nikolai Leskov, in which the heroine, unable to marry her true love, murders her husband and child in a fit of mad passion. The implied allusion was that individual terror was justified as the only way for a desperate person to shed captivity and wrench free of unbearable conditions.

To divert attention from the real reason and, at the same time, strike a blow not only at his music but also at the theme, Shostakovich was accused of "extreme naturalism" and "relishing sex." Gorky wrote, pretending not to guess, that its initiator and possibly even its author, was Stalin:

> . . . The criticism is unfounded. "Confusion"—but why? . . . The article in *Pravda* has allowed a herd of untalented people and hacks of all types to poison Shostakovich. And this is what they are doing. [Shostakovich] deserves . . . to be regarded as the most talented of all contemporary Soviet musicians.

Half the letter was taken up with impressions from his meeting with André Malraux, who was the only foreign guest allowed to see Gorky during the whole prolonged Crimean season. On March 7, Mikhail Koltsov brought Malraux and his brother to Tesseli for three days. Babel and Koltsov's wife, the journalist Yelizaveta Ratmanova, came with them. Koltsov worked in military intelligence, and his wife at the NKVD. Since every one of the visitors knew French well, only Gorky needed a translator.

He thought it necessary to convey his opinion about Malraux personally and not through intermediaries. Gorky to Stalin:

> I have heard many praiseworthy and solid things about him . . . Babel says that ministers consult with Malraux and that he is the greatest, most talented and most influential figure among the contemporary intelligentsia in the Romance countries, and that, moreover, he possesses organizational talent. Babel's opinion is confirmed by my second confidante, Maria Budberg, whom you saw at my place: she has been mingling with European writers for a long time and knows all the relationships, and opinions. She thinks Malraux is truly a person of outstanding talent.

Gorky added that Malraux is a "very talented person who deeply understands the universal importance of the work of the Soviet Union." He then listed among Malraux's shortcomings his tendency to "speak too much about trivialities as though they were important" (Malraux had drawn Gorky into a conversation concerning the works of James Joyce, about which Gorky knew little), and an even greater propensity to have his counterpart defend "a person, his creative independence, and his freedom."

By that time Stalin had already been informed that, before the trip to Tesseli, Malraux had spent an entire evening with Meyerhold in the presence of Pasternak, Babel, and Koltsov, where there had been talk of a new "world encyclopedia" on the model of Diderot, with Bukharin as its chief editor. The name of Bukharin surfaced at Tesseli too, but Gorky did not say a word about this, not suspecting that Stalin already knew. Gorky's closeness to Malraux and the attempt to secure Stalin's endorsement for their common project, the unification of European intelligentsia against fascism (when actually at that time Stalin's personal emissary, David Kandelaki, was secretly negotiating with Hermann Göring and Hjalmar Schacht—not to fight fascism but to draw closer to it), could only hasten the fatal denouement: Gorky had become obnoxious and dangerous.

He had already given Stalin what he could. The dead Gorky would automatically become an ally, but no one could vouch for a living Gorky. While his friendship with Bukharin was real, the one with Stalin was imaginary. Gorky should have been canonized as a Soviet saint and declared Stalin's best friend, which should have happened before he could do something and ruin his image.

"Stalin killed Gorky in vain," wrote Solzhenitsyn in *The Gulag Archipelago*, "by being overly cautious: he would have wound up singing the praises of 1937 as well." In principle this is true, but it's not that simple. Stalin was not afraid that Gorky would openly speak out against him or publicly condemn the impending punishment of "the enemies of the people." But the cult of the name was much less onerous than the cult of a living individual, which always remained unpredictable. It was impossible to issue a death sentence to Zinoviev and Kamenev and not expect Gorky's reaction. The mere fact that both Zinoviev and Kamenev, immediately after their arrest, had appealed specifically to Gorky, led Stalin to conclude that others would do the same. Of course, Gorky could have been isolated by denying him any letters and any dubious visitors, but Stalin at that time was not in the mood for such complications: if something suddenly did get through to Gorky, how could anyone predict the reactions of such an impulsive individual?

At a time when dozens of writers, trying to outdo each other, willingly or forcibly danced on the graves of the executed, the absence of Gorky's reaction would have been interpreted as condemning the terror. He would have naturally reacted for sure. But to bind him precisely to such a condemnation, no matter how desirable to Stalin—a text that was devoid of ambiguity, allusions, and cloudy allegories—was also not an easy thing, at the very least because one of the two main victims was Kamenev, whom Gorky honored, whom he protected, and whose innocence was obvious to him.

An option would have been to compose an indignant and damning Gorky reaction without Gorky—meaning, a falsification—and then conceal the issue of the newspaper from him wherein such a forgery would be published. That would have been too much trouble, without any guarantee of success. Under Stalin, of course, everything was possible, especially any kind of forgery. But would this not have been too much fuss? Besides, no matter how much Gorky would be prevented any contact with foreigners, it would have been impossible to exclude it completely, even as correspondence, and even under the complete control of the Lubyanka. His foreign literary colleagues would have demanded an answer. Then announce that Gorky did not wish to answer, or provide a boilerplate response for everyone, with a request not to bother him anymore? Why would all this be required, if there was a much simpler way out, by neatly removing every problem at once? Tolstoy later wrote:

> There was no way to force him to remain silent. To arrest or exile, not to mention shoot him, would have been even less likely. The idea of hastening the liquidation of the sickly Gorky "without bloodshed" through Yagoda had to have been viewed by the host in the Kremlin as the only way out.

"No person—no problem" is a formula that fits all situations in life and for all times, especially if with a single stroke several goals can be achieved at once: remove the dangerous burden and place the blame for it on those whose time had also come to be removed—and not just from the scene, but from life, and to purge oneself from any suspicion at the same time. In doing so justify the sword of retribution that had cut off millions of heads and which would cut off millions more. This was a grandiose scenario worthy of comrade Stalin, and that only he was capable of pulling off!

There was not enough room on one throne for two idols. One of them had to relinquish his seat. The second had not succeeded in removing the first; now the first had to overthrow the second, thereby transferring him to the ranks of his great and immortal associates.

At the end of March, Gorky modestly observed his next—and last—birthday. Yekaterina Pavlovna and Timosha, the constant Kriuchkov and two writers came to Tesseli to spend the day with him. One of them, Vsevolod Ivanov, was a reliable and true friend; the other, Pyotr Pavlenko, an "entrusted person" of the NKVD.

Not long before this, and also in March, Mura had shown up in Tesseli with the intention of staying with Gorky until his birthday, an occasion they had celebrated many times together, but the quarrel, mentioned in the previous chapter, prevented this from happening. Nevertheless, she preferred to act as if nothing had happened.

However, Mura's last letter to Gorky, sent in April (without a specific date) from London, is rife with those same professions of love as in all the previous ones: "My dear friend, it is now almost a month since I have left you and yet it seems that I will wake up, come to disturb you at your desk, help work in the garden and everything else that makes life pleasant. Somehow this trip struck me at how inseparable and valuable my relationship to you is, my dear."

"My relationship to you" is completely possible, but not "Your relationship to me." And Mura was smart enough to understand this perfectly well. It seems that her presence was already problematic for Gorky, but without her it was strange and uncomfortable. Was this, in addition to everything else, what filled him with such melancholy on his latest birthday, which he had always celebrated happily with Mura—and not that long ago!—in Sorrento?

Andreeva, understanding that she was not destined to be at this family celebration, sent an aloof, officially cordial letter. Letters came as well from Valentina Khodasevich, Aleksei Tolstoy, and Mikhail Koltsov. Stalin refrained from greetings, as did Yagoda. He had not even answered the last Gorky letter addressed to him, wherein he had asked, for the umpteenth time, to free Viktor Serge from exile and send him abroad. This break in the correspondence between "bosom buddies" is very portentous: did Yagoda realize that Gorky guessed his betrayal, and did Gorky punish himself for having drawn Max into a dangerous political game, becoming an unwilling accomplice in his death?

A troubling but irrefutable reason to draw Gorky from seclusion had finally appeared. It was reported from Moscow that both granddaughters had come down with the flu, which at that time was considered a dangerous illness; moreover, it was exactly the same diagnosis as the one originally made for Max.

Now no one could have stopped him—neither warnings from his physicians nor Lipa's resistance: on May 26, Gorky left Tesseli, and on the following day he arrived by train in Moscow. The history of this trip, like all trips connected with him in the final period of his life, is full of mysteries and contradictions.

Some sources maintain that he had left in a hurry because he was already ill in the Crimea, that his health was getting worse, could not get the proper care locally and that Lipa did not put up any resistance at all—on the contrary, she insisted on his immediate departure (Nina Berberova's version).

According to other information, he became sick only on the way to Moscow. "It was hot in the train." said Timosha. "They opened the windows and he caught cold."

According to the version used at the trial, Gorky left in good health and did not catch cold in the train, but his arrival was *intentionally* timed to coincide with his granddaughters' illness: he walked into their room and "on the second or third day came down with the flu, which very quickly degenerated into lobar pneumonia" (trial testimony by Dr. Levin).

There is yet another version that Gorky caught cold visiting his son's grave and Nadezhda Alliluyeva's at the same time: it was a sunny but windy day.

As in the case with Max, the circumstances leading to Gorky's illness are murky and contradictory. Yet in both cases the mysterious origin of the disease leads to the same result: lobar pneumonia. Either the result came from the same stimulus, or the external symptoms of a lung infection masked a different illness which had been perfected in the secret and sinister laboratory of poisons.

Even more symptomatic is the confusion in dates. Timosha, an unreliable witness, dictated the following recollection:

> Aleksei Maksimovich went straight from the train station to Malaya Nikitskaya, up to the second floor to see his granddaughters, spoke with them for some time, then removed books he needed from the library. Some he took with him, left the librarian a note and, without delay [!], left for Gorki.

Meanwhile, on the following day, May 28, he was still in Moscow and none other than that same Timosha was showing him her paintings, which she could hardly have forgotten about. He met with the leadership of the Young Communists and the chief editor of the newspaper *Komsomolskaya Pravda*; he received a dear guest, Nikolai Burenin, an old friend who had come from Leningrad. In the middle of the night they sat in his library and listened to a Beethoven string quartet on the gramophone.

From the reminiscences of the artist Korin it is known that Gorky intended to visit him after returning from the cemetery: he had learned from someone that there was another artist, Mikhail Nesterov, present, whose birthday was to have been celebrated a few days later, and before leaving the city he was planning to congratulate him personally. But Timosha, whom he had asked to call Korin and notify him of his arrival, said that no one picked up the phone in Korin's studio (Korin and Nesterov were inseparable there).

Did she place the call at all? Gorky was most certainly prevented from having undesirable meetings. And Korin's attempts to see him were unsuccessful: "the secretaries on duty" said over the phone that "no one is allowed to see Gorky." Valentina Khodasevich, in Moscow at the time, was told the same thing. In her later memoirs (*Portraits in Words*) she wrote,

> I understand that my presence in Gorki would be considered undesirable, but who . . . why? To this day I do not understand, and this is very unpleasant. If at least I knew that Aleksei Maksimovich was not surprised by my absence, it would have been easier.

But what, specifically, is incomprehensible here? Any extra witness, any person close to Gorky, whom it would have been difficult to prevent having contact with the sick man, if he really was ill, was an undesirable person.

The illness is considered to have begun on June 1. It is precisely this date that was mentioned in the official announcement by *Pravda*. It was confirmed by the distinguished Soviet doctor, Professor Nikolai Burdenko, who had spoken with Gorky at the end of May—"several days before his illness." In other words, up to June 1, Gorky showed no symptoms of sickness at all. But "professor-philosopher" Yudin, a Party apparatchik, NKVD employee and secretary of the Union of Writers, whom Gorky detested, declared on May 31 to a circle of acquaintances that Gorky was deathly ill and had no hope of surviving.

The illness began to develop according to the same scenario as with Max: "flu, complicated further by a flow of catarrhal changes in the lungs and deterioration of cardiac activity." The difference was that lobar pneumonia was "discovered" almost immediately with Max, while the same diagnosis was carefully concealed from Gorky; using his many years of experience as a lung patient, he concluded as much by himself a few days later.

All in all, seventeen physicians, almost all prominent in their own right, from Moscow and Leningrad gathered at Gorky's bedside. Why did they all mislead him? Perhaps they did not want to worry him? But Gorky had suffered from lung infections many times, so this could not have been a frightening surprise for him. Moreover, this diagnosis was not only concealed from him alone, but also from his close friends and family too. Or was the strictest ban on the truth mandatory for everyone?! If so, then what was the goal? Gorky trusted only Levin and Speransky—both never left him. But they kept silent too.

The most thorough scholars of Gorky's life, in describing the atmosphere that had developed on Malaya Nikitskaya and in Gorki, noted that "someone's evil will could be felt in the events that took shape around" him: "the atmosphere of a cage, under constant observation where no one feels free . . ., but [everyone] felt the presence of someone's evil will" (A. Spiridonova).

A body of evidence is kept in the secret files of Gorky's archive, which, taken as a whole, gives a sinister picture of almost mystical foreboding of the fatal outcome. In the first days of the illness some people made anonymous phone calls to Gorky's Moscow home, and to Gorki on the Kremlin telephone, asking where to send wreaths and telegrams of condolences (and several telegrams did in fact arrive!); they pronounced mysterious phrases that made the Moscow house superintendent who answered the telephone tremble ("Help us, you swine!" "Did you get what you wanted, you scoundrels?"); unannounced visitors presented an order from the regional architect to take over the "vacated" house . . . Everyone understood the absurdity of these demands—the mansion on Malaya Nikitskaya belonged to the Kremlin and not the regional architect—but the more absurd they were, the more alarming they became. A photographer was sent from the magazine *Teatr i dramaturgiia* (Theater and Drama) to Malaya Nikitskaya to take a picture of Gorky's office as an illustration for the obituary, as the photographer said when asked. It is curious that there was an outpouring of condolences and visits on June 8, when there was still nothing predicting a tragic end. It is possible that the desired finale had been scheduled for precisely that day. The nightmarish and base spectacle clearly betrayed the guiding hand of its backstage director and his unmistakable signature, unlike anyone else's.

Professor Lidiya Spiridonova relates one more ominous and symptomatic event: "On the third day of Gorky's illness, June 3, when there were still no threatening bulletins about the condition of the writer's health, his archive was removed from the house on Malaya Nikitskaya. Koshenkov, apparently, had been specially sent away for several hours on shopping errands, so that he would be unable to call Gorki and ask if this was being done with the permission of Aleksei Maksimovich. Incidentally, the telephone number 2-88-60, as was revealed later, was out of service from May 31 to June 8, but the superintendent had used it, convinced that everything was alright." Thus, quickly and stealthily, tens and maybe hundreds of files, where various papers from Gorky's office were stuffed helter-skelter and then bound with twine, were removed. The confiscation of the archive could only mean that the owner was not expected to return.

Ivan Koshenkov kept diary entries practically up to the minute. It should be remembered that he worked for the NKVD, but was denied access to its most hallowed secrets. He kept the entries for his own benefit, and not on somebody's orders; he had in fact once tried his hand at becoming a writer on Gorky's suggestion. There was undoubtedly something explosive in his diary of seventy-four manuscript pages, if the author deemed it necessary to bury it in the ground! Unearthing it in 1947, Koshenkov burned it, after rewriting it, now with only sixty-seven pages, and then gave it to the Gorky archive. The poet Oleg Chukhontsev, acquainted with Koshenkov, had been allowed to read an edited version of the diary. But Koshenkov did not say which entries he eliminated.

Regarding the archival find mentioned above, Professor Spiridonova recently gained access to some very mysterious documents in the secret archive, confirming the missing entries in Koshenkov's diary. It turned out that during two weeks in June employees of the service staff at Gorki fell ill one after the other: the superintendent, his wife, the cook—seven people in all, everyone diagnosed with angina. They all displayed symptoms similar to those observed in Gorky. These people had had no contact with him and could not have become infected by him, yet others close to him and who were constantly in contact with him did not get sick at all. All these individuals were taken for some reason to the house on Malaya Nikitskaya, not to the hospital, and did not get any medical help at all: without special instructions the Kremlin doctors could not remain so indifferent. There was a certain logic at work, since the traditional treatment of angina probably had no relationship to the disease from which all seven persons were suffering.

It may be assumed that the source of infection was the food prepared only for Gorky and which he barely touched. According to an old Russian tradition, the "menials" are given the leftovers—don't let anything go to waste! A habit that had apparently not been foreseen. Modified buttermilk from a mixture of pneumococci and staphylococci could have caused such symptoms. To a strong and healthy body it probably would not have been fatal, but it would have destroyed one already undermined and emaciated with a weakened immune system. The toxicology laboratory of the NKVD had developed the widest variety of poisons with different effects, depending upon the given case.

On June 6, *Pravda* began publishing weekly bulletins on the condition of Gorky's health. The same bulletins were published during Lenin's pre-death agony, and it would be repeated seventeen years later when Stalin had only hours to live. The country and the world were being prepared for the master's death. But his condition on June 5, when the first bulletin was issued and, according to information we have now, was still not critical, and in recent years Gorky had already experienced something similar at least twice. If it was still only a normal "cold with complications" (even serious ones), then it was too early to panic. But some informed people knew whether Gorky was doomed or not.

He had felt only the first symptoms of indisposition when Mura immediately flew in. Who had informed her of the illness, who had immediately issued her a visa and organized the flight? In spite of Berberova, who had doubts about the possibility of her landing, it is a fact: secret documents preserved in the archive confirm that Mura got to Berlin and from there arrived in Moscow on a flight of the German-Soviet airline company Deruluft.[*] She had a reserved seat as well on a return flight on June 24.

The zoologist George-Phillip Wells, son of H. G. Wells, who accompanied his father on his trips to Russia in 1920 and 1934, published *Herbert Wells in Love*, based on his father's *Fragments of an Autobiography*, where it is clear that

---

[*] Deutsch-Russische Luftverkehrsgesellschaft, a German-Soviet joint enterprise founded in November 1921.

Mura was in London at the end of May 1936 and suddenly "began to feel a strange lethargy. She in fact began to sob, which was not like her at all. She was gripped with a desire to leave on her own for France. . . . The newspapers reported that Gorky was fatally ill in Moscow and several days later," continued Wells, "I received a telegram from her in Russia. I don't think that when she left for France she intended to go to Russia; she went to him unexpectedly."

Being either naïve or completely ignorant of Soviet reality, Wells, now an old man, held on to the illusions that helped maintain his dignity and pride. Mura flew into Moscow on June 5, before any foreign or even Soviet newspapers had published the first reports about Gorky's illness. More likely than not, she went directly to Germany from London. From France via Berlin she simply could not have reached Moscow that quickly. "The desire to leave on her own for France" was one of those myths that have accompanied her throughout her life, a fairy tale for Wells. She left London, already knowing the reason why and what her final destination would be, and she sobbed. That her tears were genuine should not be in doubt.

In December 1973, at a meeting in Moscow with philologists and historians of literature, Mura stated that she had flown in even earlier—three weeks before Gorky's death, that is, almost the same day Gorky returned from Tesseli. This is patently false, because the date of her arrival is precisely established. We can understand, of course, why she misled Wells, but was it only Wells? And why?

The widely known version that Gorky requested Stalin's permission to summon Mura to say goodbye to her is pure apocrypha—it is possible that this rumor was started on purpose, following at least two goals: to confirm that at this time Mura was still the closest person to Gorky and that Gorky from the very beginning, knew the lethal outcome of his illness. In the meantime, after his return from Tesseli and up until Mura's arrival, Gorky did not see Stalin, and his steadfast enmity lately toward her excluded any such request.

He could not have done this, since Lipa, who was a true godsend to him in his final years, could not stand the sight of Mura—Gorky's special summons would have been an open affront to Lipa. And, finally, there was not the slightest need to "beg" at the highest levels for Mura to arrive: she had already traveled to Moscow more than once, as she pleased, and without Gorky's invitation.

In organizing Mura's trip on this occasion, the Lubyanka was after the same result: to secure Gorky's archive. It is very likely that Mura had brought another part (but only a part!). An oblique confirmation of this is the fact that on June 24 she did not fly out. Kriuchkov wrote a letter to the Moscow agency of Deruluft with a request to refund the cost of the ticket paid for by Mura, because she was going to be busy with "the organization of a number of matters connected with the literary legacy of A. M. Gorky."

What "matters" could she have "organized," other than to sort out the papers she had brought? For everything else there was a special commission and even a special institute, of which Gorky was the director up until he died. He was replaced by Kriuchkov right after his death.

H. G. Wells also confirms the direct link between her visit to the dying Gorky and the fate of the archive. "She did something incomprehensible with his papers," wrote Wells in *Fragments of an Autobiography*, not intended for publication during his lifetime. "She had carried out the promise to him long ago. There were probably documents which were not supposed to end up in the hands of the OGPU, and Mura had hid them in a reliable place. She probably knew something and had promised not to say anything about it to anyone. And I'm convinced that she kept her promise."

Probably, probably . . . Even more probable is the fact that she was playing several sides at once. She did not want to let Gorky down, and did not. She was fearful of the Lubyanka and toyed with it (with Yagoda personally, to be more precise) as much as she could—feigned, dodged, reassured, teased. But most of all she thought of herself. She knew what a treasure she possessed, and she also knew that probably no one could use it.

Gorky's condition worsened with every hour. The best physicians in the county gathered at his bedside, tormenting him with endless injections in an effort to buck up his flagging strength. He was all black and blue but bravely bore his suffering. Kriuchkov's manuscript memoirs contain this noteworthy phrase: ". . . if they had not treated him, but left him in peace, maybe he would have recovered."

Decades later, in 1990, an expert medical commission checked the correctness of Gorky's treatment on the basis of the history of the illness, preserved in the KGB archive. A report by Professor V. V. Tomilin, head of the Central Forensic Medical Laboratory of the USSR Ministry of Defense, and with the participation of Professor V. G. Popov and academician A. G. Chuchalin, acknowledged that the treatment was correct, which also "rehabilitated" their late colleagues. Academician Yevgeni Chazov, who treated all the Kremlin leaders in the 1970s–1980s, supported their viewpoint.

No matter how great the authority of the experts, their investigation does not carry much historical significance. Even if all entries in the history of the disease exactly correspond to reality (the history of Max's illness, by the way, according to prosecutor Vyshinsky, was nonexistent—now it too has been found but it is impossible to determine what Max's illness was and how he was treated), then one may only speak of a correct treatment with a precise diagnosis. Where, however, is the guaranty that Gorky was treated for the illness he had, and not for something else?

On June 8, the doctors pronounced Gorky's condition to be critical, and suddenly a call came from the Kremlin: Stalin, Molotov, and Voroshilov had left for Gorki. The informer was undoubtedly Yagoda—he was almost constantly in the house, although he did not enter the room where the tormented Gorky lay slumped in a chair. (Incidentally, there is another problem: why during the height of the Great Terror, unprecedented in its scale, did Yagoda, the chief of state security, never leave the home of the sick writer? Not for one day or two, but practically for two weeks!) Simultaneously ("by pure coincidence") Professor Speransky had also left for Gorki to take part in an autopsy of the body(!).

Learning that the leaders were on their way, Gorky tried to lift up his spirits somewhat and Lipa, at her own risk but with Levin's consent, administered a huge dose of camphor, like she had done many times in the past. The result was mind-boggling. Stalin had expected to see, if not already a corpse, then at least a dying person, but instead he saw a man still very much active. Speransky explained this unexpected turnabout by the shock of joyous excitement that overcame the patient at the news of a visit by his high-ranking guest. Mura also actively supported the exact same version. But apparently no one else did, it appears . . .

Gorky did not want to speak about his illness, but steered the conversation to the publication of *A History of the Civil War*, *A History of the Two Five-Year Plans*, and other current events. Stalin demanded wine and the three leaders, drinking to the health of "the great proletarian writer," left for Moscow.

Their visit was repeated two more times.

On June 10, showing up around midnight, the doctors did not allow the leaders to see the dozing Gorky—Stalin departed, leaving behind a note: he regretted that the mean-spirited "quacks" (his expression) had prevented their friendly visit.

On June 12, the leaders came again. Spending seven or eight minutes with Gorky with the doctors' permission, they had to listen to the writer's thoughts about contemporary French literature and the condition of the French peasantry: this is reported only by Mura, who overheard their conversation through the slightly open door.

This wild and grotesque farce organized. The wine that Stalin called for to drink to the health of his great friend; the foolish question, "Who is that female monk dressed in black next to the patient's bed" about Mura, whom he knew (he had seen her before with Gorky, meaning he remembered—his visual, and not only visual, memory was infallible); and the jokes like those of a slightly drunk henchman? That kind of tone in conversation with Gorky, even when he was in good health, was generally characteristic of Stalin, allowing him to avoid discussion of any serious questions.

Mura and Speransky, enriched by the eloquent details of Levin's "memoirs," maintained that Gorky kept an issue of the newspaper with the published draft of the "Stalinist" constitution under his pillow. After reading it over, he supposedly said, "Here we are all busy with nonsense, and in the country now even the stones are singing." Gorky's trademark high style is reproduced very accurately, but the many appropriate details bring to mind the Russian proverb, "He lies like an eyewitness." Lipa, the constant sick-nurse and governess, categorically denied that Gorky had any such newspaper under his pillow. She said that he had practically no strength to read anything. Gorky, nearing death, wrote twice in a faltering hand, "I can't read anything."

On June 8, those closest to him came to say goodbye to Gorky—it was too obvious for him not to have understood. Andreeva was not among them: she was waiting for the news at a completely different dacha outside Moscow. But the heavy quantity of camphor Lipa gave him had returned Gorky to life, creating the illusion of real improvement. "They pulled him from the clutches of death," joyously reported Kriuchkov to Koshenkov by telephone. But Gorky's strength again weakened, and the doctors wavered between despair and hope. However, the powerful organism which had overcome all thinkable and unthinkable illnesses, which had wracked Gorky his whole life, continued its duel with death.

By June 16, such an obvious improvement had set in that both the doctors and close friends decided that the crisis had finally passed. During the night of the seventeenth, however, the situation suddenly and abruptly changed, without any apparent reason. Gorky began gasping for breath; his pulse was irregular, his temperature fluctuated wildly. His lips turned blue, with spittle and bubbles issuing from his mouth. The doctors did everything possible to keep his heart running, but they treated the consequences of the disease and not the disease itself, the result rather than the cause. Did they know, incidentally, the nature of their patient's illness? By a strange coincidence (again "by pure coincidence") Kriuchkov got drunk on the evening of the sixteenth. Although Stalin had personally warned him that he would "answer for everything," no one could rouse the dead drunk Kriuchkov.

Just like Pavlov, who died in February, Gorky tried—for the sake of science—to jot down his pre-death feelings in his notebook. At first he wrote some disconnected thoughts in different colored pencils as they came to him in his delirium. The strangest entry is on June 6–7:

There appeared . . . people frightened by the need to live differently. They assiduously and captiously looked for signs of innovation. Some kind of demanding power-seekers crawled out from the cellars . . .

On the ninth, he could only record the date, but dictated the text: "The end of the novel the end of the hero the end of the author." He was referring to his unfinished *Klim Samgin*: the lines of the novel, hero and author coincided, prematurely cut short.

At 11:10, on the morning of the eighteenth, everything was over.

H. G. Wells immediately reacted with a telegram from London: "One of the great figures put forth by the revolutionary process in Russia has left for eternity. A writer of the world has passed away. His works remain an unsurpassed masterpiece." But he also observed that "Gorky and I had different views of the position of the writer in the USSR." Chaliapin learned about the death of his accursed friend on an ocean liner and immediately broadcast his reaction on radio, full of love, devotion, and sorrow. Among those who sent condolences were Romain Rolland and dozens of others, including George Bernard Shaw, the "old blaggard," as Gorky had characterized him. Mikhail Sholokhov, who by his own admission could not stand Gorky for the last five years, grieved at "the huge loss."

Gorky's body had not yet been removed from Gorki when Yagoda personally sealed off all the rooms, running his eyes quickly over the papers that seemed the most important to him, those which had not yet been taken away. From now on the name of Gorky and every one of the lines he had written belonged unequivocally to the Kremlin.

27.

Tragedy as Farce

Another thread to the story only adds to the mystery of Gorky's death many other nebulous mysteries. We are referring to Louis Aragon, Elsa Triolet, and André Gide being called to Moscow to the dying Gorky, not together, but separately.

According to the established version, Gorky had asked Koltsov in March to summon the French writers immediately, because he had something extremely important to tell them. Having accepted this version as indisputable, everyone has wondered what Gorky wanted to tell his confidantes. Why had he specifically chosen them? And what secrets did he take with him to the grave?

There supposedly is some logic to this version: all the writers mentioned happened to be in Moscow in June but not one of them met with Gorky. Koltsov was in Tesseli in March, meaning that hypothetically he could have hand-delivered Gorky's letters to his French colleagues. Other historians still hope to find these letters, which they claim will make it possible to understand what revelations Gorky planned to announce to the world community.

All of this smacks of obvious apocrypha. If the letters had existed, they would have come to light a long time ago. Aragon would have published them, at least during those intervals when he was quarreling with the Kremlin, or he would have quoted at least part of them. No one who has worked in the Aragon-Triolet archive has found any traces, although Aragon did claim that Gorky, through Koltsov, simply "showered" him with letters desperately beseeching him to come, meaning that there were many, very many of them... "It's two months already,"* wrote Aragon later, "that Gorky has been summoning us, and each summons sounds more and more as if it can't be put off."

---

* Since the beginning of April.

Scholars who have worked with the Aragon-Triolet archive in France claim that there are no letters or telegrams from either Gorky or Koltsov to Aragon in 1936. According to the same version, it turns out that Koltsov was the intermediary secretly involved with the "conspirator" Gorky, who was planning to let Aragon in on something that was not made public. But Koltsov was Stalin's trusted agent, a "Party soldier" who worked with military intelligence and the GRU and would have been obliged, not only by inclination but also out of duty, to show any letters to his bosses. It also means the copies would definitely have been in Gorky's Lubyanka file. The legend of Gorky's letters to Aragon was part of such insistent claims as fact that writer and historian Edvard Radzinsky unconditionally and without citing, naturally, a single source, asserted that "Yagoda had delivered Gorky's letter to Louis Aragon to the Boss, in which Gorky asked the great poet to come immediately to say good-bye." But, despite this, it was assumed that Stalin had given Yagoda instructions… These categorical and totally unfounded statements ensure that myths live on.

Something else is indisputable: Aragon and Triolet, as well as Gide, had indeed been invited to Moscow, first by Koltsov, then by Ehrenburg. The information about Gide's invitation is more concrete, although very lapidary. From recently published letters by Ilya Ehrenburg it is obvious that the invitation to Gide had been made, if not in March, then without a doubt in April. On May 9 Ehrenburg cheered Koltsov with the following message from Paris: "Gide is going for sure on June 15." According to the French writer Pierre Herbard, Gide's relative, who had flown in with him, Koltsov had told Gide to come quickly precisely because Gorky was in "bad" shape. And suddenly Ehrenburg asked him to delay his arrival because Gorky had improved! Meanwhile, a meeting of the secretariat of the international association of antifascist writers opened on June 19 in London, where Ehrenburg played the leading role, but which Gide was supposed to have chaired. Ehrenburg made sure that Gide flew to London from Moscow but, against all logic, asked him to delay his arrival by several days.

Apparently, the question of Gide's arrival, on a specific day, so upset Koltsov (but was it really Koltsov?), that on June 9 Ehrenburg asked his secretary in Moscow, Valentina Milman, to convey the following words to him immediately: "Everything is alright with the old man." This conspiracy, unusual for Ehrenburg, emphasizes how much importance was attached to this visit. It is obvious that Koltsov and Ehrenburg, even more so, were simply following instructions from higher up, without taking into account what was behind these orders. If Gide's invitation had no connection to Gorky's imminent death, then all this fuss is incomprehensible, as was the urgency of his arrival at a specific time and not "in general."

Finally, in Moscow the date of Gide's arrival was entered as June 18, the day of Gorky's death! Was it mystical coincidence or a deliberate choice?

Even more enigmatic is Aragon's extremely strange statement made almost thirty years later, in 1965, in the novel *La mise à mort*, an unusual genre for such a document. His purposefully complex style, involving both imaginary and real heroes—under their own names—where, for the benefit of literary experimentation, time and consciousness are uninterruptedly mixed, real events alternate with imaginary ones, and Aragon himself, narrating the story in the first person, also appears in the character of a certain Antoine, and Elsa Triolet is encrypted as the singer Fuger, probably has one main goal: Aragon needed the stylistic jumble to confuse the reader, to code his thoughts in a strange manner and, in the final analysis, drown the truth of the sinister events of June 1936 in it.

> [In 1936] the telegram from Michel [Koltsov] "Gorky asks you to speed up your arrival" reached us in London. I was continuing work on the novel [*Les Beaux Quartiers*] on a Soviet ship under magnificent skies, everybody was on deck, the sailors singing to an accordion… Michel was working for *Pravda* at the time, before the war in Spain. André Gide was in Moscow.

Thus Aragon describes his trip to Moscow. True, Gide was not present, but this error is nothing compared to everything else. So, Koltsov, at Gorky's behest, asked Aragon to hurry up, and what did Aragon choose for his hasty trip—the slowest form of transport, the steamship *Felix Dzerzhinsky*. "I really wanted for this trip to go on and on," admitted Aragon. "My novel was nearing completion."

The majestic beauty of the white nights not only accompanied the spellbound Aragon throughout the trip, but also awaited him in Leningrad, where he showed no hurry to rush to Moscow. There was an even better reason to remain awhile longer in the magical city on the Neva: Lili Brik, Elsa's sister, was living there now, along with her husband Vitaly Primakov, the deputy commander of the Leningrad military district.

The Parisians spent eight to ten days at the fabulous Primakov mansion outside the city, enjoying long walks along the Neva and even longer, truly Russian, tea drinking sessions in Primakov's shady park, often visited by the district commander, Marshal Mikhail Tukhachevsky himself—Aragon conversed with him in English, defending the position of the French Communist Party from the marshal's critical attacks. There was no mention of Gorky at all, although by the 6th of June, as we recall, the newspapers were publishing bulletins about his health every day, each one more alarming than the previous. But the special guests were in no hurry to see their dying friend.

> When, after a stop in Leningrad, we arrived in Moscow, on the 16th or 17th of June, it was already too late. Aleksei Maximovich's health had deteriorated. Michel wanted, however, for us to see him. Terrible. Gorky told him... He insisted that we arrive quickly, he wanted to tell us something... What? How would I know? He'd tell us himself. The following day, taking the risk on himself, Michel came for us in a car... [...] June 18. [...] A guard at the gates. Shady park. We were not allowed in, Michel got out of the car to discuss the situation, showed his documents, his identification card from *Pravda*. [...] Michel was unhappy, called someone on the phone, he was promised... Unhappy or disturbed? "He's waiting for you... he told me yesterday...to bring them to him...as soon as they arrive... [...] He loved both of you very much. The last thing I heard from him was your names. He wanted to see you so much."

In 1977, twelve years after the publication of *La mise à mort*, Aragon returned to the same theme, not in a novel but in his newly edited diaries of 1936–1937. This strictly documentary genre, where the protagonists have their real names and where actual events are described, does not justify any lies through imagery, style, metaphor and other literary devices as in a novel. Now the date of arrival in Moscow was specified as being June 18, and the hour spent in Gorki became five hours during the afternoon... But here is the rub: by this time Gorky's body had long since been removed to the city, and there was absolutely no need to wait by the closed gates for permission to enter the house.

Who lied to whom and why: Koltsov to Aragon, Aragon to his readers, or all of them together to one another? Aragon and Triolet arrived in Moscow not on the day of Gorky's death and not the day before (June 17), but early in the morning of the 15th, as announced in the newspapers. Captivated by the white nights, they still had three days to see Gorky if that is what he truly desired. "During those days he was at Gorky's side," wrote Aragon about Koltsov. That wasn't the case, since Koltsov saw Gorky for the last time on March 1. Every single person whom Gorky saw between May 27 and 31 has been identified, and Koltsov is not among them, but starting June 1 no one was allowed to see Gorky at all, except for his very closest friends (Yekaterina Pavlovna, Timosha, Mura, Lipa, Kriuchkov, Nightingale and the children) the doctors— and the leaders as well, but just for a few minutes.

"Aleksei Maximovich wanted to see you so much he was waiting for you right up until the last minute." Aragon repeated these words by Koltsov several times. If he was doing so simply to raise his prestige, then this is only half the problem, but what if Koltsov had simply lied to him? And why did Gorky specifically choose Aragon, whom he barely even knew: he had seen him once in his life, among foreign guests at the first congress of Soviet writers. And why did Aragon so deliberately and stubbornly delay his arrival in Moscow? If he had been ordered to delay, why is he silent about this? Why does he consciously mix up the dates? And, finally, what compelled him to write these insane lines in a description of Gorky's funeral: "Koltsov told us to stand next to him right behind the government leaders, and we went in together, that's what Gorky wanted…?"

The subject of "Gorky's funeral" does not end with those lines by Aragon. He returned to it again forty years later in his diary notes, as "an eyewitness," devoid of literary flourishes. Now Aragon stated that after "the ceremony on Red Square," where only farewell speeches were pronounced, the casket with Gorky's body (a casket and not an urn, which he saw with his own eyes, standing in the honor guard!) set off for Novodevichy Cemetery and he, Aragon, and Elsa followed it in a long procession, stretching out for several kilometers. The following morning, it turns out, he and Elsa visited Gorky's grave at the cemetery, close to—as he describes with topographical precision—the graves of Gogol, Chekhov, and Mayakovsky.

So just what is the significance of this unending chain of lies, beyond any lapses of memory? Neither peculiarities of style nor genre can explain that secret that undoubtedly lays hidden behind the history of Aragon's and Triolet's unhurried journey to Gorky's funeral and Aragon's description overflowing with numerous contradictions, confusion and obvious absurdities. And how to explain Aragon's final confession, not apropos of anything in particular: "On our way back [from Moscow in September 1936], Elsa and I swore to each other never to go back there again"? Only because this coincided with another tragedy which personally touched his family; in August 1936 Aragon's brother-in-law (his "beau-frère") Vitaly Primakov, husband of Lili Brik, Elsa's sister, was arrested?

Another prominent French guest, André Gide, also arrived only when he had been ordered to—June 17 at 5:30 in the afternoon (there was no flight to Moscow on the 18th). He was met at the airport by the same Koltsov, Aragon and Triolet (who supposedly had arrived in Moscow a day later!), Boris Pilnyak and Babel, who had written his mother and sister that day, "Gorky's health continues to be bad, but he is fighting like a lion. […] In the last two days the doctors have more hope than before."

Like Aragon and Triolet, Gide also took his time in reaching Gorky, who "wanted to see him so much," but he made it to the funeral in order to deliver his passionate speech, translated by Koltsov, from the tribune of Lenin's mausoleum. Only one year later André Gide would tell the truth about the happy life of the Soviet people in his book *Return from the USSR: Afterthoughts on My Return*, but there would not be a single word in it about the man who had invited him to Moscow, nor what had motivated that strange invitation.

It is easy to fall into temptation and take the wrong path: Gorky supposedly planned to tell his confidantes something so important that Stalin, fearing exposure, ordered that the apostate be liquidated. This is more the subject of an ordinary detective novel than anything resembling the truth. It is clear to anyone that Gorky could have told the world whatever he wanted through Malraux—not only Koltsov but also Babel, who spoke French like a true Parisian, were suitable as translators. It is clear that as confidantes Koltsov and Aragon were very dissimilar candidates: Gorky had already begun to recover from his former blindness and naiveté.

At the same time, the fact that Aragon and Gide were invited to Moscow is not in dispute, and these invitations were most likely made by telephone, not in writing or through third parties, as in the case with Ehrenburg. But historians have erroneously accepted the invitations from Koltsov as invitations from Gorky: Koltsov was only speaking in his name and Gorky could hardly have had the slightest inkling of this. There is no evidence of any kind that even indirectly indicates something else.

In fact, the initiator was a man who preferred the shadows: Stalin, who in those June days needed Aragon and Gide, not Gorky, and had no need at all for them to come. Koltsov probably suggested their names to Stalin: of all the prominent Western writers who were "friends of the Soviet Union" at that time (before the Spanish Civil War) he communicated more closely with the French than with anyone else. He could count on them coming without fail. Lili Brik could attract her sister Elsa, which also meant Elsa's husband, Louis Aragon, as well. Everything was calculated down to the smallest detail by the highly professional hunter of human souls.

Why did the "Supreme Leader of all Peoples" need them so much? We will probably never have a satisfactory answer. The question, incidentally, should be more specific: why were they needed *at first* and then suddenly no longer needed? Which version of Gorky's death were they called upon to confirm to the whole world, to sanctify by their authority? When and how was the original draft revised, and why were "the witnesses," who were already on their way, forced to change roles and hurry up at a snail's pace? And why even later did they so steadfastly deviate from the truth and not admit being drawn into Stalin's intrigues? New archival finds will possibly add some links to the still inconclusive chain of indirect clues and bring us closer to solving the riddle of Gorky's death.

All medical documents—the history of the illness, the death warrant, forensic medical "expertise" at the 1938 trial, the retrospective expertise of 1990 and others—are full of contradictions and fail to answer, even falsely, the central question of how, in particular, Gorky died. He had been treated for tuberculosis his entire life, but this disease is not mentioned at all in the forensic report of Dr. I. V. Davydovsky. The final diagnosis pronounced during his lifetime, established by a committee of doctors, was the following: "hemorrhagic pneumonia on the basis of bronchiectasis,* sclerosis, and emphysema." The medical warrant concerning the cause of death mentions grippe, which caused complications "in connection with an acute infectious process in the lower portion of the left lung."

When the "killer doctors" were sentenced, there was reference to some "grave illness" without any explanation. Not a word was said about poisoning—moreover, Professor Pletnev, responding to a completely different question from the prosecutor, suddenly found it necessary to emphasize that "no outside poisons of any kind had been introduced," even though no one had asked him about poisons—but Vyshinsky, on the contrary, without any connection to what the defendants and experts had just been questioned about, very strangely mentioned, in the summation for the prosecution about the role of poisons in world history, filled with examples of undesirable individuals having been poisoned by rulers.

Meanwhile, in the autopsy report there is not a single word about symptoms of poisoning, and at the trial the "experts" were not asked about the possibility of Gorky having been poisoned. Gorky's brain was taken for safekeeping to the Institute of the Brain, but the idea of analyzing it for traces of toxins was not even raised (by the way, no one knows to this day what happened to it, or what the results of the investigation were). Finally, the official medical conclusion completely unprofessionally mentions some kind of "serious infection" resulting in death, and an "acute infection" in the autopsy report, even though the highly qualified doctors probably knew that an infection "in general"—not serious, not acute, not light—does not exist, but that there are different, specific, kinds of infections leading to one specific illness or another.

---

* A widening of the respiratory passages, resulting in very serious illness, including recurrent respiratory infections, disabling cough, shortness of breath, and hemoptysis (coughing up blood).

It is not all that difficult to explain this confusion. Gorky's poisoning in 1936 was not made public, because in medical documents of that time there could not be even a hint of such foul play. But in 1938 the secret weapon of the Lubyanka remained hidden by the strictest secrecy, therefore the mechanism of murder, imputed publicly to Levin and Pletnev, could be anything, even if patently absurd and causing bewilderment on the part of any doctor, except for what it could really be. Neither Levin nor Pletnev were allowed access to the most sacrosanct of the Lubyanka secrets, therefore they could not have participated in Gorky's poisoning, and had they assumed *such* guilt they would have only entangled themselves completely, and would have been forced to name not only the Lubyanka's secret poisons about which they knew nothing, but also the usual, traditional ones, the traces of which could have been detected by any pathologist.

Only in the first half of the 1990s did the secrets become relatively accessible. Soviet justice (again in secret) had barely mentioned them back in the mid-1950s when a member of the old Lubyanka hierarchy was sentenced. The secrets turned out to be so hideous that the strictest classification was again placed on them.

The first toxicological laboratory in the USSR was created back in 1922 and called the "Special Office" (the Bolsheviks adored the word "special") under Lenin's patronage. During the first years it was headed by Ignaty Kazakov, who would become a defendant at the third Great Moscow Trial. After the death of Dzerzhinsky, the laboratory was run by his Lubyanka protégé Vyacheslav Menzhinsky, who even built a second lab at his dacha and worked there diligently. Another toxicological laboratory was later created under the auspices of the so-called "special group of particular designation" (among "insiders" it was called "Yasha's group" after the name of its chief Yakov Serebryansky); the main (but not only) task was to develop a venom to poison Trotsky. Imported poisons could not be relied upon—they were ineffective and, even worse, traceable.

The details of the Lubyanka's toxicological laboratory to this day remain one of the most carefully guarded secrets. The only certainty is that over the course of several years special poisons had been created there, leading to instant or agonizing death with a simulation of different illnesses and without leaving any visible traces in the body. As is now known from the still classified but already partially accessible archival documents of this laboratory, experiments were conducted on a combination of various pathogens to effectively act on a weakened organism.

Prominent specialists holding the highest scientific degrees took part in the experiments on living persons and their murders. Among them were the microbiologists and future corresponding members of the Academy of Sciences David Talmud and Sergei Muromtsev, Professor Grigori Mayranovsky and others. The country's future chief oncologist and president of the Academy of Medical Sciences, Nikolai Blokhin, who actively promoted the rehabilitation of Mayranovsky, when he had been symbolically sentenced (after Stalin's death)—not for killing people, but for keeping poisons at his home— was also involved in this work.

The laboratory, part of the Lubyanka department, was run by two generals—Naum Eitingon (in charge of the operation to murder Trotsky) and Pavel Sudoplatov, whose revealing book *Special Tasks* (*Intelligence and the Kremlin*, in the Russian version), is known throughout the world. Hundreds of people, among them Raoul Wallenberg, were murdered using the poisons from this laboratory. If Gorky was "assisted" in his death (it becomes increasingly difficult to doubt this), then a better method could not have been used.

Having accelerated Gorky's disease, the initiators hoped a natural course of events would take over, considering that Gorky, tormented by a multitude of woes, was truly close to the end. Any one of his illnesses, asserts Professor Chazov, could lead to the fatal outcome. Yet his body held up. When this became obvious to everyone, "nature" was then helped along, most likely on June 16: on that day a change for the better already appeared to be irreversible. But during the night everything was suddenly reversed again. Even the physicians could not have had a hand in the final act. The "game" with Aragon and Gide was explained, apparently, by the fact that the planned course of "operations" was constantly falling out of step, and corrections to it had to be made on the fly.

Nothing is easier than to arrive at the simplest of conclusions, namely that Gorky died a natural death, and any speculation about his murder can be attributed to that bloody mystification spawned by the Lubyanka during the Great Terror. Gorky, who truly was seriously ill, could have indeed died at any moment and without any ill-intentioned intervention. If, nonetheless, the more serious researchers agree to the version of an induced death, it is not because they have a passion for detective novels, but because all the indirect clues taken as a whole, especially those that became known only recently, make it impossible to ignore.

An attempt at analysis conducted from a purely medical standpoint (Viktor Topolyansky, a doctor, recently undertook it) is not promising. The physicians who attended to Gorky do not need belated rehabilitation—without a doubt, they are not guilty of anything. Gorky's death needs to be considered in its overall historical context, because of the role he played in Stalin's policy in the mid-1930s. Yagoda's toxic lab was a loyal helper to the leader in many of his ideas. It turned out to be true in this case as well.

Unfortunately, we cannot get around this bloody page in Soviet history—one of many—without examining the farcical versions that only discredit the serious efforts of many people who have attempted to search for the carefully hidden truth. Literary critic Vadim Baranov has been stubbornly insisting for years that Mura assumed the role of administering the poison because she wanted to grab Gorky's inheritance and Stalin, who had promised her something, could have encouraged her to commit a crime, threatening her with severe punishment if she refused.

This scandalous version is best suited for a cheap detective novel. In an attempt at entertainment, Baranov even invented a whole scene whereby Stalin, in a tête-à-tête Kremlin conversation, convinces Mura to become a murderess and gives her the poison—a scene impossible to imagine even in a nightmare. Many sins have been attributed to Mura, but there is absolutely nothing to justify the assumption that, even out of fear, she could have murdered the person to whom she was linked for fifteen years of her life. Stalin was a tyrant and an executioner, but not a common thief, teaching killers "to take care of" undesirables.

A former Soviet spy, Colonel Leonid Kolosov, who spent many years plying his trade in Italy, was enlisted in support of this latest version. In turn he "declassified" a conversation with his colleague, the journalist Mikhail Tseitlin (pseudonym "Mikhailov"), who in the 1950s and 1960s headed the international department of *Izvestiia*: it was under cover as a correspondent of this newspaper that Kolosov did his spying in Italy. The reliability of their "confidential conversation" is subject to doubt from the opening lines: Kolosov characterizes Tseitlin as Gorky's literary secretary, which he was not—all the literary and nonliterary secretaries of the master are known by name, and Mikhailov-Tseitlin is not among them. In fact, Tseitlin was the manager of *Literaturnaya gazeta*, with a relationship to the secret political department of the main directorate of state security. In a declassified report by the leaders of this department, Molchanov and Petrovsky, it was noted that Tseitlin was practically the "only head of the newspaper."

That description already quoted, but in a different context, is perfectly apt for Tseitlin's confidential story to Kolosov: he lies like an eyewitness. Moreover, Kolosov turned Gorky into a corpse a month after he actually became one (July 18 instead of June 18), and he placed the man at a different location. As Mikhailov-Tseitlin told Kolosov:

I found myself in the magnificent Ryabushinsky mansion on Kachalova street,[*] next to Kriuchkov. I was within his reach, so to speak. Suddenly there was some kind of commotion, and then Yagoda appeared, together with Maria Ignatyevna [...] Everyone was ordered out of the room where the sick writer lay. Aleksei Maximovich's conversation with Mura lasted for about forty minutes. Then the door opened, she came out and, accompanied by Yagoda and his bodyguards, left the house. The physician in charge came out and in a trembling voice announced to us that Gorky had passed away. I left [...]. A glass of water stood on Aleksei Maximovich's night table. But it disappeared immediately after.

Even authors of second-rate detective novels can come up with better material than this. First of all, Gorky got sick and died in Gorki, not at his Moscow residence. Neither Tseitlin nor anyone else was within Kriuchkov's "reach," since Kriuchkov, together with Mura and Lipa, was constantly at the patient's side so that no one could "reach" him. Gorky could not have spoken with anyone for forty minutes, let alone for even a few minutes, before his death, because up to the end he was unconscious and only managed to wheeze out a few sounds in delirium. There were four attending physicians, not one. After Gorky died, Mura did not leave the house but remained motionless alongside the lifeless body. Aleksandr Afinogenov, a writer who was in Gorki, wrote in his diary that "Mura, aged and gone to seed, sat there." Yagoda rushed to Gorki, but did not leave there until sometime later.

That a literary scholar who knows every minute of every hour of the final thread of Gorky's life takes this espionage nonsense seriously is truly incomprehensible! One hopes that General Kolosov acted more professionally in his regular job and did not send unverified reports to his Lubyanka boss.

No one could initiate Mura to the mysteries of the Lubyanka's secret laboratories. Even if she had agreed to this, without knowing which poison was being discussed, the pincers of the Lubyanka would have reached out to her no matter where she went: the executor of such an order could not remain alive, moreover abroad. In any case it would have been much simpler to arrange an automobile accident or some other catastrophe for her than finishing off Trotsky with an ice axe in his Mexican fortress.

In general, there was no need at all to involve an extra participant, and someone highly unreliable at that. What need was there to get Mura to come from London when Gorky's house was already full of Lubyanka agents? The victims were not treated with poison as they were in Shakespeare's day. Like kitchen products, all medicines were prepared and delivered by the Lubyanka. In a typical package and bearing a special label anything could be brought to

[*] Malaya Nikitskaya.

Gorki, and even Lipa—not to mention the doctors!—could have unknowingly administered the fatal toxin to Gorky with a clear conscience. The careful way the suspicion of poisoning was avoided at the trial speaks for itself. "Quantitatively and *qualitatively* all medicines were obtainable," Pletnev stated at the trial at the prosecutor's bidding, deflecting at the same time the idea of the existence of a poisons laboratory.

In repudiating the hypothesis of Mura as murderess, one cannot forget, however, her unbridled desire to take over Gorky's archive and his royalties. There are at least two documents confirming that Mura had prepared Gorky's last will and testament in her favor and, after being rejected by him, signed it herself by forging his signature; she had done so more than once in Germany and Sorrento. Apparently this happened when she had the opportunity to be alone with him (between June 12 and 16), but Lipa, following her intuition, did not allow her to see Gorky. Lipa personally saw the forgery; Yekaterina Pavlovna not only saw it but during the funeral attempted to give it to Stalin. He did not take it but turned it over "to someone else." To whom? There was no further reaction. The "will" disappeared and has not been found to this day.

Legally it had no value, even if Gorky had signed it: without a notary's certification it would have been considered invalid. Moreover, Stalin would not have turned over a single line written by Gorky even to his legal heirs: everything was to become "universal property." What Mura was counting on is difficult to say: she was supposedly an intelligent person but never figured out what Stalin's power represented.

In any event, the will was apocryphal and did not exist for Darya or Mura. Gorky died without having apportioned or resolved anything: if the Party, the government and comrade Stalin personally did not take it into consideration while he was living, would they really acknowledge it after his death?

But, despite all these conjectures, there is one indisputable fact that cannot be ignored. Right up until the beginning of the Second World War, Mura had definitely received money for all of Gorky's foreign editions and for the performance of his plays in other countries. A letter was found in the archive, which the then director of the main literary publishing house in the USSR (Goslitizdat), Solomon Lozovsky (subsequently deputy People's Commissar of Foreign Affairs and executed in 1952 in connection with the Jewish Anti-Fascist Committee), sent to Stalin and Molotov, confirming this with absolute certainty. Clearly not initiated into the secrets of the Kremlin and Lubyanka, Lozovsky wrote,

> Budberg handled the representation of Gorky's interests abroad. It was not only about the loss of several thousand pounds sterling but about the fact that

Baroness Budberg is a suspicious type. After being subjected to a search in Sorrento in 1925, it became known that she is an agent of the [British] Intelligence Service. She holds several hundred of Gorky's letters and several manuscripts, which she has hidden away. Now this cunning woman has set herself up as the comfort of Herbert [H. G.] Wells with the clear intent of continuing her nefarious deeds behind this writer's back.

One can imagine how Stalin and Molotov enjoyed a good laugh reading (if they actually read it!) these revelations from a wounded Soviet publisher, where some kind of truth, especially about Gorky's letters and manuscripts, and the facts they both knew very well is mixed in with unverified and falsely interpreted rumors. Is it any surprise that both Stalin and Molotov did not bother to answer the cry from the soul of the director of Goslitizdat? But one thing is indisputable: the royalties for Gorky's writings in foreign currency were deposited into Mura Budberg's accounts. Gorky's death again spurred interest around the world in his writings, and there were more editions of his works and plays than in the past. Thus, Mura's attempts to obtain the coveted document were completely rational.

How could all this have happened in countries where, to avoid extremely unpleasant consequences, ownership rights and the recipient of monies are carefully checked? The way the so-called will was drawn up negates its legitimacy, not to mention its already dubious legality. Moreover, a copy of any legally composed will remains where it was executed and confirmed (at the Moscow notary's office in this case). But there is no such copy at either the notary's office, in Gorky's archive or in the archive of the former Office for Copyright Protection (now called the Russian Copyright Agency), which was the sole recipient of foreign royalties of Soviet authors. Could foreign publishers at their own risk have paid Mura according to a piece of scribbled paper signed by the dying Gorky? For a long time I could not resolve this question.

And then it came to me! There was no will in the legal sense of this word. What Gorky scholars and people close to him, in plain language, called a will, was not that at all. It was nothing more than a new power of attorney to obtain money (she had many old ones which she had used over several years), signed by Gorky (genuine or forged) and which the Lubyanka—with Stalin's consent, of course—certified with the proper stamp; the power of attorney itself was translated into English (and, perhaps, not only English). The validity of the document, according to Soviet law (and pedantic foreign lawyers could only be guided by that), was for three years. This is how Mura made a living off Gorky's work up to the summer of 1939.

Strictly speaking, the death of the principal automatically annuls the further validity of the power of attorney. But in the absence of objections from legal heirs this formality can be ignored. In any case, the fact that, beginning with the 1940s there were no further "bonuses" in Mura's favor, means the paper she had used as Gorky's will was no longer valid. Had there been a will, she would have been the beneficiary until her death. She had obtained what she could. The archive was much more valuable. But she could not make use of this, as already discussed. She feared retribution. And she could not break her word to Gorky.

Is that all? That is all.

He had saved himself from the Leninist terror, but Stalin's terror, which he met halfway indifferently and lightheartedly, overtook him and finished him off.

Not one of Gorky's messianic ideas came to fruition.

The role which he had dreamed of playing was unsustainable under both Lenin and Stalin.

In the niche of the Kremlin wall is interred not only the secret of his life, but also the mystery of his death, one of the most terrible in the endless litany of bloody Soviet mysteries. And no one, it seems, will ever be able to solve them with absolute certainty.

28.

Maxim Gorky's Second and Third Deaths

After returning to Moscow and Stalin's gilded cage, Gorky, while alive, no longer belonged to himself. But even in death he belonged exclusively to the Party and the government. The sad ritual reserved to families of disposing of the bodies of their loved ones was not possible for Gorky and his family. Comrade Stalin's unfettered love for the great proletarian writer and his best friend deprived them even of this.

ALEKSEI MAXIMOVICH GORKY is engraved in gold lettering on a black plaque, covering the niche in the Kremlin wall where the urn with his ashes was placed. In truth the ashes are those of Aleksei Maximovich Peshkov, but the life of the writer M. Gorky went on even after his death. At the March 1938 trial he was officially proclaimed the best and most loyal friend of comrade Stalin. Vyshinsky, like the defendants who had read their confessions from pieces of paper aloud, spoke so often, so ardently and so passionately about this friendship and this loyalty that any thought of false sincerity seemed inconceivable, except perhaps only to the most obtuse listeners.

Stalin had every reason to doubt the sincerity of Gorky's "love" and no reason at all to believe in his loyalty. According to the testimony of Aleksandr Orlov, the former Lubyanka official who fled to the United States and quoted his NKVD colleagues from Moscow (Orlov was in Spain at the time), Yagoda personally sorted out the papers left by Gorky and found some manuscripts that he found very alarming. Among them was allegedly a diary where, in particular, there was the following entry about Stalin: "A flea increased one thousand times its size would be the most terrible and invincible creature on earth." It was this entry that supposedly elicited Yagoda's response: "No matter how much you feed a wolf, it will always look to the woods."

This secondhand evidence is confirmed by some firsthand evidence that coincides perfectly with what Orlov wrote. The writer Gleb Aleksandrovich Glinka (1903–1989), a descendant of Russian aristocrats who gave the world the great composer, was a member of the literary group *Pereval* (Passing) and a regular contributor to Gorky's journal *Nashi dostizheniia* (Our Achievements), was captured at the front during the Second World War and ended up in the United States where he wrote his memoirs.

In his words, the secret Gorky diary is neither apocryphal nor the fantasy of a Lubyanka general who defected, but truly existed and was found not by Yagoda but by a commission of writers led by Vasily Bobryshev, editor of *Nashi dostizheniia*. Glinka belonged to the commission as well. He saw the thick notebook with an oilcloth cover. Quickly leafing through the diary and running his eyes over the text, the members of the commission handed it over to Bobryshev in horror; he immediately summoned a KGB officer, and everyone who read it had to sign a non-disclosure agreement.

"It immediately became clear," wrote Glinka in America, "that the entire diary consisted of merciless criticism of the big shots in the Kremlin. In the very first pages it was written that if a common vile flea is increased some thousandfold, it will turn into the most horrible creature on earth, and nothing would be strong enough to keep it in check. According to the diary's author, Stalin is such a flea, blown up to unbelievable proportions by Bolshevik propaganda and the hypnosis of fear."

The second half of the diary, as Gleb Glinka testified, was "something like an appeal, or a cry, about how the absence of resistance to all this horror was unacceptable, that even the strongest people, falling into the web of the Bolshevik system, were doomed to spiritual extinction."

The image of lice was very much part of Gorky's style and had been used by him more than once for different reasons in his last years. There is another version that all these papers, including Gorky's diary, if there really was such a thing, were destroyed on Stalin's orders, but this version is not very plausible. Material that was even more dangerous for the regime was preserved in full and has survived to this day. Stalin did not consider himself nor his regime as temporary and did not see the need to justify himself in the face of future accusers; he loved to preserve documents because they could come in handy someday. Thus, if such papers existed, they would probably still be available. The existence of the diary, therefore, was never denied by any of the official Gorky scholars, or any Party functionaries or representatives of the intelligence services. They all simply skirted the question in silence, as if what Orlov and Glinka said did not exist at all. This diary (actually, notes rather than chronological entries but still called a diary) is most likely in the Lubyanka files or in a closed portion of the bottomless Gorky archive.

The debunking of Gorky, however, began almost immediately following his death, which indirectly confirms the version that the leadership considered him guilty of something nevertheless. All three of the journals he created—*Nashi dostizheniia*, *Kolkhoznik* (Kolkhoz Worker) and *SSSR na stroike* (The USSR on the Construction Site)—were already shut down two weeks after his funeral. A significant number of editorial employees, even typists, not to mention Bobryshev himself, were arrested. Writers attached to Gorky—Vladimir Kirshon, Mikhail Chumandrin and others—died in the Lubyanka (only one of this Chekist group, the prose writer and playwright Aleksandr Afinogenov, got off with a brief expulsion from the Party and the Union of Writers; he fell victim to the German bombing of Moscow in October 1941). The book about the White Sea Canal, published when Gorky was editor, and even the trip by "non-Party" writers to that NKVD construction site, which Gorky had organized, were condemned. The writers he had supported and defended were defamed and arrested, followed by execution or, at best, exile, just as those whom he characterized negatively in personal letters to Stalin and the Central Committee were to occupy all the command positions and become the arbiters of other writers' fate. A collection of memoirs about Gorky, prepared to coincide with the fifth anniversary of his death, was banned by the censor: from easily decipherable hints the reader could understand that Gorky was in fact not the very sincere, loving and loyal friend of Stalin.

In 1941, four days before Hitler's Germany attacked the USSR, the fifth anniversary of Gorky's death was observed in accordance with a special decree from the Politburo. Many articles were published in all the main newspapers, but not a word was said about how he was killed by the dastardly Trotsky-Bukharin traitors which, until then, the Soviet press had incessantly droned on about. It was perfectly clear that to attract attention again to his murder was considered undesirable.

The declassified part of Stalin's archive provides written evidence that at the end of his life he had conclusively reexamined his relationship to Gorky the writer, his best and most powerful friend. And perhaps, more accurately, he simply stopped pretending, having expressed, albeit not publicly, his true feelings concerning at least part of Gorky's creative legacy. We must admit that Stalin showed a greater understanding of literature in the end.

A collection of Gorky's poems was being readied for publication in 1951. The mock-up of the book was sent to Stalin for approval. A page from a Gorky short story, on which twenty years previously Stalin had written that he preferred Gorky to Goethe, was also reproduced. Stalin crossed out the photograph with his autograph three times in blue pencil, both front and back. The same fate befell a photograph showing Stalin and Voroshilov listening to Gorky read the story. A few poems were also crossed out (and therefore excluded from the book) with red and brown pencil marks (Stalin probably looked at the mock-up on different days), including "Song of the Falcon," which millions of schoolchildren had to memorize. It should be said that all the Gorky's "masterpieces" that Stalin excluded share an incredible lack of taste.

This had no bearing, however, on Gorky's canonization. From a person and writer who had lived a difficult life, changed his ideological and political orientations many times and who left far from equally valued works, he had been turned into a monument and was awarded his place in the gallery of departed idols by the Kremlin as the great proletarian writer and founder of socialist realism. This was his second death, like that of Mayakovsky, according to Pasternak's incisive observation, who had been transformed by Stalin into the best and most talented writer.

The interest in Gorky fell steadily among readers, despite every effort by crude Soviet propaganda, since what they were allowed was not the best in his vast literary production, but the most primitive and tasteless—mainly, his rhythmic prose like "Song of the Falcon" and "Song of the Stormy Petrel" (even after Stalin had categorically expressed his thoughts regarding these "songs"), as well as his feeble articles praising the land of victorious socialism. The result was an inevitable and strong aversion to the writer who deserved a completely different posterity.

The Communist regime had barely been overthrown when a sharp switch occurred: Gorky's name was mentioned only in a negative context. It remained just as much of a cult, only the other way around. Gorky was avenged posthumously for what he was not guilty of. Yesterday's idol had turned into a monster, which he never was, no matter how one relates to him.

A few years later and another great turnaround took place.

Today, with signs of a Soviet restoration becoming obvious, even to the West which has preferred to ignore this for a long time, and as the resurrection of the Stalinist past proceeds full steam ahead, a new era of Gorky's ascent has begun—but now tragicomically, more as a farce, as it was just before his death. Again his image is being imposed, but it is impossible to tell what kind of image—not as a victim of his own delusions and Stalinist perfidy, but as a beacon of the totalitarian era, a standard of its greatness and not its nightmare. Following his second death, M. Gorky, writer and person, is subjected to yet a third for the restoration of fairness. He definitely did not deserve this ignominy.

Less than two years after Gorky's death, YEKATERINA PAVLOVNA PESHKOVA was destined to experience another loss: the Political Red Cross, her favorite child to which she had given twenty years of her life, saving many people from death and alleviating the conditions of many more in the prisons and camps, was closed. Among those she freed from the Gulag was the lover of the White Admiral Kolchak, Anna Temireva, who wrote about Yekaterina Pavlovna in her memoirs: "She managed until late in life to pre-serve absolute purity of soul and imagination, [...] faith in people and a heart full of love. And a complete absence of sentimentality and sanctimoniousness." Several more letters telling how Yekaterina Pavlovna, against all logic and in the midst of the Great Terror, managed to free political prisoners from the Lubyanka, are also in my archive.

It is highly unlikely that the name of Gorky alone can explain the unique opportunities that Peshkova had for almost twenty years under four all-powerful Lubyanka bosses: Dzerzhinsky, Menzhinsky, Yagoda and Yezhov. She took the secret of her unusual status to the grave, without leaving, it seems, any memoirs, either written or oral.

Yet when Yezhov closed the Political Red Cross, those she had rescued from prisons and fished out of camps and exile were arrested again almost without exception and executed. She remained untouchable, outliving Gorky by twenty-nine years and passing away in 1965, during the Brezhnev era. She was eighty-seven. MIKHAIL NIKOLAEV, whom she married after Gorky, died in 1947 at the age of sixty-five.

MARIA FYODOROVNA ANDREEVA was appointed director of the Moscow House of Scientists in 1931, a position she retained until her retirement in 1948. Gorky's death affected her greatly—she immediately aged by several years. She was gravely ill for months, but the doctors who never left her side managed to get her back on her feet. She never again engaged in any political or government activity. Academics and professors gathered at her old palatial residence on Prechistenka, where Andreeva created the necessary conditions for business meetings and pleasant leisure, and during the war years supplied them with food.

Scientists who enjoyed worldwide recognition called her their kind genie. I heard this myself from many of them. No one ever brought up her participation in dirty, if not downright criminal financial operations of the Bolsheviks before 1917, which many times resulted in a fatal outcome for totally innocent victims. Most likely no one even knew about them, so there was nothing to remember. She celebrated her eightieth birthday at the House of Scientists she was so fond of and died soon after in 1953. Although she did not meet anyone from Gorky's family after his funeral, she did take part in many soirées dedicated to his memory.

At the turn of the twentieth century Lenin had given her the nickname of "Phenomenon," and there truly was something phenomenal about her fate. The product of a privileged and intellectual background, a wonderful actress and a beauty who turned the heads of the most prominent and talented of her peers, she had rushed into the adventurous life of embittered and obsessed subversives, who stopped at nothing in their quest to seize power. And she dragged her beloved Gorky into this vile swamp, ruining both his and her own life.

Nina Berberova's book *Iron Woman* (published in English as *Moura: The Dangerous Life of the Baroness Budberg*) tells the story of MARIA IGNATYEVNA BUDBERG (Mura) in detail, although it is filled with errors. Right up until her death, Mura painstakingly concealed her visits to Moscow between 1933 and 1936, and not only did she keep quiet about them, but in conversations with different people she categorically denied having any meetings with Gorky after she said goodbye to him in Istanbul. It is clear that she had promised to keep these visits secret, and in her fear of the Lubyanka she kept her word even after the secrets had long since been revealed. Incidentally, she certainly did not seek to advertise her closeness to Soviet intelligence, which let her into Moscow unhindered. There is even a version that she would enter the Soviet Union with false passports, prepared for her by the OGPU. The whole truth about this will probably never be known.

In 2002 in England the cipher communications of British agents who had followed Mura at least since 1927 were declassified. They called her a "spy, lesbian, boozer" (British plainclothes detectives were clearly being hasty in their assessment of Mura's lesbianism). They remarked that she traveled to Moscow when she felt like it, indicating that the secret of her visits to Moscow between 1933 and 1936 was no secret at all. She was hailed as the "Red Mata Hari" and an agent of several intelligence agencies at the same time. The British embassy in Moscow sent regular reports to London about her, and not only to the Foreign Office but also to MI-5. In turn, the British agency reported that Mura was an employee of Soviet intelligence, and a highly dangerous one at that, for she could drink a great deal without losing her head.

There are absolutely no signs whatsoever that Mura continued to carry out the delicate assignments of the Lubyanka after the Great Terror: after all, she was Yagoda's creature and for this alone should have joined the ranks of "unreliable comrades." However, even after his downfall, someone continued to supply her with visas for trips to Moscow. Continued interest in her on the part of the NKVD can be explained by the fact that she was still a source of some valuable information. Most likely she continued to keep some very important secrets about Gorky and, more importantly, his letters and documents. In order to get at them it was better to maintain good relations with her than sever them altogether.

The latest archival findings testify to the fact that the interest of the "competent" organs in Gorky's documents she was holding onto did not abate until at least the 1950s. In hopes of enticing from Mura the remains of the archive, Lev Nikulin was recruited in London (1958). From his "report notes" (which he stamped "Secret") to the Central Committee it is evident that Nikulin carried out delicate assignments for his former (and permanent!) masters, diplomatically depersonalized but very practical ("I have been assigned, as you know...," he addressed his "dear comrades"). The recipients of his "secret reports," of course, knew what he had been assigned to do and by whom.

The following year they met again in Paris. At the time Mura was helping her new friend, the English publisher and future member of the House of Lords, George Weidenfeld, who wanted to establish connections with Soviet authors and publishing organizations. She used the growing interest being shown in her to arrange a trip for herself and Weidenfeld to Moscow to secure the necessary copyrights of Soviet scientists for her friend for next to nothing.

The Kremlin powers regarded these arrangements very coolly, and Mura again returned to her former tactics; she began claiming that the archive ("a small suitcase with manuscripts and Gorky's letters") was kept on her estate at Aegviidu Kalliyav outside Tallinn where it was burned when Nazi troops arrived there. This version was subsequently defended by Mura's daughter, Tatyana Aleksander, who visited Moscow in 1993.

Nikulin managed to obtain from Mura several Gorky autographs, drawings and photographs, but not one of these rarities had any relationship to the sought-after archive. Among the materials brought back by Nikulin, essentially proving that he had tried very hard to carry out his task, was an unknown photograph of Gorky, unpublished to this day, posing against the background of an antiques store, confiscated in 1919–1920 by his "Expert Commission." The only positive result of Nikulin's efforts consists in the fact that now we reliably know that at least a part (apparently the most important part) of Gorky's "suitcase" remained with Mura even after 1936—no pressure of any kind worked on the "iron lady," no fear of the Lubyanka made her part with the treasure entrusted to her.

Mura's marriage to NIKOLAI BUDBERG, from whom she separated in 1922, was formally annulled four years later (N. Budberg resettled in South America and died in Rio de Janeiro in 1972 at the age of eighty-seven). Mura was free but, no matter how much H. G. Wells tried to convince her to marry him, she rejected his offer just as earlier she had rejected Gorky. No one can say precisely why. Wells left her $100,000. Had they married, she would have received more, but this was enough for her to open a literary agency in London after Wells' death .

As she had no professional skills, and the business turned out badly, Mura continued to translate Gorky's works, as well as those of other writers whom Gorky had recommended, but insofar as he had more often than not recommended extremely mediocre writers, and Mura's personal taste left a great deal to be desired, these manuscripts failed to attract the attention of publishers. Those that did had no success among readers. Moreover, her translations could serve as an example of how not to translate. Mura omitted not only words and expressions which she did not understand but whole paragraphs, even pages, if her translation required even the slightest effort.

"All London" knew her, but she had few friends. One of her closest friends was Salomeya Andronnikova, whom Anna Akhmatova celebrated in her poetry. Her husband, the lawyer Galpern, also an émigré, was a Soviet agent. It is possible that they followed each other without knowing anything about each other: a favorite device used by the Soviet intelligence services.

The mysterious and uniquely virtuous life of Mura Budberg served as the plot for the film *British Agent* starring Leslie Howard and Kay Francis, which guaranteed the film a wide audience. Unfortunately, the vast majority of people know Mura only through this film, although her real life is a thousand times more interesting and entertaining than this commonplace film version with its numerous fictions and absurdities.

After a twenty-year interruption Mura and George Weidenfeld visited Moscow in November 1959, and then she was in Moscow as a guest of Yekaterina Pavlovna and Timosha a few more times: in 1961, 1962, 1963, 1965 (at Peshkova's funeral), 1968, and, for the last time, in 1973. On one of her trips she went up the Volga with Timosha and Liudmila Tolstaya. In 1968 she participated in official ceremonies on the occasion of the hundredth anniversary of Gorky's birth.

In September 1974 Mura went to see her son, who lived near Florence. Her arrival was marked by a truly mystical event, were it not for the fact that it was completely real, adding to the image of this truly iron woman. She had just arrived when suddenly—naturally, "by pure coincidence"—the trailer in which she was transporting her belongings caught fire. What belongings these were is not difficult to guess: manuscripts and her entire personal archive. One can only imagine how many of Gorky's autographs and materials were included. Someone correctly observed that many intelligence agencies, historians and literary scholars would have paid dearly for the contents of that trailer. Mura did not allow the fire to be extinguished; admiring the flames and convinced that nothing remained of the contents in the trailer, she returned home and for the first time in many years fell asleep without sleeping pills or alcohol.

Two months later, on November 2, 1974, in the eighty-third year of her life, she died in the Italy she and Gorky loved so much, closing the fateful circle of the Stormy Petrel and the Iron Woman: he did not succeed in tearing himself away from his Moscow cage, but Mura went to Italy to die without him.

One of those attached to Gorky and Mura, the Red playboy and bon vivant, LEV NIKULIN (Olkonitsky), continued to write his false and blatant propaganda novels while regularly traveling abroad, where his former friends in the Russian literary emigration greeted him with open arms. All things considered, they figured out who was sending Nikulin on these journeys and why, but for some reason did not attribute any importance to it. On the other hand, decent people back home knew where he worked and avoided him. "Writers are of different types," wrote Ilya Ehrenburg very concisely and fearlessly in a letter to top Party functionary Aleksandr Shcherbakov. "Maxim Gorky is one thing, and Lev Nikulin is another."

It was no coincidence that an epigram like "Tell me, Cain, where's Abel? Tell me, Nikulin, where's Babel?" and others similar to it made the rounds in Moscow. In addition to his literary pseudonym he unquestionably had a Lubyanka alias, and possibly more than one. In his memoirs and in conversation Nikulin loved to present himself as being close to Gorky, whose literary ambitions the great proletarian writer not only blessed but to whom he bared his soul. He was the first to be allowed to look at his archives by the Lubyanka, so that he could write a novel, *Mertvaia zyb'* (Swell), glorifying the successes of Soviet intelligence in the 1920s. Nikulin died in 1967 at the age of seventy-six, leaving behind dozens of published and more than one unpublished book. They have been sitting on shelves, unread, for a long time now.

LIPA—Olimpiada Dmitrievna Chertkova—did not leave the Gorky home, even though she was given her own apartment in Moscow. In 1934 Gorky had arranged a small "personal" pension for her, giving her some independence. The brief memoirs that she dictated, and which remained for many decades in a closed part of the Gorky archive, are distinguished by their simplicity, disingenuousness, and truthfulness. "Red-haired Lapa" (another nickname given her by Gorky was "Lipa, good weather") turned out to be worthy of Gorky's trust and love. "I began my life with a midwife," Gorky remarked not long before his death, "and with a midwife I end it." In his words, Lipa, whom he also tenderly called Chertovka, was a "soft broom" who shook from him the "accumulated dust." All her remaining years were filled with the memory of this. Lipa died in 1951. She was seventy-three.

The life of TIMOSHA—Nadezhda Alekseevna Peshkova—ended dramatically. Her cold and captivating beauty apparently concealed something sinister, condemning to death not only everyone attracted to her, but also bringing only torment to herself.

After all the ups and downs connected with Max, Tolstoy, and Yagoda, Timosha also dreamed of a quiet harbor, finding it in the talented philologist Ivan Luppol, who headed the Institute of World Literature after Gorky's death. Luppol's writings on the French Enlightenment and the classics of French literature were highly regarded by specialists. Gorky had also noticed him and kept him close by. Clearly playing to Stalin's hand, Luppol proclaimed Gorky the heir to Goethe in his work "Problems of Contemporaneity," personally edited by Gorky and read at the Paris Congress in 1935. In January 1939 Luppol became an academician. It appeared as if he were destined for great things in his career, and for Timosha it was a quiet life without reverberations.

In August 1940 Timosha and Luppol, full of optimism, left for a vacation in the Caucasus, from which Timosha returned alone some time later. Luppol had been arrested, and Timosha, after being briefly detained, was released: it is possible that Stalin had given the order—Gorky's closest relative could "count" only on him.

On the morning of June 22, 1941, the academician V. I. Vernadsky, unaware that at dawn on that same day the Nazis had invaded the Soviet Union, made the following entry in his diary:

> I. K. Luppol suffered on account of Gorky. It was said he was shot. He was the husband of the widow of Gorky's son. [Both] were arrested in connection with the fact that during a search of some baroness, an old acquaintance of Gorky, in Derpta [Tartu], his diaries were found, criticizing the activity of the Soviet government. [...] Gorky extracted a promise from the son's widow that she would send these diaries from the baroness [to him]. Luppol was an educated person, not nice, but one of the few cultured government figures. From Romanians.

This entry contains many small errors, which is inevitable when rumors are the only source of information. But the fact that they have given rise to the history of the notorious Mura suitcase, the contents of which are connected with seditious

Gorky remarks, and that the rumors spread far beyond the boundaries of a small circle, says a great deal.

Vernadsky's testimony should be treated with all seriousness: he was in contact with many well-informed people, and the chronology provides at least some logic to his information. In July 1940 Soviet troops occupied Estonia, and the NKVD emissaries had a very good idea of what to look for and where. Thus it is highly probable that the "suitcase" had not burned at all following the entry of the Nazis a year later, but was delivered to the Lubyanka with all its contents, although the most valuable items or, at a minimum, something very essential was hidden by Mura and preserved for the flames which enveloped the trailer from London many years later outside Florence.

Among the charges against Luppol, nothing was said about Mura's suitcase or about Gorky. According to the usual Lubyanka scheme of things, he was accused of participation in a Trotskyist organization that had organized terrorist acts. In July 1941, slightly more than two weeks after the outbreak of the war, he was sentenced to be shot but, in defiance of the long established order, the sentence was not carried out. On June 23, 1942—on the same day as the sentence for the great geneticist Nikolai Vavilov—Luppol's death sentence was commuted to twenty years in the camps, and from a prison in Saratov he was transferred to one of the Mordovka camps where he died from dystrophy on May 26, 1943. He was forty-seven.

Luppol's posthumous rehabilitation took place in May 1956. Timosha was alive, though she was not the one who petitioned the authorities for his rehabilitation, but his legal wife Maria Yevtikhievna (in spite of the strict rules which existed under Stalin, this wife of an "enemy of the people" not only was not banished from Moscow, but kept her former apartment in the privileged writers' building on Lavrushinsky Lane). Her petition was supported by Yekaterina Peshkova and Ilya Ehrenburg—in all documents concerning Luppol, Timosha's name is completely absent.

Professor Vyacheslav Ivanov, son of the writer Vsevolod Ivanov (also not indifferent to her) and who knew Timosha well, maintains that Stalin was in love with her, which to a great degree explains the tragic fate of all her close friends. Timosha's next partner in life after Luppol, the architect Miron Merzhanov, whose work could mostly be seen in the government dachas around Moscow and in the Caucasus, was arrested. He designed Stalin's dacha in Kuntsevo on the outskirts of Moscow (1934), where nineteen years later the tyrant passed away, as well as the dachas of Kalinin, Voroshilov and others among his loyal advisors. For his efforts Merzhanov was rewarded with eleven years in the camps, obtaining his release only in 1960.

After his arrest in 1949, Timosha did not remain alone for long—she spirited away the husband of the daughter of the ornamental "president" of the USSR, Mikhail Kalinin. His son-in-law, Vladimir Fyodorovich Popov, was a prominent railway engineer. Soon after he teamed up with Timosha, becoming either her fifth or sixth husband, his number came up too. He was lucky: Stalin died soon after, and Popov spent only a year and a half in the Gulag; after his release, he did not return to Timosha. Timosha passed away in 1971 in the seventy-second year of her life.

Gorky's grandchildren are alive and well to this day.

At the end of the 1940s MARFA married Sergo, the son of Lavrenty Beria, at the same time as her classmate and best friend Svetlana Allilueva married for a second time, the son of Stalin's favorite, Andrei Zhdanov. Sergo was arrested with his father in June 1953, and on the same day Marfa, pregnant with her third son, was placed under house arrest along with other members of the family. Her incarceration lasted for twenty-four days and ended only after the energetic interference of Yekaterina Pavlovna, who managed to get through to Molotov. After Sergo was freed—deprived of the right not only to live but even to appear in Moscow—Marfa traveled a few times for short visits with her husband, but their marriage was not destined to last.

Sergo was coerced into taking the maiden name of his mother, Gegechkori. He was also deprived of his patronymic and called Sergei Alekseevich, not Lavrentievich. He was only able to obtain his legal patronymic and even his surname shortly before his death in 2002. Sergo was considered an outstanding specialist in the field of space technology. Sergo and Marfa's three children have the surname of Peshkov. The great humanist writer and the great executioner have common descendants—the great-grandchildren of Gorky are also Beria's grandchildren. Fate could probably not have thought up anything more sinister, absurd, and symbolic. Incidentally, Pushkin and the chief of the Russian gendarmes, Dubbelt, had grandchildren in common—history repeats itself and can no longer surprise us.

Marfa has lived her whole life in isolation, remaining aloof from any kind of publicity, but her name suddenly resurfaced recently. In May 2004 she sold at auction part of her grandfather's heritage: books from Gorky's library delivered to Timosha after his death. It is an absolute mystery why they did not end up in the collection of the Gorky museum, where his entire library was sent. Only thirty-six books in all were sold: bibliographic rarities from the eighteenth and nineteenth centuries, albums and runs of journals, a significant part of which are not held in any library in Russia. An anonymous buyer paid more than $300,000 for them at auction.

DARYA was, and still is, an actress in the Vakhtangov Theater, featured in very modest roles. She was married to an actor from the same theater, Aleksandr Grav. Gorky loved both grandchildren very much, but related to them differently. Nonetheless, they both remember their grandfather to this day and are filled with the most tender feelings for him.

VARVARA TIKHONOVA passed away in Paris in 1950 when she was sixty-four years old. She had lived with dignity during the years after Gorky had left her, never turning to anyone for help and dying in proud poverty. Not long before her death she burned all of Gorky's letters to her. Without a doubt, of all the women who had entered his life and were later abandoned, he was more a scoundrel and cad to her than anyone else. He did not simply replace her with another, more loved and more needed, but tossed her out to the whims of fate. There are absolutely no signs pointing to any reason, let alone a cause, for this. NINA TIKHONOVA, the pupil of the great Russian ballerina Olga Preobrazhenskaya (1871–1962) in emigration and a soloist in the ballet, became a French star, opened her own school in Paris, and received one of the highest awards of France, the Order of Arts and Literature. Only in the 1970s did she visit Moscow and Leningrad. Nina died in Paris in 1993.

In spite of serious illnesses, ANDREI SHAIKEVICH continued to work, combining two rather unrelated professions, that of engineer and ballet historian. He lived to the age of sixty-nine and died in Paris in 1972.

NATALIA GRUSHKO, like millions of her countrymen and -women, was crushed by the millstone of the Great Terror. What could she have been accused of, who prevented this talented failure who had so passionately responded to the outbursts of her heart? Both her sons were sent to the front at the beginning of the war to "buy off the guilt" of their mother—and both perished. But she survived, and continued to live in complete obscurity in Paris until the beginning of 1974, when she died at the age of eighty-three.

ZINOVY PESHKOV probably had no personal contacts with his adoptive father after 1927, or, if there were any contacts after that date, there is no trace of any, although there is evidence, thus far unsubstantiated, that Zinovy visited Gorky in later years in Sorrento. It is assumed that neither Gorky nor he made these visits public knowledge, just as with Mura and her trips to Moscow. About twenty years ago it became known that in the summer of 1930 Zinovy, while in Strasbourg, received a letter from Gorky from Sorrento. There is no information as to where this letter is. News of the death of his adoptive father put Zinovy in a deep funk, as evidenced from the memoirs of eyewitnesses and his own published reaction.

The one-armed Zinovy had a brilliant career as a very active participant of the French Resistance, an associate of de Gaulle, ambassador of France to China and head of its mission to Japan with the rank of ambassador. He died in 1966 at age 82, a French general and recipient of the Great Cross of the Legion of Honor. His last love, the French writer and Goncourt laureate Edmonde Charles-Roux, keeps his memory. His daughter, that is, Gorky's adopted granddaughter, Yelizaveta, who fell in love with Ivan Markov, a Soviet spy working under cover of the USSR embassy in Rome and married him, acquired Soviet citizenship and moved to the Soviet Union in the very midst of the Great Terror at the end of 1937. Almost immediately after, Markov was arrested and shot, and Yelizaveta spent time in the Gulag.

There is an unconfirmed version that Zinovy, with the help of French intelligence, with whom he was closely linked, dashed into Moscow incognito in 1939 to rescue his daughter and succeeded with the help of Yekaterina Pavlovna Peshkova. Zinovy's arrival in Moscow is doubtful, but Peshkova's assistance cannot be discounted, because after the war Yelizaveta ended up in the "regime" city of Sochi, a Black Sea resort considered governmental because of its proximity to the dachas of Stalin and his circle. For many years she lived in a wooden barracks until the Gorky Archive secured a tiny one-room apartment for her. Her older son died in an automobile accident, and the younger, Gorky's great-grandson named Aleksei in his honor, is a journalist who lives and works in Moscow.

VALENTINA KHODASEVICH became a very prominent theatrical artist and actively worked with different theaters of Moscow and Leningrad. She died in 1970 at the age of 76. Her husband DIDI—ANDREI ROMANOVICH DIDERIKHS, also a close friend of Gorky's—died in Tashkent where he had evacuated his family in 1942. Valentina married again, to their common friend, the artist Viktor Basov, but he died after only four years.

VLADISLAV KHODASEVICH and NINA BERBEROVA, who left Sorrento in 1925, settled in Paris. A few years later they split up. In the meantime, the correspondence between Khodasevich and Gorky, who highly valued the great talent of this poet, continued. His subjective and vibrant reminiscences of Gorky are a valuable source for understanding this deeply contradictory and complex personality. Khodasevich died in 1939.

With the beginning of the war Nina Berberova resettled in America, where she wrote many books in different genres, securing her worldwide renown. Her most famous book is also the first and essentially only biographical novel about Mura Budberg, *Iron Woman*, published in many languages under various names (in English it was published as *Moura: The Dangerous Life of the Baroness Budberg*). Berberova left a laconic but extremely plastic portrait of Gorky, with whom she had spent three years under the same roof: "The penetrating stare of blue eyes, soft voice with coughing, movement of the hands—very smooth, clean and even, his whole appearance that of a tall, stooped person with a sunken chest and straight legs. He had a condescending, not always pleasant smile, a face which could become mean (when his skin turned red and the cheekbones moved under his skin), he had the habit of looking over whoever he was talking to when he was asked a sharp or unpleasant question, drumming his fingers on a table or, not hearing, singing something. At every new meeting with a new person to whom he wanted to ingratiate himself, the tone of his conversation, even the movements that accompanied it, were a form of affectation and not based upon any direct feeling. Besides this, he had the innate charm of an intelligent man, unlike other people, who lived a great, difficult, and wonderful life."

Nina Berberova never changed her views, remaining a steadfast opponent of any kind of slavery. She maintained both her physical and spiritual strength until an advanced age, amazing her acquaintances with the fast cars she loved to drive to the end of her life. Not long before her death, she visited the Soviet Union during Gorbachev's perestroika (1989), where she was given a triumphant reception. She died in 1993, having cheerfully observed her ninety-second birthday.

ALEKSANDR TIKHONOV successfully skirted the Great Terror while working as an editor in various publishing houses. He left behind a slim volume of memoirs called *Time and People* (under the pseudonym of A. Serebrov). It contains many eloquent portrait sketches, but it is impossible to extract any information from this book, even though he knew a great deal and was not only a witness to, but also a participant in, the most interesting events. He wrote his memoirs about this as well, figuring that they would reach his descendants, and kept them in a secret drawer of his writing table, not trusting any archives. Once when he opened this drawer, he discovered it was empty: the manuscript had been stolen. It is probably filed somewhere in the secret archives of the Lubyanka.

Tikhonov immersed himself again and again into the whirlpool of new passions, and each time with the same outcome. His last romance was with the beautiful actress Maria Strelkova, who left him for the arms of another beautiful actor. Tikhonov died in 1956 at age 77, struck down with paralysis and having lost all contacts with Varvara and Nina.

"NIGHTINGALE"—Ivan Nikolayevich Rakitsky—remained close to Gorky's family constantly since 1918. He died in 1942 at age 59.

Immediately following the death of Gorky, GENRIKH YAGODA was given an apartment in the Kremlin—there was no higher honor than this. He moved in right away from the private residence specially built for him on Milyutinsky Lane. Now he awaited his inclusion in the Politburo, which Stalin, leaving for summer vacation before the onset of the Zinoviev-Kamenev trial, had announced to him with the words, "You have deserved it."

It turned out that he deserved something completely different: a telegram arrived from Stalin, who was in Sochi, with orders to replace Yagoda with Nikolai Yezhov as the People's Commissar of Internal Affairs. Two days before his fall from grace, Yagoda had managed to give Mura, via Kriuchkov, 400 pounds sterling, meaning that up to the end of September 1936 she was still in Moscow, "putting in order" Gorky's archive. Meanwhile, H. G. Wells asserts that he spent only three weekends without Mura. It is doubtful that his memory failed him so badly: after all, he had composed the "fragments" of his autobiography only five years after these events. It is very probable that Mura, in order to avoid any conflict with Wells, left Moscow in the summer of 1936 and then returned once again: Yagoda could have supplied her with an unlimited number of visas, as well as with the money required to take these trips. She really wanted to return that archive…

On the day of Yagoda's arrest—March 28, 1937—his Kremlin apartment, his office at work, his dacha, and two private secret hiding places, were all searched. The search lasted without interruption for nine days, and the written inventory of confiscated items fills up many pages. Hundreds of bottles of rare wines, innumerable antiques (altogether some 10,008 items), fur coats, men's suits, women's undergarments, perfume, and so on, testify to the wide variety of tastes and interests of their owner. But the most remarkable item in this list is the absence of any foreign currency or diamonds, although Soviet currency was in abundance, and valuables consisted of only five gold watches. It is also known how easily he made use of hard currency, which he never accounted for to anyone. Some historians maintain that Yagoda could have kept his currency reserves at one of his dachas, for example, at the Giltishchev dacha outside Moscow, on the Leningrad highway, where he often secluded himself during the day with Timosha and which he abandoned after having been deprived of his post as the People's Commissar of Internal Affairs. He could hardly have thought that this hideaway was so reliable and that the long arm of his NKVD colleagues would not reach him. More likely than not he kept the money at Timosha's place: the probability of her being subjected to a search was negligible and Yagoda knew this.

Not long before his demise, as we remember, Yagoda had bragged to Gorky that he was "tearing the throat" of others. Now, without complaining of fatigue and nerves, Stalin cold-bloodedly ripped him apart. Sentenced to be shot to death on March 13, 1938, Yagoda, according to an official announcement, was executed on March 15. However, Zimin, chief of the Lefortovo prison, who was also subsequently arrested and survived in the Gulag until Khrushchev's "thaw," told investigators in 1956 that at least until January 31, 1939 (the day on which Zimin was arrested in his office), Yagoda was still being held in a secret isolation cell of this prison, not by name but by number (102), and that from time to time the secret prisoner was visited by Yezhov and Malenkov. Having discovered this sensational information in an archive, I immediately published my find and then returned to it in print several times, requesting to be allowed to check it in a section of the Lubyanka archive that was kept off-limits to me. No reaction of any kind followed, although prison ledgers for those years have been preserved in full. The archive of the former KGB of the USSR refuses to cross-check it with its sources to this day.

In contrast to all the other participants of the Great Moscow Trials, Yagoda has thus far not been rehabilitated, although he was condemned not for the arrests and executions of innocent people, which would have been justified, but for espionage and other mythical crimes in accordance with the general pattern of those years for all the victims of the Great Terror. It cannot be excluded that this seeming absurdity is rather easily explained: the accusation for the murder of Gorky and Max (and perhaps not only them) was nevertheless justified. Yagoda was not accused of the murders supposedly committed by doctors with

Kriuchkov's complicity, but for those which he organized and realized with the help of the sinister poisons laboratory.

Yagoda's sister, Esfir Znamenskaya, was shot three months after her brother's execution, and the same fate befell another sister, Liliya, one month later. Their father, mother, and sister Rozaliya died in the camps. Only the sisters Frida Fridlyand and Taisiya Mordvinkina, as well as Yagoda's son, also named Genrikh, survived the Gulag. Like Beria's son, the younger Genrikh was also forced to change both his patronymic and surname. We do not know what happened to him after that.

MOTYA the policeman—MATVEI SAMOILOVICH POGREBINSKY— appointed head of the NKVD of the Gorki region while Gorky was alive, did not wait for the inevitable arrest but committed suicide immediately following the arrest of Yagoda in the spring of 1937 at the age of 42. He left a posthumous letter to Stalin: "With one hand I turned criminals into honest people, and with the other I was forced, subordinating myself to Party discipline, to hang the label of criminals on the noblest revolutionary figures of our country." Pogrebinsky, who had been proclaimed "an enemy of the people" without an investigation or a mock trial, was posthumously rehabilitated in 1956.

LEOPOLD AVERBAKH, his sister IDA—Yagoda's wife—the deputy prosecutor of Moscow and all others from the same circle, naturally, shared a common fate. In 1932 Gorky had written to Stalin about Averbakh, "… This is a highly intelligent, talented person, who has still not turned as is necessary and who needs to be instructed. He needs to be taken care of. He is very overworked, he has neuritis and terrible neurasthenia from fatigue." Stalin listened to Gorky's advice and "took care of" Averbakh once and for all so that he never again overworked himself or was overly fatigued: he had him executed.

IDA AVERBAKH-YAGODA outlived her husband by two months. The young wife of KRIUCHKOV—Yelizaveta Zakharovna Medvedovskaya, who had influenced him no less than Andreeva had in the past, was also destroyed: Kriuchkov, apparently, was a very weak-willed person, which made it much easier for Yagoda to manipulate him. Yagoda had once wanted to make Yelizaveta his concubine and informer, but it did not work. Where he failed, his successors did not. Not long before Yelizaveta's arrest a writer (whose identity to this day remains carefully guarded) was sent to seduce her, and then informed the Lubyanka in excruciating detail about everything she had confided to him during their secret trysts. Kriuchkov's father, a veterinarian, was also shot. His sister Margarita died in an insane asylum where she had been locked up. Kriuchkov's daughter Aina was miraculously saved by Stalin's favorite, Aleksandr Fadeev, but their five-year-old son Petya hid in a forest eating nuts and carrots from country gardens while his family searched for him. He died in 2002, several months before his seventieth birthday.

KRIUCHKOV and DOCTOR LEVIN were shot on March 15, 1938, along with the "Ivanoviches" so dear to Gorky—BUKHARIN, RYKOV, and other participants of the third (and final) public show trial during the Great Terror. One of Levin's sons, Vladimir, was shot right after his father; a second, Georgi, was sent to Norilsk in the Far North in September 1938, and his aged wife to Kazakhstan.

To this day the version provided by the German socialist Brigitta Gerland, also a prisoner of the Gulag who escaped from the Soviet Union and told of meeting PROFESSOR PLETNEV, sentenced to twenty-five years' imprisonment in one of the camps, still enjoys widespread currency in the West. He told her that Gorky had been poisoned with chocolates specially prepared for him by the NKVD.

This version is not apocryphal, nor created by Brigitta Gerland's imagination, but a lie deliberately circulated by the Lubyanka, the objective not being to create disinformation about Gorky's death, but about Pletnev's happy camp life. A multitude of "eyewitnesses" who "met" famous people long since executed in the Gulag conveyed happy news of this sort to their relatives.

In fact, Professor DMITRI PLETNEV, who managed to write a scientific monograph of about 250 pages in prison (it disappeared), was secretly executed on September 11, 1941, in the Medvedovsky forest outside Orel three weeks before its occupation by the Nazis, on orders from Beria and approved by Stalin. Among the other 156 people executed there at the same time was OLGA KAMENEVA. The works of Dmitri Dmitrievich Pletnev, one of the greatest Russian cardiologists of the nineteenth century, are still studied today in all medical schools around the country.

MIKHAIL KOLTSOV was arrested on December 12, 1938, and shot on February 2, 1940: he was being groomed to be one of the main defendants in the trial of the diplomats but the trial did not take place, and the country's top journalist was sentenced and secretly executed. Before his arrest Koltsov had managed to publish a book written on Stalin's instructions: *Stormy Petrel: The Life and Death of Maxim Gorky*, where it was repeated many times that he was "the closest friend of the great Stalin," and that "Gorky hated and despised the right-wing apostates who had sold out to Fascism." The book also tells in great detail how Gorky hated and despised the "Ivanoviches"—Bukharin and Rykov. Knowing full well that he had slandered both Gorky and those who had "sold out," Koltsov was attempting to save his own skin. He failed.

Koltsov's common-law wife, the German communist Maria Osten (Grossgener), who valiantly rushed to Moscow from abroad to save her husband, would be tortured and executed in 1942, but his official wife, the journalist Yelizaveta Ratmanova, who also spent time with Koltsov at Gorky's in Tesseli and supplied the intelligence services with information about their conversations, would avoid that fate: instead of falling victim to the Great Terror, she would soon marry Mikhail Styrikovich, a prominent Soviet thermal physicist and later academician. After Koltsov was rehabilitated (1954), she put in a claim for the rights to his literary heritage, but was turned down. Actually it was illegal, but ethically totally justifiable. Koltsov's cousin, Boris Yefimov (Fridlyand), would not only survive but remain, as before, a popular caricaturist and employee of *Pravda* who branded the objects of his caricatures "enemies of the people" and American "warmongers" and received the highest government honors for it. As these lines are written, he is still thriving at the age of 104, full of inexhaustible creative energy.

ISAAK BABEL was arrested on May 16, 1939, and executed on January 27, 1940, a week before Koltsov. From recently declassified archival materials, it is clear that the Lubyanka began collecting a file on him long before his arrest. A secret agent told the NKVD in September 1936 about Babel's statement regarding the outcome of the trial against Kamenev and Zinoviev: "I believe that this is not a fight of counterrevolutionaries, but a fight with Stalin based upon personal relationships." That statement alone was enough to seal his doom. Another agent, nicknamed "Emmanuel," in July 1936 reproduced Babel's reply to the question of whether he could be arrested too: "During the old man's [Gorky's] lifetime, this was impossible. And now it is also difficult." As we see, there was no difficulty at all, and during the "old man's" lifetime it was just as possible as it was after his death.

In contrast to Maria Osten, the fate of Babel's civil wife, the engineer Antonina Pirozhkovaya, had a happy ending. She was not victimized, and in 1996 she moved to the US to be with her grandson, who had emigrated there earlier. She lives in America to this day. In the US she shared her reminiscences about Babel, in particular his view of Gorky, whom he knew and understood well. "Aleksei Maximovich," Babel told his wife, "was depressed by the situation which Yagoda had created around him. Yet it was completely incomprehensible why he did not take any measures whatsoever to counter it. His house and dacha were under constant surveillance by the NKVD. He said nothing but only drummed his fingers on the table [in despair]." Apparently, Babel did not understand Gorky well enough. He had not taken into account his weak will, fatigue and helplessness.

The closeness of GRU employee Koltsov to the authorities (to Voroshilov mostly, but to Stalin too), and Babel's personal closeness to Yezhov were, without a doubt, among the most important reasons which led them to a tragic end. Babel used to visit Yezhov and had an affair with his wife Yevgenia Khayutina (she edited one of Gorky's journals)—he probably knew something though not that much, but back then to know even a little was not a good thing. Yezhov poisoned his wife himself, since she naturally knew a lot, and then his own turn came. He outlived Babel by a week and was executed on the same day as Koltsov.

Such was the fate of Gorky's two dear guests who had visited him in March in Tesseli. The third one accompanying them, as we remember, was ANDRÉ MALRAUX. There are grounds to believe that almost immediately after Gorky's death Koltsov recruited him in Spain to work for Soviet military intelligence (GRU). A recently decrypted telegram from the Soviet ambassador in Spain, Marcel Rosenberg (also executed shortly thereafter), dated July 26, 1936, in Stalin's name and People's Commissar of Foreign Affairs Maxim Litvinov, provides indisputable evidence of this. The telegram was sent by so-called "special code," which excluded the possibility of anyone becoming acquainted with it, except for the addressees and the cipher officer. Stalin read the telegram, as evidenced by the note in his hand. After Koltsov disappeared behind the thick walls of the Lubyanka, Malraux's work for the GRU ceased. In any event, no signs of it have surfaced so far. Concerning his espionage activity, albeit short-lived, for the Kremlin, French biographers of this outstanding writer and statesman prefer to remain silent. Malraux's later attitude toward the country of workers of the whole world, on the contrary, is well known.*

Among the unending number of victims of the Great Terror is ALEKSANDR AROSEV. "Almost everyone with whom I talked in Moscow," recorded Romain Rolland in his diary, "reacted negatively, saying 'He's a fool.' He is no fool, but the irreparably tactless moves he makes because of his wounded pride, become dangerous blunders. As a result, he lost his position as ambassador [to Czechoslovakia]. I am afraid that for this same reason he will also lose his position at VOKS [All-Union Society for Cultural Ties Abroad]"

Arosev not only lost his position, he also lost his head. He was accused of being a member of a "diversionary terrorist organization" planning to assassinate Stalin and Molotov. Why Arosev did not kill them, while meeting regularly with them (Molotov was his closest friend), has remained a mystery. Together with Arosev, according to the accusation, Ilya Ehrenburg, Aleksandra Kollontai, and many others who avoided the chalice of poison were also involved: Stalin considered them to be more valuable to him alive than dead.

Having learned about the arrest of Arosev from Russian émigré newspapers, Romain Rolland courageously rushed to his defense. He was not hindered by the fact that Stalin had already ignored his previous letter of March 18, 1937, following the arrest of Bukharin. "Allow me," wrote Rolland, "to remind you of a name dear to us both, that of our friend Maxim Gorky. I often saw Bukharin at his place, I saw their close friendship. Let the memory of it save Bukharin! In the name of Gorky, I ask you to spare him." Stalin did not react to this cry from the heart, but Rolland decided to try one more time, having taken seriously, it seems, Stalin's gallant assertion of his willingness to be at Rolland's complete disposal: "Arosev," he wrote to Stalin, "always displayed total loyalty and devotion to you. [...] He spoke of you with love and pride." Stalin did not respond to this letter from August 4, 1937, either, just as he ignored all the other letters Rolland had addressed

---

* André Malraux was an ardent follower of General Charles de Gaulle during the Second World War, served as de Gaulle's minister of cultural affairs from 1958 to 1969, and was a vocal anti-communist.

to him. Arosev was executed on February 9, 1938, before he had reached the age of 48.

The fate of IVAN GRONSKY turned out more favorably. Despite his closeness to Stalin, he came to Bukharin's defense in 1937 and was arrested two weeks later. He was the only one from the upper echelons of the Kremlin who was not shot in the back of the head for having raised his voice, but he spent seventeen years in a Siberian camp instead. Someone who heard his oral memoirs in 1959 stated that Gronsky remained "a fossil who had accidentally escaped from some Mesozoic era of the revolution," a hardheaded and fanatical Stalinist. He died in 1985, having lived long enough to celebrate his ninetieth birthday.

MARIA ROLLAND (MARIA KUDASHEVA, née Cuvillier), lived happily with her husband until his death (1944), preferring neutral Switzerland during the war to Nazi-occupied Paris. She did not leave any written memoirs, although she could write (she was a very promising poet in her youth) and had something to say. Incidentally, the great Russian philosopher Nikolai Berdyaev was the uncle of her first husband Sergei Kudashev, and among her lovers were not only famous Frenchmen, but also Vyacheslav Ivanov, the great poet of Russian Symbolism.

In putting together various testimonies and my own conversations with Maya Bernard Duhamel, I reached the conclusion that her Lubyanka curator in Paris was a certain Louis Gibarti, *aka* Lazslo Dobos, from the Hungarian network of Comintern spies. In 1989 Babette Gross, the girlfriend of the German anti-Stalinist and communist Willi Münzenberg, who was liquidated by hit men sent from Moscow, admitted to American historian Stephen Cohen that Maya was employed for many years by the Soviet secret police and that she completely controlled Rolland, who followed all her wise and tender advice. Madame Marie Rolland died in Paris in 1985 at the age of 90.

After Gorky, ALEKSEI TOLSTOY occupied the position of patriarch in Soviet literature. He was showered with all kinds of plausible and implausible honors, became an academician, and received, in addition to Gorky's mansion on Malaya Nikitkinskaya, his own "small wing." Stalin tenderly called him "our Soviet count." Tolstoy participated in various Stalinist actions, in particular becoming a member of the commission which "confirmed" that the mass murder of Polish officers in Katyn was carried out by the Nazis and not the Soviets.

Timosha and Tolstoy's young wife, Liudmila Ilyinichna, became friends and often met for lunch or dinner at Tolstoy's elegant dacha in the government's suburban Moscow settlement of Barvikha, where eminent composers, musicians and "necessary people" went. Aleksei Tolstoy died long before the end of the war, in February 1945, at age 62, and his likeness is to be found in a bronze sculpture near his "wing," a reminder of who was the more important master of that fashionable residence.

ALEKSEI SPERANSKY avoided repressions of any kind while continuing to forge his brilliant scientific career. Although his grandiose projects "for prolonging life" and the creation of a kind of universal remedy for conquering all diseases naturally turned out to be nonsense, he became an academician in 1939. Gorky's favorite child, the Institute of Experimental Medicine, was quietly closed in 1944, and the Academy of Medical Sciences, of which Speransky was a member, was created instead. He lived to 73 and died in 1961.

IVAN MARKOVICH KOSHENKOV remained, after the death of his master, the house superintendent at Malaya Nikitskaya. After Kriuchkov was shot, he attempted suicide by slitting his wrists. Timosha saved him by stopping the flow of blood and calling an ambulance in time. After release from the hospital, Koshenkov returned to his home in the country where he most likely buried his diary, although he later stated that he had done this in the suburban Moscow garden in the fall of 1941 when German troops were approaching Moscow. In a previous chapter it was mentioned what kind of "reworking" it was subjected to. The contents of the diary, which are now known (it was declassified and published in 2001), do not give any indication of how it could have been of interest to the Nazis and why it had to be buried not only from them but from the Lubyanka comrades as well. Maybe, and this is most likely the case, the contents of the original, uncorrected, diary were different from what was eventually published, and that would explain the undesirability of it falling into the "paws of the enemy." Koshenkov died in 1960.

In 1957, on the wave of events following the Twentieth Party Congress, a timid attempt was made to at least partially deliver the country from the overload of "Gorky" on maps, street names, factories, theaters and parks. The residents of the city of Gorki were especially active, asking the Kremlin to return their former name of Nizhny Novgorod. The "engineers of human souls," as Stalin called Soviet writers, were against it: they "strongly requested" (in their letter to Khrushchev) to preserve the "universally known, wingèd, and bright name of Gorky."

Obscure writers like the anti-Semite Kochetov and the Lubyanka employee Kozhevnikov were united with the noble and incorruptible Kornei Chukovsky and Aleksandr Tvardovsky in this sacred outburst of emotion. Almost forty years had to pass before Nizhny Novgorod got its name back, and the name of Gorky almost disappeared completely from the toponymy. Now in Moscow only part of the former troupe that broke off from the Art Theater and the "central park of culture and rest," where Communist Party veterans love to gather, still carry his name. Incidentally, it cannot be ruled out that while the restoration of cultural symbols from the Soviet era is being revived (though not, of course, on the same scale) his name will be as well—not the name of a great writer but the "flagship of Socialist Realist literature." *Literaturnaya gazeta*, the creation of which he had nothing to do, restored his image in its logotype in 2004. The monument to Gorky outside the Belorussian train station has remained in place, with its entirely fitting inscription: "From the Government of the Soviet Union."

And there are still numerous versions, legends, conjectures, rumors, true and false testimony, accurate and dubious memoirs—an ever-growing flood of the most variegated information—which continue to stimulate and inevitably attract interest to one of the most tragic figures in Russian literature.

Gifted with a rare talent, he voluntarily placed himself not at the service of literature, but at the service of politics, entangling himself in those nets which the Kremlin and Lubyanka intriguers had set for him.

In contrast to millions of other victims of the Great Terror, he voluntarily, and even willingly, placed his own head on the executioner's block and submissively waited for the blade to fall. In this rests his tragedy and in this too is the justification to future generations who will probably not forget the prophetic, cannibalistic formula sprung from his own pen: "If the enemy does not surrender, he must be destroyed."

ARCHIVAL SOURCES

PRESIDENT'S ARCHIVE (AP RF)
Fond 45, inventory 1, files 718 and 719
STATE ARCHIVE OF THE RUSSIAN FEDERATION (GARF)
Fond 3316, inventory 2, file 1613
Fond 5446, inventory 27, file 14
RUSSIAN STATE ARCHIVE OF SOCIAL AND POLITICAL HISTORY (RGASPI)
Fond 17, inventory 137, file 45
Fond 57, inventory 1, file 64
Fond 75, inventory 1, files 144 and 145
Fond 82, inventory 2, file 976
Fond 558, inventory 11, file 214
CENTRAL ARCHIVE OF THE FEDERAL SECURITY SERVICE (TsA FSB RF)
Fond 3, inventory 1, file 56
Fond 3, inventory 3, file 65
AUTHOR'S PERSONAL ARCHIVE

BIBLIOGRAPHY

Archive of M. Gorky
Vol. 13 – Gorky and Son
Vol. 15 – Gorky and Romain Rolland
Vol. 16 – Gorky and M. I. Budberg
Andreeva, M. F. *Perepiska. Vospominaniia. Stat'i. Dokumenty.* (Correspondence, Reminiscences, Articles, Documents). Moscow, 1969.
Aragon, Louis. *La mise à mort.* Ed. Gallimard, Paris, 1965.
——. *Bezumnye strelki vremeni. Ispoved' frantsuskogo pisatelya.* (The Insane Hands of Time. Confessions of a French Writer). Voprosy literatury, 1998, No. 5.
Aleksander, Tatyana. *An Estonian Childhood.* London: Cape, 1987.
Annekov, Yuri. *Dvevnik moikh vstrech* (Diary of My Meetings), Vols. 1 & 2, Moscow, 1991.
Babichenko, D. L. *Pisateli i tsenzory* (Writers and Censors), Moscow, 1993.
Baranov, Vadim. *Tri pis'ma k "vozhdiu narodov."* (Three Letters to the "Leader of the Peoples"). *Pravda,* August 12, 1990.
——. *Bezzakonnaya kometa* (Illegal Comet). Moscow, 2001.
Barakhov, V. S. Gor'kii. *Poslednie dni zhizni* (Gorky. The Final Days of His Life). *Literaturnaia gazeta,* June 12, 1989.
——. *M. Gor'kii. Poslednie stranitsy zhizni* (M. Gorky. The Final Pages of His Life). *Voprosy literatury.* 1990, no. 6.
Basinskii, Pavel. *Pochemu avtor "Nesvoevremennykh myslei" reshil vernut'sya v Rossiiu* (Why the Author of "Untimely Thoughts" Decided to Return to Russia). *Literaturnaia gazeta,* 2004, No. 15.
Berberova, Nina. *Zheleznaya zhenshchina* (published in English as *Moura: The Dangerous Life of the Baroness Budberg*), New York, 1981.
——. *Kursiv moi. Avtobiografiia* (published in English as *The Italics Are Mine*). Moscow, 1996.
——. *Liudi i lozhi* (People and Lies). Moscow, 1997.
Blok, A. *Issledovaniia i materialy* (Investigations and Materials). Leningrad, 1987.
Blium, A. B. *Sovetskaia tsenzura v epokhu total'nogo terrora. 1929–1953* (Soviet Censorship in the Era of Total Terror. 1929–1953). Saint Petersburg, 2000.
Bobrinev, V. *"Doktor Smert'," ili Varsonof'evskie prizraki* ("Doctor Death," or The Spectres of Varsonofiev), Moscow, 1997.

Chernigovskii, Dmitrii. *Sovetskaia khronika Ivana Bunina. V knige: Mikhail Roshchin, Ivan Bunin* (The Soviet Chronicle of Ivan Bunin. In the book Mikhail Roshchin, Ivan Bunin). Moscow, 2000.

Chukovskii, Kornei. *Dnevnik (1901–1929)* (Diary, 1901–1929). Moscow, 1991. *Dnevnik (1930–1969)*. Moscow, 1994.

Conquest, Robert. *The Great Terror.* Firenze, 1974.

Frezinskii, B. *Sud'by Serapionov* (The Fates of the Serapion Brothers). Saint Petersburg, 2003.

Gerling-Grudzinskii, G. *Sem' smertei Maksima Gor'kogo* (The Seven Deaths of Maxim Gorky). *Kontinent*, München, 1976, No. 8.

Gromov, Yevgenii. *Stalin. Vlast' i iskusstvo* (Stalin. Power and Art). Moscow, 1998.

Gronskii, Ivan. *Iz proshlogo* (From the Past). Moscow, 1991.

———. *Beseda o Gor'kom* (A Conversation about Gorky). *Minuvshee*, no. 10, Moscow, 1992.

Istoricheskii arkhiv, 1995, nos. 2 and 3 (*Zhurnal dezhurnykh sekretarei I. V. Stalina*) (The Journal of I. V. Stalin's Secretaries on Duty).

Ivanov, Vyacheslav V. *Zagadka poslednikh dnei Gor'kogo* (The Mystery of Gorky's Final Days). *Zvezda*, 1993, no. 1.

———. *Pochemu Stalin ubil Gor'kogo* (Why Stalin Killed Gorky). Voprosy literatury, 1993, no. 1.

Khlevniuk, O. et al. *Stalinskoe politbiuro v 30-gody* (Stalin's Politburo in the 1930s). Moscow, 1995.

Khodasevich, Vladislav. *Belyi koridor* (The White Corridor). New York, 1982.

———. *Nekropol'* (Necropolis). Moscow, 1996.

Kh'etso, Geir. *Maksim Gor'kii. Sud'ba pisatelia* (Maxim Gorky. The Writer's Fate). Moscow, 1997.

Kovalev, Valentin. *Dva stalinskikh narkoma* (Two of Stalin's People's Commissars). Moscow, 1995.

Kolosov, Leonid. *Sobkor KGB. Zapiski razvedchika i zhurnalista* (KGB Special Correspondent. Notes of an Intelligence Agent and Journalist). Moscow, 2001.

Korolenko, Vladimir. *Dnevnik. 1917–1921* (Diary 1917–1921). *Pis'ma*. Moscow, 2001.

Kostikov, V. M. *Gor'kii i emigratsiia* (M. Gorky and Emigration). *Novaia i noveishaia istoriia*, 1990, no. 1.

Kuskova, E. K. *Tragediia Maksima Gor'kogo* (The Tragedy of Maxim Gorky). *Novyi zhurnal*, 1954, no. 8.

Latyshev, A. G., *Rassekrechennyi Lenin* (Declassified Lenin). Moscow, 1996.

Literaturnoe nasledstvo. Vol. 70, Moscow, 1963. *M. Gor'kii i sovetskie pisateli* (M. Gorky and Soviet Writers).

Lockhart, Bruce R. H. *Istoriia iznutri. Memuary britanskogo agenta* (History from Within. Memoirs of a British Agent). Moscow, 1991.

Loginov, V. *Teni Stalina* (The Shadows of Stalin). Moscow, 2000.

M. Gor'kii v vospominaniiakh sovremennikov. V 2-kh tomakh (M. Gorky in the Recollections of His Contemporaries. In 2 volumes). Moscow, 1981.

M. Gor'kii i XX vek. Gor'kovskie chteniia (M. Gorky and the 20th Century. Readings on Gorky). Nizhny Novgorod, 1998.

M. Gor'kii i R. Rollan. Perepiska 1916–1936 (M. Gorky and R. Rolland. Correspondence 1916–1936). Moscow, 1996.

M. Gor'kii, Pro et contra (M. Gorky, Pro and Contra). Saint Petersburg, 1997.

M. Gor'kii i ego epokha. Vypusk 4-i (M. Gorky and His Epoch. Fourth edition). Moscow, 1995.

M. Gor'kii, Neizdannaia perepiska (M. Gorky, Unpublished Correspondence). Moscow, 2000.

Mann, Klaus. *Na povorote* (At the Crossroads). Moscow, 1991.

Maslov, A. *Smert' ne postavila tochku* (Death Did Not End It). Moscow, 1999.

Nakoriakov, N. N. *Vospominaniia o Gor'kom* (Reminiscences of Gorky). *Istochnik*, 2003, No. 5.

Neizvestnii Gor'kii. Sbornik (The Unknown Gorky. A Collection). Moscow, 1994.

Neizvestnie pis'ma Gor'kogo A. Fransu i A. Rykovu (Gorky's Unknown Letters to A. France and A. Rykov). Shpion TsRU, 1993, No. 1.

Nike, M. *K voprosu o smerti Gor'kogo* (Concerning the Death of Gorky). *Minuvshee*, vol. 5. Moscow-Saint Petersburg, 1991.

Orlov, Aleksandr. *Tainaia istoriia stalinskikh prestuplenii* (The Secret History of Stalin's Crimes), New York, 1983.

Pavlov, Viacheslav and Frezinskii, Boris. *Il'ia Erenburg v 1932–1935* (Ilya Ehrenburg from 1932–1935). Saint Petersburg, 2001.

Parkhomovskii, M. *Syn Rossii, general Frantsii* (A Son of Russia, A General of France). Moscow, 1989.

Pil'niak, E. and Antonov, V. *Byl li zagovor protiv Stalina?* (Was There a Conspiracy Against Stalin?). *Oktiabr'*, 1994, No. 3.

Povartsov, S. *Prichina smerti—rasstrel* (Cause of Death—Execution). Moscow, 1996.

Primochkina, N. *Pisatel' i vlast'* (Writer and Power). Moscow, 1998.

——. *Gor'kii i pisateli russkogo zarubezh'ia* (Gorky and Russian Émigré Writers). Moscow, 2003.

Prishvin, Mikhail. *O Maksime Gor'kom* (About Maxim Gorky). *Druzhba narodov*, 1993, no. 6.

Radzinskii, Edvard. *Stalin* (Stalin). Moscow, 1997.

Rolland, Romain. *Moskovskii dnevnik* (Moscow Diary). *Voprosy literatury.* 1989, nos. 3–5.

S dvukh beregov. Russkaia literature XX veka v Rossii i za rubezhom. Sbornik. (From Two Shores. Russian Literature of the 20th Century in Russia and Abroad. Collection). Moscow, 2002.

Slonimskii, M. *Dnevnikovye zapisi* (Diary Entries). *Neva*, 1987, no. 12.

Smirnova, L. *Gor'kii i Lenin. Razrushenie legendy* (Gorky and Lenin. Destruction of the Legend). *Voprosy literatury.* 1993, no. 5.

Sokolov, B. *Narkomy strakha* (People's Commissars of Fear). Moscow, 2001.

Solomon, Grigorii. *Vblizi vozhdia. Svet i teni* (Near the Leader. Light and Shadows). Moscow, 1991.

Spiridonova, L. *M. Gor'kii: dialog s istoriei* (M. Gorky: A Dialogue with History). Moscow, 1994.

——. *M. Gor'kii: novyi vzgliad* (M. Gorky: A New Look). Moscow, 2004.

——. *Plennik "nelepogo doma"* (Prisoner of an "Absurd House"). *Rodina*, 2000, No. 8.

Tikhonova, Nina. *Devushka v sinem* (The Girl in Blue). Moscow, 1992.

Topolianskii, V. *Vozhdi v zakone. Ocherki fiziologii vlasti* (The Leaders in the Law. Sketches of the Physiology of Power). Moscow, 1996.

——. *M. Gor'kii umer sam ili ego umertvili?* (M. Gorky died on his own or was he killed?) *Literaturnaia gazeta.* 1996, no. 24.

——. *Restavratsiia legendy ob otravlenii M. Gor'kogo* (Restoration of the Legend about the Poisoning of M. Gorky). *Literaturnaia gazeta.* 1997, no. 4.

Vokrug smerti Gor'kogo. Dokumenty, fakty, versii (Concerning the Death of Gorky. Documents, Facts, Versions). Moscow, 2001.

Voitinskii, Vladimir. *Gody pobed i porazhenii. V dvukh tomakh* (Years of Victories and Defeats. In two volumes). Berlin, 1924.

Volkogonov, Dmitrii. *Trotskii. V dvukh tomakh* (Trotsky. In two volumes). Moscow, 1992.

——. *Lenin. V dvukh tomakh* (Lenin. In two volumes). Moscow, 1994.

——. *Triumf i tragediia. I. V. Stalin. V chetyrekh tomakh.* (Triumph and Tragedy. I. V. Stalin. In four volumes). Moscow, 1989.

Weill, I. *Maksim Gor'kii. Vzgliad iz Ameriki* (Maxim Gorky. A View from America). Moscow, 1993.

Shentalinskii, Vitalii. *Raby svobody* (Slaves of Freedom). Moscow, 1995.

Zelinskii, Kornelii. *Vospominaniia* (Reminiscences). *Minuvshee*, no. 10, Moscow, 1992.

——. *Odna vstrecha u M. Gor'kogo* (One Meeting at M. Gorky's). *Voprosy literatury,* 1991, no. 5.

Index

Abramovich, Lev, 91
Adamovich, Georgi, 123
Afinogenov, Aleksandr, 385, 391
Agranov, Yakov, 86, 122
Akhmatova, Anna, 109, 123, 145, 252, 272, 320, 395
Alberti, Rafael, 320
Aldanov (writer), 170
Aleksandr II, Tsar, 101, 286
Alekseev, Georgi, 111
Alekseevna, Nadezhda (Timosha), 138, 249
Alliluyeva, Nadezhda (Stalin's wife), 223, 248, 277, 365
Amfiteatrov, Aleksandr, 110
Anderson, Sherwood, 200
Andreev, Andrei, 5, 331
Andreev, Leonid, 20–21
Andreeva, Maria, 21, 24, 29–32, 34–48, 53–56, 65–68, 70–74, 79–81, 84, 91, 97–101, 105–6, 108–9, 114, 118, 133, 138, 141, 143–44, 159–60, 162–63, 169, 188–91, 204, 250–52, 359, 365, 373, 393, 404
Andric, Ivo, 318
Andronnikova, Salomeya, 395
Andropov, Yuri, 113
Annenkov, Yuri, 77, 123, 154, 241
Antovsky, Osif, 293
Aragon, Louis, 320–21, 324, 340–41, 375–80
Arosev, Aleksandr, 340, 344, 348, 407–8
Asch, Sholom, 142, 318
Avdeenko, Aleksandr, 291, 360–61
Averbakh, Ida Leonidovna, 249
Averbakh, Leopold, 249, 260–61, 269, 273, 299–300, 404
Azef, Evno, 34

Babel, Isaak, 181, 209–10, 263, 271–73, 281, 286–89, 303, 320–21, 341, 362, 379–80, 396, 406
Bagryana, Elisaveta, 318
Bakayev, 105, 117
Balmont, Konstantin, 198–99
Baranov, Vadim, 384
Barbusse, Henri, 148, 207, 268, 271, 303, 336, 338, 349–52
Barshev, Nikolai, 343
Barsheva, Liudmila, 343

Basov, Viktor, 401
Bécaud, Gilbert, 328
Bely, Andrei, 140, 159
Benkendorf, Countess. See Budberg, Baroness
Benkendorf, Ivan Aleksandrovich, 70, 97
Benkendorf, Maria. See Budberg, Baroness
Benoit, Aleksandr, 14, 57
Benoit, Pierre, 241, 289
Berberova, Nina, 66–67, 70, 77, 131, 135–36, 150, 161, 163, 165–66, 172, 177, 242, 259, 287–88, 292, 354, 365, 369, 393, 401–2
Berdyaev, Nikolai, 154, 178, 408
Beria, Lavrenty, 6, 399
Blagin, Nikolai, 336–37
Bleklov, Kostya, 249, 263
Bloch, Jean-Richard, 148, 228, 320–21
Blok, Aleksandr, 13, 99, 110–11, 118–23, 126, 129, 141, 168, 198, 267
Blokhin, Nikolai, 383
Blukher, Vasily, 314
Bobryshev, Vasily, 390
Bogdanov, Aleksandr, 156
Bogomolov, 234
Bonch-Bruevich, Vladimir, 62, 280
Bosch, Hieronymous, 303
Bostanzhoglo, Vasily, 111
Brandes, George, 152, 317
Braude, I., 311
Brecht, Bertold, 340
Brezhnev, Leonid, 113, 393
Brik, Lili, 355, 377, 379–80
Brod, Max, 340
Broglio, Princess de, 145
Brusilov, Aleksei, 114
Bubnov, A., 263
Budberg, Baroness (Maria Ignatyevna [Mura] Zakrevskaya) (formerly Countess Benkendorf), 70–73, 97–101, 103–9, 114, 127, 132–33, 135–37, 138, 143–44, 148, 150, 157, 159, 161, 163, 166–67, 173–74, 181, 182, 184–88, 191, 200–201, 204, 210–11, 213, 218, 224, 228, 237, 240, 250, 255–57, 261, 266, 270, 276–77, 288–89, 292, 293, 295, 316–19, 343, 352–55, 360, 362, 364–65, 372–73, 378, 384–88, 393–98, 400–402
Budberg, Nikolai, 106–7, 395

Budyenny, Semyon, 210, 263
Bukharin, Nikolai, 8, 147–48, 151–53, 177,
    201–5, 213–14, 227, 233, 238–39, 242–43,
    271–74, 287, 296, 299, 314, 319, 322, 324,
    344–45, 348, 355–58, 362–63, 391, 405,
    407–8
Bulgakov, Sergei, 154, 198, 273, 320
Bunakov-Fundaminsk, Ilya, 34
Bunin, Ivan, 13–15, 39, 133, 198–99, 216, 235,
    294, 343
Bunina, Vera, 39
Burago, Kazakh Lidiya, 145
Burdenko, Nikolai, 367
Burenin, Nikolai, 31, 366
Burmin, Dmitri, 282
Butov, P., 125

Cahoon, A., 73
Casanova, 201
Chaadayev, Pyotr, 242
Chaliapin, Fyodor, 14, 86, 94, 100, 129, 138,
    149, 180, 216–17, 237, 243–46, 280–81,
    303, 374
Chamberlain, Neville, 199
Chapygin, Aleksei, 224
Charles-Roux, Edmonde, 145, 400
Chayanov, 246
Chazov, Yevgeni, 371, 383
Chekhov, Anton, 8, 14, 28–29, 70, 96, 101,
    242, 267, 269, 379
Chertkova, Olimpiada Dmitrievna (*aka* Lipa),
    191
Chesterton, G. K., 216
Chubar, V., 5
Chuchalin, A. G., 371
Chukhontsev, Oleg, 368
Chukovskaya, Lidiya, 199
Chukovsky, Kornei, 51, 61–62, 68–72, 77, 88–
    92, 101, 110, 121, 129, 134, 137, 169, 176,
    190, 194, 199–200, 205, 207–8, 292, 409
Chumandrin, Mikhail, 391
Claudel, Paul, 339
Cohen, Stephen, 408
Comon, Combette de, 145
Cremier, Benjamin, 318
Curie, Marie, 148, 152

Dan, Fyodor, 151, 356
Dantes, George-Charles, 221
Danton, 324
Danzas, Julia, 221, 265
Davydovsky, I. V., 381
De Gaulle, Charles, 400
Delvari, 63

Diderikhs, Andrei (Didi), 67–68, 79, 132, 135,
    181
Diderot, Denis, 362
Dimitrov, Georgi, 350–51
Dobrowen, Issay, 86
Dobuzhinsky, Mstislav, 14
Dostoyevsky, Fyodor, 197, 242, 332
Dovgalevsky, Valeriyan, 244–45
Dreiden, Simon, 134
Dreiser, Theodore, 200
Dubbelt, L., 399
Duhamel, Bernard, 339
Duhamel, Georges, 148, 201, 228, 339
Duhamel, Maya, 408
Duranty, Walter, 311
Durnovo, Nikolai, 297
Durtain, Luc, 228, 339, 341
Dybenko, Pavel, 86
Dzerzhinsky, Felix, 48, 63–64, 71, 73, 78, 83,
    86, 88, 91, 102–3, 105, 109, 113, 153–54,
    159, 175–81, 187, 382, 392
Dzhugashvili, Josef Vissarionovich. *See* Stalin,
    Joseph

Efroimson, Vladimir Pavlovich, 358
Ehrenburg, Ilya, 140, 160, 235, 320–21, 324,
    376, 380, 396, 398, 407
Eichenvald (literary critic), 170
Einstein, Albert, 152, 233
Eitingon, Naum, 383
Eluard, Paul, 340

Fadeev, Aleksandr, 272, 286, 297–99, 324, 404
Farrère, Claude, 86
Fedin, Konstantin, 149
Feit, Andrei, 34
Feldbein, Lev, 312
Fersman, Aleksandr, 52, 114
Feuchtwänger, Lion, 201, 340
Figner, Vera, 101
Firin, Semyon, 269
Fomin, V., 156
France, Anatole, 13, 115, 148, 150–51, 216,
    317, 324
Frank, Leonhard, 201
Frank, Semyon, 154
Fridlyand, Frida, 404
Frunze, Mikhail, 179
Fyodorov, Lev, 83, 263, 266
Fyodorovna, Maria, 31, 36, 39, 41, 44–45, 68–
    69, 71, 89, 97, 98, 103, 133, 144, 188–89,
    239

Gabe, Dona, 318

Gabrilovich, Yevgeni, 273
Galpern, 395
Galsworthy, John, 115, 160, 201, 216, 317
Ganetsky, Yakov, 179–82, 202
Garibaldi, 167
Geintse, Maria ("Molecule"), 67, 135
Gerland, Brigitta, 405
German, Yuri, 273
Gerzoni, Doctor, 90
Gezzi, Francesco, 228–30
Gibarti, Louis (*aka* Lazlo Dobos), 408
Gide, André, 5–6, 340–41, 375–77, 379–80, 383
Ginzburg, Saul Moiseevich, 60
Gippius, Zinaida, 52, 60, 69, 76, 90, 133
Glavlit. *See* Volin, Boris
Glazunov, Aleksandr, 100, 129
Glebova-Kameneva, Tatyana, 213, 333
Glinka, Gleb Aleksandrovich, 389, 390
Goethe, Johann Wolfgang von, 255, 391, 397
Gogol, Nikolai, 242, 379
Gorbachev, Mikhail, 125, 310, 402
Gorbov, Aleksandr, 125
Göring, Hermann, 333, 363
Graf, Oskar Maria, 320
Grave, Aleksandr, 399
Grinberg, Zakhar, 93
Gromov, Mikhail, 337
Gromova, Vera Alekseevna, 190
Gronsky, Ivan, 247–48, 297, 315, 319, 350, 408
Gross, Babette, 408
Grossman, Vasily, 273
Grushko, Natalia, 96–99, 135, 251
Grzhebin, Zinovy, 55–58, 60, 88–89, 130, 133, 150, 163
Grzhebins, 135
Gumilev, Nikolai, 69–70, 74, 77, 122–26, 129, 141, 168

Hamsun, Knut, 201, 317
Hardy, Thomas, 317
Hauptmann, Gerhardt, 115, 152, 201, 317
Herbard, Pierre, 376
Herriot, Eduard, 148
Hitler, Adolf, 161, 318, 328, 333, 391
Hoover, Herbert, 114
Huxley, Aldous, 340

Ibañez, Vicente Blasco, 115
Ilyinichna, Maria, 123
Ilyinsky, Grigori, 297
Inber, Vera, 291, 320
Ioffe, Abram, 266
Ionov, Ilya, 54, 59–61, 172, 176

Ipatyev, Vladimir, 114
Ivanov, Georgi, 110
Ivanov, Vsevolod, 134, 273, 281, 290–92, 338, 364, 398
Ivanov, Vyacheslav, 87, 134, 178, 188, 308, 398, 408
Ivanovich, Aleksei, 152, 205, 239, 299, 300
Ivanovich, Nikolai, 205, 239
Izgoev, Aleksandr, 111, 154

Joyce, James, 362

Kadyan, A., 123, 124
Kaganovich, Lazar, 5, 8, 263, 267, 273, 279, 294, 299–300, 325, 327–28, 344, 350, 358
Kalinin, Mikhail, 6, 114, 136, 337, 398
Kamenev, Lev, 8, 55, 91, 99, 114, 118, 120, 135–36, 153, 160, 213–14, 265, 271, 274, 282, 296, 314–16, 319, 327, 329–34, 346, 350, 356, 363, 402, 406
Kameneva, Olga Davydovna (Bronstein), 55, 333, 405
Kaminskaya, Olga Yulievna, 26–28, 261–62
Kaminsky, Anatoly, 230
Kandelaki, David, 333–34, 363
Kanner, Grigori, 267
Kant, Immanuel, 161
Kaplan, Fanny (Dora), 22–23, 150
Karpinsky, Aleksei, 114, 356–57
Karsavin, Lev, 154
Karsavina, Tamara, 217
Kashchenko, V., 66
Kassil, Lev, 325
Kataev, Valentin, 273
Kaverin, Veniamin, 324–25, 345
Kazakov, Ignaty, 382
Kerensky, Aleksandr, 15, 115, 118, 145
Kerzhentsev, Platon, 188
Khalatov, Artemi, 197, 207, 210, 251, 255, 258
Khariton, B., 125
Khayutina, Yevgenia, 406
Khlebnikov, 81, 209
Khodasevich, Valentina (Merchant Lady), 67–68, 79, 86, 87, 89, 95–96, 99, 131, 135, 181, 301, 348–49, 365–66, 401
Khodasevich, Vladislav, 36, 48, 55, 63, 74, 117, 128, 156–58, 160, 161, 166, 174–76, 196, 237, 401
Khodorovsky, Iosif, 305
Khrushchev, Nikita, 4–5, 7, 87, 205, 403, 409
Kibalchik, Volodya, 286
Kirov, Sergei, 263, 307–8, 312–13, 328–30, 333, 357
Kirsanov, Semyon, 322

Kirshon, Vladimir, 391
Kishkin, Nikolai, 114–15
Kizevetter, Aleksandr, 154
Klychkov, Sergei, 181
Knipper, Olga, 29
Kochetov, V., 409
Koestler, Arthur, 336
Kokoshkin, F., 90
Kolchak, Aleksandr, 145, 264, 392
Kollontai, Aleksandra, 86, 189, 294, 407
Kolosov, Leonid, 384–85
Koltsov, Mikhail, 5, 335, 338, 341, 362, 365, 377–80, 405–7
Kondratyev, N., 156, 246
Konopleva, Lidiya, 23, 150
Konstantinovich, Dmitri, 90
Konstantinovich, Gavriil, 90
Korin, Pavel, 190, 343, 366
Korolenko, Vladimir, 14–15, 74, 92, 113, 121, 129–31, 141
Korsak, Boleslav, 26
Koshenkov, Ivan, 248, 303, 305, 368, 373, 409
Kovalenko, Aleksandr Mikhailovich, 37
Kozhevnikov, V., 409
Krandievskaya, Natalia, 342–43
Krasin, Aleksandr, 77
Krasin, Leonid, 15, 30, 31
Krestinsky, N., 162
Kriuchkov, Aina, 404
Kriuchkov, Pyotr (PePeKriu), 44, 56, 67, 72, 97–100, 108, 144, 160, 163, 167, 174, 182, 189–90, 192, 206–8, 230, 237, 239–40, 248, 253–55, 256, 260–65, 267, 272, 289, 293–95, 300–310, 325, 330, 340–42, 345–46, 348, 353–54, 364, 370–71, 373, 378, 385, 402–4, 409
Krupskaya, Nadezhda, 54, 125, 154, 161, 198–99, 204, 234
Krzhizhanovsky, Gleb, 125
Kudashev, Sergei, 408
Kudasheva, Maria, 229, 338–40, 346–48
Kuibyshev, Valeriyan, 218, 332
Kukolevsky, I., 156
Kuprin, 235, 294
Kurella, Alfred, 315, 350
Kursky, Dmitri, 151, 153, 255
Kuskova, Yekaterina, 114, 154, 178, 215
Kustodiev, B., 57
Kusurgasheva, Alma, 301

Ladyzhnikov, I., 126, 150
Lagerlöf, Selma, 201, 340
Lakshin, Vladimir, 87, 349
Langevin, Paul, 228

Lapshin, Ivan, 154
Lenin, Vladimir Ilyich (V. I. Ulyanov), 3, 5–9, 11–13, 15–23, 25, 30–31, 37–39, 46–57, 60–64, 73, 78, 81, 84–93, 99–100, 102–3, 108–9, 111–31, 133–37, 139, 141–47, 149–56, 159, 161–63, 166–73, 176–80, 193–94, 199, 202–5, 209, 211, 214–16, 219, 225–26, 234, 251–52, 256, 262, 265–67, 272, 279, 282, 298–301, 308, 315, 321, 331, 335, 337, 356, 359, 369, 382, 388, 393
Leonov, Leonid, 274
Leskov, Nikolai, 361
Levin, Dan, 305, 306
Levin, Lev, 6, 252, 282, 302–5, 307, 309, 311, 340, 348–50, 365, 367, 372–73, 382, 405
Levine, Isaac Don, 201
Levitan, I., 57
Lewis, Sinclair, 216
Lilina, Zlata (Bernstein), 54
Lipa (Chertkova, Olimpiada Dmitrievna), 191–92, 203, 208, 218–19, 250, 261, 277, 285, 293, 305, 346, 348, 353, 365, 370–73, 378, 385–86, 397
Litvinov, Maxim, 81, 317, 407
Liverovsky, A., 17
Lockhart, R. Bruce, 71, 106, 185–87, 211, 240, 261
London, Jack, 13
Long, Ray, 175, 255–57, 337
Losev, Aleksei, 259
Lossky, Nikolai, 154
Lozinsky, M., 125
Lozovsky, Solomon, 386
Lunacharsky, Anatoly, 19, 54–55, 80, 93, 119–20, 129, 150, 153, 195, 203–4
Lunts, Lev, 149
Luppol, Ivan, 397–98
Lutokhin, Dalmat, 180, 235
Luxemburg, Rosa, 13

Machiavelli, Niccolò, 328
Maclean, Sir Fitzroy, 311
Maeterlinck, Maurice, 317
Magda, 348
Maierova, Maria, 318
Makhlin, 89
Maksimovic, Desanka, 318
Malevich, 209
Malinovskaya, Yelena, 29–30
Malraux, André, 320, 322, 324, 340, 362, 380, 407
Malyantovich, Pavel, 17, 18, 102, 253
Mandelstam, Osip, 74, 145, 273, 320
Mann, Heinrich, 201, 233, 340

Mann, Thomas, 201, 216, 340
Manukhin, Ivan, 41, 62, 76, 90–91, 94
Marguerite, Victor, 148
Marinetti, Filippo Tommaso, 318
Markov, Ivan, 400–401
Marshak, Samuil, 273, 289
Martinson, Moa, 320
Martov, Yuli, 151
Marx, Karl, 78, 201, 315, 321, 356
Masaryk, Tomas, 115, 166
Mashirov, A., 125
Maslov, P., 17
Maupassant, Guy de, 243
Mayakovsky, Vladimir Vladimirovich, 13, 140, 194–96, 198, 206, 209, 219, 243, 322, 355, 379, 392
Mayranovsky, Grigori, 383
Mechnikov, I., 83
Medvedovskaya, Yelizaveta Zakharovna, 404
Mekhlis, Lev, 332
Melgunov, Sergei, 202
Merchant Lady. *See* Khodasevich, Valentina
Merezhkovsky, Dmitri, 50–52, 56–57, 133, 202, 216, 235, 294, 317
Merzhanov, Miron, 398
Meyerhold, V., 209, 287, 362
Michurin, Ivan, 306
Mikhailovich, Nikolai, 90–91, 123
Mikhailovna, Valentina, 68
Mikoyan, Anastas, 5, 250
Milman, Valentina, 376
Mints, Isaak, 282
Mizinova, Lika, 96
Moiseevich, Lazar, 328
Molchanov, 384
Molecule. *See* Geintse, Maria
Molotov, Vyacheslav, 5–6, 8, 119–20, 162, 267, 271, 283, 325, 337, 340, 344, 350, 357, 372, 386–87, 399, 407
Mordvinkina, Taisiya, 404
Morgan, J. P., 145
Morozov, Pavel (*aka* Pavlik), 284, 334
Morozov, Savva, 12–13, 30–31, 39, 192, 207, 251
Moussinac, Leon, 341
Mukhina, Vera, 290
Münzenberg, Willi, 408
Munzer, Thomas, 167
Mura. *See* Budberg, Baroness
Muravyov, Nikolai, 102
Muromtsev, Sergei, 383
Mussolini, Benito, 164, 172, 188, 196

Nansen, Frithof, 114

Nazvanov, M., 125
Nemirovich-Danchenko, Vladimir Ivanovich, 32, 39, 133, 267, 287–88
Nesterov, Mikhail, 366
Nesterovskaya, Anastasia, 90
Nezlobin, K., 43
Nezval, Vitezslav, 320
Nicholas, Tsar, 90
Nietzsche, Friedrich, 161
Nightingale. *See* Rakitsky, Ivan Nikolaevich
Nikiforov, Georgi, 274
Nikitin, A., 17
Nikolaev, Mikhail, 44, 101, 144, 251, 393
Nikulin, Lev, 241, 273, 289–92, 325, 394–96
Ninochka, 66, 107, 130, 136, 158
Nizhinskaya, Bronislava, 217, 250
Nosik, Boris, 339

Odoevtseva, Irina, 123
Oksman, Yulian, 96, 98
Oldenburg, Sergei, 18, 52, 92, 114, 149, 196
Olesha, Yuri, 321
Ordzhonikidze, G., 5, 204, 263, 361
Orlov, Aleksandr, 312, 389–90
Osadchy, Pyotr, 215, 231–32
Osinsky, 156
Osorgin, Mikhail, 154, 180
Osten, Maria (Grossgener), 405–6
Ostrovsky, A., 251

Panferov, Fyodoryodor, 290, 298–99, 324, 332, 340, 360
Paramonov, Boris, 83
Parandowsky, Jan, 318
Parvus, Aleksandr, 12
Pasternak, Boris, 140, 159, 230, 253–54, 272, 320, 321, 322, 324, 325–27, 341, 345, 355, 362, 392
Pasternak, Leonid, 230
Pauker, Karl, 4
Pavlenko, Pyotr, 364
Pavlov, Ivan, 14, 83, 263, 356–57, 373
Pavlovna, Yekaterina Peshkova, 5, 28–45, 65–67, 69, 73, 99–103, 105–6, 108–9, 111, 113–14, 117, 123, 130–32, 137, 139, 144–45, 150, 159, 163–64, 166, 170–71, 173–80, 186, 188–92, 204, 209, 215, 222, 251, 253, 259, 300–303, 305–6, 306, 309, 339, 342–43, 346–48, 353–55, 359, 364, 378, 386, 392, 395, 398–99, 401
PePeKriu. *See* Kriuchkov, Pyotr
Peretti, de (French Minister of Foreign Affairs), 146
Peretts, Vladimir, 297

Peshkov, Aleksei Maksimovich (Maxim Gorky), 3, 26, 31, 39, 62, 98, 139–40, 144, 194, 211, 216–17, 227, 253, 262, 272, 280, 285, 303, 314, 330, 342, 361, 366, 368, 389

Peshkov, Zinovy Alekseevich (*see also* Sverdlov, Zinovy Mikhailovich), 144–45, 196, 249, 288, 400

Peshkova, Nadezhda (Timosha), 220, 397

Peshkova, Yekaterina. *See* Pavlovna, Yekaterina Peshkova

Peters, Yan, 71, 73

Petrovsky, 384

Petrov-Vodkin, Kuzma, 93, 145

Petzold, Maria Valentinovna, 217

Pilnyak, Boris, 86, 140, 223–24, 252, 273, 317, 320, 379

Pinkevich, Albert, 53

Pirozhkovaya, Antonina, 406

Plato, 161

Platonov, A., 273, 320

Platten, Fritz, 18

Pletnev, Dmitri, 6, 305, 381–82, 386, 405

Pogrebinsky, Matvei (Motya), 220, 240–41, 348, 404

Pogrebov, N., 125

Postyshev, P., 271, 361

Potapenko, Ignaty, 96, 251

Preobrazhenskaya, Olga, 217, 400

Primakov, Vitaly, 377, 379

Prishvin, Mikhail, 205, 269–70

Prokopovich, Sergei, 17, 114–16, 154

Pugacheva, Alla, 301

Pyatigorsky, Yuri, 79

Radek, Karl, 152, 266, 319, 322, 324, 328, 356

Radlov, Sergei, 63

Radomyslskaya, Liya, 55

Radzinsky, Edvard, 273, 376

Rakitsky, Ivan Nikolaevich ("Nightingale"), 67–68, 79–81, 95, 108, 138, 144, 166, 218, 261, 289, 378, 402

Ramzin, Leonid, 232–33

Rasputin, Grigori, 94

Ratmanova, Yelizaveta, 362, 405

Reilly, Sidney, 71, 106

Reinbot, A., 251

Remizov, Aleksei, 93, 94

Riola, Lika, 36

Rodzhers, Henrietta, 86

Roerich, Nikolai, 14

Röhm, Ernst, 328

Rolland, Madeleine, 147

Rolland, Romain, 13, 27, 141–42, 147–48, 152, 159–60, 166–67, 186, 198–99, 201, 216, 228–30, 233–34, 235, 236, 258, 266, 268, 286–87, 293–94, 303, 317, 327, 328, 338–40, 343–50, 352, 374, 407–8

Romains, Jules, 148, 318

Romanov, Grand Duke Konstantin, 90

Rozanov, Vasily, 94

Rozenfeld, Boris, 333

Rozenfeld, Nikolai, 333

Rozenfeld, Nina, 333

Rozenfeld, Samuil, 91

Rozhdestvensky, Vsevolod, 110

Rozhkov, Menshevik Nikolai, 110–12

Rubinstein, Ida, 217

Rudzutak, Yan, 271

Rumyantsev, Nikolai, 41–42

Ruskin, John, 161

Russell, Bertrand, 99, 152, 283

Ryabushinsky, Pavel, 259

Ryabushinsky, Stepan, 248, 315, 385

Rybnikov, 156

Rykov, Aleksei, 8, 151, 152, 177, 182, 204–5, 213–14, 238–39, 242, 287, 296, 299–300, 316, 405

Ryutin, Martemyan, 278, 299

Sadoveanu, Mihail, 318

Saint-Exupéry, Antoine de, 336

Savostin, Mikhail, 81, 136

Schacht, Hjalmar, 363

Schmit, Nikolai, 12, 31

Schmit, Yelizaveta, 31

Schnitzler, Arthur, 201

Schopenhauer, Arthur, 161

Seifulina, Lidya, 273

Selishchev, Afanasy, 297

Selvinsky, Ilya, 325

Semashko, Nikolai, 37, 113, 203

Semenov, Grigori, 23, 150

Serafimovich, Aleksandr, 261, 298

Serebryakov, Z., 145

Serebryansky, Yakov, 382

Serge, Viktor, 286–87, 344–45, 365

Sergeevna, Nadezhda, 275

Shadurskaya, Zoya, 189

Shaikevich, Anatoly, 65, 107, 158

Shaikevich, Andrei, 131, 400

Shaikevich, Fyodor, 250

Shaikevich-Tikhonova, Varvara Vasilyevna, 65, 68, 99–100, 107, 250, 400

Shakespeare, William, 11, 99, 385

Shaw, George Bernard, 143, 152, 201, 233, 269, 340, 374

Shcherbakov, Aleksandr, 324, 327, 334, 336–38, 355, 396

Shekhtel, Fyodor, 248
Shestov, Lev, 154
Shingarev, A., 90
Shkapa, Ilya, 318–19, 353
Shklovsky, Viktor, 74, 291
Shmidt, Otto Yulevich, 321
Sholokhov, Mikhail, 5, 98, 252–53, 273, 374
Shostakovich, Dmitri, 345, 361–62
Shukhaev, Ivan, 14, 145
Shvernik, Nikolai, 266
Sinclair, Anthony, 115
Sinclair, Upton, 200–201, 233, 268, 340
Sinelnikov, A., 43
Sinitsyn, Sergei, 138
Skorokhodovaya, Olga, 283
Skvortsov-Stepanov, Ivan, 203
Slavatinsky, 88
Slepnev, Mavriki, 337
Slonimsky, Mikhail, 75
Slutsky, Abram, 312
Smith, Richard R., 255
Smolyaninov, 156
Solomon, Georgi, 136, 193
Solovyev, Vladimir, 161, 242
Solzhenitsyn, Alexander, 363
Somov, C., 145, 234
Sorel, Georges, 152
Sorin, V., 145
Sorokin, Pitirim, 154
Speransky, Aleksei, 263, 283, 302, 305, 367, 372–73, 408, 409
Speransky, Mikhail, 297
Spiridonova, Lidiya, 256, 367–68
Stalin, Joseph (Josef Vissarionovich Dzhugashvili), 3–9, 26, 85, 116, 120–22, 136, 170, 173, 179, 194–97, 199–210, 213–18, 222–27, 237–40, 243, 245–49, 251–60, 262–63, 265–68, 271–74, 277–83, 286–87, 290–300, 303–4, 306–25, 327–35, 337–41, 344–47, 349–52, 354–65, 369–73, 376, 380, 383–84, 386–92, 397–99, 401–9
Stalin, Svetlana, 341, 399
Stanislavsky, Konstantin, 14, 32, 39, 110–11, 204, 267, 287
Stasova, Elena, 266
Stavsky, Vladimir, 297
Steklov, Vladimir, 14
Stendhal, 201
Stepanovich, Nikolai, 70
Stepun, Fyodor, 154
Stetsky, Aleksei, 297
Stomonyakov, B., 162
Strelkova, Maria, 402
Struve, Nikita, 146

Styrikovich, Mikhail, 405
Sudeikin, 57, 145
Sudoplatov, Pavel, 383
Sukhanov, Nikolai, 15, 86, 231, 246
Surkov, Aleksei, 355
Suvarin, Boris, 241, 271–73, 347
Svanidze, Yekaterina "Alesha", 333
Svechnikov, V., 222
Sverdlov, Yakov, 144–46, 163, 249
Sverdlov, Zinovy Mikhailovich, 144
Sytin, Ivan, 43

Tagantsev, Vladimir, 122–24
Talmud, David, 383
Taratut, 31
Tatlin, Vladimir, 209
Taylor, 167
Temireva, Anna, 392
Tennyson, Alfred, Lord, 161
Terekhov, Georgi, 125
Tikhonov, Aleksandr (Serebrov), 41, 65–69, 77, 107, 110, 121, 134–35, 158, 168, 173, 175–76, 192, 207, 250, 265, 292, 402
Tikhonov, Andrusha, 67
Tikhonov, Nina Aleksandrovna, 67, 140, 217, 400
Tikhonova, Varva Vasilyevna. *See* Shaikevich-Tikhonova, Varvara Vasilyevna
Tikhonovs, 66–68, 99, 207
Tikhvinsky, Mikhail, 168
Tilge, Susanna, 351
Toller, Ernst, 318
Tolstaya, Aleksandra, 115
Tolstaya, Liudmila, 396
Tolstaya, Timosha, 396
Tolstoy, Aleksei, 5, 28, 114, 140, 156, 159, 261, 269, 280, 291, 324, 341–43, 354, 364–65, 408
Tolstoy, Ivan, 58
Tolstoy, Leo, 7, 115, 161, 201, 242
Tomilin, V. V., 371
Tomsky, Mikhail, 203, 214, 242, 299
Tonkov, Vladimir, 53
Topolyansky, Viktor, 357, 383
Tovstonogov, Georgi, 99
Trenev, Konstantin, 209
Tretyakov, S., 320
Triolet, Elsa, 163, 320, 375–79
Troekurov, 234
Trotsky, Leon, 16, 51, 55, 73, 120, 136, 152, 155, 169–70, 173, 194, 196, 213, 238, 253, 256, 287, 291, 316, 332, 356, 382–83, 385, 391
Tseitlin, Mikhail, 384

Tsvetaeva, M., 140, 145
Tukhachevsky, Marshal, 377
Tupolev, Anatoly, 335–37
Turgenev, Ivan, 242
Tvardovsky, Aleksandr, 241, 409

Ukhanov, Konstantin, 206
Ulrikh, Vasily, 310–11
Ulyanov, V. I. *See* Lenin, Vladimir Ilyich
Ulyanova, Maria (Lenin's sister), 5, 161
Ulyanovs, 124
Umansky, Konstantin, 316–17
Unshlikht, Iosif, 153

Vaksberg, Matvei, 358
Vasilyev, Pavel, 264
Vavilov, Nikolai, 358, 398
Veresayev, Vikenty, 197
Verhaeren, Emile, 13
Vernadsky, Vladimir, 17, 125, 308, 356–57, 397–98
Verne, Jules, 161
Vertinsky, Aleksandr, 97
Vidal, Annette, 351
Vildrac, Charles, 148, 228, 339
Vinaver, Mikhail, 102, 111, 178
Vinogradov, Aleksandr, 305
Vladimirsky, 156
Vodpyanov, Mikhail, 337
Volin, Boris (*aka* Glavlit), 197, 202
Volina, Margarita, 262
Volkogonov, Dmitri, 154
Volnov, Ivan, 93
Volodarsky, Moisei (Goldstein), 61
Voloshin, Maximilian, 178
Volynsky, Akim, 88, 125
Voronsky, Aleksandr, 156, 182
Voroshilov, Klim, 8, 204, 233, 254–55, 263, 271, 325, 337, 344–46, 372, 391, 398, 406
Vorovsky, Vatslav, 108, 139, 141
Vrangel, P., 145
Vvedensky, Aleksei Andreevich, 138
Vyrubova, Anna, 93
Vysheslavsky, Boris, 154
Vyshinsky, Andrei, 6, 207, 309–11, 371, 381, 389

Wallenberg, Raoul, 383
Webb, Sidney, 152
Weidenfeld, George, 394–95
Wells, George-Phillip, 369
Wells, H. G., 13, 99–100, 104, 115, 122, 143, 152, 160, 187, 191, 201, 204, 211, 233, 240, 261, 270, 276–77, 295, 318–19, 327, 340, 354, 369–71, 374, 387, 395, 402

Yagoda, Genrikh, 5–6, 8–9, 200, 206–7, 215, 218–22, 224, 226–27, 239–42, 243–49, 252, 255, 260–61, 263–65, 269, 272, 277–89, 290–91, 294, 299–300, 302–12, 317, 319, 330, 333, 341–43, 345–49, 354–55, 357, 360–61, 364–65, 371–72, 374–76, 384–85, 389–90, 392–94, 397, 402–4, 406
Yakovlev, Aleksandr Nikolaevich, 310
Yakovlev, Vasily, 281
Yakovlevich, Vladimir, 349
Yavorsky, Y., 124
Yefim Shaikevich, 65
Yefimov, Boris (Fridlyan), 406
Yeliseyev, 74
Yevdokimov, 117
Yevseevich, Grigori, 59, 62
Yevtikhievna, Maria, 398
Yezhov, Nikolai, 312, 332, 358, 392, 393, 402–3, 406
Yudin, Pavel, 301, 323, 367
Yurovsky, 156

Zaitsev, Boris, 49, 50, 89–90, 114
Zakharova, Yelizaveta, 189, 239
Zakrevskaya, Maria. *See* Budberg, Baroness
Zakrevsky, 70
Zaks, Samuil (*aka* Gladnev), 55–57
Zamkov, Aleksei, 290
Zamyatin, Yevgeni, 86, 93, 121–23, 156, 224, 252
Zaslavsky, David, 331–32
Zazubrin, Vladimir, 224
Zelinsky, Korneli, 272, 274
Zenkovsky, Vasily, 154
Zhdanov, Andrei, 5, 263, 324, 399
Zimin, 403
Zinoviev, Grigori, 8, 19–20, 54–55, 57, 59–64, 72–75, 80, 86, 91–93, 105, 111–13, 116–17, 120, 123–24, 126, 131, 148, 152, 169–70, 173, 176, 188, 194, 196, 274, 296, 316, 330–33, 350, 356, 363, 402, 406
Znamenskaya, Esfir, 404
Znamenskaya, Liliya, 404
Znamenskaya, Rozaliya, 404
Zorin, Leonid, 96, 314, 347
Zorin, Sergei, 152
Zoshchenko, Mikhail, 291, 320, 327
Zweig, Stefan, 27, 186, 201, 268, 303